SESSIONS ROLL 1550

GUIDE

TO THE

LANCASHIRE
RECORD OFFICE

R. SHARPE FRANCE, M.B.E., D.Litt.,M.A.

I.S.B.N. 0 902228 52 8

LANCASHIRE COUNTY COUNCIL
PRESTON
1985

First edition 1948
Second edition 1962

PRINTED BY T. SNAPE, PRESTON.

Foreword

Among the first tasks undertaken by the Lancashire Record Office when it was established in 1940 was the preservation and sorting of the splendid series of Quarter Sessions records which survive for Lancashire. A measure of the success of the venture was that the Record Office soon established itself as the custodian of an ever widening range of archives of official and ecclesiastical bodies, of business and private individuals. Today the strong rooms contain records occupying approximately six and a quarter miles of shelving. These accrue at the rate of some eight hundred feet of shelving each year. The variety and scope of the documents so preserved reflect the rich heritage of the people of Lancashire and their important contribution to the development of the social, cultural and economic life of the nation.

The continuing and rapid increase in interest in national and local history and genealogy means that the facilities provided by the Lancashire Record Office for consultation of the records are in constant use. During 1983 some 8,000 people consulted approximately 45,000 documents. Some were academics or were engaged in work connected with studies in school or higher education. Many enquiries were for legal purposes, but the vast majority of those using documents were simply interested in the history of their own family or community.

The publication of this third edition of the *Guide to the Lancashire Record Office* provides an indispensable tool for those wishing to consult the records. It provides a summary of all archives deposited at the Office up to and including 1976. The daunting task of compilation has been undertaken by the first County Archivist, Dr. R. Sharpe France, who retired in 1976, and to whom I am happy to have this opportunity to pay tribute.

A knowledge of the past is essential if we are to understand the present and plan successfully for the future. Much of that knowledge is derived from written records. The foresight of the Lancashire County Council in establishing and maintaining the Lancashire Record Office is worthy of praise, as is the public spirit of those individuals and organisations who have generously deposited their archives for use by the public. If this valuable work is to continue with equal success in the future I would urge the owners of documents to deposit their papers with the Record Office for the benefit of present and future generations.

Simon Towneley

Her Majesty's Lord Lieutenant and
Custos Rotulorum in the County
of Lancaster

Introduction

The Lancashire Record Office came into existence in 1940 and moved in 1975 to the present premises which provide excellent facilities for the storage and conservation of records and for their consultation by individuals and groups. It has been appointed by the Lord Chancellor as a repository for various classes of public record under section 4 of the Public Records Act 1958 and been recognised as a repository for manorial and tithe documents by the Master of the Rolls under section 114A(7) of the Law of Property Act 1922 and section 36(2) of the Tithe Act 1936, as amended by section 7(1) of the Local Government (Records) Act 1962. It is also a Diocesan Record Office for the dioceses of Blackburn, Bradford and Liverpool under the provisions of the Parochial Registers and Records Measure 1978, and holds certain ecclesiastical records for the dioceses of Chester and Manchester; moreover it is approved for the deposit of records of the Roman Catholic arch-diocese of Liverpool and the dioceses of Lancaster and Salford. The County Council is the archive authority for Lancashire by virtue of the powers conferred on it by the Local Government (Records)Act 1962 as amended by the Local Government Act 1972. The Lancashire Record Office therefore contains many documents relating to the history of Lancashire which have been deposited or given by public spirited organisations and private individuals and by other local authorities.

The *Guide*, which divides records into the standard categories of public, official, ecclesiastical and private classes, provides as complete a summary as possible of all archives deposited to the end of 1976, but it should be noted that their inclusion does not imply that they have all been catalogued. For accessions subsequent to 1976 users are referred to the *Annual Report* and/or *Lists of Accessions* published by the record office. Copies of these are available in the search room and may also be found in the main branches of local libraries in Lancashire and record offices throughout the country.

The County Council pursues an active policy of record acquisition and the County Archivist will be happy to inspect and advise on any documents and to receive new accessions. These may be in the form of long term loans when the owner retains his title to the documents, or in the form of gifts.

Users of the record office are asked to note the following procedures which may affect their visits and their use of the archives.

Documents of less than 50 years old, in some cases more, may not be open for consultation; those in an unfit state of preservation may be unavailable until they have been conserved, and uncatalogued collections will generally be withheld until they have been fully processed. In cases where microfilm copies are available original documents will not normally be produced. It should be noted that a letter in advance will often make a visit to the record office more profitable by enabling the staff to alert enquirer to the extent of what is and what is not available for research purposes.

Photographs and photocopies can be supplied at reasonable charges but the County Archivist reserves the right to refuse permission for copies to be made, especially when the safety of the document would be placed in jeopardy. Copying of documents deposited by private owners is, of course, subject to their approval. Permission to publish documents, either in text or facsimile form, should be sought from the County Archivist.

Contents

Part I — Public Records

COURTS OF QUARTER SESSIONS
LANCASHIRE

Part II — Official Records
COUNTY COUNCIL

Part III — Parochial Records

Part IV — Ecclesiastical Records

CHURCH OF ENGLAND DIOCESAN AND
ARCHIDIACONAL

Part V — Deposited Collections

xiv

xv

Part I

Public Records

The records summarised in Part I of this Guide are deposits under section 4(1) of the Public Records Act, 1958, and presentations under section 3(6) of that Act. With respect to these records the Public Records Act, 1967, requires that certain of them be closed to inspection until they are thirty years old; some classes are closed for longer periods.

COURTS OF QUARTER SESSIONS LANCASHIRE

Under the Crown Courts Act, 1971, Courts of Quarter Sessions and Assize were replaced on 1 January 1972 by Crown Courts administered by central government. This resulted in the recent deposit of Quarter Sessions records later in date than those listed below, which are, in general, closed to public inspection and are yet to be catalogued. Enquiries with regard to these records should be made to the County Archivist.

I. THE COURT IN SESSION

Sessions Rolls (QSR)

1588–92, 1601–06, 1608–09, 1615–42, 1646–1729, 1736–41, 1744–49; for 1550 see DDHi Miscellaneous, p. 000.

These documents are in effect the minutes of the court, being formally compiled after the Sessions from the memoranda in the order books. They consist of long parchment membranes fastened at the head and then rolled. In 1750 the Sessions Rolls were discontinued, the order books taking their place as the final record of the court.

The rolls for 1588–1606 have been edited by James Tait for the Chetham Society (New Series, Vol. 77, 1917).

1

Order Books (QSO/2)

1626–43, 1646–66, 1668–70, 1672–75, 1677–1702, 1704–1971.

This series, beginning as the memoranda books of the Clerk of the Peace, became, in 1750, the final record of the court.

Draft Order Books (QSO/1)

1815–17, 1935–65

Petitions (QSP)

1648–1908

There is a small number of gaps for individual Sessions. Included in this numerous class are documents relating to poor relief, repair of roads and bridges, appointment of parish constables and high constables, coroners' accounts, applications for registration of dissenters' meeting-places, militia accounts, gaol accounts, warrants for payment of accounts for the transport of army baggage, calendars of prisoners, and a great variety of other matters.

Earlier petitions will be found in the Recognizance bundles.

Recognizances (QSB/1)

1605–06, 1623–43, 1646–58, 1660–1834

Though consisting principally of bonds for appearance at Sessions to answer charges or to prosecute, other matters are to be found in these bundles, such as informations, depositions, highway diversion papers and plans, calendars of prisoners, and (to 1648) petitions.

Recognizance Books (QSB/2)

1583–84, 1796–1839

The latter are in the nature of an index to the Recognizances themselves.

For Alehouse Recognizances see page 11.

Calendars of Prisoners (QJC)

All Sessions 1821–69, 1889–1967
Preston Sessions only 1870–75

These give the place and date of the session, the name, age and state of education of the prisoner, the offence, and the sentence.

Earlier calendars will be found among the Petitions and Recognizances.

Indictment Rolls (QJI/1)

1605–06, 1619, 1626–42, 1646–1869

These consist of the actual indictments and jury panels.

Indictment Books (QJI/2)

1619–26, 1629–36, 1642, 1646–53, 1660–73, 1679–85, 1686–92 (DDKe 2/2), 1700–19, 1743–49, 1760–71

These process books of indictments give the names, abodes, and occupations of defendants, their offences and pleas, together with other cognate information.

Estreats of Fines (QJE)

1626, 1628–31, 1633–43, 1646–76, 1680–82, 1685–92, 1695–98, 1703–05, 1721–28, 1730–54, 1760

These are notes of the fines and amercements, extracted from the Sessions Rolls, which were to be levied by the high constables and remitted to the Chancellor of the Duchy of Lancaster. Among them are rolls of 1650 relating specifically to alehouses, and 1651 non-attendance at church.

Appeals (QJX)

John Ferrers, in claim for loss of money stolen at Prestwich by highwaymen, 1668.

Most appeal papers are to be found in the Petition bundles.

(QSV 55) Rating Appeal Committee for Amounderness, Blackburn, and Leyland Hundreds, minutes 1929–40.

Insolvent Debtors' Papers (QJB)

1678, 1690–91, 1696, 1704, 1712–20, 1725–57, 1761–65, 1769, 1772, 1774–76, 1778, 1781, 1794, 1797, 1801, 1804, 1806, 1809, 1811–15, 1822–24

These consist mainly of the schedules of real property, personal property, and debts owing to the prisoners who claimed release from gaol under the long succession of Acts for that purpose.

Riot Depositions (QJD)

1826–93

These are the sworn statements of witnesses in cases of civil disturbance. Many relate to labour troubles and prize-fighting.

See also among the records of the Clerk of the Peace, page 20.

Attendance Books (QSA)

1952–71

Preston Quarter Sessions Mess Committee (QSV)

Minutes 1940–72, visitors' book 1906–21, correspondence 1897–1915, 1953–58, 1966, 1971

3

II. ADMINISTRATION

Highways and Bridges (QAR)

Much information on the building, rebuilding, and repair of bridges and repair of highways will be found in the Sessions Rolls and Order Books, as well as in the Petitions.

Highway Committee minutes, 1878–89
Contracts for repair and rebuilding of bridges: Ribchester 1775, Ribble 1779 (see also DDX/51/2), Staley 1781, Lancaster 1783, Hindsford 1861, Agecroft 1862
Contracts for upkeep of bridges: Amounderness 1740, 1750, Leyland Hundred 1745, 1752, West Derby Hundred 1759
Penwortham Bridge Committee: minutes and papers 1885–86
Accounts: Whalley and Fiendsforth bridges 1634, Radcliffe bridge 1699, Ancoats bridge 1699; cash-book for West Derby Hundred bridges 1846–93
Certificates of road repairs, Salford Hundred 1738–43
Reports on Blackburn Hundred bridges 1876–89
Plan Books (bridges): 1777 (North Lonsdale), 1805 (the whole county), 1860 (Blackburn Hundred)
Returns of all minor bridges in the county, township by township, 1801

Diseases of Animals (QAC)

Returns of infected places 1866.
Licences to hold markets, exhibitions, and sales 1867–68
Minutes of the Cattle Plague Committee are to be found in the Sessions Order Books.

Finance (QAF and CT)

General

General Finance Committee minutes 1845–89
Kirkdale Finance Sub-Committee minutes 1851–89
Lancaster Finance Sub-Committee minutes 1850–89
Preston Finance Sub-Committee minutes 1845–89
Salford Finance Sub-Committee minutes 1842–89
Reports of Finance Committee 1844–80
Treasurers' abstract of accounts 1799–1889
Treasurers' statements of account 1828–39, 1842–45
Bank books 1832–45
Orders for reimbursement on militia affairs 1803–14
Mortgages for building New Bailey Prison, Salford 1788–90
Registers of mortgages 1854–62, 1867–70
Manchester Assize Court mortgages 1861–86
Police mortgages 1878–1901

4

Annual accounts 1845–48; see also *Annual and Adjourned Sessions Proceedings* to 1889 in Search Room
Personal accounts ledger 1850
Impersonal accounts ledger 1850
Account books 1850, 1863–64
Cash book 1850–54
Journal 1850
Register of loans 1848–96, 1867–77
Ledger 1848–50
Diseases of Animals: accounts recouped from boroughs 1870–98
Lunatic Asylums loan accounts 1848–72
Treasurers' estimates 1872–1903
Police enquiries re pensions 1889–1902
Miscellaneous returns to House of Commons 1850–95

A large number of vouchers and bills are to be found in the Petition bundles.

County Rates

Rate Basis Committee minutes 1849–88
Assessment books 1814, 1828, 1841, 1845
Assessment returns 1883
Assessment memoranda 1816–37
Assessments 1841–84
Rate rolls 1852–62, 1864–68, 1878, 1881
Poor rate returns 1800–17

Gaols, Houses of Correction, etc.

The original county gaol was Lancaster Castle. In the Order Books and Petitions are many references to its upkeep and government. The first House of Correction for the county was established at Preston in 1617 on the site of the friary, the present gaol, on a new site, being built in 1789. The Manchester House of Correction was established in 1657, being succeeded by the New Bailey in 1787 and Strangeways in 1864. The House of Correction at Kirkdale was built in 1819, being followed by the present Walton gaol in 1855.

Title deeds (QGB): Lancaster 1788–1880, Preston 1714–1903, Liverpool 1847–81, Manchester 1783–1881
Lancaster Castle Committee minutes (QAL) 1783–1848
Plans (PP): Lancaster, Liverpool, Preston; (DDX/70) Lancaster extension *c.* 1841
Reports by governors, chaplains and surgeons (QGR): Lancaster, Preston, Liverpool, Manchester 1823–67 (with a few gaps)
Rules (QGV): Lancaster 1826–44, Preston 1793–1867, Liverpool 1840–66, Manchester 1826–46
Visiting Committee minutes (QGG): Preston 1910–46

Charity trustees' minutes (QGP): Preston 1890–1946
Registers of prisoners (QGP): Preston 1883, 1903
Reformatory and Industrial Schools Committee minutes (QAB)
1880–88

Licensing (QAD)

Licensing committees minutes 1872–1974
Returns of public houses 1890, 1904
Compensation reports 1907–48

Lunacy (QAM)

Lancaster (see also Hospital Records, page 000)

Building contract 1813–14
Specifications 1813–14
Accounts prior to appointment of Treasurer 1810–12
Building vouchers 1811–18
Orders for payment of maintenance 1816–18
Maintenance accounts 1823–97
Building and furnishing accounts 1823–91
Wage books 1850–62, 1873–98
Attendants' wages 1877–83
Bills passed for payment 1863–1902
Register of receipts 1875–79
Ledgers 1877–1913
Accounts with townships and guardians 1816–18, 1824–92
Registers of admissions 1816–24, 1845–59, 1870–90
Indexes to registers of admissions 1845–1923
Registers of private patients 1880–1912
Quarterly admission synopses 1816–74
Reports of Medical Officer 1816–40, 1845–48
Registers of cases 1826–1943
Reports of autopsies 1876–81
Registers of discharges and deaths 1850–1944
Register of patients recovered 1888–1911
Registers of deaths 1837–45, 1875–87, 1903–54
Register of burials 1832–54
Letter-book 1878–83
Diet book 1883–89
Magistrates' visiting book 1829–70
Registers of escaped patients 1895–1915
Staff changes 1890–98
Committal warrants 1816–63

Prestwich:

Board minutes 1853–1948
Building Committee minutes 1847–50

6

Admission orders, case-books, wage-books, notices of admission and discharge, registers of deaths, absence books, and committee minutes 1850-1934

Rainhill:
Title deeds 1623-1808

Whittingham (see also Hospital Records, page 000):
Miscellaneous papers, rules, plans 1867-83

Settlement registers of pauper lunatics 1826-93

Reports on all asylums 1852-88

Militia (QAS)

Standing Militia Storehouse Committee minutes 1855-89:

Proceedings and reports 1853-58
Contracts, deeds etc. (Preston, Everton, Warrington, Burnley, Fleetwood, Bolton, Liverpool, Manchester, Wigan, Salford, Radcliffe, Lancaster) 1854-71
Correspondence 1853-84
Accounts 1854-61
Reports 1856-60
Plans (PM) Everton, Preston, Warrington, Burnley, Salford, Bury 1837-78

Police (QEC and QEV, see also Police Records, page 58)

County Constabulary Committee minutes 1840-89

Rules 1842

Report on Police superannuation funds 1875

Report on intemperance 1877

Charge books: Bacup division 1861-71, Blackburn Higher division 1860-71, Bury division 1898-1900, Kirkham division 1858-72, Manchester division 1842-54, 1894-95, Ormskirk division 1894-96, Prescot division 1848-53

Occurrence book: Bolton division 1846-65

Summons books: Amounderness division 1843-62, Bacup division 1861-71, Blackburn Higher division 1861-67, Bolton division 1844-62, Leyland division 1869-75, Manchester division 1847-54, 1859-62, Prescot division 1843-55

Combined charge and summons books: Bolton division 1852-60

Sectional occurrence books: Cliviger 1891-96, Eccleston 1896-1902, Failsworth 1895-1902, Fulwood 1887-95, Galgate 1884-98, Haydock 1889-98, Hindley 1888-96, Ince 1888-92, 1894-99, Littleborough 1877-98, Ramsbottom 1894-98, Skerton 1878-82, West Derby 1893-96

7

Headquarters: contracts, plans and accounts 1877

Garstang Police Station: building tenders and papers 1852–54

Accrington Borough Police: charge books 1884–89

(MBBa) Bacup Borough Police: Chief Constable's general orders 1887–91, report books 1887–1933

Other Committees

General Purposes Committee minutes (QAG) 1858–78

Parliamentary Committee minutes (QAP) 1853–89

Provisional Courts Committee minutes (QAH) 1945–46

Quarter Sessions Advisory Committee minutes (QSV) 1945–47

Minutes of Miscellaneous Committee (QAV/1): adulteration of food 1872–76, County Analyst 1886–87, accommodation of pauper lunatics 1877–78, Hundred of Salford relief 1880, Justices' Clerks Act 1877, salaries and pensions of asylum officials 1883–88

Reports of Special Committees (QAV/3): county expenditure 1845 and 1849, public bridges 1849, Salford House of Correction 1850, prisons accommodation and discipline 1852, Justices' Clerks' fees 1856, Coroners Acts 1860, state of Manchester House of Correction 1783, county rate 1863, pauper lunatics' accommodation 1867, billeting militia regiments 1867, adulteration of food Acts 1874

Liverpool County Sessions House Committee minutes (QGB 3/5) 1884–86

County Probation Committee minutes (QAA) 1945–46

III. ENROLMENT, REGISTRATION AND DEPOSIT
CHARITIES AND SOCIETIES

Charities (QDC)

The Act of 26 Geo. III *c.* 58 (1786) required ministers and churchwardens to send returns of charities to the Clerk of the Peace, who was to transmit them to Parliament. The Clerk of the Peace was, under 52 Geo. III *c.* 102 (1812), to register memorials describing the property of every charity. 16–17 Vict. *c.* 137 (1853) required trustees to deliver to him copies of their annual statements of account.

Returns 1787–88 (Lancashire section, pp. 567–626, of printed *Abstracts of Returns of Charitable Donations*, 1816)

Memorials 1813–44

Accounts 1854–59, 1862–68, and 1870–72 for Henshaw's Bluecoat School, Prestwich-cum-Oldham only

In the Record Office Library are bound sets of the Lancashire sections of the *Charity Commissioners' Reports*, 1820–29 and 1898–1905, giving much detail relating to each charity, and the *Digest of Endowed Charities*, 1869

Loan Societies (QDS/1)

(Including Friendly, Sick and Burial, and Building Societies.)

Various Acts and amendments, from 33 Geo. III *c.* 54 (1793), required the depositing with the Clerk of the Peace of a variety of documents.

Bonds of Treasurers 1794–1862

Notices of Removal 1826–83

Register of Rules 1837–97

Original Rules 1800–91 (including the literary and scientific institutions of Ormskirk 1851 and Blackburn 1844; mechanics' institutions of Burnley 1844, Ashton-under-Lyne and Dukinfield 1844 and 1863, Radcliffe and Pilkington 1844, Warrington 1846, Lancaster 1850, Colne 1852; Manchester Concert Hall 1843, Manchester Botanical and Horticultural Society 1843, Manchester Natural History Society 1843, Preston Law Library 1844, Preston Institution for the Diffusion of Knowledge 1844, Manchester Royal Exchange Library 1878, Ulverston Young Men's Literary Institute 1869, Liverpool Medical Institution 1879, and Warrington Museum and Library 1891)

Alteration of Rules 1813

Freemasons (QDS/2)

The Unlawful Societies Act, 39 Geo. III *c.* 79 (1799) exempted from its provisions regular lodges of Freemasons on condition that each lodge certified its members' names to Quarter Sessions annually.

Returns 1799–1803; 1824 (Manchester Lodge of Affability); 1837 (Eccles St. John's Lodge and Ringley Lodge of Charity)

Savings Banks (QDS/3)

The Act of 57 Geo. III *c.* 130 (1817) with amendments required the depositing with the Clerk of the Peace of transcripts of the rules of Savings Banks and Annuity Societies.

Rules 1817–51

Register of rules 1781–1851

DEFENCE

The 1795 Act required 589 men for the Navy from Lancashire, and the Acts of 1796 required 5,160 men for the Army and 763 for the Navy.

Returns of men for the Army and Navy from every township in the county under the Acts of 35 Geo. III *c*. 5 (1795) (QDV/26) and 37 Geo. *cc*. 3 and 4 (1796) (QDV/1).

GAME PRESERVATION

Under the Act of 9 Anne *c*. 27 (1710) it was necessary for a lord of a manor to register with the Clerk of the Peace the appointment of the one gamekeeper allowed by the Act at any one time. This Act was repealed, but registration continued, by 1–2 William IV *c*. 32 (1831). The registers are useful in giving the names of lords of manor at definite dates.

Registers (QDG/1) 1711–1967 (see also page 19)

HIGHWAYS

Highways have been stopped and diverted under a succession of Acts, principally 8–9 Will. III *c*. 16 (1697), 13 Geo. III *c*. 78 (1773), 55 Geo. III *c*. 68 (1815), and 5–6 Will. IV *c*. 50 (1835).

Enrolments of Inquisitions *ad quod damnum* (QAR 5–15) Preston 1756, Leyland 1757, Wrightington 1760, Ince Blundell 1766; see also Recognizance Rolls.

Justices' Orders and Certificates (QSD) 1836–1971

Earlier Orders will be found in the Recognizance Rolls and for later see p. 36. To about the year 1800 sketch plans are included, which later become more detailed and better executed.

JURORS (QDF)

Under the Act 7–8 Will. III *c*. 32 (1696) petty constables were to return annually to Quarter Sessions lists of men between 21 and 70, township by township, who were qualified to serve on juries. Subsequent Acts, especially 3 Geo. III *c*. 25 (1730) and 6 Geo. IV *c*. 50 (1825), altered the qualifications. These useful lists give the men's ages, occupations and places of abode.

Lists (under Act of 1696): Amounderness and Blackburn Hundreds 1696, Warrington Division of West Derby Hundred 1708

Lists (under Act of 1730): almost complete for 1776, 1778, 1781, 1784, 1792–1812, 1814–24

Lists (under Act of 1825): complete for 1825–32

LICENSED TRADESMEN

Alehousekeepers (QSB/3)

The Act of 5–6 Edw. VI c. 25 (1552) required licensed victuallers to enter into a recognizance of good behaviour, which was to remain on record at Quarter Sessions. By 26 Geo. III c. 31 (1753) the Clerk of the Peace was also to keep a register of the bonds. This system was terminated by the Act of 9 Geo. IV c. 61 (1828).

Returns (Hundred by Hundred, with varying completeness) 1619–21, 1627–37, 1641–42, 1646–52, 1654–57, 1660–62, 1665, 1667, 1669, 1672, 1677, 1681, 1683–84, 1690, 1692, 1701, 1717, 1720, 1727–42, 1744, 1746–48, 1750–68, 1770–1813, 1815–28

Registers 1822–29

Badgers

Badgers, or itinerant sellers of corn, fish, butter or cheese, when licensed at Quarter Sessions, had, under the Act of 5 Eliz. I c. 12 (1563), to enter into a recognizance.

Registers (QDV 30 and 32) 1621–22, 1635; see also Recognizance and Petition Rolls

PARLIAMENTARY ELECTIONS

Land Tax Assessments (QDL)

The Act of 20 Geo. III c. 17 (1780) declared that none should vote at county elections who was not assessed to the Land Tax. It was necessary therefore that a duplicate of the assessment for each township be sent to the Clerk of the Peace annually. The information given consists of the proprietor's name, the occupier's name, the amount of tax payable, and the rental, for each property taxed.

1780: Salford Hundred only
1781–1831: complete
1832: Lonsdale, Blackburn, and Salford Hundreds only

Electors (EL)

The Representation of the People Act 2–3 Will. IV c. 45 (1832) enlarged the county franchise and instituted printed registers of electors. Further enlargements were brought about by Acts of 1867, 1885, 1918, 1928, 1945, 1948, and 1969.

Registers—
Under Act of 1832: 1832–60, 1866
Under Act of 1867: 1868, 1870, 1875, 1880, 1885
Under Act of 1885: 1886, 1890, 1895, 1900, 1905, 1910, 1915
Under Act of 1928: 1934, 1939

11

Under Act of 1945: 1945, 1946
Under Act of 1948: 1950, 1955, 1960, 1963–71
Under Act of 1969: 1971–74

Disputed Elections (QDE)

Under the Act of 10 Anne *c.* 31 (1711) the poll-books at disputed elections were ordered to be delivered to the Clerk of the Peace to be kept among the Quarter Sessions records.

Preston 1826; included are poll-books, registers of voters, tally-papers, correspondence, etc.; see also Houghton MSS., p. 228.

Boundary Commissions

Reports 1832, 1867, 1885, 1915 (in Record Office Library)

POVERTY AND CRIME

Vagrants

The Acts of 17 Geo. II *c.* 5 (1744) and 59 Geo. III *c.* 12 (1819) controlled the deportation of vagrants to Scotland and Ireland. Large numbers of the latter passed through the hands of the Lancashire justices and there has been preserved a series of registers of such vagrants sailing from Liverpool. The information given includes their names, whether accompanied by wife, number of children, name of ship, and often the county from which they had been sent.

Registers (QDR) 1801–02, 1811–14, 1818–35

There is of course much information on vagrancy in the Sessions Order Books and Petitions.

Convictions (QGC)

By long-established practice, convictions under summary jurisdiction out of Sessions were often forwarded to the Clerk of the Peace. Convictions of special cases were dealt with by specific Acts, i.e. tanners not paying duty, 9 Anne *c.* 11 (1710), beggars, 17 Geo. II *c.* 5 (1743), swearers of profane oaths, 19 Geo. II *c.* 21 (1746), pawnbrokers, 39–40 Geo. III *c.* 99 (1800), and juvenile offenders 10–11 Vict. *c.* 82 (1847).

Recusants (QGC/2 and QDV/5 and 6) 1679 and 1682

Tanners 1710

Liverpool Beggars 1818–19

Manchester and Salford Pawnbrokers 1810

Swearers of Profane Oaths 1757 (QGC 2/4 and QSV/14)

Juvenile Offenders 1847–81

12

Tyburn Tickets

Under the Act 10–11 Will. III c. 23 (1699) persons apprehending and successfully prosecuting a felon were entitled to a certificate freeing them from serving parochial offices, such certificate to be enrolled with the Clerk of the Peace.

Tickets (QDV/24) 1765–73; see also p. 14

Transportation (QGT)

The Acts of 4 Geo. I c. 11 (1718) and 6 Geo. I c. 23 (1720) required the contractors for transportation to enter into a bond.

Bonds 1836–43

PROPERTY

Corn Rents (AT)

Under various local Acts the awards made in connexion with the establishment of corn rents in certain ecclesiastical parishes were to be deposited with the Clerk of the Peace. Attached to the awards are detailed plans of the townships constituting the parishes.

Cockerham 1839

Lancaster 1833 (with alterations of 1835, 1855, 1875 and 1896)

St. Michaels-on-Wyre 1824

Deeds of Bargain and Sale (QDD)

The Act of 27 Hen. VIII c. 16 (1535) required deeds of bargain and sale to be enrolled within six months of completion in one of the courts at Westminster or with the Clerk of the Peace of the county where the property lay. The Act of 5 Eliz. I c. 26 (1562) allowed enrolment in the Palatinate Courts of Lancaster, Chester, and Durham.

Deeds 1585, 1588–1620, 1622–42, 1646–56, 1658–60, 1662–69, 1671, 1677–81, 1686, 1687, 1691, 1692

Enclosure Awards and Agreements (AE, except when otherwise shown)

By Act: Ashton-under-Lyne 1841, Astley 1764, Barnacre-with-Bonds 1772, Barton-upon-Irwell 1856, Billinge 1877, Billington, Wilpshire, and Dinckley 1791, Borwick 1819, Broughton-in-Furness 1847, Carnforth 1864, Cartmel 1809, Caton 1818, Childwall and Woolton 1813, Chipping, Mitton, and Ribchester 1812, Chorley 1768, Church Coniston 1858, Claife 1799, Claughton-in-Amounderness 1731, Claughton-in-Lonsdale 1806, Clayton-le-Moors 1797, Clitheroe 1788, Crosby and Litherland 1816, Croston 1775, Culcheth 1751, Edgworth 1797, Egton-with-Newland 1823, Ellel 1757, Entwistle, 1860, Farington 1833, Farnworth and Kearsley 1798, Forton 1786, Fulwood 1817, Gleaston 1859, Hale and Halewood 1803, Halton 1800, Harwood 1801, Hawkshead, Monk Coniston and Skelwith 1862, Hesketh-with-Becconsall 1870, Hopwood 1815, Hornby 1804, Horwich 1821, Ince-in-Makerfield 1890, Kirkby Ireleth 1831, 1867, Lathom and Skelmersdale 1781, Layton-with-Warbreck 1769, Little Harwood 1776, Little Urswick 1822, Longton 1761, 1821, Lostock 1808, Lower Darwen 1780, Lowton 1765, Nether Kellet 1815, Newton (Manchester) 1805, Oldham 1804, Osmotherley 1862, Oswaldtwistle 1776, Over Darwen 1896, Over Kellet 1805, Penketh 1868, Pennington-in-Furness 1827, Pilling 1867, Quernmore 1817, Radcliffe and Ainsworth 1812, Rawcliffe and Stalmine 1833, Ribbleton 1870, Rumworth 1817, Scotforth 1809, Tatham 1858, Thornton-le-Fylde 1806, Tonge-with-Haulgh 1818. Trawden and Colne 1821, Tunstall 1825, Ulverston 1813, Walton-on-the-Hill and Fazakerley 1763, Warton and Silverdale 1817, Wavertree 1769, Westhoughton 1727, Whittington 1817, Wiswell 1790, Woolston-with-Martinscroft 1849, Worsley 1768, Worsthorne-with-Hurstwood 1848, Yealand Conyers and Yealand Redmayne 1778

By Agreement: Adlington 1763, Astley 1737, Broughton-in-Furness 1771 (CCE 1/117), Cuerden 1804 (DDTa 323), Farington 1705, 1784, Finsthwaite 1727 (DDPd 26/227), Golborne 1763, Great Harwood 1762 (DDHe 75/6), Haighton 1810, Hindley 1727 (DDB 72/53), Howick 1763 (DDHe 80/1), Leyland 1724, 1748, Litherland 1718, Longton 1818, Lytham 1608, Oldham 1604, Orrell 1666 (DDBa 11/21), Rusland 1842 (DDAa 238), 1861 (DDAr 246), Satterthwaite 1849, Spotland 1812, Thornham 1691, Thornton (Sefton) 1742, Warton-with-Lindeth 1740 (PR 2768/2), West Derby 1753, Westhoughton 1642, 1685

Miscellaneous Deeds (QDD)

1718–1971

Under the Act of 3 Geo. I c. 18 (1717) it was necessary for the wills of Roman Catholics and all deeds relating to their property to be enrolled by the Clerk of the Peace. The series is complete to 1820. A handlist of Roman Catholics' wills is in the searchroom. From about 1790 other documents of great variety requiring enrolment have been added to this class; these relate *inter alia* to the following matters:

Certificates of convictions (Tyburn Tickets) under 10–11 Will. IV c. 23 (1699)

Certificates of annuities and rent charges under 3 Geo. III c. 24 (1763)

Sheriffs' inquisitions as to the value of land required for public utilities under particular Acts

Appointments of canal trustees and commissioners under particular Acts

Rules of the High Court concerning weirs under 28–29 Vict. *c*. 121 (1865)

Bye-laws relating to the rivers Mersey and Lune under particular Acts

Notifications of alterations to river banks under particular Acts

Appointments of returning officers under 2–3 Will. IV *c*. 45 (1832)

Grants of Borough Quarter Sessions under 5–6 Will. IV *c*. 76 (1835)

Appointments of assistant Poor Law commissioners under 4–5 Will. IV *c*. 76 (1834)

Orders establishing Poor Law unions under 4–5 Will. IV *c*. 76 (1834)

Orders for government and valuation of Poor Law unions under 4–5 Will. IV *c*. 76 (1834)

Declarations of additional polling places under 6–7 Will. IV *c*. 102 (1836)

Orders establishing registration districts under 6–7 Will. IV *c*. 86 (1836)

Appointments of Income Tax commissioners under 5–6 Vict. *c*. 35 (1842)

Nominations of sheriffs and coroners and their deputies, under various Acts

Orders for formation of coroners' districts under 7–8 Vict. *c*. 92 (1844)

Accounts of election expenses under 17–18 Vict. *c*. 102 (1854)

Oaths of Judges in Bankruptcy under 24–25 Vict. *c*. 134 (1861)

Orders creating highway districts under 5–6 Will. IV *c*. 50 (1835) and 25–26 Vict. *c*. 61 (1862)

Arrangements between railway companies under particular Acts

Certificates of fitness of industrial schools under 24–25 Vict. *c*. 113 (1861)

Orders for construction of piers under particular Acts

Judgments of commissioners concerning fisheries under 28–29 Vict. *c*. 121 (1865)

Orders relating to detached portions of townships under 39–40 Vict. *c*. 61 (1876) and 45–46 Vict. *c*. 58 (1882)

Appointments of perpetual commissioners under 3–4 Will. IV *c*. 74 (1833) for taking acknowledgments by married women of deeds executed by them

PUBLIC UNDERTAKINGS

Boats and Barges (QDV 16)

The Act of 35 Geo. III *c*. 58 (1795) required the registration of all vessels exceeding 13 tons burden used on inland navigations.

Register 1795

Parliamentary Plans (PD)

Under Standing Orders of the House of Commons, first made in 1792, "a map or plan of such intended cut, canal, aqueduct or navigation, with a book of reference, shall be deposited for public inspection at the office of the Clerk of the Peace of every county, before the 11th of November previous to the application to Parliament." In due course other types of public utility were included in the provision. The following list gives the date of the earliest deposited plan in each class. It should be noted that some of the schemes never came to fruition:

Bridges 1813
Canals 1792
Docks and harbours 1810
Drainage 1854
Gasworks 1837
Electricity works 1882
Markets 1822
Piers 1862
Railways 1822
Reclamation of land 1800
Roads 1807
Town improvements 1843
Tramways 1869
Waterworks 1798

Turnpike Trusts (QDT)

By the Act of 3 Geo. IV *c*. 126 (1822) a copy of each turnpike trust's statement of account was to be sent annually to the Clerk of the Peace. Under specific Acts the treasurers of trusts were required to deposit a bond of indemnity with the Clerk of the Peace.

Accounts 1822–90 (90 trusts)

Bonds of Treasurers 1798–1825

RELIGION

Oaths and Declarations (QSJ)

The Test Act of 25 Car. II *c*. 2 (1673) required each person holding civil or military office (save the lesser parochial ones) to receive the sacrament according to the Church of England and to deliver to Quarter Sessions a certificate to that effect. At the same time they were to take the oath against transubstantiation. Other Acts rendering necessary the taking of oaths to support the Act of Settlement, to abjure the Stuarts, not to injure the Church of England, and of allegiance, were passed in 1714, 1722, 1778, 1791, and 1812.

Sacrament certificates 1673–1829

Oaths against Transubstantiation 1673–87, 1692, 1711–55

Act of 1714 1714–22

Persons refusing 1716–44

Act of 1722 1723

Subscriptions of dissenters to the Thirty-nine Articles (QDV/2) 1726–82

Act of 1778 1778–91

Act of 1791 1791–1867

Not to injure the Church of England 1828–76

Miscellaneous Oaths 1673–1886; (QJB/6) Jan. 1677/8

Papists in Prescot division taking and refusing oaths (QSV/7) 1744–45.

Sectarians (QDV/9)

In 1829 the House of Commons required from each township "the number of places of worship, not of the Church of England, distinguishing as far as possible of what sect or persuasion, and the total number of each sect."

Returns (original) 1829

Papists (QDP)

The first Jacobite rebellion resulted in the passing of the Act of 1 Geo. I c. 55 (1715) which required every papist to register his name and details of his real property with the Clerk of the Peace, to be subscribed personally or by attorney at Quarter Sessions. In most instances both the original return and the enrolment have been preserved. The first six rolls (1717) have been published by the Record Society of Lancashire and Cheshire, Vols. 98 and 108.

Registers and returns 1717–76, 1778–83, 1788

Warrants of attorney 1717–27; thereafter the warrant is filed with the return

Places of Worship (QDV)

The Toleration Act, 1 Will. and Mary c. 18 (1688) allowed Protestant Dissenters to hold their meetings openly, provided the

17

meeting places were registered with the bishop, the archdeacon, or Quarter Sessions. A subsequent Act, 52 Geo. III *c*. 155 (1812) required the places to be notified to the alternative authorities. It was not until the Act of Geo. III *c*. 32 (1791) that some of the provisions of the Toleration Act were extended to Roman Catholics, conditional upon their registering their places of worship, their priests, and their schoolmasters.

Register of Dissenters' meeting houses 1689–1852

Returns of Roman Catholic chapels 1791–97

Register of Roman Catholic chapels, etc. 1791–1851

TAXATION

Corn Tax (QDV/21)

The Acts of 29 Geo. III *c*. 58 (1789) and 31 Geo. III *c*. 30 (1791) provided for the payment of a duty on foreign corn, and established inspectors who were to take oaths of office, to be enrolled with the Clerk of the Peace, and to certify returns of corn prices.

Oaths of inspectors 1789–98

Certificate of price returns 1801–02; see also Sessions Order Books

Hearth Tax

By the Act of 13–14 Car. II *c*. 10 (1662) an annual payment of 2s. was required from every householder for each firehearth. Poor persons were exempt.

Returns (QDV/14): Salford, Huncoat, and Manchester 1664

Exemptions (QDV/18 and 19) Ainsworth, Birtle, Butterworth, Castleton, Middleton, Swinton, Thornham, Urmston, and Worsley 1664

Microfilms of the original returns in the Public Record Office are available (MF 27–29, 35)

Land Tax (See page 31)

Poll Tax

Returns: Bolton division of Salford Hundred, 1678

Tax Commissioners (QDV/27)

Under the Act of 46 Geo. III *c*. 65 (1806) all local commissioners for the collection of taxes had to enrol with the Clerk of the Peace their certificate of appointment.

Certificates 1806–15

Game Duty (QDG)

Acts of 24 Geo. III *c.* 43 (1784) and 25 Geo. III *c.* 50 (1785) required all who kept dogs, guns, etc. for the taking of game to register with the Clerk of the Peace and take out a certificate annually; see also page 10.

Registers 1784–89

Correspondence 1805–07

Hairpowder Duty (QDH)

The obligation to take out an annual certificate with duty of a guinea was imposed on users of hairpowder by the Acts of 35 Geo. III *cc.* 49 and 112 (1795).

Registers 1795–97

Correspondence 1795–96

VARIOUS

The following documents, though perhaps not strictly to be included among Documents Deposited, have long been placed in that division.

Returns made in 1655 of persons in Blackburn Hundred taking up arms against Parliament in 1641 (QDV/11)

Rental of bailiffs of Salford Hundred (QDV/12) 1677

Registers of parish constables (QDV/20) 1632–37, 1650–58, 1660–64

Association in support of William III (QDV/10) 1696; published 1921 as the *Lancashire Association Oath Rolls*, ed. W. Gandy

IV. JUSTICES OF THE PEACE

Commissions of the Peace (QSC)

Issued under the Palatinate of Lancaster seal, these formal documents give the names, but not usually the abodes, of the Justices.

Commissions 1598, 1602, 1604, 1620, 1627–42, 1646–50, 1658, 1664–73, 1675–79, 1682–1727, 1730, 1731, 1733–37, 1739–42, 1744, 1745, 1747–49, 1752, 1753, 1756–58, 1761, 1763, 1766, 1769, 1772, 1777, 1780, 1814, 1820, 1828, 1830, 1835, 1838, 1840, 1844, 1849, 1852, 1859, 1868, 1921, 1961, 1974

Lists

These give the abode and date of qualification: 1821–23, 1825, 1826, 1828–1974

Qualifications (QSQ/1)

The Justices' Qualification Act of 18 Geo. II *c*. 20 (1745) provided that no one should be a Justice of the Peace unless he was possessed of an estate worth at least £100 a year and took an oath to that effect. This qualification has been altered by subsequent Acts.

Oath Books 1745–1906

V. CLERK OF THE PEACE

Many official papers and letters, 17th and 18th *c*., are in Lord Kenyon's muniments (DDKe).

Appointments (CPG)

The Clerk of the Peace for Lancashire was appointed under the seal of the Duchy of Lancaster. From the end of the 18th century until 1879 the office was a sinecure operated by deputies.

Grants and Deputations 1796, 1800, 1825, 1826, 1838, 1858

Precedents. etc, (CPV)

"Articles to be given in Charge at the Sessions of the Peace," *c*. 1610
Formulary and Memoranda Book compiled between 1750 and 1770

Fees and Accounts (CPF)

Order of Duchy Court relative to fees (CPV) 1664
Accounts of fines and fees 1800–18, 1839–43, 1852–56
Accounts of deputies with Sessions 1811–31
Cash accounts of deputies 1813–25
General accounts of Thomas Birchall 1815–22
Accounts relating to riots at Manchester and Rochdale 1829

Inventories of Records (CPA)

c. 1808, 1872, 1907

Riot Papers (CPR)

Ashton-under-Lyne 1868–69
Blackburn 1878
Bolton 1868
Ince 1881
Leigh 1868
Rochdale 1868
Stalybridge 1863
Wigan 1859

Correspondence (CPC)

General 1836–38
Coroners 1860–80

Barrow-in-Furness (QBA)

Court record book, appeals register, legal-aid register, index of jurors, general files, case files 1962-71

Blackpool (QBL)

Court record book, appeals register, legal-aid register 1948-71, case files 1952-68

THE COURT OF ANNUAL GENERAL SESSIONS

In 1798, under the provisions of the Act of 38 Geo. III *c*. 58, the Lancashire Justices were empowered to hold a special annual session at Preston for the purpose of dealing with purely administrative business which concerned the county as a whole. Up to the last quarter of the 18th century an extra-legal meeting for similar purposes had taken place yearly "at the Sheriff's Table" at Lancaster Assizes. See Historic Society of Lancashire and Cheshire, Vol. 96, 1944.

Proceedings at the Sheriff's Table (QSV/11): 1628, 1661-94; for 1577-86 see DDF Official.

Sessions Act papers (QSV/8): 1785-98

Minutes (QSG): 1798-1890

Preston Sessions House (QSV/9, 12): Building accounts and plans 1825-30

COURTS OF PETTY SESSIONS (PS)

Amounderness Division (PSAm): Minutes 1842-45, 1895-97

Barrow-in-Furness Borough (PSBa): Court registers 1922-40, juvenile court register 1936-39, licensing register 1874-1949

Blackburn Hundred (PSB1): Minutes 1918-41, chairmen's notebooks 1956-68, court registers 1880-1940, Employers and Workmen Act 1875, plaint book 1876-1915, court files 1949-67, bonds and orders 1953-61, committal and appeal papers 1959-68, licensing minutes 1872-1934, licensing registers 1931-60, licensing files 1953-66, Explosives Act 1875, registers 1904-59, juvenile court register 1933-41, juvenile court minutes 1944-54, probation files 1953-63, register of bastardy orders 1861-67, instalment registers 1958-64, collecting officers' account books 1947-56

Blackburn Borough (PSBk): Minutes 1900–46, court registers 1914–50, bastardy orders 1845–72, 1880–85, 1890–91, 1912–26, maintenance orders 1886–1935, approved school orders 1905, 1906, 1942, 1968, licensing registers 1872–1932, register of licences referred 1905–10, club register 1903–62, dog-licence register 1934–39, licensing lease register 1936–51, probation registers 1908–57, adoption registers 1927–60, lunacy registers 1934–60, poor prisoners' defence list 1931–64, registers and cash books 1911–14, 1933–37, seal matrices 19th century

Bolton County Division (PSBo): Minutes and orders 1869–1956, court registers 1919–43, juvenile court register 1933–55, magistrates' oath books 1896–1968

Church Division (PSCh): Minutes 1919–40, court registers 1880–1941, court files 1953–60, licensing registers 1940–60, licensing files 1944–60, juvenile court minutes 1933–47, probation orders 1938–52, probation committee minutes 1926–50

Colne Borough (PSCo): Minutes 1918–20, draft minutes 1910–31, licensing and probation committee minutes 1914–44

Colne County Division (PSCo): Court register 1905–15

Darwen Division (PSDa): Minutes 1906–41, court registers 1881–84, 1915–51, court files 1944–67, committal and appeal papers 1961–67, licensing minutes 1881–1947, licensing registers 1905–65, licensing files 1904–31, 1954–67, juvenile court registers 1933–53, fees and fines book 1924–54, highways orders 1948–67, Explosives Act 1875, register 1904–53

Garstang Division (PSGa): Minutes 1880–1913, 1921–43, court registers 1885–1951, licensing registers 1872–87, 1925–56, bastardy orders 1859–73, daybook 1879–80, letterbook 1940–42

Hornby Division (PSHo): Minutes 1927–50, court registers 1896–1955, licensing registers 1872–1957, juvenile court minutes 1933–57, juvenile court register 1934–54, adoption register 1932–49, cashbook 1903–29

Kirkdale Division (PSK): Court registers 1885–1955, juvenile court registers 1941–55, juvenile panel 1933–64, probation minutes 1927–59, warrant books 1930–42, maintenance orders 1946–55, fees and fines 1949–54, arrears 1949–57, licensing registers 1953–62, licensing plans 1903–61, club registers 1903–28, music register 1949–61

Kirkham Division (PSKh): Court register 1940–53

Lancaster Borough (PSLa): Court registers 1889–99, 1907–15, 1918–21, 1928–57, licensing registers 1903–26, 1950–62, music registers 1889–1958, club registers 1903–62, juvenile court registers 1933–57

Leyland Hundred (PSLe): Leyland court minutes 1842–75, 1884–1922, Chorley, Croston, Rufford, and Standish court minutes 1839–59, 1870–71, 1875–1921, Leyland court registers 1880–1929, Chorley, Croston, Rufford, and Standish court registers 1880–1929, all divisions court registers 1929–67; licensing registers: Hundred 1872–78, Leyland 1878–1922, Chorley, Croston, Rufford, and Standish 1878–1901, 1903–16, 1918–23, 1926–44; bastardy allegations 1852–57, daybook 1878–80, juvenile court registers 1934–55

Lonsdale North Division (PSLN): Minutes 1867–1937, court registers 1854–78, 1884–91, 1893–1937, licensing registers 1872–1927, plans of Ulverston court 1870–71

Lonsdale South Division (PSLS): Minutes 1889–92, 1893–1911, 1913–42, court registers 1880–1924, 1927–55, licensing registers 1872–88, 1903–50, club register 1903–53, register of sureties 1881–85, juvenile court registers 1934–55

Manchester County Division (PSMa): Minutes 1868–1948, committee minutes 1935–49, letterbook 1910–15

Middleton Division (PSMd and PSMi): Minutes 1859–88, court registers 1880–1929, chairmen's notebooks 1889–99, 1908–20, bastardy information book 1859–87, recognizances 1860–1920, beerhouse convictions 1872–87, mission and charity-box accounts 1897–1907, Middleton and Tonge subdivision minutes 1889–99, 1908–20

Morecambe Borough (PSMo): Minutes 1922–25, 1928–30, court registers 1919–32, ledger 1921–69

Ormskirk Division (PSOr): Court plan c. 1850

Preston Borough (PSPr): Court registers 1916–30, plans of public houses 1887–1950, plans of theatres, cinemas, etc., 1898–1957

Rochdale Borough (PSRo): Court registers 1840–1929, 1933–36

St. Helens Borough (PSSH): Adult registers 1882–1939, register of offenders 1908–10, licensing registers 1882–1913, 1916, 1923–27, 1933–37, licensing minutes 1903–15, lists of licensed victuallers 1882–1901, compensation statements 1906–15, club registers 1903–32, Employers and Workmen Act 1875, plaint and minute book 1891–1901

CORONERS' COURTS (CR)

Blackburn 1919
East Lancashire 1950–72
Preston 1920–74
Rochdale 1911–42

Salford 1925, 1926, 1928, 1937–55

West Derby 1882–1974 (including treasure trove files for Kirkby 1953

Ormskirk 1949

St. Helens 1913

Up Holland 1921

For the manorial coroners of Hale and Prescot see pp. 193 and 173 respectively and for Walton-le-Dale see *De Hoghton Deeds and Papers*, p. 193; for borough of Clitheroe see p. 44.

COUNTY COURT RECORDS

Blackburn (DDX/168): plaint book 1841–43

Clitheroe (CYC): letter books 1822–54, cause lists 1847–50, 1854, 1855, 1858, court orders 1847–52, 1855, summons lists 1853–54, 1856–58, day books 1822–32, 1833–55, ledgers 1820–51, debt book 1824–49, expenses book 1852–59, monthly accounts 1849–55, minute books 1833–46, 1853–54, memorandum books 1850–56

PALATINATE OF LANCASTER RECORDS

Assize Rolls (PPLC): 1664, 1668, 1669, 1672, 1673

Calendars of Crown Prisoners (QJC): 1801–29, 1832–37; (DDX/255) 1767

Miscellanea (DDCm): correspondence 1818–19, assize statistics 1798–1818, commutation of death sentence orders 1819–42, rules of court 1831–70, fiats for additions to commissions of the peace 1838–40, cause lists 1853–74, depositions 1852–72, jury lists 1869–75, judgment roll 1869–75, prothonotary's letter book 1853–55, writs 1377–79, 1860–68, fines 1469–1504, assignment of gaol 1793, insolvent debtors' papers 1809–24; (DDPr) seal-keeper: fiats for additions to commission of the peace 1786–1808, accounts 1760–68, 1771–93, correspondence 1767–93; (DDPd) seal-keeper's correspondence 1791–1822

APPEALS TRIBUNAL 1916–1917 (TA)

Forms and memoranda: group and class systems administration, list of tribunal members, circular letters, list and plan of areas, notices to farmers, notes on cases, lists of certified occupations, regulations, conscientious objection applications, Home Office and Board of Trade pamphlets

PROBATE RECORDS*

Reference should be made to the *Handlist of Genealogical Sources* published by the Lancashire Record Office.

Diocese of Chester (Lancashire south of the Ribble, with the addition of the chapelry of Saddleworth, co. York).

Act Books (supra): 1580–88, 1590–92, 1596–1644, 1649, 1660–95, 1719, 1722, 1723, 1728–41, 1765–1858

Act Books (infra): 1660, 1661, 1663, 1666, 1667, 1729–40, 1765–1800, 1826–58

Entry Books: 1684–1770

Registers (supra): these are full copies of the wills, 1838–58

Fee Books (supra and infra): 1722–29, 1737–47, 1754–82, 1789–1808; up to 1777 these books contain details of the majority of probate acts and thus are a useful substitute for the missing act books.

Caveats (supra): 1587–1602

Rural Deans' Court Books: 1799–1802

Original wills, inventories, administrations, and tuition bonds, executors accounts', depositions, etc.: 1487–1858 in three series, supra, infra and contentious cases.

Indexes: a variety of original indexes have been printed by the Record Society of Lancashire and Cheshire for the period 1487–1825.

Archdeaconry of Richmond (five Western deaneries, of which Amounderness and Furness were wholly in Lancashire, Copeland wholly in Cumberland, Kendal partly Lancashire, partly Westmorland, and Lonsdale partly Lancashire, partly Westmorland, and partly Yorkshire West Riding).

Act Books and indexes: Amounderness 1670–72, 1719–1858, Copeland, Furness, Kendal, and Lonsdale 1712–1858

Original wills, inventories, administration and tuition bonds, etc.: 1457–1858

Registers: Copeland, Furness, Kendal and Lonsdale 1697–1706, 1697–1731, 1810–11

Indexes: indexes of the Lancashire items 1457–1858 have been printed by the Record Society of Lancashire and Cheshire.

---

* See Jones, B.C., *The Lancashire Probate Records*, Hist. Soc. Lancs. & Ches. Vol. 104 (1952).

Manorial Peculiar of Halton

Original wills, inventories, administration and tuition bonds: 1615–1815

Register: 1743–1806

Lancaster Probate Registry

Registers: 1858–1938

Liverpool Probate Registry

Registers: 1858–1940 (up to 1875 severely damaged)

Principal Probate Registry

Calendars: 1858–1928

TITHE

Diocese of Blackburn (DRB): tithe awards and plans (many with altered apportionments and certificates of redemption):

Adlington 1842, Aldcliffe 1847, Alston 1837, Altham 1842, Anderton 1844, Arkholme-with-Cawood 1848 and 1849, Ashton-with-Stodday 1842, Barnacre-with-Bonds 1839 and 1846, Barton 1847 (photo), Bilsborrow 1840, Bispham 1845, Bispham-with-Norbreck 1848, Bolton-le-Sands 1846, Borwick 1846, Bretherton 1838, Briercliffe-with-Extwistle 1850, Brindle 1839, Broughton 1839, Bryning-with-Kellamergh 1839, Bulk 1843, Burnley 1846, Burrow-with-Burrow 1849, Cabus 1844, Cantsfield 1846, Carleton 1838, Carnforth 1846, Caton 1843, Catterall 1846 and 1847, Charnock Richard 1842, Chatburn 1845, Chipping 1840, Chorley 1839, Claughton-in-Amounderness 1839, Claughton-in-Lonsdale 1847 (photo), Clayton-le-Woods 1838, Cleveley 1844, Clifton-with-Salwick 1840, Clitheroe 1842, Cockerham 1850, Colne 1842, Coppull 1842, Croston 1837, Cuerden 1839, Dalton 1837, Dilworth 1837, Downham 1850, Dutton 1837, Duxbury 1843, Eccleshill 1843, Eccleston 1841, Ellel 1845, Elston 1837, Elswick 1839, Euxton 1847, Farington 1839, Farleton 1848, Fishwick 1843, Forton 1846, Foulridge 1842, Freckleton 1838, Fulwood 1847, Goosnargh-with-Newsham 1849, Great Eccleston 1838, Greenhalgh-with-Thistleton 1838, Gressingham 1845, Grimsargh-with-Brockholes 1841, Habergham Eaves 1842, Haighton 1840, Halton 1839, Hambleton 1839, Hardhorn-with-Newton 1838, Heapey 1845, Heath Charnock 1842, Heaton-with-Oxcliffe 1838, Hesketh-with-Becconsall 1839, Heskin 1837, Heysham 1838, Hoghton 1841, Holleth 1840, Hornby 1848, Hothersall 1838, Howick 1840, Ightenhill Park 1839, Inskip-with-Sowerby 1839, Kirkham 1837, Kirkland 1847,

Lancaster 1845, Layton-with-Warbreck 1838, Lea, Ashton, Ingol, and Cottam 1838, Leck 1846, Leyland 1838, Little Eccleston-with-Larbreck 1839, Little Hoole 1839, Longton 1839, Lytham 1840, Marsden 1849, Marton 1839, Mawdesley 1837, Medlar-with-Wesham 1839, Melling-with-Wrayton 1849, Middleton 1844, Much Hoole 1839, Nateby 1844, Nether Kellet 1840, Nether Wyresdale 1839, Newton-with-Scales 1838, Osbaldeston 1850, Over Kellet 1840, Overton 1844, Over Wyresdale 1848, Padiham 1839, Parbold 1837, Penwortham 1839, Pilling 1845, Pilling Lane 1847, Poulton-le-Fylde 1839, Poulton, Bare, and Torrisholme 1839, Preesall-with-Hackensall 1847, Priest Hutton 1846, Preston 1840, Quernmore 1844, Ramsgreave 1849, Ribbleton 1843, Ribby-with-Wrea 1839, Ribchester 1838, Roeburndale 1849, Rufford 1839, Samlesbury 1849, Scotforth 1844, Shevington 1843, Silverdale 1846, Singleton 1839, Skerton 1841, Slyne-with-Hest 1845, Stalmine-with-Stainall 1841, Standish-with-Langtree 1842, Tarleton 1840, Tatham 1848, Thornley-with-Wheatley 1840, Thornton-le-Fylde 1839, Thurnham 1843, Trawden 1844, Treales, Wharles, and Roseacre 1840, Tunstall 1846, Twiston 1843, Ulnes Walton 1837, Upper Rawcliffe-with-Tarnacre 1840, Walton-le-Dale 1839, Warton-with-Lindeth 1846, Weeton-with-Preese 1840, Welch Whittle 1842, Wennington 1849, Westby-with-Plumptons 1840, Wheelton 1846, Whittingham 1850, Whittington 1848, Whittle-le-Woods 1840, Winmarleigh 1849, Withnell 1840, Woodplumpton 1838, Worthington 1843, Wray-with-Botton 1849, Wrightington 1841, Yate and Pickup Bank 1851 (photo), Yealand Conyers 1846, Yealand Redmayne 1846

Diocese of Carlisle (DRC): tithe awards and plans:

Aldingham 1846, Angerton 1806, Dalton-in-Furness 1842, Dunnerdale 1849, Hawkshead, Monk Coniston, and Skelwith (part) 1847, Kirkby Ireleth 1842, Lowick 1849, Osmotherley 1849, Pennington 1840, Seathwaite 1839, Subberthwaite 1849, Ulverston 1850, Urswick 1839 and 1849

Diocese of Liverpool (DRL): tithe awards and plans (many with altered apportionments and certificates of redemption):

Abram 1844, Aintree 1845, Allerton 1839, Altcar 1848, Ashton-in-Makerfield 1839, Aspull 1841, Aughton 1848, Bickerstaffe 1841, Billinge 1843, Birkdale 1845, Bold 1840, Bootle-cum-Linacre 1839, Burscough 1846, Burtonwood 1839, Childwall 1846, Cronton 1843, Croxteth Park 1838, Cuerdley 1842, Culcheth 1838, Dalton 1842, Ditton 1844, Downholland 1843, Eccleston 1840, Everton 1846, Fazakerley 1846, Formby 1845, Garston 1841, Golborne 1838, Great Crosby 1844, Great Sankey 1839,

Haigh 1796, Hale 1841, Halewood 1843, Halsall 1845, Haydock 1839, Hindley 1839, Houghton, Middleton, and Arbury 1840, Huyton 1850, Ince Blundell 1844, Ince-in-Makerfield 1841, Kenyon 1839, Kirkby 1839, Kirkdale 1840, Knowsley 1847, Lathom 1846, Lathom Newburgh 1846, Litherland 1845, Little Crosby 1844, Little Woolton 1848, Lowton 1838, Lunt 1845, Lydiate 1844, Maghull 1840, Melling 1840, Much Woolton 1840, Netherton 1845, Newton-in-Makerfield 1839, North Meols 1839 and 1840, Ormskirk 1845, Orrell 1841, Orrell and Ford 1845, Parr 1843, Pemberton 1848, Penketh 1840, Poulton-with-Fearnhead 1840, Prescot 1847, Rainford 1841, Rainhill 1843, Rixton-with-Glazebrook 1840, Roby 1849, Scarisbrick 1839, Sefton 1845, Simonswood 1840, Skelmersdale 1839, Southworth-with-Croft 1837, Speke 1844, Sutton 1808, Tarbock 1847, Thornton 1845, Toxteth Park 1847, Up Holland 1845, Walton-on-the-Hill 1847, Warrington 1837, Wavertree 1846, West Derby 1838, Whiston 1842, Widnes 1808, Wigan 1838, Windle 1808, Winstanley 1838, Winwick-with-Hulme 1838, Woolston-with-Martinscroft 1840

Diocese of Manchester (DRM): tithe awards and plans (many with altered apportionments and certificates of redemption):

Ainsworth 1838, Alkrington 1838, Anglezarke 1849, Ardwick 1844, Ashworth 1840 (photo), Astley 1846, Atherton 1839, Barton-upon-Irwell 1849, Bedford 1847, Birtle-cum-Bamford 1845, Blackley 1844, Blackrod 1841, Bradford 1845, Broughton 1844, Burnage 1845, Bury 1837, Butterworth 1846, Chadderton 1840, Cheetham 1846, Chorlton-cum-Hardy 1847, Chorlton-on-Medlock 1849, Cowpe Lenches, New Hall Hey, and Hall Carr 1839, Crompton 1845, Crumpsall 1846, Denton 1849, Didsbury 1845, Droylsden 1847, Elton 1838, Failsworth 1845, Farnworth 1850, Flixton 1843, Gorton 1844, Great Heaton 1839, Great Lever 1845, Halliwell 1851, Harpurhey 1846, Haughton 1845, Heap 1838, Heaton 1845, Heaton Norris 1848, Hopwood 1840, Horwich 1851, Hulme 1854, Kearsley 1855, Kirkmanshulme 1846, Levenshulme 1844, Little Bolton 1845, Little Heaton 1846, Little Hulton 1844, Lostock 1849, Manchester and Beswick 1849 (photo), Middle Hulton 1844, Middleton 1839, Moss Side 1849, Moston 1848, Newton 1846, Oldham 1848, Openshaw 1844, Pennington 1847, Pilkington 1841, Pilsworth 1838, Prestwich 1839, Radcliffe 1841, Reddish 1846, Rivington 1850, Royton 1847, Rumworth 1849, Rusholme 1848, Spotland 1845, Stretford 1838, Thornham 1839, Tonge 1839, Tottington Higher End 1838, Tottington Lower End 1842, Tyldesley-with-Shakerley 1847, Urmston 1842, Walmersley-with-Shuttleworth 1838, Westhoughton 1850, Westleigh 1846, Withington 1848 (photo)

HOSPITAL RECORDS (HR)

Accrington Victoria Cottage Hospital: organizing committee minutes 1894–98, house committee minutes 1911–15, 1919–48, staff meeting minutes 1940–48, employers' hospital fund committee minutes 1944–48, annual reports 1898–1945, registers of in-patients 1898–1920, 1925–32, 1936–41, 1949–54, registers of out-patients 1936–51, operations books 1916–22, 1926–65, press cuttings 1946–51

Blackburn Queen's Park: registers (chronological) 1885–1913, (alphabetical) 1894–1949, sub-committee minutes 1930–48, reports to committees 1927–45, birth registers 1936–47,1950–52, death registers 1914–30, 1938–51, inmates' property registers 1914–33, children's registers 1921–43, visitors book 1948–60, registers of mechanical restraint 1906–59, registers of seclusion 1914–59, index of officers 1882–1942, wages receipt books 1916–22, offences and punishment book 1933–46, obstetric record 1939–44, register of probationer nurses 1941–51, suppliers' register 1942–48, pupil midwives, register 1944–50, inventories 1947, operations record 1920–39, register of Lunacy Act patients 1920–59, psychiatric patients' ward reports 1957–64

Blackburn Royal: board and committee minutes 1857–1958, annual reports 1865–1947, operations book 1924–56, accident books 1939–57, in-patients registers 1930–38, 1942–54, out-patients' registers 1930–53, indices to registers 1926–53, financial records 1885–1957, press cuttings 1911–45, visitors' reports 1920–41, mortuary book 1948–59, dispensary stock book 1895–1901, register of domiciliary visits 1920–32, dental register 1925–39, joint consultative staff committee minutes 1950–52, physiotherapy register 1954–56, East Lancashire workpeople's hospital fund minutes 1938–49 and reports 1945–46

Burnley Joint Board: annual reports 1927–45

Burnley Victoria: minutes 1890–1946, annual reports 1886–1947

Chorley: minutes 1893–1946, committee minutes 1910–48, annual reports 1834–1947, in-patients' registers 1927–43, 1945, press cuttings 1883–1909, 1924–47

Clitheroe: management committee minutes 1949–67, administrative officers' minutes 1957–67, finance and establishment sub-committee minutes 1949–67, supplies sub-committee minutes 1957–67, building sub-committee minutes 1957–67, financial records 1954–61, creed registers 1935–68, institution day books 1938–49, 1951–57, birth register 1950–51, death register 1950–69, admission and discharge registers 1934–72, daily report books 1958–64, register of mechanical restraint 1901–48, medical examination book 1945–49, medical officers' report books 1926–55, register of dangerous drugs 1935–52, visitors' books 1934–51, case book 1934–48, casualty book 1953–67, cash register 1897–1961.

Colne: minutes 1900–48, annual reports 1900–47; (MBCo) Jubilee Hospital register 1900–18

Earby (UDEa): minutes 1925–41, admittance books 1941–48, financial papers 1925–48

Fylde, Preston, and Garstang Joint Board: minutes 1896–1918

Horwich, Westhoughton, and Blackrod Joint Board: minutes 1900–39, ledgers 1901–09, 1915–28

Lancaster Moor: casebooks: general 1826–57, 1859–65, men 1865–1911, women, 1865–1910; case notes: men 1911–43, women 1911–44; medical registers 1915–38, pauper registers 1907–43, registers of discharges and transfers 1907–30, register of departures 1931–44, death registers 1911–54; see also QAM/1

Ormskirk, Lathom, and Burscough Joint Board: minutes 1901–31, ledgers 1902–25

Padiham (UDPa): committee minutes 1907–34

Preston Sharoe Green: admission registers: under Lunacy Acts 1926–48, persons of unsound mind 1943–48; maternity register 1935, staff register 1930–48, mortuary register 1936–43

Preston Lostock Hall: register of nurses 1922–48, register of servants 1922–48

Prestwich Polefield Hall: finance committee minutes 1915–19

Whittingham: minutes 1873–1947, admission registers 1873–1930, reception orders 1873–1930, salary records and miscellanea 19th and 20th century

INSURANCE COMMITTEES (IC)

Barrow-in-Furness: minutes 1912–41, registers of payments to doctors 1933–48, record of drug testing cases 1925–32, doctors' account book 1930–43, cash book 1912–43, ledger 1913–49, correspondence 1913–34

Blackburn: minutes 1912–38, 1943–48, register of payments to doctors 1948, cash book 1939–48, ledger 1913–39

Blackpool: (all before 1936 destroyed by fire): minutes 1936–48, registers of payments to chemists 1936–46, register of payments to doctors 1936–48, cash book 1936–48

Bolton: minutes 1913–48, register of payments to doctors 1942–48, ledger 1913–48, press cuttings 1912–19

Bootle: minutes 1912–48, register of doctors 1914–24, register of claims 1913–39, register of payments for drugs, etc., 1916–29, register of payments to doctors 1914–45, cash book 1912–31

Burnley: minutes 1912–48, cash book 1934–47, press cuttings 1913–30

Bury: minutes 1939–48, cash book 1943–46, register of sealed documents 1914–48, superannuation files 1928–47

Lancashire: minutes 1912–48, registers of payments to doctors 1921, 1924, 1926, registers of payments for drugs, etc., 1916, 1919, 1923, 1928, 1932, wages book 1914–19, superannuation statements 1924–41

Oldham: minutes 1913–48, cash summaries 1912–49

Preston: minutes 1912–48, cash books 1936–49, salaries book 1938–48, registers of payments to doctors 1936–49, government circulars 1913–16, 1920–24, 1928–48

Rochdale: minutes 1937–48

St. Helens: minutes 1912–16

Southport: minutes 1912–48

Warrington: minutes 1913–48, register of payments to doctors 1913–38, registers of payments to chemists 1927–43, cash books 1912–44, ledger 1912–49, invalided men attendance system 1917–20

Wigan: minutes 1912–48

LAND TAX COMMISSIONERS (LT)

Blackburn division: declarations of secrecy 1842–99

Ormskirk division: appeal minutes 1873–92, 1905–36

Wigan division: minutes and oath books 1797–1907

LAND TAX AND VALUATION OFFICERS (LT)

Amounderness division: assessment books 1916–36

Blackburn division: assessment books 1936–49

Leyland division: assessment books 1922–36

Warrington division: assessment books 1851–52, 1929–49, analysis of commercial property 1950

LOCAL PENSIONS COMMITTEES (LP)

Barrowford: minutes 1908–29

Birkdale: minutes 1908–12

Blackburn Rural: minutes 1918–32, register of claims 1908–31, correspondence 1934–47

Brierfield: minutes 1908–27, register of claims 1908–23

Fleetwood: minutes 1927–31

North Ribble: minutes 1918–31

Ormskirk: minutes 1924–42

Rishton: minutes 1908–30, register of claims 1923–28, correspondence 1921–47

NATIONAL COAL BOARD (NC)

Ackers, Whitley and Co., Wigan area, officials' wages books 1897–1920

Alkrington Colliery: mines and brickworks particulars of sale 1875–78, 1896

Ashton Moss Colliery Co.: press cuttings 1875–1915

Astley and Tyldesley Coal and Salt Co.: measurement of coal got 1882–92, legal papers 1846–1918, plans 1863–1922, solicitors' accounts 1867–74, 1893–97, correspondence and miscellanea 1868–1924

Atherton Collieries: pension fund minute book 1930–53, sick and burial society and pension fund accounts 1944–55; (DDX 991) ledger 1821–72, journal 1868–72

Bickershaw Collieries: officials' wages books 1920–30, 1936–41, 1943–46, other wages books 1938–39, 1942–47

Blainscough Colliery Co.: sick and relief society account book 1938–54

Bridgewater Collieries: salaries journals 1824–1924, wages records 1826–33, 1840–69, cash books 1769–70, 1772–83, 1789–94, 1798–99, 1807–15, 1818–21, 1838, 1840–51, 1854, 1856–57, 1900–04, 1920–29, general accounts 1763–1810, 1844–50, abstracts of accounts 1829–37, letter books 1878–96, production output 1886–97, sales contracts 1908–35, prices for getting coal 1903–16, heavy items of cost 1908–17, 1921–28, mine rents and royalties 1913–22, general ledger 1909–31, valuation 1914, register of debenture holders 1925–33, general journal 1911–14, 1921–34, estate rental 1923–29, estate ledger 1921–30, legal documents 1803–1910, agents' notebooks 1873–74, 1878, correspondence and papers 1807–1920, later records 1921–48, Bridgewater Wharves papers 1921–34

Clifton and Kearsley Coal Co. (including Outwood Colleries and Pilkington Colliery Co.): share registers 1909–29, private ledgers 1885–1929, private journals 1885–1929, cash book 1928–30, balance sheets 1885–1928, expenses accounts 1912–13, stock books 1896–1928, wages and salaries records 1912–31, farm accounts 1910–29; Outwood Collieries: register of members 1909–25, private ledger and journal 1909–29, balance sheets 1909–28, stock books 1909–28, wages books 1907–31; Pilkington Colliery Co.: register of members 1907–24, private ledger and journal 1908–29, balance sheets 1908–28, monthly trading accounts 1913–29, stock book 1912–18, costs of sinking Astley Green pits 1907–13

Cliviger Coal and Coke Co.: cash books 1846–1935, impersonal ledger 1890–1928, capital accounts 1856–1933, sales ledgers 1849–1947, delivery ledgers 1855–57, 1861–70, 1888–1946, day books 1870–75, bad debts ledgers 1853–1931, pit day books 1855–59, 1879–80, get books 1855–64, rent and gas books 1871–1942, goods received books 1855–59, 1876–85, 1914–27, invoices 1865–1914, receipts 1887–1903, 1910–51, wages books 1852–81, wages sheets 1881–1902, pit production committee minutes 1945–47, correspondence and papers 1820–1938.

Collins Green Colliery Co., Warrington: letter book 1896–1907, reports of accidents 1936–44.

Richard Evans and Co., Ashton-in-Makerfield: list of shareholders c. 1880–1900, deed registers 1889–91, c. 1920, legal documents 1851–1923, agency books c. 1855–c. 1914, rent books 1889–1946, letter books c. 1877–99, letters and papers 1877–1900, photograph albums 1912–45, prices book 1897–1929, Old Boston colliery canteen committee minutes 1942–52, Lyme colliery explosion papers 1930, water supply papers 1876–1901; see also DDPk

Fletcher, Burrows and Co., Atherton: monthly pit sales 1886–87, dispute photograph 1893, analyses of wages 1902–14, price lists 1908

Garswood Hall Colliery Co., Ashton-in-Makerfield: minutes 1893–1937, wages books 1924–47, cash book 1929–42, sales and purchases book 1931–42, non-employees subscription lists 1939–41; see also DDGe

Hargreaves Collieries: George Hargreaves and Co. Accrington and Rossendale: general balances 1895–1933, coal ledgers 1871–89, 1916–32, rentals *c.* 1870–1947, register of boys 1917–25, wage books 1909–50, daily tub book 1847–69, compensation correspondence 1916–39, mine inspection book 1932–38, 1961; John Hargreaves Ltd., Burnley and Habergham Eaves: annual returns 1893–1902, balance sheets 1911–35, private accounts 1915–33, stock and plant records 1834–72, 1904–32, valuations 1913, 1920, rentals 1904–47, weekly output books 1930–37, prices, wages and agreements 1891–1944, press cuttings 1893–97, 1903–05, 1941–46; Hargreaves Collieries Ltd.: debenture records 1932–48, cash books 1934–40, output and stock books 1937–43, wages books 1936–46, deputation minutes 1910–47, pithead bath records 1932–52, contract agreement book 1937–49, correspondence 1932–52, deeds 1495–1946.

Hulton Colliery Co.: ledgers 1886–1935, journals 1907–35, output books 1916–18, 1930–42, agents' reports 1943–46, tax books 1916–30, disaster enquiries 1911, 1917

Andrew Knowles and Sons, Manchester: salaries journals 1894–1921, office wages 1927–30.

Lancashire Associated Collieries: Central Coalmines Scheme 1930–38, reports 1932–48, accounts 1936–46, lists of collieries 1935–45, sales records 1935–40, lists of employees 1937–49, staff pension fund minutes 1937–49, social club minutes 1937–50

Lancashire Foundry Coke Co. Altham: debtors' ledger 1930–35, wages books 1930–42, agreements 1930, 1940

Landgate Colliery Co.: production committee minutes 1941–45

Manchester Collieries: shareholders' meeting papers 1930–38, legal documents 1921–46, reports 1934–45, officials' meeting papers 1938–46, ledgers 1928–46, journals 1929–45, cash books 1929–47, private journal 1930–46, profit and loss books 1931–46, valuations 1931–42, rentals 1929–47, get books 1929–44, wages and salaries 1902–14, 1929–38, pension fund minutes 1930–54, safety records 1937, 1941–46, conciliation records 1941–46, welfare records 1928–51, chairman's miscellanea 1928–42

Moss Hall Coal Co., Wigan: statements of value 1904–43, wages book 1912–14

Pearson and Knowles Coal and Iron Co, Wigan: quantity books 1883–1937

William Ramsden and Sons: debit ledger 1915–35

St. Helens Collieries Ltd.: journals 1934–45, wage sheets 1945–47, report on merger 1933

34

J. and R. Stone and Co., Ashton-in-Makerfield: articles of association 1911–51, annual reports 1923–49, legal papers 1887–1944, ledgers 1869–1945, day books 1869–78, cash books 1900–42, goods received book 1898–1910, purchase journals 1933–52, private accounts 1887–1930, balance sheets 1925–34, 1946–52, royalties book 1889–1932, voucher books 1869–93, 1947–49, get books 1878–82, 1892–95, 1933–42, wagon day books 1873–88, engineers' letter book 1922–26, analysis reports 1922–48, memoranda book 1878–1942, surface time book 1887–88, 1931–49, stoppage books 1880–91, wage books 1870–84, 1921–47, correspondence 1918–54, personal financial records 1900–53

Sutton Heath and Lea Green Collieries Co., St. Helens: wages agreement books 1911–49, get book 1943–53, Lea Green miners' relief society minutes 1933–64

Sutton Manor Collieries, St. Helens: miners' welfare fund papers 1934–43; see also DDSm

Towneley Coal and Fireclay Co.: rental 1915–48, fines book 1912–58

Tyldesley Coal Co.: memoranda book 1884–1912, agents' reports 1890–94

Wigan Coal and Iron Co.: get records 1866–1930, sales records 1903–39, brick sales book 1904–51, legal papers 1879–1936, letter book 1923–25, clock face reports 1924–42; see also DDX/129

Wigan Coal Corporation: statistics 1944–45, classification book 1945–46, costs records 1931–46

Wigan Junction Co.: wages book 1914–16

SHIPPING RECORDS (SS)

Crew lists of ships registered at Fleetwood, Lancaster, and Preston 1863–1913.

Crew lists of fishing vessels registered at Fleetwood 1884–1914

Part II

Official Records

COUNTY COUNCIL

County Councils were established under the Local Government Act 1888, and that for the County Palatine of Lancaster ceased to exist on 31 March 1974, following the Local Government Act 1972. It was replaced by the Lancashire County Council on 1 April 1974, which administers a considerably reduced area. The achievements of the 'old' County Council are chronicled in *The History of Lancashire County Council 1889 to 1974*, edited by J. D. Marshall, 1977.

Minute books (CCM) 1889–1974

Attendance books (CCA) 1939–56

Bye-laws (CCB) 1909–60

Orders (CCO) 1889–1974

Year books (CCY) 1891–1974

Notices of motion (CCN) 1889–1958

Registers of deeds (CCR)

Registers of documents sealed (CCR) 1889–1947

Highway diversion orders (CSD) 1972 to date

COMMITTEES

Minutes, etc. of the following committees and sub-committees of the County Council:

Agricultural Committee (CM) 1919–47 and its sub-committees: Accounts (CAM) 1920–47, Alt Drainage (CFM) 1923–30, County Livestock and Horse-breeding (CKM) 1921–32, Croston Drainage (CBM) 1920–31, Cultivation (CEM) 1919–21, Diseases of Animals (CDM) 1920–47, Glazebrook Drainage (CGM) 1929–32, Husbandry (CSM) 1921–42, Land Drainage (CLM) 1919–47, Overton Drainage (COM) 1920–36, Small-holdings and Allotments (CHM) 1920–47, Spen Dyke Drainage (CIM) 1925–33

Air Raid Precautions Committees (ARP): Precautions 1938–39, Emergency 1939–45, Joint Accounts 1939–49; Home Office circulars 1939–45, Ministry of Health circulars 1940–44, County Control Centre (RC) (incident reports, message books, raid warnings, unexploded bomb records, register of requisitioned premises, etc.) 1939–45

Capital Allocations Committee (CMA) 1971–74

Chairmen's Committee (GCM) 1918–31

Children's Committee (CWM) 1946–70, its area sub-committees (CWO) 1952–70: and other sub-committees (CWS): Boarding-out and Homes Management 1947–70, Adoption Case 1961–70, Finance and General Purposes 1970, Approved School Management 1968–70, Special Residential Establishments 1970, Children and Young Persons Act 1963, 1964–70, Boothstown Remand Home (EUM) 1946–70

Civil Defence Committee (DCM) 1949–68

Co-ordination Committee (GM) 1931–53; Architects' Department sub-committee (GMS) 1939–47

County Horse-breeding Committee (HRM) 1911–20

County Pensions Committee (CPM) 1928–47

County Rate Committee (CRM) 1901–29

Diseases of Animals Acts Committee (DAM) 1904–1919; Acting sub-committee (DAS) 1905–08

Diseases of Animals Acts and Smallholdings Committee (DAM) 1951–70

Establishment Committee (XM) 1947–73

Estates and Industrial Development Committee (IDM) 1970–74; Smallholdings sub-committee (IDS) 1972–73

Executive Cattle Plague Committee (CNM) 1889–1904; district sub-committees (CNS) 1889–93

Finance Committee (FM) 1889–1974 and its sub-committees: Audit (FAM) 1907–53, Building Policy (FOM) 1970–73, Central Vehicle Maintenance (FYM) 1956–59, County Buildings (FXM) 1898–1912, 1942–53, County Hall Redevelopment (FHM) 1959–69, County Mess (FMM) 1942–55, County Records (FVM) 1941–74, Disciplinary (FIM) 1959–68, Estimates (FNM) 1948–72, General Purposes (FGM) 1953–70, Lancaster Division (FLM) 1850–1942, Local Taxation Licences (FTM) 1922–70, Preston Court-house (FCM) 1898–1903, Preston Division (FPM) 1845–1942, Registration of Births and Deaths (FBM) 1930–53, Salford Division (FSM) 1842–

1942, Superannuation (FFM) 1924–45, Travelling Expenses (FEM) 1948–49, West Derby Division (FDM) 1851–1942; wage-book of County Office cleaners, etc. (FW) 1888–1965, inventory of County Offices (FXV) 1878–91

Financial Adjustments Committee (JM) 1889–1905

Fire Services Committee (KM) 1947–74, General Purposes and Accounts sub-committee (KMS) 1948–62

Health Committee (HM) 1947–69 and its sub-committees: Ambulance and Health Services Transport (HTM) 1947–70, Ambulance Special (HUM) 1957–67, Disciplinary (HVM) 1950–61, Division No. 7 (HDM) 1948–74, Family Unit Accommodation (HYM) 1960–69, Finance and General Purposes (HFM) 1970–73, Mental Health (HSM) 1947–70, Nursing Service (HNM) 1947–70, Social Service Co-ordination (HSC) 1967, Welfar Services (HWM) 1948–70, Welfare Services Special (HXM) 1956–68

Highways and Bridges Committee (MBM) 1893–1974 and its sub-committees: Advisory (MBA) 1945–62, County Planning (MPM) 1930–48, Disciplinary (MBD) 1968–69, Liverpool and East Lancashire Road (MEM) 1927–35, Widnes-Runcorn Bridge (MBC) 1946–62

Lancashire Education Committee (EM) 1903–73 and its sub-committees: Accidents (EIM) 1952–53, Accounts (EFM) 1903–48, Agricultural (EAM) 1905–72, Air Raid Precautions (ECM) 1938–42, Architectural (EBM) 1905–72, Boothstown Remand Home (EUM) 1942–70, Camp Schools (EES) 1947–63, Defective Children (EMS) 1920–24, Disciplinary (EWM) 1961–73, District Administration (EDM) 1904–17, Evening Schools and Classes (EGM) 1905–07, Farm (EAS) 1904–53, Further Education (EHM) 1903–72, General Purposes (EJM) 1948–72, Horticultural (EAS) 1911–14, Libraries (ELM) 1924–67, Primary and Secondary Education (EEM) 1903–72, Pupil Teachers' Centres (ENM) 1904–09, Revision (ERM) 1919–31, Scholarships (ESM) 1903–71, School Health (EMM) 1908–72, School Meals (EQM) 1946–70, Secondary Day Schools (EOM) 1904–09, Special Schools (EES) 1952–72, Teachers' Training Colleges (ETM) 1904–08, Youth (EYM) 1940–72

Divisional Executive Committees*: Ashton-under-Lyne (EXA) various committees 1905–13; Chorley (EXCh) 1945–74; Darwen (ExDa) 1945–68; Eccles (EXEc) 1945–65, reports 1903–26, newspaper cuttings 1905–36; Farnworth (EXFa) 1951–

---

* In the case of a borough, reference should also be made to the records of that borough.

38

65, other committees 1903–51, sub-committees 1903–48, salaries register 1929–47; Flixton (EXF) various committees 1925–39, staff books 1928–45, staff returns 1915–46; Fulwood (EXP) 1945–50, sub-committees 1903–45, school files *c.* 1945–*c.* 1964, staff papers 1947–66, correspondence 1945–68; Kearsley and Little Lever (EXLL) sub-committees 1927–45; Poulton-le-Fylde (EXK1) district committee 1912–44; Lytham St. Annes, (EXK1) sub-committee 1940–47; Prescot (EXPr) 1945–69 other committees 1903–70; Ramsbottom (EXRm) sub-committee 1909–45; Rishton (EXRi) 1945–64, other committees 1903–64, staff registers 1885–68, evacuation papers 1939–43, correspondence 1934–46; Thornton and Fleetwood (EXTF) various committees 1903–48; Tottington and Ainsworth (EXTo) various committees 1905–45; Ulverston (EXU1) 1928–70

Reports of the Chief Education Officer (EKR) 1904–73, County Librarian (ELR) 1930–66, Medical Superintendent of Schools (EMR) 1909–71

Libraries Committee (YR) reports of the County Librarian 1966–72

Local Pension Committee (LPM) 1908–28 and its sub-committees (LPS): Barrowford 1908–29, Birkdale and district 1908–12, Blackburn district 1918–32, Brierfield 1908–27, Fleetwood 1927–31, North Ribble 1918–31, Ormskirk 1924–42, Rishton 1908–30

Lunatic Asylums Committee (LAM) 1889–91 and reports (LAR) 1889–90

Midwives Act Committee (MAM) 1904–38

Midwives, Maternity and Child Welfare Committee (MWM) 1938–48 and its Wartime Nurseries sub-committee (MWS) 1942–46

Parliamentary Committee (NM) 1889–1974 and its sub-committees: General Purposes (NGM) 1968–69, Industrial Development (NIM) 1961–72, Local Government Act (NLM) 1894, Review of County Districts (NLR) 1930–33; reports on Review of County Districts (NLM) 1930–33

Planning Development Committee (PDM) 1944–45

Planning Committee (PLM) 1947–74 and its sub-committees: Control of Development (PLS/2) 1948–69, Development Plan PLS/3) 1950–69, General Purposes (PLS/1) 1948–49, Industrial Development (PDI) 1952–59, Moveable Dwellings (PLS/4) 1953–54, White Walls Industrial Estate Management (PDW) 1955–64

Public Assistance Committee (PAM) 1929–48 and its sub-committees: Central Relief (PRM) 1930–48, Contracts (PCM) 1933–48, Emergency (PEM) 1940–43, General Purposes, Finance, and Institutions (PGM) 1930–48

Area Committees:

Ashton-under-Lyne Area (PU/16) Board and sub-committees 1930–46

Blackburn and Clitheroe Area (PU/5): Guardians' Committee 1930–48, Boarding-out sub-committee 1930–47, Coplaw View Management sub-committee 1930–48, Management committee 1937–40, Relief Repayments sub-committee 1930–48, Church Relief sub-committee 1941–48, Clitheroe Relief sub-committee 1940–48, Darwen Relief sub-committee 1939–48, Rishton Relief sub-committee 1939–48

Burnley Area (PUZ): monthly reports on children boarded out 1922–45, register of children in certified schools 1903–47, register of old age pensions 1943–48, receipt and expenditure books 1946–48

Fylde and Garstang Area (PU/3): Guardians' committee 1930–45, Cottage Homes sub-committee 1930–45, Fylde Institution sub-committee 1930–44, Garstang Institution sub-committee 1936–39

Haslingden Area (PU/7): Guardians' committee 1930–44

Lancaster Area (PU/2): General committee 1930–35

Leigh Area (PU/13): Guardians' committee 1930–47, Public Assistance committee 1929–38

Ormskirk Area (PU/8): General committee 1930–46

Prescot Area (PU/12): General committee 1941–43
Rochdale and Bury Area PU/11): Guardians' committee 1930–42

Wigan Area (PU/9): Relief sub-committee 1931–35

Public Health and Housing Committee (PHM) 1889–1970 and its sub-committees: Blind Persons Act (PJM) 1941–48, Housing (PBM) 1920–23, Maternity and Child Welfare (PMM) 1918–38, Water and Sewerage (PWM) 1931–48, 1955–64, Public Health Analyst (PAR) reports 1926–73, Medical Officer of Health (PHR) reports 1889–1971

Selection Committee (SEM) 1948–72

Small Holdings and Allotments Committee (SHM) 1892–1919, 1948–51; register of applications from ex-servicemen (SHV) 1918–31

Social Services Committee (SWM) 1970–74 and its sub-committees:
Approved School Management (SWS/1) 1971–73, Special
Residential Establishments (SWS/2) 1971–73

Technical Instruction Committee (TIM) 1891–1903 and its sub-
committees: Agricultural (TIS/1) 1899–1903, Farm (TIS/2)
1894–1902; reports of the Director of Technical Instruction
(TIR) 1891–1903

Transport Committee (TPM) 1964–74

Tuberculosis Committee (TM) 1913–48; Sanatoria sub-committee
(TSM) 1922–48; reports of the Central Tuberculosis Officer
(TR) 1914–47

War Charities Act Committee (WRM) 1940–47

War Pensions Committee (WPM) 1916–20; Finance and General
Purposes sub-committee (WFM) 1919–21

JOINT COMMITTEES AND BOARDS

The minutes, etc. of a number of Joint Committees and Boards,
on which the County Council has or had representation, are in the
Record Office.

Air Raid Distress Fund (ARD) 1940–49

Co-ordination Committee for Liverpool Overspill (LOM) 1966–73

County Rate Joint Committee (CJM) 1891–1929

County Valuation Committee (VM) 1927–50; Appeals sub-committee (VAM) 1935–39, minutes of sub-panels of valuers (VSM)
1931–48

Joint Committee for New Lancashire County (NCM) 1972–73

Lancashire Inebriates Act Board (IM) 1899–1924 and its committees:
Farm (IFM) 1905–24, Finance (IAM) 1901–24, House (IHM)
1904–24, Sites and Works (ISM) 1900–04

Lancashire (Asylum) Mental Hospitals Board (HBM) 1891–1948 and
its committees: Area Mental Welfare Services (HBS/5) 1945–
48, Ascertainment (HBS/7) 1938–48, Contracts (HBS/4)
1921–48, Finance and General Purposes (HBS/1) 1891–1948,
(HBS/8) 1915–22 and (HBS/3) 1915–48, Mental Deficiency
Acts (HBS/2) 1914–48; reports (HBR) 1891–1938, year books
(HBY) 1924–48

Lancashire River Authority (LRA) reports 1964–74

Lancashire Rivers Board (LRM) 1939–44 and its committees:
Finance and General Purposes (LRS/1) 1939–51, North
Regional (LRS/2) 1939–50, South Regional (LRS/3) 1939–50.
See also WBR/1 p. 62

Lancashire and Western Sea Fisheries Joint Committee (SFM) 1900–29 and its sub-committees (SFS): Finance and General Purposes 1891–1900, 1915–30, Finance 1900–15, General Purposes 1900–15, Scientific 1895–1919, Southern Division 1891–92

Mersey and Irwell Joint Committee (BMM) 1891–1939 and its sub-committees (BMS): Chemical 1893–1926, Consulting 1892–1926, Finance 1895–1939; Epitome of Actions book (BMV) 1893–1936

Onward (North West Building Consortium) Officers' Committee (OM) 1965–74

Police (formerly Standing Joint) Committee (SJM and POM) 1889–1969 and its sub-committees: Building Programme (SJP) 1938–46, General Purposes, Police Accounts and Pensions (SJS) 1942–56

Probation Area Committees (PNM) 1949–65

Ribble Joint Committee (BRM) 1891–1939

Road Safety Committee (RSM) 1947–64

Voluntary Hospitals Committee (VHM) 1921–25

War Agricultural Committee (WAM) 1915–18 and its sub-committees: Cultivation (WCM) 1918–19, Executive (WEM) 1916–19

Wigan and District Mining and Technical College Joint Committee (WTM) 1954–72 and its sub-committees: Finance and General Purposes (WTS) 1954–63, Staffing (WTE) 1954–65

BOROUGH COUNCIL RECORDS

Until their dissolution in 1974, boroughs were the oldest record-keeping local authorities in England. Their powers were variously defined by prescriptive usage, royal charters, and occasionally by Act of Parliament until 1835. In that year the first Municipal Corporations Act established a uniform constitution for boroughs, which were subsequently known as Municipal Boroughs to distinguish them from the larger authorities, called County Boroughs, which were established under the Local Government Act of 1888. The records listed below also include those of predecessor authorities, where relevant, such as local boards of health, established at various dates under the provisions of the Public Health Act, 1848, and of Improvement Commissioners appointed under specific Acts. For an account of the legislative framework see B. Keith-Lucas and P. G. Richards, *A history of local government in the twentieth century*, London, 1978. Under the terms of the Local Government Act, 1972,

Municipal and County Boroughs ceased to exist on 31 March 1974, and were superseded by District and Metropolitan District Councils.

Accrington (MBA) minutes 1902–62, committee minutes 1860–78, street-lighting inspectors' minutes 1841–45, education miscellanea 1903–49, ledgers 1862–1963, housing records 1924–56, mortgage registers 1862–1949, overseers' minutes 1898–1918, rate books 1845–53, property owners' ledger 1926–50

Ashton-under-Lyne (MBAs) education committee minutes 1919–51; (PUA) rate-books 1836–90

*Bacup (MBBa) minutes 1863–82, committee minutes 1865–1913, burial board minutes 1858–82, relief funds committee minutes 1881–86, overseers' minutes 1910–27, valuations 1881–1921

Blackpool (CBBl) rate-books 1844–1912, valuations 1858–1911, Board of Health accounts 1873–75, overseers' minutes 1895–1903, civil defence records 1938–73, fire service records 1933–74, transport records 1897–1960 (DDX25) grant of manor of Layton 1554

Burnley (CBBu) council and committee minutes 1889–1974, education committee minutes 1940–55, abstracts of accounts 1902–60, water managers' reports 1883–1939, medical officers reports 1906–34 and 1955–63

Bury (CBB) minutes 1846–76

Chorley (MBCh) minutes 1854–1961, committee minutes 1853–1948, lighting inspectors' minutes 1832–53, lifeboat committee minutes 1895–99, minutes etc., re Gilchrist Lectures 1885–1900, minutes re memorial to Lt. Gen. Feilden 1885–96, clerks' letter books 1857–1967, and correspondence files 1914–69, education letter book 1887–1901, surveyors' letter books 1884–1947, ledgers 1832–50, and plans 1848–1950, 'The Poor's Book' 1814–45, church rate books 1810–18, other rate books 1811–75, 1881–1961, valuations 1863–1939, bye-laws 1877–1960, burgess rolls 1881–1914, financial records 1854–1972, sewerage records 1854–1909, plans 1848–1950, specifications 1880–1930, deposited plans 1872–1949, planning records 1925–36, overcrowding survey 1939–65, medical officers' reports 1931–71, statutory registers 1871–1965, mortgage records 1854–82, cemetery records c. 1880–1944, sale particulars 1870–1950, register of printing 1902–66, petition for incorporation 1880

---

* additional unlisted deposits not included here.

*Clitheroe (MBC, DDX/19 and DDX/28) enclosure award 1788, rentals 1696–1843, commons marking books 1764–1779, leases of borough lands 1666–1851, election papers 1601–1868, court of pleas papers 1583–1833, court of enquiry papers 1590–1830, court leet papers 1593–1834, recognizances 1590–1820, letters of attorney 1585–1623, bail bonds 1751–1819, affidavits 1761–1820, papers concerning surrender of charters 1684–85, constables' accounts and papers 1662–1811, overseers' accounts and papers 1704–1834, surveyors of highways 1764–92, bailiffs' accounts 1617, 1678, 1694, 1723–1829, Land Tax assessments 1737, 1750, call books for election of bailiffs 1635–1812, poll for election of bailiffs 1747, parish church repair accounts 1818–24, census returns 1801, 1831, militia lists 1763, 1802, 1815, 1817, process books 1608, 1629, 1641, jury lists 1636–63, window tax assessment 1767, coroners' inquests 1795–1801, building bye-law deposited plans 1859–1948 ; (DDX54) contested election papers 1780 (see also DDFr, p. 176)

Colne (MBCo) minutes 1875–95, committee minutes 1876–1903, letter books 1880–94, burial board minutes 1858–97, rate books 1860–1910, valuations 1867, 1898, 1913, ratepayers' meeting minutes 1792–97, 1861–75, 1881–97, firemen's wage book 1887–99, education committee minutes 1926–45, water department log-books accounts etc., 1889–1963

Darwen (MBDa) minutes 1930–45, manor court rolls 1658, 1670, 1671, 1768–1809, boundaries 1364, rental 1591, schedule of leases 1761, conveyances 1563–1882, plan of Bull Hill estate *c.* 1820

Fleetwood (MBF) minutes 1842–64, committee minutes 1842–1964, Whitworth Institute minutes 1873–88, Fielden Library minutes 1888–1906, flood-relief committee minutes 1927–32, war emergency committee minutes 1939–45, financial records 1843–1914, contracts and agreements 1842–67, valuation and rate books 1843, 1844, 1858, 1868, 1876–94, registers of sealed documents 1895–1942, 1955–71, clerks' letter books 1843–1970, mayors' letter books 1949–69, clerks' private letter books 1907–34, foreshore papers 1799–1905, 'general letters' 1872–1907, gasworks papers 1873–1937, papers *re* moving of shingle 1878–80, Local Government Board correspondence 1878–1901, new market papers 1889–94, ferry papers 1890–1934, Jubilee clock papers 1897, tramway papers 1897–1938, steamship papers 1898–1919, miscellaneous papers 1883–1939, Association of Port Sanitary Authorities minutes and papers 1908–15, Parliamentary Bills, Acts, and related papers 1807–

---

* additional unlisted deposits not included here.

1947, licensing committee registers 1885–1959, sewerage papers 1891–1916, war records 1939–45, register of common lodging-houses 1881–1936, register of cowkeepers, etc., 1899–1926, flood disaster papers 1927–28, building plans 1885–1948.

Garstang (DDX386) charter 1679, record book 1663–1887, accounts 1873–1910

*Haslingden (MBH) minutes 1875–1953, committee minutes 1875–1953, letter books 1892–1964, financial records 1891–1967, overseers' accounts 1783–86, vestry minutes 1790–1896, surveyors' minutes and accounts 1875, valuations 1850–1956, survey 1850, rate books 1858–1951, medical officers' reports 1875–1962, sanitary inspectors' reports 1891–1962, surveyors' reports 1891–1951, surveyors' letter books 1910–69, street works records 1877–1962, housing records 1875–1959, tramway records 1898–1946, education minutes 1892–1943, school attendance records 1885–1937, electricity records 1915–33, cemetery records 1896–1938, baths records 1934–50, planning records 1912–53, plans 1849–1965, relief-fund records 1914–64, Personal Service League records 1934–47, World War records 1916–19, A.R.P. records 1938–45, (PUH) overseers' minutes 1895–1927, overseers' financial records 1856–88, 1895–1927

Heywood (MBHe) minutes 1875–81, committee minutes 1864–1928, rate books 1821–1915, lighting accounts 1864–67

*Lancaster (MBLa) minutes 1891–1967, abstracts of accounts 1850–1970, valuation lists 1808–1956, rate books 1801–1961, financial records 1815–1927, overseers' records 1823–80, general incoming correspondence 1903–18, letters from Local Government Board 1908–15, letters from government departments 1912–18, letters *re* war effort 1914–18

Lytham St. Annes (MBLs) Lytham: committee minutes 1847–1922, ratepayers' meeting minutes 1853–98, nuisance reports 1865–68; St. Annes-on-Sea: minutes 1878–88, 1902–06, committee minutes 1878–1906, overseers' minutes 1904–27

Middleton (MBM) minutes 1861–86, committee minutes 1864–94, burial board minutes 1860–1911, overseers' accounts 1773–81, vestry minutes 1860–95, surveyors' minutes 1857–61

Morecambe and Heysham (MBMo) minutes and committee minutes 1852–94, burial board minutes 1873–95, cemetery orders book 1883–87, survey 1824

---

* additional unlisted deposits not included here.

Mossley (MBMy) minutes and committee minutes 1864–1965, accounts 1865–1956, rate books 1869–1950, valuations 1894–1963, overseers' accounts 1895–1927, surveyors' reports 1888–1901, health reports 1914–24, education committee minutes 1908–11, 1925–45, clerks' correspondence 1926–61, mayors' correspondence 1932–35, mortgage registers 1864–91, gas finance 1864–1936, housing finance 1924–43, waterworks finance 1876–1943, plans 1870–1951

Nelson (MBNe) committee minutes 1894–1972, technical school syllabuses 1891–1910, 1913–16, 1922–23, 1930–31, 1936–37, water department letter books 1894–1931, day books 1872–1934, wages books 1881–1967, ledgers 1910–49, account books 1926–48, miscellanea 1865–1957, medical officers' reports 1931–69; (DDBd) correspondence 1861–99; education committee minutes 1909–26, 1930–34, annual reports 1911–29, school medical officers' reports 1908–33, inspectors' reports 1898–1941, letter books 1893–1932, letters received 1893–1930, registers of labour certificates 1901–19

Preston (CBP) minutes 1836–1946, committee minutes 1836–1968, borough court records 1860–1963, oath books 1815–1935, burial board draft minutes 1861–64, fire brigade log books 1949–73, medical officers' reports 1947–57, departmental reports 1878–1921, year books 1951–74, tenancy registers 1907–37, contracts registers 1911–32, waterworks records 1890–1967 and plans 1816–1931, old-age pensioners' records 1908–46, local Acts papers 1805–1906, Ribble Navigation reports 1822–1907, Ribble Navigation Companies' early records 1806–1946, minutes 1837–85, letter books 1860–85, financial records 1837–1901, contracts 1838–1908, arbitrations 1843–1907, pilotage and regulations 1806–98, dredging papers 1836–1926, accidents to shipping papers 1822–1932, legal papers 1799–1926, Ribble Branch Railway records 1869–98, records of vessels owned 1838–1914, miscellanea 1760–1915; (DDX685) deeds of Church Street property 1679–1826

Prestwich (MBPr) minutes 1866–96, committee minutes 1857–1906, vestry minutes 1863–99, letters received 1884–89, ledger 1867–88, rate book 1914

Radcliffe (MBR) minutes and committee minutes 1866–1907, rate books 1867–1900, valuations 1882–1910, overseers' letter books 1885–88, deeds 1791–1965

*Rawtenstall (MBRa) ledgers 1876–86, 1898–1900, 1916–19, expenditure estimates 1897–1917, abstracts of accounts 1893–1903,

* additionnl unlisted deposit not included here.

education ledgers 1920–43, rate books 1848–1935, survey 1839, valuations 1868, 1874, 1883–87, 1895

Rochdale (CBR) minutes 1830–58, committee minutes 1829–63, select vestry minutes 1824–1907, Buersill Local Board minutes 1870–72, militia ledger 1814–15, register of motor cars 1919, rate books 1795–1929, valuations 1850–1909

Stretford (MBS) minutes 1868–1919, committee minutes 1968–1942, records of civilian war deaths 1939–45, miscellanea 1868–1945.

URBAN DISTRICT COUNCIL RECORDS

Urban district councils were created as a result of the Local Government Act, 1894, and absorbed the functions of local boards of health established at various dates under the provisions of the Public Health Act, 1848. The records of both authorities are included below. For an account of the legislative framework see Central Office of Information, *Local Government in Britain*, London, H.M.S.O., 11th ed., 1980. Urban district councils ceased to exist on 31st March 1974, and were superseded by District Councils under the provisions of the Local Government Act, 1972.

Adlington (UDAd) minutes 1872–97, food-control committee minutes 1917–20, local fuel and lighting committee minutes 1918–19, valuations 1879–93, local tribunal minutes 1915–18, ratepayers' meeting minutes 1835–1930, miscellanea 1855–1919

Audenshaw (UDAu) minutes 1880–1912, committee minutes 1879–1910, surveyors' reports 1876–93, ledger 1880–82, returns to government departments 1882–1938, nuisance committee minutes 1859–60, ratepayers' meeting minutes 1860–74

Barnoldswick (UDBk) minutes 1890–1971, housing committee minutes 1923–24, local pension sub-committee minutes 1908–22, and letter books 1913–31, committee report books 1954–61, legal papers 1877–1925, contracts 1890–1957, clerks' correspondence 1892–1952, letter books 1897–1922, year books 1941–74, bye-laws 1891–1960, press cuttings 1902–38, 1946–50, ledgers 1895–1949, abstracts of accounts 1911–73, miscellaneous financial records 1891–1955, valuation lists *c.* 1870–*c.*1950, rate books 1892–1951, medical officers' reports 1897–1963, hospital fund minutes and papers 1918–48, local food control committee cash books 1939–47, electricity department records 1919–46

Barrowford (UDBa) minutes 1892–1900, committee minutes 1892–96, ledgers 1893–98, measurements of roads 1874, account book of William Hargreaves, schoolmaster 1774–95

Bispham-with-Norbreck (UDBs) minutes 1903–18

Brierfield (UDBr) minutes 1868–1974, committee minutes 1869–74, rate books 1868–1961, ledgers 1868–1968, financial statements 1879–83, valuations 1895, 1929, 1934, overseers' minutes 1898–1926, engineers' letter books 1914–41, abstracts of accounts 1915–73, overseers' balances 1903–29, estimates 1952–62, housing inspection registers 1913–35, death registers 1910–42, gas regulations 1904–20, register of workshops 1906–26, inventory of British Restaurant 1943, register of new houses 1936–52, newspaper cuttings 1971–72

Carnforth (UDCa) minutes 1821–1956, committee minutes 1880–1961, valuations 1838–1956, rate books 1831–1958, health registers 1933–38, surveyors' books 1896–1952, clerk's letter book 1920–26, ledgers 1894–1965, overseers' accounts 1802–51, surveyors' accounts 1847–95, manor rents accounts 1839–58

Chadderton (UDCd) minutes and committee minutes 1873–95, letter books 1893–1900, rate books 1852–1905, valuation 1874, bath committee minutes 1895–1904, horse and provender committee minutes 1895–1908, technical instruction committee minutes 1895–1903, overseers' accounts 1844–47

Church (UDCh) minutes and committee minutes 1879–96, 1955–59, 1964–65, ledgers 1879–95, rate books 1851–1964, valuations 1869–1934, school attendance committee minutes 1893–1909, war memorial committee minutes 1917–23, clerk's correspondence 1896–1961, bye-laws 1881–1906, accounts 1879–1962, surveyors' records 1878–1955, health reports 1942–67, terrier of property 1908–66, wartime records 1915, 1939–45

Clayton-le-Moors (UDCl) minutes and committee minutes 1864–1973 letter books 1873–96, ledgers 1864–1967, overseers' accounts 1810–12, vestry minutes 1907–15, rate books 1838–1960, valuations c. 1850–1934, nuisance committee minutes 1859–1964, library subscription register 1862–92, letter from local Government Board 1876–1909, Mercer's charity accounts 1884–1936, distress fund minutes 1908–09, relief committee minutes 1914–19, volunteer training corps papers 1916–19, war charity papers 1941–45, newspaper cuttings and notices 1875–1928, air-raid distress fund papers 1940, Mercer Museum papers 1809–62, autobiography of John Mercer, clerks' correspondence 1895–1966, register of outworkers 1908–11, register of workshops 1935–51, petroleum register 1940–67, annual statements of account 1878–1960, mortgage register 1928–38, surveyors' reports 1903–65, surveyors' letter book 1912–20, street works records 1863–1965, housing records 1911–64, health reports 1898–1967, war records 1915–27, 1939–43, Mechanics Institute committee minutes 1856–1921, joint cemetery board minutes and other records 1885–1965, joint sewerage board minutes 1893–1971

Crompton (UDCr) minutes of Board of Directors 1839–52, surveys 1623, 1799, valuation 1837, highways overseers' accounts 1833–43, Board of Surveyors accounts 1843–55

Croston (UDCn) minutes 1891–1934, ledgers 1890–1934, letter books 1895–1921, valuations 1867–1934, rate books 1910, 1920, 1930, building plans 1887–1933, report on sanitary condition 1931, demolition bonds 1921–23, loan sanctions 1888–93, bye-laws 1905, 1924, correspondence 1929–1905, 1929–34, financial statements 1890–1932, local food control committee letter books 1917–22, deeds of Horseshoe Inn 1799–1885

Dalton-in-Furness (UDDa) minutes 1873–95, committees' reports 1880–91, letter books 1871–93, ledgers 1873–96, bill books 1871–96, accounts 1876–93, reports 1878–99, rate books 1873–95, declarations of owners and occupiers 1873–93, notices 1879–99, registers of owners and proxies 1878–94, legal diaries of clerks 1881–1944, burial board minutes, ledgers and letter books 1860–95

Denton (UDDe) minutes 1871–97, committee minutes 1866–1907, letter books 1861–1905, rate books 1847–90, valuations 1780, 1871–80, 1884, 1903, annual statements of account 1884–99, overseers' accounts 1860–90, health reports 1890–1903; Haughton: minutes 1877–83, committee minutes 1877–84, rate books 1850–90, valuations 1878–94, register of labour certificates 1884–1906, title deeds 1695–1961

Droylsden (UDDr) minutes 1863–1922, committee minutes 1867–96, letter books 1889–91, rate book 1826–34, ratepayers' meetings minutes 1864–1927, mortgage register 1864–1912, newspaper cuttings 1892–1925

Earby (UDEa) minutes and committee minutes 1909–42, clerks' files 1738–1967, bye-laws 1929–39, press cuttings 1921–46, ledgers 1921–61, account books 1913–22, abstracts of accounts 1925–46, valuations 1828–1950, rate books 1882, 1915, 1931, 1941, 1951, 1961, health reports 1939–67, fire brigade records 1906–42, electricity records 1931–45, hostel records 1942–45, register of slaughterhouses 1927–35, shops register 1935–40, complaints book 1947–63, housing reports 1951–64, cemetery burials 1887–1960, water company records 1891–1921

Failsworth (UDFa) minutes and committee minutes 1863–94, health report 1891

Formby (UDFo) minutes 1905–27, committee minutes 1906–45, ledgers 1905–16, 1924–70, rate books 1930, 1940, 1950, 1960, valuations 1925, 1929, 1934, 1938, abstracts of accounts 1952–58, financial statements 1906–16, vestry minutes 1888–1905, parochial committee minutes 1894–1903.

Fulwood (UDFu) minutes and committee minutes 1880–1967, ledgers 1864–1960, valuation lists 1911–34, rate books 1925–65, mortgage registers 1866–1940, medical officers' reports 1896–1972, water supply records and plans 1882–1932, sewerage records 1886–1932, highway records 1891–1936, clerks' letter books 1919–31, poor law overseers' ledgers 1826–39

Great Harwood (UDGh) minutes 1863–98, committee minutes 1864–1933, ledgers 1864–69, 1880–1949, rate books 1864–1963, valuations 1872–1955, wages books 1901–51, health reports 1907–70, financial records 1881–1972, mortgage register 1908–40, street improvements, allotments and other registers 1925–69, Mercer Hall building records 1915–65, plans 1906–66, clerks' files 1897–1957, acts and orders 1867–1909

Huyton (UDHu) minutes 1877–94, committee minutes 1877–1900, ledgers 1878–97, financial statements 1884–1904, letter books 1880–98, measurements of roads and footpaths 1879, air-raid reports 1939–44

Kirkham (UDKi) minutes 1845–1932, ledgers 1880–1916, committee minutes: building and plans 1880–1925, finance 1880–1923, fire engines 1882–1941, highway and general purposes 1880–1923, lighting 1880–1935, recreation 1899–1940, sanitary 1893–1923, coronation 1911, Kirkham and Wesham Joint Sewerage 1912–49

Lathom (UDLa) minutes 1872–1931, committee minutes 1908–30, rate books 1914, 1925, 1930, ledgers 1872–98, valuations 1909, 1915, 1918, 1922, mortgage records 1900–31

Lees (UDLe) minutes and committee minutes 1872–99, ledgers 1860–96, rate books 1864–80, 1895–1904

Leyland (UDLl) minutes 1863–1959, fire brigade drill books 1903–32, festival programmes and papers 1931–68, war savings committee minutes and papers 1940–59, deposited plans 1948–65, ledgers 1880–92, over-crowding survey 1935, committee reports 1914–26, local government reorganisation records 1972–73

Litherland (UDLd) minutes 1863–96, highways assessments and accounts 1780–1885

Littleborough (UDLi) minutes 1870–93, committee minutes 1879–98, letter books 1870–93, ledgers 1870–92, financial statements 1871–1902, ratepayers' meeting minutes 1819–85, newspaper cuttings 1882–97, bye-laws 1888–1906, relief committee minutes 1862–66, Chicago fire relief committee minutes 1871; relief and fund papers: Armenian 1896, Indian famine 1897–1900, South African war 1899–1902, war memorial 1918–22, Gresford colliery 1934, cancer campaign 1936, air-raid distress 1941

Longridge (UDLo) minutes and committee minutes 1879–1968, ledgers 1895–1965, valuations 1929–59, rate books 1914–62, building bye-law plans 1909–48, letters *re* drinking fountains 1887–88

Milnrow (UDMi) minutes 1875–91, committee minutes 1881–1928, ledgers 1870–96

Newton-le-Willows (UDNe) minutes 1855–97, committee minutes 1855–1903, surveyors' reports 1865–1911, letter books 1859–95, ratepayers' meeting minutes 1841–1915, overseers' accounts 1839–98, rate books 1856–1904, 1943–50; deeds and papers relating to Astley, Bedford, Billinge, Cronton, Golborne, Lowton, Newton-in-Makerfield, Pennington, Poulton with Fearnhead, Prescot, Tyldesley, and Warrington 1657–1878

Ormskirk (UDOr) minutes and committee minutes 1861–1968, rate-books 1900–45, ledgers 1852–1917, valuation 1923, reports 1921–28, 1943–68, register of lodging-houses 1879–1910, register of slaughterhouses 1851–1955, overcrowding survey 1936, Town Clerks' Historic Ormskirk collection 1696–1970, seal registers 1938–1971

Oswaldtwistle (UDOs) minutes 1863–75, 1880–1965, committee minutes 1863–1965, letter books 1898–1910, ledgers 1882–1900, 1911–63, rate books 1839–1961, sanitary inspectors' records 1893–1963, planning records 1923–1953, plans 1865–1970, flood relief accounts 1964, gas and water records 1908–65, library correspondence 1903–61, Queen Victoria Jubilee Nursing Association executive committee minutes 1907–48

Padiham (UDPa) minutes 1874–1974, committee minutes 1874–1927, ratepayers' meeting minutes 1831–86, 1891–97, press cuttings 1873–1956, correspondence 1920–70, valuations 1885–1973, rate books 1914–73, ledgers 1874–1967, overcrowding survey 1936, coronation committee minutes 1902, war records 1916–26, 1939–54, sealed documents 1877–1966, contracts 1926–61, agreements 1846–1970, bye-laws 1911–64, gas and water records 1876–1927, mortgage registers 1874–1935, workmen's compensation papers 1905–09, burial board and cemetery records 1857–1974, local Acts papers 1874–1964, financial

51

records 1875–1974, wages and salaries records 1927–74, surveyors' stores records 1949–74, housing records 1908–69, water records 1875–1968, annual reports 1922–59, the Hargreaves-Veevers Historic Padiham collection of photographs, prints etc., 1820–1973

Poulton-le-Fylde (UDPo) minutes 1900–48, committee minutes 1900–48, clerks' files 1900–70, valuations 1921, 1928, 1934, rate books 1896–1966, ledgers 1900–61, register of workshops 1921–25, dairy register 1954–57, gas records 1888–1949, ratepayers' association minutes 1922–32, building bye-law plans 1898–1947; (DDHa) burial board letter books 1903–1933.

Preesall (UDPl) minutes, committee minutes and reports 1901–74, clerks' correspondence 1925–53, ledgers 1900–68, valuations 1897–63, rate books 1896–1971, slum clearance papers 1928–37, war memorial papers 1919–73, joint burial board minutes and papers 1856–1967

Prescot (UDPr) minutes 1867–92, committee minutes 1874–86, bye-laws 1868, 1888, drawings of old town hall 1954

Rainford (UDRf) general purposes and sanitary committee minutes 1873–1908, ledgers 1881–93, bye-laws 1873. These are the sole survivors of a fire.

Ramsbottom (UDRa) minutes 1873–92, committee minutes 1873–94, burial board minutes 1873–97

Rishton (UDRi) minutes 1882–1973, committee minutes 1882–1973, ledgers 1882–1958, overseers' minutes 1908–26, photographs of town *c*. 1900, registers of plans 1883–1947, electricity records 1915–22, maps and plans 1891–1967

Royton (UDRo) minutes and committee minutes 1863–70, 1880–95, ledgers 1872–94, burial board minutes 1870–97, vestry minutes 1843–97, surveyors' minutes 1837–63, rate books 1845–1900

Skelmersdale (UDSk) minutes 1874–1968, finance committee minutes 1881–1968, other committee minutes 1880–1968, ledgers 1899–1950, war relief fund minutes and accounts 1915–21, rate books 1901, 1914, 1930, 1940, 1950, 1960, press cuttings 1921–50, 1964–73, seal register 1954–68

Thornton Cleveleys (UDTh)minutes and committee minutes 1900–69, letter books 1902–68, rate books 1902–61, overseers' letter book 1901–06, ledgers 1900–45, abstracts of accounts 1935–72, valuations 1929–62, health reports 1900–72, sanitary inspectors' journals 1940–71, overcrowding survey 1936, maps and plans 1925–64, private street works register 1925–32; Thornton, Bispham, and Carleton joint sewerage board minutes 1902–09, 1912–37, letter books 1902–09

Tottington (UDTo) minutes and committee minutes 1896–1902, rate books 1887–1900, press cuttings 1894–1901, Tottington and Ainsworth relief committee minutes 1914–19

Trawden (UDTr) minutes 1863–1960, committee minutes 1927–60, mortgage register 1869–1926, rate books 1865–1961, year books 1895–1967, letter books 1910–25, correspondence files 1897–1967, ledgers 1869–1956, valuations 1865–1956, survey 1846, deposited plans c.1880–1920, planning papers 1890–1965, surveyors' accounts 1814–16, 1837, 1844–45, health reports 1912–69, overcrowding survey 1937, register of slaughter-houses 1925–51; relief and fund minutes and papers: local distress 1914–18, Belgian famine 1916–17, war charities 1916–18, war memorial 1919–22, Hartley hospital 1925–34, war comforts 1939–48

Turton (UDTu) minutes and committee minutes 1873–94, 1902–21, 1925–57, letter books 1878–1913, war relief committee minutes 1914–15, Bolton and district regional planning committee minutes 1926–41, 1946–48, miscellanea 1865–88, abstract of title to Turton Tower 1835–90

Up Holland (UDUh) minutes 1872–80, 1901–68, ledgers 1917–56, valuation 1934, rate books 1914, 1940, 1960, register of assistance to private enterprise 1923–29, seal registers 1953–68, property register 1866–74

Urmston (UDUr) minutes 1894–1931, committee minutes 1895–1948, burial board minutes 1890–95, accounts 1895–1933; (CSU) drainage committee minutes 1906–11, 1917–33

Walton-le-Dale (UDWd) minutes 1877–1953, committee minutes 1877–1953, reports to council 1930–74, contracts 1880–1935, agreements 1882–1932, correspondence 1823–1935, letter books 1888–1933, year books 1901–51, press cuttings 1911–74, ledgers 1877–1945, auditors' reports 1885–1931, account books 1883–1938, cash books 1897–1945, mortgages 1880–1939, wages books 1932–61, valuations 1861–1963, rate books 1909–66, health reports 1898–1960, sanitary inspectors' letter books 1912–24, 1932–39, register of slaughterhouses 1892–1948, building plans books 1878–1965, building applications 1945–54, overcrowding survey 1935, housing papers 1923–48, private street works books and papers 1904–71, waterworks and sewerage papers 1877–1958, gas and electricity papers 1877–1949, surveyors' correspondence 1903–52, miscellaneous plans 1885–1959, town planning papers 1927–45, monthly returns of births 1877–1907, omnibus licences books 1903–19, Chorley motor omnibus joint committee minutes 1924–28, fire and war damage papers 1938–44, evacuation papers 1939–45, air-raid reports 1939–44, civil defence papers 1938–68, relief fund appeals 1946–57, local government reorganization papers 1969–70

Wardle (UDWa) minutes and committee minutes 1882–87, 1890–97, ledger 1886–89, poor rate 1829, valuation 1834, ratepayers' meeting minutes 1840–94, mill valuation 1883

Whitworth (UDWh) minutes 1896–1937, committee minutes 1874–1955, letter books 1898–1916, year books 1904–63, ledgers 1894–1945, education minutes 1896–1910, 1918–30, surveyors' accounts 1839–74, ratepayers' meeting minutes 1896–1910, 1918–30, seal registers 1904–47, lighting committee minutes 1869–74, overseers' minutes 1895–1927, burial board ledger 1876–82, press cuttings 1939–62, valuations 1895–1950, rate books 1900–51, returns of births and deaths 1894–1920, infectious diseases certificates 1895–1914, sanitary inspectors' journals 1929–49, building plans 1874–1923, housing records 1920–53, tramway records 1882–1932, electricity records 1904–19, burial board minutes etc., 1875–1960, miscellanea 1831–1953

Withnell (UDWi) minutes and committee minutes 1893–95, ledger 1893–97, rate books 1891–92

RURAL DISTRICT COUNCIL RECORDS

Created under the provisions of the Local Government Act, 1894, rural district councils superseded rural sanitary authorities which had been established under the Public Health Act, 1872. Based as they were upon the unions of parishes set up under the Poor Law Amendment Act of 1834, they were often coextensive with the ancient territorial divisions known as hundreds, although their administrative functions were entirely modern. Their records are noted below. For an account of the relevant legislation see Central Office of Information, *Local Government in Britain*, London, H.M.S.O., 11th ed., 1980. As in the case of urban district councils and municipal boroughs, rural district councils were superseded on 1st April 1974 by district councils.

Barton-upon-Irwell (RDBa and SAM) minutes 1872–1933, ledgers 1873–94, finance committee minutes 1928–33, rating committee minutes 1927–33, parochial committee minutes 1895–1933, Flixton surveyors' reports 1905–15

Blackburn (RDBl) minutes 1873–1961, committee minutes 1901–61, ledgers 1937–61, rating survey 1913, valuations 1934, 1945–49, rate books 1951–53, 1960, public health registers

1913–65, overcrowding survey 1936, public health reports 1928–67, plans register 1891–1946, deposited plans 1927–48. Mellor parochial committee minutes 1891–93

Bowland (RDBo) minutes and committee minutes 1923–51, clerks' papers 1891–47, ledgers 1911–62, valuations 1929, 1932, 1950–61, rate books 1940–41, 1951–61, 1970–71, housing inspections 1934–35, overcrowding survey 1935–36, sanitary inspectors' journals 1947–70, health reports 1949–64, milksellers' register 1926–32, meat inspection records 1939–50, 1954–68, petroleum register 1906–22, factory register 1937–71, register of planning applications 1934–49

Burnley (SAE and RDBu) minutes 1872–82, 1891–94, highway agreements 1883–1940, deposited plans 1883–1948, rate books 1867–1926; (RL) Leeds and Liverpool canal rating committee minutes 1889–92, and papers 1890–1906

Chorley (SAC and RDCh) minutes 1880–1967, committee minutes 1896–1967, clerks' letter books and correspondence 1872–1964, year books 1924–1968, ledgers 1873–1957, valuations 1863–1939, rate books 1851–1951, rating letter books 1927–1961, health reports 1901–59, sanitary reports 1916–57, register of deaths 1940–53, overcrowding survey 1937, housing records 1936–61, surveyors' records 1899–1966, water records 1881–1947, sewerage records 1890–1939, plans 1879–1957, omnibus records 1925–38; (RHC) highway committee minutes 1899–1914; and ledgers 1899–1915

Clitheroe (SAA and RDC) minutes 1880–94, abstracts of accounts 1953–73, year books 1958–59, 1963–73

Fylde (SAF) minutes 1873–94

Garstang (RDG) minutes 1873–1964, rating committee minutes 1926–60, valuation lists 1896–1934, rate books 1841–1928, clerks' letters 1932–38, year books 1895–1974, ledgers 1882–1947, medical officers' reports 1889–1972, building bye-law plans 1893–1948, housing records 1910–55, electricity records 1922–52, sewerage and water supply records 1891–1930, railway records 1848–1906, war records 1939–46, plans 1947–72, press cuttings 1899–1912

Haslingden (SAH) minutes 1872–83, letter book 1873–80, Haslingden parochial committee minutes 1874–75

Lancaster (SAL and RDLa) minutes 1872–96, committee minutes 1897–1928, letter books 1881–95, 1907–17, ledgers 1905–40, financial statements 1922–38, abstracts of accounts 1905–11, valuations 1879–1974, rate books 1840–1927, register of empty properties 1930–40, surveyors' and sanitary reports 1882–1952, surveyors' memoranda book 1896–1927, surveyors' letter books 1883–99, building plans 1859–1955, sanitary inspectors' letter books 1906–35, register of licences 1927–61, journal of nuisances 1934–49, canal-boat inspections 1929–38, register of infectious diseases 1910–35, highway papers of Heaton, Scotforth, Over Wyresdale, Ellel, Yealand, and Warton 1896–1927, marriage notice book (Lancaster registration district) 1920–54, plans of William Atherton's estate in Preston 1813, plans of Greenbank estate, Preston 1817

Lunesdale (RDLu) sub-committee minutes 1912–30, valuation 1934, surveyors' reports 1895–1909, health statistics 1945–54, register of dairies 1946–49, annual reports 1951–71, year books 1907–25, 1963–64, press cuttings 1910–16, 1932–39

Ormskirk (SAO) minutes 1872–94

Prescot (SAP) minutes 1873–98

Preston (RDP) minutes 1878–1971, committee minutes 1895–1972, ledgers 1917–66, valuation lists 1928, 1933, rate books 1934–61, medical officers' reports 1896–1948, overcrowding survey 1936, building bye-law plans 1897–1965, Grimsargh parish council minutes 1894–1927, local tribunal minutes 1916–18, evacuation records 1939–46, reports to water committee 1937–59, press cuttings 1901–20; (RHP) surveyors' monthly reports 1904–42

Sefton (SAD and RDSe) minutes 1885–1932, ledgers 1924–32

Warrington (SAW) minutes 1872–77, 1883–98, ledgers 1873–85, surveyors' reports 1880–1904

West Derby (SAD) minutes 1885–97, ledgers 1873–94

West Lancashire (RDWL) minutes 1895–1968, committee minutes 1877–1968, clerks' correspondence 1924–48, financial records 1889–1969, contracts 1927–42, rate books 1939, summaries 1934–54, building records 1927–48, building bye-law plans 1900–60, medical officers' reports 1891–1935, West Lancashire rural housing survey records 1947–58

Whiston (previously Prescot) minutes 1873–98

DEFENCE OF THE REALM

Lieutenancy (L)

General

Minute books 1796–1831, commissions 1797–1862, correspondence 1771–1899, letter books 1798–1908, finance 1798–1810, 1855–63, nominal rolls 1798–1908, lists of deputies 1796–1866, enrolment books 1811–27, militia storehouse papers 1853–56, militia acts 1852–61, miscellanea 1796–1815

Property Qualifications (QSQ/3)

These are properly Quarter Sessions documents, to be kept by the Clerk of the Peace under the Acts of 31 Geo. II, *c* 25 (1757) *et seq.*

Deputy lieutenants, 1757–82, 1803–08

Militia officers, 1760–78, 1780–1808

Provisional cavalry officers, 1797–98

Amounderness Sub-division

Minute books 1806–52, nominal rolls 1823, enrolment books 1790–1831, finance 1811–16, 1852, cavalry book 1796–98, miscellanea 1852–54

Leyland Sub-division

Minute book 1952, nominal rolls 1807–31, enrolment books 1803–31, finance 1811–16

Prescot Sub-division

Acceptance of rules 1807, oath book 1816

Miscellaneous

Royal Lancashire Volunteer Regiment (DDX/124), muster roll 1795

Royal Field Artillery (DDX/152), "A" battery, 330th Brigade, official diary 1917–18

Manchester Military Association (DP/288), minutes, accounts, etc., 1782–84

Loyal Kirkham Volunteers (DDX/190), minutes, correspondence etc., 1798

Leyland and Ormskirk Militia (DP/375), orderly book 1809–13

Preston Volunteer Training Corps (DDX/11), minutes 1915–23

Home Guard (HG)

5th County of Lancaster (Preston County) Battalion, location and commanders of companies, "B" company part I orders 1940–44, battalion part II orders 1942–45, photographs, list of ammunition shelters 1944, defence works 1945, brief history 1945

8th County of Lancaster (Preston) Battalion, battalion part II orders 1940–44, instructional handbook, Lancashire Territorial Army Association, final strength returns 1944

41st County of Lancaster Battalion, nominal rolls, officers 1941–44. and women 1943–45

42nd County of Lancaster (Irlam) Battalion, nominal roll "B" company 1942–43

47th County of Lancaster Battalion, nominal rolls "B" and "C" companies 1944

48th County of Lancaster Battalion, casualty book "C" company 1941–43, nominal rolls of "B" and "H" companies 1940–42, HQ company 1940–42, women 1943 and cadet messengers 1943

49th County of Lancaster Battalion, nominal roll of officers 1941–44

51st County of Lancaster (Ashton-under-Lyne) Battalion, nominal rolls of "B" company 1941–42, HQ company 1942–44, Northern Aircraft 1942, Waterworks Transport 1942, L.M.S. Railway 1942, L.N.E. Railway 1942, Denton Sheet Metal 1942, National Gas 1942, Electricity Works 1942, A. V. Roe Ltd., 1942

55th County of Lancaster Battalion, No. 3 company commanders' record book, nominal rolls of No. 3 company 1940–42, and No. 4 company 1944

63rd County of Lancaster Battalion, nominal roll "A" company 1940–44

Burnley Home Guard, book of enrolments, etc., 'E' company 1943–44, nominal rolls "A," "B," "C," "D," "E," "F," and HQ companies 1940–44

Rawtenstall Home Guard, HQ company attendance register 1944

In and out transfers, various battalions, 1942–45

SHRIEVALTY (HS)

Grand Jury, Lancaster assizes, minutes 1800–1933

Undersheriff, papers and accounts 1813–14

Writs, 1783–91

POLICE RECORDS

Accrington (MBA) charge books 1884–89

Ashton-under-Lyne (PLA) charge books 1933–43, misconduct book 1931–47, force list 1884–1940

Bacup (MBBa) general orders 1887–91, chief constables' reports 1887–1933; (PLA) register of constables 1888–1946, discipline book 1920–46, pay books 1913–43, personal records 1888–1938, memoranda 1863–76

Barrow-in-Furness (CBBa) register of constables 1881–1920, chief
constables' reports 1912–18, reports on diseases of animals
1883–1956, reports on common lodging houses 1929–56,
reports on pleasure and ferry boats 1932–53, police surgeons'
reports 1924–48

Blackpool (PLB) general orders 1887–1957, police orders 1912–66,
chief constables' reports 1912–25, 1931–36, 1947–59, wartime
instructions 1938–45, examination and service records 1887–
1919

Burnley (PLBu) general orders 1909–64, chief constables' reports
1897–1921, pay receipt books 1892–1938, duty book 1887–98,
conduct book 1915–33, defaulters book 1887–1962, cash books
1925–45, requisition books 1924–56, charges registers 1887–
1964, refused charges book 1920–43, court books 1903–65,
occurrence books 1924–63, convicts report book 1899–1935,
convicts' photograph books 1907, 1919, registers of habitual
criminals 1909, 1911, 1920, register of summonses 1929–32,
crime register 1964–65, register of beersellers 1887–91, register
of beerhouse keepers 1889–96, register of licensed victuallers
1890–1923, fire brigade requisition book 1891–1933, register of
cases for Quarter Sessions 1912–35, papers re National Minority
Movement 1925–35, diaries of Detective Dyke 1930–32, cotton
strike papers 1931–32, royal visit papers 1938, pedlars' certificates 1932–65, papers re Auxiliary Police Association and
Womens' Auxiliary Police Corps 1941–48, register of persons
sent to gaol 1911–58, marine storekeepers' licences 1946–65,
Royal Lancashire Agricultural Show papers 1948, opencase
mining papers 1949–55, register of service 1887–99

Lancashire (PLA) general orders 1840–1939, standing orders 1936–40,
daily strength book 1916–29, memorandum books 1887–1914,
1920–42, fire brigade memoranda 1938–42, circular book 1894,
prisoners' photograph book 1866–92, register of force 1884–
1940, newspaper cuttings 1852–1934, letter books 1943–65,
1883–1915, returns book 1877–83, sergeants' examination
results 1911–50, convictions registers 1874–1908, register of
constables 1931–46, examination books 1840–1925, photograph
books 1880–1950, transfer books 1912–66, promotion examination results 1926–66, gratuities books 1890–1933, posting books
1877–1951, swearing in book 1879–1937, appointments of probation officers 1908–36, educational qualifications 1920–69, wartime orders 1914–18, confidential security memorandum books
1939–42, Home Office circulars 1939–46, ARP memoranda,
1935–43, wartime memorandum books 1939–40, numerical
registers 1840–1930, personnel records 1860–1969, annual
reports 1964–75, press cuttings 1893–1936

Divisional records: Accrington occurrence book 1926–29, charge books 1889–1929, summons books 1900–30; Askam occurrence books 1940–42, 1947–52; Church letter book 1909–24, summons book 1919–27, charge book 1918–30; Clayton-le-Moors occurrence book 1924–30; Clitheroe occurrence book 1919–30, summons book 1914–29, charge books 1905–30; Dalton-in-Furness occurrence book 1939–41, 1948–50; Golborne charge book 1932–46; Grange-over-Sands occurrence books 1939–41, 1948–51; Great Harwood occurrence books 1923–28; Greenodd occurrence books 1939–41, 1947–50; Hawkshead occurrence books 1939–41, 1948–55; Manchester charge book 1939–43; Rishton occurrence book 1924–29; St. Helens (QEV) day book of P.C. Jones 1876; Ulverston occurrence books 1940, 1949–51; Westhoughton occurrence books 1896–1903, charge books 1933–38; Whalley occurrence book 1924–29; Wigan (QEV) defaulters' register 1862–1911

Little Lever (PLA) miscellanea 1911–60

Preston (CBP) chief constables' reports 1923–64, licensing reports 1957–58, Home Office circulars 1884–1907, duty book of P.C. Jones 1913, file *re* women police 1936–47, file *re* crown inspections 1936–48

St. Helens (CBSH) chief constables' reports 1918–20, 1926–54, 1956–67

Southport (CBSo) charge books, court books, cuttings books, reports, miscellanea 1870–1946

Warrington (CBWa) chief constables' reports and returns 1895–1912, crimes register 1928–35, charge register 1937–38, posters and handbills 1831–63

Wigan (PLWi) general orders 1889–1931, chief constables' reports 1930–69, criminal returns 1917–45, charge sheets 1932–67, wages books 1908–67, pay analysis books 1952–66, occurrence books 1944–67, force summonses 1933–39, cash book 1954–62, disbursement books 1944–57, day book 1929–35, appointment book 1878–1915, watch committee reports 1938–69, leave book 1931–47, insecurity book 1955–60, licences register 1921–68, newspaper cuttings 1922–48

TURNPIKE TRUSTS

These were established by individual Local Acts.

Blackburn and Addingham (DDBd 57) accounts 1817–72, correspondence 1855–73

Blackburn and Burscough Bridge (Walton-le-Dale) (TTE) minutes 1755–93, accounts 1755–1803

Blackburn and Cocking End (DDX 680) accounts 1845–80

Blackburn and Preston (TTJ) case for promoter 1824, minutes 1824–42

Bury, Haslingden, Blackburn, and Whalley (TTA) minutes 1789–1827, 1847–75, second district minutes 1810–20, memoranda book 1820–40

Clitheroe and Blackburn (TTB) minutes 1845–81, mortgage book 1823–71

Colne and Broughton (DDBd 57) accounts 1823–76, correspondence 1823–76, plans 1825–40, minutes 1823–76, miscellanea 1829–76

Haslingden Private Lane (DDX 118/123) agreements 1830, 1833, minutes 1830–76, accounts 1830–76, contracts 1831–72

Heywood (TTH) minutes 1800–76, accounts 1790–1820, 1837–43, mortgages 1790–1860

Manchester and Ashton-under-Lyne (UDDr) minutes 1851–85, letter book 1869–77, plan of Droylsden roads 1857

Penwortham and Wrightington (DDH) mortgages 1825–27, various 1856–64

Prescot and Liverpool (TTG) minutes 1726–89, plans 1820

Preston and Garstang (TTD) minutes 1751–82

Rochdale and Edenfield (DDX 613) mortgage 1796

Skipton and Colne (TTI) index to orders 1756–74, minutes 1787–1836, correspondence 1809–17, 1831–59, mortgages 1756–1834, accounts 1806–59

Ulverston and Carnforth (TTK) mortgages and leases 1820–76, accounts 1823–78, correspondence 1819–70, various 1819–76

Wigan and Preston, North of Yarrow (TTC) minutes 1832–59, mortgages (DDL) 1823–34

HIGHWAY BOARDS

The Act of 25–26 Vict. *c*. 61 (1862) authorized the Justices to set up highway boards compulsorily by the combination of parishes. They were abolished by the Local Government Act of 1894, which allowed postponements.

Cartmel (HBC) minutes 1877–99, accounts 1877–99, ledgers 1877–99

Childwall (HBA) minutes 1885–98

Flixton, Urmston, and South Barton (HBB) minutes 1876–81, 1887–95

Garstang (HBG) minutes 1863–95; (RDG) ledgers 1863–95

Hawkshead (HBH) minutes 1892–99, ledger 1892–99, letter books 1892–99

High Furness (HBF) minutes 1892–99, finance committee minutes 1893–99, ledgers 1893–99

Leyland Hundred (HBL) minutes 1865–99, ledgers 1887–99, papers 1867–91

Low Furness (HBU) minutes 1892–99, finance committee minutes 1892–99, various committees minutes 1893–99, ledger 1892–99, correspondence 1892–99, papers 1892–99

Ormskirk (HBO) minutes 1864–90

Prescot (HBP) minutes 1882–89

Sefton (HBS) minutes 1864–99

Southport (HBN) minutes 1893–99

Walton-le-Dale (UDWd) minutes 1848–67, accounts 1831–51, 1866–77

DRAINAGE AUTHORITIES (CS and WBR)
(See also Joint Committees p. 41)

Alt Drainage Commission: act 1779, minutes 1801–1923, letter books 1906–21, account books 1868–91, surveys 1815–1907, memoranda book 1866–79, plans 1818–1920, reports 1872–1904, miscellanea 1791–1893; (DDM 2) commissions 1771, plan 1778, accounts 1788–96, report 1798, miscellanea 1771–1928

Croston Drainage Commission: act 1800, minutes 1800–1919, 1933–77, account books 1836–1903, plan 1845; (PR 1243) accounts 1907–26

Hesketh Estate (Flood Defences) Commission; minutes 1918–74, rate books 1933–64

Lancashire River Authority: minutes 1964–74

Lancashire River Board: minutes 1951–65

Longton Drainage Committee: minutes 1943–74, rate books 1952–57

Overton Drainage Commission: minutes 1897–1928, account book 1898–1920, plans 1897, 1919

Ribble, Calder, Hodder, Irwell, and Mersey Commission: commission 1674, estreats 1678–79

River Douglas Catchment Board: minutes 1931–51, ledgers 1931–40

River Wyre Catchment Board: minutes 1931–51, expenditure book 1944–52

Slyne Valley Drainage Commission: minutes 1911–19

South Fylde Drainage Board: minutes 1947–77, rate books 1947–64

Thurnham and Cockerham Internal Drainage Board: minutes 1949–77

Urmston and Flixton Drainage Committee: minutes 1906–11, 1917–33

BOARDS OF GUARDIANS OF THE POOR

These Boards were established by the Poor Law Amendment Act of 4–5 William IV, *c.* 76 (1834), and ceased under the Local Government Act 1929.

Ashton-under-Lyne (PUA) constitution 1837, minutes 1837–1930

Barton-upon-Irwell (PUE) constitution 1849, minutes 1849–1930, out-door relief lists 1850–70

Blackburn (PUK) minutes 1837–1930; committee minutes: finance 1863–97, finance and salaries 1897–1928, stores 1899–1930, school attendance 1877–1903, cottage homes 1900–30, workhouse farming 1890–1922, boarding-out 1910–30, and miscellaneous committees 1897–1925; general ledgers 1837–1930, parochial ledgers 1864–1927

Burnley (PUZ) constitution 1836, minutes 1837–1930; committee minutes: assessment 1862–1920, workhouse building 1871–77, school attendance 1877–97, and general 1879–1905; valuation lists 1875–1929, registers of children 1904–10, 1928–45, ledgers 1938–1929

Bury (PUB) minutes 1840–1930, returns of paupers relieved 1871–1900, returns of guardians and officials 1870–1915, voucher book (CBB) 1848–58, bills (CBB) 1848–51

Chorley (PUX) minutes and committee minutes 1838–1947, valuations 1863–1920, punishment records 1872–1948, letter books 1877–95, 1918–30, ledgers 1843–1927

Clitheroe (PUC) minutes 1837–1902, 1905–30; committee minutes: buildings 1870–74, school attendance 1877–86; letter books 1843–1940, ledgers 1838–47, 1874–1908, township account books 1838–1909, relief order book 1924–30, creed register 1914–34, birth and death registers 1867–1914

Fylde (PUF) minutes 1845–1930; committee minutes: assessment 1862–1927, workhouse 1864–1930, finance 1906–30, children's homes 1908–19, boarding-out 1911–46, cottage homes 1920–30

Garstang (PUY) minutes 1837–1930; committee minutes: assessment 1862–64, school attendance 1877–1903, workhouse management 1908–14, house 1914–30; ledgers 1902–30

63

Haslingden (PUH) minutes 1838–1930; committee minutes: workhouse 1865–70, infirmary 1898–1905, boarding-out 1911–20; letter books 1838–1902, lists of guardians and officers 1839–1921, valuations 1880–82, year-books 1904–29, overseers' balance sheets 1856–88, 1917–25

Lancaster (PUL) constitution 1839, minutes 1839–1930; committee minutes: workhouse 1840–45, 1919–28, children's home 1910–28, finance 1889–1928, assessment 1862–1934, general 1928–30; letter books: assessment 1866–69, registration 1841–44, general 1845–69, 1887–1920; lists of guardians and officers 1840–1904, ledgers 1918–30, abstracts of accounts 1892–1903, 1912–13, overseers' balance sheets 1903–25, relief books 1894–1945, vaccination records 1857–66, 1885–1915, pauper lunatic records 1865–1923

Lunesdale (PUN) minutes 1869–1900; committee minutes: assessment 1868–96, school attendance 1877–97; letter book 1869–71

Manchester see Swinton Industrial School p. 90

Oldham (PUO) minutes 1847–1901, assessment committee minutes 1862–1942, valuations 1914, 1929

Ormskirk (PUS) minutes 1837–1930, assessment committee minutes 1896–1912

Prescot (PUP) minutes 1837–1930; committee minutes: assessment 1862–81, finance 1894–1911, general 1872–1930, school attendance 1877–1903

Preston (PUT) minutes 1838–1930, assessment committee minutes 1907–27

Rochdale (PUR) minutes 1845–1900; committee minutes: building 1868–77, general purposes 1874–78, parliamentary 1887–93, various 1863–65, 1892–1900, visiting 1874–94, workhouse 1851–87

Ulverston (PUU) minutes 1836–1930; committee minutes: assessment 1862–1927, general 1890–1918, house 1920–24, house and children 1927–30; ledgers 1836–76, registers of rating objections 1891–1929, letter books 1869–1930, parochial ledger 1911–27

Warrington (PUV) minutes 1837–1900

Wigan (PUW) minutes 1837–1930; committee minutes: assessment 1863–75, removal 1888–95, school attendance 1877–1903, workhouse 1884–96, various 1896–1930; ledgers 1838–61, abstract of expenditure 1877–96

MEDICAL COMMITTEES (MCP)

Preston Local Dental Committee; minutes 1947–74

Preston Local Medical Committee: minutes 1936–74, cash books 1949–74

Preston Local Optical Committee: minutes 1948–74

ELECTRICITY BOARDS

Mid-Lancashire Electricity District Advisory Board (EY) board minutes 1924–48, engineering advisory committee minutes 1924–37, finance committee minutes 1924–42, special committee minutes 1924–31, correspondence 1924–48, letter books 1924, circulars 1924–48, financial records 1925–48, conference of Joint Electricity Authorities records 1926–48, Conjoint Conference of Public Utility Associations records 1936–47, Electricity Commission reports 1923–46, Electricity Commission correspondence 1927–48, South-east Lancashire Electricity Advisory Board records 1922–31, miscellanea 1924–47

GAS AND WATER RECORDS

Accrington and District Gas and Water Board (MBA) minutes 1894–1919, finance minutes 1930–37, stock and debenture books 1863–1950, ledgers 1897–1931, treasurers' accounts 1939–49, wages books 1931–58, printed accounts 1892–1967

Fylde Water Board (WBF) minutes 1860–1974; committee minutes, agenda, ledgers, letter books, gauge books, reservoir statistics, rainfall returns, plant books, order books, registers of transfers, stock and mortgages register, loan and debenture addresses, Bowland log sheets, rent book, special rates book, Dunsop and Langden refraction survey, superannuation fund book, cash book, press cuttings, etc.

Nelson (MBNe) Water Department: stock book 1872–1920, letter books 1894–1931, day books 1872–1934, wages books 1881–1967, ledgers 1910–49, account books 1926–48, annual reports 1914–19, 1929–30, plans 1891–1906, miscellanea 1865–1957

Padiham (UDPa) water miscellanea 1885–1968; Gas, Light, and Coke Co. deed 1846, share register 1850–76, ledgers 1866–76

SCHOOL BOARDS

The School Boards were set up under the Act of 33–34 Vict., c. 75 (1870), and were superseded by the Education Committees following the Act of 2 Edw. VII, c. 72 (1902)

Bacup (MBBa) school attendance committee minutes 1892–1903

Barrowford (SBB) minutes 1887–94, 1900–02, miscellany book 1885–1905

Belmont (SBA) minutes 1896–1903

Blackpool (SBBp) minutes 1899–1903; committee minutes: finance and general purposes 1899–1903, buildings and sites 1899–1903

Briercliffe-with-Entwistle (SBD) minutes 1889–1903

Burtonwood (SBJ) minutes 1876–1903

Dalton-in-Furness (SBC) lease of Lindal and Marton schools, 1895

Edgworth United (SBE) minutes 1874–1903

Fleetwood and Thornton (SBQ) (established in 1878 they became separate boards in 1895): minutes 1878–1903, ledgers 1878–1903, account books 1878–99, mortgage registers 1880–1902, letter book 1878, average attendance books 1889–1903, miscellaneous papers 1879–1903, Blakiston Street school contracts, etc. 1879–1902, Chaucer Road school contracts, etc. 1901–03, Copse Road school plans and papers 1896–1900, Fleetwood Testimonial school contracts, etc. 1847–96, London Street school plans and papers 1896–1900, Thornton school contracts, etc. 1878–1902, miscellaneous papers 1875–1910

Forton United (SBF) minutes for formation of board (PR 1406) 1874, minutes 1875–1903, attendance book 1896–98

Great Sankey (SBG) minutes 1884–1903

Hambleton (SBH) minutes 1877–1903

Lancaster (DDHd) committee minutes 1897–1902, teachers' applications 1895–1902

Littleborough (SBL) minutes 1900–03

Nelson (MBNe) minutes 1893–1903, ledgers 1893–1903

Pendleton (Clitheroe) (UDPa) minutes 1894–1903

Pleasington (SBP) minutes 1876–1903 (continued to 1926)

Prescot (SBO) minutes 1896–1904

Royton (SBR) minutes 1879–1903; committee minutes: science and technological 1889–90, school attendance 1877–1906

Salford (SBN) report 1891–94

Skelmersdale (SBK) minutes 1877–1903

Southworth-with-Croft (SBM) minutes 1875–98

Tottington Higher End (SBT) minutes 1882–95 (merged with Walmersley and Ramsbottom)

Trawden (SBV) minutes 1896–1903

Ulnes Walton (PR 747 and 252) minutes 1878–1900

Ulverston and Mansriggs (SBU) bonds 1898–1901, prosecutions 1878–1903

Walmersley and Ramsbottom (SBX) minutes 1895–98, committees' minutes 1895–1903

Walmersley and Shuttleworth (SBW) minutes 1878–95 (merged with Walmersley and Ramsbottom)

Worsthorne (SBZ) minutes 1893–1903 (continued to 1911)

SCHOOL RECORDS

Abram (SMA) colliery schools log books 1882–1944

Accrington (MBA) quarterly reports 1903–16, register of pupil teachers 1903–18, register of salaries and appointments 1903–20, record of absences of teachers 1903–20, register of staff 1904–37; (PR 2890) St. James's infants log books 1863–1908, managers' minutes 1886–98, 1903–58; (SMAc) St. James's boys and girls log book 1863–99, St. James's boys admission register 1924–58, Hargreaves Street log book 1914–17, Wesleyan log book 1863–1905, Technical admission register 1900–11, Woodnook Secondary handicraft centre log book 1921–46, Woodnook Secondary mixed log book 1937–66, St. John's infants log books 1872–1952, St. John's punishment book 1907–23, St. Mary Magdalene's log books 1884–1940, St. Peter's log books 1871–1961, St. Matthew's (ESP) plans 1924, St. Peter's admission registers 1902–51, Peel Park infants log books 1893–1955, Peel Park infants admission registers 1898–1954, Hyndburn Park Secondary log books 1923–66, Hyndburn Park Council log books 1906–55, St. Oswald's R.C. log books 1866–1949; (ESP) plans pre 1944, St. Oswald's R.C. admission registers 1895–1935, Hannah Street log books 1884–1963; (SP) plans: St. James's 1857, St. John's 1881, Christ Church 1843–55

Adlington (SMAd) Council (Congregational to 1908) log books 1879–1961, Council admission registers 1895–1939, Council correspondence and reports 1878–1939, National (later C.E.) log books 1863–1956, National admission registers 1886–1948; (SP) National plans 1840–57

Aighton, Bailey, and Chaigley (CUCg) Walkerfold trustees' minutes 1851–93, papers 1893–1922, repair accounts 1792–1806; (SMCy) Walkerfold log books 1876–1911, 1924–60, admission register 1878–1959

Aldingham (DRCh 37/41) nominations of masters 1691–1716; (SP) Dendron plan 1862

Alston (DDTs) College deeds and papers 1870–83

Altham (SMA1) C.E. log book 1869–1921; (PR 2819) National cash books 1871–1903

Anderton (SP) St. Joseph's R.C. plan 1871

Ashton-in-Makerfield (SP) St. Thomas's plan 1850; (PR 2927) Seneley Green apprentices 1817–79; (ESP) Cansfield Grove plan 1923

Ashton-under-Lyne (SMAs) Albion log books 1871–1926, Charlestown Independent log book 1909–28, Charlestown junior log books 1871–1923, Christ Church log books 1863–1968; (ESP) Darnton Road plans 1923, Hurst Council managers' minutes 1910–27, Hurst Methodist managers' minutes 1869–82, Hurst National log books 1863–1914, Hurst St. John's log books 1873–1936, Mossley Road log book 1926–64, Park Bridge log book 1914–62, Park Bridge managers' minutes 1955–62, Practical Instruction Centre log book 1928–35, Ryecroft British log book 1902–12, St. Peter's log books 1872–1933, Trafalgar Square log books 1896–1964, Waterloo New Connexion correspondence, reports etc. 1872–1938, West End Council log books 1912–61, Youth Committee minutes 1941–46; (SP) Charlestown plan 1846

Ashworth (SMI) log book 1884–1906; (PR 2914) registers 1846–58, 1918–21

Aspull (SMAp) C.E. log books 1868–1924, C.E. admission registers 1875–1943, New Springs C.E. log books 1873–1928, New Springs C.E. admission registers 1874–1948; (ESP) Infants plans 1909

Astley (SP) plan 1847

Atherton (SP) plans: National 1840, Bag Lane 1871, Bolton Road 1871

Audenshaw (SMAw) Council (British to 1903) log books 1863–1949, Council managers' minutes 1903–09, Methodist log books 1869–1960, Poplar Street log book 1914–57, Secondary log book 1957–64

Aughton (SMAu) R.C. log books 1869–1955, admission register 1897–1968, Parochial log book 1880–1928, minutes 1835–1939 and notices, correspondence etc. (including Sunday School) 1816–80; (EXOk) Christ Church managers' minutes 1913–30

Bacup (SMBb) Mount log books 1863–1917, admission registers 1884–1933, reports 1909–39, Tunstead C.E. log books 1863–1939, Western Primary log books 1902–49, admission registers 1911–55; (SP) plans: Christ Church 1859, Wesleyan 1860–61

Balderstone (SMB) C.E. log book 1871–1922, admission register 1875–1917, Mellor Brook C.E. log book 1948–62

Bardsea (SMBx) log books 1871–1936, admission register 1886–1936

Barnoldswick (SMBr) C.E. log books 1885–1946, Gisburn Road log books 1907–68, admission registers 1929–68; (ESP) plans: National 1903, Rainhill Road *c.* 1903

Barrow-in-Furness (SP) plans: Hindpool 1864, St. Mary's R.C. 1870

Barrowford (SMBa) Bradley log books 1953–69, Secondary (formerly Congregational) log books 1871–1969, St. Thomas's log book 1869–1914; (SP) plan n.d.; (UDBa) accounts of William Hargreaves, schoolmaster, 1774–95; (EXNe) Council managers' minutes 1935–45; (ESP) Central plan 1907

Barton-in-Amounderness (SMNe) Newsham R.C. log book 1863–1910

Bashall Eaves (ESP) C.E. plan 1903

Bedford (SP) plan n.d.; see also Leigh

Bickerstaffe (SMBa) C.E. log books 1863–1938, admission registers 1860–1938, summary registers 1874–1946; (EXOk) C.E. managers' minutes 1938–68

Billinge (SMBi) C.E. log books 1874–1948, managers' minutes 1870–99, plans 1901, 1910, returns and reports 1900–33; (SP) plans: Birchley R.C. n.d., National 1872; (UDBw) C.E. accounts 1892–1902; (ESP) Elementary plan 1911

Billington (PR2965) cash book 1901–14, miscellanea 1796–1838; (SP) plan n.d.

Bispham (DDX 285) Durning's Free Grammar school minutes 1693–1911, log books 1875–1915, account books 1876–1949, letter books 1910–39, records of admission 1875–93, deeds 1691–1862, inspectors' reports 1884–1912, correspondence, etc. 1845–1925, school magazine 1897–1916; (EXOk) Durning's managers' minutes 1955–71

Blackburn (DDBk) Grammar foundation deed 1514, letters patent 1567, minutes 1590–1867, agreements etc. 1586–1660, accounts 1660, 1683–88, 1789–1869, registration slips 1820–42, legal papers 1585–91, correspondence 1746–1855, applications for teaching posts 1803, 1807, 1808, 1812, 1819, 1845, 1849, deeds of lands in Mellor and Samlesbury 1301–1475, plans 1837, miscellanea 1704–1913; (SP) plans: All Saints' 1871, Bank Top 1855, Christ Church 1857, Holy Trinity 1841–72, St. John's 1844, St. Michael's 1848–71, St. Peter's 1871, Wesleyan 1860, St. Thomas's 1866, Wensley Fold n.d.; for other schools in Blackburn see p. 98.

Blackley (SP) plans: Barnes Green 1862, Infants n.d.

Blacko (SMBk) Board log books 1875–1928; (EXNe) Council managers' minutes 1935–45

Blackpool (SMBp) Bispham Endowed log books 1877–1961, admission registers 1866–1958, Claremont log books 1907–69, admission registers 1942–64, honours books 1926–65, punishment book 1949–70, outline history 1907–68, Devonshire Road log books 1903–48, admission registers 1928–59, attendance books 1957–66, honours book 1926–65, Grammar admission register 1907–24, fees register 1906–21, applications for admission 1910–18, newspaper cuttings 1933–55, Highfurlong Open-air (formerly Widnes Open-air) log book 1928–64, Marton Baines' Endowed log books 1874–1926, admission registers 1937–50, photographs 1896–1963, Palatine log book 1913–37, admission registers 1913–40, teachers' time book 1939–48, reports 1914–58, Revoe log books 1900–56, managers' minutes 1903–36, admission register 1940–46, visitors' book 1901–37, outline history 1907–53, St.John's log books 1867–1921, admission registers 1865–1936. managers' minutes 1904–17, Thomas Road log books 1903–61, managers' minutes 1903–25, Waterloo Road log book 1904–36, managers' minutes 1904–35, Wesleyan log book 1878–92

Blackrod (SMBl) National log books 1863–1959, admission register 1915–47, accounts 1845–1900, Scot Lane log books 1869–1956, admission registers 1890–1946, managers' minutes 1903–10, returns and reports 1896–1922; (SP) plans: National 1845, Scot Lane 1868; see also Rivington and Blackrod (ESP) Scot Lane plans 1908

Blawith (SMBw) Parochial receipts and sales 1916–52, stocks and stores 1933–51

Bold (SMBo) Bold Heath C.E. log books 1876–1968, admission registers 1876–1968, managers' minutes 1905–37, cash books 1876–1903, plans 1874, 1926, punishment book 1911–35, stock books 1943–68, miscellanea 1873–1968

Bolton (DP 280) programmes 1815–22; (DRCh 37/17) nominations of masters 1726–47; (FRM) Friends' Adult minutes 1894–1916; (SP) plans: All Saints' 1845–56, Christ Church 1857, Emmanuel 1851–71, Holy Trinity 1854–59, St. George's 1864, St. Mark's 1860, SS Peter and Paul R.C. 1858

Bolton-by-Bowland (ESP) Endowed plan 1903

Bootle (SP) plans: St. Alexander's n.d., St. John's n.d.

Bowland Forest (ESP) plans: Thornyholme R.C. 1903, Whitewell 1904

Bradford and Beswick (SP) plan 1864

Bretherton (DDCm) book containing "a true description . . . of the first rysinge or beginninge of the School of Bretherton" 1652–98, deeds and papers (land in Eccleston, Bretherton, Accrington and Musbury) 1628–1774; (PR 2851) trustees' minutes 1654–1776, correspondence 1813–79, accounts 1835–1909, cash book 1879–89, reports 1885–1925

Briercliffe (SMBc) log books 1890–1958, admission registers 1890–1956, Evening log book 1893–1958, admission register 1893–1917; (SP) St. James's plan 1854; (EXNe) Council managers' minutes 1925–45

Brierfield (SMBr) Congregational log books 1881–99, Council log books 1905–31, managers' minutes 1904–27, Holy Trinity R.C. log book 1895–1921, admission register 1912–54, National log book 1874–1902, Wesleyan log book 1885–1901

Brindle (SMBd) log book 1864–1925, admission register 1876–1926, trustees' minutes 1868–82, deeds 1865–75, accounts 1906–42, correspondence 1916–48; (SP) plans 1864–77; (DDCm) appointments of trustees 1715–1802; (ESP) Gregson Lane plan 1904.

Broughton-in-Furness Domestic Subjects Centre record and syllabus book 1953–59, Aulthurside C.E. log books 1875–1958, admission registers 1875–1958, stocks and stores 1949–58

Burnage (SP) plan 1859

Burnley (DDBd) parish school papers 1890–1902; (RCBt) St. Aloysius R.C. log book 1863–1902

Burscough (SMBu) Methodist log books 1871–1936, admission registers 1871–1939, managers' minutes 1870–1903, centenary papers 1971, R.C. accounts 1881–85 and papers 1848–1911, St. John's log books 1871–1921, 1944–66, admission registers 1925–66, managers' minutes 1891–1935; (EXOk) Practical Instruction Centre managers' minutes 1913–51, St. John's managers' minutes 1935–61, Wesleyan managers' minutes 1903–56

Burtonwood (PR2720) building accounts 1605, teachers' salaries 1608–1797

Bury (DDBy) Grammar deeds 1369–1856, building accounts etc. 1761–1800, estate papers 1665–1876, registers 1923–61, examination questions 1831–56, inspection reports 1907–13, trustees' minutes and accounts 1840–67, apprenticeship indentures 1732–1854, and many printed *ephemera*.

Butterworth (DDRo) deeds and papers 1726–1915, correspondence 1792–1915

Carleton (SME) log book 1875–97

Carnforth (ESP) Elementary plans 1912

Cartmel (PR) masters' bonds 1709–1844, receipts and accounts 1843–82, correspondence 1844–82, deeds 1605–1882, miscellanea 1845–80; (DRCh 37/27) nominations of masters 1716–1832; (SMCx) fourth year log book 1952–58, admission register 1954–58, schemes of work 1957; (EXU1) special subjects centre managers' minutes 1928–58; (SP) plans: Grammar n.d., National 1859

Cartmel Fell (SMCa) log books 1873–1971

Castleton (SP) All Souls' plan 1872

Caton (DDX 600) accounts 1862; (DDGa) rules of Brookhouse girls n.d.

Chadderton (SMCh) Bourne Street log book 1893–1910, Busk Wesleyan log book 1904–24, Christ Church log books 1909–38, Cowhill log book 1894–1905, Drury Lane log books 1894–1926, Denton Lane log book 1904–21, Eaves Lane log book 1921–70, Middleton Junction Wesleyan log books 1874–1968, trustees' minutes 1873–95, Mills Hill log books 1894–1922, Pupil Teacher Centre log book 1899–1906, Stanley Road log books 1901–54. (SP) Hollinwood plan n.d.; (ESP) Park Street plan 1924

Charnock Richard (SMCk) log books 1861–1933, plan 1858, illuminated address 1914; (ESP) Christ Church plan 1896

Chatburn (SMCb) log book 1901–57

Cheetham (SP) St. Marks' plan 1872

Chorley (SMCc) St. George's log books 1863–1909, St. Mark's log book 1929–64, St. Peter's log books 1881–1970; (UCh) Unitarian teachers' accounts (giving names of children) 1768–1857; (SP) plans: Parochial 1834–57, St. George's 1856, St. Mary's R.C. n.d., St. Peter's n.d.

Chorlton-on-Medlock (SP) plans: St. Luke's 1861, St. Saviour's 1857

Church (SMCu) Ernest Street log book 1872–1914; (SP) plan 1859; (EXRi) Church and Oswaldtwistle managers' minutes 1929–34

Claife (SMCf) High Wray log books 1877–1931, admission register 1877–1922, Sawrey C.E. log book 1967–69

Clayton-le-Moors (SMCl) All Saints' log books 1881–1915, admission register 1915–37. managers' minutes 1880–1903, receipts and sales 1914–66, medical reports 1932–52, British log book 1871–1912, Mount Pleasant log book 1912–25, Oakenshaw Wesleyan log books 1863–1912, St. James's log books 1863–1938, admission register 1893–1953, cash book 1911–57, school pence and teachers' salaries accounts 1879–1911, St. Mary's R.C. (formerly St. Edward's) log books 1871–1946; (SP) plans

1856–70; (PR 2983) Enfield Infants accounts 1867–87; (EXRi) Arthur Street managers' minutes 1907–12, Mount Pleasant managers' minutes 1911–39 (ESP) Mount Pleasant plans 1908, 1931

Clayton-le-Woods (SP) plan 1871

Clifton-with-Salwick (SMCs) managers' minutes 1903–33

Clitheroe (DDX 22 and 28 and DX) Grammar minutes 1700, 1844–78 accounts 1680–1825, 1834–52, 1854–1915, rentals 1854–1915, leases 1730–1847, Endowed Schools Commission papers 1864–71, deeds and papers relating to the school and its property in Clitheroe, and Almondbury, Easby, Hellifield, Honley, Skipton, Thornton-in-Craven, co. York 1554–1896, log book of *Dolphin* of Lancaster 1774–78; (PR) National minutes 1839–1903, St. James's infants deeds and papers 1839–59; (SMCi) Low Moor log book 1913–53, St. James's log books 1863–1965, admission registers 1916–33, punishment book 1900–23, honours book 1912–64; (SP) plans: St. James's 1840, St. Mary's (n.d.); (EXRi) Nursery managers' minutes 1947–51

Cliviger (SMK) Holme log book 1890–1933, admission register 1890–1958, plans 1889–99, Mereclough log books 1872–1930

Cockerham (PR) deeds and papers 1793–1831, accounts 1830, 1859–68. (SP) plans 1859–82

Colne (SMCo) Black Lane Ends log book 1899–1924, admission register 1899–1924, Christ Church log books 1871–1939, Church log books 1908–28, reports on religious instruction 1885–1924, Emmott minutes 1903–12, log book 1873–1912, Exchange Street log book 1898–1928, George Street log book 1901–02, Laneshaw Bridge log book 1912–53, Lord Street infants log books 1900–59, admission registers 1900–55, Lord Street junior log books 1902–51, admission register 1928–67, National log books 1863–1908, minute book 1903–13, Park Secondary log books 1900–72, Primett Bridge log books 1887–94, 1903–67, admission registers 1929–60, Skipton Road log book 1900, Stanley Street log book 1882–1900, admission register 1886–1900, Unsectarian log book 1886–1900, Waterside National minutes 1903–23, cash book 1866–91, log books 1863–1907, Wesleyan log book 1899–1913; (SP) Christ Church plan 1840; (DDBd) Infant minutes and papers 1834–42, Adult Evening papers 1863–64, Grammar foundation papers 1880–1920 and rebuilding papers 1812; (ESP) Secondary plan 1929

Colton (SMCt) Bouth log books 1873–1937, admission registers 1873–1937; (PR 2850) C.E. cash book 1886–95; (SP) Finsthwaite plan 1873; (SMFi) Finsthwaite log books 1875–1970, admission register 1946; (EXUl) Finsthwaite managers' minutes 1853–70, Haverthwaite managers' minutes 1954–70

Coniston (SMCn) Practical Instruction Centre record book 1955–59

Coppull (PR 2865) National log book 1892–1910, admission register 1904–38, Chapel Lane letter book 1910–17; (SP) plan 1862

Croft see Southworth

Crompton (SP) plans: High Crompton 1846, St. James's n.d., Shaw 1859

Cronton (SMCr) managers' minutes 1894–98, correspondence 1930–56, plans 1922, 1928

Crosby (DDX 892) Waterloo Grammar drama programmes 1939–71, sports programmes 1954–68; (ESP) Waterloo Elementary plans 1912, 1931; Secondary plans 1910; see also Great Crosby

Croston (SMF) Church log books 1871–1931; (PR) minute and account book 1661–1851, deeds 1668–1804

Culcheth (SP) plans: Lately Common n.d., Risley Presbyterian 1850–55

Dalton (SMD) log book 1878–1908, reports and returns 1899–1967

Dalton-in-Furness (EXUl) Council managers' minutes 1928–56, Dowdale's managers' minutes 1949–61, Grouped County managers' minutes 1939–64; (SP) plans 1860–67

Darwen (SMDa) Avondale Road log book 1931–47, Belgrave British log books 1888–1933, Blackburn Road Wesleyan log books 1892–1933, Blacksnape log book 1869–1923, returns and correspondence 1902–23. Bolton Road British log books 1869–1914, Duckworth Street log books 1868–1966, admission registers 1933–66, Earcroft C.E. log books 1865–1963, managers' minutes 1903–14, Highfield Congregational log books 1891–1937, admission registers 1945–66, Hoddlesden St. Paul's log books 1862–1944, managers' minutes 1904–06, Hollins British log books 1871–1966, admission registers 1944–46, Holy Trinity log books 1863–1938, managers' minutes 1903–16, Lower Chapel British log books 1869–1966, St. Barnabas's managers' minutes 1903–17, St. Cuthbert's log books 1871–1944, managers' minutes 1903–14, St. Edward's R.C. managers' minutes 1905–21, St. George's managers' minutes 1904–13, St. James's log books 1873–1924, managers' minutes 1903–11, St. John's log books 1866–1924, admission registers 1916–52, managers' minutes 1904–16, St. Joseph's R.C. log books 1873–1958, managers' minutes 1905–13, Sandhills British log books 1877–1914, Tullyallan Open-air log books 1926–55, Technical women's admission register 1913–22, Wesleyan Central log books 1871–1923, managers' minutes 1878–96; (PR 2878) St.

James's minutes 1878–92, accounts 1882–1903, reports etc. 1881–97

Deane (PR) minutes and accounts 1787–1868, miscellanea 1881–91, deeds (Tottington) 1657–1878; see also Rumworth

Denton (SMDe) Haughton Green County log book 1929–71, Russell Scott log books 1882–1917, reports and correspondence 1881–96, Trinity Wesleyan log books 1874–1913; (SP) Christ Church plan n.d.; (ESP) Duke Street plans *c*. 1910

Didsbury (DRCh 37/43) nominations of masters 1699–1722; (SP) plans 1851–59

Downham (SMDo) log books 1879–1966

Droylsden (SMDr) Littlemoss C.E. log books 1873–1911, 1958–64; (SP) St. Mary's plan n.d.; (ESP) Moorside Council plans 1906

Dunnerdale-with-Seathwaite (SMDu) Seathwaite admission register 1874–1946, receipts and sales 1926–47

Dunnockshaw (SMDu) Clowbridge Baptist Evening log book 1893–1921, Clowbridge National log books 1903–62, managers' minutes 1941–62, Council log books 1869–1972, admission registers 1867–1972. (EXRi) Council managers' minutes 1906–35, Evening managers' minutes 1905–39

Earby (SMEa) County log books 1897–1962, admission registers 1910–46, returns and reports 1895–1930, Evening Institute returns 1897–1902, Kelbrook County log books 1871–1937, admission registers 1896–1946, Springfield log book 1899–1964, admission registers 1939–60; (ESP) plans: Board 1905, Grammar 1904, Kelbrook *c*. 1903, Riley Street 1903

Eccles (SMEc) Beech Street admission register 1922–53, Evening log book 1903–11, Parish log books 1866–1933, admission registers 1887–1939; (SP) Parish plans 1854–65; (ESP) Secondary plan *c*. 1910

Eccleston, Chorley (SMEn) C.E. admission register 1915–54

Eccleston, Prescot (SMEs) Christ Church log book 1871–1909; (SP) St. Thomas's plan n.d.; (DDCs) Hill deeds and papers 1798–1960; (EXPr) Bleak Hill managers' minutes 1951–70, Council managers' minutes 1911–51, Lane Ends managers' minutes 1939–70; (DDX 932) Grammar governors' minutes 1879–1938

Edgworth (SMEd) Children's Home log books 1886–1953, Evening log book 1895–1955, admission register 1910–54, St. Anne's log books 1866–73, Wesleyan log books 1863–1973, admission registers 1881–1957, punishment book 1910–40, Wesleyan Evening log books 1874–1913; (SP) Wesleyan plan 1861; (F RM 16) proposals for Friends' School 1802

75

Egton-with-Newland (SP) Penny Bridge plan 1867; (DDTy) letters and papers 1859–1900

Ellel (SP) plan 1858

Elton (SP) plans: All Saints' 1846, St. Stephen's n.d.

Euxton (PR 2902) trustees' minutes and accounts 1839–1939; (DDSh) papers 1853–61

Everton (SP) plans: Emmanuel 1870, Kensington 1865, R.C. 1871, St. Chrysostom 1854–56, St. George's 1871, St. Peter's 1855–79, St. Saviour's n.d.

Failsworth (SP) plan n.d.

Farington (SMG) New log book 1874–1940, Temporary Council managers' minutes 1939–53; (ESP) Junior plans *c.* 1920

Farnworth (SMFa) Francis Street log books 1904–33, Green Bank Nursery log books 1930–37, Queen Street Domestic log book 1931–51, Queen Street Training Seminary (later Council) log books 1872–1950, minutes and accounts 1838–56, absent teachers register 1905–43, damages book 1906–32, punishment book 1936–55, St. Thomas's log books 1870–1939, Wesley log book 1903–14; (SP) St. John's plan n.d.

Finsthwaite see Colton

Fleetwood (EXTF) Grammar governors' minutes 1928–64, Provided managers' minutes 1903–57, Secondary managers' minutes 1921–28; (SP) R.C. plan 1841

Flixton (SP) plan n.d.; (DDS1) lease 1672

Formby (SMFo) St. Peter's (formerly Female) book of deeds, accounts, etc. 1833–58, log book 1892–1950, admission register 1896–1904, 1927–35, cash book 1877–1903

Forton (SMFt) County log books 1863–1949, reports 1879, 1882, 1889–1925

Foulridge (SMFr) Evening log book 1900–32, National log books 1863–1949; (SP) plan n.d.

Freckleton (SP) plan 1867

Fulwood (SMFu) Evacuee's log book 1939–45, St. Vincent's R.C. stock book 1956–59, Watling Street managers' minutes 1907–38; (PR) Cadley deeds 1714–22

Garstang (SP) R.C. plan 1857

Garston (SP) plans: Aigburth 1859, National 1865–71

Gisburn (ESP) Council plan 1903

Gisburn Forest (SMGi) Tosside reports and returns 1878–1939; (ESP) Tosside plan 1903

Golborne (SP) plan 1869

Goodshaw (SMGd) Board log book 1897–1922, Council (formerly Baptist) log books 1886–1972, Evening log book 1896–1905

Goosnargh (SMGo) Oliverson's log book 1879–93, governors' minutes 1879–1918, managers' minutes 1903–12, deeds and papers 1658–1895, Whitechapel managers' minutes 1927–51, miscellanea 1888–1927

Gorton (SP) plans: Longsight St. John's 1857, St. Francis R.C. 1860, St. Patrick R.C. 1869

Great Crosby (SP) plans: National n.d., R.C. 1859–72; (DDB1 12) letter *re* fees 1810; see also Crosby

Great Eccleston (SMGe) St. Mary's R.C. admission register 1879–1949; (RC Ec) St. Mary's R.C. log book 1863–1905

Great Harwood (SMHa) British log books 1866–1909, Catholic boys log book 1938–43, Evening admission register 1945–48, National log book 1863–1904, St. John's log books 1889–1973, admission register 1930–64, Technical admission registers 1936–45; (EXRi) Barn Meadow managers' minutes 1906–09, Western managers' minutes 1909–20

Great Marton (PR 1296) deed for school site 1854

Great Sankey (SP) plan n.d.

Greenhalgh-with-Thistleton (SMEp) Esprick log book 1965–74

Gressingham (SMGr) log book 1919–37

Grindleton (SMGn) Lane Ends log book 1898–1945; (ESP) plans: Lane Ends 1903, National 1903

Habergham Eaves (SP) plans: All Saints' 1870, Holy Trinity 1867, Parochial 1845–55

Halewood (SMHw) Boys log book 1898–1934, Girls log books 1866–1926, admission register 1854–80, stock and stores books 1913–50, Infants log books 1893–1926, stock and stores book 1913–26. (SP) plan 1847 (EXPr) Mackett's managers' minutes 1962–69, Plantation managers' minutes 1967–70, Secondary managers' minutes 1967–70

Halliwell (SP) plans: Jubilee n.d., St. Peter's 1857

Halsall (PR 258) terrier 1760

Halton (SMHn) National log book 1863–1925, managers' minutes 1891–1952, letters 1863–1910; (SMAh) Aughton Burton's log book 1907–51

Hapton (SMHp) Bridge National log books 1872–1942, managers' minutes 1873–1954, admission register 1924–70, plans of alterations 1910, MS history, Evening admission register 1906–25;

(SP) plan n.d.; (EXRi) Council managers' minutes 1911–44, Evening managers' minutes 1906–25; (ESP) National plan 1909

Harwood (SP) Christ Church plan n.d.; (EXDa) Wesleyan managers' minutes 1896–1956

Haslingden (SMHs) Baxenden Wesleyan log books 1863–1939, stock and stores book 1921–40, Bury Road British log book 1894–1915, Bury Road Evening log book 1908–33, admission register 1932–45, Bury Road National log books 1894–1915, Central log books 1875–1937, managers' minutes 1915–31, stock and stores book 1932–44, Ewood Bridge National log books 1902–59, Grammar fee book 1925–33, Grane National log book 1878–1913, Helmshore Council log book 1919–41, managers' minutes 1909–31, Helmshore Evening log book 1896–1915, admission register 1912–14, Mechanics' Institute British log book 1870–1902, St. James's log book 1931–40, admission register 1901–40, reports and papers 1884–1939, Technical admission registers 1932–45, Technical and Evening Institute cash book 1895–1901, fee book 1919–33, Wesleyan log book 1863–1915, registers of pupil teachers 1905–08; (SP) plan 1870; (ESP) plans: Grammar 1937, Central 1938, Technical 1908, 1920, 1927

Haverthwaite see Colton

Hawkshead (DRCh 37/59) nominations of masters 1691–1829; (DDSa 14) lease 1721

Haydock (SP) plan 1865

Heapey (SP) White Coppice plan n.d.

Heaton (SP) St. John's plans 1856–69

Hesketh-with-Beconsall (SP) plan 1871

Heyhouses (SMHe) Sabden Board log books 1894–1945, admission registers 1894–1932

Heywood (SMI) Heap Bridge National log book 1873–1922, Heady Hill log book 1945–64, Hill Street log book 1905–06, Hornby Street log book 1863–1909, Queen Street British log books 1871–1906, Regent Street log book 1909–23, St. James's log book 1863–1909, St. John's log books 1867–1929, Wesleyan log book 1878–1906; (PR 2904) St. Luke's managers' minutes 1893–1903; (SP) plans: St. John's n.d., St. Luke's Mount Street n.d., St. Luke's William Street 1856–59

Higham (SMHi) C.E. log books 1873–1961, Methodist log books 1870–1967; (PR 2863) C.E. building papers 1835–39, account book 1873–77; (EXRi) Council managers' minutes 1897–1967, Evening managers' minutes 1905–48

Higher Booths (SP) plans: Crawshaw Booth Wesleyan n.d., Love-clough n.d.

Hindley (SMHd) All Saints' National log books 1863–1925, Hindley Green C.E. reports and papers 1897–1904, Hindley Green Council log book 1927–70, St. Benedict's R.C. log books 1869–1924; (SP) plans: St. Benedict's R.C. 1858–61, St. Peter's 1872; (DDX 740) Hindley and Abram Grammar admission registers 1856–1937, letter books 1887–1926, staff register 1882–1934, accounts 1880–1902, returns and reports 1882–1946, exercise books 1857–59, mine rents 1890–1919, coalmine plans with coal got 1892–1927

Hoghton (SMHo) log book 1903–26, admission register 1874–1918

Hopwood (SMI) British log book 1869–96

Horwich (SMHr) Albert Street log book 1915–50, British log books 1882–1932, Girls Senior log books 1931–59, Methodist log books 1887–1915, St. Catherine's log book 1893–1926; (CUHo) British managers' minutes 1897–1908, letters and papers 1895–1908; (ESP) Chorley New Road plan 1895

Howick (SMP) C.E. Girls log book 1878–1904, Mixed managers' minutes 1904–53

Hulme (SP) plans: St. George's 1871, St. John's 1855, St. Mark's 1853–64, St. Mary's 1864–68, St. Michael's 1862, St. Philip's 1858, St. Stephen's 1867

Hulton (PR 2168) managers' minutes 1887–1927, correspondence etc. 1886–1943

Huncoat (EXRi) Council managers' minutes 1905–29, Evening managers' minutes 1905–26

Hutton (ESP) Grammar plans 1923–34

Huyton (EXPr) Central managers' minutes 1934–45, Malvern managers' minutes 1952–55, Modern managers' minutes 1945–54, Page Moss managers' minutes 1942–54, Park managers' minutes 1923–54, Twig Lane managers' minutes 1934–54

Ince-in-Makerfield (SMIn) Belle Green log books 1869–1940, admission register 1938–56, St. William's R.C. log books 1876–1960; (SP) plan 1849

Inskip (SP) plans 1862–67

Kearsley (SMKe) Moor National log books 1863–1965, admission registers 1871–1929, new building papers 1912–17, photographs of old boys 1914–16, West Domestic Centre log book 1913–35, West Handicraft Centre log book 1913–59; (SP) Moor plan n.d.; (ESP) Secondary plans 1935, 1963

Kirkby (SMKi) Rushy Hey log book 1957–68, admission register 1957–67; (EXPr) Brookfield managers' minutes 1955–60, Cherryfield managers' minutes 1953–63, Millbrook managers' minutes 1956–60, Overdale managers' minutes 1959–60, Park Brow managers' minutes 1954–60, Quarry Green managers' minutes 1956–60, Ruffwood managers' minutes 1958–60, Rushy Hey managers' minutes 1956–60, Simonswood managers' minutes 1954–60, Westvale managers' minutes 1956–60

Kirkdale (SP) plans: St. John's R.C. 1877, St. Lawrence's 1872, St. Mary's 1843–68, St. Paul's 1871

Kirkham (SMKw) The Willows R.C. reports 1865–88, letters and circulars 1866–98, examination schedules 1872–97, plan n.d.; (DDD and PR) Grammar deeds 1602–1809, memoranda book 1832, building account book 1807–08, Girls' Charity accounts 1760–1840, 1795–1893; (EXK1) Kirkham and Wesham Council managers' minutes 1910–45, Kirkham and Wesham Handicraft Centre log book 1910–57; (ESP) Elementary plans 1909

Kirkland (SMGa) managers' minutes 1903–54, account book 1903–47; (PR 2449) correspondence, returns etc., 1768–1824, cash book 1871–1904, plans and tenders 1875

Knowsley (EXPr) Longview Primary managers' minutes 1938–70, Longview Secondary managers' minutes 1945–70, Maypole managers' minutes 1942–63, Nine Tree, Brookside, Croft, and Cantril Farm managers' minutes 1967–70, Stockbridge managers' minutes 1951–70, Woolfall managers' minutes 1956–70

Lancaster (SMQ) Dallas Road log books 1912–66, Dallas Road Women's Home Training Centre log book 1924–26, Domestic Science log books 1902–31, Girls' Charity log book 1876–96, Middle Street log book 1899–1939, St. Anne's log books 1863–1972, admission registers 1906–72, managers' minutes 1953–72, punishment book 1931–72, term test record 1955–71, St. John's managers' minutes 1904–23, St. Luke's log books 1871–1963, St. Mary's National log books 1880–1939, Scotforth National log books 1868–1944, admission registers 1875–1922, managers' minutes 1877–1915, Scotforth Open-air log book 1923–27, Skerton Evening log book 1919–34, Wesleyan log books 1877–1912; (SP) plans: British n.d., National 1855–60, St. John's 1867, St. Thomas's 1847; (DDX 116) Grammar magazines 1893–1964

Lathom (SMLa) Evening log book 1897–1916, St. James's log books 1863–1964, medical reports 1913–45; (SMNw) Newburgh log books 1870–1945; (SP) St. James's plan 1870; (EXOk) Park managers' minutes 1903–63, St. James's managers' minutes 1902–57

Lea, Ashton, Ingol, and Cottam (SP) plans: Ashton n.d., Lea n.d.; (ESP) Lea Greaves Lane plan 1952

Lees (SMAs) Zion British reports 1856, 1860

Leigh (SMLh) Church Street Baptist log book 1878–1909, Windermere Road log book 1908–32; (SP) Parish plan n.d.; see also Bedford and Westleigh

Levenshulme (SP) plan n.d.

Leyland (SMLe) Earnshaw Bridge St. John's log book 1919–51

Litherland (SMLi) Holy Sepulchre R.C. log book 1887–1933, St. Philip's log book 1910–29

Littleborough (SMO) Evening log books 1896–1928, Lake View Children's Hospital log book 1952–63, Shore log books 1869–1963; (SP) plans: C.E. 1843, Dearnley n.d., Shore 1873; (ESP) Summit plan c. 1900

Little Hoole (SML1) Dob Lane log books 1863–1949; (ESP) Walmer Bridge plans 1936

Little Hulton (SP) St. John's plans 1863–71

Little Lever (SMLv) Senior log books 1934–67, Wesleyan log books 1885–1934; (SP) plan 1848

Little Woolton (SP) plan n.d.

Liverpool (DDX 58) Picton's Academy exercise book 1843

Livesey (SMLs) Feniscowles log books 1907–27, admission registers 1907–45, St. Francis' (formerly Immanuel) log books 1866–1911, managers' minutes 1903–63; (PR 2846) Feniscowles trustees' minutes 1888–1929, correspondence and accounts 1874–1913; (EXRi) Feniscowles Council managers' minutes 1907–26

Longridge (SMLn) British managers' minutes 1903–55, Smith's C.E. log books 1869–1959, returns etc. 1924–38, punishment book 1935–43, inventory 1941; (SP) plans 1858–66; (ESP) Smith's C.E. plan 1935, special subjects centre plan 1915

Longton (SMLo) C.E. log books 1877–1925, Council managers' minutes 1925–51; (DDLa) minutes and accounts 1793–1863; (ESP) New Longton Infants plans pre-1944

Lowick (DDLk 10/34) agreement to establish school 1757; (SP) plan 1856

Lowton (SP) plan 1869

Lydiate (SP) R.C. plan n.d.

Lytham (SMJ) Endowed log books 1874–1975, admission registers 1874–1975, reports 1877–1964, teachers' agreements 1878–1925, returns 1910–25, St. Peter's R.C. log book 1863–87; (SP) St. John's plan n.d.; (DDB 74/9) Seafield handbill c. 1850; (DDTs) accounts of Seafield pupil 1882–84; (EXK1) Cookery Centre log books 1940–57; (RCLy) St. Peter's R.C. papers 1865–1959; (DDX 103) Lytham (School) Charities minutes 1845–99, accounts 1750–1886

Maghull (SMMa) C.E. log books 1901–35, managers' minutes 1839–1947, miscellanea 1838–1939

Manchester (SP) Collyhurst plan; (RCMa) St. Augustine's R.C. managers' minutes 1903–38, accounts 1868–72; (RCMc) St. Chad's reports 1858–65, cash book 1879–82; (DDX 185) minute books of "the gentlemen educated at the free grammar school" concerning a monument to Charles Lawson, High Master, 1807–09, with letters, etc., 1749–1836

Marsden (SP) Lomeshaye plan n.d.

Mawdesley (SMMw) Methodist log book 1931–71; (SP) R.C. plan 1857

Mearley see Pendleton

Middleton (SMM) All Saints' log books 1866–71, admission registers 1877–1927, Bowlee Methodist log books 1876–1967, New Jerusalem log books 1863–1910, Providence Congregational log book 1890–1910, Rhodes Council admission register 1938–53, Wood Street Wesleyan log book 1874–1910; (SP) plans: C.E. n.d., Rhodes n.d.; (DDX 655) Grammar foundation charter 1572 (photocopy)

Milnrow (SMMi) New Hey British log books 1881–1914, New Hey St. Thomas's log book 1917–35, Ogden Endowed log books 1879–1965, managers' minutes 1904–65, admission registers 1881–1965, reports and returns 1878–1927; (SP) plans: National 1840, New Hey n.d.

Morecambe (SMMc) Poulton Board (later Central and Euston Road) log books 1877–1973, admission registers 1895–1973, summary registers 1942–73, reports 1905–50, school meals attendances 1966–73, record cards 1960–73; (SP) Poulton plan 1855

Mossley (SMMo) Micklehurst All Saints' log books 1863–1956; (DDX 296) Miss Lotherington's school exercise books and prospectuses 1866–68

Moston (SP) plan 1843

Much Hoole (DDPr 77) case re schoolmaster's stipend c. 1790; (PR 2892) memoranda 18th cent.

Much Woolton (SP) plan 1847

Musbury Helmshore (SMHs) Evening log book 1896–1915, admission registers 1912–14, fee book 1925–29

Nateby (PR 2979) cash book 1874–1903, reports, returns etc., 1874–97, accounts 1897–1907

Nelson (SML) Bradley log books 1895–1952, Bradshaw Street log books 1908–58, Carr Road log books 1874–1924, Edge End Senior log book 1932–48, Junior Instruction Centre log books 1935–37, Leeds Road log books 1878–1938, Railway Street log books 1889–1908, Reedyford Wesleyan log book 1885–1910, St. John's log books 1863–1945, admission registers 1869–1954, St. Joseph's R.C. log book 1896–1927, St. Joseph's Evening log book 1898–1921, St. Mary's managers' minutes 1897–1900, St. Paul's log books 1879–1958, admission registers 1879–1953, reports and returns 1879–1925, Scotland Road log books 1881–1904, Walverden log book 1899–1922; (ESP) Secondary plans 1922.

Nether Wyresdale (SMX) Dolphinholme log book 1865–1917

Newchurch-in-Pendle (SMNc) C.E. log books 1873–1907, 1925–54, reports and returns 1877–1903, 1925–60, admission register 1900–62; (DDBd) St. Mary's building papers 1872–77

Newchurch-in-Rossendale; (SP) Edgeside plan 1871; see also Bacup

Newsham (SMNb) R.C. log book 1863–1910

Newton, Manchester (SP) All Saints' plans 1853, 1860

Newton-in-Makerfield (SMNe) All Saints' log books 1867–1950, admission register 1918–64, Earlestown C.E. log book 1863–1912, admission register 1899–1922, St. Peter's log book 1865–88; (SP) plans: Earlestown 1857, St. Mary's R.C. n.d., St. Peter's 1859, Wargrave n.d.

Newton-with-Scales (DDNw) Blue School trustees' accounts 1707–1861, plans 1781 etc., master's testimonials 1799, inventories 1776–1822, apprenticeship indentures 1712–1877, deeds (Freckleton, Kirkham, Newton-with-Scales, Warton, Weeton-with-Preese, Thistleton, Norbreck, Great and Little Eccleston 1371–1863.

North Meols (SP) Churchtown plan n.d.; (EXOk) Banks Methodist managers' minutes 1955–64, Banks St. Stephen's managers' minutes 1960–67

Oldham (SP) plans: Coldhurst 1855, Glodwick 1854, Greenacres Moor n.d., St. Mary's R.C. 1858, St. Peter's 1845, St. Stephen's 1871, St. Thomas's 1872, Waterhead n.d.; (RCO1) St. Mary's R.C. managers' minutes 1911–22

Old Laund Booth (SMOd) Fence C.E. log books 1863–1968

Openshaw (SP) plan n.d.

Ormskirk (DDX 191) Grammar governors' minutes 1612–1952, accounts 1612–1952, admission register 1889–1910, fees register 1894–1904, letter books 1909–20, memoranda books 1920–29, inspectors' reports 1887–1921, deed 1625–1916; (SMOk) United Charities log books 1863–1952, admission registers 1888–1952, punishment book 1902–46, reports, returns etc. 1863–1933; (SP) United Charities plan 1872; (EXOk) Girls' Council managers' minutes 1923–37, Senior Council managers' minutes 1938–47, United Charities managers' minutes 1913–52

Orrell (SMOr) Holgate Independent log book 1883–1921, MS. history 1970; (SP) Lamberhead Green Wesleyan plan 1858; (ESP) Holgate's plan 1911, Far Moor plans 1911

Osmotherley (DRCh 37/132) appointment of master 1741; (SMOm) Broughton Bank admission register 1876–1955

Oswaldtwistle (SMOs) Cockerbrook log book 1907–18, Hippings Wesleyan log books 1863–1934, admission registers 1889–1955, Hippings Vale C.E. log books 1887–1961, punishment book 1900–08, Holy Trinity log books 1871–1930, Knuzden St. Oswald's log books 1863–1929, admission register 1877–1928, Moor End log book 1930–38, New Lane log book 1892–1915, St. Mary's R.C. log book 1872–1959, admission register 1912–58, history 1948, St. Paul's log books 1883–93, 1924–46, Stanhill St. Matthew's log books 1887–1930, United Methodist log books 1885–1930; (SP) plans: Belthorn n.d., Cabin End 1859, New Lane n.d.; (EXRi) Belthorn Independent managers' minutes 1955–65, Church and Oswaldtwistle managers' minutes 1929–34, Special Subjects Centre managers' minutes 1911–23, West End managers' minutes 1913–29

Over Kellet (DDX 103) appointment of grammar trustees 1698

Overton (SP) plan 1871

Over Wyresdale (SMAy) Abbeystead Cawthorne's Endowed trustees' minutes and accounts 1684–1908, log books 1879–1932, admission register 1868–95, plan 1928, reports 1879–1922

Padiham (SMPd) Cross Bank Wesleyan log book 1907–24, Green C.E. log books 1875–1927, 1949–63, admission register 1901–09, St. John's R.C. log books 1874–1970, St. Leonard's log books 1869–1945, admission registers 1928–68, cash book 1873–76, Secondary governors' minutes 1958–66, Technical admission registers 1915–47, Wesleyan log books 1910–68; (SP) plan 1857; (PR 2863) St. Leonard's trustees' minutes and accounts 1822–63, Girls and Infants log book 1863–91, senior mixed log books

1891–92, 1897–1960, infants log books 1891–1933, managers' minutes 1907–45, managers' accounts 1908–42, admission registers 1911–57, returns 1910–39, miscellanea 1756–1962; (UDPa 17/45) Technical reports and papers 1891–1905; (EXRi) County secondary managers' minutes 1953–66, Cross Bank Council managers' minutes 1907–18, St. Leonards' Secondary managers' minutes 1903–58; (ESP) Elementary plans 1908, St. Matthew's plan pre-1941

Parbold (SMPa) Douglas National log book 1879–1928, miscellanea 1880–1924

Parr (SP) plans n.d.; see also St. Helens

Paythorn (SMPy) log books 1908–76 (ESP) Newsholme plan 1903

Pemberton (SP) plans 1870

Pendlebury (SMPn) St. Augustine's log book 1906–48 (SP) St. John's plan n.d.

Pendleton and Mearley (SMPe) log book 1912–45, admission register 1863–1943, attendance registers 1868–88, 1922–39, Sunday school attendances 1874–86; (PR 2994) miscellanea 1837–1952

Pendleton, Salford (SP) plans: Charlestown n.d., St. Paul's n.d., Weaste Lane 1847, Wesleyan n.d.

Penketh (SP) Wesleyan plan n.d.

Penwortham (SMP) Cop Lane managers' minutes 1903–53, correspondence, plans etc. 1919–53, council managers' minutes 1939–53, End infants log book 1878, attendance register 1876–79, accounts, reports etc., 1875–79, Middleforth accounts etc., 1860–87; (ESP) junior plan 1950

Pilkington (SMPi) Besses-o'th' Barn British log books 1878–1920, Park Lane British log books 1862–1920; (DDX 759) Stand grammar vouchers 1786–1811, trustees' proceedings 1797–98, 1822–23, application for mastership 1798, contract for fittings 1913; (SP) plans: Stand All Saints' 1871, Stand Lane n.d.; (ESP) Higher Lane plans 1914, Stand secondary plans 1937

Pilling (SP) plan 1855 (SMPl) Eagland Hill log books 1953–58

Pleasington (SBP) Board log book 1878–1933; (PR 2653) accounts 1831–62, miscellanea 1824–79

Poulton-le-Fylde (UDPo) Evening log book 1898–1907; (DDHu) Baines' governors' minutes 1904–41, accounts 1881–1924, letter books 1882–1912, 1920–32, reports 1882–1929; (PR 2831) C.E. report 1874–97; (EXTF) Hodgson senior managers' minutes 1932–56

Poulton-with-Fearnhead (SP) Padgate plan 1843

Prescot (SMPs) Handicraft Centre log book 1926–42; (DDPs) Grammar accounts 1678–88, deeds and papers 1686–1960, admission register 1903–37, press cuttings 1909–37, grant-of-arms 1933, log book 1877–1901; (EXPr) Council managers' minutes 1904–70, Further Education Centre managers' minutes 1945–70, Girls' Grammar governors' minutes 1955–70, Grammar governors' minutes 1950–70; (ESP) Secondary plan 1922.

Preston (SMPr) All Saints' log books 1863–1937, Ashton Methodist log books 1893–1957, managers' minutes 1904–58, Ashton St. Andrew's log books 1887–1958, admission register 1904–37, managers' minutes 1904–72, Ashton St. Michael's log book 1904–59, admission register 1926–59, Bairstow Street Temporary log book 1939–45, admission register 1939–45, Barlow Street Wesleyan managers' minutes 1894–1904, Brockholes County Secondary log book 1965–75, photographs 1968–75, Christ Church log books 1862–1968, admission registers 1917–69, punishment book 1896–1935, Deepdale County Secondary log book 1928–64, photographs 1961–64, Domestic Subjects Centre log books 1908–65, Eldon Street Council log books 1886–1959, admission registers 1917–59, Eldon Street Higher Grade log book 1892–98, Eldon Street Wesleyan log book 1866–1904, Emmanuel log book 1866–1904, English Martyrs R.C. log books 1871–1965, admission registers 1871–1965, Falcon Street Handicraft Centre log book 1939–58, Fishwick Council Senior log book 1936–64, admission registers 1936–59, photograph albums 1951–62, Fishwick St. Mary's log book 1877–97, Frenchwood County Secondary miscellanea 1933–58, photographs 1933–64, Grimshaw Street British log books 1868–1928, Hincksman Memorial Methodist log books 1862–1953, admission register 1916–58, Holy Trinity log books 1882–1970, admission registers 1932–70, Maitland Street Manual Training log book 1908–58, Orchard Methodist log book 1909–32, Parish Church log books 1878–1928, admission register 1878–1955, Plungington Road National log book 1902–39, admission register 1902–11, Ribbleton Avenue Methodist log book 1884–1927, admission register 1941–60, St. Augustine's R.C. log book 1863–1965, admission registers 1876–1951, St. Barnabas' log book 1873–1910, St. Cuthbert's log book 1939–60, admission registers 1911–59, St. Ignatius's R.C. log books 1919–63, admission registers 1891–1965, St. James's log books 1872–1938, St. Jude's log books 1894–1957, admission registers 1914–57, St. Luke's log books 1870–1959, admission register 1904–59, St. Mark's log books 1864–1958, admission register 1919–58, St. Mary's log books 1880–1948, admission register 1894–1946, St. Mary Street Methodist log books 1871–1959, admission registers

1875–1959, St. Matthew's log books 1887–1959, admission registers 1900–58, St. Paul's log books 1862–1937, St. Peter's log books 1875–1946, admission registers 1925–46, St. Saviour's log books 1880–1940, admission registers 1925–59, managers' minutes 1904–59, St. Thomas's log books 1872–1956, admission registers 1936–56, St. Thomas's Evening log book 1900–05, St. Wilfrid's R.C. admission registers 1871–1957, Wycliffe Memorial log book 1939–43, admission register 1939–43; (CBP) Barlow Street managers' minutes 1907–09, Deepdale Council managers' minutes 1910–38, Deepdale Modern governors' minutes 1928–43, Moor Park Open-air managers' minutes 1919–30, Nursery managers' minutes 1931, Special managers' minutes 1931–53, Youth Employment Bureau annual reports 1950–70, Director of Observatories reports 1951–72, attendance committee complaints books 1889–1941, register of school meals 1914–48, school attendance returns 1927–53, register of child entertainers 1932–37, clog register 1935–45, register of casual employment 1940–50; (SP) plans: All Saints' 1853, Christ Church 1857, Emmanuel 1872, English Martyrs R.C. n.d., Orchard Street Wesleyan 1857, St. Ignatius's R.C. n.d., St. James's n.d., St. Luke's 1861, St. Mary's 1846–56, St. Matthew's n.d., St. Paul's 1853–57, St. Peter's 1859, St. Peter's Brook Street 1855, St. Thomas's 1845–55, St. Wilfrid's R.C. n.d., Trinity 1843; (PR 2972) St. Jude's managers' minutes 1904–55; (DDX 465) Mill Hill Ragged contribution book 1926–45; (DDX 725) National 1st annual report 1816; (PR 2900) Queen Street Ragged subscriptions 1859–66; (PR 1490–92) Bluecoat registers, memoranda and accounts 1703–1926; (PR 2315) Trinity correspondence etc. 1878–95; (PR 2845) miscellanea 1702–1956; (DDX 4) Cambridge House index of pupils 1932–58, miscellanea 1928–55

Prestwich (SP) Rooden Lane British plan 1853

Quernmore (DDQ) log books 1863–1950, managers' minutes 1923–58; (SP) plan 1857

Radcliffe (SP) plans: Bank Top n.d., Close Wesleyan n.d., St. Joseph's R.C. 1857; (ESP) St. Paul's plans 1885

Rainford (SMRf) Crank Hill National log books 1868–1932, admission register 1869–89, cash books 1874–1930, reports and papers 1873–1925, National log books 1864–1940, admission registers 1869–1921, managers' minutes 1875–1955, cash books 1880–1921, reports and papers 1901–25, plans c. 1900, National Continuation log book 1896–1912; (EXPr) Bushey Lane managers' minutes 1958–70, C.E. managers' minutes 1955–63, Crank Hill managers' minutes 1959–70, Longton Lane managers' minutes 1954–70, Senior Council managers' minutes 1940–70

Ramsbottom (SMR) Buckhurst log book 1914–60, Evening log book 1893–1932, St. Andrew's log books 1868–1968, managers' minutes 1922–61, cash book 1928–51, specification 1873, Turn log books 1880–1968, Wesleyan log books 1863–1948, admission registers 1877–1933, account book 1890–1902, schemes of work 1941–44, returns and papers 1900–39

Rawtenstall (SMRa) Alder Grange log books 1920–73, Belmond Special reports 1953, 1957, Cloughfold log books 1868–1946, admission register 1936–59, Constable Lee St. Paul's log books 1868–1963, Cowpe Council log books 1912–66, Crawshaw Booth St. John's log books 1863–1972, Evening log book 1897–1900, Lea Bank Secondary log books 1926–71, Lumb National log books 1871–1953, Townsendfold log books 1883–1902, 1924–57, Handicraft Centre log books 1909–25, Water log books 1876–1962, admission register 1915–55, punishment book 1900–01, Wesleyan log books 1863–1937, Whitewell Bottom log books 1889–1960; (SMGd) Goodshaw Baptist log books 1886–1972, Goodshaw Board log book 1897–1922, Goodshaw Evening log book 1896–1905; (MRo) Longholme Wesleyan minutes 1868–1904

Read (SMRe) Congregational log books 1888–1929

Reddish (SP) St. Joseph's R.C. plan 1857

Ribby-with-Wrea (SMWr) Endowed log book 1878–1909, managers' minutes 1848–1907, accounts 1848–84, Girls' log book 1879–93, admission register 1895–1921, reports 1859–64, accounts 1884–1917, miscellanea 1877–1953; (DDD and DDH) accounts 1716–1848, deeds 1571–1825, correspondence 1715–55

Ribchester (SMRb) Evening log book 1899–1926, Knowle Green British log books 1872–1962, admission registers 1882–1961, managers' minutes 1954–62, register of evacuees 1939, National log books 1872–1922, admission registers 1872–1960, managers' minutes 1910–47, cash book 1878–96; (SP) plan 1871

Rishton (SMRi) Evening log book 1894–1934, admission registers 1938–54, Methodist log books 1867–1927, plan *c.* 1860, Primitive Methodist log book 1908–43, admission register 1889–1943, SS. Peter and Paul's log books 1867–1953, Secondary log book 1942–61.

Rivington and Blackrod (DDX 94) Blackrod: deeds 1609–1823, vouchers 1802–75, accounts 1736–1875, correspondence 1800–46, minutes 1849–76, legal papers 1847–49; Rivington: accounts 1574–1711, vouchers 1794–1842, correspondence 1725–1861, registers 1575, 1836–75, memoranda book 1615–1857, statutes 1570, 1714, miscellanea 1571–1868; Rivington and Blackrod

Grammar: accounts 1884–89, mark book 1893–94, examination results 1904–10, committees' minutes 1882–89, admission registers 1905–45, library register 1882–1906, nominal register 1882–90, miscellanea 1560–1945; and see above, Blackrod

Rochdale (SMNo) Bagslate Wesleyan log books 1871–1929, Greenbooth log books 1867–1931, Lanehead Wesleyan log book 1874–1928, Red Lumb log book 1906–30; (SP) plans: Buersill n.d., Hamer St. John's 1862, Newbold St. Peter's 1871, Parochial n.d., St. Albans n.d., St. Chad's n.d., St. Mary's n.d.; (DRCh 37/110) nomination of Grammar master 1755

Roughlee Booth (SMRo) log book 1882–1925

Royton (SBR) Board log book 1897–1912, Central Board log book 1900–19, Wesleyan log book 1891–1909; (SP) St. Paul's plan n.d.

Rufford (SMRu) C.E. log books 1878–1937, punishment book 1900–45.

Rumworth (SP) Deane plan 1851

Rusholme (SP) Trinity plan n.d.

Sabden (EXRi) Council managers' minutes 1903–58, Evening managers' minutes 1905–48; see also Heyhouses

St. Annes-on-Sea (EXKl) Council managers' minutes 1923–54

St. Helens (SP) plans: Church Street n.d., Cowley's n.d., Duke Street n.d., Parr Mount 1858–67, St. Joseph's R.C. 1857, Wesleyan n.d.; see also Parr and Sutton

Salesbury SMSa) C.E. log books 1888–1966, admission registers 1867–1948, reports and returns 1868–1931; (PR 2885) building minutes 1805–13

Salford (SP) plans: Brindle Heath 1858, Great George Street 1859, Lower Broughton National 1858, Lower Broughton St. Andrew's 1871, Lower Broughton St. Nicholas's n.d., St. Bartholomew's 1844–66, St. Matthias's 1841, St. Peter's R.C. n.d., St. Simon's 1855, Stowell Memorial 1871

Salterforth (SMCo) log books 1872–1970, plans 1910; (ESP) National plan 1904

Samlesbury (RCSa) Sowerbutts Green diary of work 1875–80

Sawley (SMSy) County log books 1877–1976, report 1969; (ESP) Council plan 1903

Scarisbrick (SMSb) County log book 1876–1909, admission register 1876–97, punishment book 1926–42, building accounts 1816–17, trustees' minutes 1875–92, cash books 1875–1903, correspondence 1876–1940; (EXOk) Council managers' minutes 1926–74

Scorton (SMSc) British log books 1863–1966, admission register 1858–94, R.C. log books 1875–1951

Sharples (SP) Astley Bridge plan 1858; (UDTu) Belmont National managers' minutes 1875–98, cash book 1886–98

Shevington (ESP) Broad o'th' Lane plans 1922–24

Silverdale (SP) plan 1854

Simonstone (PR 2863) specifications, accounts and subscription letters 1837–57

Simonswood see Kirkby

Skelmersdale (SMSm) Barnes Road log books 1880–1923, Blaguegate Wesleyan log books 1872–1967; (EXOk) Barnes Road managers' minutes 1903–24, Blaguegate Methodist managers' minutes 1903–51, C.E. managers' minutes 1926–66, Council managers' minutes 1924–51, County Secondary managers' minutes 1957–67, Practical Instruction Centre managers' minutes 1951–54

Skelwith (SMSk) Brathay C.E. log books 1863–1970

Slaidburn (ESP) plans: Brennand's 1904, Girls 1903

Southport (SMSo) Christ Church Higher Grade Boys managers' minutes 1898–1904, Christ Church National drawing c. 1840, St. Andrew's Higher Grade Girls managers' minutes 1888–1916; (SP) plans: Christ Church 1854, St. Paul's 1863, Trinity 1856–60

Southworth-with-Croft (SP) Croft plan 1854

Spotland (SP) St. Clement's plan 1853

Stainton-with-Adgarley (SMSt) C.E. log book 1904–27, admission register 1904–27

Stalmine-with-Staynall (SP) plan n.d.

Standish (DDX 211) pupils' Latin speeches 1775–77

Staveley (SP) plan 1875; (DDTy) letters and papers 1828–1909

Stretford (PR 81, 82) deeds 1845, 1865; (SP) plans 1843–64

Sutton (SP) plans: National 1863, Peasley Cross Holy Trinity 1856, St. Anne's 1868

Swinton (PUG) industrial schools: institution admission and discharge books 1846–48, 1850–1934, school admission and discharge books 1892–1926, indices 1848–1935, master's journal 1922–29. (These schools were established by the Manchester Board of Guardians)

Tarleton (SMTa) C.E. managers' minutes 1912–38, Central managers' minutes 1930–49, Domestic Science cash books 1954–62; (EXOk) County manager's minutes 1949–69; (ESP) Council plans 1928

Tatham (SMTt) St. James's log book 1876–1914, managers' minutes 1903–69, building agreement 1875, school-farm papers and accounts 1882–1958

Thornley (EV 6) report 1938

Thornton-le-Fylde (DDPb) deeds 1735–1806; (EXTF) Baines's managers' minutes 1948–53, Provided managers' minutes 1903–48, Secondary managers' minutes 1948–56

Thurnham (SMTh) Evening log book 1905–06, Glasson Dock C.E. log books 1863–1925, R.C. log books 1887–1953; (RCTm) R.C. managers' minutes 1913–53; (SP) Glasson plan 1860

Tockholes (SMTk) National log books 1869–1939; (PR 2763) reports 1875–89, letters 1844–1952, managers' papers 1950–58

Tonge-with-Alkrington (SP) plan 1860

Torver (SP) plan 1872

Tottington (SMTo) Evening log book 1899–1920, Greenmount Primary log books 1863–1970, admission register 1926–70, reports 1902–39, Hawkshaw Lane St. Mary's day log books 1870–1927, and evening log books 1895–1924, Laurel Street Evening Institute admission register 1945–46, Practical Instruction Centres managers' minutes 1930–45, Wesleyan log books 1867–1925, managers' minutes 1903–35; (SP) Edenfield plan 1860; (ESP) Council plan 1927

Trawden (SMTr) Council punishment book 1926–48, Evening log book 1908–10, National log book 1876–94, Wesleyan log book 1875–95, Winewall log books 1880–1910; (SP) plan 1840; (EXNe) Council managers' minutes 1935–45; (DDBd) National building papers 1841–43

Turton (PR 2864) St. Anne's managers' minutes 1879–1903

Tyldesley (SMTy) Girls' Council log books 1926–35; (SP) plan 1857; (ESP) Darlington Street plan 1892

Ulnes Walton (SMUw) log books 1874–1976, admission register 1878–1976, managers' minutes 1903–14, miscellanea 1846–1962, photographs 1955–73; (PR 252, 747) deeds 1844, 1846

Ulverston (DRCh 37/132) appointments of masters 1718, 1741; (SMUl) C.E. log books 1863–1962, admission registers 1897–1931, R.C. managers' minutes 1895–1924, returns, agreements etc. 1882–1907, Sandside log books 1885–1963, admission registers 1917–63, punishment book 1928–31, caretaker's diary

1950–63; (SP) plan n.d.; (PR 2847) C.E. reports, accounts, letters etc., 1818–1901; (EXUl) Grammar governors' minutes 1944–61, Grouped County managers' minutes 1928–62, Stone Cross managers' minutes 1951–52, Victoria managers' minutes 1948–67; (ESP) Sandside plans 1884

Up Holland (SMUp) Digmoor log books 1877–1968, managers' minutes 1939–68, Grammar reports 1871–75, St. Thomas's log books 1863–1968, admission registers 1859–1966, punishment book 1900–58, reports 1876–1928, appointments of teachers 1901–41; (SP) plans: Girls' 1848, Roby Mill 1875; (DDX 305 and DDLm) Grammar governors' minutes 1877–1916, rental 1884–1909, reports 1910–34, log book 1915–33, rules 1710, deeds 1616–1805; (ESP) Crawford plans 1914

Upper Allithwaite (PR 2803) Lindale trustees' minutes 1839–59, managers' minutes 1890–1903, building papers 1837–38

Upper Holker (SP) Brow Edge plan n.d.; (DRCh 37/24) Brow Edge appointments of masters 1716–1809; (PR 2850) Brow Edge deeds 1821–96; (ARR 13/3) Brow Edge dispute over mastership 1724–28; (DDX 284) Brow Edge deeds etc. 1678–1906

Urmston (SMUr) Council managers' minutes 1924–36, Grammar governors' minutes 1923–41, Pupil Teachers' Centre staff register 1892–1922

Urswick (DDX 279) foundation letters patent 1585; (DRCh 37/135) appointments of masters 1698–1788

Waddington (ESP) C.E. plan 1905

Walmersley-with-Shuttleworth (SMW) Shuttleworth National log books 1863–1928; (SP) Shuttleworth plans 1858–67

Walton-le-Dale (DDHo) receipts 1753–90; (SMWa) Brownedge R.C. attendance register 1961–64, Council managers' minutes 1929–50, Higher Walton C.E. log books 1866–1954, admission registers 1895–1969, Lostock Hall Domestic Subjects Centre cash book 1957–59; (SP) plans: National n.d., St. Aidan's n.d., School Lane 1869–71; (ESP) Lostock Hall plans 1906

Walton-on-the-Hill (SP) plan 1870

Warrington (DDKe) Grammar foundation deed 1526; (DDLi) Grammar correspondence 1818–25; (DDWr) Blue Coat trustees' minutes 1821–32, 1853–68, deeds 1615–1899, accounts 1785–1907, plans *c*. 1800, masters' reports 1853–67, 1883–1903, miscellanea 1712–1886; (SP) plans: British n.d., Female Practising n.d., Heath Side St. Pauls' 1853–70, Mount Practising 1870, Orford n.d., Parochial 1870, St. Alban's R.C. 1870, St.

Anne's 1862, St. Elphin's training 1853, St. Paul's Bank Quay 1866, St. Paul's John Street 1864

Warton-in-Lonsdale (SMWl) Infants' log book 1931–69; (DRCh 37/138) Grammar appointments of masters 1704–65

Wavertree (SP) plans: Holy Trinity 1866, St. Bridget's 1874, St. Mary's 1871

Weeton-with-Preese (SMWe) National and Evening log book 1863–1903

Wesham (SMWm) St. Joseph's R.C. log books 1890–1960, admission registers 1890–1941; see also Kirkham

Westby (SMWb) St. Anne's R.C. log book 1869–1960, reports, returns etc., 1884–1941, plan 1894

West Derby (SP) plans: Parochial 1860, Stanley St. Anne's n.d., Whitefield Road n.d.

Westhoughton (SMWa) Central log book 1915–57, admission register 1915–52, Fourgates St. John's log books 1877–1940, Leigh Road log book 1913–68, Wingates St. John's log books 1863–1969; (SP) plans: Parochial 1858, Wingates St. John's n.d.; (PR 2176) deeds 1745–85, trustees' resolutions 1809–12

Westleigh (SP) plan 1872; see also Leigh

Whalley (SMWh) National log books 1862–1946, admission registers 1870–1946; (DDX 250) Grammar letters patent 1571, list of schoolmasters 1630–1864, nominations 1764, 1788, miscellanea 1716–1864; (DDX 333) master's licence 1716

Wheelton (SP) plan n.d.

Whiston (SMWt) Halsnead admission registers 1872–82, 1911–42, visitors' book 1898–1922; (EXPr) Central managers' minutes 1928–55, Halsnead managers' minutes 1940–70, Higher Side managers' minutes 1964–70, Modern managers' minutes 1945–70, Willis managers' minutes 1960–70

Whitefield see Pilkington

Whittington (SMWf) log books 1863–1972, admission register 1889–1972

Whittle-le-Woods (SMWw) C.E. log books 1863–1957, reports etc. 1870–1936; (SP) plans: National n.d., South Hill R.C. n.d.; (RCSh) South Hill R.C. accounts 1871–88

Whitworth (SMWz) Hallford Congregational log book 1872–1928, managers' minutes 1888–1928, St. Bartholomew's log books 1863–1967

Widnes (SMWd) Dock National log books 1862–1965, letters 1839–41, 1859–60, Farnworth National attendance register 1845–50, cash books 1884–1903, miscellanea 1844–1916; (SP) plans: Dock National 1861, Dock St. Mary's n.d., Farnworth 1844–63, St. Patrick's R.C. n.d.; (SMBp 10) Open-air log book 1928–39; see also Blackpool

Wigan (SP) plans: All Saints' 1866, National and Blue Coat 1857–66, Presbyterian 1867, St. Andrew's Martland Bridge n.d., St. John's R.C. n.d., St. Joseph's R.C. 1873, St. Mary's R.C. n.d., St. Patrick's R.C. 1856, St. Thomas' Clayton Street 1870, St. Thomas's National 1871, Wesleyan 1850–54

Windle (SP) Moss Bank plan n.d.

Winmarleigh (DDX 589) lease 1903

Wiswell (SMWx) Barrow Congregational log books 1881–1962, National log books 1873–1963, admission register 1891–1963; (EXRi) Barrow Congregational managers' minutes 1911–49

Withington (SP) St. Paul's plans 1843–68

Woodplumpton (SMWo) Catforth National managers' minutes 1873–1955, Catforth St. Robert's R.C. log book 1930–68, admission register 1881–1968, returns etc. 1960–68; (SP) plans: Catforth n.d., Catforth St. Robert's R.C. n.d., C.E. n.d.; (PR 2930) Catforth accounts 1859–84; (DDX 399) deeds 1699–1861

Worsthorne (SMWs) Council managers' minutes 1911–25; (SP) plan n.d.; (EXNe) Council managers' minutes 1925–45, Mereclough managers' minutes 1925–30

Wray-with-Botton (SMN) C.E. log book 1909–30

Wrightington (ESP) Elementary plan 1909

Sarah Walmsley's Charity (DDHo) for education of children in Lancashire and for schoolmaster in parishes of Kirkham, Poulton, and St. Michaels: accounts 1703–91

The Hulme Trust (DDX 391): these documents relate to the manor of Astley, which included lands in Bedford and Tyldesley: manorial court rolls 1564, 1567, 1569, 1571, 1572, 1608, 1623, 1654, 1744–46, title deeds 1385, 1522–1891, enclosure award 1764, inquisitions *post mortem* Adam Mort 1631, Thomas Mort 1638

Part III

Parochial Records (PR)

Ecclesiastical and civil parish records have been received from a great variety of sources, including parish, rural district and urban district councils, incumbents and private individuals. Although the Local Government Act of 1894 vested the existing civil records in the new urban district and parish councils, comparatively few were in fact removed from their original custody. This was possibly occasioned by the fact that in Lancashire the great majority of ecclesiastical parishes comprised many townships, or civil parishes. It has therefore been felt that all parochial records, ecclesiastical and secular, could more conveniently be combined in one list.

In 1981 the Record Office began to implement the Parochial Registers and Records Measure, 1978, and was appointed Diocesan Record Office for the whole of Blackburn Diocese and for the rural deaneries of North Meols, Ormskirk and Prescot within Liverpool Diocese, as well as for that part of Bradford Diocese which was incorporated into Lancashire in 1974. The surveys under the Measure have led to a very significant growth in holdings of parish records; this increased level of deposit is likely to continue for a number of years.

The list below is accurate to 1976. Information on more recent accessions of parish registers is incorporated in the current edition of the *Handlist of Genealogical Sources* and references to other classes of parish document are to be found in the cumulative index to parish records.

Entries relating to ecclesiastical parishes containing more than one township are distinguished by an asterisk.

Accrington registers 1596–1895, township accounts 1691–1800, churchwardens' accounts and vestry minutes 1804–70, select vestry minutes 1847–53, situations of graves 1846–55, church extension committee minutes 1886–1905, church-officers' meeting minutes 1917–53, banns books 1808–18, 1856–75, 1928–70

Adlington St. Philip's mission (splinter sect) registers 1900–34

Aighton, Bailey and Chaigley valuations n.d.

Ainsworth registers 1727–1812, pew dispute 1855, Chancery case re land for chapel 1839

Alston-with-Hothersall churchwardens', overseers' and constables' accounts 1712–1838, township meeting minutes 1845–82, rate books 1840–62, highway accounts 1819, 1823, 1880–81, poor rate receipt and payment book 1839–48, workhouse account books 1822–38, valuations (PUT) 1884, 1898–1910

Altcar registers 1664–1809, surveyors' accounts 1714–72, churchwardens' accounts 1774–1888, freeholders lists 1771, 1773, valuations 1901–07

Altham registers 1596–1934, graveyard schedule 1903–38, chapelwardens' accounts 1843–1908, registers of services 1906–45, church council minutes 1914–30, war memorial committee minutes, etc 1919–21

Anderton ratepayers' meeting minutes 1884–98, parish council minutes 1901–73, township meeting minutes 1821–45

Anglezarke financial records 1839–47, 1868–1907

Arkholme-with-Cawood baptismal registers 1828–64, surveyors' accounts 1837–59, valuations 1838–40, 1849, 1874, 1880, 1885, 1889

Ashton-in-Makerfield (UDAs) township minutes 1741–1834, highway accounts 1818–63

Ashton-under-Lyne vestry minutes 1720, 1742–53, 1764–66, 1772–79, 1782, 1792–96, poor-stock accounts 1697–1708, lists of churchwardens and overseers 1683–1895, churchwardens' accounts 1689, 1691, 1695, 1696, 1703, 1705, 1713–15, 1717, 1718, 1778, 1780, church ley 1778–79, subscriptions for bells 1779, overseers' accounts 1698, 1718, poor assessments 1691, 1694–96, 1701, 1703, 1706, 1710, 1718, 1719, 1723–25, 1727, 1728, 1730, 1732, 1733, 1748, 1775, 1778, window-tax assessment 1744, conscription order 1804, census returns 1811, freeholders' list 1825, constables' accounts 1832–35, miscellanea 1701–53

Ashworth registers 1813–1958, grave book 1853–1940, pew rents 1860–73, churchwardens' accounts 1864–1970, service registers 1917–50, parochial church council minutes 1921–45

Aughton churchwardens' accounts 1737–1828, surveyors' accounts 1737–78, overseers' accounts 1737–1840, constables' accounts 1738–1856, surplice 1839–60, vestry minutes 1771–1904, taxation list 1787–1814, church goods 1787, list of overseers 1738–75, list of constables 1670–1751, list of churchwardens and overseers 1670–1741, list of taxpayers 1725–26, list of surveyors 1692–1743, apprenticeship register 1803–37, tithe award 1848, list of briefs collected 1701–27

Balderstone registers 1751–1906, churchwardens' accounts and vestry minutes 1898–1970, St. Saviour's registers 1835–58, service registers 1836–60

Barley (DDBd) survey c. 1824

Barnacre-with-Bonds parish council minutes 1894–1916, valuations 1817, 1851, 1862–82, 1896–1907, overseers' accounts 1766–1868, select vestry minutes 1821–37, rate books 1834–46, highway accounts 1853–63, bastardy orders 1802–11, settlement orders 1804–38, miscellanea 1807–27

Barrowford (DDBd) valuation 1847

Barton-in-Amounderness (PUT) valuations 1885, 1888–96, 1898–1910

Barton-upon-Irwell letters to overseers of Dalston, Cumberland 1816–19, workhouse account book 1821–22; (DDX 65) apprenticeship indenture 1782

Bickerstaffe churchwardens' accounts 1708–1828, constables' accounts 1712–1831, overseers' accounts 1711–1839, surveyors' accounts 1713–1828, ratepayers' meeting minutes 1839–1925, land-tax assessments 1763–69, apprenticeship registers 1803–37, apprenticeship indentures 1716–1824, settlement papers 1691–1765, Ormskirk workhouse papers 1732–1839, miscellanea 1674–1840, list of constables 1720–43, association to prosecute felons 1792, church deeds and papers 1843–1925

Billinge registers 1696–1899, churchwardens' accounts and vestry minutes 1771–1856, parish meeting minutes 1708–61, pew book 1718, blanket-money accounts 1803–1934, papers re patronage dispute 1765, application to erect gallery 1823, pewholders c. 1824, settlement papers 1679–1811, overseers' papers 1707, 1795, 1808, 1810, 1813

Billington registers 1733–1962, parsonage papers 1868–92, apprenticeship indentures 1722–1825, overseer's accounts 1742–1833, constables' accounts 1742–1827, surveyors' accounts 1779–1815, bastardy orders 1786–1823, poor claims from workhouses, etc. 1820–36, correspondence 1790, 1821–33, distress inventories, etc. 1751, 1820–34, rate precepts 1785, 1798, 1820–35, removal orders 1711–1834, settlement certificates 1700–1823, coucher-book of miscellaneous papers 1557 to late 19th century, Little Harwood survey 1735, rate books 1824–29, 1858–59, petition against alienation of Langho chapel 1688, miscellanea 1588–1872, parish council minutes 1894–1931, deeds of play area 1924–70, coronation papers 1953

97

Bilsborrow valuations 1863–96; (RDG) 1897–1928

Birkdale (DDln 63) accounts of churchwardens, constables, overseers and surveyors 1735–1832

Birtle-cum-Bamford (CBR) parish council minutes 1928–33

Bispham township meeting minutes 1722–1808, 1839–94, township accounts 1722–1808, churchwardens' accounts 1844–46, 1851–54, constables' accounts 1750, 1766, 1809, 1812–18, 1821–35, 1840–51, overseers' accounts 1757, 1766, 1809–35, 1838–40, 1845–46, surveyors' accounts 1808–52, financial statements 1895–1917, land-tax assessments 1799–1810, 1812–14, 1868, 1871, window-tax assessments 1799–1803, 1805–7, 1809–10, other tax assessments 1801–12, poor rate assessments 1838–40, highway rate assessments 1842–50

*Bispham-with-Norbreck registers 1599–1935, preachers' register 1879–1913, churchwardens' accounts 1886–1909, miscellanea 1872–1937, parish magazines 1888–95, constables' and overseers' accounts 1794–1839; (DDX 1) select vestry minutes; (CBBl) general and poor rate books 1897–1911, lighting rate books 1899–1902, valuations 1897–1902

*Blackburn coucher books of miscellaneous papers: Balderstone 1684–1862, Billinge (Blackburn) Schools 1831–50, Blackburn All Saints 1837–65, Blackburn St. Clement's school 1841–64, Blackburn St. Peter's 1817–63, Blackburn Trinity 1835–61, Blackburn Trinity Sunday School 1839–56, Blackburn National and Sunday schools 1838–66, division of parishes 1849–61, Bamber Bridge St. Saviour's 1824–60, diocesan education board 1839–51, Great Harwood 1680–1865, Lower Darwen 1824–61, Mellor Brook 1833–69, Salesbury 1806–61, Tockholes 1649–1863, Walton-le-Dale 1714–1873, Witton 1832–61, Sancroft Trust 1683–1895, Society for the Promotion of Christian Knowledge 1815–65, Society for the Propagation of the Gospel 1819–38. Curates' receipt books 1752–96, National and Sunday school minutes 1829–63, poor stock and bible accounts 1694–1801, churchwardens' accounts 1713–1813, church rebuilding papers and accounts 1818–35, Sancroft Trust deeds 1688–1829, poor and bastardy papers 1695–1825, apprenticeship indentures 1695–1825, highway papers 1621–1753, church rate books 1818–33, churchyard papers 1649–1815, letters to overseers of Dalston, Cumberland 1832, Enclosure awards: Billington, Wilpshire and Dinckley 1791, Little Harwood 1776, Lower Darwen 1780; (DDX 391) rectory rentals and accounts 1752–64; (PR 3001) St. John the Evangelist registers 1789–1975, banns books 1929–73, service registers 1926–75, minutes 1888–1936, miscellanea 1890–1963; (PR 3002) St. Michael and All Angels registers 1839–1937, banns books 1927–67, service registers 1907–45, minutes 1920–48, correspondence 1837–1902, miscellanea 1845–69

Blackley (DDX 829) chapel quarterage book 1762

Blacko (RDBu) rate book 1826

Blackpool Holy Trinity registers 1837–1956, church papers 1836–41, St. John's registers 1821–1970, banns books 1874–1941, 1948–67, service registers 1897–1958, vestry minutes 1860–1921, churchwardens' accounts 1927–67, correspondence 1871–1958

Blackrod registers 1607–1944, conveyance of chapel 1581, faculty for rebuilding 1766

Blatchinworth and Calderbrook (CBR) valuations 1862–94; (UDLi) highway accounts 1780–1871

Blawith overseers' accounts 1871–1913

Bleasdale valuations 1863–96; (RDG) 1897–1928; (PR) ratepayers' meeting minutes 1877–95, parish council minutes 1894–1937, library committee minutes 1890–93, 1899–1929, coronation minutes 1902, letter books 1895–1958, financial records 1892–1959

Bold ratebooks 1914–34

Bowland Forest parish meeting minutes 1894–1945

Bradshaw (UDTu) parish council minutes 1894–98, overseers' accounts 1867–98

Bretherton plan of church 1840, churchwardens' accounts 1848–54, church rates 1858–84, pew rents 1872–74, township accounts and papers 1719–1884, rate books 1829–83, farm accounts 1840–66, minutes of Council on Education 1851–58, Sunday school registers 1932–48, service registers 1872–1952, seating plan 1898, apprenticeship indentures 1744–1832, militia lists 1817, 1823, agreement for prosecution of felons 1745

Briercliffe-with-Extwistle (DDBd) poor book 1754–55

Brindle registers 1558–1861, churchwardens' accounts 1775–1895, vestry minutes 1818–63, tithe award 1838, plan of church 1867, faculty for rebuilding of chancel 1869

Broughton-in-Amounderness registers 1653–1848, church and parish accounts 1715–81, churchwardens' accounts 1705–1838, select vestry minutes 1821–40, visitation returns 1817–18, apprenticeship indentures 1694–1826, register of apprentices 1804–26, settlement certificates 1698–1746, removal orders 1694–1828, bastardy bonds 1715–87, bastardy orders 1737–1833, overseers' accounts 1780–90, 1812–38, constables' accounts 1812–38, list of constables 1802–05, 'fire money' lists 1818–45, list of overseers

1827–40, nominations of guardians 1837–40, appointments of overseers 1725–1834, poor rate books 1812–39, church rate books 1813–25, 1831, 1832, highway assessments 1739–1841, highway papers 1819–39, assessed tax instructions 1807–39, assessment lists 1813–39, land-tax assessments 1811–39, militia lists 1813–31, tithe list 1809, tithe papers 1813–39, subscribers to Christmas banquet 1825–44, charity papers 1690–1828, jurors lists 1826–40, voters lists 1832–39, freeholders lists 1813–27, census returns 1821–41, deeds of Goosnargh, Barton, Woodplumpton, Broughton, Sowerby, Haighton, and Longton 1433–1758, letters to James Tuson, schoolmaster, 1815–43, select vestry papers 1822–39, parish council minutes 1894–1928 and accounts 1895–1965

Bryning-with-Kellamergh parish council minutes 1894–1934, overseers' accounts 1885–1910

Burnley survey and plans of curacy c. 1896, St. John the Baptist's registers 1878–1934, St. Margaret's marriage registers 1898–1968

Burrow-with-Burrow overseers' accounts 1817–70

Burscough registers 1832–1931, churchwardens' accounts 1708, 1767–73, account of sacrament money 1773, constables' accounts 1707, 1708, 1718, 1758, 1771–73, overseers' accounts 1717, 1729, 1759, 1771–74, settlement and bastardy papers 1693–1798, apprenticeship indentures 1725–1832, surveyors' accounts 1707–79, rating assessments 1680–1771, miscellanea 1720–1850; (DP 437) town book 1770–1850

*Bury select vestry minutes 1823–30, fever relief book 1789–90, voluntary subscriptions to government 1798, workhouse book 1787–96, poor assessment books 1789, 1794–96, monthly relief book 1789–95, weekly relief book 1790–95, relief account book 1809–12, filiation account book 1820–30, churchwardens' and overseers' voucher book 1819–24, justices' warrants 1750–1850, bastardy bonds 1679–1808, settlement certificates and bonds 1689–1842, settlement adjudication orders 1804–07, examinations of poor 1797–1848, filiation orders 1689–1846, removal orders 1691–1858, apprenticeship indentures 1675–1856, box certificates from friendly societies 1798–1816, letters 1822–23, Elton census returns 1801, (Microfilm) registers 1590–1948, overseers' accounts 1692–1832

Butterworth (DDX 188) church ley for Lordship Side 1777–78; (CBR) valuations 1868–94; (UDMi) ratepayers' meeting minutes 1850–95

Cabus poor rate assessment 1863, valuations 1869–96; (RDG) 1896–1929

Cantsfield poor rate assessments 1876–79, 1886–94, 1896, valuations 1883, 1887, 1893, agricultural rate valuation 1896

Carleton township account book 1786–1839, parish meeting minutes 1894–1934, report on footpaths 1930; (UDPo) parish council minutes 1910–34, rate books 1910–15

*Cartmel vestry books 1847–94, overseers' papers 1798–1882, charity papers 1658–1936, manorial papers 1610–1833, enclosure commissioners' minutes 1796, surveys and valuations 1825–58, plans 19th century, land-tax assessment 1789, miscellaneous deeds 1668–1847

Castleton rate book 1789–90; (CBR) select vestry minutes 1837–94, occupiers c. 1820, rate books 1795–99, 1820–99, valuations 1863–99; (UDMi) surveyors' accounts 1851–79

Caton registers 1585–1864, accounts of churchwardens, overseers, constables, surveyors, etc. 1714–1805, vestry minutes 1790–1824, parsonage plan 1844, church plan 1864, workhouse accounts 1830–41, poor rate assessments 1851–83, sanitary rate assessment 1880–81; (DDGa) poor rate assessments 1727, 1785, 1791, 1803–08, 1833, highway rate book 1859, land-tax assessments 1763, 1796

Catterall valuations 1863–96; (RDG) 1898–1929

Charnock Richard church plan 1859, accounts and papers 1859–1908, parish council minutes 1894–1960, precept book 1895–1957, parsonage plan 1861

Chatburn accounts of overseers, churchwardens, surveyors and constables 1797–1856, vestry and ratepayers' meeting minutes 1846–94, survey 1820; (DDX 28) poor rate assessments 1836–37, 1879–86

Chipping registers 1559–1950, churchwardens' accounts 1847–1912

Chorley registers 1548–1856, letters to overseers of Dalston, Cumberland 1826

Church registers 1633–1948, churchwardens' accounts 1710–64, vestry minutes and accounts 1766–1845

Claughton-in-Amounderness survey and valuation 1848, valuation 1863, parish council minutes 1894–1946; (RDG) valuations 1897–1929

Claughton-in-Lonsdale registers 1701–1840, township memoranda book 1701–1804, churchwardens' accounts 1828–47, vestry minutes 1828–90, workhouse agreement 1829, parish council minutes 1952–61

Clayton-le-Moors registers 1840–63, churchwardens' accounts 1840–74, 1911–14, service registers 1906–13, vestry minutes 1863–84, St. James' School-church register 1882–1906

Cleveley valuations 1862–74, poor rate assessment 1906; (RDG) valuations 1898–1929; (PR2953) Shireshead registers 1829–1946

Clifton-with-Salwick parish council minutes 1894–1917, overseers' accounts 1885–1909, Lund marriage registers 1840–63, vestry minutes and churchwardens' accounts 1841–1923, service registers 1893–97, 1914–51

Clitheroe registers 1570–1843, banns book 1823–47, church rate assessments 1809–17, bellringing agreements 1810–17, church-wardens' accounts 1656–1802, vestry book 1752–1801, bells and clock correspondence 1843–48, graveyard extension papers 1859–62, parsonage correspondence 1845–59, plans 1826–27, rebuilding papers, licences and papers of the Rev. J. H. Anderton 1826–66, Sunday school accounts 1836–80, report on condition of St. Mary's 1893. St. James' registers 1839–1919, banns book 1861–1934, service registers 1894–1937, churchwardens' ac-counts 1848–94, church missionary society collection book 1839–93, mutual improvement society minutes 1877–79, Sunday school minutes 1853–70, attendance book 1850–65 and class book 1868–90; (DDX 28) select vestry minutes 1829–34, poor rate assessments 1789, 1799, militia list 1802, rate books 1828, 1839, tithe collection books 1871–94, 1901–25; (DDX 150) Sunday school sick society minutes 1847–62, 1928–49, accounts 1868–1949

Cliviger Holme registers 1756–1953, banns books 1839–65, 1902–63, service registers 1908–22

*Cockerham registers 1595–1930, churchwardens' accounts 1738–1899, vestry minutes 1822–1923, corn-rent accounts 1825–1906, minutes of association for distribution of bibles 1836–49, rate-payers' meeting minutes 1872–1901, overseers' books 1799–1821, 1835–36, 1840–59

*Colne registers 1811–17, service registers 1877–1939, confirmation registers 1924–37, churchwardens' accounts 1703–1819, 1869–1902, vestry minutes 1834–1942, church papers 1815–1953, letters and accounts 1822–1957, faculties 1857–1961, burial ground plans and papers 1858–1900, missions committee minutes 1926–58; (DDBd) surveyors' accounts 1767–1827

*Colton (DDMc) rate books 1729, 1761, 1772, 1776

Coppull parish council minutes 1894–1955, registers 1757–1966, service registers 1948–62, Sunday school accounts 1844–55

Croft registers 1833–1966, preachers registers 1894–1911, vestry minutes and churchwardens' accounts 1845–1900, parochial church council minutes 1921–38

Crompton (UDCr) survey of commons 1623, survey 1799, valuations 1828, 1837, surveyors' accounts 1833–55, minutes of the board of directors 1839–52

Cronton mission-church plans 1905–26, papers and accounts 1905–37, apprenticeship indentures 1719–1835, surveyors' accounts 1718–74, 1799–1865, bastardy papers 1710–1831, settlement papers 1726–1836, militia papers 1795–1802, overseers' accounts and papers 1718–1853, constables' accounts 1718–1837, rate books 1796–1808, 1838–50, 1924–34, charity accounts 1758–78, miscellanea 1688–1838

Crosby registers 1749–1893 (transcript DDX 219)

*Croston registers 1538–1948, churchwardens' accounts and vestry minutes 1681–1842, valuations 1724, 1806–28, terriers 1718, 1722, 1757, rent rolls 1793–1828, constables', overseers' and surveyors' accounts 1717–1855, banns book 1814–29, register of churchings 1753–79, Sunday school and school of industry minutes and accounts 1801–70, rectory deeds and papers 1427–1893, faculties 1744–1800, plans 1798–1844, Croston relief committee minutes 1863, miscellanea 1619–1871, Croston Finney papers 1597–1726, census returns 1801, 1811

Crumpsall (DDX 177) valuation 1798

Culcheth township accounts and papers 1702–1880, rate books 1813, 1823, 1828–35, 1840–56; see also Newchurch-in-Culcheth

Dalton parish council minutes 1894–1937, parish accounts 1896–1948

Darcy Lever (UDTu) ratepayers' meeting minutes 1864–66

Darwen St. John's registers 1865–1927, banns books 1865–76, 1919–27, parish magazines 1866–1925, church guild minutes 1881–98, vestry minutes 1895–1919, St. James's registers 1781–1931, churchwardens' accounts 1833–88, vestry minutes 1872–1933, church council minutes 1902–07, accounts 1899, 1913–23, parochial workers' committee minutes 1935–42, pew deeds 1784, 1795, survey 1851, rent book 1820–47

Davyhulme parish council minutes 1910–33

*Deane creation of parish (DDHu) 1541; registers 1637–1890, churchwardens' accounts 1723–1916, churchwardens' minutes 1818–1935, churchwardens' order book 1807–11, seat rate accounts 1869–84, offertory book 1914–23, parochial church council minutes 1920–36, Heaton new church minutes 1891, faculties and conveyances 1786–93, Heaton church papers 1878–94, Horwich chapel deeds (land in Tottington) 1722–88, miscellanea 1754–1906

Dilworth poor rate assessment 1842, highway assessment 1871, highway accounts 1883

Ditton church plans *c.* 1874

Downholland constables' accounts 1704–97, overseers' accounts and papers 1733–1832, memoranda books 1682–1870, papers re death of John Hughes 1726, apprenticeship indentures 1716–90, workhouse inventory 1740, subscription to suppress rebellion 1745, inventory of horned cattle 1750, parish council minutes 1894–1963, accounts 1895–1969, papers 1894–1924

Dunnerdale-with-Seathwaite (DDMc) township accounts 1774, 1776

Dutton rate books 1842–44, 1847–52, 1855–59, valuation 1858, tithe rentals 1838, 1870, land-tax assessor's and collector's warrant and instructions 1852

Easington overseers', surveyors' and constables' accounts 1719–1872, constables' papers 1719–1868, settlement and removal papers 1719–1844, apprenticeship indentures 1735–1838, bastardy papers 1718–1843, rate assessments 1739–1907

Eccleshill parish council minutes 1955, accounts 1942–71, correspondence 1899–1971, poor rate receipts and payments 1838–46

*Eccleston (Chorley) registers 1603–1932, churchwardens' accounts 1712–64, 1801–88, churchyard plans 1875, *c.* 1850, 1892; (DRB 4) church papers 1545–1740

Eccleston (Prescot) rate books 1914–34

Edgworth (UDTu) rate payers' meeting minutes 1888–94, parish council minutes 1894–98, overseers' accounts 1867–98, poor rate 1914, highway accounts 1860–68

Egton-with-Newland valuations 1885–92; (DDMc) poor rate 1710, 1711, land-tax 1740, 1757

Ellel registers 1828–1933, service registers 1870–93, 1906–17, faculties and papers 1740–1873, apprenticeship indentures 1731–1811, township papers 1741–1810

Entwistle (UDTu) ratepayers' meeting minutes 1888–94, parish meeting minutes 1894–98, overseers' accounts 1867–98, valuation 1892

Euxton registers 1774–1926 (for 1711–73 see Leyland), miscellanea 1724–70; (DDCm) churchwardens' accounts 1715, poorhouse accounts 1717, 1731–34, 1736

Farington highway rates 1844–47, highway accounts 1853–56, parish council minutes 1894–1946

Fishwick settlement certificates 1714–80, bastardy orders 1812–26, removal orders 1827, miscellaneous accounts 1826–27

Flixton overseers' minutes 1866–1911, parish council minutes 1894–1933

Formby registers 1710–1941

Forton valuation 1863, poor rate assessment 1906; (RDG) valuations 1897–1928

Freckleton select vestry relief applications 1831–34, marsh assessments 1830–32

Fulwood overseers' minutes 1751–1820, 1846–89

*Garstang registers 1567–81, register of burial in woollen 1678–91, banns register 1780–1872, memoranda of christenings and burials 1819–25, 1835–52, draft registers 1768–83, churchwardens' accounts 1734–1800, 1807–63, vestry minutes 1808–65, special sermons 1757–1857, churchwardens' vouchers 1785–92, faculties 1782–1929, east window fund 1868–78, restoration committee minutes 1866–69, vestry accounts 1864–1939, surrogates' accounts 1763–67, miscellanea 1784–1880, church defence committee minutes 1895, Butter vault papers 1899, names of servicemen 1914–19, Bilsborrow parish papers 1924–29, Sunday school papers and roll-book 1828–34, 1912–22, plan of churchyard 1821, valuations 1863–81, 1896–1909; (DDPd) advowson deeds and papers 1569–1862, ordinations, etc. 1753–1891, parish accounts and papers 1657–1939, terriers 1716–1825, Garstang chapel papers 1753–1822, Stout House deeds and papers 1904–30, Calder Vale church papers 1861–86, Claughton tithe papers 1723–1846, Cabus church rates 1850–69; (DDX 386) select vestry minutes 1815–25; (RDG) valuations 1911–29

Goodshaw registers 1732–1899, churchwardens' and overseers' accounts 1691–1744, 1816–44, vestry minutes 1818–96, select vestry minutes 1821–27

Goosnargh registers 1639–1948, churchwardens' accounts 1845–1932, list of churchwardens 1607–1882, churchyard enlargement 1870, overseers' accounts 1796–1822, minutes of twenty four-men 1634–1939

Great Crosby registers 1749–1861

Great Eccleston valuations 1863–83; (RDG) 1896–1928

Great Harwood registers 1547–1948, apprenticeship indenture-1723–1819, removal and settlement papers 1699–1826, churchwardens' accounts 1727–89, constables' accounts 1741–89, surveyors' accounts 1758–86, overseers' accounts 1732–1834, Sunday school register 1822–26, window-tax assessment 1762, survey 1805, relief registers 1825–35, relief subscriptions 1842, poor-stock deeds 1681–1838

Greenhalgh-with-Thistleton accounts of overseers, constables and surveyors 1741–1838

Grimsargh-with-Brockholes consecration deed 1726

Habergham Eaves committee minutes 1836–41

Hale rate books 1929, 1934

Halewood overseers' accounts 1702–45, surveyors' accounts 1703–42, constables' accounts 1701–79, apprenticeship indentures 1704–1827, settlement and removal papers 1694–1825, bastardy papers 1704–1809, militia orders 1808, miscellanea 1693–1850, rate books 1913–35, parish council minutes 1935–65, accounts 1895–1965, coronation committee minutes and accounts 1951–54, sound-film of coronation festival 1953

*Halsall registers 1662–1844, school terrier 1760, accounts of churchwardens, constables, overseers and surveyors 1694–1885, vestry minutes 1694–1894, terriers 1738, 1778, 1825, church restoration papers 1822–24, faculties 1884–97, agreements for prosecution of felons 1808, 1829, tithe papers 1791, church-rate books 1850–89, poor-rate books 1844–74

Halton registers 1592–1949, churchwardens' accounts 1867–1910, deeds 1686–1759, banns registers 1824–1947, parochial church council minutes 1920–45

Hambleton registers 1695–1949, endowment deed 1689, valuations 1863–79, 1884–96, select vestry minutes 1824–27, parish council minutes 1894–1913, ratepayers meeting minutes 1852–59, 1896–1937, township papers 1769–1851

Hapton valuations 1885–95

Harwood (UDTu) ratepayers' meeting minutes 1888–94, parish council minutes 1895–98, overseers' accounts 1822–38, 1867–98, rate books 1887–98

Haslingden survey and rate book 1798

Haverthwaite war memorial committee minutes and papers 1919–48, homecoming and memorial fund papers 1940–49

Hawkshead, Monk Coniston and Skelwith ratepayers' meeting minutes 1877–92, overseers' accounts 1836–48, surveyors' accounts 1829–93, poor-rate assessments 1836–96, highway-rate assessments 1844–91

Haydock township accounts 1741–1828

Heap vestry minutes 1885–1921; see Heywood

Heapey registers 1813–1914, churchwardens' accounts and vestry minutes 1858–92, (for registers 1711–1812 and miscellanea 1729–1917 see Leyland)

Heysham letter to overseers of Dalston, Cumberland 1837

Heywood registers 1745–1906, church papers 1824–94, building committee minutes 1858–65, pew papers 1859, offertory accounts 1862–78, organ paper 1867–69, organ committee minutes 1867–69, churchwardens' accounts 1877–1922, church council minutes 1879–84, 1907–17, parish magazine 1866–94, Sunday school union minutes 1891–1904, 1912–29

Higham-with-West Close Booth papers re clandestine Wesleyan burials 1855–56, St. John's church papers 1872–76, parish council minutes 1894–1967, accounts 1937–70, correspondence 1942–68, miscellanea

Hoghton for registers 1781–1812 see Leyland

Holleth valuations 1873–96, poor-rate assessment 1906; (RDG) valuations 1897–1922

Hollinfare see Rixton-with-Glazebrook

Hoole registers 1673–1960, churchwardens' accounts and vestry minutes 1812–71

Hornby registers 1742–1805, terriers 1752, 1789, registers of Roman Catholics 1782, 1787, 1790, churchwardens' accounts 1730–1800, 1804–39, vestry minutes 1821–39, church rate 1838, plan of chapel lands 1797

Horwich registers 1660–1841, churchwardens' accounts 1820–1901, overseers' accounts 1817–25, boundary particulars 1824–42, poor-rate book 1856

Houghton, Middleton and Arbury constables' accounts 1734, 1737, 1738, 1748

Ince Blundell survey and valuation 1849

Inskip-with-Sowerby valuations 1863–96; (RDG) 1897–1928

Kirkby rate books 1929, 1935, chapelwardens' accounts 1717–18

*Kirkham registers 1540–1855, churchwardens' accounts 1735–1819, vestry minutes 1735–1934, terrier 1778, pew rents 1823, organ book 1770–1841, memoranda book 1553–1850, overseers' accounts 1754–1839, constables' accounts 1754–1816, surveyors' accounts 1754–1812, rate books 1812–36, apprenticeship indentures 1717–1826, settlement certificates 1707–1829, removal orders 1705–1832, bastardy orders 1791–1801, miscellanea 1713–1844

Kirkland valuations 1862–96, parish council minutes 1894–1955; (RDG) valuations 1897–1928

Knowsley rate books 1912–35

Lancaster overseers' letter books 1809–19, 1837–40, letters to overseers of Dalston, Cumberland 1813, St. John's parochial church council minutes 1920–24

Latham constables' order for collection of money for forces 1650

Layton-with-Warbreck overseers' accounts 1818–39; (CBBl) rate books 1844–76, valuation 1855

Lea, Ashton, Ingol and Cottam: Lea parish council accounts 1896–1947, letter books 1914–35, street-lighting papers 1938, 1953–56, coronation papers 1953

*Leyland registers 1651–1878, baptisms of dissenters and papists 1720–41, banns books 1823–1909, churchwardens' accounts 1815–19, 1823–1912, vestry minutes 1831–1924, church fabric faculties and papers 1591–1956, churchyard papers 1847–1937, queries re church customs 1722, terrier 1728, tithe papers 1912–36, glebe papers 1751–1938, miscellanea 1733–1957; (Microfilm) registers 1736–1947, vestry minutes 1748–1871, churchwardens' accounts 1823–70, St. James: churchwardens' vouchers 1863–70, miscellanea 1858–95, survey 1819, township accounts 1737–58, parish meeting minutes 1748–72; (DDF) settlement papers 1736–41, workhouse papers 1780; (DDX 48) survey of churchyard 1932

Lindale; see Upper Allithwaite

Litherland (SMLi) St. Philip's parish magazine 1887–97

Little Harwood rate books 1838, 1873–94, valuation 1883

Little Heaton (MBPn) ratepayers' meeting minutes 1852–94

Little Hulton (DP) proclamations 1815–30, notices 1820–26, licences, correspondence, etc. 1815–32, poor relief papers 1817–30; (DDX 149) apprenticeship indentures 1743

Livesey: Feniscowles registers 1836–1970, coucher books 1833–1906, churchwardens' accounts 1836–92, coronation committee minutes and papers 1953

Longridge registers 1760–1925, vestry minutes 1783–1838, parochial accounts 1878–1923, plans 1891–1900, specification for new tower 1841, confirmation registers 1895–1911

Longton registers 1754–1948, papers 1772–1956, brass band minutes, etc. 1926–47, Sunday school accounts 1836–57, 1923–30, ratepayers and vestry minutes 1879–1909, overseers' and workhouse account book 1833–39, parish council minutes 1894–1958, playing-fields committee minutes 1935–37, annual meeting minutes 1894–1958, accounts 1897–1957

Longworth (DDHu 42) overseers' accounts 1765–1839; (UDTu) ratepayers' meeting minutes 1852–67, 1890–94, parish meeting minutes 1894–98, overseers' accounts 1867–98

Lostock poor rate books 1851–81, highway rate books 1851, 1856, 1864, 1868, 1870, 1872, valuations 1880–91

Lytham registers 1679–1908, apprenticeship indenture 1780

Maghull registers 1729–1919, churchwardens' accounts 1755, 1830–1903, church papers 1750–1957, township accounts 1749–1840, vestry minutes 1823–35, apprenticeship indentures 1823, 1824, associations for prosecution of felons 1699, 1832–36, overseers' accounts 1824–40; (SMMa) parish-hall trustee's minutes 1906–34, site deed 1907

Marsden (DDBd) valuation 1836

Marton ratepayers' meeting minutes 1878–99, parochial committee minutes 1886–91, 1910–34, parish council minutes 1894–1934, lighting minutes 1925–33, vestry minutes and accounts 1873–1909

Mawdesley parish council minutes 1894–1934, accounts 1896–1956, correspondence 1898–1949

Melling-with-Wrayton association for prosecution of felons 1777, hair-powder certificates 1795, apprenticeship indenture 1801, subscriptions to Indian famine relief fund 1897–1900

Mellor parish council minutes 1894–1971, accounts 1943–69, correspondence 1953–68

Moston select vestry minutes 1825–38

Myerscough valuations 1863–94; (RDG) 1897–1929

Nateby ratepayers' meeting minutes 1879–94, parish council minutes 1894–1942, accounts 1896–1967, correspondence 1930–67, coronation committee minutes and papers 1902, papers re marriage of Dorothy Bretherton 1913, valuations 1815, 1862–96, poor rate assessment 1906; (RDG) valuations 1897–1929

Nelson Little Marsden registers 1813–1958, banns books 1904–51, finance register 1899–1905, church institute minutes 1893–1951, subscription book 1893–1906

Nether Kellet valuation 1898

Nether Wyresdale valuations 1863–96; (DDX 264) tithe collection book 1860–1922; (RDG) valuations 1897–1929

Newchurch-in-Culcheth registers 1599–1865, births of papists and presbyterians 1702–19, churchwardens' accounts 1845–97

Newchurch-in-Pendle registers 1721–1856, index of bishops' transcripts 1574–1813, banns book 1788–1871, chapelwardens' accounts 1735–1837, overseers' accounts 1805–16

Newchurch-in-Rossendale settlement certificates 1698, 1741, poor rates 1751, 1757

Newton-in-Makerfield (DDX 153) apprenticeship indentures 1785–1837, bastardy orders 1812–43, friendly society certificates 1801–32, plan 1745, gas rate collectors' accounts 1856–57, miscellanea 1897–1929, removal orders 1834–57, settlement certificates 1721–67

Newton-with-Scales township papers 1688–1801, parish council minutes 1894–1934, overseers' accounts 1885–1910; (DDNw) associations for prosecution of felons 1763, 1802, constables' precepts, warrants, etc. 1754–1831, militia orders 1803–32, bastardy papers 1718–1830, apprenticeship indentures 1712–1877, overseers' accounts 1753–1838, settlement papers 1711–1832

North Meols parish council minutes 1919–57, letter books 1928–34, accounts 1913–43

Oldham rate assessments 1747–1867, overseers' accounts 1854–1900, valuation 1893; (DDX 783) St. Mary's plan 1880

Openshaw township minutes and accounts 1831–49, survey 1840, rate book 1842

*Ormskirk registers 1557–1852, register indices 1743–1877, banns books 1821–34, churchwardens' accounts 1776–1888, churchwardens' minutes 1876–79, vestry minutes 1819–1937, statistic of services 1812–73, schedule of gravestones 1877, ruridecanal meeting minutes 1906–35

Out Rawcliffe highway accounts 1848–56, valuations 1863–95; (RDG) valuations 1897–1929

Over Kellet registers 1653–1948, faculty 1765, list of briefs 1710, fees book 1795–1861, Easter dues 1835–46, constables' accounts 1809–15, churchwardens' accounts 1816–39

Overton registers 1722–1902, churchwardens' accounts and parish meeting minutes 1771–1834, 1838–45

Over Wyresdale registers 1724–1813

Padiham registers 1573–1887, churchwardens' accounts 1623–53, 1706–1927, parochial church council minutes 1920–26, miscellanea 1672–1906, plans 18th century, tithe books 1784, 1788, 1803, 1823–57, apprenticeship indentures 1702–75, township accounts and papers 1678–1829, parochial library accounts and papers 1839–55, relief committee papers 1824–27, letters re

110

postal services 1796–1803, Trafalgar subscriptions 1805, Waterloo subscriptions 1815, Canon Mills testimonial fund minutes 1911–12, St. Matthew's licence 1873, congregation meeting minutes 1892–1901

Parbold overseers' accounts 1838–48, ratepayers' meeting minutes 1852–94, rate books 1848, 1850, 1853, 1855, 1856, 1858–62, 1865, 1867–70, 1872–75, 1877, 1880, 1881, 1883–91, 1893–99, valuation 1872, parish council minutes 1894–1952, social club committee minutes 1893–95, war memorial committee minutes 1944–55, letter book 1895–1928, accounts 1895–1941, Douglas registers 1809–1953, service registers 1897–1962, vestry, etc. minutes 1895–1963, churchwardens' accounts 1910–48, miscellanea 1765–1973; (DDX 1167) faculty for gallery in Douglas chapel 1801

Pendleton (Salford) overseers' relief list 1818

Pendleton (Whalley) burial register 1888–1956, banns book 1919–39, service registers 1897–1919, 1926–35, vestry etc. minutes 1924–64, financial records 1847–1966, Sunday school registers 1840–51, reading-room minutes 1900–09, faculties 1893–1958

Pennington-in-Furness church book: overseers' accounts, vestry minutes etc. 1672–1827, parish council minutes 1894–1955, accounts 1896–1941, rate books 1883, 1918, 1919

Penwortham registers 1857–1937, service registers 1872–1914, churchwardens' accounts 1833–67, parochial church council, etc. minutes 1888–1918, poor rate assessments 1837, 1861

Pilkington rate books 1770–75, 1783, 1789, 1797, 1800, 1804, 1806, 1808, 1810, 1811, 1813, 1815, 1817–21, 1826–30, 1835, 1837, 1838, 1850, 1852, 1853, 1860–66, 1873–77, valuations 1863, overseers' accounts 1731–90, overseers' letter book 1842–58, ratepayers' meeting minutes 1808–27, 1846–76, Outwood surveyors' accounts 1811, Whitefield lighting committee minutes 1861–66, nuisances act committee minutes 1856–60

Pilling registers 1630–1761, 1798–1951, licence to teach 1716, agreement for new chapel 1716, township accounts 1776–1820, vestry minutes 1853–95, valuations 1864–1907; (DDX 264) tithe collection books 1876–78, 1894–1923; (DDX 484) chapel papers 1621, 1716; (DDX 934) rate book 1842–43, valuation 1842; (RDG) valuations 1912–28

Pleasington apprenticeship indentures 1731–1829, bastardy papers 1769–1831, poor-law papers 1738–1829

*Poulton-le-Fylde registers 1591–1854, banns books 1823–77, churchwardens' accounts 1764–97, vestry minutes 1708–1927, pew rents 1856–99, contribution roll 1645, settlement certificates

1696–1812, removal orders 1704–1821, poor accounts 1708–1831, apprenticeship indentures 1711–1826, bastardy papers 1721–1822, workhouse agreements 1731–66, miscellanea 1674–1819, select vestry minutes 1836–73; (UDPo) parish council minutes 1894–1900

Preesall-with-Hackensall valuations 1865–82, 1896–1902; (DDBo) valuation 1830

*Prescot churchwardens' accounts 1663–1786, marriage bonds and licences 1683–1813, certificates of burial in woollen 1689–90, subscriptions for Christian slaves in Algiers 1690, index of papists c. 1740, orders for rebuilding steeple 1797, miscellanea 1678–1785 .

*Preston registers 1611–1969, twenty-four men's minutes 1644–1891, churchwardens' accounts 1723–69, church rates 1850–55, miscellanea 1840–92, churchyard extension 1804, glebe deeds 1738–1835, service registers 1935–62, clergy papers 1919–45, benefice papers 1854–1949, church fabric papers 1852–1956, pew papers 1684–1960, inventories 1907–41, accounts 1820–56, parochial church council minutes 1920–53, Sunday school minutes 1839, 1905–46 and registers 1856–59, 1869–1915, mission accounts 1899–1938 and correspondence 1921–38, church and parish extension papers 1846–1925, bellringing rules 1817, diary of clerical attendance at workhouse and house of recovery 1848–64, yearbooks 1924–34, parish magazines 1893–1965, magazine committee minutes 1946–56; (DDHo) various deeds, papers and plans 1470–1855, Christ Church: registers 1857–70, banns books 1923–58, service registers 1880–90, 1894–1903, 1921–39, accounts 1887–1947, parish magazines 1872, 1895–1960, sale-of-work committee minutes 1891, vestry and parochial church council 1894–1911, pew rents 1902–24, Sunday school minutes 1892–98, 1930–39, papers re fabric 1903–31, pew plan 1843, inventory 1907, St. Andrew's: registers 1837–1941, banns books 1938–72, service registers 1883–1933, war memorial committee minutes 1953–54, St. George's: wardens' accounts 1745–1867, 1917–36, miscellanea 1726–1918, St. James's: registers 1846–1952, banns books 1866–81, 1913–49, 1957–70, service registers 1876–1967, vestry minutes 1906–15, parochial church council minutes 1948–57, church papers 1840–1967, preachers register 1875–1940, faculties 1894–1927, girls' Sunday school registers 1912–26, St. Jude's: registers 1893–1953, banns book 1922–52, service registers 1902–64, vestry minutes 1888–1921, parochial church council minutes 1910–62, pew rents 1902–25, churchwardens' accounts 1906–16, 1935–64, confirmation register 1940–62, St. Paul's: registers 1860–1959, banns books 1911–75, confirmation books 1916–74, service registers 1869–1975, vestry minutes 1832–1922, parochial church council minutes 1886–1922, 1930–38, 1952–70, pew rents 1848–57, 1920–49, offertory books 1920–28, accounts 1929–49, bible class registers 1895–1909, 1921–50, institute committee minutes 1917–30, mission hall minutes 1935–39, social club minutes 1925–39, electoral rolls 1920–31, 1950–74, photograph albums 1867, 1879, Sunday school minutes 1842–1929, accounts 1886–1917 and registers 1869–1939, parish magazines 1871–1955, St. Barnabas mission service registers 1872–93, St. Peter's: registers 1862–1970, banns books 1864–1973, vestry book 1898–1922, pew books 1924–50, service registers 1922–73, churchwardens' accounts 1837–69, 1872–1911, 1914–40, vestry minutes 1913–73, parochial council minutes 1943–76, St. Saviour's: registers 1868–1969, service registers 1868–1970, vestry minutes and accounts 1869–1928, inventory 1882, parochial church council minutes 1920–29, sketch of Leeming Street chapel c. 1850, sale of chapel 1859, plan c. 1868, consecration 1868, register of preachers 1868–59, scrapbook 1869–1945, incumbents' income returns 1929–42, biographical index of parishioners c. 1950, Trinity: council minutes 1925–52, registers 1815–1951, banns book 1901–51, service registers 1926–51, vestry minutes 1842–52, parochial miscellanea 1815–1959, building minutes, deeds, accounts, bazaar papers, etc. 1813–78, Sunday school accounts 1830–46, vestry minutes 1813–75; (DDPr) assessment, accounts, etc. 1778–1836, apprenticeship indentures 1736–1878

Priest Hutton valuations 1818–28

Quernmore (DDQ) settlement papers 1846–52, surveyors' accounts 1800–33, 1852–60, select vestry minutes 1830–49, notices 1833–49

Rainford registers 1719–1881, vestry minutes 1788–1826, 1872–1913, churchwardens' accounts 1871–1912, constables' accounts 1776–87, bastardy accounts 1790–1810, overseers' accounts 1806–27, poor rate books 1838–45, 1848–51, 1853–58, highway rate books 1842, 1844, 1848, 1849, 1851–53, 1858, rate collecting book 1855–60, land-tax assessment 1842

Rainhill rate books 1913–35

Read parish council minutes 1894–1966, financial records 1896–1956, allotments register 1896–1921

Reedley Hallows (RDBu) rate books 1885–1921

Ribbleton poor rate assessments 1868–69

Ribby-with-Wrea registers 1847–1909, service registers 1887–96, 1912–32, vestry minutes 1886–1944, inventory 1914, articles of enquiry 1906, church and school deeds 1722, 1757, benefice papers 1847–1965, faculties 1921–67, miscellanea 1892–1975, rate assessments 1776–86, ratepayers' meeting minutes 1865–95, parish council and committee minutes 1894–1957, accounts 1895–1956; (DDD) accounts and miscellanea 1715–61

*Ribchester registers 1598–1812, banns books 1824–37, 1872–1956, select vestry minutes 1650–1769, 1804–1951, churchwardens' accounts 1660–1845, terrier 1828, affidavits for burial in woollen 1678–81, poor rate assessment 1839; (DDHo) deeds and papers 1406–1864

Rishton overseers' minutes 1908–26, overseers' papers 1703–80, rate books 1839, 1847, 1848, 1879, 1880, 1885, 1886, 1894–97, valuations 1838, 1876, 1884, 1886, 1894, 1896

Rivington registers 1703–1876, parsonage repair accounts 1823–53, chapelwardens' accounts and vestry minutes 1732–1907

Rixton-with-Glazebrook Hollinfare registers 1654–1812

Rochdale (DDCi) glebe leases 1761–1945

Roughlee Booth (RDBu) rate books 1867, 1877–1923, valuations 1872, 1876, 1881

Rufford registers 1673–1853, banns book 1850–1913, churchwardens' accounts 1811–78, vestry minutes 1825–97, poor rate assessment 1838, rate books 1841, 1856–87, constables' accounts 1837–95, church rate books 1851–86, ratepayers' meeting minutes 1873–78, coronation committee minutes 1902, 1911, drainage accounts 1902–26, mole and rat catchers' book 1884–87

Rusland surveyors' accounts 1768–1836

Sabden miscellanea 1902–70, parish council minutes 1894–1970, correspondence 1939–73, accounts 1911–67, footpaths survey 1950, register of allotments 1918–45; (PUZ) valuations 1925–28

St. Helens registers 1713–1925, vestry minutes and accounts 1814–59, lists of briefs 1722–38, 1813–15, pew lists 1723–49

*St. Michaels-on-Wyre registers 1707–1950, churchwardens' accounts 1729–1934, vestry minutes 1729–1877, wheat prices 1805–1914, valuation of Upper Rawcliffe 1819

Salesbury registers 1809–1938, building subscriptions 1805–13, plan c. 1807, subscriptions for new church c. 1860

Salford overseers' papers 1717–98, apprenticeship indentures 1710, 1730, 1754, 1758, 1761

Samlesbury registers 1678–1902, ratepayers' meeting minutes 1829–1958, valuation 1834; (DDX 291) pew faculty 1785

Satterthwaite highway assessments and accounts 1889–92

Scarisbrick township book 1702–51

*Sefton registers 1597–1780, 1783–1899, township accounts 1718–1830, poor rate book 1888–90

Sharples highway accounts 1887–94; (UDTu) Belmont parish council minutes 1894–98 and poor rate book 1914, Higher End vestry minutes 1881–94 and surveyors' accounts 1868, 1877–96

Shevington overseers' ledger 1838–48, ratepayers' meeting minutes 1852–94, parish council minutes 1894–1927, letter book 1895–1902, accounts 1914–26, rate books 1842, 1846–50, 1852–54, 1856–62, 1864–95, sanitary rate books 1884, 1895–98, 1902, valuations 1872, 1874

Shireshead; see Cleveley

Silverdale ratepayers' meeting minutes 1838–95, parish council minutes 1894–1931

Simonswood overseers' accounts and papers 1720–1839, bastardy orders 1732–1819, assessments 1782–1841, apprenticeship indentures 1719–68, ley books 1780–96, militia papers 1765–1831

Southport Christ Church registers 1821–1947, banns books 1837–1928, parochial church council minutes 1920–66, accounts 1920–50, vestry minutes 1874–1969, memoranda 1888–1939, ledger 1918–32, St. Andrew's registers 1872–1969, banns books 1872–90, 1933–52, parochial church council minutes 1923–69, accounts 1894–1911, pew rents 1903–12, confirmation register 1905–17, churchwardens' minutes 1905–23, Brotherhood minutes 1906–13, parish magazines 1889–1913, 1915–21, 1923–36, 1941–42

Speke rate books 1926, 1931

Spotland (CBR) select vestry minutes 1824–26, 1830–31, 1870–95, occupiers c. 1820, 1867–90, overseers' accounts 1884–95, rate books 1776–1891, valuations 1865–94; (DDX 183) church rate assessments 1826–29

Stalmine-with-Staynall valuations 1864–81, 1883–95, burial board draft minutes 1858–77; (UDPl) burial board papers 1854–60; (RDG) valuations 1896–1928

*Standish registers 1560–1812, churchwardens' minutes and accounts 1679–1839, overseers' accounts 1820–38

Staveley constables' accounts 1746–1816, overseers' accounts 1746–1829

Stretford registers 1599–1855, list of churchwardens 1711–76, church rebuilding papers 1717–18, list of overseers 1694–1746, consecration of St. Matthew's 1842

115

Tarbock overseers' accounts 1746–1811, township accounts 1811, bastardy papers 1724, 1767, rate books 1929, 1932, 1935, ratepayers' meeting minutes 1856–94, parish council minutes 1894–95, surveyors' accounts 1809–59

Tarleton township meeting minutes 1836–94

*Tatham registers 1813–1947, churchwardens' accounts 1751–1918, vestry minutes 1842–1918, Easter dues 1750–64, 1809–30, tithe collections 1810–34, tithe agreements 1814–46, church papers 1794–1954, township accounts 1751–1828, township papers 1789–1900; (Microfilm) settlement certificates 1789–1814, examination of settlers 1816–22

Tatham Fell registers 1745–1934, terriers 1767, 1778, 1876, Sunday school accounts 1817–48, Sunday school registers 1863–76, faculties 1738–1935, churchwardens' accounts 1742–1934, vestry minutes 1865–1936, analyses of infant mortality 1831–40, parochial statistics 1915–28, lists of parish officers 1671–1844, overseers' accounts 1742–1843, surveyors' accounts 1771–86, constables' accounts 1742–1837, poor rate receipts 1823–44

Thornham (CBR) overseers' accounts 1829, rate books 1856–86, valuations 1850, 1880

Thornton (Sefton) township meeting minutes 1830–90, 1892–1901, parish council minutes 1894–1940, rate book 1881–83, accounts 1874–1917, survey and valuation 1848, perambulation of boundaries 1900, miscellanea 1894–1914

Thornton-le-Fylde apprenticeship indentures 1721, bastardy bond 1724; (UDTh) parish council minutes 1894–1900, survey 1804; (DP 409) highway accounts 1811–31; (DP 411) highway accounts 1832–36

Thurnham valuations 1838–53

Tockholes township accounts 1764–68, 1838–48, township minutes 1886–94, constables' papers 1694–1852, apprenticeship indentures 1730–1815, highway accounts and papers 1711–1894, poor-law papers 1668–1854, church accounts and papers 1837–1946, population book 1905, parish council minutes 1894–1969, accounts 1894–1949, letter books 1936–46, air-raid census 1938

Tottington highway accounts 1893–95

Tunstall poor rate assessments 1890–91, 1893–96, valuations 1888, 1893, 1897

Turton registers 1719–1927, vestry minutes 1779–93, churchwardens' accounts 1841–1911, faculty for rebuilding 1840, letter to overseers of Dalston, Cumberland 1838; (UDTu) select vestry minutes 1852–96, overseers' minutes 1898–1927, rate books 1824–29, 1914, overseers' accounts 1843–44, 1874–1902, highway accounts 1856–59, 1862–73, valuation 1866

Ulnes Walton overseers' accounts 1868–1909, poor rate assessment 1837

Unsworth registers 1730–1840, trust deed 1728, consecration deed 1730, commission for new gallery 1787

Up Holland registers 1600–1901, vestry minutes 1790–1970, churchwardens' accounts 1724–1927, faculties 1770–1898, licences to curacy 1882–96, church fabric papers 1786–1884, restoration committee minutes 1881–90, new vicarage correspondence 1898–1901, settlement certificates 1769–73, removal orders 1769–86, bastardy bonds 1769–86, extract of Naylor baptisms 1790–1835

Upper Allithwaite "The book of the poore" 1674–1767, Lindale registers 1734–1817, accounts 1733–1832, rebuilding minutes and accounts 1825–30, chapelwardens' accounts 1828–1914, institute committee minutes 1890–1907, institute accounts 1869–1902, salary accounts 1742–1842, overseers' accounts 1813–94

Upper Holker constables' and overseers' accounts 1732–1836, list of landowners to serve parish offices 1732–1808, Poor Close accounts 1728–47

Upper Rawcliffe-with-Tarnacre valuations 1863–87, 1892–96; (RDG) 1897–1928

Urmston vestry minutes 1870–1921

Waddington overseers' records 1738–1871, constables' accounts 1741–1803, surveyors' accounts 1737–1814, 1844–65, land-tax assessments 1847–51

Walton-le-Dale registers 1653–1912, memoranda and lists of parish officers 1703–96, churchwardens' accounts 1799–1877, vestry minutes 1817–1930, pew book and plan 1816, relief of distress committee minutes and census 1862–64, bell catalogues 1877, 1879, correspondence with bellfounders 1879–80, bill book 1877–99; (UDWd) vestry minutes 1826–66, ratepayers' meeting minutes 1870–94, overseers' minutes 1901–27, vestry accounts 1827–33, valuations 1821, 1832, 1848; (DDHo) letters and papers 1685–1754

Wardleworth (CBR) rate books 1833–85, valuations 1862–93

Warrington St. Paul's registers 1831–1906, All Saints register 1887–96, letters to overseers of Dalston, Cumberland 1827–37; (DDX 215) removal orders 1700, 1754

Warton-in-Amounderness registers 1848–52, consecration papers 1725, miscellanea 1722–1850, parish council minutes 1894–1932, overseers' accounts 1885–1908

Weeton-with-Preese overseers' accounts 1885–1910

Westby-with-Plumpton overseers' accounts 1885–1909, parish council minutes 1894–1914

Westhoughton poor rate books 1840–55, 1857–79, 1881–82, church rate books 1846, 1847, 1860–62, burial rate book 1856

*Whalley registers 1538–91, churchwardens' accounts 1636–1868, sacrament money accounts 1732–1814, faculties 1747–1812, rectory deeds 1616–1799, church restoration committee minutes 1890–91, apprenticeship indentures and papers 1681–1880, parish council minutes 1894–1925; (DDX 336) apprenticeship indentures 1748, 1762

Wheatley Carr Booth (RDBu) rate books 1925, 1926

Wheelton survey 1835

Whiston rate books 1913–34, financial statements 1901–54, account books 1895–1959, correspondence 1895–1941

Whitewell registers 1713–1868, churchwardens' accounts 1816–62, church rate books 1851–52

Whittington registers 1558–1764, church-brief collections 1664–91, appointments of clerk and schoolmaster 1690, 1695, church subscriptions 1871–74, overseers' accounts 1861–76, surveyors' accounts 1808–37, 1866–80, valuation 1869, mole rate book 1889–92

Whittle-le-Woods registers 1830–1956, parish council minutes 1929–69, accounts 1936–64; (DDSh 25) township book 1620–1818, valuation 1795

Whitworth (UDWh) ratepayers order book 1831–74, overseers' accounts 1895–1925

Widnes Farnworth registers 1538–1897, churchwardens' accounts c. 1690–c. 1890, receipts for brief collections 1717–61, confirmation registers 1893–1917, communion statistics 1903–18, parish magazines 1891–1914, register of preachers 1915–22, plans 1826, 1846, 1872, 1878, contract for new gallery, etc. 1824, faculty and plan for restoration 1894, memorial window papers 1904–28, curacy fund papers 1913–16, grave plans 1816, c. 1900, c. 1920, 1928, parish boundary papers 1908–09, St. Ambrose trust deed 1883, consecration papers 1883–84, correspondence 1917–19, 1929–34, trustees' minutes 1919–32, St. John registers 1914–19, preachers register 1914–42, plans c. 1914, building papers 1913–

14, St. Mary registers 1858–1910, plans 1909, histories of church
c. 1960, 1970; (CCV) churchyard inscriptions

Windle rate books 1927, 1928, 1935

Winmarleigh valuations 1864–96, poor rate assessment 1906; (RDG)
valuations 1896–1928

Winstanley township book 1754–1921

Winwick-with-Hulme parish council minutes 1906–65; (DDX 153)
descriptions of inhabitants 1851

Wiswell vestry minutes 1858–63

Woodplumpton registers 1604–1879, banns book 1824–91, register of
apprentices 1811–15, overseers' accounts 1700–42, 1771–1818;

Worsley (DDX 125) valuation 1815

Worston (DDX 204) township meeting minutes 1867–1922

Worthington rate books 1855, 1859, 1860, 1862–63, 1867–97, valuations 1872–74, parish council accounts 1895–1954

Wray-with-Botton parish council minutes 1895–1957, Holy Trinity
building accounts 1834–43, letter books 1837–63, 1876–92,
correspondence 1845–1901

Wrightington overseers' accounts 1838–48, vestry minutes 1852–94,
parish council minutes 1894–1910, 1923–73, charity papers
1894–1963

Yealand Conyers highway rate book 1889, collectors' monthly
statements 1854–67, 1875–1903, surveyors' accounts 1885–91

Yealand Redmayne ratepayers' meeting minutes 1878–94, valuation
c. 1895, financial records 1895–1962, clerks' correspondence
1912–57, highway rate books 1857–63, 1869–80, 1882–89,
collectors' monthly statements 1858–1903, surveyors' accounts
1874–90

Part IV

Ecclesiastical Records

CHURCH OF ENGLAND DIOCESAN AND ARCHIDIACONAL

The complicated diocesan history of Lancashire is discussed in *The Victoria History of Lancashire*, vol. II, since the publication of which the diocese of Blackburn has been created from the northern part of the diocese of Manchester. For probate records see page 25. Searchers may also consult the *Handlist of Genealogical Sources*, published by the Lancashire Record Office.

Archdeaconry of Lancaster (ARL) articles of enquiry 1896, 1901, call books 1869–71, 1873–75, 1877–79, 1881–83, 1885–88, 1890, 1896–97, appointment of registrar 1870, papers concerning portrait of the Ven. Archdeacon John Hornby 1887

Archdeaconry of Liverpool (DRL) list of churchwardens 1854–81

Archdeaconry of Richmond (Western Deaneries of Amounderness, Copeland, Furness, Kendal, and Lonsdale); (ARR) processes of citation 1687–1746, 1768, 1786–1806, call books 1670–1837, compert books 1665–68, 1670, 1673–76, 1679–83, 1685–89, 1692, 1693, 1695, 1697–1705, 1707–12, 1714–33, 1735–41, 1743–47, 1749–50, 1753, 1756–60, 1763, 1765–66, 1769–70, 1772–74, 1776–79, 1781–82, 1784–85, 1789–90, 1792–93, 1796, act books 1708–20, 1730–48, writs of excommunication 1703, 1719–32, 1766, fee books 1745–87, presentments of churchwardens (Lancashire parishes only) 1635–1846, sequestration orders 1788–1807, censuses of Broughton-in-Amounderness and Kirkham 1676, and Preston 1679, churchwardens' declarations (Lancashire parishes only) 1841, 1843, 1846, 1850, forms of prayer and proclamations 1798–1807, marriage bonds and affidavits (printed to 1755 by the Record Society of Lancashire and Cheshire) 1648, 1651, 1661–1854, 1861, cause papers (assessments, adultery, clergy, church officers, schoolmasters, defamation, faculties, matrimony, pews, probate, tithes, etc) 1530–1838, state of churches 1782

Diocese of Blackburn (DRB)

Bishops' transcripts of parish registers (chapelries follow the mother-parish); an asterisk denotes gaps within the indicated period. Where transcripts exist of dates earlier than the surviving registers the date of the latter is given in square brackets.

Bispham 1676–1718*, 1720–1849; Blackpool 1826–58*

Blackburn 1606–1747*, 1749–1837; Blackburn St. John 1813–46, Blackburn St. Paul 1830–40, Blackburn St. Peter 1821–38, Balderstone 1751–1853*, Balderstone St. Saviour 1836–53*, Great Harwood 1628–1739*, 1741–1856, Langho 1772–1846, Lower Darwen 1829–32, Over Darwen 1723–1836, 1856, Over Darwen Trinity 1829–34, Salesbury 1813–38*, 1873–76, Samlesbury [1678], 1623–1751*, 1753–1845, Tockholes 1728–1830, Walton-le-Dale [1641] 1609–1739*, 1741–1854, 1870–89, Walton-le-Dale Bamber Bridge 1837–46, Walton-le-Dale Higher Walton 1871–82*

Bolton-le-Sands 1676–1707*, 1710–1841, 1843–89*; Over Kellet 1682–1709*, 1712–1865

Brindle 1621–87*, 1690–1861

Chipping 1678–93*, 1697–1870, 1872–81*

Chorley 1630–1756*, 1758–1830, 1832–47*, 1865–71*; Chorley St. George 1836–54*, Chorley St. Peter 1851–58*

Cockerham 1673–1718*, 1721–1869, 1871–1902*; Ellel [1832] 1753, 1830, 1841–71, Shireshead 1830–60

Croston 1607–89*, 1691–1873; Bretherton 1841–46, Hesketh-with-Becconsall 1803–44, Mawdesley 1841–46, 1871–83*, Rufford [1669] 1632–1777*, 1793–1828*, Tarleton 1723–1822, 1825–54

Eccleston 1616–85*, 1690–1847, 1849–50; Douglas 1722–1845, 1847–55*, Wrightington 1857–62

Garstang 1679–1718*, 1721–1861, 1863–1903*; Pilling 1688–1719*, 1721–1861, 1864–78*

Halton 1673–1710*, 1712–1869; Aughton 1856–63, 1865–82

Heysham 1676–1715*, 1717–1804, 1806–68

Hoole [1673] 1662–1706*, 1709–57, 1759–1846

Kirkham 1678–1718*, 1721–1860, 1864–1932*; Goosnargh 1673–1718*, 1720–1866, Hambleton 1813–66, Lund 1840–41, 1843–82, Treales 1858–79, 1882–87, Warton 1726–32, 1755–71, 1773–83, 1846–58*, Whitechapel 1819–30, 1835–71

Lancaster 1675–1718*, 1721–50*, 1752–1814, 1816–57*; Lancaster St. Anne 1843–62, Lancaster St. John 1842–59, Lancaster St. Thomas 1845–59, Admarsh (Bleasdale) 1815–39, Caton 1673–1716*, 1718–1859, Fulwood 1865–68, Fulwood Garrison 1850–61*, Glasson 1840–80, Gressingham 1676–1712*, 1714–1858, 1863–88, Overton 1813–31, 1836–38, Poulton-le-Sands 1746–72, 1774–75, 1792, 1794, 1813–36, 1839–42, Quernmore 1856–88, 1904–06, Skerton 1843–67*, Stalmine 1678–1734*, 1736–1861, 1863–78, Wyresdale 1813–80*

Leyland [1653] 1622–86*, 1737–1826, 1828–44*; Euxton 1737–1837*, Heapey 1737–1833, Hoghton 1788–1848*, 1871–83*, Withnell 1841–46

Lytham 1678–1718*, 1720–43, 1745–1834, 1845

Melling 1677, 1689–1710*, 1713–1849, 1851–53; Claughton 1716–30*, 1732–69, 1771–91, 1793–1800, 1802–62, Hornby 1742–54*, 1818–47, 1851–61, 1863–76

Penwortham [1857] 1608–1706*, 1741–1813, 1815–55, 1857–70; Farington 1841–45*, Longton [1813] 1758–1813, 1815–55, 1857–70

Poulton-le-Fylde 1679–1718*, 1721–1857, 1859–68; Marton 1751–1836, Thornton 1837–40

Preston 1616, 1671–1718*, 1729–34, 1736–82, 1813–44; Preston Burial Ground 1858–61, Preston St. Paul 1867–75, Barton 1850–69*, Broughton 1671–1718*, 1721–1861, 1863–70

Ribchester 1676–1718*, 1721–1802, 1804–39; Longridge 1813–39

St. Michaels-on-Wyre 1677–1718, 1720–1878, 1881–88; Great Eccleston Copp 1813–40, 1844–75*, Inskip 1849–79, 1882–83, Out Rawcliffe 1838–45*, Woodplumpton 1674–1723*, 1726–1861, 1863–82*

Standish 1611–1701, 1708–1861; Adlington 1839–46, Coppull 1793–65

Tatham 1676–1706*, 1708–1872; Tatham Fells 1813–72

Tunstall 1689–99*, 1701–1838, 1843, 1874; Leck 1859–68*

Warton 1637, 1673–77, 1689–1708*, 1710–1835, 1837–59*; Carnforth 1877–96*, Silverdale 1822–35, 1837–38, 1844–1911*, Yealand Conyers 1822–35, 1837–38, 1844–55, 1885–1911*

Whalley 1605–85*, 1688–1739, 1741–1800, 1802–46, 1848–75*; Accrington 1614–1739*, 1742–1868, Altham 1614–1739*, 1742–1848, Bacup 1793–1846, Burnley 1572–1726*, 1728–1847, Chatburn 1838–46, 1871–77*, Church [1633] 1600–1739*, 1741–1836, 1838–46, Clitheroe 1572–1739*, 1741–1841, Clitheroe St.

James 1848–54, Colne 1602–1700*, 1702–39, 1741–1829, Downham [1653] 1606–1739*, 1741–70, 1772–1839, 1841–85*, Fence 1837–46, 1872, Goodshaw Booth 1801–04, 1812–38, Haslingden [1620] 1603–1701*, 1703–39, 1741–62, 1764–1844, Holme 1792–1800, 1802–05, 1807–45, 1901–04, Marsden 1813–24, 1826–42, Great Marsden 1850–54, Little Marsden 1848–54, Newchurch-in-Pendle 1599–1635*, 1663–1739*, 1741–1836, Newchurch-in-Rossendale [1653], 1606–98*, 1700–39, 1741–51, 1753–1848, Oswaldtwistle 1848–54, Padiham 1609–41*, 1663–87*, 1691–1783, 1785–91*, 1793–1840, 1843–73*, Rawtenstall 1838–47, Trawden 1846–74, Tunstead 1843–48, Whitewell 1756–61, 1763–77*, 1810–43

Whittington 1664–1713*, 1715–99, 1801–04, 1807–41, 1851, 1874, 1876

Terriers: Accrington 1825, Bacup 1825, Blackburn 1663, 1747, Bolton-le-Sands 1691, 1701, c. 1715, 1738, 1742, 1778, 1788, Brindle 1663, 1684, 1701, 1704, 1712, 1728, 1747, 1760, 1766, Burnley 1825, Chipping (charities) 1722, Claughton 1778, 1788, Cockerham 1783, Croston 1722, 1728, Darwen 1783, Eccleston 1663, Garstang 1738, 1743, 1744, 1746, 1749, 1752, 1753, 1755, 1760, 1766, 1770, 1778, 1789, Goodshaw 1821, Great Harwood 1778, Halton 1698, 1700, Heysham 1697–99, 1706, 1708, 1710, 1713, 1719, 1721–32, 1778, Hoole 1696, Hornby 1789, 1829, 1832, Kirkham 1698, 1701, 1716, 1778, 1814, 1825, Leyland 1728, Longton 1814, Lytham 1778, 1788, Melling 1691, 1778, 1779, 1783, 1789, 1804, Newchurch-in-Pendle 1778, Newchurch-in-Rossendale 1702, Padiham 1813, Penwortham 1789, Poulton-le-Fylde 1743, 1749, 1752, 1774, 1776, 1778, 1783, 1813, Poulton-le-Sands 1778, Preston 1663, Ribchester 1665, 1728, St. Michaels-on-Wyre 1733, Samlesbury 1778, Stalmine 1760, 1770, 1778, Standish 1663, 1665, 1778, 1804, 1825, Tarleton 1728, Tatham 1693, 1695–99, 1701, 1709, 1712, 1716, 1722, 1729–88, 1798, 1803, Tatham Fell 1778, 1813, Tunstall 1698, 1709–27, 1733, 1743, 1753, 1760, 1766, 1770, 1778, 1783, 1788, 1814, 1820, Warton 1695, 1698–1701, 1707, 1709, 1716–18, 1728, 1778, 1825, Whittington 1700, 1701, 1709, 1716, 1718, 1722, 1723, 1725, 1731–76, 1778–91, 1794, Woodplumpton 1689, 1740, 1825

Visitation records 1937–67, affidavits 1961–67

Diocese of Carlisle (DRC)

Bishops' transcripts of parish registers (chapelries follow the mother parish; an asterisk denotes gaps within the indicated period).

Aldingham 1638–1711*, 1713–1848, 1850–64, 1866–77; Dendron 1803–73*

123

Cartmel 1664–1711*, 1714–1878; Cartmel Fell 1857–83, Field Broughton 1859–85*, Flookburgh 1859–69, Grange 1857–70, Height (Quaker) 1865–94*, Staveley 1857–73

Colton 1664–1722*, 1724–1854, 1856–70; Finsthwaite 1725–1830, 1832–55, 1857–91, Haverthwaite 1855–87, Rusland 1852–54, 1856–69, 1874–89

Dalton-in-Furness 1676, 1689–93, 1695–1703, 1705–1871; Walney 1856–74

Hawkshead 1689–1710*, 1712–1807, 1810–64; Brathay 1837–54, 1856–84, Colthouse (Quaker) 1865–94*, Satterthwaite 1766–1854, 1856–1903, 1905–14

Kirkby Ireleth 1723–1838, 1855–77; Broughton-in-Furness 1673–1712*, 1714–1896, Seathwaite 1737–1856, Woodland 1834–56*

Pennington 1689–1712*, 1715–1870

Ulverston 1635–1708*, 1710–1841, 1856–59; Blawith 1746–1875, Coniston 1689–1716*, 1718–1843, 1845–48*, 1850–80, Egton-with-Newland 1813–68, Lowick 1740–70, 1777–1873, Swarthmoor (Quaker) 1865–93*, Torver 1692–1712, 1715–1800, 1802–44*, 1846–71, Ulverston Trinity 1832–68*

Urswick 1634–1712*, 1714–1841, 1855–70; Bardsea 1856–59*

Terriers: Aldingham 1727, Broughton-in-Furness 1709, 1738, 1778, 1825, Cartmel 1698, 1701, Colton 1775, 1783, Coniston 1778, Dalton-in-Furness 1698, 1778, 1783, Finsthwaite 1743, 1778, Hawkshead 1698, 1701, 1778, 1783, Lowick 1698, Pennington 1698, 1778, 1788, Torver 1778, n.d., Urswick 1698, 1708, 1716, 1778

Diocese of Chester (MF 5-9)

diocesan visitations 1578–1684 (microfilm).

Diocese of Liverpool (DRL)

Bishops' transcripts of parish registers (chapelries follow the mother-parish, an asterisk denotes gaps within the indicated period).

Altcar [1664] 1663–95*, 1699–1745, 1748–1862

Aughton 1606–41*, 1662–84*, 1690–1882

Childwall 1602–15*, 1628–38*, 1664–85, 1690–1869; Garston 1813–47, Grassendale 1868–79, Hale 1604–40*, 1668–1893, Halewood 1839–71, Much Woolton 1826–74, Speke 1876–80, Wavertree Holy Trinity 1806–90, Wavertree St. Mary 1856, 1873–82

Halsall 1606–40*, 1664–85*, 1690–1893; Lydiate 1841–53*, Maghull 1610–37*, 1663–89*, 1729–1868, Melling 1610–37*, 1664–85*, 1690–1857, 1871–77

Huyton 1604–29*, 1637–41, 1664–85*, 1693–1868; Knowsley 1844–83

Liverpool [1660] 1604–41*, 1663–69, 1673–1867; All Saints 1835–38, All Souls (Vauxhall) 1854–84, Christ Church 1799–1837, 1851, Holy Trinity 1802–06, 1809–43, St. Alban (Bevington) 1846–83, St. Andrew 1815–61, 1873–74, St. Anne (Richmond) 1773–92, 1800–42, St. Catherine 1831–41, St. David 1827–32, St. George 1734–1862, St. John 1773–1852, St. Luke 1831–48, 1868–74, St. Mark 1815–43, St. Martin 1829–56, St. Mary (Blind Asylum) 1829–49, St. Mary 1829–64, St. Matthew 1798–1831, 1851, St. Matthias 1843, St. Michael 1826–63, St. Paul 1769–1881, St. Peter 1704–1868, St. Philip 1816–60, 1868, 1879–81, St. Simon 1837, St. Stephen 1801–69, St. Thomas 1750–1875

North Meols 1606, 1620–39*, 1663–85*, 1690–1708, 1712–1838; Southport Christ Church 1822–39, Southport Holy Trinity 1874–75, Southport St. Paul 1881, Southport St. Stephen 1878–80

Ormskirk 1604–41*, 1657–66*, 1668–1841; Scarisbrick 1853–86

Prescot 1602–41*, 1664–1832, 1835–51; Great Sankey 1769–83, 1800–80, Parr Holy Trinity 1869–88, Rainford [1718] 1702–06, 1723–1849, 1855–65, Sutton 1849–61, Whiston 1868–70, 1892–94, Widnes Farnworth 1604–41*, 1664–91*, 1694–1873, Windle St. Helens 1813–55

Sefton 1619–41*, 1663–1855; Great Crosby 1749–1869, Great Crosby Waterloo 1841–47, 1868–70, Litherland Seaforth 1855–59, 1873–77

Walton-on-the-Hill 1625–40*, 1666–1880; Breck Holy Trinity 1848–53, Bootle Christ Church 1866–78, Everton St. Augustus 1830–39, Everton St. George 1814–60, Everton St. Peter 1850–54, Formby St. Luke [1711] 1620–41*, 1663–84*, 1690–1839, Kirkby [1678] 1610, 1629–37*, 1664–85*, 1714–1848, Kirkdale St. Aidan 1869–76, Kirkdale St. Mary 1826–43, 1855–59, Toxteth Park St. Clement 1841–56, Toxteth Park St. James 1775–1843, Toxteth Park St. John 1868–83, Toxteth Park St. Michael 1816–93, Toxteth Park (Quaker) burials 1864–97, Toxteth Park St. Paul 1838–77, West Derby [1737] 1697, 1723–28*, 1736–1871, West Derby St. Ann 1832–46, West Derby St. John (Knotty Ash) 1852–58, West Derby St. John (Tue Brook) 1871–81, West Derby St. Mary 1832–73, West Derby St. Stephen 1851–54

Warrington 1596, 1600–41*, 1670*, 1693–1853; Warrington Holy Trinity 1850–54, Warrington St. Paul 1831–56, Burtonwood 1682–1728*, 1732–1876, Rixton Hollinfare 1757–1870, Poulton Padgate 1841, 1846–61

125

Wigan 1600, 1613–41*, 1658–1712*, 1721–1869; Wigan St. Catherine 1841–46, 1876–93, Abram 1838–72, Billinge 1722–69, 1772–1856, Dalton 1870–77, Hindley 1722–33, 1738–1844, 1876–79, Up Holland 1619, 1629–41*, 1663–95*, 1697–1854, 1876–79

Winwick 1600–41*, 1666–1889; Ashton-in-Makerfield 1698–1854, Culcheth Newchurch 1609, 1619, 1700–1854, 1860–93, Culcheth Glazebury 1878–80, Golborne 1854–72, Lowton 1737–1885, Newton-in-Makerfield St. Peter 1737–1868, Newton-in-Makerfield Emmanuel 1845–55, Southworth-with-Croft 1845–92

Terriers: Ashton-in-Makerfield 1814, Aughton 1663, 1696, 1701, 1705, 1709, 1712, 1716, Bickerstaffe 1895, Childwall 1728, 1770, Great Crosby 1825. Hale 1778, 1825, Halsall 1696, 1709, 1738, 1742, 1778, 1789, 1825, Hollinfare 1778, Huyton 1696, 1729, 1733, Kirkby 1686, 1712, 1714, 1717, 1718, 1720–23, 1726, 1728, 1733, 1778, 1789, 1799, Liverpool 1706–17, Lowton 1814, Maghull 1778, 1825, Melling 1709, 1747, 1770, 1825, Newchurch-in-Culcheth 1814, North Meols 1696, 1729, 1733, Ormskirk 1663, 1696, 1705, 1814, Sefton 1663, 1701, 1705, 1709, 1712, 1715, 1722–24, 1728–30, 1742, 1754, Up Holland 1811, Walton-on-the-Hill 1686, 1733, 1738, 1742, 1747, 1754, 1757, 1759, 1760, 1763, 1765, 1766, 1778, Warrington 1663, 1701, 1712, West Derby 1778, Wigan 1814, Wigan St. George 1814, Winwick 1701, 1899

Diocese of Manchester (DRM)

Bishops' transcripts of parish registers (chapelries follow the mother-parish; an asterisk denotes gaps within the indicated period).

Ashton-under-Lyne 1594–1640*, 1670–1722*, 1728–1816, 1824–32; Christ Church 1846–56, St. James 1867–1904, St. Peter 1826–30, Hey 1868–69, Lees 1758–1846, Mossley 1773, 1777, 1784–1838, Stalybridge 1782–90, 1793–95, 1798–1820

Bolton-le-Moors [1587] 1573–1641*, 1670–95*, 1705–1872; Emmanuel 1847–52, Holy Trinity 1853–56, St. George 1801–47, St. John 1849–54, Belmont 1850–55, Blackrod [1607] 1606–13*, 1633, 1641, 1670, 1696–1700, 1716–27*, 1730–1863, Bradshaw 1853–76*, Harwood 1840–65, Little Lever 1806–46, Rivington [1703] 1637, 1639, 1721, 1725–51*, 1753–1855, Tonge 1848–51, Turton 1813–40, 1848–54, Walmsley 1845–47, 1870–76

Bury 1603–41*, 1661–76*, 1683–95*, 1702–11*, 1738–1873; St. John 1790–1867, St. Paul 1845–67, Edenfield [1728] 1717, 1731–45*, 1747–1836, 1841–45, 1856–77, Elton All Saints 1843–46, 1858–67, Elton St. Stephen 1882–94*, Heywood 1807–17*, 1819–42, Holcome 1730–50*, 1752–1860, Ramsbottom 1850–54, Tottington St. Anne 1799–1862, Walmersley 1838–67

Deane [1637] 1613–40*, 1670–80*, 1682–1885; Farnworth St. John 1836–45, Farnworth St. James 1866–80, Halliwell St. Luke 1871–79, Halliwell St. Peter 1840–43, Horwich 1749–94*, 1796–1846, 1871–83, Peel 1807–47*, Westhoughton 1755–1839

Eccles 1613–41*, 1672–1711*, 1726–1864; Barton St. Catherine 1843–62, Ellenbrook 1781–1852 (for 1758–73 see Leigh), Pendlebury 1842–55, Pendleton 1777–1862, Swinton 1792–1863, Walkden 1839–59, Worsley 1848–49

Flixton 1606–41*, 1670–1721*, 1723–1834, 1842–47

Leigh 1602–41*, 1660–86*, 1690–1846; Astley [1760] 1724–1842, 1848–54, Atherton 1724–1846, Bedford 1840–55, Ellenbrook 1758–73, Tyldesley 1825–47

Manchester 1614, 1634–39, 1672–96*, 1708–1851; All Souls 1840–47, St. Anne [1736] 1712–38, 1763, 1810–45, St. George 1818–31, St. James 1788–1838, St. John 1769–1846, St. Mary 1806–45, St. Matthew 1837–45, 1855–82, St. Michael 1800–13, 1829–32, St. Paul 1822–43, St. Peter 1795–1839, SS. Simon and Jude 1844–47, Ardwick 1752–55, 1761–1843, Blackley 1721–35, 1733–1819, 1829–32, 1838–41, Cheetham St. Mark 1806–40, Cheetham St. Luke 1839, 1848–54, Cheetham St. Thomas 1855–70, Chorlton-cum-Hardy [1737] 1639, 1753–84*, 1798–1830, 1833–42, Chorlton-on-Medlock All Saints 1820–34, Chorlton-on-Medlock St. Luke 1814–40, Denton St. Lawrence 1700, 1723–1841, 1845–48, Denton Christ Church 1848, 1851–55, Didsbury 1603, 1619–28*, 1637–39, 1670–82*, 1721–1864, Gorton 1676–84*, 1721–1846, Heaton Norris 1779–1802, 1808–39, Hulme 1828–41, Moss Side 1850–63, Newton [1723] 1721–1839, Openshaw 1839–42, Salford Sacred Trinity [1794] 1635–41*, 1665–84*, 1721–37*, 1746–1836, 1885–89, Salford Christ Church 1842–46, Salford St. Philip 1833–40, Salford St. Stephen 1808–16, 1823–43, Stretford St. Matthew 1665–95*, 1722–28, 1737–74*, 1777–1847, Stretford St. Thomas 1838–63, Withington 1842–47

Middleton 1609–41*, 1662–90*, 1721–1847, 1865–74; Ainsworth 1731–1835, 1857–74, Ashworth 1813–69, Hopwood 1829–39

Oldham 1604–41*, 1665–86*, 1688–1700, 1702–06*, 1709–1844; St. James 1830–48, St. Peter 1768–1848, 1865–71, Coldhurst Holy Trinity 1848–75, Hollinwood 1782–1854, Waterhead Holy Trinity 1847–50, Werneth 1847–54, Chadderton St. John 1846–54, Chadderton St. Matthew 1848–54, 1873–75, Crompton 1723–1837, 1848–54, Royton 1758–1846, 1858–80

Prestwich [1603] 1599–1641*, 1670–1713*, 1721–1854, 1865–83; Ringley 1773–1847, Stand 1827–46, Unsworth 1792–1828, 1831–45

127

Radcliffe 1604–48*, 1665–1700*, 1721–1868; St. Thomas 1819–78

Rochdale 1599–1639*, 1661–1703*, 1710–1839; Littleborough 1758–1844, Milnrow 1750–1847, 1873–77, Saddleworth 1612–41*, 1673–1700*, 1722–1846, Saddleworth Dobcross 1787–1842, Saddleworth Friarmere 1784–1846, Saddleworth Lydgate 1788–1846, Spotland 1837–43, Todmorden [1666] 1625–32*, 1671–1713*, 1715–1832, Wardleworth St. James 1821–31, 1848–58, Wardleworth St. Mary 1747–1839, 1848–55, Whitworth [1763] 1752–1846, Wuerdle 1834–44, 1848–57

Graveyard inscriptions (with plans): Eccles St. Mary, Manchester Collegiate, Manchester St. Anne, Manchester St. John, Manchester St. Mary, Manchester St. Peter, Manchester Chorlton All Saints, Manchester Didsbury St. James, Oldham St. Mary, Ramsbottom St. Paul

Terriers: Ashton-under-Lyne 1663, 1666, 1696, 1722, 1728, Astley 1778, Blackley 1825, Blackrod 1789, Bolton-le-Moors 1696, 1728, 1747, Bury 1663, 1696, 1713, 1728, Chorlton 1814, Deane 1705, 1728, 1777, 1778, 1825, Eccles 1663, 1696, 1701, 1705, 1709, 1716, Ellenbrook 1701, Flixton 1728, 1757, 1778, Gorton 1832, Heaton Norris 1814, Horwich 1778, Lees 1778, Leigh 1742, 1782, 1789, Manchester St. John 1778, Manchester St. Mary 1778, Middleton 1663, 1664, 1728, Milnrow 1835, Peel 1813, Prestwich-with-Oldham 1663, 1696, 1778, 1813, Radcliffe 1663, 1705, 1709, 1728, 1778, Rivington 1778, Rochdale 1662, 1783, Saddleworth 1701, 1705, 1709, 1712, 1728, Todmorden 1747, 1778, 1780, Westhoughton 1814

Church Commissioners (DDCc) Bury rectory estate deeds 1805–1971, Bretherton church deeds of Barrowford 1715–26, plans of many former parsonages 1815–1951, deeds of Ashton Park, Preston 1710–1919, and of Levenshulme and Sharples 1619–1732

ROMAN CATHOLIC

Archdiocese of Liverpool (RCLv):

Those records which date before 1894 may be classified broadly into parochial, diocesan, interdiocesan, and educational records and include, *inter alia*, visitation returns from 1830, mission, parish, and schools balance-sheets from 1780, schools' religious examination and inspection returns 1858, 1864, various records of the Northern and Lancashire Vicariate, the state of the diocese 1847–96, mission deeds from 1664, Lea mission papers from 1790, Blackburn Trust deeds from 1589, visitation diaries of Bishop Goss 1855–67, parochial census returns 1855, mission accounts 1890–94, letter-books of Bishops Goss 1855–72, O'Reilly 1877–94, and Whiteside 1894–1902, an extensive collection of correspondence including the Holy See, most of the English bishops, John Lingard, E. W. Pugin, Gerard Manley Hopkins, William Rathbone, etc. There are also very many other documents, either individual or in small groups, bearing upon the administration of the diocese.

Parochial:

Accrington (RCMf) microfilm registers: Sacred Heart 1871–1941, St. Anne's 1897–1941

Ardwick (RCMf) microfilm registers: St. Aloysius' 1863–1941

Ashton-under-Lyne (RCMf) microfilm registers: St. Anne's 1871–1941, St. Mary's 1870–1914, Workhouse 1884–1916

Aspull (RCMf) microfilm registers 1898–1941

Aughton (RCAu) registers 1798–1856, confirmations 1803–44

Bamber Bridge (RCBB) St. Mary's registers 1764–1855

Barrowford (RCMf) microfilm registers: SS. Peter and Paul's 1902–41

Barton-upon-Irwell (RCBI) Holy Cross registers 1793–1857; (RCMf) All Saints' microfilm registers 1845–1941

Billington (RCBg) St. Mary's registers 1837–73

Birchley (RCBi) St. Mary's register 1792–1855, confirmation 1825, rent-charge on Potter's estate 1781

Blackbrook (RCBl) registers 1771–1857, confirmations 1813, 1825, 1831, 1835

Blackburn (RCMf) microfilm registers: St. Alban's 1856–1927, St. Joseph's 1874–1939, St. Peter's 1889–1942

Blackley (RCMf) microfilm registers: Mount Carmel 1871–1941, St. Clare's 1929–41

Blackrod (RCWJ) register 1732–38

Bolton (RCBo) SS. Peter and Paul's registers 1794–1859, confirmations 1838; (RCMf) microfilm registers: St. Edmund's 1861–1941, St. Mary's 1856–1941, St. Patrick's 1866–1941, SS. Peter and Paul's 1856–1941

Bradford (RCMf) St. Brigid's microfilm register 1879–1940

Brierfield (RCMf) Holy Trinity microfilm register 1896–1941

Brindle (RCBr) registers 1722–1875

Broughton, Salford (RCMf) microfilm registers: St. Boniface's 1892–1941, St. Thomas's 1875–1941

Brynn (RCBm) register 1776–1822, confirmations 1821

Burnley (RCBT) St. Mary's registers 1820–55; (RCMf) microfilm registers: Christ the King 1929–41, St. Augustine's 1896–1941, St. John's 1892–1941, St. Mary's 1871–1941, St. Mary Magdalene's 1887–1941

Burscough (RCBu) registers 1793–1856, confirmations 1821–38, chapel accounts 1882–1901, school accounts 1881–85, school papers 1866–88, mission census 1914, minutes of the Conference of St. John held at the Willows, Kirkham 1864–79, chaplain's register of St. George's industrial school, Liverpool 1875, Liverpool diocesan mission fund reports 1874–93, pastoral letters of bishops of Liverpool 1873–1924, reports of Liverpool ecclesiastical education fund 1875–93, correspondence and papers of James Peter Coghlan, printer, 1770–78, 1791–1800 with, *inter alia*, Roman Catholic dignitaries of Britain and France

Catforth (RCCa) financial papers 1871–1948, miscellanea 1880–1955, correspondence 1873–1956

Cheetham Hill (RCMf) microfilm registers: St. Chad's 1867–1941, St. William's 1895–1904

Chorlton-on-Medlock (RCMf) microfilm registers: Holy Family 1876–1908, Holy Name 1868–1941, St. Augustine's 1870–1941

Claughton-in-Amounderness (RCCl) presbytery archives 1685–1761, Rev. John Barrow's correspondence and papers 1757–1814, Rev. Robert Gradwell's correspondence and papers 1795–1834, Rev. Henry Gradwell's correspondence and papers 1818–61, Rev. Robert Gradwell's correspondence and papers 1855–99, accounts of clergy general fund 1787–1803, accounts of Sion House, Lisbon 1816–24, life of Rev. Robert Gradwell, life of Thomas Fitzherbert-Brockholes, history of Claughton mission, Mawdesley Estate deed 1662–1890, Goosnargh Estate deeds 1729–1916

Clayton Green (RCCg) registers 1822–56

Clayton-le-Moors (RCCm) St. Mary's registers 1815–76, confirmations 1819–71, grave receipts 1881–1905, Sunday school attendances 1844–71

Clitheroe (RCCo) SS. Michael and John's registers 1798–1865, confirmations 1802–52

Colne (RCMf) Sacred Heart microfilm registers 1871–1941

Coniston (RCCs) *status animarum* 1866–78, visitation papers 1875, 1925, 1930

Croft (RCCr) register 1795–1856

Crompton (RCMf) St. Joseph's microfilm registers 1874–1941

Croston (RCCn) registers 1780–92, Culcheth family births 1650–55, inventory of church 1708

Crumpsall (RCMf) St. Anne's microfilm registers 1917–41

Culcheth (RCCu) register 1791–1825

Darwen (RCMf) microfilm registers: Sacred Heart 1878–1941, St. Joseph's 1871–1941

Didsbury (RCMf) St. Ambrose's microfilm registers 1933–41

Droylsden (RCMf) St. Stephen's microfilm registers 1935–41

Eccles (RCMf) microfilm registers: St. Mary's 1879–1941, Weaste All Souls' 1896–1941; see also Barton-upon-Irwell

Eccleston (Prescot) (RCPn) Portico registers 1753–1848

Euxton (RCEu) registers 1740–1895, letter-books (building) 1864–84, 1908–16

Failsworth (RCMf) St. Mary's microfilm registers 1871–1941

Farnworth (RCMf) Our Lady of Lourdes microfilm registers 1913–41

Fernyhalgh (RCFe) accounts 1728–1846, historical accounts, schedule of gifts 1701–23, registers 1771–1856, pew accounts 1830–48, correspondence 1686–1864, deeds and papers 1682–1937

Formby (RCFo) registers 1796–1853, confirmations 1803–31, correspondence *re* financial affairs of the Rev. Wilfrid Carr 1921–22

Garstang (RCG) SS. Mary and Michael's registers 1788–1897, Mumfod Trust papers 1782–1897, Greystoke Trust correspondence 1886, Dewhurst Benefaction papers 1685, 1897, miscellanea 1868–1971

Garswood (RCGa) registers 1798–1867, confirmations 1838

Goosnargh (RCGo) registers 1770–1855, accounts 1817–35, correspondence 1830–37, draft sermons 1765–81

Gorton (RCMf) Sacred Heart microfilm register 1902–41

Great Crosby (RCGo) register 1826–55, confirmations 1838, 1844

Great Eccleston (RCEc) accounts 1861–69, correspondence 1853–68, registers 1772–1857, subscription lists 1864–68

Haigh (RCMf) Our Lady's microfilm registers 1870–1941

Haslingden (RCMf) Immaculate Conception microfilm registers 1876–1941

Hawkshead (RCCs) St. Michael's *status animarum* 1866–78

Heaton Norris (RCMf) St. Mary's microfilm register 1866–1942

Heywood (RCMf) St. Joseph's microfilm registers 1858–1941

131

Hindley (RCHi) registers 1758–1855, confirmations 1774, 1826–48, names of people cured by the hand of the Rev. Nicholas Postgate 1850–52, chapel building accounts 1788–91

Hornby (RCHy) St. Mary's registers 1762–1855, census 1763, confirmations 1813, 1821, 1831, bills and receipts 1777–95, correspondence 1754–1930, miscellanea 1728–1907

Hulme (RCMf) St. Lawrence's microfilm registers 1927–41

Ince Blundell (RCIn) registers 1785–1861

Ince-in-Makerfield (RCIm) registers 1787–1817

Irlam (RCMf) St. Theresa's microfilm registers 1874–1941

Kirkham (RCKi) registers 1775–1855, census books 1860–69, 1878, notice books 1875–79

Lancaster (RCLa) *bullae* of appointments of bishops 1924–62, St. Peter's registers 1784–1855, miscellanea 1752–1900

Lea (RCLe) registers 1775–1841

Lees (RCMf) St. Edward's microfilm registers 1874–1941

Leigh (RCLh) registers 1778–1843

Levenshulme (RCMf) St. Mary's microfilm registers 1859–1941

Leyland (RCLl) registers 1845–64, memorabilia concerning mission 1824–91

Little Crosby RCLc) registers 1801–56, confirmations 1849

Little Hulton (RCMf) St. Edmund's microfilm registers 1898–1941

Longridge (RCMf) St. Wilfrid's microfilm registers 1869–1941

Lytham (RCLy) St. Peter's registers 1753–1856, banns books 1874–82, notice books 1873–85, finance papers 1856–1958, synodal papers 1855–1946, miscellanea 1722–1939, centenary committee minutes 1939–61, sick-club minutes 1857–1912, census 1880

Manchester (RCMa) St. Augustine's registers 1820–55, building accounts 1868–72; (RCMc) St. Chad's registers 1772–1850, notice books 1863–91; (RCMm) St. Mary's registers 1794–1855; (RcLy) St. Mary's building accounts 1835–61; (RCM) St. Patrick's registers 1832–72; (RCMf) microfilm registers: Ancoats St. Alban's 1865–1941, Ancoats St. Anne's 1875–1941, Ancoats St. Michael's 1877–1941, Goulden Street St. Joseph's 1885–1903, Longsight St. Robert's 1915–41, Longsight St. Joseph's 1888–1941, Miles Platting St. Edmund's 1877–1941, Mulberry Street St. Mary's 1870–1941, St. Casimer's 1904–31, St. Patrick's 1870–1941

Mawdesley (RCM) register 1812–46

Mossley (RCMf) St. Joseph's microfilm registers 1871–1941

Moston (RCMf) St. Margaret Mary's microfilm registers 1935–41

Nelson (RCMf) microfilm registers: Holy Saviour 1902–41, St. George's 1922–41, St. Joseph's 1884–1941

Newsham (RCNe) registers 1774–96, 1815–16, 1855–76

Oldham (RCOl) St. Mary's registers 1829–55; (RCMf) microfilm registers: Hollinwood Corpus Christi 1877–1941, Our Lady and St. Patrick's 1870–1941, St. Anne's 1878–1928, St. Mary's 1871–1941

Orrell (RCOr) register 1774–1848, confirmations 1813, 1821, communicants 1803, 1804, 1810–25

Osbaldeston (RCOs) St. Mary's registers 1836–93

Oswaldtwistle (MCMf) St. Mary's microfilm registers 1894–1941

Padiham (RCMf) St. John's microfilm registers 1870–1941

Pendlebury (RCMf) St. Mark's microfilm registers 1923–41

Pleasington (RCPl) St. Mary and John's registers 1817–53

Poulton-le-Fylde (RCPo) registers 1814–51

Rawtenstall (RCRa) St. James the Less registers 1836–55; (RCMf) St. James the Less microfilm registers 1868–1941

Ribchester (RCRi) St. Peter and Paul's registers 1783–1865; (RCMf) St. Peter and Paul's microfilm registers 1865–1941

Rishton (RCMf) St. Charles' microfilm registers 1887–1942

Rochdale (RCRo) St. John's registers 1822–73; (RCMf) microfilm registers: St. John's 1873–1941, St. Patrick's 1860–1941

Royton (RCMf) SS. Aidan and Oswald's microfilm registers 1883–1941

Rusholme (RCMf) St. Kentigern's microfilm registers 1926–41

St. Helens (RCLo) registers 1785–1856

Salford (RCMf) microfilm registers: Mount Carmel 1877–1941, St. John's 1856–1941, St. Joseph's 1875–1941, St. Peter's 1868–1941

Samlesbury (RCSa) St. Mary's registers 1793–1869

Scarisbrick (RCSk) registers 1773–1856, confirmations 1831–1852

Scorton (RCSc) registers 1774–80, 1795–1855, letters and papers 1785–1904

Singleton (RCPo) register 1831–56

South Hill (RCSh) register 1772–1827, club minutes 1897–1910, school accounts 1871–88, letter concerning benefactions 1809, 17th century sermon book

Standish (RCSt) St. Marie's registers 1742–1864, communicants 1770–1841, Standish coal accounts 1746–80

Stretford (RCMf) microfilm registers: St. Anne's 1859–1941, St. Hugh's 1938–41

Swinton (RCMf) microfilm registers: St. Charles's 1923–41, St. Mary's 1867–1941

Tatham (RCHy) Robert Hall registers 1757–1817

Thornley (RCTh) St. William's registers 1800–40

Thurnham (RCTm) SS. Thomas and Elizabeth's registers 1785–1855, press cuttings 1858–1948, pastoral letters 1853–1917, correspondence 1785–1940, miscellanea 1860–1925, apprenticeship fund accounts 1787–1917

Ulverston (RCUl) St. Mary's registers 1812–97, new church subscriptions 1874–76, pew church accounts 1895–1907, miscellanea 1862–1926

Urmston (RCMf) English Martyrs' microfilm registers 1892–1941

Walton-le-Dale (RCMf) St. Patrick's microfilm register 1856–1942

Warrington (RCWa) registers 1771–1855

Weld Bank (RCWb) registers 1802–55, confirmations 1803–38, burial society accounts 1856–1918, letters and papers of Bishop Edward Diconson 1735–46

Wesham (RCWh) miscellaneous papers 1883–1958

Westby (RCWe) registers 1763–1816, 1820–44, building papers 1861–1932, inventories 1792, 1860, correspondence 1806–66, Haydock pedigree 1774–1849

Wigan St. John's (RCWj) registers 1740–1860, building accounts 1818

Wigan St. Mary's (RCWm) registers 1819–84

Woolston (RCWo) registers 1771–1875, Easter communicants 1827–34, registration at Quarter Sessions 1837

Wrightington (RCWr) registers 1795–1879, confirmations 1813–76

Yealand (RCY) St. Mary's registers 1762–1930, notes on mission 1761–1860

Transcripts of registers (DDX 241): Aughton 1798–1830, Bedford 1778–1828, Birchley 1792–1849, Bolton-le-Moors 1794–1809, Brynn 1776–1822, Burscough 1793–1830, Chorley South Hill 1772–1827, Chorley Weld Bank 1802–15, Clitheroe 1798–1839,

Crosby 1801–39, Croston Hall 1757–1819, Eccleston Portico 1753–1816, Euxton 1740–1815, Formby 1796–1837, Garswood 1798–1822, Hindley 1758–1830, Ince-in-Makerfield 1787–1817, Ince Blundell 1785–1825, Kirkby Gillmoss 1757–1860, Kirkham Willows 1827–55, Lancaster 1837–1923, Liverpool Seel Street 1788–1837, Lydiate 1791–1843, Manchester Mulberry Street 1794–1825, Manchester Rook Street 1772–1840, Mawdesley 1820–40, Ormskirk 1750–1848, Orrell 1774–1848, Preston St. Mary's 1768–1820, Poulton-le-Fylde 1831–51, Scarisbrick 1713–1824, Standish 1755–1836, Walton-le-Dale Brownedge 1764–1845, Warrington 1774–1850, Widnes Appleton 1771–1854, Wigan 1732–1822, Windle Blackbrook 1771–1834, Woolton 1756–1856, Wrightington 1795–1889

Lancashire Infirm Secular Clergy Fund (RCCF) administrative and financial papers 1672–1936, correspondence 1736–1919, miscellanea 1770–1957

Transcripts of documents relating to Roman Catholics in Lancashire 1697–1796; (RCV) from originals at Ushaw and Up Holland

Photocopies of documents relating to Jesuit churches in Lancashire 1693–1890 (RCSj)

CONGREGATIONAL

Congregational Union of England and Wales (CUEW) books of hosts 1912, 1931, books of guests 1912, 1931, books of delegates 1931, county survey question sheets 1959–60

Evans Trust (CUL, CUEv) correspondence 1912–51, reports 1908–25

Lancashire Congregational Union (CUL) agreement for formation 1786, articles of association 1898, 1910, 1918, minutes 1806–92 year books 1867–1973, executive committee minutes 1845–1932, cash books 1801–05, 1896–1906, 1916–61, missionary committee minutes 1965–72, correspondence 1934–73

Lancashire Congregational Union, Liverpool District (CULv) minutes 1866–1905, 1956–72

Lancashire Congregational Union Lay Preachers' Association (CUL) minutes 1899–1904, 1944–64, Liverpool District minutes 1897–1947

Lancashire Congregational Ministers' Provident Society (CUL, CUM) minutes 1844–1931, reports 1843–1902, finance papers 1920–55

Lancashire Congregational Women's Guild of Christian Service and Fairhaven Home of Rest (CUL, CUWo) minutes 1899–1954, register of guests 1916–33, inventory 1950

Cheshire Congregational Union (CUCu) minutes, reports and correspondence 1959–64, Women's Guild of Christian Service minutes 1948–72, Stockport and Macclesfield minutes 1949–72, League of Service (Bowdon area) minutes 1949–72

Local churches:

Abram (CUAb) deacons' minutes 1927–68, account book 1927–70, members' roll 1939–57, correspondence about closure 1967–71

Accrington (CUAc) Oak Street register of members 1839–64, communion registers 1914–65, deacons' minutes 1921–52, church meeting minutes 1921–69, church aid and missionary society minutes 1881–1901, Higher Antley Street deacons' minutes 1952–69, Park Road deacons' minutes 1913–32

Alkrington (CUAk) building committee minutes 1927–29

Ashton-under-Lyne (CUL and CUAs) Independent registers 1815–51, Ryecroft registers 1815–1967, schedule of deeds 1924, church meeting minutes 1849–84, 1921–67, deacons' minutes 1867–1953, members' roll 1925–67, communion registers 1925–51

Ashton-under-Lyne and Oldham District (CUAo) district meeting minutes 1968–72

Barrowford (CUBw) registers 1861–1917, 1922–74, church meeting minutes 1862–1975, deacons' minutes 1913–68, pew rentals 1883–1928, 1940–64, miscellanea 1863–1958

Barrow-in-Furness (CUBa) Hindpool Road deacons' minutes 1881–1931, accounts 1882–1931, pew rental 1898–1917

Blackburn (CUBl) James Street church meeting minutes 1837–1961, committees' minutes 1864–1961, deacons' minutes 1873–1961, accounts 1910–61, miscellanea 1842–1961, Band of Hope minutes 1914, 1925–34; (CUL) Park Road church meeting minutes 1920–64, deacons' minutes 1892–1901, 1922–34, 1953–65, trustees' minutes 1872–1948, members' roll 1857–1959, register 1936–65

Blackburn District (CUBk) annual and autumnal meeting minutes 1830–1972, district committee minutes 1913–72, council minutes 1965–72

Blackpool (CUBp) Bethesda miscellanea 1819–70

Bolton (CUBt) Bank Top minutes 1912–56. Derby Street church meeting minutes 1868–1970, deacons' minutes 1907–66, Sunday school minutes 1909–46, finance committee minutes 1926–51, members' lists 1868–1964, communion register 1918–65, baptismal register 1959–70, miscellanea 1876–1970; (CUL) Mawdesley Street church meeting minutes 1807–58, 1888–1962, deacons' minutes 1864–1962, deaconesses' minutes 1893–1923, committees' minutes 1852–1961, trustees' minutes 1891–1955, registers 1809–67, 1889–1960, sick and burial society minutes 1836–1912, members' lists 1845–1912, cash book 1865–80, burial ground plan n.d.

Bolton and Farnworth District (CUBn) ministers' and deacons' committee minutes 1941–72, ministers' Fraternals minutes 1937–72, miscellanea 1934–72

Bootle (CUBo) Emmanuel deacons' minutes 1871–1964, church meeting minutes 1871–1964, registers 1877–1964

Broughton, Salford (CUBr) church meeting and deacons' minutes 1916–20, 1942–55, committee minutes 1907–19, members' roll 1855–1950, registers 1855–1960

Burnley (CUBy) Thursby Road church meeting minutes 1914–47, deacons' minutes 1890–1946, committees minutes 1899–1941, accounts 1935–47, members' roll 1914–38, registers 1911–47

Bury (CUBu) Bethel trust deed 1883, Castle Croft members' register 1915–67, women's guild minutes 1933–65, annual reports 1935–40, Kay Street mission school deeds 1908, 1914

Castleton (CUCa) appointment of trustees 1903

Caton (CUCn) church meeting minutes 1952–63, deacons' minutes 1960–62, cash book 1943–62, members' list 1946–58

Chaigley (CUCg) Walker Fold minutes 1831–93, accounts 1873–93, registers 1801–84, miscellanea 1800–1950

Chorley (CUCh) Hollinshead Street deeds 1783–1910

Colne (CUCo) church minutes 1857–1971, deacons' minutes 1886–1971, committees minutes 1860–1971, members' lists 1811–1972, attendance registers 1849–68, 1889–1976, registers 1825–1976; (DDSp) correspondence, etc. 1927–65

Darwen Group (CUDa) minutes 1945–72

Droylsden (CUDr) church, deacons' and committee minutes 1856–79, members' rolls 1856–82, 1904, 1934–48, accounts 1860–79, 1893–1966, registers 1856–1969, choir minutes 1918–51, miscellanea 1859–1969

Eccles (CUEc) King Street church meeting minutes 1908–65, deacons' minutes 1925–65, committees minutes 1908–63, communion attendance book 1937–63, registers 1908–64, Sunday school minutes 1882–1965, amateur dramatic society minutes 1944–53

Edgworth (CUEd) church meeting minutes 1900–45, members' list 1880–1948, graveyard schedule 1869–1908, register 1885–1928, historical notes 1771–1855

Greenhalgh-with-Thistleton (CUK) Cornah Row trustees' and committee minutes 1853–1972, account book 1931–73, cash book 1967–72

Halton (CUHa) church meeting minutes 1890–1964, building committee minutes 1895–98

Horwich (CUL) Lee Lane attendance registers 1918–41, register 1840–80, members' roll 1898–1927, committee minutes 1849–1972, financial records 1838–1942, record of seatholders 1879–1905, graveyard records 1880, 1920–56

Lancaster (CULa) Bowerham correspondence 1904, Dolphinholme trust deeds 1881, 1888

Littleborough (CULt) Summit church meeting minutes 1853–1972, deacons' minutes 1890–1972, members' roll 1853–1927, registers 1853–1972, account book 1927–73, ladies' guild minutes 1919–33, Sunday school accounts 1894–96, Sunday school journal 1891–99, teachers' meeting minutes 1883–1915

Liverpool (CULi) Great George Street church meeting minutes 1812–1936, deacons' minutes 1822, 1876–1934, trustees' minutes 1822–92, registers 1811–1966, members' lists 1819–1916, teachers' minutes 1835–52, lay agency minutes 1854–59, advisory committee minutes 1923–25, literary and debating society minutes 1869–80, accounts 1834–1964, pew rentals 1841–43, 1862–74, miscellanea 1821–1964; Bethesda church meeting minutes 1824–53, school committee minutes 1820–36, Sunday school teachers' minutes 1832–33, building committee minutes 1836, registers 1803–1904; Crescent church meeting minutes 1854–1933, deacons' minutes 1848–77, 1904–09, 1933–45, chapel debt committee minutes 1841–43, weekly offering committee minutes 1880–82, committees minutes 1849–1940, pew rental 1841–59, school committee minutes 1839–77, accounts 1840–1959, miscellanea 1841–1968; Hanover Street registers 1830–46; Hartington Road cash book 1963–65; Newington church meeting minutes 1854–71, pew rentals 1845–70, cash book 1851–57, register 1837–53; Stanley church meeting and deacons' minutes 1858–1946, members' roll 1859–75, register 1859–93

Liverpool District (CULv) annual meeting minutes 1866–1905, annual and autumnal meeting minutes 1956–71, committee minutes 1964–72, chairmens' bible 1906–73

Livesey (CUCt) Cherry Tree deeds 1894, 1900

Manchester District (CUMb and CUMc) minutes 1852–1964, executive committee minutes 1904–71, finance committee minutes 1906–66, association minutes 1893–1910, mission board minutes 1896–1902, evangelists' committee minutes 1891–

95, Salford sub-committee minutes 1905–12, cash books 1894–1945, correspondence, etc. 1916–66, salaries and wages books 1952–61, women's auxiliary minutes 1939–51, miscellanea 1960–72, articles of association 1907

Morecambe Bay District (CUMo) minutes and committee minutes 1967–72

Oldham (CUL) Derker church meeting minutes 1866–1966, deacons' minutes 1880–89, 1915–66, Sunday school minutes 1881–90, 1903–65, Sunday school registers 1870–1923, members' list 1874–1915, registers 1883–1966, offerings record 1874–85, accounts 1895–1923, 1935–40, baptism certificates 1897–1966

Oldham Board (CUOl) minutes 1893–1967

Ormskirk (CUOr) church meeting minutes 1828–47, 1869–1973, committees' minutes 1834–38, 1921–22, deacons' minutes 1917–73, members' rolls 1828–46, 1943–70, registers 1848–76, 1943–70, pew rentals 1843–60, accounts 1843–80, sewing-meeting day-book 1922–58, treasurers' correspondence 1965–71, Sunday school minutes 1862–88, 1905–18, accounts 1829–90

Padiham (CUL) Horeb church meeting minutes 1895–1930, building committee minutes 1896–1910, miscellanea 1896–1935

Pendleton, Salford (CUSa) Broad Street church meeting minutes 1858–1900, register 1836–1959, trust deed 1858, finance committee minutes 1911–19, mining correspondence 1924; (CUPe) Charleston church meeting minutes 1855–72, deacons' minutes 1892–1971, committees minutes 1864–1920, Sunday school minutes 1843–89

Preston and Fylde District (CUPf) Fylde ministers' fraternal minutes 1942–73, magazine accounts 1946–71, Jubilee filmstrip 1956, women's committee minutes and accounts 1957–72, Women's Guild correspondence 1957–70, accounts 1929–72, District meeting minutes 1818–1908, 1968–72, London Missionary Society minutes 1930–72, Women's Guild of Christian Services minutes 1946–56, Association of Lay Preachers minutes 1961–72

Rainhill (CURa) church meeting minutes 1891–1974, deacons' minutes 1891–1974, Sunday school minutes 1940–69, Women's Guild minutes 1970–73, members' roll 1891–1907, register 1891–1908, accounts 1906–49, 1952–69, Sunday school anniversary collections 1939–66

Rochdale (CURo) Providence deacons' minutes 1865–76, trustees' minutes 1895–1946, Instruction Society minutes 1867–79, cash book 1914–34, graveyard schedule 1807–55, architect's report 1891, correspondence 1899–1958

St. Helens (CUSh) Toll Bar mission building committee minutes 1919–48

Salford Central Mission (CUSm) ways and means committee minutes 1906–09, youth committee minutes 1925–49, correspondence, etc. 1948–64

Salford (CUSa) Chapel Street committee for management of singing minutes 1836–38, Richmond church meeting minutes 1928–64, deacons' minutes 1912–64, building society minutes 1926–47, Sunday school minutes 1855–68, 1907–39, bazaar committee minutes 1870–77, cash books 1843–63, 1924–64, deeds 1848–88, members' roll 1863–1955, school building accounts 1871, papers about W. L. Sheldon legacy 1947–62, register 1917–52

Southport (CUSo) Chapel Street church meeting minutes 1824–62, deacons' minutes 1890–1906, committees minutes 1895–1901, graveyard schedule 1824–72, members' roll 1807–86, interments 1824–31, Sunday school cash book 1894–1930; Eastbrook Lane graveyard schedule 1834–68; Hawkshead Street church meeting minutes 1882–84, 1892–1903, 1915–27, 1947–58, deacons' minutes 1892–1903, registers 1883–1909, 1925–68, committees minutes 1891–1954, sisterhood minutes 1915–35; Lord Street church meeting minutes 1963–66, deacons' minutes 1968–72; Portland Street church meeting minutes 1871–1927, 1945–57, deacons' minutes 1940–57, Sunday school minutes 1931–48, members' roll 1871–1905, registers 1871–1964; West End church meeting minutes 1939–62, deacons' minutes 1956–62, Sunday school cash book 1907–58

Stretford (CUSt) Chester Road church meeting minutes 1832–1931, 1946–60, deacons' minutes 1950–58, members' lists 1832–65, 1870–74, 1907–37, committee minutes 1949–57, Sunday school minutes 1911–29, registers 1832–50, 1912–58, pew rental 1860–67, cash books 1855–68, 1910–60, collection accounts 1890–1910, attendance registers 1857–70, articles found under foundation stone

Tyldesley (CUTy) deacons' minutes 1959–68

Ulverston (CUUl) church meeting minutes 1852–58, 1879–1961, deacons' minutes 1870–89, 1893–1921, 1927–66, committee minutes 1872–1922, registers 1868–77, 1918–68, cash book 1920–55; Friends of Soutergate chapel minutes 1834–40

INGHAMITE

Colne (InCo) church meeting minutes 1896–1974, trustees' minutes 1880–1918, choir minutes 1909–31, Sunday school minutes 1883–1940, Band of Hope and Adult Temperance Society minutes 1897–1921, church representatives' minutes 1947–61, registers 1827–1974, financial records 1825–55, Sunday school registers 1880–89, 1900–39, 1952–53, new chapel building fund records 1898–1912, trustees' letter book 1911–18, miscellanea 1839–1959

METHODIST

(P = Primitive, U = United, W = Wesleyan)

Accrington (MMr) marriage registers: Abbey Street W 1905–63, Baxenden W mission room 1922–60, Union Street W 1860–1955, U Free Church 1907–39

Bacup (MMr) marriage registers: Mount Pleasant W 1900–51, Stacksteads Booth Road 1943–51, Thorn 1948–62, Wesley Place W 1899–1961; see also Rossendale

Barley (MNe) P minutes 1889–1922, Sunday school registers 1897–1929, Barley Green W minutes 1884–1942

Barnoldswick (MMr) marriage registers: Calf Hall Road 1933–63, Station Road P 1913–64

Barrowford (MNe) P circuit minutes 1893–1935, station account books 1907–35, missionary account book 1926–37, chapel aid account book 1910–20, centenary fund record 1907, schedules and reports 1894–1932, Sunday school schedules 1933–36, account book 1845–59; Higherford W minutes 1823–95, account books 1865–1927; (MMr) Zion P marriage registers 1903–58

Blackburn (MMr) marriage registers: Alton Street W 1899–1964, Benson Street W 1914–70, Clayton Street W 1899–1958, Harwood Street W 1904–58, Higher Audley P 1928–72, Kidder Street W 1927–64, Paradise Lane U 1931–69, Trinity W 1879–1964, Waterfall U 1923–44, Zion P 1926–38

Blackpool (MBp) Circuit minutes 1903–13, committee minutes 1875–1934, accounts 1891–1925; Adelaide Street W circuit minutes 1921–39; W North circuit minutes 1934–41, 1952–66, accounts 1934–50; Bispham W trustees' minutes 1901–34; Ebenezer P trustees' minutes 1914–28, registers 1933–72; Newton Drive New Connexion trustees' minutes 1898–1967, register 1904–67; North Shore W trustees' minutes 1875–1906, ledger 1889–1916; Raikes Parade W trustees' minutes 1886–1908, committees minutes 1903–65, Sunday school minutes 1930–54, Forces canteen minutes 1940–44, register 1890–1942; Springfield New Connexion register 1890–1955; Trinity U trustees' minutes 1881–1966, committees minutes 1908–58, cash books 1891–1970, collection books 1900–72, registers 1903–72, Sunday school minutes 1897–1966, admission register 1934–71, accounts 1864–

74, 1880–1916, 1934–70, staff registers 1934–79, Band of Hope minutes 1887–1911, accounts 1904–14; (MMr) marriage registers: Adelaide Street W 1935–72, Grasmere Road P 1926–66, Maybell Avenue P 1929–56, Newton Drive U 1913–66, Rawcliffe Street W 1906–71, Shaw Road U 1915–55

Brierfield (MMr) Burnley Road P marriage register 1920–55

Burnley (DDX 888) Brunswick town and temperance mission minutes 1886–97, assistant missionary's diary 1895–98; (MMr) marriage registers: Accrington Road W 1932–67, Brunswick 1942–62, Central W 1932–65, Claremont Street U 1909–61, Fulledge W 1902–59, Hanover U 1910–58, Manchester Road W 1932–70, Mount Zion 1935–37, Queensgate W 1915–68, Rehaboth 1952–61, Stoneyholme 1933–65

Chorley (MMr) marriage registers: Ebenezer P 1909–68, Railway Street U 1899–1941

Clayton-le-Moors (MMr) Barnes Street P marriage registers 1911–61

Clitheroe (MMr) marriage registers: Moor Lane U 1926–42, Waterloo W 1922–62

Cliviger (MMr) W marriage registers 1907–65

Colne (MCo) Circuit minutes 1822–83, accounts 1810–98, plans 1822–68, members' lists 1837–82; Albert Road W trustees' minutes 1789–1806, 1815–37, 1852–91, seat accounts 1777–1886, 1901–49, leaders' accounts 1778–1868, 1905–06, 1917–21, stewards' accounts 1877–1931, collection journals 1869–1926, treasurers' accounts 1889–1932, quarter-day disbursements 1830–36, War comforts fund 1914–19, Sunday school minutes 1864–77, attendance register 1811–45, 1899–1913; Skipton Road P choir committee minutes 1909–16, 1951–56; Waterside P Sunday school service plan 1857; (DDSp) Collingwood Street W trustees' minutes 1880–1932, P trustees' minutes 1911–40, Sunday school minutes 1897–1906; (MMr) marriage registers: Bunkers Hill 1936–71, Collingwood Street W 1898–1959, Ebenezer P 1909–61, Mount Zion U 1899–1951

Croston (MPr) Emmanuel U trustees' minutes 1874–1960, accounts 1903–30, correspondence 1902–16; (MMr) Emmanuel U marriage registers 1928–60

Darwen (DDX 509) W Sunday school minutes 1840–55; (MDa) marriage registers: Blackburn Road W 1909–65, Bolton Road W 1885–1952, Duckworth Street U 1899–1940, Lynwood 1934–67, Redearth Street P 1912–60

Fleetwood (MFl) Circuit minutes 1902–31, 1934–60, accounts 1881–1934, women's auxiliary accounts 1922–71; Elm Street W trustees' minutes 1909–53, collection journals 1914–19, 1928–55, accounts 1905–69, members' list 1930–52, Sunday school minutes 1947–67, Sunday school roll 1914–15, guild minutes 1947–63, sisterhood minutes 1931–63, poor stewards' accounts 1930–63, correspondence 1905–39; Mount P trustees' minutee 1902–36, leaders' minutes 1871–80, 1927–37, circuit committes minutes 1873–79, 1883–86, Sunday school accounts 1888–1910, Sunday school registers 1863–98; North Church Street W trustees' minutes 1902–51, committees' minutes 1878–1956, accounts 1846–1905, 1935–58, foreign missionary society minutes 1896–1949, choir minutes 1935–70, youth club accounts 1952–57, Sunday school minutes 1846–57, 1928–71, accounts 1920–72; (MMr) marriage registers: Elm Street W 1930–63, North Street W 1900–71

Freckleton (MMr) Preston Old Road P marriage register 1920–65

Great Harwood (MMr) marriage registers: Jubilee U 1912–66, Mount Zion U 1910–49

Halsall (MMr) marriage register 1950–75

Haslingden (MMr) marriage registers: Blackburn Road 1956–70, Grane Road P 1902–56, Helmshore W 1923–62, Old W 1905–61, Salem U 1899–1961

Higham (MMr) W marriage registers 1906–70

Horwich (DDX 84/3) New Chapel Sunday school register 1842–65

Kearsley (MMr) Ringley W marriage register 1902–61

Lancaster (MMr) marriage registers: Brock Street U 1903–35, Moor Lane P 1926–64, Skerton 1950–55

Morecambe (MMo) Circuit minutes 1928–34, missionary committee minutes 1922–34; Clarence Street U trustees' minutes 1878–1964, leaders' minutes 1880–1965, committees minutes 1874–77, 1907–11, 1936–39, 1950–65, Sunday school minutes 1937–61, accounts 1874–1964, registers of preachers 1877–1918, members' lists 1892–1924; Green Street W accounts 1874–79; Heysham new site W trustees' minutes 1935–44; Pedder Street P trustees' minutes 1907–24, register 1936–42; Torrisholme W trustees' minutes 1877–1952; West End W trustees' minutes 1903–46, cash books 1934–56; (MMr) marriage registers: Clarence Street U 1932–65, Parliament Street P 1927–74, Sandylands U 1921–75

Nelson (MNe) W Circuit minutes 1865–1967, Manse Trust minutes 1897–1951, plans 1865–1972, Hartley Trust minutes 1932–34, local preachers' minutes 1888–1933, foreign missionary minutes 1904–50, temperance committee minutes 1926–60, Sunday school council minutes 1912–46, class-leaders' minutes 1911–17, stewards' accounts 1865–1938, foreign missionary accounts 1872–1909, schedule books 1916–56, trust schedule books 1903–39; U Circuit minutes 1894–1910; Bradley Hall W trustees' minutes 1913–55, account books 1900–61; Carr Road W trustees' minutes 1865–1967, account books 1848–1967; Church Street P trustees' minutes 1896–1964, account books 1940–58; Cooper Street W trustees' minutes 1881–1964, account books 1885–1951; Hollins Road Sunday school minutes 1952–72; Netherfield Road P trustees' minutes 1907–37, account books 1918–41; Newbridge P account books 1892–1946; Railway Street W trustees' minutes 1908–64, account books 1881–1964; Reedyford W trustees' minutes 1864–1961, account books 1867–1964, Sunday school register 1878–1950; Regent Street U trustees' minutes 1891–1964, account books 1946–65, members' register 1899–1916; Scotland Road P account book 1918–42; Southfield W trustees' minutes 1914–49, account books 1931–70; Stanley Street U trustees' minutes 1869–1934, account book 1870–1950; Temple Street W trustees' minutes 1898–1948, account books 1937–71; (MMr) marriage registers: Bradley Hall W 1908–59, Netherfield Road P 1925–35, Railway Street W 1908–64, Regent Street 1943–61, Stanley Street 1933–46, Trinity W 1908–74, Zion P 1900–64

North Lancashire District (MNl) overseas mission minutes 1932–62

Oswaldtwistle (MMr) marriage registers: Foxhill Grove P 1912–67, Melbourne Street P 1906–53, Moscow Hill U 1910–54, York Street W 1910–66

Padiham (MMn) marriage registers: Church Street W 1851–1967, Hall Hill W 1888–1951

Poulton-le-Fylde (MBp) W trustees' minutes 1889–1928, deeds 1924–67, collection journals 1929–51, film of building of new chapel 1967

Preesall (MFl) Knott End P trustees' minutes 1931–67, committee minutes 1924–32, collection journal 1905–14, Sunday school minutes 1923–59

Preston (MPr) W Circuit minutes 1866–1918, trust schedule books 1867–1924, stewards' book 1873–93, committee minutes 1893–1945, local preachers' minutes 1897–1914, Sunday school minutes 1912–52, youth reports 1945–66; P Circuit minutes 1890–1940; Fylde Road and Moor Lane Circuit minutes 1939–52; Preston A Circuit minutes 1942–60; Ashton W trustees' minutes 1892–1925, account books 1891–96; Bray Street W poor-stewards' accounts 1926–65, Sunday school minutes 1934–64, cradle roll 1938–59; Eldon Street P trustees' minutes 1939–59; Fylde Road P trustees' minutes 1886–1962, Sunday school minutes 1929–61; New Chapel trustees' minutes 1891–94, treasurers' accounts 1896–1913, 1943–62, men's committee minutes 1952–53; North Road W trustees' minutes 1892–1955, leaders' minutes 1867–94, building minutes 1836–40, trustees' accounts 1843–1909, poor-stewards' accounts 1862–67, treasurers' account 1932–60, Sunday school minutes 1887–1912; (MMr) marriage registers: Ashton W 1921–59, Barlow Street W 1928–68, Deepdale P 1925–47, Edward Street W 1932–52, Fylde Road P 1924–61, Marsh Lane W 1899–1961, Moor Lane U 1924–52, North Road W 1933–55, Orchard U 1907–51, St. Mary Street W 1899–1964, Saul Street P 1907–43; (DDPr 138/ 17) Lord Street W register 1804–36

Rawtenstall (MMr) marriage registers: Cloughfold W 1922–68, Haslingden Road U 1900–36, Jubilee P 1917–65

Rishton (MMr) marriage register 1909–63

Rossendale (MRo) Rawtenstall Circuit minutes 1866–1972, stewards' accounts 1866–1910, 1934–71, committee minutes 1896, 1918– 70, youth council minutes 1959–68, collection schedules 1866– 85, 1908–24, 1929–67; Bacup Circuit accounts 1924–40; Bacup and Waterfoot Circuit minutes 1940–43, accounts 1940–43; Circuit amalgamation papers 1925–43; Cloughfold W trustees' minutes 1874–1972, leaders' minutes 1899–1969, collection journal 1880–1908, Sunday school minutes 1877–94, 1904–65, Sunday school registers 1870–1906; Jubilee P trustees' minutes 1913–67; Longholme W trustees' minutes 1920–61, treasurers' accounts 1892–1929, 1941–62, ledger 1908–40, seat rents 1940 61, Sunday school registers 1826–80, 1950–73, Sunday school minutes 1875–1960; Loveclough Providence U trustees' minutes 1914–54, accounts 1860–1949, seat rents 1946–60, plans 1867– 1905, death certificates 1853–79, marriage certificates 1928–33, 1943–52; Rakefoot W stewards' books 1811–58, 1944–69, collection journal 1937–49, Sunday school minutes 1928–54; Salem U minutes 1891–99, 1905–66; Springside W trustees' minutes 1924–68, leaders' minutes 1914–55, collection journals 1949–67, accounts 1950–67; Sunnyside P Sunday school minutes 1872–84; Townendsfold P trustees' minutes 1929–70, leaders' minutes 1907–69, collection journals 1893–99, 1920–30, correspondence 1928–71; Water Eden U trustees' minutes 1941– 56; see also Bacup, Rawtenstall

St. Annes-on-the-Sea (MMr) South Drive P marriage register 1921– 68

Samlesbury (MMr) marriage register 1934–49

Skelmersdale (MMr) Knowle Brow W marriage register 1924–67

Thornton-le-Fylde (MFl) P trustees' minutes 1878–1942, leaders' minutes 1934–60, accounts 1878–1906, 1935–65

Trawden (MCo) W accounts 1844–87, register 1818–23; (MMr) Bethel P marriage register 1914–60

Whalley (MWh) W trustees' minutes 1869–1952, foreign mission minutes 1891–1957, accounts 1840–1957, class books 1813–1904, circuit plans 1818–98

Withnell (MMr) W marriage register 1915–66

UNITARIAN

Ainsworth (UAi) minutes and letters 1813–14, deeds 1719–93

Bolton and District Ministers' Fraternal (UBo) minutes 1878–1914, 1919–74, miscellanea 1932–79. This covers all Lancashire except Manchester.

Chorley (UCh) abstract of title 1665–1751, miscellanea 1755–1839, rebuilding papers 1803–1928, letters re appointments 1897–1903, balance sheets 1904–19, receipts for teaching expenses (with names of pupils) 1768–1857

Preston (UPr) members' meeting minutes 1827–77, committee minutes 1877–1948, fellowship minutes 1924–31, cash books 1898–1938, pew rents 1907–65, charity distribution accounts 1732–1808, Sunday school minutes 1922–50, women's league minutes 1945–63, miscellanea 1706–1971, history 1672–1947, press cuttings 1937–40

FREE CHURCH COUNCILS

Morecambe and Heysham (DDX 625) Free Church Federal Council minutes 1933–66, cash book 1919–66

SOCIETY OF FRIENDS

(DDX 448) Abstracts of title to premises in Manchester, Liverpool, Hardshaw, Westhoughton, Langtree, Wigan, Ashton-in-Maker-field, Penketh, Southport, Chester, Holt, and Wrexham 1597–1842; plans of Todmorden meeting-house c. 1800, Manchester Mount Meadow c. 1835, Oldham Turf Lane c. 1835; Marsden monthly meeting accounts 1740–1857, Hollin Hall rental 1837–54

Marsden Monthly Meeting (FRM) minutes (men) 1678–1966, rough minutes (men) 1803–40, minutes (women) 1678–1889, rough minutes (women) 1824–1905, minutes of ministry and elders 1787–1876, minutes of ministry and oversight 1877–1906, sufferings books 1653–1720, 1764–1871, lists of members 1812–89, membership book 1893–1953, certificates of removal 1723–1896, registers of certificates sent 1818–1924, registers 1654–1913, disownment papers 1701–1853, ministers' travel certificates 1731–1867, reports of committees 1782–1889, correspondence with other monthly meetings 1754–1892, marriage consent papers 1726–1888, epistles from yearly meetings 1715–1878, minutes of quarterly meetings 1746–1913, minutes of yearly meetings 1802–34, epistles of women friends 1785–1873, miscellaneous correspondence 1776–1874, accounts 1787–1920, record of public gifts 1737–1879, list of deeds, etc. 1844, report on trust property 1916, account of Hopkinson and Thomasson families 1792

Bolton preparative meeting minutes 1829–57, 1881–1938

Crawshawbooth preparative meeting minutes (men) 1696–1918, minutes (women) 1698–1937

Edgeworth and Bolton preparative meeting minutes 1776–1956, accounts 1771–1906, book catalogue 1779, building accounts 1771, plans 1795, 1802, men's class minutes and accounts 1922–40

Marsden preparative meeting minutes (men) 1696–1952, minutes (women) 1698–1874

Oldham preparative meeting minutes (men) 1860–1934, minutes (women) 1856–71

Radcliffe preparative meeting minutes 1833–1964

Rochdale preparative meeting minutes (men) 1808–88, minutes (women) 1808–70

Sawley preparative meeting minutes (men) 1747–1808, minutes (women) 1763–91

Todmorden preparative meeting minutes (men) 1737–1870, minutes (women) 1707–96

Trawden preparative meeting minutes (men) 1734–83, 1788–1821, minutes (women) 1799–1812

Preston Monthly Meeting (FRP) minutes (men) 1724–1903, minutes (women) 1761–1886, minutes of ministry and oversight 1839–1901, book society minutes 1854–61, certificates of removal 1801–58, certificates to other meetings 1745–1826, certificates from other meetings 1760–1861, accounts of Freckleton estate 1724–94, registers 1651–1837, miscellaneous correspondence 1734–95, disownment notices 1752–1838, yearly meeting minutes 1697–1791, quarterly meeting minutes 1722–98, miscellaneous pamphlets and reports 1672–1857

Freckleton preparative meeting minutes 1760–76

Fylde preparative meeting minutes 1711–83

Preston preparative meeting minutes (men) 1764–92, 1839–96, minutes (women) 1857–86, cash book 1862–93, lists of members 1858–82

Wyresdale preparative meeting minutes (women) 1817–39

148

Part V

Deposited Collections

CHARITIES

Ashton-in-Makerfield (PR 2927) apprentice stock minutes 1817–79

Aughton (PR 61) Sutch's accounts 1787–1855

Bickerstaffe (PR 432, 433) Watkinson's accounts 1798–1803, 1818–83

Billington (PR 2965) poor stock orders and accounts 1672–1838

Bispham (PR 2596) Peter Lathom's distribution 1857–71

Blackburn (PR 1549) Livesey's miscellanea 1732–1866

Blackrod (DDX 23) Popplewell's deeds 1820–33; (PR 2967) deeds 1803–70, accounts 1830–1906

Bold (PR 2897) distribution book 1828–85

Bolton (DDX 23) Popplewell's deeds 1820–32

Brindle (DDX 705) Henry Gorton's trust deed 1700

Broughton-in-Amounderness (PR 1889) Hoghton's, Petticoat, Newsham's, Noblett's, Talloner's, Bascow's and Threlfall's miscellanea 1659–1825

Burscough (PR 1269–73) John Houghton's, Peter Lathom's, and William Sutch's lists of recipients 1797–1826

Bury and Tottington (DDWo) Guest's deeds (Elton) 1615–1873

Chatburn (DDX 28) charitable society accounts 1816–35

Chorley (DDX 761) Hoghton of Astley trust deed 1841

Claughton-in-Amounderness (RCCl) clothing accounts 1818–1904, Henry Barton's accounts 1819–70

Clayton-le-Moors (UDCl) Mercer's accounts 1884–96

Cronton (PR 605) accounts 1758–78; (PR 2968) Glover's, Kirkdale's, and Windle's papers 1752–67, Glover's correspondence 1895–1902

Croston (PR) Croston's almshouses deeds 1693–1865, Hough's miscellanea 1721–1825, Master's bequest 1765, Layfield's miscellanea 1711–62, Norris' bequest 1741; (PR 2844) Layfield's deed 1762; (DDF) Dandy's deed 1668

149

Cuerden (PR 67) Burscough's accounts 1792–1893

Deane (PR 2191) John Guest's deed 1831

Dilworth (PR 2945) Frances Roade's minutes and papers 1914–19

Downholland (PR 2956) distributions 1806–70

Golborne see Lowton

Halsall (PR 267, 271) Stanley's donation 1783–1827, Watkinson's donation 1819–50

Halton (PR 2788) memorandum and account book 1738–1823

Haslingden (MBH) clothing accounts 1797–1828

Hornby (PR 2896) Elizabeth Thornton's will 1742 and accounts 1826–38

Kirkham (DDPr 1) Grimbaldeston's apprenticeship indentures 1804; (DDD) Harrison's minutes and accounts 1880–1905, Barker's minutes 1678–1842, accounts 1851–80

Leyland (DDF) Rigby's almshouses deeds 1639; Farington's almshouses deed 1690, memoranda book 1854–89, and accounts 1853–77; Banister's deed 1632, memoranda book 1754–1891; Osbaldeston's deed 1737, notice 1850; (PR 2908) Balshaw's papers 1892–1917, Crooke's schedule of deeds 1770–1847, church-room accounts 1914–15

Longridge (PR 2939) Richard Houghton's accounts 1848–1912

Lowton and Golborne (DDX 891) Leadbeater's deeds and papers 1572–1973, minutes 1889–1973, balance book 1888–1972; (PR 344–8) Leadbeater's accounts 1687–1851, Byrom's accounts 1687–1791

Lydiate (DDX 96) Gore's deeds 1620–1903, accounts 1678–1895

Maghull (PR 2922) poor fund deed 1846, minutes 1882–1933

Manchester (DDSl) Robert Sutton's clothing accounts 1688–1920

Marton (PR 1294) Jolly's deed 1784

Middleton (DDX 193) Stocks' deed 1692, accounts 1692–1789, apprenticeship indentures 1692–1880

Parbold (PR 2821) Gillibrand's accounts 1868–1903, Peter Lathom's accounts 1960–64

Pennington-in-Furness (PR 2843) Fell's and Ashburner's minutes and accounts 1904–30

Poulton-le-Fylde (DDPr) Baines' apprenticeship indentures 1718–1818

Preston (PR 1443) list of "pious and charitable gifts" 1605–1729, Houghton's deed 1819; (PR 2845) Smith's bread and Peploe's benefaction papers 1898–99, W. B. Rideal correspondence 1938–45, Brown's bread correspondence 1947–48, accounts of Langton's or Kings 1762–1920, Brown's 1921–33, Jane Stanley's 1932–33, Rigby's 1785–1845, 1877–1932; (PR 2952) Catherine Pennington's distribution 1871–1907

Ribchester (PR 2905) Dob Hall distribution 1792–1807, 1845–98, Waterworth's distribution 1848–79, Harriet Quartley's disbursements 1880–1933 and statements of account 1876–87

Rufford (PR 1191) Peter Lathom's accounts 1839–78

Rumworth (PR 2181) John Laithwaite's deed 1760

St. Michael's-on-Wyre (PR) Terlway's deeds 1693–1862, bread abstract of title 1759–60

Silverdale (PR 69, 70) accounts 1850–1924

Staveley (PR 172) poor money accounts 1784–1846

Thornton (PR 1845, 1848) Homes's will 1695, accounts 1918–30

Tottington see Bury

Up Holland (PR 2907) deeds and papers 1671–1899, accounts 1927–64; (PR 2454) united charities minutes 1899–1925, letter book 1910–18, register of applications 1899–1926, accounts 1899–1941, Fairclough's letter book 1885–99, register of recipients 1877–98, accounts 1849–99, Mawdesley's accounts 1868–95

Upper Allithwaite (PR 2803) Lindale: Lawrence Newton's accounts and papers 1591–1904, Miles Taylor's accounts and papers 1663–1801, 1864–69; (PR 863) Miles Taylor's accounts 1782–1858

Walton-le-Dale (PR 2948) Thomas Crook's distribution 1688; (DDHo) Hoghton's deeds 1729–33; (DDX 994) Burscough's deed 1667

Warton-in-Lonsdale (DDX 205) Mansergh's apprenticeship indentures 1844–48

Whalley (PR 2777) Poor Stock accounts and papers 1661–1944, Clothing accounts and papers 1822–55; (PR 2929) Adam Cottam's will 1838, minutes and accounts

Whiston (PR 2968) account book 1830–61, Hawarden's correspondence 1895–96, Oliver Lyme's correspondence 1895–97, 1937–40, Ashton's correspondence 1902, 1905, 1932–51

Whittle-le-Woods (DDX 761) Lady Hoghton's almshouses deeds 1841

Widnes (PR 2897) Bread dole and Garnet's flannel accounts 1892–1917, correspondence 1896–1929

Woodplumpton (DDX 88) Hollowforth accounts 1781–1820

Peter Lathom's Charity (DDX 92) will 1701, deeds, etc. 1656–1925, survey 1810; (DDF 783) rental 1757

SOCIETIES

Agricultural Societies:

Ashton-under-Lyne and District (NCGh) allotment holders' association minutes 1938–39

Clitheroe (DDX 793) agricultural association minutes 1862–81

Edgworth (PR 2864) agricultural society minutes 1908–27

Haslingden (DDX 118) agricultural society subscription books 1865, 1867, 1870, 1872–73

Lancashire County Herb Committee (DDX 64) minutes 1942–46, reports 1942–45

Newton-with-Scales (DDNw) marsh-owners' accounts 1901–20

Preston and Fulwood (DDX 218) horticultural society minutes 1925–60, press cuttings 1938–60

Rochdale (DP 389) agricultural society minutes 1876–80

Rufford (PR 1187) horse, cattle and poultry show minutes 1900–26

Building Societies:

Colne (DDBd) Union club house-building society ledger and day book 1816–31

Longridge (DDH) building societies agreement 1793, accounts 1793–1804, 1799–1814

Oldham (DDHe) building societies: Coach and Horses minutes and accounts 1889–91, Guenacres Moor minutes 1884–1903, Swan minutes 1890–1901, accounts 1874–1909

Church Societies:

Cartmel (PR 2803) Bible association minutes 1833–44

Colne (PR 2950) Society for the Propagation of the Gospel minutes 1919–35

Eccleston, Chorley (DDX 1077) St. Mary's mothers' union scrapbook 1970

Padiham (PR 2863) Sunday school teachers' association minutes 1909–16

Preston (DDX 926) Sunday schools' association minutes 1910–51, reports 1882–1913, guild papers 1902, 1922, 1952, Whit Monday papers 1925–39; (PR 2845) Church of England men's society minutes 1907–25, Church missionary association minutes 1922–34

Wigan (PR 2907) clerical society minutes 1873–95

Educational Societies:

Bacup (MBBa) mechanics' institute subscription books and ledgers 1861–1908

Blackpool (DDX 706) literary and scientific society minutes and reports 1898–1961

Clitheroe (PR 2484) St. James's mutual improvement society minutes 1877–79

Colne (MBCo) pupil-teachers' association minutes 1901–03

Haslingden (MBH) mechanics' institute minutes 1846–50, young mens' institute minutes 1854–60

Liverpool (DDX 824) juvenile reformatory association minutes 1855–1924, 1934–56, letter books 1872–1919, log books 1909–54, admission registers 1892–1955, licence register 1900–14, medical reports 1903–11, 1926–34, punishment books 1909–24, various registers 1904–40; (CULi) Great George Street Congregational literacy and debating society minutes 1869–80

Much Woolton (DDX 411) mechanics' institute and library minutes, accounts, reports, etc. 1846–1904

Over Wyresdale (SMAy) mutual improvement society minutes 1881–82

Preston (PR 2951) Christ Church mutual improvement society minutes 1889–96

Salford (RCBt) Diocesan school association minutes 1897–1908

Widnes (PR 2897) pastoral aid society letter book 1916–17; SPCK account book 1915–16

Friendly and Charitable Societies:

Amalgamated Weavers' (DDX 1138) approved society minutes 1912–36, membership records 1912–33

Barrow-in-Furness (DDX 524) working-men's provident tontine minutes 1914–46, subscription book 1932–49

Billington (PR 2965) Langho sick society cash book 1852–73

Broughton-in-Amounderness (DDX 830) Catholic charitable society minutes 1851–1933, registers of members 1812–1947, mass registers 1857–92, 1920–53, register of recipients 1853–63, cash book 1914–50, rule books 1792–1839

153

Chipping (DDX 814) Oddfellows' minutes 1885–1963

Chorley and District (DDX 984) workpeople's central hospital fund minutes 1925–49

Clitheroe (DDX 418) John Taylor's friendly society, minutes, letters, etc. 1827–69, Sisterly love society rules 1816

Cliviger (NCCl) miners' relief society minutes 1899–1927, rules 1898–1924, registers of members 1881–98, letter book 1899–1931, ledgers 1899–1935, cash books 1881–1936, contribution books 1881–1925, claims record 1881–82, 1934–47; (NCHa) Holmes Chapel Sunday school sick society registers 1905–33

Darwen (PR 2878) St. James's sick and burial society minutes 1844–78

Downham (DDX 28) friendly society subscription book 1824–47

Kearsley (DDX 669) Harrison, Blair and Co., manufacturing chemists, sick and life club minutes 1918–24, accounts 1918–24, rules 1874

Lancashire and Cheshire (NCLm) miners' welfare committee minutes 1928–48, Blackpool convalescent home minutes 1928–48

Lancaster (DDX 69) William IV lodge of Oddfellows minutes and register 1831–50

Lea (DDX 433) Oddfellows' minutes 1916–50

Lindale (PR 2803) provident society accounts 1860–78

Livesey (PR 2846) sick club minutes 1880–83, accounts 1832–52, papers 1880–81

Lytham (RCLy) sick club minutes 1876–1912, accounts 1885–1912

Preesall (DDX 479) tontine minutes 1900–26

Preston (DDX 857) district Oddfellows minutes 1859–1900; (DDX 433) Duke of York lodge of Oddfellows minutes 1818–38, Pleasant Retreat lodge of Oddfellows minutes 1856–76, 1913–23, registers 1836–92, balance sheets 1838–42, declaration books 1871–91, 1909–31, proposition book 1854–1916; (DDHs) Horrockses weavers' sick club subscription book 1882–1945

Rochdale (DDX 261) Lower Place sick and burial society minutes 1842–65

Rossendale (NCHa) collieries accident and burial society minutes 1898–1906, rules 1925, cash books 1874–93, 1902–13, financial statements 1905–56

St. Michaels-on-Wyre (DDX 911) friendly society admission book 1845–1941

Slaidburn (DDX 814) Oddfellows minutes 1841–1909

Tarleton (DP 389) Oddfellows contribution book 1842–60

Tockholes (PR 2762) friendly society papers 1832–88

Walton-le-Dale (PR 2948) friendly society papers 1859–69; (DDX 516) friendly society minutes 1857–58, treasurers' bonds 1863, 1866

Whitworth (DDX 177) Hall Fold sickness and burial society minutes 1851–76

Widnes (PR 2897) sick society papers 1898–1917

Worsley and Walkden Moor (NCBw) friendly society minutes 1840–1903, financial records 1840–1930

Yorkshire West Riding (CUWy) independent provident society minutes 1869–1948

Music and Stage Societies:

Blackpool (DDX 3) children's pantomime programmes 1916–60; (DDX 706) glee and madrigal society papers 1892–1931, musical festival programmes 1901–65

Eccles (CUEc) King Street congregational amateur dramatic society minutes 1944–53

Prestwich (DDX 380) amateur operatic and dramatic society minutes and accounts 1918–37

Political Societies:

Clitheroe (DDX 800) Conservative association minutes 1909–47, cash book 1885–98, letter book 1913–15, balance sheets 1876–90, 1918–28, year books 1961–65, election expenses files 1910–45

Crosby (DDX 806) Conservative and Unionist association minutes 1901–63, miscellanea 1925–45

Garstang (DDFz) Primrose league minutes 1894–1911, register 1897–1909, cash book 1894–1911

Lancashire and North Western (DDX 960) Association of Clerks of urban district councils minutes 1947–74

Lancashire (DDX 952) Rural district councils' association minutes 1959–74, correspondence 1964–74, cash books 1938–67

Lancashire (DDX 954) Urban district councils' association minutes 1964–74, annual conference proceedings 1930–72, letter books 1905–30

Newton Heath (DDX 1014) Parliamentary debating society minutes 1882–83

North Western (DDX 988) Society of town clerks minutes 1931–74

155

North Western (DDX 1048) Students' society of the institute of municipal treasurers and accountants minutes 1933–50

Preston (DDX 575) Suffragette's illuminated addresses *c.* 1913, accounts of women's social and political union 1966, letter about suffragettes in Preston 1967; (DDCm) Leguleian society minutes 1824–34

Prosecution of Felons:

Barton-in-Amounderness (DDX 702) deed 1802

Bickerstaffe (PR) 1792

Caton (DDGa) 1817

Clifton-with-Salwick (DDH) deed 1801

Freckleton (DDX 194) deed 1754

Halsall (PR) 1808, 1829

Hambleton (PR 3013) deed 1785

Lowton (PR) 1825

Melling-with-Wrayton (PR 2898) deed 1777

Newton-with-Scales (PR) 1763, 1802

Penwortham and Howick (DDR) 1801

Prescot (DDCm) 1814

Turton (UDTu) account book 1789–1856

Social Societies:

Altham (PR 2819) Boy scouts' log book 1939–48

Ashton-under-Lyne (DDX 432) Society for the blind minutes and ledgers 1895–1951

Barrow-in-Furness (DDX 764) Samaritans' annual reports 1971–75

Bilsborrow (DDX 1054) Women's institute scrapbooks *c.* 1975

Bolton (DDX 764) Samaritans' annual reports 1965–72

Burnley (DDX 345) Association for care of young girls reports 1884–1958

Clitheroe (DDX 344) District club minutes 1914–60

Colne (DDX 682) Temperance society and band of hope minutes 1889–95, 1904–35, speakers' plans 1898–1938, accounts 1888–1951

Davyhulme Park hospital student nurses' association minutes 1930–39

Denton (UDDe) Lads' club papers 1893–95

Earby (UDEa) Nanny association minutes 1939–49, miscellanea 1940–49

Formby (DDX 832) Citizens' advice bureau case books 1965–70, correspondence 1965–70

Garston (DDX 1033) District nursing association minutes 1873–1948, reports 1910–40, correspondence 1901–51

Kirkland (DDX 598) Churchtown men's club minutes and accounts 1932–66

Lancashire (DDX 978) Community council entries for "Early Recollections" essay contest 1964

Lancashire (WI) Federation of women's institutes minutes 1920–65, agenda and reports 1944–70, circulars 1934–64, programmes 1924–68, miscellanea 1924–69; Jubilee scrap books 1965: Allithwaite, Arkholme and Gressingham, Bilsborrow, Broughton (Preston), Calder Vale, Cartmel, Downham, Eccleston (Chorley), Foxfield, Hambleton, Kirkham, Leck, Pendleton (Whalley), Rusland, Samlesbury and Cuerdale, Warton Crag, Wrea Green, Wrightington; minutes: Kirkland 1921–58, Pilling Lane and Preesall 1935–39

Lancashire (CPRE) Branch of the council for the protection of rural England minutes, reports, and correspondence 1933–63

Longridge (PR 2939) Church Lads' Brigade minutes and accounts 1922–36

Manchester (DDX 764) Samaritans' annual reports 1965–69

North East Lancashire (DDX 345) Association of Girl Guides reports 1917–64

North West Lancashire (DDX 867) Association of Girl Guides commissioners' minutes 1918–59, county committee minutes 1918–29, annual meeting minutes 1918–48, training committee minutes 1930–45, executive committee minutes 1950–63, Barrow district minutes 1920–46, Preston division minutes 1946–52, annual reports 1923–71, miscellanea 1920–71; (DDX 950) miscellanea 1916–70

Oswaldtwistle (UDOs) Queen Victoria jubilee nursing association minutes 1907–48, District nursing association minutes 1907–48

Padiham (DDX 345) District nurse fund prospectus 1881, annual reports 1882–1929; (PR 2863) Clothing society registers 1851–72

Penwortham (SMP) Clothing club miscellanea 1846–87

Preston (DDX 135) Citizens' advice bureau filing cards 1949; (PR 2951) St. Peter's temperate society minutes 1912–23; (DDX 465) Rechabites' minutes, accounts, etc. 1885–1945; (DDX 764)

157

Samaritans' annual reports 1970–73; (DDX 982) Productivity society minutes 1953–73; (DDX 1149) Historical society minutes 1947–51

Rainford (SMRf) Social club minutes 1922–24

Southport (DDX 1087) 3rd Southport scouts' log books 1924–27

Ulverston (DDX 784) Ulverston association accounts 1824–40

Walton-le-Dale (PR 2948) Temperance society minutes 1884, 1936–40, cash book 1885–1918, pledge book 1884–1937

Whittle-le-Woods (RCSh) Catholic club minutes 1897–1910

Whitworth (UDWh) Nursing association minutes 1931–45, clerks notes 1931–47, ledgers 1933–41, miscellanea 1931–47

Sports and Pastimes:

Aughton (DDX 183) Races subscription list 1764

Blackpool and Fleetwood (DDX 734) Yacht club minutes 1907–09, 1912–14, regatta registers 1910–14, 1924–29

Burnley (CUBy) Thursby Road tennis club minutes 1928–36

Fulwood (DDX 103) racecourse minutes 1790–1829

Haslingden (DDX 118) Crubden coursing company rules 1841

Lancaster (DDX 1016) Canal trust minutes, papers and plans 1963–66

Nelson (PR 2938) St. Paul's cricket club cash book 1937–48

Oldham (DDX 653) Photographic society minutes 1867–85, 1890–1957, accounts 1890–1951, letter book 1884–97, miscellanea 1867–1968

Prescot (PR 2968) Amateur bowling league minutes 1927–43, accounts 1936–46

Preston (DDX 146) Union hunt subscription list 1770

Rochdale (DDX 183) Hounds kennel book 1841–66

Ribble, Hodder and Calder (DDX 61) Fishery protection association minutes 1858–66

River Calder (DDBd) Riparian owners' minutes 1897–98, 1932–37

Ulverston (PR 2847) Book club rules 1756

Whitworth (DDX 177) Natural history society minutes 1900–05

TRADE UNIONS

Agriculture: National Union of Agricultural and Allied Workers (DDX 1045) district and branch (Lancashire, Cumberland and Westmorland) minutes and papers 1921–74

Footwear: Rossendale Union of Boot, Shoe, and Slipper Operatives (DDX 1160) minutes 1895–1968, conciliation board minutes 1927–62, departmental minutes, etc. 1957–69, cash books and contribution ledgers 1895–1969, general ledger 1905–09, dispute, strike and distress pay book 1910–22, general federation of trade unions (assurance) contribution ledger 1938–47, shoe-making price surveys 1909–13 and lists and agreements 1899–1956, magazine *Unity* 1926–70 and company files 1912–74

Painters: National Society of Painters (DDX 1090) Padiham branch minutes 1938–63, members' register 1893–1970, account book 1936–40

Teachers: National Union of Teachers (DDX 1074) Lancashire county association minutes 1919–73

Textiles:

General Union of Lancashire and Yorkshire Warp Dressers (DDX 1141) minutes 1894–1918, rules 1919, report on price list for chain beaming 1944

Accrington and District Weavers' Association (DDX 1138) minutes 1929–51, obituary book 1892–97, accounts 1908–18, 1939–48, membership and contribution records 1913–46, receipts 1930–67, letter books 1920–69, price calculation book 1929–54, miscellanea 1920–49

Accrington and District Textile Trades Association (DDX 1138) minutes 1939–55, accounts 1907–31

Bamber Bridge Branch, Preston and Districts Association of Power-loom Overlookers (DDX 1151) minutes 1949–55, draft minutes and accounts 1959–61, contribution and superannuation books 1933–63, benefits book 1914–63

Barrow-in-Furness Branch, National Union of Dyers, Bleachers and Textile Workers (DDX 1069) minutes 1956–62, attendance register 1968–74

Blackburn Association of Power-loom Overlookers (DDX 1128) committee minutes 1858–1960, trustees' minutes 1887–1916, executive minutes 1888–1972, sub-executive minutes 1890–1913, letter books 1936–48, ledgers 1927–51, accounts 1861–1951

Blackburn and District Weavers', Warpers' and Winders' Association (DDX 1078) minutes 1903–49

Chorley Branch, Preston and District Association of Power-loom Overlookers (DDX 1151) minutes 1878–1919, rules 1878–1965, letter books 1920–25, correspondence 1947–72, account books 1878–1972, balance sheets 1940–74, contribution and superannuation books 1892–1971, record of members' declarations 1884–1960, members' book 1920, miscellanea *c.* 1926–44

Chorley and District Branch, Northern Counties Textile Trades Federation (DDX 1151) minutes 1948–70, rules 1906

Church and Oswaldtwistle Textile Trades Federation (DDX 1138) minutes 1907–38, rules 1907

Church and Oswaldtwistle Weavers' Association (DDX 1138) minutes 1890–1948, priced sample book 1917

Colne Branch, Nelson and District Association of Warp Dressers (DDX 1141) minutes 1895–98

Darwen Weavers', Warpers', and Winders' Association (DDX 1078) minutes 1888–1957, reports 1886–1960, death-money book 1897–1951; Textile Manufacturing Trades Federation minutes 1909–14

Great Harwood Association of Power-loom Overlookers (DDX 1128) committee minutes 1912–72, members' minutes 1913–68, membership records 1891–1970, contribution books 1915–66, cash books 1916–72, notice of claims book 1910–57

Haslingden Branch, Amalgamated Textile Warehouse Workers' Association (DDX 1140) minutes 1907–45, accounts 1907–61

Haslingden Operative Spinners' Association (DDX 1134) minutes 1868–1963, contribution books 1876–1950, accounts 1886–1959, balance sheets 1920–66, stoppage pay book 1888–1912, correspondence and papers 1867–1976, rule books 1909–76, miscellanea 1889–1956

Longridge Branch, Preston and District Association of Power-loom Overlookers (DDX 1151) minutes 1889–1967

Manchester and Rochdale and District Warp Dressers' Association (DDX 1141) cotton control payments 1917

Nelson and District Association of Warp Dressers and Preparatory Workers (DDX 1141) minutes 1892–99, 1910–51, collectors' records 1922–46, contribution records 1936–47, active service register 1914–19, membership notifications 1947–57, correspondence 1928–30, 1958–71, rules 1929–73, price list 1916

Nelson, Colne and Darwen Chain Beamers' Association (DDX 1141) unemployment register 1914–32

North Lancashire Card, Blowing Room, and Ring Spinners' Association (DDX 1102) minutes 1913–65, accounts 1900–66, contribution records 1866–1968, members' register 1915–56, stoppage books 1914–61, reports 1902–53, miscellanea 1874–1968

Preston and Districts Association of Power-loom Overlookers (DDX 1151) central records: minutes 1892–1957, secretaries' journals 1921–35, almanacs 1889–1977, rules 1905–71, letter books 1921–51, correspondence 1920–69, compensation claims records 1910–48, cash books and accounts 1893–1976, contribution and superannuation records 1899–1977, N.H.I. benefits register 1916, out-of-work payments book 1932–38, delegation book 1920–63, members' registers c. 1900, club cash books 1898–1963, miscellanea 20th c.

Preston and District Textile Warehouse Operatives (DDX 1142) minutes 1906–43, contribution books 1906–59, unemployment benefit registers 1917–40, financial records 1906–57, membership registers 1907–57, registers of short-term unemployment 1920–21, correspondence and agreements 1920–60, agenda 1920–70, press cuttings 1927–38

Preston Amalgamated Textile Warehousemen (DDX 836) minutes 1906–43, contribution books 1906–59, benefits registers 1917–40, financial records 1906–62, members' registers 1907–57, correspondence 1920–59

Preston Powerloom Weavers', Warpers', and Winders' Association (DDX 836) account book 1889–94; (DDX 1089) minutes 1864–1959, burial society minutes 1861–68, membership records 1866–1941, collection lists 1902–35, cases and complaints books 1904–64, correspondence 1860–68, stoppage books 1887–1938, contribution books 1895–1940, wages papers 1906–45, legal papers 1894–1926

Preston Textile Trades Federation (DDX 1089) minutes, accounts and attendance registers 1907–65

Rawtenstall Calico and Paper Stainers' Union (DDX 658) minutes 1891–1928

Rochdale Branch, Amalgamated Weavers' Association (DDX 1123) including general council agenda c. 1890–c. 1965, central committee minutes 1944–62, correspondence 1913–49, extensive working papers c. 1890–1972, accounts c. 1900–c. 1967

Woodworkers:

Burnley Lodge, Operative Joiners and Carpenters (DDX 333) minutes 1850–73

Padiham Branch, Amalgamated Society of Woodworkers (DDX 1090) minutes 1891–1933, entrance book 1891–1938, benefit books 1877–1961, transfer book 1911–46, account book, 1898–1966

EMPLOYERS' ASSOCIATIONS

Coal:

Southwest Lancashire Coal-owners' Association (DDX 381) minutes, accounts and correspondence 1898–1955; (NCSw) accounts 1910–54

Lancashire and Cheshire Coal Association (NCLc) minutes 1926–27, committee minutes and papers 1911–45, correspondence 1928–44, circulars 1910–44

Textiles:

Accrington and District Cotton Spinners' and Manufacturers Association (DDX 1115) minutes 1896–1960, correspondence 1912–60, financial records 1912–60

Blackburn and District Cotton Manufacturers' Association (DDX 1115) minutes 1877–1966, reports 1942–71, rules 1897–1931, letter books 1906–51, correspondence 1932–74, papers of Frank Longworth, J.P. 1928–46, questionnaire returns 1935–57, circulars 1908–61, financial records 1903–55, levy records 1899–1950, wage and price lists 1860–1950, dispute books 1945–54, price calculation books 1891–1933, costing books 1913–18, trade statistics 1924–60, re-organisation compensation records 1959–60, wartime records 1940–41, miscellanea c. 1850–1970, minutes of Cotton Spinners' and Manufacturers' Association (Manchester) joint meetings 1927–35

Burnley Master Cotton Spinners' and Manufacturers' Association (DDX 1145) minutes 1894–1963, ledgers 1912–1963, subscription book 1945–60

Chorley Cotton Manufacturers' Association (DDX 1116) minutes 1914–63, letter books 1942–64, correspondence 1922–63, rules and agreements 1886–1933, financial records 1913–63

Clitheroe Cotton Employers' Association (DDX 1115) minutes 1906–64, correspondence 1930–51

Colne and District Coloured Goods Manufacturers' Association (DDX 1145) minutes 1888–1963, ledgers 1920–63, subscription book 1948–61

Colne Master Spinners' and Manufacturers' Association (DDSp) levy book 1953–61

Great Harwood Masters' Association (DDX 1115) minutes 1893–1922, letter book 1893–1924

Haslingden Cotton Manufacturers' Association (DDX 1115) balance sheets 1966–69

Nelson and District Manufacturers' Association (DDX 1145) minutes 1891–1963, letter books 1938–63, ledgers 1916–63, subscription book 1925–63

North Lancashire Textile Employers' Association (DDX 1116) minutes 1838–1961, reports 1901–55, letter books 1853–1962, circulars 1946–52, correspondence 1919–63, Preston Guild and Exhibition files 1882–1952, commonplace book 1924, lists of officers and members 1927–69, memoranda books 1919–40, financial records 1897–1967, sundry rules 1896–1969, price lists and agreements 1887–1958, memoranda and articles of association 1900–26, handbooks and year books 1905–57, miscellanea 1826– c.1969, cotton industry re-organization correspondence 1959–63

Padiham Master Cotton Spinners' and Manufacturers' Association (DDX 1145) minutes 1890–1963, ledgers 1890–1963, subscription books 1922–61

Various rule books, price lists and miscellanea 1891–c.1964, register of weaving price calculations 1914–49 (DDX 1145)

BUSINESS RECORDS

Architects and Surveyors:

Lancaster (DDX 641) Spencer E. Barrow, architect, plans and papers 1912–16

Liverpool (DDX 162) Culshaws, surveyors, plans (covering a wide area of Lancashire, Wirral etc.) 1927–1915

Auctioneers, Valuers and Estate Agents:

Colne (DDX 671) R. H. Berry and Sons, auctioneers and valuers accounts 1884–1940, sale books 1870–1949, press cuttings 1878–1915, valuations 1883–1960

Liverpool (DDSu) Williams and Sutcliffe, estate agents, letter books 1847–1961, accounts 1844–51, 1937–61, plans and memoranda 1800–91

Preston (DDIm) Jabey Jones and Son, auctioneers, sale and valuation books 1850–1920. (DDX 74) E. J. Reed and Sons, auctioneers, plans and particulars of sale of properties throughout Lancashire 1783–1950

Bakers:

Pendleton, Salford (DDX 1043) James Royle, baker, ledger 1858–84

Banks:

Colne, (DDBd) Savings Bank ledgers, returns etc. 1844–77

Preston Bank (DX) character books 1834–37

Rufford (DDX 129) Penny Bank withdrawal book 1859–72, day books 1859–80, account books 1859–83

Brewers:

Blackburn (CYC) Thomas and John Holden account books 1852–56. (DDX 223) partnership agreement: Dutton and Haworth 1807; Johnson, Taylor, and Chadwick 1832

Clitheroe (CYC) James Haworth account books 1845–49. Bury (DDWo) Crown correspondence, deeds etc. 1888–1910. Manchester (DDX 808) Land and Lomax partnership deeds 1846–59. Preston (DDX 687) Cardwell's deeds and papers 1898–1900, (DDX 816) Glover Street deeds 1728–1923

Brickmakers:

Oldham (DDRe) brickworks accounts 1822–45. Warrington (DDX 614) Brick and Tile Co. papers 1904–11

Builders:

Bretherton (PR 2851) Henry Hodge's accounts 1816–25. Huyton (DDX 401) J. Whittaker & Son ledgers 1864–68, 1889–1938, debt book 1907–15, work book 1893–96, materials-used book 1930–39, funeral bill books 1929–37. Blackburn and Whalley (DDG) Richard Thompson & Son letter book 1848–58. Preston (DDX 202) J. Todd account book 1860–68

Canal:

Lancaster (DDX 1052) Canal workmen's job book 1841–45, report book (including drownings) 1900–12, bills register 1906–17, wind and water records 1904–42, fire-equipment book 1905–17, fire-drill book 1917–49, wages books 1900–31, horse-sickness book 1932–48, insurance book 1915–42, circulars 1914–18, agreement registers 1870–1948, miscellaneous files 1792–1949. Manchester Ship Canal (DDX 101) correspondence and papers 1882–87; (DDBe) papers, plans, pamphlets etc. 1881–1925

Cheese Factors:

Preston (DDTh) Ernest Threlfall, Son & Co. account books 1878–1961, letter books 1903–15, correspondence 1887–1963, local society papers 1894–1914

Chemists:

Kearsley (DDX 669) Harrison Blair & Co., manufacturing chemists, papers and plans 1833–1933. Openshaw (DDX 808) Bowers and Peate partnership deed 1876. (DDX 684) Fishers of Preston prescription books 1870–1967, day books 1912–55

Coach Builders:

Preston (DDX 460) W. Harding & Co. wages books 1914–18, drawings and photographs of coaches, carts, cars etc. c.1880–1955

Coal:

Ashton-under-Lyne (DDX 614) Hurst papers 1778–1860. Atherton (DDLi) papers 1876–84; (DDX 991) ledger 1821–72, journal of Hubert Fletcher, esq. 1868–72. Burnley (DDX 502) Peter Pickup and father, coal investigators, accounts and memoranda 1818–49, work diary 1866, survey book (N.E. Lancs.) 1787–1880. Chadderton (DDX 809) section of Stockfield pit c.1890. Clayton-le-Moors (DDLx) papers 1659–1843, plan c.1780, banksmen's weekly bills 1793–1803, stock book 1848. Crompton (DDX 614) lease of Mountain Mine 1857. Eccleston, Prescot (DDSc) accounts 1754–57, 1770–73. Great Harwood (CYC) account books 1865–71. Hulton (NCHu) account books 1886–1935. Oldham (DDX 614) papers 1736–1874. Rainford and Up Holland (DDX 1041) Victoria and Albert deeds 1849–56. St. Helens (DDSn) Sutton Manor minutes, accounts and papers 1904–56. Skelmersdale (DDX 92) Crow Orchard statements and valuations 1874–77, 1881–85; White Moss statements and valuations 1877–1909. Shevington (DDSc) agreements 1679, 1770. Wigan (DDX 127) Coal and Iron Co. papers 1870–96. Winstanley (DDBa) accounts 1676, 1766. Worthington (DDEl) Blainscough account books 1873–1932

Co-operative Society:

Sabden (DDX 715) Industrial Society minutes 1895–1966, accounts 1914–66, nomination book 1914–61

Drapers:

Fleetwood and Brazil (DDX 503) John Cottam's letter book 1856–69. Nelson (DDBd) William Crook's accounts 1843–62

Electricity:

Blackpool (DDX 786) pamphlets and papers 1893–1943

Engineers:

Bury (DDHl) Robert Hall and Sons, machinery manufacturers, wage books 1844–1949, home account books 1865–1940, foreign account books 1869–1904, miscellanea 19th and 20th c., bill books 1877–93, sundries order books 1887–89, stock and plant books 1854–1973, ledgers 1874–77, loom order books (with drawings) 1865–75, plans and catalogues 19th and 20th c. Haslingden (DDX 118) Laneside Foundry papers 1845–66.

St. Helens and Widnes (DDX 1041) Robinson and Cooks, engineers, partnership deed 1884, dissolution 1898. Preston (DDX 438) W. and J. Foster Ltd., knitting-machine manufacturers, account books 1889–1946, diaries of James Foster 1862, 1866, business and moral precepts of James Foster 1864, letter and essay on the Isaac Lamb of Michigan knitting-machine 1896. Manchester (DDX 178) Chas. Chapman & Sons, journals of borings 1870–1922. Eccles (DDX 260) Nasmyth, Gaskell & Co., machine maker partnership deeds 1842, 1843, 1850

Entertainment:

Morecambe (DDX 1017) account book of Sunday sailings to Blackpool 1908. Oldham (DDRe) Colosseum account book 1901–03, Empire ledger 1899–1915, Grand account book 1913–17, Theatre Royal daily returns 1884–85. Preston (DDTs) Theatre Royal correspondence, accounts and deeds 1867–79, (DDCm) Pleasure Gardens accounts and reports 1876–84.

Farming:

Bretherton (PR 2851) William Hodges' accounts 1880–86

Fishing:

Fleetwood (DDX 303) Mellings Ltd., trawler owners, settling books 1905–38, wages book 1925–29, accounts 1931–44; Lune Steam Fishing Co. director's minutes 1906–14

Gas:

Carnforth (DDX 791) director's reports 1887–1913. Chorley (MBCh) share register 1820–49. Darwen (DDBd) minutes and papers 1840–55. Fleetwood (DDX 1135) letters and papers 1839–1912. Garstang (DDX 256) minutes 1879–1949, shareholders' returns 1935–48. Leyland and Farington (DDX 256) minutes 1862–1949, accounts 1921–56. Littleborough (DDX 791) minutes 1938–47. Longridge (DDX 256) minutes 1866–1942, accounts 1901–50, mortgages 1883–1935 Morecambe (MBMo) Gas Co minutes 1858–70. Padiham (UDPa) minutes 1852–63, 1875–76, share register 1847–76, Poulton-le-Fylde (DDHa) articles of association 1885, papers 1888–1903. Preston (DDX 256) minutes 1815–70, letter book 1815–18, secretary's accounts 1815–17, agenda books 1863–1945, account books 1819–1948, correspondence 1820–1949. Prescot (DDCs) minutes 1859–66, inspectors' accounts 1836–67

Grocers:

Clitheroe (CYC) Bentley and Harrison cash books and ledgers 1846–54, unidentified ledgers 1842–48, 1851–54, 1867–71. Leigh (DDX

749) Henry Shovelton accounts and papers 1864–90. Manchester (DDX 808) partnership deeds: Gould and Wright, tea merchants 1858; Gould, Wright and Davies, tea and coffee merchants 1871. Preston (DDPr) Rawcliffe and Baines partnership deed 1767. Wigan (DDX 778) E. H. Monks, wholesale grocers, cornmillers and merchants account books 1875–78, 1883–86, 1939–67, employment contract 1888. (DDP) unidentified account book 18th c.

Gunpowder:

Haverthwaite (DDX 116) Lowwood Gunpowder Works solicitors' letters 1858–63. (DDLo) cash books 1798–1839, day books 1801–40, balance accounts 1800–20, wages books 1808–23, journals 1810–11, bank books 1798–1828, blacksmith's accounts 1835–42, cartage accounts 1815–38, cooperage accounts 1825–31, postage books 1825–31, lists of debts 1814–17, magazine accounts 1825–31, gunpowder accounts 1804–26, cartage and boatage accounts 1829–34, bills and receipts 1798–1846, letters 1798–1840

Hosiers:

Salford (DDX 1009) unidentified sale book 1651–62

Hotels:

Singleton (DDX 559) Miller Arms spirit stock books 1904–28. Blackpool (DDX 318) Wellington accounts 1852–1905

Insurance:

Oldham (DDRe) Sun Life book of policies and accounts 1877–1911

Iron:

Clitheroe (CYC) Robert Clark, iron and brass founder account books 1837–59. Colton (DDMc) Backbarrow Iron Co. account books 1728–45, deeds and papers 1712–54. Wigan (DDX 127) Coal & Iron Co. papers 1870–96. Backbarrow and Pennybridge Furnace (DP 373) accounts 1763–80. Spark Bridge and Duddon Ironworks (DDX 192) accounts 1750, 1755–65, 1772–79

Joiners:

Penwortham (DDX 526) J. R. Taylor, joiners and wheelwright, accounts 1856–73, 1891–1942, letter book 1902–07. Ulverston (DDX 524) unidentified joiner and builder, accounts 1834–42

Law:

(see also Solicitors' Accumulations p. 172f.) Colne (DDBd) John Bolton, attorney, ledgers and accounts 1782–1806; Bolton and

Hargreaves, solicitors 1845–70; William Hartley, and Hartley and Pilgrim, solicitors, cash books and papers 19th and 20th c. Liverpool and Preston (DDX 766) J. J. Somerville, barrister, business diaries 1930–56, ledgers 1936–62, cash books 1946–67. Preston (DDP) Paul Catterall, solicitor, business and personal papers 17th to 19th c., (DDX 103) Wilson, Rawstorne & Wilson account books 1810–39, 1824–26

Linoleum:

Lancaster (DDX 909) Shrigley and Williamson, painters and gilders, and James Williamson and Son, linoleum manufacturers, account books 1837-69, dispatch books 1845–62, order books 1838–53, receipt books 1837–52, wages books 1837–45, gilder's time book 1840–42, machinery correspondence, etc. 1863, 1900–16

Millers:

Nelson (DDBd) Flour Milling Co. directors' minutes 1892–1901

Milliners:

Manchester (DDX 808) Batho, Taylor and Ogden partnership deed 1904, (DDX 239) M. Nicholson & Co. deeds of partnership and dissolution 1845

Newspapers:

Liverpool (DDX 260) *Daily Post and Journal* purchase and management agreement 1874

Paper:

Bleasdale (DDJa) Oakenclough Paper Mill sales ledgers 1828–78, purchase books 1831–1903, cash books 1875–77, 1891–1932, letter books 1898, 1903–06, wages books 1874–86, 1898–1925, sample books 1892–1940, blacksmith's accounts 1843-60. Darwen (DDX 691) Potter & Co., wallpaper manufacturers, partnership deeds 1853–1900, patents 1850–57, legal papers 1807–85

Plumbers:

Colne (DDBd) Battinson & Whitaker, plumbers and ironmongers deed of partnership 1816. Bacup (DDX 335) Shepherd, Swire & Markham, partnership deed 1896.

Printers:

Blackpool (DDX 1051) Henry Maxwell & Co. wage books 1892–1909. Leyland (DDX 930) H. Threlfall Ltd., account books 1907–30, stock books 1914–27. Oldham (DDX 818) unidentified, samples of great variety 1760–1830

Quarries:

Billinge (PR 203) John and Henry Mather, and Henry Sephton, quarrymen, deed of partnership 1797. Colne (DDBd) Blakey accounts and correspondence 1871–85. Egerton (DDX 492) Walsh's sand quarry account book 1880–1922

Railways:

Liverpool and Southport (DDX 972) Dick, Kerr and Co , Preston, contract for electrification 1903. Longridge to Hellifield (DDB) correspondence 1917–24. Shipley to Colne (DDB) notices, letters etc. 1846–55

Surgeons:

Kirkham (DDPr) William Loxham account book 1756–73, (DDS) William Knipe and Thomas Shaw partnership deed 1838

Tailors:

Manchester (DDX 808) Muirhead and Percival partnership deed 1896

Tanners:

Beckhead (DP) William Gibson letter book 1827–43. Warrington (DDX 614) F. W. & Jas. Reynolds ledger 1853–71

Textiles, Calico Printers:

Adlington (DDX 389) Alexander Hargreaves, pattern and wages book 1838–47. Clitheroe (CYC) Primrose Printworks ledgers 1810–26, 1837–53; (DDX 28) Bridgewater Printworks recipe books 1835. Ramsbottom (DDX 924) Turnbull & Stockdale wages books 1907–36, machinery account book, account books 1908–56, order books 1935–40

Textiles, Cotton:

Accrington (DDX 812) Bury Bros. private ledger 1866–1923, private stock book 1901–23. Atherton (DDLi) Albion Mill papers c.1890, Mather Lane Spinning Co. papers 1903–08. Blackburn (DDX 513) R R. Jackson account books 1900–40; (DDX 577) register of under-18s. at cotton factory 1842- 44; (DDX 868) Thomas & Richard Eccles, cotton weavers, pattern books 1898–1970, order books 1906–25, design books 1932–72, private ledger 1897–1953, inventories 1901, 1912, stock books 1931–55. sample books 1912–14, directors' minutes 1897–1937; (DDX 868) books and papers of Ewood Mill 1929–62, Primrose and Waterfall mills 1889–1964, Cardwell mill 1920–61, Alston mill 1930–66, Albion mill 1898–1975; (DDX 1041) Rodgett & Brierley, cotton-spinners, partnership and deeds 1839–49. Bolton (DDBx) Joshua Bamber & Co., cotton-waste merchants, articles of association 1886, balance sheets 1898–1933, 1954–70, wage books 1908–55, private ledgers 1917, 1933; Bolton Cotton Waste Co., minute book 1935–55, private ledger 1935–43, balance sheets 1946–54; Edwin Cooper, cotton waste merchant, balance sheets 1965–70; W. A. Openshaw & Co., cotton spinners, balance sheets 1954–70; Cannon Bros., cotton spinners, minutes 1920–38, ledgers 1899–1938, accounts 1929–37, extension papers 1917–24; Croal Spinning Co., minutes 1907–55, balance sheets 1955–70. Clayton-le-Moors (DDLx) James Lomax and William Mercer, partnership deed 1783. Colne (DDBd) Walk mill accounts and valuations 1818–31, pricing books 1904 24, inventories 1917, 1923, 1937, miscellanea 1896–1952; Edward and Pickles Riley & Co., cotton weavers, pricing books 1904–24, inventories 1917, 1923, 1937, order schedules 1896–89, miscellanea 1899–1956. Eccleston, Prescot (DDSc) factory papers 1784–93. Farington (DDX 819) Wm. Bashall & Co., ledgers and accounts 1834–1927. Great Harwood (DDX 868) Wm. & John Thompson, cotton spinners, nominal ledgers 1922–63, sales book 1926–55, private ledger 1918–31, expenditure books 1941–56. Kirkham (DDS) Fylde Manufacturing Co., twills, minutes 1875–82. Liverpool (DDX 1041) Rodgett & Co. cotton brokers partnership deed 1862. Manchester (DDX 2) Bryce, Smith & Co., pattern books 1801–93, account books 1844–69, laboratory trials 1894. Oldham (DDX 614) cotton factory papers 1842–56; (DDRe) Hartford mill, loan holders deposit book 1919–31. (DDX 869) Osborn Mill Co., cotton spinners, minutes 1922–57, shareholders' minutes 1915–53, share and loan books 1889–1957, financial records 1889–1969, wages books 1907–12, 1936–55, stock and yarn books 1918–67, holiday account books 1939–50, plans and tenders 1887–1948; Gresham Mill Co., cotton spinners, minutes 1948–57, register of directors 1903–62. (DDX 1014) Granville Mill Co., miscellanea 1884–87. Oswaldtwistle (DDX 868) John Fish Ltd., cotton-weavers, letters patent 1852, minutes 1874–1947, share registers 1874–1948, out-letter book 1902–07, private ledger 1881–1964. Preston (DDX 819) Daniel Arkwright Ltd., minutes 1900–08; (DDX 842) T. & W. McGuffog, cotton-spinners, letter book 1882–87, bills register 1871–86; (DDHs) Horrocks, Crewdson & Co., ledgers 1799–1945, journals 1812–1947, cash books 1823–1953, bill books 1811–17, 1833–36, pattern books c. 1900–62, day books 1933–60, pay book 1859–62, salaries and pensions books 1881–1911, weavers' sick fund book 1886–1946, private wages 1900–26, Royal Infirmary fund book 1919–29, cost analysis books 1886–1920, expenses book 1904–27, stock book 1870–87, balance sheets 1836–42, 1890–1919, plans c. 1810–c. 1950, wear-and tear account book 1839–77, strike papers 1853, machinists' accounts 1800–05, partnership papers 1801, 1870–75, price lists

170

1844–80, index of child employees 1852–82, directors' attendance book 1896–1904, trade correspondence 1818–60, Thomas Miller's letter book 1836–48, bills of exchange 1795–96. Preston, Cuerden, Farington and Higher Walton (DDX 819) G. & R. Dewhurst Ltd., stock accounts 1838–87, other accounts 1837–1940, letter books 1875–89. Radcliffe (DDBx) Black Lane Mills Co., cotton-spinners, balance sheets 1909–41, 1946–70, ledgers 1907–53, minutes 1907–39. Turton (DDAs) records of Ashworth's mills 1815–1905. Walton-le-Dale (DDCm) Lostock Hall spinning mill valuation 1876; (DDX 938) Lostock Hall Spinning Co., minutes 1874–78. Whalley (DDG) S. Longworth & Co., 19th and 20th c. records. Whitworth (DDX 639) Facit Mill Co., minutes 1904–26, 1941–62, inventory 1920, stock books 1956–67

Textiles, Wool:

Bury and Heywood (DDX 823) James Kenyon & Son, woollen weavers, purchasing journals 1834–70, production books 1820–79, accounts 1824–92, letter books 1866–1906, price lists 1867–1905, Crumble mill deeds 1714–1826

Thread Manufacturers:

Manchester (DDX 358) Ermen & Engels, partnership deeds 1862–74.

Water:

Haslingden and Rawtenstall (DDX 951) Waterworks Co., contracts 1862–63; Irwell reservoirs scheme papers and plans 1832–33; Padiham (UDPa) Waterworks Co., minutes 1854–75, share register 1854

Miscellaneous:

(DDX 614) agreement re manager of tartaric acid works, Bury, 1851. (DDHa) Shard Bridge Co., Hambleton, reports 1890, 1914, mortgage 1904, strengthening 1909. (DDX 118) Haslingden Great George Street Public Accommodation Co., papers 1851–79. (DDBd) Barrowford Industrial and Commercial Co. and Co-operative Manufacturing Co., liquidators' accounts, reports, etc. 1857–67. (DDCa) account book of Giles Pooley, London merchant 1653–58, of unidentified English merchant at (?) Leipzig 1638–39, and of Tarleton coastal trader 1752–55. (DDX 239) partnership deeds of Marsh & Francis, stoneware merchants, 1845 and Thompson & Marshall, commission agents, 1845, both Manchester. (DDX 142) R. Blezard & Sons, millwrights, Preston account books 1838–41, 1851–61, 1868–1900. (DDX 218) Preston telephone subscribers 1882

SOLICITORS' DEPOSITS

Ascroft, Whiteside & Co., Blackpool (DDA)

Title Deeds: Claughton-in-Amounderness 1734–1856; Freckleton 1741, 1829; Great Marton (water-mill) 1731–1800; Greenhalgh 1735–1882; Kirkham 1723–1850; Lea 1713–1830; Newton-with-Scales 1742–1851; Poulton-le-Fylde 1716–90; Ribby-with-Wrea 1820–39; Treales 1755–1802; Weeton-with-Preese 1772–1816; Westby-with-Plumpton 1766; Woodplumpton 1725–1859

Miscellaneous: Agreement for sale of copper of *Foudroyant* 1897; Wadman family certificates 1755–1838; inventory of Thomas Lewtas of Poulton 1774; apprenticeship indentures: cooper 1719, blacksmith 1829, tailor 1742

Baldwin, Weeks & Baldwin, Clitheroe (DDX/8)

Title Deeds: Colne 1563, 1736, 1775; Goldshaw Booth 1584–1777; Hapton 1785; Haslingden 1718–76; Higham 1769, 1776; Higher Booths 1788; Manchester 1801; Read 1634; Trawden 1681, 1798

Legal Papers: Volume of decrees, etc., relating to Honour of Clitheroe 1609–66; commission of bankruptcy, Thomas Dixon of Clitheroe, corn-merchant 1825; summons of George Culter for killing game 1815; commission of bankruptcy, Henry Armistead of Sabden, innkeeper 1831; case on repair of bridge over Ribble, *c.* 1811

Correspondence: James Pickup's cotton factory, Burnley 1806

Ecclesiastical Papers: Survey of Whalley glebe 1769–75; assessment for repair of Haslingden church 1788

Official Papers: County rate precept 1765; assessment for Higher Booths land-tax 1826–27

Accounts: John and Christopher Hargreaves estates 1808–11; James Hoyle, Bashall farmer 1807–34

Miscellaneous: Inventory of Widow Tillotson of Colne 1700; goods of Thomas Croysdale of Burnley 1827; rules of Sabden Charitable Society 1799–1829; rules of Preston Borough Court *c.* 1800

Boote, Edgar & Co., Manchester (DDEd)

Title Deeds: Bury 1887–1972; Castleton and Heywood 1811–1962; Chipping 1774–1866; Farnworth: Britannia Works 1838–1966; Garston 1790–1927; Great Sankey 1783–1964; Kearsley 1851–1973; Manchester 1740–1964; Manchester and Pendleton 1695–1958; Milnrow 1877–1975; Oldham 1716–1974; Preston 1858–

1965; Prestwich 1955–67; Rochdale 1944–68; Salford 1896–1960; Turton 1959–75; Withington 1920–61

Clarke, Oglethorpe, Lancaster (DDO)

Title Deeds: Cockerham 1543–1792; Forton 1773–1800; Heysham: Trumacarside 1686–1719, various 1658–1827; Lancaster: St. John's pew 1755–1824; Hardhorn-with-Newton 1657–1829; Hornby Honour 1731; Poulton and Thornton 1730–61; Preesall-with-Hackensall 1708–1810; Scotforth 1754–1849; Skerton 1764–1808; Thornton-le-Fylde 1672–1843; Yealand Redmayne 1623–1837; Caton, Overton, Ellel, Poulton-le-Sands, Morecambe, Singleton, Out Rawcliffe 1741–1939

Estate Papers: Cockerham boundaries 1636, 1702, 1751, 1798; survey of Jacksons in Hackensall 1790

Correspondence: Drainage of Marton mere 1732; slaving voyage to Virginia 1752

Legal Papers: Inquisition on bounds between Cockerham and Winmarleigh 1563; exemplification of customs of Cockerham (1362 and 1483) 1579; Lune fisheries 1795–1800; Adam Thornborrow's plantation in Berbice, West Indies 1822–1903; Burscough moss 1753

Plans: Cockerham 1745, c. 1780

Accounts: Ministers' accounts of Garstang rectory 1538–39, 1543–44; Cockerham manor 1540–41

Miscellaneous: Lancaster apprenticeship indentures 1832–76; conveyance of ship *Alice* of Ulverston 1809; apprenticeship indenture, Richard Dobson to Liverpool sailor 1723

H. Cross & Co., Prescot (DDCs)

Manorial: Bold: court-books 1783–1814, 1844–50; Burtonwood: court-books 1783, 1789, 1793, 1794, 1796, 1797, 1799, 1802, 1816, call-book 1795; Prescot: coroners' inquisitions 1847–59, court rolls 1510–1714

Title Deeds: Ashton-in-Makerfield 1639–1857; Aspull 1656–1840; Blackrod 1627, 1806; Burtonwood 1700–1850; Cronton 1688–1853; Ditton 1671–1829; Eccleston 1663–1849; Haydock 1779; Heath Charnock 1843–56; Huyton 1598–1856; Knowsley 1636–1801; Parr 1711–1866; Prescot 1741–1860; St. Helens 1797–1879; Scarisbrick 1773; Sutton 1637–1848; Whiston 1616–1747; Windle 1712–1866

Marsh family properties in Aughton, Eccleston, Knowsley, Prescot, Rainford, Rainhill, Sutton, and Wavertree 1700–80

Family Papers: Atherton estates in Prescot, Rainhill, and Whiston 1800–61; Bold pedigree 1722; Chorley pedigree *c.* 1774

Correspondence: Various 1803–67; dispute concerning pollution at Parr 1849–53; Plumbe's estate, Prescot 1749–66

Ecclesiastical Papers: Childwall rectory and tithes 1558–1833; faculty to enlarge Prescot church 1817; estimates for repair of Eccleston tithebarn 1814; Prescot parish: tithe-meeting minutes 1842–47; appointment of collectors for fund for Burtonwood minister and schoolmaster, with receipts 1694

Legal Papers: West *v.* Chantler (Anderton, co. Chester, salt) 1813; Williams *v* Master (debt) 1767–73; Hatton *v.* Gerard (debt) 1815–16; Pole *v.* Gerard (Ashton coal) 1813–21; Eccleston Hill school 1837–61; Patent Alkali Co. *v.* overseers of Eccleston (rates) 1852; Le Blanc process 1883

Official Papers: Prescot: gas-inspectors' accounts 1836–67, minutes 1859–66. Agreements for prosecution of felons, Ashton-in-Makerfield 1814, Prescot 1814. Royal Lancashire Militia, Prescot subdivision nominal rolls and papers 1802–53. Parr Mill Bridge rebuilding contract, plans, etc. 1824–34

Business Papers: Partnership, etc., papers: Mackay, West & Holt, glass manufacturers 1829–37; Southern & Southern, drapers 1786; Churchill & Spencer, alkali manufacturers 1844–47; Thomas Spencer, earthenware manufacturer 1848–54. Petition of Prescot and district watchmakers against duties 1798, papers of Robert Bolton, Wigan brassfounder 1752–1808; Warrington tobacconists' partnership 1786

Plans: Yew Tree, Eccleston 1817; Cuckstool Nook, Prescot 1839; Hanging Bridge, Sutton 1819; Roby Hall 1829; Prescot Hall estate 1869

Rentals: Childwall rectory 1783, 1785, 1788; Patten's Fylde estate 1809–15; Col. Fraser of Ravenhead 1820–44

Accounts: Erection of Prescot market house 1808–09; Anderton (co. Chester) salt works 1810–12; Mrs. Fraser of Ravenhead 1816–45; unidentified farmer 1819–25

Miscellaneous Papers: Enclosure at Aspull 1763, 1798; survey of waste lands enclosed in Sutton 1806–24

W. J. Dickson & Sons, Kirkham (DDD)

Deeds: Bryning Hall 1612–1823; Broughton (Preston) 1811, 1816; Burscough 1770; Catterall (including mills) 18th and 19th c.; Clifton marsh 1856; Elswick 1750; Fleetwood 1871–1883; Freckleton 1634–1871; Fulwood 1824; Goosnargh 1765; Great

Eccleston 1684; Greenhalgh-with-Thistleton 1612–28; Hambleton 1739, 1775; Hardhorn-with-Newton 1692–1745; Kirkham 1639–1896; Larbreck 1571–1731; Little Bolton 1848; Lytham 1886; Poulton-le-Fylde 1839; Preston, 1533, 1753–1819; Ribbywith-Wrea, 1622–1883; Roseacre 1673–1775; Walton-le-Dale 1675–1695; Warton 1710–1876; Meathop, Westmorland 1602–1740. (Many of these refer to the properties of Kirkham grammar school.)

Correspondence: Descriptive letter from Rio de Janeiro 1821

Ecclesiastical Papers: Licence for enclosing pew in Kirkham church 1676; faculty for pew in Kirkham church 1740

Plans: Kirkham property of Christ Church, Oxford 1843–48

Rentals and Accounts: Kirkham, rental 1748; Kirkham bailiff's accounts 1744–45

Miscellaneous: Inventories: John Kirkham of Larbreck, tanner, 1694; Nicholas Sharples of London, innkeeper, 1716

Kirkham apprenticeship indentures 1721–49; circular advocating Humane Societies 1789; Freckleton and Newton marsh-owners: minutes 1855–1901, accounts 1841–69, various papers 1746–1919; solicitor's diaries of W. J. Dickson 1857–1900; partnership agreement, Kay & Birley, Kirkham, flax-spinners, 1851; Richard Bradkirk's South Sea Company papers 1720–29; Birley family papers including deeds of Aughton, Bryning-with-Kellamergh, Freckleton, Kirkham, Bolton, Lytham, Ribbywith-Wrea, Warton-in-Amounderness, Woodplumpton 17th to 19th c.; Kirkham association for prosecution of felons 1814

Finch, Johnson & Lynn, Preston (DDL)

Title Deeds: Adlington 1305–1781; Anglezarke c. 1230–1754; Bretherton 1723; Burrow 1607–1850; Cantsfield 1807–40; Catterall 1832; Chorley 1715–1828; Didsbury 1683–1763; Dilworth 1797, 1802; Eccleston (Croston) 1697–1847; Elswick 1703; Freckleton 1726; Garstang 1728, 1752; Goosnargh 1642–1839; Greenhalgh-with-Thistleton 1703, 1731; Haighton 1590; Hambleton 1739–1823; Hardhorn-with-Newton 1777–1817; Heath Charnock 1569; Hindley 1647–1752; Kirkham 1767; Lancaster 1619–1786; Layton-with-Warbreck 1719–1842; Lea, Ashton, Ingol, and Cottam 1667; Leck 1634–1827; Leyland 1624–1834; Liverpool 1745–96; Marton 1738–1841; Mawdesley 1298–1785; Newton-with-Scales 1808; Out Rawcliffe 1724–67; Over Wyresdale 1709–28; Pilling 1839; Poulton-le-Fylde 1793–1844; Preston 1798–1857; Ribby-with-Wrea 1688, 1689; Rufford 1761–72; Scotforth 1722–1820; Shevington 1358–1835; Stalmine 1684–1821; Thornton-le-Fylde 1754–1829; Tockholes c.

1250–1823; Ulnes Walton 1790–1829; Walton-le-Dale 1674–1846; Wheelton 1754–97; Whitefield 1820–31; Whittingham 1511–1819; Wigan 1696; Withnell 1615–1754; Worthington *c.* 1250–1684

Estate Papers: Requests for sods, stone, etc., from Adlington waste 1666–1731; statement of the custom in Stalmine-with-Stainall 1787; agreement for repair of Hipping Hall, Tatham 1757

Correspondence: Letters concerning Manchester School of Design 1837–38; letter describing battle of Culloden 1746

Ecclesiastical Papers: Faculty for rebuilding Leck chapel 1739

Rentals and Accounts: Rentals of Gibson property in Lancaster 1797–1830; executors' accounts of Rev. Richard Prescott of Up Holland 1797–1811

Miscellaneous: Inquisitions *post mortem*: James Aughton of Adlington 1598, Robert Fleetwood of Wesham 1642; circular on opposition to removing assizes from Lancaster 1823; mortgages of tolls of Wigan to Preston turnpike 1823–34; grant of freedom of Lancaster to John Bannister of Bentham, co. York 1711; warrant to arrest straggling seamen 1756; apprenticeship indenture, Robert Whitaker of Walton-le-Dale, combmaker 1781; Adlington enclosure agreement 1763; reports of Lancaster canal committee 1852–61; precepts for bridge repair in Blackburn Hundred 1745; French interim passport for Sir William Bretherton 1840

Francis & Co., Cambridge (DDFr)

The Clitheroe papers of the 1st Earl Brownlow: deeds 1561–1802, Swan Inn papers 1719–48, Ridiough's burgages papers 1737–82, mill papers 1663, 1822, burgage papers 1772–1834 (including agreements, letters, lists of burgages, surveys, plans), borough papers 1620–80, election papers 1661–1830, Clitheroe and Preston turnpike papers 1865.

Miscellaneous Deeds: Hapton 1375; Holme, co. York 1656; Gisburn co. York 1723

Hamer & Park, Poulton-le-Fylde (DDHa)

Title Deeds: Carleton, Hambleton, Larbreck, Layton, Lea, Marton, Pilling, Poulton-le-Fylde, Thornton-le-Fylde 1720–1914

Hart Jackson & Sons, Ulverston (DDHj)

Title Deeds and Miscellaneous Papers: Aldingham 1709–1888; Blawith 1651–1815; Broughton East 1636–1829; Broughton-in-Furness 1783–1866; Cartmel 1586–1867; Dalton-in-Furness 1702–1836; Dunnerdale 1602–1779; Egton-with-Newland 1597–

1849; Flookburgh 1776; Grizedale 1587–1744; Hawkshead 1661–1765; Kirkby Ireleth 1691–1808; Lancaster 1748–1918; Lowick 1690–1809; Osmotherly 1711–1836; Pennington 1616–1873; Rusland 1721; Satterthwaite 1576–1778; Ulverston 1552–1885; Urswick 1748–1817

Other counties: Ulpha, Cumberland 1664–1901; Halifax co. York, 1792–1862; North Carolina 1753–65

Correspondence: John Wilkinson, ironmaster, to James Stockdale 1778–95; James Watt, engineer, to James Stockdale 1785–1803; James Stockdale from West Indies 1777; Samuel Smiles to James Stockdale 1860–65

Ecclesiastical Papers: Faculty for Ulverston pew 1700; Ulverston rectory papers 1836–64; Torver chapel papers 1860–64; licence to John Trant, curate of Flookburgh 1730

Family papers: Cartmel, Rawlinson, Rigge, and Petty families (inc. title deeds) 1551–1870

Manorial: court books of Muchland and Torver 1740–60, 1781–1845, 1849–1921

Plans: South Pennington 1821; Kirkby Low Demesne *c.* 1810; Crookland, Dalton-in-Furness 1872

Business Papers: Ulverston Mining Company, partnership 1840, dissolution 1866; patent for printing machinery, Stephen Soulby, Ulverston, 1852; agreement for sale of Thorphinsty charcoal 1760

Official Papers: Building of bridge, Newland, 1812; Lower Allithwaite land-tax assessment 1737; Leven fishery papers 1865–86; Kent, Bela, Winster, Leven, and Duddon Fishery Board proceedings 1881–1912; Satterthwaite assessments 1652–1707; Lonsdale subsidy roll 1623

Rentals: Ulverston rectory 1801–65

Accounts: Halton and Leighton furnaces and Caton forge 1752–56; Whitrigg ironworks 1779; schooner *Bee* 1844–50

Miscellaneous: The historical and antiquarian collections of James Stockdale, author of *Annals of Cartmel*; James Stockdale's geometry exercise book, Mr. Wood's school, Whitehaven, 1810; certificate of service, Charles Gray Rigge, R.N., 1829–67

Hill & Son, Ormskirk (DDHi)

Manorial: Clayton-le-Woods; verdicts 1674, 1802

Dalton: court roll 1507, verdicts 1812–24

Lathom: court book 1791–1811, verdicts 1753, 1754, 1757–60, 1762, 1763, 1765–73, 1775–90, 1810–17, call-books 1753–57, 1763–68, 1772, 1774–78, boundaries 1662, 1663, 1767

Ormskirk: boundaries 1662, 1693

Skelmersdale: verdicts 1812–24

Up Holland: court rolls 1362, 1371, 1423, 1524, 1526, 1532, 1538, 1595–1601, 1605–17, 1651, 1668, 1671–76, 1678, 1680, 1682–84, 1686–88, 1691, 1692, 1694–96, 1698–1701, 1709–16, 1719, 1721, 1723, 1726, 1728, 1735, 1737, 1740, 1743, 1756–61, 1764, 1766–69, 1773–75, 1777, 1779, 1782, 1784–87, 1789, 1793, 1795, 1799, 1801–04, 1806, 1810–47, 1849, 1850, 1852–62, 1864–67, 1874, 1875, 1877–80, 1882–92, 1901–28; court books 1599–1603, 1607–15, 1619, 1620, 1622, 1623, 1630, 1633, 1640, 1747–1892; verdicts 1709, 1711, 1723, 1728, 1737, 1739, 1743, 1757, 1812–33, 1839; call-books 1707, 1709–13, 1719, 1737, 1739, 1743, 1757, 1820–47; roll of customary tenants c. 1550; compoti (Up Holland, Kellet, Chorley, Lancaster, Wigan ,Aughton, Cuerdley, Halewood, and Samlesbury) 1420–21, 1428–30, 1432–33, 1438–39, 1500

Rentals: Clayton-le-Woods, Dalton, Lathom, Melling, Skelmersdale, Up Holland, and Westhoughton 1791–1803, Dalton 1827–34, Lathom 1817–34, Skelmersdale 1827–34

Miscellaneous: Marriage settlement of Hugh, son of Richard Jollybrand of Lathom, to Isabel, daugher of Hugh Mason of Lathom 1581; tithe awards (printed) Lathom and Melling 1839; account of comptroller to Lord Stanley 1460; Quarter Sessions roll (see frontispiece) 1550; elevation c. 1780 and plans c. 1870 of Lathom House

Holden & Wilson, Lancaster (DDHd)

Deeds: Allithwaite 1829–1917; Bolton-le-Sands 1871–1903; Borwick 1648–1871; Burrow 1800; Carnforth 1736–1888; Caton, Forge mill 1883–96; Ellel 1746–1877; Forton 1779–1902; Halton 1752–1886; Lancaster 1598–1920; Morecambe and Heysham 1863–1915; Over Kellet 1682–1880; Poulton, Bare and Torris-holme 1642, 1817–1883; Priest Hutton 1666–1896; Scotforth 1716–1891; Overton 1707–1808; Penwortham 1859; Preesall 1800; Preston 1865; Quernmore 1821; Roeburndale 1848; Skerton 1586–1899; Thurnham 1867–1893; Tunstall 1800; Warton 1794–1884; Wennington 1904, Pritt family deeds 1822–65. Sharp family deeds: Borwick, Carnforth, Priest Hutton, Scotforth, and Warton 1678–1935

Miscellaneous: Coroners' records 1898–1934; Lancaster Amicable Society: account-book 1857–1905, letter-book 1903–05; Lancaster Building Society papers 1896–98; Lancaster Printing Company papers 1901–02; Lancaster Railway Carriage Company papers 1880–1902; report on Heysham as harbour 1865; Morecambe Tramways papers 1888–1917; partnership agreement, Sharp, Fletcher & Co., ironfounders 1881; Slyne-with-Hest Building-land Syndicate letter-books 1898–1918; Thurnham Hall rental 1884–93, valuation 1868

Houghton, Craven & Co., Preston (DDH)

Title Deeds: Ashton-in-Makerfield 1565–1654; Bailey 1769–1839; Barton (Preston) 1752; Bolton 1797–1810; Bretherton 1804; Brindle 1650; Broughton (Preston) 1755–62; Burnage 1722, 1750; Caton 1703–1911; Charnock Richard 1706; Chipping 1815; Chorley 1719–1915; Claughton (Garstang) 1694–1824; Clayton 1659, 1812; Croston 1731; Dilworth, Lum mill 1762–1810; Eccleston (Prescot) 1795; Everton 1770; Fazakerley 1777, 1785; Fishwick 1756–61; Forton 1800; Freckleton 1774–1899; Golborne 1746–77; Goosnargh 1735–1859; Haigh 1730–84; Haighton 1671–1859; Hesketh-with-Becconsall 1767; Heskin 1691–1900; Hoghton mill 1824; Lancaster 1834–45; Lea 1822; Leyland 1760–73; Liverpool 1760–77; Longton 1712; Much Hoole 1722–1873; Musbury 1832; Newton-in-Makerfield 1793; Newton-with-Scales 1790; Osbaldeston 1784; Over Darwen 1828; Over Wyresdale 1757; Penwortham 1697; Pleasington Hall 1692, 1792; Preston 1738–1852; Samlesbury 1702, 1707; Skerton 1831; Ulverston 1749–1838; Upper Rawcliffe-with-Tarnacre 1597–1795; Walton-le-Dale 1584–1803; Walton-on-the-Hill 1733–1810; Wheelton 1785; Whittle-le-Woods 1729; Withnell 1728–1831; Woodplumpton 1773–1849; Yate Bank 1771

Legal Papers: Ribble weir at Brockholes 1757; commissions of bankruptcy, William Stephenson of Preston, linendraper 1816, Joseph Myers of Preston, wine merchant 1823; brief for new road from Westhoughton to Heath Charnock 1826; Ribble salmon fisheries 1755

Official Papers: Appointment of deputy-lieutenant 1839; letters patent for transfer of records to new sheriff 1840

Ecclesiastical Papers: Lease of part of St. Michaels-on-Wyre chancel 1737; Hoghton tithes 1827–28; faculty for gallery in Samlesbury church 1790; particulars of burials and pews in Chorley church 1635–58; sale of land in Goosnargh for curacy of Wyresdale 1735

179

Election Papers: Tallies, briefs and various papers in Preston disputed elections 1826 and 1868

Surveys: Valuations of Worsley Close Wood, Chorley 1795, 1798 and part of Hall i' th' Wood estate, Chorley 1800; survey of Preston and Ribbleton *c.* 1825

Rentals: Pleasington 1824, 1827–29

Plans: Crompton's estate in Chorley *c.* 1720; Redbank in Chorley 1804; Ogden Brook weir in Haslingden 1786; Munday's well, Preston 1832; Walton and Fazakerley enclosures 1698; Atherton and Crompton lands in Walton, Fazakerley, and West Derby 1769, 1777, 1784; Hoghton factory 1819; Martin Mere drainage 1828; Bimpson's in Heskin 1560; Dilworth 1813–36

Miscellaneous: Papers in Preston collection for Indian Famine Fund 1859; inventories of James Smith of Ashton-in-Makerfield and his wife 1788; Haighton Green and Cow Hill enclosure award 1813; patent and other papers for power-loom of Johnson and Kay, Preston 1805–26; partnership and dissolution agreements, Munday and Munday, Preston machine-makers 1837, 1841; inventories of Thomas Balshaw and John Cooper of Walton-le-Dale 1731, 1716; dissolution of partnership, Jackson, Stephenson and Swainson, Walton-le-Dale calico-printers 1809; subsequent partnership agreements 1811, 1815, 1818; Hoghton cottonmill sale catalogue 1826; Longridge Building Societies' account-books and papers 1793–1805

Apprenticeship indentures: Stalmine-with-Staynall 1774, Preston 1774–1804, Penwortham 1781, Farington 1782, 1787, Inskip 1782, Walton-le-Dale 1785, Woodplumpton 1783, Chester 1789

The papers of Richard Cookson of Goosnargh: Accounts: Whittingham Easter-roll 1695; Goosnargh church-ley 1775; Whittingham poor-tax 1777; Goosnargh rate-book 1845; Goosnargh mill accounts 1832–1839; Goosnargh, Whittingham, and Barton tithe-rent books 1853, 1875, 1876, 1878–85; Goosnargh school: register 1846–47; accounts 1832–36, 1868–72

"Black Book" Goosnargh school 1858–60

Memoranda books 1871–74

Census: various 1831–81

Manuscripts of unfinished history of Goosnargh, *Goosnargh Past And Present, Goosnargh Rambler.* etc.

O. Ladyman, Preston (DDLa)

Manorial: Longton: court-books 1744–49, 1757–63, 1765–73, 1781, 1815, 1816, 1827–31, 1842, 1849; estreats 1745, 1765–71, 1826; call-books 1744–48, 1815, 1816; deputations of stewardship 1780, 1816

Title Deeds: Blackpool 1797; Bury 1787–1806; Croston 1743–84; Eccleston (Croston) 1627–1802; Haighton 1704–85; Longton 1802; Standish-with-Langtree 1785; Preston 1782, 1832

Plans: Norris estate in Croston 1835; Longton Marsh 1838; Shawes estate in Preston 1802; Lancaster road, Preston *c.* 1835

Surveys: Thornton estate in Croston and Eccleston 1779; Lea 1783

Accounts: Thomas and Joseph Brockholes of Claughton 1742–76

Miscellaneous: Rules of Croston Union Society 1825; Longton Marsh: enclosure papers, leases, etc., 1776–1893; sale of deer from Stonyhurst 1777; inventory of William Yates of Trafford Hall 1813; grants of arms: Fazakerley of Chorley 1830, Hornby of Winwick 1863; oaths taken at Preston Quarter Sessions 1719–75; affidavits concerning damage to vessels coming to Preston 1826–34; commission in bankruptcy, William Woodcock of Preston, timber and wine merchant 1827; conveyance of pew in Preston church 1832; St. Michaels-on-Wyre tithes: surveys, assessments, etc. 1814–15

Peace & Ellis, Wigan (DDEl)

Title Deeds: Abram 1785–1904; Ashton-in-Makerfield 1770–1888; Aspull 1804–66; Blackrod 1873–74; Butterworth, Clegg Hall 1852–78; Coppull 1840; Culcheth 1696–1762; Golborne 1629–1788; Heskin 1711–31; Hindley 1802–64, Ranicars 1711–93; Hindley Green 1791–1824; Liverpool 1774–93; Lowton 1608–1856, Peel Ditch 1682–1787, Guests 1662–1856, Holcrofts 1698–1752; Orrell 1725–43; Pemberton 1688–1852; Tyldesley 1685–1824; Up Holland, Big Moor 1656–1870; Urswick 1731; Westhoughton 1806–74; Wigan 1654–1891, Wigan Lane 1780–1825, Standishgate 1671–1825, Scholes 1688–1824, Bridge Hey 1676–1771, Jollys House 1633–1816, Mesnes Lane 1809–34, Tickles House 1807–21, Scholes cottonmill 1791–1810, Wigan Lane factory 1792–1803

Leases: Aspull 1860, Hindley 1865–89, Pemberton 1853, Skelmersdale 1798–1829, Southport 1818–69, Up Holland 1875, Westhoughton 1805, Westhoughton mill 1898–99, Wigan 1818; Coalmines in Adlington 1910, Aspull 1910, Blackrod 1910, Coppull 1886, Hindley 1852–95, Rainford 1848–66, Shevington 1836, Wigan 1845–1910, Worthington 1910)

Family Papers: Settlements, wills, correspondence, etc.: Baldwin of Adlington 1794–1842, Heron and Penson of Wigan 1820–1910, Jolly of Wigan 1633–1848; list of heirlooms at Wrightington Hall 1881

Pearson & Pearson, Kirkby Lonsdale (DDPe)

Title Deeds: Cantsfield 1593–1907; Sefton 1696–1726. Other counties: co. York: Burton-in-Lonsdale 1598–1903; Thornton in Lonsdale 1601–1898. St. Vincent (W. Indies) 1784

Survey: Burton-in-Lonsdale (co. York), Cantsfield, and Tunstall 1768

Plan: Cantsfield 1865

Miscellaneous: Lancaster, admission of burgesses, 1724

Pilgrim & Badgery, Colne (DDBd)

Title Deeds: Barley with Wheatley Booth 1651–1910; Barrowford 1525–1866; Blackburn 1659–1852; Blackpool 1797–1873; Briercliffe-with-Extwistle 1493–1849; Burnley 1622–1854; Clayton-le-Dale 1608–1849; Clitheroe 1641; Colne 1550–1913; Dinckley c.1300; Foulridge 1613–1855; Goldshaw Booth 1622–1869; Habergham Eaves 1691–1819; Haslingden 1614–1862; Heysham 1726–1861; Higher Booths 1705–1824; Liverpool 1737–1842; Marsden 1570–1892; New Laund Booth 1770–1833; Newchurch-in-Rossendale 1690–1792; Old Laund Booth 1671–1800; Over Darwen 1846; Padiham 1719–1852; Tatham 1726; Tottington 1761; Trawden 1549–1873; Barley and Wheatley Booth 1619, 1889; Worston 1793, 1844; Yate and Pickup Bank 1782–1872; Little Marsden; other counties: Skipton (co. York); Salterforth (co. York)

Family Papers: The principal families referred to in this collection are Driver, England, Foulds, Hargreaves, Sagar and Worswick; Trustill family (inc. Brierfield Mills) 1854–1919; Ecroyd family, inc. Farrer Trust c.1900; will and coat of arms of William Farrer; Astley family, Trawden 1830–1930 inc. Heirs House estate 18th–20th c.; Folds family inc. sale of Wrea Green Manor House 1873

Correspondence: Foulridge tithe 1848–53; Hargreaves of Heirs House, family affairs in England and Georgia, U.S.A. 1817–70; Marriott property in Marsden 1792–1867; Trawden enclosure 1820–57; Tatham enclosure 1850–53; sale of Burnley militia barracks 1883–84; Burnley curacy 1812–1901; Colne Methodist Society 1814–15. There are large numbers of letters, etc., not yet sorted relating to East Lancashire turnpike trusts and railways, and the Leeds and Liverpool canal, late 18th to 19th c.

Legal Papers: Barrowford mill 1853; Barrowford bridge widening 1815–16; Swinglehurst v. Robinson (Clough estate) 1809–16; Chipping roads 1896–99; Tillotson v. Hargreaves (Abraham Hargreaves will) 1804–23; Walton v. Hartley (Marsden) 1786;

Wycoller boundaries 1616–1788; presentation to Burnley church 1725, 1814; Oldham-Ripponden turnpike 1853–57; correspondence, etc., about Barrowford School 1893–1932; Gargrave footpath case 1925; petitions opposing creation of Earby U.D. 1908; Nelson Water bills 1888, 1918; Colne Grammar School foundation 1880–1920

Business Papers: Partnership agreement: Hargreaves & Hargreaves, Blackburn attornies 1856; Colne arcade papers 1881–87; Over Darwen Gaslight Company, minutes and papers 1840–55; reports of Evona Investment Co., Salt Lake City 1914–20; Colne Savings Bank 1844–74; weekly lists of closing share prices at Liverpool Jul.–Dec. 1842 and railway share prices Jan.–Dec. 1843; Messrs. Bolton & Hargreaves, solicitors, 1845–70; Colne Water Estates 1860–1940; inventory and valuation of contents of Nelson Inn 1856; Union Club House Building Society, Colne 1816–31; correspondence, etc., about purchase of Colne Gas Co. by the local Board 1877; Astley's Brewery inc. terrier of public houses 1888–1924; celebrations in Burnley and Colne of the marriage of Prince of Wales 1863; partnership papers Wm. Ecroyd & Sons late 19th c.; school bills, Pembroke House, Lytham c.1890; Calf Hall Shed Co., Barnoldswick late 19th and early 20th c.; North Western Central Railway (never built) c.1890; Colne Amusements Ltd., and King's Theatre, Colne 1911–20; Palace and Empire Picture Theatres, Haslingden 1914–17; Wm. Hartley and Messrs. Hartley & Pilgrim 19th & 20th c.

Ecclesiastical Papers: Burnley: list of subscribers 1714; division of seats 1722; deeds 1719–1837; faculty for alterations 1872; Haslingden: allocation of pews 1778; Trawden, papers 1843–44; Colne: chapel revenue papers 1632–1909 with correspondence 1750–1891

Plans: Barrowford: Park Hill and Mill Holme, c.1790; Colne: Sagar pasture c.1752, Standroyd c.1800, Townend Meadow 1841, Leech House c.1880, Hothole Croft 1824, Greenfield mill 1825, 1842, Heyroyd 1845; Blakey Hall 1791, c.1800; Marsden: Spring-Gardens, Hagg, and Lenches 1836, Sagar & Hartley's lands 1845, Catlow 1873, Edgend c.1850; Newchurch-in-Rossendale: Wolfenden c.1830; Over Kellet, Hall Garth estate 1904–24; Rochdale: Hamer Bottoms 1868; Yate and Pickup Bank: Quaker Fold 1859; New Laund Booth highways 1815

Rentals: Burnley curacy rentals 1821–25, 1837, 1878–87; Hargreaves estates in Barrowford and Colne 1804–13, 1823–66

Accounts: Hargreaves accounts 1804–68; Burnley church and school 1798–1802; William Crook of Nelson, draper, 1843–62; John Dewhurst of Padiham, brassfounder, executors', 1850–53

Miscellaneous: Agreement for public clock in Colne 1841; Colne Patriotic Fund, Foulridge subscriptions 1854; inventories: John Pollard of Foulridge, farmer, 1819, Matthew Pollard of Lower Bradley, yeoman, 1827, Robert Shepherd of Oldham, yeoman, 1813, Thomas Thornber of Vivary Bridge 1848, Mrs. Ingham Walton of Barrowford 1879, John Whalley of Trawden 1854; inquisitions *post mortem*: Robert Briercliffe of Briercliffe 1617, James Foldes of Trawden 1635, William Sagar of Marsden 1617; numerous probate documents; exercise books Whitefield House Academy, Roby *c.*1846

Plant, Abbot, & Plant, Poulton-le-Fylde (DDPb)

Title Deeds: Bispham-with-Norbreck; Carleton; Greenhalgh-with-Thistleton; Hambleton; Kirkham; Lytham; Marton; Pilling; Poulton-le-Fylde; Preston; Staining, Hornby's Charity 1721–52; Thornton-le-Fylde; inc. school 1735–1806; Westby 1656–1861;

Miscellaneous: Blackpool Sunday School Sick Society accounts 1835–40; lawyers' diaries 1827, 1830–38, 1840–52

Robinson & Sons, Blackburn (DDX/223)

Title Deeds: Accrington 1836; Billington 1780, 1801; Blackburn 1750–1890; Blackpool 1799, 1867; Church 1734–1849; Dutton 1758, 1781; Freckleton 1777; Great Harwood 1777, 1779; Haslingden 1817; Haulgh 1766; Heywood 1785; Hutton 1785; Livesey 1784; Manchester 1789; Padiham 1791, 1811; Pendleton 1647, 1811; Pleasington 1604–1709; Preston 1808; Ribchester 1690–1765; Rishton 1817; Turton 1780; Urmston 1695–1870; Whalley 1833–60; Yate Bank 1681

Ecclesiastical Papers: Whalley tithes: deed of association 1810, accounts 1834–35, various 17th and 18th century papers; survey of archbishop of Canterbury's Lancashire lands 1616

Business Papers: Dissolution of partnership, Wilkes & Peel, cotton manufacturers 1799. Award concerning Canal New Mills, Blackburn 1870; partnership agreements: Dutton & Haworth, Blackburn brewers 1807; Hornby, Newsham & Haworth, Blackburn cotton-manufacturers 1826, 1829; Hornby, Newsham & Kenworthy, Blackburn cotton-manufacturers 1834; Johnson, Taylor & Chadwick, Blackburn brewers 1832; correspondence of Manchester agent of Leeds and Yorkshire Assurance Co. 1842–43

Miscellaneous: Inventories of William Rishton 1669, Elizabeth Rishton 1672, of Friarhill in Accrington; contracts for building Blackburn and Over Darwen railway stations 1847, and Blackburn goods warehouse 1848; Blackburn disputed election: briefs, depositions, etc., 1868; Colne, Foulridge, and Pendle Forest rental 1772–73; army papers of Capt. Thomas Gartside of Manchester 1801–59

Satterthwaite & Swainson, Lancaster (DDX/70)

Plans: Addington estate in Kellet 1781, 1806, 1808; Brockholes weir on Ribble 1806; lands in Halton and Caton 1796; Conder mill in Scotforth and Quernmore 1829; manor of Caton Hall 1777 (from original of 1626); parts of Aughton and Caton 1786 (from original of 1745); Skerton new weir on Lune c.1800; Scarthwaite in Quernmore 1821; the Lune at Halton and Caton 1795

Miscellaneous: Records relating to Lune fishery at Halton 1782; commission of bankruptcy, Richard Tomlinson of Lancaster, shoemaker, 1817; Torrisholme moss drainage award 1789; surveys of Halton 1799 and Nether Kellet 1821; book containing verdicts of manors of Cockerham 1732–47, Hornby 1731–53, Tatham 1732–53, and Holme 1732–37, and Preston Patrick 1733–38, Westmorland; Lancaster elections: John Wilson Patten accounts 1830, and his agent's minute-book 1847

Shuttleworth, Dallas & Crombleholme, Preston (DDCm)

Title Deeds: Caton 1849–73; Chipping; Goosnargh; Hardhorn-with-Newton 1725–1885; Liverpool 1725–98; Lytham 1855–66; Osbaldeston 1702–1864; Pendleton (Whalley); Preston 1841–65; Singleton 1757–1863; Thornley; Walton-le-Dale 1718–1876; Weeton-with-Preese 1753–1864; Whittingham 1640–1732; Woodplumpton 1801–1909

Legal Papers: Blackburn, rectory, manor, and commons 1341–1842; marriage settlement of Richard Willis of Halsnead to Lucy Atherton 1819–41; exchequer order for payment of Forton tithes 1679; agreement for Winckley Square, Preston 1807, and for Preston dispensary 1810

Family Papers: John and William Gregson, Liverpool 1807–63 with account books 1821–52; Latham family, Wigan 1733–1835 inc. letters from Philadelphia 1760–70

Correspondence: Preston militia fund 1844–59; Preston Pleasure Ground (inc. accounts) 1876–84

Miscellaneous: Conditions for sale of Halton properties 1834; costs of Hallé Orchestra's visit to Preston Guild 1862

Turner & Smith, Preston (DDTs)

Title Deeds (other than Barton Estate, see below): Alston 1780–1887; Balderstone 1813–87; Barrow-in-Furness 1870; Blackpool 1855–95; Brindle, Roman Catholic chapel 1839–54; Broughton (Preston) 1602–1887; Carnforth 1825; Claughton-in-Amounderness 1874; Clayton-le-Dale, Showley Hall 1680–1866; Clitheroe 1868; Dutton 1655–1720; Fishwick 1868; Fleetwood 1851–87; Freckleton 1727–1860; Fulwood 1626–1720; Grimsargh 1803–87; Kirkham 1813–1909; Liverpool 1842–80; Lytham 1881–88; Manchester 1850–90; Newton-with-Scales 1810–48; Preston 1629–1884; Ribchester 1780–1872; Salford 1850–90; Walton-le-Dale 1815–63; Whittingham 1704–1862; other counties: Cumberland, Sebergham 1766–1841; Derbyshire, New Mills 1849–62

Family Papers: Chadwick of Preston (later of Essex and Worcestershire): deeds and correspondence 1774–1890; Fielding of Ribchester: farming ledger 1817–50, correspondence 1826–96, plan of Seed Green 1855, deeds 1820–70; Roskell of Preston: correspondence and accounts 1825–68; partnership agreement Arrowsmith & Roskell, bankers, 1825; abstracts of bank ledgers 1833–60; Shepherd of Liverpool: accounts, deeds, etc., 1840–80; Threlfall of Broughton and Lytham: correspondence (brewery, railways, etc.) 1860–95; Walmsley of Showley in Clayton-le-Dale: correspondence, etc., 1780–1820

Business Papers: Longridge: Building Society papers 1822–35; Preston: Marsh Lane Foundry, liquidation papers 1865–80; Theatre Royal, correspondence, playbills, accounts and deeds 1867–79; various inns, correspondence and deeds 1812–97

Barton (Preston) Estate (see also p. 329): Manorial: Barton court books 1769–1831; title deeds: Barton 1545–1899, Bilsborrow 1603–1887, Chipping 1603–1720, Goosnargh 1553–1887, Ribbleton 1602–1720, Woodplumpton 1594, Barbon, Westmorland, 1817; leases 1669–1729; tithe leases 1611–82; settlements 1598–40; inquisitions *post mortem* Thomas Barton 1554, 1604

Plans: Whittingham Lower End *c*.1780

Miscellaneous: Higher Brockholes farm, Grimsargh: farm-diaries and accounts 1920–22; Teebay of Preston, account-book 1760–81; Preston apprenticeship indentures 1820–50; Ribchester National school: correspondence, deeds and plan 1871–72

Slater, Heelis and Co., Manchester (DDSl)

Title Deeds: Salford estate Ackers-Shakerley 1648–1922; Flixton School 1672; Radcliffe and Pilkington Gas Co. 1845; Chorley

Colliery Co. 1910–26; Ashton-under-Lyne, Bury, Kearsley, and Whitworth 1790–1900

Winder and Holden, Bolton (DDHw)

Deeds and papers of Pilkington and Andrews estates in Ainsworth, Little Lever, Middleton and Rivington c.1300–c.1880. Westhoughton colliery deeds 18th and 19th c. Deeds of Greene's estate in Leigh 18th to 20th c. Plans of Kearsley Moss 19th c.

Witham, Weld & Co., Liverpool (DDWw and DDX/754)

Title Deeds: Anderton, R.C. school 1871; Clayton-le-Woods 1814–73; Crosby 13th to 20th c.; Darcy Lever, Dove Bank; Halliwell The Boot; Quernmore 1794; Wheelton, Windy Harbour 1683–1796

Legal Papers: Grant of wreckage at Formby 1670; the Ogle Roll c. 1602, copies of deeds of property in Whiston

Manorial: Crosby court rolls, 16th to 19th c.; Sefton halmote rolls 1299–1412

Family Papers: Weld Blundell family inc. Herbert Weld Blundell, African traveller 1880–1930 and estate papers, inc. Bowland, 18th & 19th c.; Molyneux Seel of Huyton 19th c.; Scarisbrick estate 19th and 20th c.; Fitzherbert-Brockholes family and estate 18th and 19th c.; Peter Atherton of Liverpool, machine-maker and inventor 1790–1850; Standish of Standish 1785–1889; Towneley of Towneley 1762–1922; Marsland of Habergham Eaves 1813–97

Woodcock & Sons, Bury (DDWo)

Title Deeds: Accrington 1730–1875; Ainsworth 1864; Birtle 1753–86; Blackburn 1796–1856; Broughton (Salford) 1787; Bury: Chesham estate 1681–1869, Lees estate 1601–1845, Union foundry 1805–82, St. Paul's church 1842, various 1795–1877; Castleton: Chamberlane estate 1783–1855; Chadderton 1638–1827; Cheetham 1825–46; Chorlton-on-Medlock 1838–67; Cliviger 1795–1870; Elton: Cobhouse Nabb 1731–1851, Hall de Hill 1766–1831, Woodrode 1597–1750, various 1698–1834; Farnworth 1878; Habergham Eaves 1855–59; Harwood: Christ Church school 1850; Heap 1788–1833; Great Heaton 1602–1825; Hindley: Ranicars estate 1730–1900; Horwich 1699–1877; Kearsley 1808–29; Little Hulton 1809; Liverpool 1843–60; Lower Booths 1832; Manchester 1776–1802; Newchurch-in-Rossendale 1731–1902; Pendleton (Salford) 1836–39; Pilkington 1698–1848; Quarlton 1812; Salford 1724–87; Spotland 1696–1870; Tottington Higher End 1723–1850; Tottington Lower End 1688–1862; Walmersley-with-Shuttleworth: Burrs tenement

187

1708–1833, Baldingstone school 1716–1822, Craggston tenement 1704–1825, Patmoss Methodist chapel 1842–58, various 1800–85; Worsthorne-with-Hurstwood 1795–1870

Leases: Birtle-with-Bamford 1829–60; Bury: Hampson mill 1813–22, Butcher Lane mill 1847, Stanley mill 1850–57, Redivales mill 1877, Chesham land 1876–1904, various 1779–1877; Edgworth coalmines 1815; Elton 1714–1889; Heap and Heywood 1821–80; Hindley coalmine 1896; Pilkington 1810–71; Prestwich 1745–70; Spotland 1882; Walmersley-with-Shuttleworth 1772–1863

Mortgages: Elton to Blackburn road-tolls 1824–25; Heap poor-rates 1855–56; Unsworth cotton-mill 1844–50; Whitworth Manufacturing Company 1867–72

Plans: Bury: Brickhouse estate 1850; Cheetham, disputed land 1835; Elton: Hall de Hill estate 1784, Summerseat 1809; Heap: Schofields estate 1838, 1839; Kearsley: Stoneclough 1873; Little Hulton: smithy 1809; Pilkington: Smethurst estate 1848; Tottington Higher End: Holhouse 1780; Tottington Lower End: Lower Ashenbottom 1826, Wash estate 1828, Dick Field estate 1841, Foul Coats 1841; Walmersley: Rowlands estate 1848

Rentals: Sir W. H. Clerke's estate, Bury, 1809–17

Surveys: Elton:Hall de Hill 1763, 1784, Summerseat 1809, Elton 1780; Harwood 1798; Heap: Schofields estate 1838; Tottington Higher End: Holhouse 1780; Tottington Lower End: Wash estate 1828, Lower Ashenbottom 1826, Dick Field estate 1841, Foul Coats 1841; Walmersley: Rowlands estate 1848

Charity Papers: Bury: Robert Shepherd's charity, apprenticeship indentures 1672–1750, candidates for relief 1744–67, appointments of trustees 1687–1852

Business Papers: Lancashire and Yorkshire railway, branch line in Radcliffe, Cheetham, Prestwich and Pilkington: reports, valuations, deeds, etc., 1875–82; Bury & Tottington District railway: report, accounts, etc., 1882–88; Southport Waterworks: correspondence, reports, accounts, etc., 1876–1901; Bury Crown Brewery: correspondence, deeds, etc., 1888–1910; various businesses in Bury, mainly cotton firms: correspondence, deeds, sale catalogues, etc., 1820–90

Ecclesiastical Papers: Copies of baptismal registers, Dundee Independent Chapel, Holme 1699–1730, 1800–37

Miscellaneous: Wills, late 17th to late 19th c., with index 1755–1839; 18th and 19th c. papers of many families, especially Hamer of Summerseat, Kay of Bury, Openshaw of Bury, Ormerod of Rossendale, and Shaw of Bury

Woodcock & Sons, Haslingden (DDX/118)

Title Deeds: Bacup 1814–1929; Edenfield 1816–95; Edgworth 1834–1921; Habergham Eaves 1826; Haslingden 1614–1948; Lower Booths 1769–1910; Manchester 1786–1882; Mellor 1635–1830; Musbury 1806; Newhallhey 1664–1903; Newchurch-in-Rossendale 1756–1889; Over Kellet 1925–60; Ramsbottom 1710–1867; Ramsgreave 1722–90; Spotland 1666–1905; Tottington 1613–1885; Walmersley-with-Shuttleworth 1797–1944; Bacup, Newchurch-in-Rossendale, Cowpe-with-Lench, Spotland, Accrington, Birkdale, Burnley, Rawtenstall, Littleborough 1746–1963;

Yorkshire: Waddington 1604–1891; West Bradford 1731–1920

Estate Papers: Minerals in Honour of Clitheroe 1548–1889; survey of Tottington Lower End 1794

Legal Papers: Admittances qualifying solicitors and their clerks to take surrenders in Honour of Clitheroe 1871–1911; Holden *v.* Mordacque (Halsingden Church school) 1852–57; Haslingden Gas, Light & Coke Co., 1856–58

Business Papers: Laneside Foundry, Haslingden, letter books 1842–1960, various 1845–66; partnership agreement, Nuttall & Fox, Ramsbottom and Rio de Janeiro, commission agents and merchants 1864

Official Papers: Haslingden lighting and watching, various, 1844; account for repairing road at Musbury 1824; Tottington assessments 1793–1811; Rossendale assessments 1727, 1728; Haslingden and Rawtenstall waterworks, various 1851–62

Ecclesiastical Papers: Faculty for enlarging Edenfield chapel 1739; grant of gallery in Newchurch chapel 1754; sale of pews in Edenfield chapel 1764; papers concerning footpaths through Haslingden churchyard 1876; papers concerning a pew and church-rate at Haslingden 1828, 1846

Election Papers: Haslingden: notices and songs 1875, 1888, 1890; South Lancashire: papers 1861, 1865

Accounts and Rentals: Account for measuring Tottington common 1622; Tottington rental 1662

Plans: Haslingden turnpike road 1814; Edge Side mill, Newchurch-in-Rossendale 1840; Edgworth Stone Delf 1852; land in Ainsworth 1842; Burnley 1841; Cobham estate, Rossendale *c.*1830; Hardmans mill, Newhallhey, 1861; Haslingden court-house and school *c.* 1820; lands in West Bradford, co. York 1815; road at Waddington, co. York 1801; Horncliffe estate in Tottington 1751, 1789, 1836, 1851, 1881; part of Great Harwood 1820; Crawshaw Booth, Spotland, Rawtenstall, Haslingden and Newchurch-in-Rossendale 1850–82

Miscellaneous: Agreement for right of way in Spotland 1746; Woodcock pedigree 1732–1944; apprenticeship indentures, Haslingden, Tottington 1821–99; Private Lane, Haslingden, papers and accounts 1830–76; Waddington, co. York, common, letters and papers 1801–13; cotton famine: statement 1862 and report 1863; papers of Edenfield toll contracts 1875–78; papers concerning Newchurch-in-Rossendale highway upkeep 1881–82; agreement for upkeep of road at Flaxmoss 1795; sale of schooner *Mischief* 1851

ESTATE AND FAMILY MUNIMENTS

It is, perhaps, in the class of private muniments that the public spirit has to the greatest degree manifested itself, for it is true to state that the Lancashire Record Office now houses the muniments of almost all the great Lancashire estates, as well as of a number of smaller ones. It will be noticed how many of these remained in the same families for six, seven, even eight hundred years, only occasionally descending through a female line.

Alison of Park Hall, Charnock Richard (DDAl)

This estate, based on a moiety of the manor of Charnock Richard, was in the hands of a branch of the Hoghtons of Hoghton until about 1710 when, on marrying the heiress of the Daltons of Thurnham, the name was changed to Dalton. The Park Hall estate was sold in 1789 to William German and descended to his great-grandson Henry Alison, who was county treasurer 1860–1916.

Title Deeds: Charnock Richard 1603–1818, Euxton 1655–1722, Shevington coal 1792, Up Holland 1654–1825, Welch Whittle 1691

Family Papers: Settlements 1683–1830

Estate Papers: Surveys: Charnock Richard 1665, Rough Park in Up Holland *c.*1770

Archibald of Rusland (DDAr)

The Rusland estate was founded in the 16th century by a cadet branch of the Rawlinsons of Graythwaite whose descendant sold it in 1762 to Thomas Walker whose grand-daughter carried it in 1832 to her husband Charles Dickson Archibald, of a Nova Scotia family.

Title Deeds: Colton 1545–1927, Walney Island and Low Furness 1703–1896, Nova Scotia 1856–68

Family Papers: Settlements 1690–1881

Estate Papers: memoranda on timber sales 1832–54; Northscale tenants' resolutions on rabbit-shooting and stick-gathering 1793; Rusland Hall rental 1838–53; enclosure agreements 1842 and 1861

Correspondence: Letter-books of Charles William Archibald 1869–93

Legal Papers: Law papers 1586–1636

Business Papers: Agreement for sale of iron cinders 1608; conveyances of bloomery 1720 and 1726; hammer-man's agreement 1802

Official Papers: Finsthwaite, Haverthwaite and Rusland: poor account 1700, assessment 1728, removal order 1743

Accounts: Timber accounts 1768–71, personal accounts 1882–1927

Assheton of Downham (DDHCl)

The Honour of Clitheroe was granted to George Monck, newly created Duke of Albemarle, in 1661. From him it descended to the Dukes of Buccleuch and in 1884 was apportioned to Lord Henry Scott who, in 1885, was created Lord Montagu of Beaulieu. He created the Clitheroe Estate Company in 1898, which later passed the property to Ralph Assheton, later Lord Clitheroe.

The Honour of Clitheroe: records, including court rolls and books 1311–1925, with indices 1660–1925; call books and indices 1909–25; stewards' accounts and vouchers 1760–c.1830; rentals 1884–1923; extract books 1722–1925; Barclay's map and survey 1804–10; Oddie's plan of Clitheroe 1781; 18th c. copy of 1662 survey; mineral leases and plans 19th and 20th c.; miscellanea 17th to 20th c.

The Manor of Slaidburn: records, including court rolls and books 1392–94, 1519–1925, with indices from 1660; extract books, custumals, etc., 17th to 20th c.

Clitheroe Estate Co.: directors' minutes 1898–1910, 1929–45, correspondence and miscellanea 20th c. (from the Montagu Estate Office)

Bankes of Winstanley (DDBa)

The manor of Winstanley was purchased in 1596 from Edmund Winstanley (whose family had held it from the early 13th century) by James Bankes who, although a London goldsmith, was a member of a Wigan family.

Manorial: Winstanley; court books 1665–77, 1717–95, call books 1672–76, 1716–22; Up Holland: custumal 1675

Title Deeds: Pemberton: Rawlinson's estate (including property in Fulwood) 1753–1869; Clapgate estate 1731–1828; Fairbrothers 1757–1876; Hawkley estate 1680–1847; Hawardens Estate 1760–1839; Hindley Hall, Holmes House, Longley House, Jolleys, etc., 1747; Taylors, Lamberhead Green 1685–1875; Lime Vale 1780–1867; Moss House Farm 1827–63; Norley 1700–1872; Pegges or Worthingtons Farm 1710–1855; Shelley House 1687–1853; Somerscales estate 1737–1828; Stone House 1657–1850; Turners o'th'Brook 1792–1825

Ashton-in-Makerfield: Park Lane estate 1658–1864

Billinge: Bispham Hall estate 1573–1872; Cowleys Tenement 1771–1851; Colsheds 1576–1800; Harpers or Wilsons Tenement 1655–1837; Knowles Tenement 1799–1858; Longshaw estate 1714–1877; Lime Vale 1696–1833; Marsland estate 1712–1871; Moyers Tenement 1749–1851; Strawberry estate 1811–74; miscellaneous 1570–1780

Newton-in-Makerfield: Newton Park 1624–1829

Orrell: Lower House and Round Thorn 1781–1850; Taberners or Catteralls 1641–1850; Windus cottages 1813–63; miscellaneous 1596–1757

Up Holland: Ayrefield 1553–1879; Rothwells House 1752–1860; Church Seats 1696–1822; Toppings estate 1725–1835; Tower Hill Farm and Delph 1613–1869; miscellaneous 1569–1888

Urmston: miscellaneous 1625–52

Winstanley: miscellaneous 1327–1824

Wigan: Tarleton Meadow and Barrow Meadow 1613–1849; Pottery estate 1802–73; Thompson's Pierhead 1802–53; Strines 1618–1871

Family Papers: Settlements 1601–1821; mortgages and bonds 1722–70; grant of arms, Holt of Bispham 1841; diary of William Bankes, M.P., 1660; cornet's commission of William Bankes 1666; memoranda book of James Bankes 1586–1617

Estate Papers: Register of deeds 1530–1770, survey 1776, coal leases 1792–1875; Winstanley colliery accounts 1676, 1766; plans of alterations to Winstanley Hall by Lewis Wyatt 1818–19; visit book of Winstanley tenants 1833

Legal Paper: Barton v. Holme 1750–52, Hawarden v. Bankes 1750–62, Homes v. Stanley 1801–33, Bethel v. Cross 1847–69

Charities: Eddleston's charity, Billinge 1672–1796

Ireland Blackburne of Hale (DDIb)

King John granted the manor of Hale to Richard of Meath in 1203 from whom it descended to the Irelands, then, in 1675, to the Aspinwalls through marriage. They held the property only until 1733, when another marriage brought Hale to the Greenes. A further marriage in 1752 made Thomas Blackburne of Orford owner of Hale.

Manorial: Hale: court rolls 1655, 1705, 1708, 1709, 1713, 1719–22, 1728, 1729, 1734, 1735, 1737–50, 1752, 1754, 1755, 1757–64, 1766, 1768–72, 1774–77, 1780, 1781, 1786–91, 1795, 1796, 1798, 1800, 1801; court papers 1707, 1719, 1722–24, 1728, 1729, 1733–35, 1738–50, 1752–54, 1758, 1760, 1761, 1763, 1764, 1766, 1768–72, 1774, 1775, 1777, 1779, 1781, 1787–91, 1795–97; water-bailiffs' warrants and accounts 1724–30, 1732, 1737, 1755–70, 1772, 1773, 1788, 1800, 1812; coroners' inquests 1711, 1712, 1716, 1721, 1723, 1742, 1743, 1752, 1757, 1761, 1769, 1772, 1774, 1778, 1779, 1787, 1793, 1799

Title Deeds (including leases): Hale *c.*1210–1590, leases 1321–1718; Hale Charter Roll 1203–1411; Burscough 1655; Croft *c.*1260; Culcheth *c.*1240–1542; Garston 1329–49; Lowton *c.*1280–1471; Ormskirk 1620; Penketh *c.*1240–1513; Poulton-with-Fearnhead 1382–1633; Ribby-with-Wrea *c.* 1280–1304; Sefton 1365; Warrington (Austin Friars) *c.* 1240–1780

Other counties: Cambridgeshire, Crawden 1532; London 1367; Middlesex, Edmonton 1509

Family Papers: Settlements and wills 1321–1704; bonds and acquittances 1378–1628; pedigrees: Ireland of Salop *c.*1580, Ireland of the Hutt and Lydiate *c.* 1630, Ireland of the Hutt 1589 (by Thomas Chaloner, Irish king-of-arms), Ireland of the Hutt *c.* 1600

Legal Papers: Writs and commissions 1386–1616

Ecclesiastical Papers: Hale chapel: rebuilding 1757–59, new bells 1814; Hollinfare chapel: grant of advowson 1526

Official Papers: Shrievalty accounts 1743

Miscellaneous: Letters of confraternity, Chester Dominican friary 1469; Privy Council letter to John Ireland, lieutenant of Isle of Man concerning the bishop of Man and the Book of Common Prayer 1611; release of William the Botyler to Gilbert of Culcheth and his tenants of Warrington of the need to provide a beadle 1300

Blundell of Halsall (DDBb)

Title Deeds: Liverpool 1781–1837, Ulverston parish 1624–1787, West Derby 1659–1857

193

Family Papers: Settlements, etc., 1731–1871, wills 1581–1832

Business Papers: Co-partnership agreements 1776–81

Ecclesiastical Papers: Halsall church advowson deed 1781–1853, faculty 1872

Miscellaneous: Account book of William Trenow of Liverpool 1684–1719, then of Bryan Blundell 1734–42 (including overseas trade and Bluecoat school); journal of Bryan Blundell (with ship drawings) 1687–1756

Blundell of Little Crosby (DDBl)

Robert, great-grandson of Osbert of Ainsdale (living 1160), took the name Blundell in the second quarter of the 13th century and through the marriage of his grandson David to Agnes Molyneux, heiress of Little Crosby, the estate came to the Blundells. The main line failed in 1737 on the death of Nicholas Blundell, whose heiress Frances married Henry Pippard, a Liverpool Irish merchant. Their son in 1772 took the name Blundell. For accounts of the family see: *Crosby Records*, Chetham Society, Vol. 12; T. E. Gibson, *A Cavalier's Notebook* and *Nicholas Blundell's Diary* 1702–1728; M. Blundell, *Cavalier* and *Blundell's Diary and Letter Book* 1702–1728.

Manorial: Great Crosby: halmote rolls 1461, 1586–90, 1599, 1668. 1669, 1674, 1677, 1678, 1739, 1750–53, 1756, 1770, 1771, 1774, 1775, 1791, 1795, 1797, 1798, 1802, 1821–25, 1832; minute book 1839–62; suit roll 1845–51

Little Crosby: court rolls 1557, 1565, 1568, 1570, 1574, 1576, 1580, 1589, 1591, 1604, 1606, 1616–19, 1622, 1624, 1626, 1628, 1634, 1637; court books 1657, 1658, 1660, 1665, 1671, 1673, 1698, 1702, 1704–07, 1709, 1711–13, 1718, 1828–52; estreats 1569, 1574, 1576, 1580, 1634, 1637, 1657, 1658, 1660, 1667, 1702, 1704, 1706, 1715

Title Deeds: Altcar 1799, Aughton 1329, 1404, Bickerstaffe 1412, Billinge 1720, Bold 1329, 1541, Childwall c.1200–50, Claughton-in-Amounderness 1369, Coppull 1253, Eccleston (Prescot) 1314–1544, Formby 1275, 1328, Freckleton and Kellamergh 1410, Great Sankey c.1250–1340, Halewood 1339, Hindley 1379–1684, Huyton 1417, Lathom c.1220, Litherland and Orrell c.1220–1433, Liverpool 1377–1709, Newton-with-Scales 1329, Penketh 1339–61, Rainford c.1270–1522, Rainhill 1321–1426, Sefton 1311–1411, Thornton c.1270–1773, Tyldesley c.1260–1362, Walton-on-the-Hill 1276, Much Woolton 1282, Allerton c.1280, Elswick 1321, Hale 1279, Ince Blundell c.1270–1770, Widnes 1509

Ditton, Wheathill 1615–1723, Ditton c.1250–1810

Great Crosby c.1190–1818, Little Crosby c.1220–1850, Little Crosby, Moorhouses c.1250–1720

Other Counties: Cheshire: Cuddington 1331, Noctorum 1702–37; Northamptonshire: Whittlebury 1610–67; Staffordshire: Newcastle-under-Lyme 1403–05; Shropshire: Bishops Castle 1254, Walcot 1278

Ireland: these deeds and papers, relating principally to the Dowdale and Pippard families in Dundalk, Drogheda and Dysart c.1282–1807, were transferred to the National Library of Ireland in 1948.

Family Papers: Settlements, etc., 1278–1809

Diaries: William Blundell's tour in British Isles 1805, William Blundell's tour to France, Germany and the Netherlands 1818, William Blundell's tour to the Netherlands 1821, F. Smith's voyage to Sydney 1840, John Blundell at Thirsk 1841–42, William Blundell junior's voyage to Egypt 1845–46, Agnes Smythe's tour to Europe 1842, Nicholas Blundell's honeymoon in Europe 1847–48, William Blundell's diaries 1834–54, Nicholas Blundell's diaries 1846–89, Agnes Blundell's diaries 1855, 1872, 1886, William Blundell's diary 1866, Nicholas Blundell's memoranda 1869–90

Bonds and acquittances 1390–1593, general pardon to William Blundell 1626, account of life and death of Mrs. Blundell 1707

Estate Papers: Tenants' books, giving a very detailed account of every tenement, with a great variety of memoranda and advice on management: Little Crosby, etc., 1659–1806, Ditton 1710–68

Ditton rentals 1625–29. Little Crosby and Ditton surveys 1653. Little Crosby harvest book 1748–70

Correspondence: Miscellaneous letters on many subjects, including Great Crosby school, relief of British prisoners in France, bathing machines, elections, etc., 1800–40; vestments at Crosby 1781; settlement on marriage of William Blundell 1808–09; management of the estate 1821–28; executorship of will of Capt. Henry Trafford of Croston 1816–27, ensigncy of William Blundell 1835–37; executorship of will of Charles Tempest of Broughton 1836; Capt. William Blundell and his death in Burma 1850–53

Legal Papers: Recusancy of various members of the Blundell family 1590–1679; Blundell v. Molyneux 1519–27; notes, etc., on the Jacobite plot trial at Manchester 1694

Official Papers: Appointments: William Blundell, captain, 1642, John Wood, lieutenant, 1686, William Blundell, ensign, 1836, lieutenant 1840 and captain 1849, William Blundell, major and deputy lieutenant 1811 and lieutenant-colonel, 1823, Nicholas Blundell, captain 1831, Philip Smith to be in charge of chaplains in household of Duchess of Orleans 1661

Account of arms in Little Crosby, Great Crosby, Ditton, and Warrington 1570

Estreat roll of minstrels' court of Cheshire 1703

Orders of deputy lieutenants concerning William Blundell's provision of arms 1673–75

Licence by James II to Richard and Judith Latham of Liverpool, being Catholics, to practice surgery and keep a boarding school

Accounts: Stewards' accounts 1763–77, 1807–16, 1820–52; wages books 1822–31, 1842–48; accounts of executors of Nicholas Blundell 1737–69, 1795–1806; rent ledgers 1793–1804, 1814–46; cash books 1795–1828, 1850–67; accounts of Capt. William Blundell in India 1850–52

Ecclesiastical Papers: Dispensation for marriages of Henry Blundell and Anne Leyland 1522, and of James Blundell and Margaret Butler 1515; account of making the Harkirk burial ground and the finding of Saxon coins there

Miscellaneous: Inventories of William Blundell 1638, Nicholas Blundell 1640, and Emily Blundell 1640; inventory of plate at Crosby Hall 1876

Blundell of Ince Blundell (DDIn)

Richard Blundell first appears as lord of Ince in the late twelfth century and from him it—together with the extensive properties purchased by Robert Blundell in the mid-seventeenth century— descended to Charles Robert Blundell who died in 1837, devising his property to a distant kinsman, Thomas Weld of Lulworth Castle, co. Dorset, who took the additional name of Blundell.

For an account of the family see T. E. Gibson: *Lydiate Hall and its Associations.*

Manorial: Birkdale and Ainsdale: court books 1637, 1757–94, 1814– 17; call books 1748–78, 1864–90; Formby: court books 1638–39, 1725–33

Title Deeds (including leases): Adlington 1627, Ainsdale leases 1624– 1921, Aintree (Cockersand abbey) 13th c., Allerton 1301–45, Anderton leases 1715–25, Aughton 13th c.–1822, Bickerstaffe (Cockersand abbey) 13th c., Billinge 1540–89, Birkdale 1553– 1687, leases 1598–1931, Broughton-in-Amounderness 1599– 1825, Childwall rectory 1593, Chipping 1620–1786, leases 1666–

1834, Clifton-with-Salwick 1613, Clitheroe 13th c.–1725, Colne 1556, Downholland c.1280, Edgworth 1600, Farnworth 1571, Formby 1499–1933, leases 1515–1829, Forton 1662, Great Crosby 1771, 1811, Hale and Halewood 1316–82, Halsall (St. John of Jerusalem) 12th c.–1796, Hambleton 1232, Heath Charnock 1439, Heaton 1332–1724, Horwich 1580–1715, Ince Blundell (Stanlaw and Merivale abbeys) 13th c.–1815, leases 1259–1921, Ireby 1605, Kirkby 1814, Little Crosby 13th c.–1763, Liverpool 13th c.–1561, Lostock (Cockersand abbey) 13th c.–1562, Lydiate 13th c. –1748, leases 1671–1923, Maghull c.1260–1766, Mawdesley 1513, Melling (Cockersand abbey) 1302–1623, leases 1561–1849, Much Woolton 1388, Ormskirk 1399–1751, Pendleton (Clitheroe) 1581–1608, Preston 1377–1627, leases 1543–1854, Rumworth 1563–1714, Scarisbrick 13th c.–1578, Sefton church 1684, Thornton (windmill) 1552, 1809, Tyldesley 1598–1602, Ulverston 1574, Wiswell 1459

Other counties: Chester 13th c.–1341; Essex: Southminster 1550, 1673, Little Totham and Goldhanger, 1595; Kent: Greenwich 1650; Yorkshire: West Bradford 1423–1634, Kirkby Ravensworth rectory 1544–94, Patrick Brompton rectory 1602–16

Family Papers: Wills 1443–1778, settlements 1315–1795, bonds and receipts 1363–1729, inquisition *post mortem* of William Blundell 1547, inventory of James Blundell 1542, general pardons of Robert Blundell 1487, Robert Blundell 1556, Robert Blundell 1604, and Robert Blundell 1626, inventory of heirlooms 1841 and of pictures 1931

Estate Papers (leases are shewn with title deeds): Enclosure of part of Birkdale Common for school 1769, agreement for dividing Formby sandhills 1669, agreement on flooding in Ince Blundell and Little Crosby 1713, agreement for cleaning watercourses 1758, lease books 1688–1712 and 1721

Correspondence: Various letters 1570–1831, including references to harvest boons 1623, Rivington chapel 1637, the Lydiate settlement 1725–29, Catholic emancipation 1810 and 1826

Legal Papers: Various cases 1462–1810, including Eccles and Deane tithes 1545, Smithills 1582, Ince Blundell tithes 1618, boundaries 1626, Westhoughton tithes 1701, Ainsdale warren 1719–31, Lydiate gravel 1798–1803, Ince heirlooms 1810, Preston houses 1754–68

Ecclesiastical Papers: Eccles and Deane tithes 1546–1671, agreement on vicarage of Bolton-le-Moors 1461, declaration on use of money for Formby R.C. chapel 1807, ordination of sub-deacon of Burscough priory, 1470, Eccles and Deane churchwardens' accounts 1486 and 1535

Plans: Aughton c.1770, Broughton-in-Amounderness 1813, Ince Blundell town-field 1729, Ince Blundell farms 1781–1800, 1859–64, Ince park c.1770, 1796, Ince windwill c.1800, Lydiate Hall and park c.1770, Lydiate plantations 1809, Melling Cunscough farms 1766, Formby and Birkdale c.1662, Fulwood development 1878–96, Preston 1805, 1809, Birkdale 1809

Rentals and Accounts: Rentals: General 1842–1958, Tyldesley c.1540, Sir Richard Molyneux 1539–73, Heaton 1611, Lydiate and Cunscough 1624–25, 1692, 1697, 1699, 1752–54, Ince Blundell c.1721, 1765–76, Formby and Birkdale 1738–40, 1764; accounts: general 1576–77, 1774–75, 1893–1915, estate 1763–78, stewards' 1763–1860, Anderton stewards 1704–09, Ince Hall wagesheets 1813–33, 1882–90

Surveys: Exchange between Henry Blundell and the Earl of Sefton 1769–77, Chipping 1831, Formby 1845, Ince Blundell 1861, Lydiate and Aughton 1862, Ince Blundell, Melling, Lydiate, Formby, Ainsdale, and Birkdale 1913

Charity Papers: John Goore's charity, Lydiate: appointment of new trustees 1677

Alt Drainage: Rebuilding Alt bridge 1677, papers on scouring the River Alt 1696–1702, arbitration papers 1698–1701

Foreshore papers: A large collection of miscellaneous items bearing upon foreshore rights on the southwest coast of Lancashire 1292–1901; grants and papers re development of Birkdale foreshore 1894–1910

Miscellaneous: Grant of livery of the manor of Manchester 1509, inspeximus of inquisition on boundaries of Downholland moss 1548, coroner's inquest on Richard Bucke of Sefton 1556, letters patent granting chantry lands in Lancashire, Staffordshire, Cheshire, and Yorkshire to the hospital of Savoy 1558, account of the trial and execution of the earl of Essex c.1600, order of assizes concerning settlement in strange parishes 1629; agreement with rector of Sefton on potato tithes 1789, Ainsdale church papers 1913

Bourne of Stalmine (DDBo)

Cornelius Fox of Stalmine was one of the purchasers of the estates forfeited by the Butlers of Rawcliffe for the part they played in the Jacobite rising of 1715, and it was by the marriage of his daughter and heiress to John Bourne of Wyresdale that the family acquired its interests in the Stalmine and Hackensall district. Later members had trading interests in Liverpool.

Title Deeds (including leases): Carleton lease 1729, Hambleton lease of a saltcoat 1698 and of enclosed land 1705, Hutton 1760–90, Liverpool timberyard, etc., 1787–1823, Pilling 1768–74, Preesall-with-Hackensall 1559–1803, Rawcliffe 1677–1808; Stalmine-with-Stainall 1621–1860, Thornton Stanah land 1583; other counties: Yorkshire: Westby estate 1699–1744

Family Papers: Settlements, etc., Westby 1661, 1729, Bourne 1842, wills 1783–1856

Correspondence: Various 1736–1858, rebuilding Kirkham church 1820–23, Mowbreck estate 1808–34, fishing in Upper Rawcliffe 1814, Rochdale canal 1794–1805, wreck off Stalmine 1855–59

Legal Papers: Stalmine tithes 1829

Business papers: Rochdale canal profits and losses 1792–1802

Official Papers: Stalmine tithe meeting minutes 1837, Preesall tithe meeting minutes 1837

Ecclesiastical Papers: Faculty for rebuilding Kirkham church 1821, repair of Stalmine church 1727, Stalmine church terrier 1700, Kirkham petition for endowment of church and enforced residence of clergy 1834

Plans: Kirkham church 1820–21, Stalmine hall c.1820, land in Stalmine 1826, Wyre harbour c.1840

Rentals and Accounts: Rentals: Stalmine, Preesall, Rawcliffe, and Hambleton 1843–56, Mowbreck 1834, Cornelius Bourne's estate 1806; accounts: Preesall mill 1743–48, Stalmine mill 1729–40, John Bourne's accounts 1820–33

Braddyll of Portfield in Whalley (DDBr)

The Portfield estate was acquired by John Braddyll, of nearby Brockhall, in 1580 and it remained with his descendants, along with the rest of their Whalley properties, until it was sold to James Whalley of Clerk Hill (see Greenwood of Clerk Hill p. 220).

The undermentioned documents are the only known surviving ones of this estate, having been preserved by a descendant of Richard Cottam, steward of the property in the mid-18th century.

Title Deeds: Accrington, Antley, and Donishope 1543–1622, Downham tithes and barn 1546, Haslingden waste 1557, Oswaldtwistle 1560–1674, Pendleton licence to alienate 1542, Ribchester and Dutton 1564, Samlesbury manor and hall 1686–1692, Whalley and Billington 1542–1688, Wiswell licence to alienate 1544, Worston 1624–55

Other counties: London and Middlesex: Gracechurch Street 1684, Hatton Garden 1684, Tottenham 1675–76; Yorkshire: Bowland 1517–1671

Family Papers: Appointments: bailiff of Ennerdale, Cumberland 1568, surveyor of Duchy of Lancaster woods and forests 1559, receivership of Cumberland, Westmorland, and Lancashire 1611

Pardons: unlicensed alienation, Armeston, co. Lincoln, 1595, general 1559, 1604 and 1626; settlements, etc., 1554–1688, wills 1575–1693

Ecclesiastical papers: Whalley abbey: confirmation of grant of Toxteth and Smeedon 1316, licence to grant moiety of manor of Billington 1318, confirmation of vicarage of Whalley 1331, inspeximus of plea roll concerning trespass in Rossendale 1347, exemplification of annexation of St. Michael in Castro, Clitheroe, to Whalley church 1368, exemplification of plea in chancery concerning various activities of abbot 1377, confirmation of grant of advowson of Whalley 1399, letters patent settling dispute over Bowland tithes 1482

Rentals: Rental of estates in Whalley, Billington, Dinckley, Accrington, Lancaster, Bashall, Bowland and Samlesbury 1756–73

Miscellaneous: The King's speech to Parliament 1694; appointment of deputy lieutenants 1676 and 1685

The Earl of Bradford (DDBm)
The muniments of his Lancashire estate.

Title Deeds: Adlington and Anderton 1533–1727, Bolton 1581–1815, Darcy Lever 1735–1805, Ditton and Knowsley 1386–1499, Farnworth 1563–1793, Great Lever 1595–1793, Haulgh 1533–1793, Ince-in-Makerfield 1423–77, Kearsley 1533–1793, Middleton 1533–1793, Rainhill 1381, Standish 1533–1793, Tonge 1533–1793, Walton-on-the-Hill 1453–1793

Colliery accounts: 1667–19th c.

Rentals: 17th–19th c.

Plans: Great Lever 1728, estates in Bolton, Great Lever and Farnworth 1770

Bretherton of the Hey (DDBt)
The family of Bretherton (later Brotherton) appears in Newton-in-Makerfield towards the end of the 14th century, but does not seem to have acquired the Hey until about 1520. In 1820 the estate was sold to the Leghs.

200

Title Deeds (including leases): Newton-in-Makerfield 1395–1812, leases 1552–1758, Hindley 1690–1711, Roby 1540, Westhoughton 1604–1722, Winwick 1630–1726, tithe lease 1743
Other counties: Cheshire: Crowley 1656–1809, Over Whitley 1618–70; Hampshire: Leckford 1668–1752; Wiltshire: Dunhead and Ham 1670–1810

Accounts: Bank-books: William Browne Brotherton 1800–05, Mrs. M. B. Brotherton 1812–19, Thomas Smith 1805–19

Correspondence: William Urmeston to cousin William Sale 1586, Thomas Grymesdiche, Warrington, to William Urmeston, Leigh 1597, T. H. Brotherton, Vigo Bay, to his mother 1811, unsigned to W. B. Brotherton 1815

Miscellaneous: Indulgence, Stafford hospital 1479, quietus for subsidy 1544, episcopal decree concerning burial place in Winwick church 1617, papers on recusancy of John Bretherton 1655, certificate concerning election of Sir James Forbes and Thomas Brotherton as M.P.s for Newton-in-Makerfield 1691

Stapleton-Bretherton of Rainhill (DDBt)

Deeds and papers of Rainhill, Cronton, Ditton, Sutton, and Ince-in-Makerfield 17th–20th c.

Fitzherbert-Brockholes of Claughton (DDFz)

Claughton was purchased by Roger of Brockholes in 1338 and Heaton-in-Lonsdale came to John of Brockholes by marriage about 1380. The Heskeths of Mains succeeded, through marriage, in 1751 and, again through marriage, the estate came to the Fitzherberts in 1783.

Manorial: Heaton: court papers 1736, 1759, 1767, 1768, 1775, 1778–82, 1785, 1788, 1789, 1804, 1806, 1810, 1815, 1822

Title Deeds: Claughton: Cobble Hey and Peacock Hill c.1280–1856, Cowfawes 1618–1832, The Carrs 1792–95, Mount Pleasant 1693–1860, Walkers 1693–1825, Crabtree Nook 1766–1805, Hamilton Green 1714–99, Barn Fields 1706–69, Allotments 1731–1825, Langfield House 1758–1802, Higher Birks 1602–1763, Innfield 1656–1862, Fleet Street 1555–1818, Sturzaker House 1568–1818, Walmesley Bridge 1713–1835, Claughton Green 1758–1814, Nook 1774–1850, Stubbins 1724–1874, Town Croft 1749–1830, various 1281–1580; Poulton-le-Fylde: Carr Bridge 1768–48, Fayles 1574–1770, Arley 1768–1862, Boonfalong 1789–1832, Ords Carr 1753–1815, Carr Meadow 1802–12, Bridge Meadows 1821–36, various 1326–1856

Aighton, Bailey, and Chaigley c.1290–1584, Balderstone 1657, Billington c. 1290, Bilsborrow 1637, Bretherton 1446–1540,

Carleton 1634–86, Catterall c. 1290–1876, Church 1295–1392, Cliviger 1540, Croston 1540, Freckleton 1532, Garstang 1421–1629, Goosnargh 1447–1825, Grimsargh-with-Brockholes 1414–1681, Halewood 1414–79, Hambleton ferry 1833, Heaton 1387–1878, Lancaster 1373–1770, Little Eccleston 1421–1669, Marton c. 1290, Much Hoole 1446–1525, Myerscough park 1809–16, Nateby 1704, Newsham 1546, Ormskirk 1558, Osbaldeston 1657, Oswaldtwistle 1343–92, Overton 1668–1836, Penwortham 1534, Preston 1414–1704, Rawcliffe 1704, Ribbleton 1639, Singleton 1602–1851, Tarnacre 1612, Tatham 1363–1444, Thornton 1500–1713, Warton 1538, Witton 1386–1404, Woodplumpton 1652

Family Papers: Settlements 1524–1855; wills 1587–1828; grants of arms 1783, 1875, royal licenses for change of name 1782, 1875, papers on election of William Fitzherbert-Brockholes to County Council 1888

Correspondence: From Roman Catholic bishops, etc. 1758–1803

Official Papers: Claughton survey and valuation 1730; papers on stopping-up of Claughton roads 1824

Ecclesiastical Papers: Poulton-le-Fylde Breck R.C. chapel 1822–66

Rentals and Accounts: General rentals and accounts 1766–95, 1818–64, wage-book 1854–69, stewards' accounts 1747–1800, household accounts 1783–1810, Claughton rentals 1781, 1811–13, 1816, 1823–26, Claughton and Myerscough rentals 1818–21, Mains (Singleton) rentals 1803, 1817, 1822–24; Claughton and Mains rentals 1820–21, Heaton rentals 1816, 1817, 1823, 1824, 1826, Heaton and Mains rentals 1818, 1820, 1822, 1825, 1826, Lancaster rental 1812, Heaton and Lancaster rental 1800–03

Miscellaneous: History and accounts of North Staffordshire hunt 1884–98; Garstang Habitation of Primrose League: minutes 1894–1911, register 1894–1909, cash-book 1894–1911

Earl Brownlow (DDFr)

Deeds, election papers, etc. Clitheroe 17th to 19th c.

Calvert of Broughton and Preston (DDX 1029)

Deeds and papers 1668–1895

Cavendish of Holker (DDCa)

The estate of Holker was acquired by Christopher Preston after the suppression of Cartmel priory. The eventual heiress, Catherine, married Sir William Lowther of Marske, bart., and their son married Elizabeth Cavendish, daughter of the second duke of Devonshire. In the meantime, a distant relative, Sir Thomas Preston, about 1680 gave the Furness abbey estate to the Jesuits; for which action it was forfeited and thus came to the Prestons of Holker. When the second Sir William Lowther died in 1756 he left the Holker and Furness estates to his cousins, Lords George and Frederick Cavendish. Unfortunately no trace has been found of any mediaeval documents.

Manorial: Cartmel: court books 1613, 1658–1721, 1683–1709, 1711–22, call book 1725

Title Deeds: Aldingham: Colt Park 1694–1729, Gleaston Castle 1671–1720; Allithwaite: Hampsfell and Grange Fell 1783–1802, Cartmel Town: 1610–1801 (see also Holker); Dalton-in-Furness: various properties (including watermills) 1615–1792; Holker: various properties 1523–1804, Tarbucks House 1685–1720, Turners tenement 1597–1707, Taylors 1543–1731, Richardsons 1696–1769, William Preston's 1597–1707, Cark properties 1629–1774, Twiceadays 1625–1775, Hirds House 1668–1773, Mosses 1632–1835, Bigland Scar 1783–1801, Walton Hall 1771–1801, Cark papermill and Cark and Holker cornmills 1660–1726; Kirkby Ireleth: land and slate-quarries 1751–81; Lancaster: houses 1728–49; Urswick pasturage 1808

Family Papers: Wills 1685–1828; elegy and epitaph on Thomas Preston 1679; Preston pedigree c.1700; Preston and Lowther inventories 1692–1705; pedigree of Hilton, Tyson and Stapleton families 16th c.; grant of baronetcy to William Lowther 1697; petition for William Cavendish to stand for Northern parliamentary division of Lancashire 1832

Appointments: Deputy lieutenancies 1663, 1676, 1685, 1688, 1702, captaincy of Thomas Preston 1676 and 1683, colonelcy of Sir William Lowther 1702, lieutenancy orders 1663 and 1675; nominal roll of Major Preston's Company 1684

Estate Papers: Survey of Gleaston and Colt Park 1682, diversion of road from Parkhead 1775, valuations of Furness farms 1796, valuations of Kirkby Ireleth 1772, lists of Kirkby Ireleth enfranchisements 1780

Correspondence: Estate and household administration 1726–1803, Cartmel enclosure 1792–96, Cartmel rectory 1794–97

Miscellaneous letters 1665–1805 on such subjects as Sir Thomas Lowther's attendance in Parliament 1731, schoolmaster at Cartmel Fell 1768, architectural designs 1787, rainfall at Lancaster 1784–88, Backbarrow cottonmill 1790, Staveley curacy 1793, reclamation of Kent Sands 1787, coalworks around Holker 1776, from, *inter alia*, Sir Robert Walpole, the bishops of Chester and Llandaff, and John Carr of York

Legal Papers: Papers in Saule and Gibson *v.* the trustees of Heversham school 1686, claim to forfeited Furness estate of Sir Thomas Preston 1663–96, taking of wood by lessees of iron ore pits 1707, Wollaston and Lake *v.* Preston and Lowther re claim to the manor of Furness 1711–26, Woles *v.* Hird *re* tithe customs in Dalton-in-Furness 1715

Business Papers: Letters and papers concerning trading by the schooner *Britannia* of Lancaster 1759–61; account book of English merchant at (?) Leipzig 1638–39; account book of Giles Pooley of London, merchant 1653–58; accounts of coasting venture, based on Tarleton 1752–55

Official Papers: North Lonsdale land tax assessments 1746, Allithwaite and Holker assessments 1694

Ecclesiastical Papers: Cartmel rectory: title deeds 1556–1746, valuation 1764, bushel tithe agreements 1651–1705, Easter dues 1745 and 1791, tithe corn books 1669–1767; various tithe papers 1649–1763

Dalton-in-Furness rectory: title deeds 1613–1726, tithe books 1738–63, Easter dues 1642, 1738–96, valuation 1796

Burton-in-Kendal rectory: accounts 1663–65

Plans: Cartmel mossdales 1793, Bigland and Holker roads, late 18th c.

Rentals and Accounts: Preston family estates 1663–66; Angerton moss 1682 and 1726; Thomas Preston's debts 1692–95; Sir William Lowther's estates 1702–15; Furness, Holker, and Cartmel 1711–96; Furness 1728–1916; Stainton iron-mine 1664–66; Anthony Lowther of Marske 1677–80 and his widow 1702–15; Lord George Cavendish 1765–81; J. H. Richardson's bill-book 1788–97; John Robinson's accounts 1795–1802; labourers' vouchers 1796–98; wheat-farm and dry-moulter rents of manor of Muchland 1624–1769; general account 1905–8

Charity Papers: Inquisition concerning gift by Sir Thomas Preston of all the iron-ore in Furness to poor of Dalton and Urswick 1678; various papers concerning pensions to poor of Dalton, Aldingham, and Urswick 1638–1745; appointment of Brow Edge schoolmaster 1724

Miscellaneous: Papers concerning the Lancaster election of 1768, including lists of freemen 1689–1767 and schedule of window tax 1766

Farming partnership agreement 1777

Cavendish of Brindle and Inskip (DDCv)

The manor of Brindle was held by the Gerards of Brynn from the mid-14th century until 1582 when it was sold by Sir Thomas Gerard to help to pay the heavy fine inflicted on him for his alleged support of Mary, Queen of Scots. The purchaser was William Cavendish, ancestor of the dukes of Devonshire, but it eventually passed to a junior branch of the family, the lords Chesham. Inskip belonged to the Keighleys from 1285 until the end of the 16th century when it passed by marriage to the above-mentioned William Cavendish, with whose descendants it remained until sold to the earl of Derby in 1843.

Manorial: Grant of court leet, Brindle, 1614

Title Deeds: Brindle 1568–1843; Inskip 1585–1600

Family Papers: Settlements 1747–75, mortgages 1589–1842

Estate Papers: Leases: Brindle 1591–1866, Inskip 1692–1772, Walton-le-Dale water-scheme papers 1878–82

Ecclesiastical Papers: Institution of James Starkey to Brindle 1594; Inskip tithe 1841

Plans: Great Eccleston and Inskip 1841, Walton-le-Dale water supply 1878

Clifton of Lytham (DDCl)

In 1170 the manors of Clifton and Salwick were in the possession of Walter son of Osbert, whose son William was the first to take the surname Clifton. It may well be that at the same date the manor of Westby-with-Plumpton was also held by the family, though it is not specifically mentioned in the documents until the early 1200s. In 1606 the manors of Lytham and Little Marton were acquired by purchase while the manor and rectory of Kirkham were held on lease from the Dissolution until the 19th century. Settlements made on marriages with the Molyneuxes of Sefton have resulted in documents relating to that family being found among the Clifton muniments.

See R. Cunliffe Shaw, *The Clifton Papers*

Manorial: Clifton-with-Salwick: court books 1677–91, 1702–12, 1727, 1733, 1736, 1738–46, 1748, 1750, 1752, 1756–58, 1760–65, 1768–70, 1772, 1773; call books 1736, 1737

Ellel: court rolls 1589–92, 1605, 1606, 1666, 1667, 1670

Halton (Cheshire) Honour (including Halton, Runcorn, More, Whitley, Antrobus, Cogshall, Bidston, Kelsall and Widnes): 1355–56

Kirkham: court rolls 1582, 1591, 1611–12, court books 1680–1811

Layton: call-books 1787–96, 1817–45

Little Marton: court book 1639–89

Lytham: court rolls 1504, 1514, 1517, 1518, 1522–26, 1529, 1533, 1539, 1541, 1543, 1559, 1563, 1577, 1596, 1605–08, 1610; court books 1611–1712, 1731, 1739, 1741–44, 1746, 1754, 1757–60, 1762, 1763, 1765–69, 1772, estreats 1606–17

Salford Wapentake and Portmote: court rolls 1540–41, 1546–47

Westby-with-Plumpton: court rolls 1569, 1581, 1584, 1610, court books 1611–1712

Title Deeds (including leases): Altcar 1328–1583, leases 1716–18; Ashton-with-Stodday 1343; Astley 1604; Aughton 1372; Bilsborrow 1436; Birkdale and Ainsdale leases 1618–33; Bispham-with Norbreck 1798; Blackrod 1607–08; Bleasdale 1552–1777, leases 1650–1713; Bootle-with-Linacre 1342; Broughton 1605; Bryning-with-Kellamergh 1607, leases 1561, 1604; Carleton leases 1631–1751; Caton (St. John of Jerusalem) *c.*1250; Catterall 1635, 1650; Charnock Richard 1404; Clifton-with-Salwick 1370–1880, turbary 1559, leases 1560–1827; Cuerden lease 1611; Dalton *c.*1260–1583, lease 1605; Down-holland *c.*1260–1590, leases 1588–1620; Eccleston 1627, lease 1611; Little Eccleston tithes 1661, 1680; Ellel *c.*1250 (Cocker-sand abbey), lease 1719; Elswick 1606; Euxton *c.*1270–1627; Formby 1538–1631, leases 1577–1625; Freckleton 1376, 1606; Goosnargh leases 1561–1825; Greenhalgh-with-Thistleton 1611, tithe 1530; Haighton 1794; Halsall 1379–1621, leases 1594–1621; Hambleton tithe lease 1543; Hardhorn-with-Newton 1686–1779; Heskin 1556; Heysham rectory 1574–1640; Ince Blundell 1377, 1388; Kirkby 1596; Kirkdale 1682; Kirkham 1371–1864, rectory 1610–1853, leases 1568–1850, rectory leases 1503–1850; Lancaster 1596; Lathom 1608–28; Layton-with-Warbreck 1596–1875, leases 1609, 1754–1816; Little Marton leases 1568–1877; Liverpool 1311–1787; Lowton 1406; Lydiate 1502; Lytham *c.*1190–1895, leases 1606–1869, grant to Durham priory *c.*1190, agreement on common 1608; Maghull 1467–1660; Medlar tithe 1612; Melling 1281–1634; Much Woolton 1710–1785; Newton-with-Scales leases 1561–1762; Out Rawcliffe lease 1692; Pemberton 1315; Pilling leases 1558–1621; Poulton-le-Fylde 1746; Preston 1442, 1536; Ribby-with-Wrea leases 1566–1742; Salford, grant to Merivale abbey *c.*1190; Scotforth 1547–1612; Sefton 1667, 1696; Silverdale 1614; Singleton leases 1567, 1628; Stalmine-with-Staynall 1582–1607; Standish 1608; Tarbock 1425; Thornton 1388–1489; Toxteth Park 1620; Up Holland 1506–89; Walton-le-Dale 1410; Walton-on-the-Hill 1433, advowson 1472; Warton 1574–1854, leases 1629–1824; Weeton-with-Preese lease 1771; Westby-with-Plumpton leases 1575–1826; West Derby c.1250–1722; Westleigh lease 1602; Winstanley 1362; Wrightington 1682

Other counties: Cardington, Bedfordshire 1586; Cheshire c.1220–1657; Newton-in-Martock, Somerset 1628; Lancing, Sussex 1668; Beetham, Westmorland 1505; York 1338–77, Badsworth 1477, co. York

Family Papers: Settlements 1395–1820, bonds 1490–1778, pedigrees 1466–1889, wills 1476–1832, pardons 1351, 1507

Estate Papers (leases are shewn with title-deeds): Layton Hawes award 1609, Melling commons division 1699, lease books 1688–1788; Lytham, Warton and Westby sea defence papers 1728–90; fishery papers 1675–1872, contract books 1725–90, Spen Dyke drainage 1792, lists of cottagers in Lytham 1857, brickmaking agreements 1861–62; surveys: Marton 1719–1840, Lytham 1719–1886, Westby 1719–1844, Clifton-with-Salwick 1719–1871, Layton 1816–40, Molyneux properties 1650–63; Lytham mills multure book 1714–31, team-books 1752–53; sheep-book 1705–06; commons book 1752

Correspondence: Christ Church, Oxford, requiring subscriptions towards entertaining James I, 1605; Thomas Hawarden, referring to plague in Liverpool 1652; William Clifton, from Venice, Vienna, Leghorn, and Aleppo 1676–78; news letters 1676–77; estate letters on a wide variety of subjects 1836–45, 1847–50; from J. T. Clifton, M.P., 1846–55, 1867–80; from Lady Eleanor Clifton 1866–82; from the Hon. William Lowther 1865–67; from Thomas Henry Clifton 1867–77; from Madeleine Clifton 1874, 1878–80; estate letter-book 1868–71, 1916–39; steward's letters 1816–18

Legal Papers: Re will of Cuthbert Clifton 1516, re land at Lingart in Barnacre c.1596, Molyneux sequestration 1647–58, rights on Clifton marsh c.1695, Molyneux v. Liverpool Corporation 1604, 1670, Clifton v. Lowde of Kirkham 1686–87, Butler v. Lytham priory 1531, Fleetwood v. Clifton re turbary on Layton Hawes 1607–09, quo warranto proceedings against Merivale abbey concerning Altcar 1292, legal formulary based on charters of Syon abbey c.1450

Business Papers: Lytham dock register 1815–18, Fylde Horse-breeding Co., papers 1879, Blackpool and Lytham Railway: accounts 1862–71, letters and papers 1862–70, Ribble Navigation Co., accounts 1815–23

Official Papers: Appointments: Robert Heathwaite as rural dean of Richmond, Boroughbridge, and Furness 1565, as commissary of

Richmond 1564, wardship of Cuthbert Clifton 1589, John Clifton as deputy lieutenant 1796

Subsidy rolls: Leyland Hundred 1585, 1612, West Derby Hundred 1612, Amounderness Hundred 1626, Blackburn Hundred 1626

Ecclesiastical Papers: Presentation of Hugh Halsall to Halsall rectory 1495, proceedings in Court of Arches concerning Altcar tithes 1365–68, Lund chapel papers 1532–1755, Lytham Easter rolls 1632–41, 1696–1706, 1728–67, 1789–93, Warton benefice papers 1882

Plans: Layton, Marton and Lytham c.1530; Lytham c.1610, 1789, 1812; Westby-with-Plumpton and Little Marton 1809; Clifton-with-Salwick, Warton, Layton, and Great Marton 1816; Blackpool sewerage 1876, Marton Moss 1773, St. Annes-on-the-Sea 1874

Rentals; General 1625–1822, Lytham 1588–89, Euxton, Eccleston, and Ulnes Walton 1653, Ellel 1688, lease ledgers 1757–1809, tithe rentals 1725–56, Kirkham rectory 1733–1826, arrears books 1727–56

Accounts: Stewards' accounts 1697–1796, Lytham common agistment accounts 1755, Mary Clifton's personal accounts 1727–43, sundry accounts 1735–38, 1788–91, Lytham housekeeping expenses 1768–86, 1789–91, 1801–12, Sophia Clifton's accounts 1784–1804, Juliana Clifton's accounts 1785–87, cash books 1796–1815, Lady Bridget Clifton's jointure accounts 1696–1711, servants' wages 1750–56, labourers' wages 1756–93, 1837–40, general accounts 1842–1939

Charity Papers: Lytham charities 1740–48, poor prisoners at Lancaster, deed 1640, Halsall school and poor, deed 1593

Miscellaneous: Forced loan letter 1612; inventories: viscount Molyneux of Croxteth 1654, Thomas Clifton of Westby 1657, Thomas Clifton of Lytham 1713, 1734; water-colour drawing of Lytham 1734; water-colour drawing of Lytham 1610; navigation instructions 1713; Lytham Invalids' Home papers 1878; Blackpool park papers 1890; agreements, plans and papers concerning the Clifton and Lea road 1718–1893

Walmersley-Cotham of Southport (DDCo)

Title Deeds: Claughton-in-Amounderness 1665–1925, Goosnargh 1730–1895, Windle 1756–1940

Accounts and Rentals: Rentals of above 1790–1865; accounts as above 1840–99

Legal Papers: Re above estates 1843–93

Plans: Claughton 1800, 1840, 1846, Goosnargh 1799, Windle 1820, 1830, 1867, 1872

Survey: Claughton, and Windle 1802

Lord Crawshaw of Crawshaw (DDX 821)

Brooks pedigree and family history papers 1860–1908

Family and political correspondence 1839–1904

Family settlements, wills, etc., 1875–1932

Leases and papers *re* sporting rights in the Trough of Bowland 1882–1932

Papers *re* Towneley collieries, Cliviger, 1861–1925

Wills and papers of Adamson family of Colne 1790–1899

Dissolution of partnership; Brookes of Manchester, merchants 1846

Letters patent: pipe-coupling and loom improvements 1853

Appointment of Thomas Brooks as deputy lieutenant 1884

Viscount Cross (DDX/841)

Political, official and family papers of Richard Assheton Cross 1624–1901

Crosse of Shaw Hill (DDSh)

There is some slight evidence that the Crosse family originated in Lathom, but Adam of the Cross appears in Wigan in 1277. In the next century properties were acquired in Wigan and Liverpool and shortly after 1400 in Chorley. In the middle of the 18th century Shaw Hill was built in Whittle-le-Woods

Title Deeds*: Adlington 1509, Astley 1720–54, Balderstone 1775, Bispham-with-Norbreck (including cotton factory) 1720–1827, Charnock Richard 1345, 1498, Chorley 1401–1772, leases 1772–1844, Cronton 1409, Culcheth and Kenyon 1399–1402, Fazakerley 1507–1637, Halewood 1339, Heapey chapel 1755–60, Heath Charnock 1282, Huyton 1501, Ince-in-Makerfield 1398, Kirkdale 1405, Lathom *c.*1280, 1465, Litherland 1506, Liverpool *c.*1290–1742, leases 1673–1794, Nether Wyresdale lease 1603, Parr 1412, Rivington 1338–1724, Speke 1498, Up Holland 1504, Walton-on-the-Hill *c.*1280–1561, lease 1680, Walton-le-Dale oil mill 1749, Wavertree 1497, West Derby 1498, Wigan *c.*1280–1437, Whittle-le-Woods and Clayton-le-Woods 1595–1839

---

* A schedule of some 224 of the earlier documents was printed by the Historic Society of Lancashire and Cheshire, vols. 41, 42, 43 and 45, but it contains many errors.

Other counties: Cheshire: Butley, 1560–1776, Odd Rode 1693, Haughton 1720, Norley 1724; Flint 1346; Shropshire: Gravenhangor, Drayton, Oswestry and Woore 1273–1730; Warwickshire: Brockhurst and Berkswell c.1290

Family Papers: Settlements, etc. 1314–1779; Crosse pedigrees and genealogical memoranda 19th c.; Ikin of Drayton-in-Hales, Salop, and Butley, Cheshire, pedigrees, 19th c.; Newton of Whitchurch, Salop, pedigrees 19th c.; wills 1383–1752. Inventory of Shaw Hill 1748

Appointments of various members of Crosse family to cornet 1722, lieutenant 1744, deputy lieutenant 1767, 1796, 1830, sheriff 1807, 1837

Correspondence: General 1703–1814; Euxton school 1853–61

Legal Papers: Cross v. Parker, etc., re various properties 1725; Legh v. Threlfall re Staining tithes 1732–34; Rex v. Cross re smuggling at North Meols 1740; Crosse v. Price re Liverpool Townfield c.1770

Ecclesiastical Papers: Lease of church of Llanasaph 1468; dissolution of marriage of Roger Crosse and Letitia Norris 1519; plan of burials and seating, Chorley 1635; Chorley pew deeds 1674–1732; Preston St. George's pew deed 1729; faculty for gallery in Leyland church, with pew plan 1742, 1744

Rentals: General 1637, 1811–24, Liverpool 1539, 1765–93, Balderstone 1815, Chorley, etc., 1825–37

Miscellaneous: Schedule of harness of Maykin of Kenyon 1419; descent of Edward IV from Jehosophat, 15th century; letter from Elizabeth I to the emperor of Cathay, 1602; pedigrees of European and English royalty and nobility 17th century; arguments upon judgement given to the earl of Bath 1693; Privy Council instructions on death of William IV, 1837 (See also DDX/1111)

Farington of Worden (DDF)

In 1206 Roger de Lacy gave to Robert Bussell the manor of Leyland. A daughter carried a moiety to the Faringtons who acquired the other moiety by purchase in 1617. Worden was purchased in 1534. Perhaps the most interesting member of the family was William, 1537–1610, who was comptroller of the household of three earls of Derby and was probably* the prototype of Shakespeare's Malvolio. Through him a number of Stanley documents are in this collection. Appended are the Farington documents which,

---

* *Shakespeare Association Bulletin*, vol. viii, 1932.

through marriage, went to the Huddlestons of Sawston, Cambridgeshire.

(There are many documents relating to this estate in the accumulation of the solicitors, Messrs. Houghton, Craven & Co., Preston, see p.179).

Manorial: Aspull: court-rolls 1565, 1567, 1573, 1584, 1586, 1594–96, 1599, 1601

Leyland: court-books 1775–86; orders 1618, 1625, 1626, 1637, 1650, 1651, 1681, 1683–86, 1688–94, 1696–1700, 1702, 1705, 1707, 1709, 1718; suitors lists 1659, 1665, 1683–86, 1688, 1689, 1691–94, 1765, 1787–97; call-books 1799–1803; precepts 1782–1802, 1830; verdicts 1787–1802, 1829–44; amerciaments 1770–74, 1825, 1829; inquisitions 1854–1907

Penwortham (barony, included many west Lancashire townships): court-rolls 1590, 1599–1601, 1603–19, 1622–26; court-books 1691, 1702–08, 1711, 1722–24, 1740–80, 1787, 1790, 1798; estreats 1567, 1568, 1571–78, 1587–1608, 1709–16, 1756, 1759–64, 1769–75; call-books 1705, 1706, 1724–80, 1815–51; verdicts 1799, 1839–45; inquisitions 1854, 1857–1900; constables' presentments 1702, 1705, 1707, 1709, 1711, 1718, 1719

Ulnes Walton: court-book 1578; orders 1503–14, 1533–35, 1540, 1577, 1583, 1588, 1618, 1624; call-book 1711

Title Deeds (including leases): Abram 1663; Accrington mill 1598–1616; Aighton c.1280; Aughton 1323–42; Chorley 1512, 1579; Clayton-le-Dale c.1230; Clitheroe c.1280; Croston 1349–1401, Finney lease 1726; Dinckley 1627; Dunnerdale-with-Seathwaite 1601; Eccleston (Chorley) c.1210–1602, leases 1447–1599; Euxton 1663–1758, leases 1718–45; Farington (Evesham abbey and Penwortham priory) c.1190–1580, leases 1350–1670; Heaton Norris leases 1567–91; Hesketh-with-Becconsall c.1280–1411; Howick 1366; Hutton (Cockersand and Evesham abbeys) c.1220–1550, leases 1575–97; Lathom 1330; Leigh and Pennington 1596–1723; Longton 1307–1692, leases 1376–1594; Ormskirk c.1280–1410; Preston 1323–1588; Read 1580; Salesbury 1565; Tockholes 1567; Ulnes Walton 1346–1754, leases 1332–1726; Walton-le-Dale: Baldwins tenement 1619–1761, The Mains 1623–1725; Whittingham 1621; Whittle-le-Woods c.1290–1638; Wigan 1369; Wilpshire c.1280; Woodplumpton 1330; Wrightington 1329. Penwortham: various properties 1548–1768, leases 1611–1726; Crookings 1495–1757; Lower Hall 1590–1609. Leyland: various properties c.1200–1756, leases 1318–1812; Beardsworth family properties c.1250–1671; Blackleach family properties 1535–1774; Charnock family properties

211

1571–1609; Heald family properties 1664–71; Woodcock family properties 1614–1728; The Brex 1509–1657; Dicconsons 1695–1716; Honkinton c.1230–1404; Kents 1618–51; Leyland Meadow 1561–1726; Loone Hey 1622–85; Low Fields 1454–1768; Northbrook c.1290–1596; Overhouse 1576–1600; Ten Mark Lands 1512–1610; Worden c.1300–1605. Other counties: Flintshire, Trythen Vauchen 1638; Yorkshire, Bentley 1632

Family Papers: Settlements 1406–1769; confirmation of arms 1560; pedigree rolls c.1620 and c.1640; pedigree book 1845; "Robert Bretherton's petegrie" c.1600; Bradshaw of Pennington pedigree 1698; various pedigrees and memoranda on the Nowells of Read, and Matthews of Whitby; bonds 1428–1725; catalogue of books 1746; inventory of Shaw Hall 1795; list of heirlooms 1846; visitors' book Shaw Hall, 1773–79; travel diaries, Sir William Farington 1765, 1784, Wilkinson Matthews 1834–36; school exercise books 1783; game register 1819–28; insurance policies (DDH) 1768

Appointments: Henry Cooke, canon of York 1722; James Fenton, constable of Lancaster Castle 1587 assigned to Thomas Farington 1591; William Farington. deputy lieutenant 1638, 1757, 1761; James Farington, deputy lieutenant 1842; Sir Gilbert Hoghton and William Farington, knights of the shire, 1640; Richard Farington, ensign 1675; Alexander Nowell, ensign 1704; William Farington, major 1798; James Farington, captain 1835; William Farington, sheriff, 1636, 1813; Henry Fleetwood, steward of Penwortham 1617; Henry Farington, steward of Penwortham 1505

Estate Papers (leases are shewn with title deeds): Surveys: general 1637, 1675, 1678, 1725 (plans), 1795, c.1800 (plans); Leyland 1569, 1570, 1575, 1578, 1602, 1614, 1616, 1768 (plans); Penwortham 1632, 1768; Ulnes Walton 1614, 1763; general lease-book 1731; Bryning-with-Kellamergh memoranda 1565–1578; Bretherton memoranda 1585–91; Leyland commons and moss papers 1423–1866; Leyland roads papers 1749–1863

Correspondence: Various correspondence 1541–1799 (many of the earlier ones printed in Chetham Society vols. 31 and 39); Bradshaw Civil War letters 1650–59 (printed by Hist. MSS Commission 1877); letters on affairs of Sir Thomas and Lady Hesketh of Rufford 1766–80; letters concerning Worden Hall museum 1774–1879; letters on family and antiquarian matters 1841–86; letters (in French) from M. Constancon 1785–91; letters concerning right of way through the Mains, Walton-le-Dale 1746–47; letters on the affairs of Thomas Farington 1589–1620

Legal Papers: An abnormal number of papers concerning law-suits are to be found in this collection, including Eccleston glebe 1576–1605, Leigh grammar school 1770, Longton tithes 1589–1603, Ulnes Walton manor 1580–82, Penwortham moss 16th century

Official Papers: Lancashire rate and tax book 1645; Royal Lancashire Regiment, orderly book 1794–95; tax assessments: Leyland highways 1636, Leyland Hundred land tax 1703, 1706–08, 1713, 1714, 1753; a book of loans, taxations, subsidies and musters 1559–1608; subsidy roll 1593; shrievalty papers 1636–39, 1714–1851

Ecclesiastical Papers: Blackburn: Easter-book 1565–69; Easter-roll 1586; lease by Cranmer of the rectory (with chapels) 1548, with other papers 1552–1598

Leyland: grant of church to Evesham abbey c.1155; rectory rental 15th century; charity endowment 1524; other papers 1586–1867; tithe deeds 1477–1549

Lancaster: advowson deeds 1593–1673

Plans: Leyland 1768, 1775; Hutton c.1600; Penwortham c.1590. c.1730, 1739; Ulnes Walton c.1740

Rentals: General 1430, 1505, 1553, 1559, 1570, 1573–99, 1605–10, 1626, 1635, 1636, 1648, 1704, 1705, 1729, 1733, 1740, 1742–1839; Leyland 1412, 1616, 1660, 1671, 1686, 1690, 1691, 1698–1707, 1728; Penwortham 1607, 1660. 1671, 1684, 1728, 1732–41, 1768; Ulnes Walton 1425, 1430, 1471, 1505, 1540, 1542. 1545, 1546, 1582, 1693, 1695, 1698–1707; Pennington 1705–09

Accounts: General 1695–1828, Hannah Farington's accounts 1817–29, household accounts 1744–80, workmens' wages 1574–1634, 1824–26, Littlewood estate accounts 1835–42, Richard Nowell's accounts, Altham 1744–92 and London 1761–79; Ribble fishery 1575–76

Charity Papers: Haigh: rules of The Receptacle 1775; rental of Peter Lathom's estates 1757; Leyland: almshouses 1639–1889, Bannisters 1632–1891, Dandys 1668, Osbaldestons 1737–1850, workhouse 1780

Miscellaneous: Meteorological records, Leyland, 1886–1939; Parliamentary proceedings 1629; petitioners for bridge at Penwortham 1738; Ribble fishery leases 1535, 1547, 1575, 1652; inventory of Sir Thomas Talbot, Blackburn 1562; royal orders for wearing the red rose badge by inhabitants of Penwortham, Ulnes Walton, Eccleston, and Leyland 1504, 1533, 1543; legal formulary c.1600; abstract of "evidences" 1603; Charles I's letter to William Farington and his son to go to York 1642;

213

letters-patent to John Milnes of Gloucester for "portable apparatus for exercising Human Body" 1862

Stanley Papers: Letter-book of Edward, earl of Derby 1532–39 (Chetham Soc. vol. 19); household expenses of the earl of Derby 1561–62, orders for the earl of Derby's household 1569 and the "weekely brieffements" of the earl of Derby's houses 1586–1590 (Chetham Soc. vol. 31); various deeds and papers 1570–1639, including the will of Edward, earl of Derby 1572, dissolution of marriage of Ann Stanley 1577, account of funeral of Henry Stanley 1598, surveys of lord Strange's lands 1636–41

Huddleston Papers (DDX/102)

Manorial: Leyland court-book 1568–70

Title Deeds: Leyland c.1200–1610, leases 1326–1417; Farington 1292–1581, Preston 1333–93, Ulnes Walton 1386, Croston rectory 1617

Rentals: Leyland 1542, 1570, 1589, 1591

Accounts: 1558, 1571, 1579, 1607–10

Fell of Ulverston (DDFe)

Ulverston deeds 1611–1859; family and business correspondence c.1790–1880, Robert Fell's accounts 1790–1800; Ulverston land-tax assessments 1792, 1799, 1800; Ulverston plan 1833. Deeds and papers of Caton, Overton, Tatham, Ulverston and Wray 1646–1934. Flan How, Ulverston, deeds 1788–1868

Floyd of Chorlton-cum-Hardy (DDFl)

Rev. Thomas Floyd papers 1848–75; William Henry Hope's Ceylon diary 1860–62; E. Ila Floyd (née Hope) diaries 1914–43, letters and papers 1896–1946; Rev. Thomas Earl Floyd letters and papers 1890–1937; Thomas Hope Floyd diaries and scrapbooks 1912–73, outgoing letters 1947–72, letters to parents 1902–42, incoming letters 1903–55, political leaflets 1920–70, genealogical papers and scrapbooks 1871–1937

Formby of Formby (DDFo)

The present Formby family acquired a quarter of the manor in the mid-16th century, but—although the descent is not clear—it is certain that they have held property in Formby since the 13th century. Properties in East Lancashire were brought in by marriage in 1784. There are many references to aggregation of scattered holdings among the deeds relating to Formby.

Manorial: Formby: court-books 1757–1925; order-books 1714–25, 1760–1817; call-books 1748–62, 1782, 1783, 1788–93, 1806–11, 1829, 1839, 1840, 1842

Title Deeds (including leases): Altcar leases 1641, 1764; Aughton 1719; Broughton-in-Amounderness 1489; Kellamergh and Wrea 1639–1710; Dalton *c.*1290; Downholland leases 1640–1811; Eccleston (Prescot) 1737; Formby exchanges 1752–1804; various properties *c.*1280–1856 (including windmill 1539), leases 1474–1860; Great Crosby 1752–1861; Ince-in-Makerfield 1735; Lathom lease 1805; Liverpool: Hunter Street school 1793, Trinity church pews 1796; Maghull: Richmonds Tenement 1675–1800, Mawdesley's Tenement 1769–1818, various properties 1799–1859, leases 1729–1817; Ormskirk leases 1750, 1807; Orrel lease 1737; Raven Meols 1668–1835, leases 1727–1824; Salesbury lease 1623; Scarisbrick lease 1726; Sefton 1325; Bury 1753–1811; Newchurch-in-Rossendale 1698–1808; Spotland: Brandwood 1667, Wolstenholme 1649–1685; Tottington: Lumb Hall 1754–1824, Nuttall Hall 1639–1836; Walmersley 1695–1845

Family Papers: Settlements 1486–1875; wills 1692–1859; genealogical memoranda 17th and 19th century

Appointments: John Formby, deputy lieutenant 1767; Richard Formby, deacon, 1780, priest 1784, curacy of Formby 1794, freedom of Liverpool 1798; Miles Formby, deacon 1818, priest 1818, curate at Liverpool 1821, rector of West Monkton, Somerset 1823, curate of Cothelstone, Somerset 1824; John Formby, curate of Melling 1829; Lonsdale Formby, deacon 1844, curate of Warmingham, Cheshire 1844, priest 1845, curate of Formby 1846

Estate Papers (leases are shewn with title deeds): Estimate for buildings at Downholland Hall 1792; states of culture at Downholland Hall 1819, 1821; survey of Maghull 1813; surveys of Formby 1783 and 19th century; agreements concerning Formby warren 1667–1832; depositions as to boundaries of Raven Meols 1584; inventory of Nuttall Hall 1706

Memoranda book relating to the East Lancashire properties, early 19th century

Correspondence: From Jonathan Scott, Liverpool, concerning anonymous charitable trusts 1812–31; the affairs of Willis Earle of Whiston 1820–21; the marriage settlement of Richard Willis of Halsnead 1830–31; enclosure in Formby 1854–58; the removal of a stone from York Minster to Formby church 1839; stopping-up roads in Formby 1845–58; wreck-of-the-sea at Formby and Raven Meols 1857; the Formby pedigree 1833–1901; the Hesketh of Tulketh trust 1748–1858; the affairs of the Rev. Calvin Winstanley of Liverpool 1789–1834; Mrs. Graham's trust for the Warrington clergy 1806–24; the Elton and Blackburn turnpike trust 1855; Walton church leys 1820–30

Legal Papers: "The Great Formby Cockle Case" 1867–1916, Papers on foreshore rights 18th and 19th century

Plans: Downholland c.1796; Maghull 1798–1840; Bentylee in Walmsley 1779

Miscellaneous: Grant of absolution issued from the Hospital of the Holy Trinity, Walsoken, Norfolk, 1418. Agreement by 162 tenants of Formby, Ainsdale, and Raven Meols against attempt by the rector of Walton-on-the-Hill to take tithe of potatoes and "garden stuff", 1789

Gaisford of Gresgarth (DDGa)

After being in moieties for about 300 years, the manor of Caton (Gresgarth or Grassyard being the manor house of one moiety since at least the mid-1400s) came into the hands of George Compton in 1666. It was sold several times before being acquired by Thomas Edmondson in 1806 and from him it has descended through marriage to the present owners.

Manorial: Caton: court papers 1668, 1669, 1671, 1674, 1676, 1678, 1680, 1681, 1684, 1685 1697, 1706, 1707, 1741, 1757, 1758, 1760, 1763–65, 1767, 1770, 1775, 1782, 1783, 1790, 1791, 1798

Title Deeds: Caton: manor 1675–1804, Bridge End 1615–1811, Larger Hill 1625–1762, Little Hill 1749–63, Moorside 1631–1824, Short Rakes 1675–1776, Silk Mill 1717–1805, Tenter Close 1691–1765, Town End 1623–1815, various properties 1637–1736; Quernmore: Hollinghead 1631–1812

Family Papers: Settlement 1726

Appointments: T. G. Edmondson as lieutenant in militia 1865, and captain 1869, John Edmondson as deputy lieutenant 1855, J. F. Cawthorne as master forester of Wyresdale and Bleasdale 1825, John Fenton as master forester of Quernmore, Myerscough, Amounderness and Bleasdale 1780

Estate Papers: Contracts for wall-building, enclosing and draining 1819; various accounts 1802–07; fishery papers 18th–19th c. lease of slate-quarry 1715; colliery leases 1732, 1741; timber, draining and leasing agreements 1709–1844; boundary survey 1757

Correspondence: Hathershelf to Scout road, Caton boundaries, manorial rights, Lancaster to Richmond Turnpike Trust, Caton occupation roads, Caton workhouse, Caton enclosure, North-Western Railway Co., and the Penny Bridge road, sporting rights, permission to use bridge, etc., 19th c.

Legal Papers: Cases for counsel's opinion: manorial rights, 1792, Caton Moor allotments 1873

Business Papers: Caton Bridge accounts and shareholders list 1807–82

Official Papers: Caton land tax assessments 1763, 1796; Caton rate assessments 1727, 1785, 1791, 1803–08, 1833; Caton highway rate-book 1859; game tax certificates 1815–59; assessment on Lonsdale Hundred for repair of Lancaster bridge 1748

Ecclesiastical Papers: Tithe books 1790–95, 1815, 1837–43; papers on rebuilding of Caton church 1867; papers on state of Caton church 1801–02; declaration of trust concerning tithes 1762; grant of tithes 1804

Plans: "River Loyne at Caton" 1626, Hollin Head 18th c., part of waste 1763, Tenters estate 1792, Cornthwaite's land 1804

Miscellaneous: Caton association against felons, 18th c. and 1817

Garnett of Quernmore (DDQ)

In 1630 Quernmore Park was sold by the Crown to Sir Thomas Preston of Furness, passing by marriage to Lord Clifford of Chudleigh in 1685. It remained in his family until sold to Charles Gibson of Preston in 1794 and was acquired by William Garnett of Lark Hill, Salford, in 1842, who also obtained a lease of Bleasdale from the Duchy of Lancaster.

Title Deeds: Bulk, Nightingale Hall 1650–1750; Ellel 1774–1898; Lancaster 1726–71; Preston 1611–1785; Quernmore, various properties 1756–1861, Humble Bee's Nest 1736–1866; Salford, Lark Hill 1835–45; Skerton 1655–1773

Other counties: Cumberland, Whitebeck 1593–1804; Durham, Bishop Auckland 1700–24

Family Papers: Garnett: settlements, mortgages and wills 1816–1900; miscellaneous family papers 1801–31; appointments of William Garnett as high sheriff 1879 and deputy lieutenant 1921. Gibson: miscellaneous papers 1781–1842; settlements 1742–92

Estate Papers: Quernmore: waste leases 1511–90, leases 1704–1910, surveys 1796, 1852, Eccles estate papers 1817–62, conditions of sale 1842

Bleasdale: contracts, accounts, leases and game-books 1830–1920 survey 1795

Correspondence: Garnett: various 1794–1956, Bleasdale church 1841, Grassyard shoot 1900–01, Lancaster quarter sessions 1916, shrievalty 1877–80, 1937–42, 1952, Quernmore school 1851–53, Halton church 1880–81, Quernmore tithes 1948–54, Lancaster grammar school 1858–68, Bleasdale reformatory 1856–71, Bleasdale estate 1893–97, East London work among boys 1920–27, Quernmore church 1831–61, Jamaican business 1794–1806,

217

W. J. Garnett's travels in China, Turkey, Persia, Russia, Argentine, etc. 1905–18; Bleasdale forest 1880–92

Gibson: Caton bridge 1805–30, Furness estates 1805–06, various 1822–31

Official Papers: Letters to H.M. Consul-General at Tangier 1797–1809, 1834–39

Royal Lancashire Volunteers, letter-book 1797–98, Lancaster Volunteers, minute book 1797, 3rd Royal Lancashire Militia, various 1825–54. Tyburn ticket 1813

Plans: Quernmore 1839, 1842

Rentals: Quernmore 1829–67, Liverpool 1826–45

Accounts: Quernmore general accounts 1814–77, Quernmore household accounts 1829–34, Charles Gibson's trust accounts 1824–32, Quernmore and Bleasdale general vouchers 1858–63, Bleasdale reformatory cash-books 1856–63

Miscellaneous: Salford election papers 1832, 1838; medical prescriptions 1836–50, Mrs. Mary Moore's holiday journal 1859–72, Quernmore parish magazine 1871–94

Gerard of Ashton-in-Makerfield (DDGe)

The Gerards obtained the manors of Ashton-in-Makerfield and Windle by marriage about 1330. Thomas Gerard was created a baronet in 1611 and Robert Gerard became Lord Gerard of Brynn in 1876. The Cantsfield estate came in by marriage in 1696, while as "founder's kin" they have long been connected with Repton School in Derbyshire. A Tasburgh marriage in 1780 brought in properties in Lincolnshire, London, Kent and Ireland.

Manorial: Ashton-in-Makerfield: verdicts 1636, 1637, 1650, orders 1732–61, estreats 1736–60, call-books 1806–08 (DDGe) 1872–74

Windle: court-books 1650–1761. (DDGe) 1743–1874

Title Deeds (including leases): Abram 1614–48; Adlington 1597–1619, leases 1592–1658; Ashton-in-Makerfield 1615–1878, leases 1563–1841; Aspull 1650–1812; Aughton 1691; Bardsea 1709; Billinge 1375–1877, leases 1588–1873; Blackley 1612; Brindle 1580; Childwall rectory 1582–1851; Eccleston 1648–1717; Garston 1586, 1735; Heaton 1600; Hindley 1577; Kirkby 1770; Lancaster 1729–49, leases 1659–1734; Maghull 1690; Mawdesley 1642–99, leases 1708–1813; Parr 1655–1788; Preston 1621; Rainford 1558–1701; Skelmersdale 1645; Tatham 1715; Westleigh 1706; Widnes 1792; Wigan 1610–1756, leases 1690–97; Windle 1683–1869, leases 1661–1864; Winwick 1631; Worthington 1583

Other counties: Cheshire: Ledsham 1641; Derbyshire: Etwell and Hardwick 1647; Huntingdonshire: Alconbury 1658; Middlesex: Hendon 1690; Nottinghamshire 1655–71; Staffordshire: Ashmore 1640; Yorkshire: Aysgarth 1707–03; Burton-in-Lonsdale 1591–1625

Tasburgh family deeds: Lincolnshire, Kent, London, Conge Abbey in Ireland 1612–1845

Family Papers: Settlements 1508–1827, wills 1617–1854, bonds 1600–1877, creation of baronetcy 1611, papers concerning Repton School 1654–1824, pass for Sir William Gerard from Denbigh 1646; (DDGe) pedigree c.1820

Correspondence: Letters from the Emperor of the French on his visit to Garswood 1846; Letter from Disraeli on the proposed Gerard peerage 1875

Estate Papers (leases are shewn with title-deeds): Coalmining 1653–1870 (principally Ashton, Billinge and Windle), Brynn surveys 1648, 1705, 1736, grant of free warren in Ashton and Billinge 1617, lease-book 1716–99, boundary of Ashton 1771, Bardsea moor enclosure proposals 1712, inquisition on diverting road at Carr Mill 1758

Ecclesiastical Papers: Faculty for gallery in Ashton-in-Makerfield chapel 1723; report on estates left by recusants to support religion 1692

Legal Papers: Anderton v. Aughton (manor of Adlington) 1597, Gerard v. Pegg (Aske, co. Derby) 1641, Wilson v. Ireland (manors of Southworth, Middleton, Pennington) 1650, Gate v. Langton (Hindley) 1631, Gerard v. Ryley (Standish) 1621, Haselden v. Gerard (Ashton watermill) 1585, Corbishley v. Assheton (Ashton) 1616, Franceys v. Sorocold (Westleigh) 1694, Lyon v. Tarleton (Rainford) 1592, Fearnhead v. Dennett (Widnes) 1730–46

Plans: Cuerden c.1700; Southworth, Croft, Middleton, Poulton, and Fearnhead 18th c.; Winstanley wagon-road c.1820

Rental: Bardsea 1712

Miscellaneous: Agreement concerning scholars at St. Omer 1706; articles for building Eye bridge, Ashton-in-Makerfield, 1628

Dawson-Greene of Whittington (DDGr)

Manorial: Slyne-with-Hest court-books 1746–1922, verdicts 1745–1830, call books 1759–1807; Whittington court books 1701–1933 boundary rolls 1804, 1855, rectory admittances 1758–1920

Title Deeds: Torrisholme *c*.1230, 1359, 1368, *c*.1470, 1569; Slyne-with-Hest, Whittington, Over and Nether Kellet, Silverdale, Skerton, Furness Fells 16th to 19th c., Chillington (co. Stafford) *c*.1230

Family Papers: Memoranda and diaries of Thomas Greene 1705–68, diary of Mrs. Greene Bradley 1830–31, diaries of Thomas Greene 1816–51, William Greene's notebook at Sedbergh School *c*.1754–62, parliamentary and quarter sessions notebooks of Thomas Greene 1840–65, wills and settlements 1768–1887

Estate Papers: Survey of lands of Bolton priory, co. York, late 13th c., valuations of lands in Cockerham 1815, 1822, surveys of lands in Whittington n.d., Claughton-in-Lonsdale lease book 17th to 18th c.

Correspondence: A large collection of letters mainly of the Greene and Bradley families of Slyne. Correspondents include William Hayley, Richard Cumberland, George Romney, and the Duke of Wellington 1706–1894; Robert Fagan letters *re* art collectors and Italian travel *c*.1780–1810

Official Papers: Oliver Cromwell's summons to William West to attend parliament 1653, printed declaration by James III 1743

Ecclesiastical Papers: Bolton-le-Sands: pew list and accounts 1817, Greene pew papers 1826–30, tithe dispute 1825–31, conversion of tithebarn to school 1848, south porch right of way 1848–49

Plans: Quernmore 1815, Whittington Moss n.d., Whittington Hall n.d., 1886, 1890

Rentals and Accounts: A large collection of rentals and accounts mainly of the Greene and Bradley families 1706–1893

Greenwood of Clerk Hill (DDG)

This estate, anciently called Snelleshow, belonged to Whalley abbey. In 1553 it was sold to John Crombock with whose descendants it remained until sold in 1699 to the Whalleys of Sparth in Clayton-le-Moors, in whose family it was held until being sold in 1871 to Solomon Longworth; it then came to the Greenwoods by marriage.

Title Deeds: Chatburn 1712–14; Lower Darwen 1780; Downham 1600–66, leases 1752–70; Greenhalgh-with-Thisleton 1728–45; Haslingden 1614; Marsden 1672–1746; Preston 1743; Whalley: Clerk Hill 1553–1704, Asterley 1553–1686, various properties 1553–1799; Wiswell 1544–1866; Wrightington 1657–1731. Yorkshire: Bowland 1679–1870

Family Papers: Settlements 1579–1753; mortgages 1691–99; grant of wardship and marriage of Richard Crombocke 1617, 1631; royal licence to assume names and arms of Smythe and Gardiner

1797; wills 1630–1858; extracts from parish registers relating to Gardiner family 1807–40

Estate Papers (leases are shewn with title-deeds): Survey of Asterley (Whalley) n.d., division of White Ash and Knuzden collieries in Oswaldtwistle 1737

Legal Papers: Assheton *v.* Whalley (Whalley watermills) 1691; Clayton *v.* Crombock (debt) 1699

Official Papers: Order of deputy lieutenants for Thomas Whalley to contribute to cost of armed horseman 1693. Levy of £5 for burying John Whalley in linen 1733

Plans: Clerk Hill estate 1788

Miscellaneous: Commission and interrogatories to discover boundaries of Crosedale in Bowland 1576; licence to alienate Baverstock and Clack, Wiltshire, 1618; accounts of freeholders' meeting to send address to Prince Regent 1817

Hesketh of Rufford (DDHe)

Rufford belonged, in 1212, to Chester abbey, but somewhat later it was held of the abbot by Richard Fitton, from him descending to his two daughters, one of whom married William of Hesketh. His son John became sole lord in 1318 and the estate descended regularly to Sir Thomas George Fermor-Hesketh, who was created Baron Hesketh of Hesketh in 1935.

Great Harwood was also a Fitton manor, the whole of it becoming Hesketh property in 1310. About 1290 the estate of Tottleworth in Rishton was purchased. From 1558 until 1800 the Heskeths were lords of a moiety of the manor of Croston.

When Lord Hesketh gave Rufford Old Hall to the National Trust he included a small number of documents, mainly mediaeval. These are in the Record Office (DDN) but have, for simplicity's sake been assimilated with the following survey. Another group of Hesketh documents was acquired by Col. John Parker of Browsholme (see p. 250) and there is yet a further collection in the muniments of the earl of Derby (see p. 265).

Manorial: Croston: court-roll 1588; Hesketh-with-Becconsall: court-roll 1577; Tarleton: court-rolls 1577, 1627; Wrightington: court-roll 1473; Great Harwood: grant of market 1328, grant of court-leet 1615, certificate of homage 1429; Rufford: grant of market, fair and free warren 1339 (*inspeximus* of 1573); call-books 1869–74, 1876–87

Title Deeds (including leases): Aighton, Bailey, and Chaigley 1601; Aspull 1555; Aughton (Cockersand abbey) *c.*1230–1399; Bilsborrow lease 1546; Bispham 1381–1565, leases 1742, 1779;

Bretherton c.1260–1605, leases 1366–1805; Clitheroe 1621; Crompton (Cockersand abbey) c.1200; Croston c.1280–1799, leases 1361–1779; Dalton (Cockersand abbey) c.1230; Dinckley c.1280; Dunnerdale 1613; Eccleston (Cockersand abbey) c.1200, 1520, lease 1628; Garstang leases 1672–86; Garston (Cockersand abbey) c.1210, lease (Whalley abbey) 1339; Great Harwood c.1275–1775, leases 1307–1769; Hesketh-with-Becconsall 1556–1855, leases 1554–1918; Hornby and Melling 1332; Howick c.1250–1609, leases 1510–1627; Hutton c.1290–1609, leases 1337–1621; Lathom 1505, 1516; Longton c.1280–1800, leases c.1230–1775; Lydiate c.1290; Mawdesley 1316–1846, leases 1323–1780; Much Hoole leases 1638–1781; Newton-with-Scales 1598–1806, leases 1715–69; Ormskirk 1437–1683, leases 1543–1657; Parbold c.1300–1638, leases 1593–1695; Pemberton 1422, Pendleton (Clitheroe) 1505; Penwortham 1429; Preston 1324–1641, leases 1496–1575; Rainford 1515; Ribbleton 1659–1678, leases 1672–1779; Rishton c.1250–1767, leases 1547–1763; Rufford c.1260–1815, leases 1624–1918; Samlesbury 1621–56, lease 1610; Scarisbrick (Cockersand abbey) c.1230–1732; Shevington 1330–1805, leases 1363–1846; Spotland lease 1520; Sutton (Cockersand abbey) c.1200–c.1260; Tarleton (Cockersand abbey) c.1220–1805, leases c.1202–1912; Ulnes Walton lease 1475; Walton-le-Dale lease 1788; Wigan c.1300–1595, leases 1316–1560; Wilpshire c.1290; Windle (Cockersand abbey) 1201; Winmarleigh leases 1657–1688; Wrightington c.1270–1725, leases c.1300–1785

Other counties: Cheshire: Guilden Sutton (Norton abbey) lease 1483; Gloucestershire: Little Compton lease 1824; Lincolnshire: Nocton c.1230; Shropshire: Ellesmere, Kenwick, Hodnet, Northwood, 1346–1623; Sussex: Eastbourne priory lease 1510

Family Papers: Settlements and mortgages 1338–1809; wills 1505–1821; bonds 1326–1830; pedigrees and genealogical memoranda 17th–19th century; appointment of Robert Hesketh as steward of manor of Ormskirk 1598; appointment of Sir Thomas Hesketh as deputy lieutenant 1761

Miscellaneous deeds and papers relating to the Stopforth family of Bispham etc., 1410–1610

Estate Papers (leases are shewn with title-deeds): Enclosure: Great Harwood 1759–62; Croston Finney 1601–61; Hesketh-with-Becconsall 1831–1918; Howick 1763; Longton 1760–1830; Mawdesley 1817–34; Rawcliffe 1831–37; measurement books 1821–35. Estate memoranda books 1821–35. Boundary papers 1341–1807

Surveys: Croston 1828, Great Harwood and Rishton 1803–19, Mawdesley 1820–88, Wrightington 1827, Hesketh-with-Becconsall 1794–1825

Accrington: partition of Antley 1522; Clayton-le-Moors: making mill-dam 1334; Longton: use of moss 1575; Holmeswood: building agreement 1807; Martin Mere: drainage papers 1817–1836, farm building papers 1812–27, deeds 1704–77; memoranda books "to prevent loose papers lying in the office" 1831–34; account of rabbits caught in Rufford and Tarleton 1865–73

Correspondence: Correspondence of Sir Thomas Darlymple Hesketh: the Hon. and Rev. Edmund Knox and Mrs. Lucy Pearson (family affairs) 1803–23; G. A. Legh Keck (Tarleton moss and Croston drainage) 1806–13; the rectors of Croston and Tarleton and the bishop of Chester (enlarging Rufford church) 1807–08; the rector of Tarleton and Shuttleworth & Hopkins of Preston (Rufford advowson and new gallery) 1808–24; Sir Henry Hoghton and Sir John Shelley (Brockholes tithes) 1812–13; Edward Pearson of Liverpool (bankruptcy) 1814–30; W. Miller, Preston (Martin Mere) 1823–26; J. S. Legh, Liverpool (Crook's farm, Wrightington) 1826–35; Mr. Justice Bayley (fees at Lancaster assizes) 1827–28; William Shakeshaft, Rufford (estate management) 1831–33; Lady Shelley (Shelley family difficulties) 1831–40; Joseph Sands, Liverpool ("Bone dust papers") 1836–40; William Rawstorne, Preston (Mawdesley new church) 1839; J. Burnett, Rufford (estate management) 1813–14

Rufford water supply 1897–1908; the affairs of General Despard 1823–40; constableship of Shevington 1601; Martholme tithes 1658; cottage on Shevington waste 1668; brickmaking on Shevington moor 1680; maintenance of minister at Great Harwood 1684; letter-books 1843–77

Legal Papers: Hesketh v. Thornton (Croston Finney) 1601; indictment of William Robynson, etc., for damage to Longton house 1607; various awards (Harwood common 1457, Shevington mill-dam 1480, Martholme mill 1489, Rishton and Harwood commons 1491, 1457–1536; Hill v. Halsall (Martin Hall) 1570; Nowell v. Hesketh (Harwood moor) 1601–1603; Cooper v. Standish (Shevington) 1668; France v. Hesketh (Ribbleton) 1678–83; Derby, Scarisbrick, Fleetwood and Hesketh (Martin Mere) c.1710; Hesketh v. Standish (Shevington coal) 1712; Monk v. Hesketh (Rufford) 1801

Business Papers: Ribble navigation: reports and papers 1829–59

Coal: various papers, agreements, etc., relating to coal in Great Harwood 1563–1845, Parbold 1815–16, Shevington 1666–1839, Wrightington 1688–1836

William Shakeshaft (as well as being steward to Sir Thomas Dalrymple Hesketh he was a surveyor in private practice): daybook 1803–10, account books 1824–33, correspondence 1814–33, field and measuring books (including survey of Preston 1809) 1807–40, instructions on appointment as steward 1809, will and executorship papers 1834

Official Papers: Roll of Lancashire soldiers to serve in Ireland 1600; instructions for brief for Dorchester fire 1614; rules for Shevington constableship 1601–19; Croston drainage assessment book 1800–18; notebooks of Sir Thomas Dalrymple Hesketh as chairman of quarter sessions 1819–29; Rufford apprenticeship register and agreements 1802–15; Longton, workhouse papers 1819–31

Ecclesiastical Papers: Divorce of Thomas Standish of Ormskirk and Joan Stanley 1558; indulgence from Preston friary 1479

Croston: assignment of Becconsall chapel 1559

Great Harwood: agreements with abbots of Whalley to settle disputes 1455, 1512

Rufford: lease of chantry 1378, petition for curate and order for his salary 1664, payment of rent to Chester abbey 1505, faculty for alterations 1826, tithe accounts 1819–24, consecration of churchyard extension 1853

Plans: Boundary of fishery between North Meols and Hesketh 1806; Tarleton (and parts) 1827–1905; Wrightington (and parts) 1800–1913; Hesketh-with-Becconsall (and parts) c.1770–1911; Longton (and parts) 1817–27; Mawdesley (and parts) 1820–63; Rufford (and parts) c.1720–1905; Up Holland 1805; map of Lancashire shewing Catholic chapels 1820, 1828; chart of Ribble 1890; plan of Preston 1822

Rentals and Accounts: Rental of Rufford, Great Harwood, and Kerkeby in Kendall 1461–62; general rentals 1750–1906

Steward's account-books 1722–24, 1744–46; timber account and measurement books 1840–84; blacksmith's account-books 1821–26, 1838–67; butcher's account-books 1833–36; grocers account-books 1862–82; saddler's account-books 1834–42, 1856–72; wheelwright's account-book 1824–41; chemist's account-books 1846–69; Rufford Hall day-book 1809–13; bricks account-book 1849–69; John Burnett's account-books 1811–24; building account-books 1821–23, 1832–33, 1852, 1871; carpenter's account-books 1834–38, 1843–47; labourers' account-books 1723–25, 1789–1810, 1872–88; farm account-books 1815–72; gardeners' account-books 1818–64; grooms' account-books 1818–26, 1848–52; sale-books 1816–29; Dr. Charles Dandy's accounts 1859–66; Sir Thomas Dalrymple Hesketh's personal account-books 1805–38 and bank-books 1799–1821

Charity Papers: Rufford clothing club accounts 1845–52. Rufford Old Hall school: accounts 1816–18, writing-books 1833–61, lists of scholars 1849–62

Miscellaneous: Certificates of deposits of deeds at Up Holland priory 1500 and Whalley abbey 1522; order for payment of rents to Burnley school 1586; prospectus for survey of Lancashire by P. P. Burdett of Derby 1768; *Farm-leases in the Hundred of West Derby* by William Roscoe 1811

De Hoghton of Hoghton (DDHo)

In the later 12th century Warin Bussel, baron of Penwortham, gave some of his lands to his daughter's husband, Hamon the Boteler, whose grandson Adam was the first to use the Hoghton surname. Through the marriage of Richard of Hoghton about 1320 Lea and many other properties came to the family. Walton-le-Dale, long the possession of the Langtons, was purchased from mortgages by Richard Hoghton about 1598. Sir Richard Hoghton was one of the three Lancashire baronets created in 1611.

Among the documents found in the office of the clerk of the peace were some which certainly belong to this estate. For ease of reference these (DX/1208-1268) have been assimilated with the list below. The many earlier documents were calendared by J. H. Lumby in volume 88 of the Record Society of Lancashire and Cheshire, 1936. These are not included in the following account.

Manorial: Withnell court-books 1796, 1797, 1799, 1801–06, 1808–13, 1815–18, 1822–24, 1826

Title Deeds: Alston hall 1794–1820; Hoghton 1798–1844, Moulden mill 1656–1882, Hoghton Bottoms mill 1868–70, Hoghton school 1708–28; Lea 1781–1880; Walton-le-Dale 1740–1853; Penwortham mill 1860–67; Walton mill 1830–52

Family Papers: Bold settlements and wills 1561–1728; Hoghton settlements 1708–1843; diaries of Major-General Daniel Hoghton: India 1804, Copenhagen 1807; Peninsular War 1810–11; appointment of Sir Richard Hoghton as deputy steward of Amounderness 1523; pedigrees and papers 17th–19th century.

Royal licence to resume name "de Hoghton" 1862; commissions to Daniel Hoghton as lieutenant-colonel 1804, colonel 1805; apprenticeship indenture of Henry Hoghton to John Waller, London, merchant, 1698

Estate Papers: Hoghton and Walton-le-Dale drainage 1861–65; general surveys 1802; Walton-le-Dale leases 1799–1896; Withnell leases 1729–93; Lea and Ashton leases 1785–1896; leasebooks 1707, 1759, 1801, 1805, 1807–30; requests for corpses to pass over Walton Maines 1733–1810; descriptions of boundaries: Hoghton 1697, 1719, 1773, 1814, 1839, Heapey 1655, 1715, 1746, Anglezarke 1746, Lea and Ashton 1814, Walton-le-Dale 1679, 1699; tithe assignments 1785–1843

Correspondence: Letters from Daniel Houghton, the African traveller, at Galway, Dover, and Cowes 1777–79; letters to and from Major-General Daniel Hoghton (Lord William Bentinck, Marquess Wellesley, Viscount Castlereagh, etc.) concerning India, West Indies, the Peninsular War, etc., 1801–11

Official Papers: Instructions from the earl of Derby for garrisoning Leigh, Warrington, Wigan, Preston, and Brindle 1642; registration of Walton Hall as nonconformist meeting-place 1689; papers concerning repair of Moulden Brow 1665–1706; papers concerning repair of Walton Cop 1634–1749

Ecclesiastical Papers: Request for interment in chancel of Preston church 1688–1784; letters and papers concerning Preston church: pews, churchwardens, parish clerks, the Twenty Four Men, alterations, etc. 1644–1883; letters and papers concerning Walton-le-Dale church: pews, patronage, 1685–1790; letters and papers concerning Ribchester church: parish clerks, pews, etc. 1663–1863; receipt of a bell from Threlfall chapel in Goosnargh 1581; pew in Brindle church 1688; request for assistance in building new chapel at Tockholes 1710; presentations to chapel of Broughton 1683, 1684, 1761; abstract of title to chapelry of Broughton 1581–1744

Rentals: General 1648, 1720, 1743–1853; ground-rents 1797–1849

Accounts: Hoghton and Samlesbury 1743–69; general estate 1742–1853; Sir Henry Hoghton's 1730–68

Charity Papers: Walton-le-Dale, Shuttlingfield charity accounts 1832–93; Sarah Walmsley's charity for education in Kirkham, Poulton-le-Fylde, and St. Michaels-on-Wyre parishes, accounts 1703–91

Hopwood of Hopwood (DDHp)

The first members of the family to appear in the records is William of Hopwood, who was living in 1277. From him the estates descended to Dr. Robert Hopwood who died in 1762 and after the death of his wife in 1773 they passed to Edward Gregge of Chamber Hall in Werneth, who took the name of Hopwood. It is said that the reason for this bequest was that Edward Gregge had rendered services to Dr. Hopwood during the 1745 Jacobite incursion into Lancashire.

The Chamber estate was purchased in 1646 by Henry Wrigley, a merchant, and about 1680 his grand-daughter married Joseph Gregge.

Title Deeds (including leases): Ashton-under-Lyne 1514–1758; Ashworth 1610; Birtle-with-Bamford 1610–21; Broughton (Salford) 1607–55; Chadderton 1654–90; Crompton 1519–1667; Over Darwen 1658; Elton 1656; Halliwell 1762; Little Heaton 1652–54; Hopwood 1620–50, leases 1528–1769; Liverpool 1672–1714; Manchester 1426–1737, leases 1610–1778; Middleton 1334–1705, leases 1423–1778; Moston 1632; Newton (Manchester) 1640; Oldham 1433–1681, leases 1594–1719; Pilsworth 1652–54; Radcliffe 1631–33; Ribchester, water-mill 1505; Royton leases 1650–53; Salford 1535–1652, leases 1627–50; Spotland 1653–66; Stretford 1712; Thornham lease 1598; Tottington 1653–70; Turton 1657; Urmston 1599; Urswick leases 1640–41; Wigan leases 1515–1648; Worsley 1456

Family Papers: Settlements 1430–1770; wills 1567–1776; inquisitions *post mortem* 1570–1633; grant of freedom of London to Henry Wrigley, girdlemaker, 1630; appointment of Henry Wrigley as sheriff 1650; inventory of Henry Wrigley 1658; inventory of Madam Gregg 1707; commission of Robert Gregg Hopwood as captain 1794; grants of leave to Ensign Hopwood 1825, 1829

Estate Papers (leases are shewn with title-deeds): Agreement for division of Hathershaw Moor in Thornham 1691

Legal Papers: Assheton v. Hopwood (seats in Middleton church) 1702; Taylor and Tetlow v. Booth (Horsedge in Oldham) 1624; counsel's opinion concerning coal in Oldham 1791; Wrigley v. Cudworth (north chapel in Oldham church) 1648

Business Papers: Bills of sale of John Bowker of Salford, chapman 1637; agreements concerning iron mining at Urswick 1641–42; agreement concerning calves at Walmersley 1655; list of goods bought for Henry Wrigley 1646; letter concerning shipments of wool for London 1650; bonds 1444–1782

Official Papers: Assize orders concerning taking of poor in Manchester 1629–41; agreement for enclosure of Oldham commons and dividing Oldham from Chadderton 1604; Hopwood valuation 1781–82; quarter sessions order for stopping footway in Castleton, Hopwood and Middleton 1824; Jury writ for Manchester quarter sessions 1580; declaration of loan to Parliament by Henry and Alice Wrigley c.1645; Henry Wrigley's shrievalty papers 1650–52

Ecclesiastical Papers: Certificate and plan of re-pewing Middleton church 1794; faculty for gallery in Middleton church 1713; papers concerning maintenance of minister in Oldham 1646–48; certificate of payment to minister of Shaw chapel 1654; ordinances for governing Hoghton chantry in Ribchester church 1417; dissolution of espousal of Arthur Ince and Joan Gerard of Wigan parish 1515

Rentals and Accounts: Chipping rental 17th c.

Account-book of executor of John Gregory of Rochdale, gent. 1675–83 with general account 1705–10

Account of Henry Wrigley as receiver-general in Lancashire 1648–49

Houghton of Lowton (DDHt)

The yeoman family of Houghton sprang from Newton-in-Makerfield and later acquired Sorocold and Byrom properties there and in Lowton.

Title Deeds: Newton-in-Makerfield 1649–1841; Lowton 1709–1803

Family Papers: Settlements 1699–1873; valuation of goods of William Houghton 1823; property and income tax papers 1807–81; wills 1656–1870; insurance policies 1847–69; genealogical papers 1735–1869

Correspondence: Family letters 1757–1890; letters to the Morris family of Tyldesley from their emigrant relatives in America 1829–46

Business Papers: Agreement between Richard Bradshaw of Swinton and Allen Caine of Liverpool for working a patent for improving light reflectors 1887; agreements, letters, etc., concerning the Liverpool and Manchester, London and North Western, and Grand Junction railways 1829–66

Accounts: A miller's accounts 1772–77; account-book of cotton farmed-out for spinning and weaving 1801–06; accounts of executors of John and Sarah Leigh 1870–75; miscellaneous bills 1768–1884

Plan: Thomas Houghton's land in Lowton 1831

Miscellaneous: Rules of Manchester beagles 1775; list of lottery scheme meetings 1779–80

Hulton of Hulton (DDHu)

This family is supposed to have been among the faithful vassals of Robert Banastre expelled from Wales in 1167. Certainly Iorwerth and Madoc, sons of Bleiddyn, held lands in Hulton before 1200. About two hundred years later the estates, which had grown considerably, were divided between the Hultons of Hulton and the Hultons of Farnworth, but much of the property of the latter branch returned to the senior line by purchase about 1677. William Wilbraham Blethin Hulton was created a baronet in 1905. In 1664 Ann, daughter of William Jessop, clerk of the council during the Commonwealth, married William Hulton.

Among the documents found in the office of the clerk of the peace was a box of what are certainly Hulton muniments. These (DX 535-609) have, for ease of reference, been assimilated with the list below.

Title Deeds (including leases): Ashton-in-Makerfield 1736; Barton-on-Irwell 1292; Billinge 1460; Butterworth 1280–1738; Chorley 1703; Culcheth 1420; Denton 1274–1516, leases 1579–1634, coal-leases 1739–89; Farnworth c.1300–1814, leases 1621–1787; Halliwell 1294; Harpurhey 1327–1560, leases 1562–1795; Heaton 1341–1721; Hindley 1420; Hulton c.1200–1572, leases 1444–1812; Hundersfield 1422–1588; Ince-in-Makerfield c.1290–1408; Kearsley 1326, leases 1739–84; Longworth 1622–79, Longworth Pasture 1689–93, leases 1589–1809; Manchester 1280–1785, leases 1333–1764; Mawdesley lease 1491; Oldham c.1205–1696; Ordsall 1658–62; Rumworth 1619–1817, leases 1583–1692; Salford 1650–1710; Spotland 1324–1602 lease 1592; Tyldesley-with-Shakerley 1342–1422, lease 1428; Westhoughton c.1200–1724, leases 1562–1751; Wigan 1384–1482

Other places: Bryans Town in Westmeath 1667; London 1660, 1673; "the Somer or Barmodas Ilands" 1637–43

Family Papers: Settlements c.1300–1874; wills 1486–1775; inquisitions *post mortem* 1508–1613; bonds 1419–1755; pedigrees c.1550–1802; genealogical papers 1664–1809; grant of crest 1561; general pardon of Adam Hulton 1509; grant of custody of Richard Hulton, an idiot, 1553; inventory of William Jessop of Grays Inn 1675; papers concerning bringing the corpse of William Hulton to England 1772

Appointments: William Hulton as commissioner concerning Accrington copyholders 1664; William Hulton to take affidavits 1673; William Legh as ensign 1696, 1702, captain 1707, William Hulton as sheriff 1810 and as constable of Lancaster castle 1828, 1830, 1837; William Wilbraham Blethyn Hulton as constable of Lancaster castle 1892

Estate Papers (leases are shewn with title-deeds): Agreement for partition of Bedford moss 1406; boundary between Denton and Bredbury, co. Chester 1718; trees fallen in Denton 1724; request to set up "a horse gin" in Denton 1735; request for way through fields at Denton 1741; William Hulton's claim to wastes in Farnworth and Kearsley 1796; agreement between Cockersand abbey and Richard of Hulton about wastes and woods of Westhoughton 1312; sale of timber on Hulton properties in Lancashire and Ireland 1739

General surveys 1694–1717; lease agreements 1721–34

Correspondence: Concerning the Bryans Town estate in Westmeath 1657–1743; to and from William Jessop, referring, *inter alia*, to his election to Parliament, and Hackin, a haunted house near Longworth, 1656–72; William Jessop to his daughter Ann, wife of William Hulton, 1664–75 (written from Grays Inn, Lees in Essex, Oxford, etc., these refer, *inter alia*, to plague, fire, Felsted school, political events; they contain many passages in shorthand)

Miscellaneous letters 1637–1906, including references to Blackrod school 1691–94 and labour disturbances 1819–30; enclosure of Deane Moor 1792–95

Legal Papers: Awards 1417–1556; Hulton *v.* Hulton (Bolton, Middleton, and Lever) 1499; Hulton *v.* Hulton (Westhoughton) *c.*1530; Hulton *v.* Ratcliffe (finance) 1632; Hulton *v.* Mather (Bryans Town) 1701; allowances to exhibitioners from Manchester grammar school 1791; Hulton *v.* Mosley (Halshaw Moor) 1743; Over Hulton common 1724; Longworth pasture *c.*1730; Westhoughton Snydle watering-pool and well 1712; Westhoughton Chequerbent bowling green 1722; Westhoughton common *c.*1545–1726; ballasting of ships in river Thames *c.*1660; Winwick rectory *c.*1660

Business Papers: Bolton and Leigh railway: letters, prospectus, agreements, estimates, etc. 1824–28; Rochdale and Ashton Canals: minutes and papers 1793–98

Official Papers: Warrant for arrest of named Irishmen for assaulting the constable of Bedford 1690; agreement for erecting cottage for poor on Halshaw Moor 1679; warrant for raising light-horse in Hulton 1690; assessments for paying Westhoughton township debts 1795; consent for erecting cottage on Rumworth waste 1678; letters from Henry VIII to Adam Hulton to raise men against the Scots 1523 and 1542; West Derby Hundred subsidy-roll 1558; certificate by burgomaster of Lubeck of ownership of the ship *St. John* 1647; order for discharge of Adam Hulton from sequestration 1649; order for William

Hulton to supply an armed man 1660; assize order for relief of poor of Bolton parish 1687; Privy Council order for raising recruits in Lancashire 1691; order for pressing of seamen in Lancashire 1706; sessions order on wages c.1750; papers on treatment of prisoners in Lancaster castle 1820; statement to magistrates on misgovernment of public-houses in Bury and Bolton c.1820; papers on William Hulton's election to Parliament 1820; petition to Parliament for transferring franchise of Grampound to Lancashire 1820

Ecclesiastical Papers: Papers on illness of the vicar of Bolton 1793; letters-patent creating the parish of Deane 1541; Deane terrier 1728; letters and papers concerning Deane church 1668–1829; papers concerning the Hulton seat in Manchester church c.1670–1775; petition for brief for rebuilding Westhoughton chapel 1723; grant of advowson of Drigg, co. Cumberland c.1190; certification of dispensation for marriage of Roger of Hulton 1390; mandate of provincial prior of Austin Friars for masses on death of William, prior of Cartmel 1418; dispensation for marriage of Adam and Alice Hulton 1489; composition between abbots of Fountains, Salley, and Kirkstall concerning tithes of Saddleworth 1456; confirmation of marriage of Adam Belfield and Margaret Scolefeld at Rochdale 1496; licence for marriage of Adam Hulton and Clemence Norris 1534; sentence of nullity of marriage of Anne Belfeld and Richard Leigh of Rochdale 1570; reports on number of seats in churches of Blackrod, Bolton, Bradshaw, Bury, Heywood, Little Hulton, Holcome, Rivington, Turton, and Walmsley 1814

Plans: Longworth pasture, lately improved, 1732

Rentals: General 1694–1712, 1744, 1746, 1747, 1754, 1759–64, 1773–81, 1786–95, 1797, 1805–11, 1824–28, 1830; Denton 1692; Harpurhey 1690, 1692; Over Hulton 1826–34; Longworth 1827–30; Rumworth 1690; Westhoughton 1827–30

Accounts: Steward's accounts 1701–06, 1714–37, 1741–65, 1769–91, 1821–22; colliery accounts 1700–28, 1752–65, 1769–83, 1811–14, 1819–29, 1832–36; Longworth overseer's accounts 1765–1839; timber accounts 1739–40; accounts of Madam Legh 1706–23; quietus to collectors for defence of realm 1515; receipt for £10 composition from Robert Haworth for refusing knighthood 1631; quietus to Adam Hulton, collector of Tenth and Fifteenth 1561; quietus to executors of William Legh, sheriff 1723

Miscellaneous: Grant by Henry VIII to Roger Hulton of 10 marks annuity from profits of County Palatine of Lancaster 1510; inventory of Thomas Hoghton of Lea, esq., 1592; "Several consideracions touching the government of the Navie" 1645;

exercises in ballistics by David Balldock 1682; exercises in navigation c.1682; songs and verses 1814–30; a volume of printed notices, etc., relating to Bolton area c.1840

Kenyon of Peel (DDKe)

From 1589 to 1663 the Lancashire clerkship of the peace was in the hands of the Rigbys, passing in the latter year to Roger Kenyon of Parkhead in Whalley, who had married Alice, the daughter of George Rigby of Peel in Little Hulton. That property, later known as Kenyon Peel Hall, descended to the present Lord Kenyon. Roger Kenyon was governor of the Isle of Man, M.P. for Clitheroe, and receiver-general of the Duchy of Lancaster. Lloyd Kenyon, Lord Chief Justice, was created Baron Kenyon of Gredington in 1788.

It should be stated that the present collection is additional to that published by the Historical Manuscripts Commission in its 14th Report, Appendix IV. Those documents are still in Lord Kenyon's keeping.

Manorial: Myerscough: verdicts 1693–94; Newton (Manchester) appointment of steward 1744; Rochdale: notes of inquisitions and surrenders 1619

Title Deeds: Accrington 1613–52; Aighton 1666; Ainsworth 1622–1758; Ardwick 1698; Ashton-under-Lyne, Haughton and Openshaw 1598–1700; Aspull 1630–34; Astley 1763–73; Barton-upon-Irwell 1626–1766; Billington 1567–1669; Bilsborrow and Badsberry 1724; Birtle-with-Bamford 1706; Blackley 1671; Bolton-le-Moors 1652–1759; Bradshaw 1707; Broughton (Salford) 1704–41; Bury 1631–1721; Butterworth 1647–96; Carnforth 1730; Castleton 1348–1508; Catterall 1562; Chadderton 1667–1725; Cheetham 1758; Chorley 1655; Chorlton-on-Medlock 1765; Chorlton-cum-Hardy 1650–1769; Clayton and Eccleshill 1720; Clayton-le-Moors 1711; Clitheroe 1583–1780; Coppull 1688; Cuerden, Walton-le-Dale, Clayton-le-Woods and Farington 1590–1638; Deane 1635–1778; Denton, Heaton, Kenyon and Sharples 1654–69; Dinckley 1614–52; Downham and Worston 1627; Droylsden 1714–49; Dutton and Dilworth 1652; Entwistle 1670–1749; Euxton 1718; Flixton and Urmston 1720; Furness 1675; Goosnargh 1562–1659; Gorton 1692–1829; Haigh 1606–1709; Halliwell 1604–1757; Great Harwood 1618–28; Heaton 1467–1681; Hopwood 1613; Horwich 1657; Little Hulton, Tyldesley, Worsley, Astley and Turton 1250–1837; Hundersfield, Rochdale and Butterworth 1671–1765; Ightenhill Park 1706; Ince-in-Makerfield, Aspull and Hindley 1604–1739; Irlam 1654–1744; Great Lever and Middleton 1632–1717; Lostock 1713; Lydiate 1587; Manchester 1319–1786; Mellor

1746; Moston 1765; Oldham, Crompton, Royton and Chadderton 1569–1717; Orrell 1745; Oswaldtwistle 1645; Pemberton 1397–1728; Pendlebury 1635; Pendleton (Salford) 1678–1759; Pilkington 1684; Poulton 1633; Prestwich 1668–1729; Read 1655–1668; Ribchester and Dilworth 1721; Royton 1719–41; Rumworth 1673–1717; Salford 1652–1760; Samlesbury 1626; Standish-with-Langtree 1644–1762; Thornley-with-Wheatley 1616; Trafford 1679–1736; Turton 1605–1766; Tyldesley-with-Shakerley 1638–1818; Unsworth 1714; Warrington 1526–1762; Westhoughton 1712; Whalley 1571–1677; Wigan 1479–1782; Winmarleigh 1548; Withington 1686–90; Worsley 1709–63; Wyresdale 1733

Other counties: Cheshire: Beeston 1700, Betchton 1701, Birtles 1731, Buglawton 1555, Capesthorne 1730, Chester 1623–91, Disley 1684–88, Drakelow 1587, Macclesfield 1668, Middlewich 1416, Mobberley 1751, Mottram 1622, Nantwich 1577, Stockport 1594–1660, Stretton 1715, Wincle 1738–43; Derbyshire: Hope 1741, Mellor 1707; Yorkshire: Doncaster 1707

Family Papers: Settlements 1619–1829; wills and inventories 1601–1787; bonds 1541–1767; book containing copies and abstracts of bonds and settlements 1701–65; book containing list of deeds concerning the clerkship of the peace, Dr. Roger Kenyon, Rev. Edward Kenyon of Prestwich, burgages in Clitheroe, and the Peel estate, 18th century

Estate Papers: Surveys: Milnshaw in Accrington 1617; Dalton-in-Furness 1619; Plain Furness 1620; Peel in Hulton 1657; Denton 1714; Longworth 1721, 1730; Over Hulton 1722; Tottington 1723; Westhoughton 1723–25; Wigan c.1780; Giggleswick, co. York 1605

Correspondence: Alexander Rigby of Wigan 1596–1617; Roger Kenyon of Parkhead 1609–36; George Rigby of Peel 1622–44; Roger Kenyon of Peel 1649–98; George Kenyon of Peel 1692–1728; George Kenyon II of Peel 1723–75; miscellaneous 1596–1832

Legal Papers: A large collection, including: Kenyon v. Rigby (clerkship of peace) 1660; Ellenbrook chapel in Worsley c.1690; Kenyon v. Lever (Prestwich tithes) c.1690; Assheton v. Nowell (Samlesbury, Heyhouses and Colne) c.1630; Oldfield v. Kenyon (Peel and Parkhead) c. 1690; Brandwood v. Ashley (Entwistle) 1748; Cobham v. Barlow (Eccleston, Prescot) 1737; Walmsley v. Grundy (salmon from Preston) 1764; Wolstenholme v. Schofield (Bury church) 1724. Letters of attorney 1624–1779

Business Papers: Vale Royal, Cheshire, iron-furnace agreements 1718–20; Partington, Cheshire, slitting mill agreements 1757, 1759; Ravenscroft, Cheshire, saltworks agreements 1725

Official Papers: Preston elections 1617–1768; Isle of Man shipping and customs duties 1651–93; clerkship of the peace 1610–1740*; quarter sessions 1523–1778; shrievalty and assizes 1593–1792; lieutenancy and militia 1643–89; duchy of Lancaster 1567–1729; Thieveley (Cliviger) lead mines† 1629–35; Parliament 1616–29, 1661–1720; recusancy 1591–1747; the Jacobite Plot 1684–95; Blackburn Hundred fairs and markets 1663–1714

Ecclesiastical Papers: Sketch of heraldic glass in Burnley church 17th century; list of churches and vicars in Lancashire c.1615; prayers, sermons and notes 1640–89; Bedford tithes, grants and assignments 1706–79; Eccleston (Chorley) presentation 1627, faculty 1704; Turton, memorandum of chapel endowment 18th c., Prestwich, terrier 1663, tithe lease 1668; Ringley chapel deeds 18th.

Plans: Peel in Little Hulton 1783; Worston and Downham 1593; Stockdale near Malham, co. York c.1620

Rentals: Radcliffe and Middleton 1563–74; Whalley and Billington c.1620; Oswaldtwistle tithe 1613; Hawkshead bailiwick 1619; Plain Furness 1619; Dalton-in-Furness 1619; Kenyon and Lowton 1661; Hulton and Westhoughton 1696–98; Heaton, Kenyon, Sharples, Denton, and Manchester 1725; Gorton, Openshaw, and Middle Hulton 1787–1836

Accounts: Alexander Rigby 1591–1621; George Rigby 1621–44; Beatrix Rigby 1649; Roger Kenyon of Parkhead 1610–36; miscellaneous Kenyon 1637–59; Roger Kenyon of Peel 1659–98; Dr. Roger Kenyon 1689–1728; George Kenyon of Peel 1698–1728; George Kenyon II of Peel 1729–1822; miscellaneous Kenyon 1717–68, 1868–78; account-book of William Holt, hatter, 1722–26; Roger Kenyon's accounts of writs issued by the Exchequer 1691–94

Miscellaneous: Passport from Ireland 1691; papers relating to the earls of Derby 1651–87; book of deeds, Salesbury and Clitheroe, 17th century; notebook of Latin play 17th century; recipes 17th and 18th century; petition of Sir Philip Egerton and other prisoners at Chester, affirming loyalty to William III, c.1689; petition of Roger Kenyon re office of customer of Chester c.1690; petition of Beatrix, widow of Edward Copley of Batley,

---

* See *Historic Society of Lancashire and Cheshire*, vol. 106.
† See *Record Society of Lancashire and Cheshire*, vol. 102.

co. York, for restoration of estates *c*.1665; list of animals in Great Close, Malham moor, co. York, 1619; surrender of chantry rents in Cumberland and Westmorland 1615; orders concerning Wirksworth, co. Derby, lead mines 1604

Lord Lilford of Bank Hall (DDLi)

To Lord Lilford have descended three ancient Lancashire estates—Atherton, Bank in Bretherton and Bewsey in Burtonwood.

Atherton was the possession of the Athertons from at least the early thirteenth century and remained with them until Elizabeth Atherton married Robert Gwillym of Herefordshire in the early eighteenth century. Their son Robert Vernon succeeded in 1763 and took the name Atherton, marrying Henrietta Maria, elder daughter of Peter Legh of Lyme. It was their daughter Ann Maria who carried the Atherton estate to Thomas, Lord Lilford by marriage in 1797.

The manor of Bretherton was originally owned in moieties by the Banastres. One moiety became subdivided, but was brought together again by the Heskeths of Rufford in the eighteenth century and sold to Lord Lilford about 1880. The other moiety, known as Bank, descended to Christopher Banastre, who died in 1690. His daughter married Thomas Fleetwood and their daughter married Thomas Legh of Lyme. His younger grand-daughter married James Anthony Keck of Leicestershire, from whose descendant Lord Lilford inherited Bank in 1860.

About 1264 Robert de Ferrers conveyed Burtonwood to William le Boteler who made Bewsey his seat. The Boteler estates were sold to Thomas Ireland in 1597 and passed (except Warrington, which he sold in 1628) to his daughter Eleanor, who married John Atherton, and thus they descended to Lord Lilford.

Manorial: Atherton: court-books 1838–89; court-papers 1807–32

Bewsey: court-papers 1808–34

Coppull: court-books 1664, 1769, 1777, 1793, 1796, 1797, 1802–04, 1809–12; call-book 1754

Pennington: court-books 1689–1706, 1794–1888; court-papers 1815–24

Sankey: court-papers 1806–20

Warrington: court-rolls 1523–24, 1592–93

Title Deeds (including leases): Atherton 1543–*c*.1880, leases 1616–*c*.1910; Bedford *c*.1650–*c*.1790, leases 1723–25; Bretherton leases 1759–1829; Brockholes 1432; Burtonwood 1404–*c*.1620, leases *c*.1750–1862; Coppull 1391–1802, leases 1505–*c*.1750; Liverpool *c*.1560–*c*.1680; Penketh *c*.1260–1718, lease 1625–73;

Great Sankey c.1250–1830, leases 1682–1796; Sutton 1340–c.1620; Tarleton 1718–c.1880, leases c.1750–c.1880; Up Holland 1597–1802; Warrington c.1260–1674; West Derby lease 1715; Westhoughton 1590–c.1760, leases (coal) 1796–c.1860; Westleigh 1558–1815. leases 1665–c.1910; Woolton c.1290–c.1680, lease 1699

Other counties: Cheshire 1520–1653; Herefordshire 1572–c.1790

Family Papers: Settlements 1422–1851; wills 1508–1885; papers re divorce of Thomas Ireland c.1592; award in wardship dispute 1422; grant of custody of lunatic 1587

Appointments: Thomas Ireland as bailiff of Halton and Whitley, co. Chester 1611, counsellor-at-law to Prince Charles 1623

Estate Papers (leases are included with title-deeds): Lease registers: Atherton estate 1727, c.1740, 1774, surveys 1723–1866, lease agreements 1839–94, game-book: Bank Hall estate 19th c., stewards' reports: Bank Hall and Atherton estates c.1880–c.1910, crop-records and drainage books 1803–31, papers and accounts for Little Sankey enbanking 1550–1734, Atherton estate: plantation papers 1799–1830, private-road papers 1773–1880, drainage books 1817–30, papers re damage by colliers 1775–78, papers re stewards' salary and terms of employment, Atherton, c.1785–1812, terrier of Broad Hinton, Salthorp and Quidhampton, co. Wilts. 1802, survey of Herefordshire and Monmouth estates 1760, survey of Penketh demesne c.1686, survey of Sir Alexander Rigby's estates in Layton, Duxbury, Chorley, Coppull, Poulton, Hardhorn, Carleton, Marton and Bispham c.1714

Correspondence: John Jeffreys (father of the judge) to Ireland family (finance) 1629–39, estate affairs 1718–1900, Warrington school 1810–18, turnpike roads 1818–25, Warrington Trinity chapel 1821, Westleigh parsonage 1812–85, Atherton coalmines 1824–33, railways 1824–35, Chowbent chapel 1832–33, Leigh tithes 1838–45, river pollution 1869–72, letter-books of John and Atherton Selby, surveyors, 1876–1904

Legal Papers: Warrington and Burtonwood manorial rights 1775–1806, right of appointing Warrington schoolmaster c.1812, Lilford v. Wigan Coal & Iron Co., c.1882–90, Bold v. Ireland (Burtonwood, Sankey and Warrington manors) 1600

Business Papers: Albion cotton-spinning mills; Atherton c.1890, Atherton colliery 1876–84, Mather Lane Spinning Co., Leigh 1903–08

Official Papers: Leigh improvements 1842–95, Manufacturers' Relief Committee 1843, Census 1831, Wigan and Warrington bills of mortality 1814–15, Warrington poor expenditure 1792–

95, Manchester Lying-in Hospital 1795–96, Warrington ordinances 1617, election of Warrington churchwardens c.1715, election of Burtonwood officers 1622, Herefordshire quarter sessions, county-fund papers 1693–98, Monmouthshire deputy-lieutenant's militia order 1690

Ecclesiastical Papers: Warrington advowson c.1230–1646, Leigh church 1620–1815, Atherton tithes 1704–1828; Tarleton: new chapel 1718, Primitive Methodist chapel 19th century; Leigh churchyard 1791, gallery 1817, Chowbent St. John's rebuilding c.1810–35, Sankey chapel 18th and 19th c.

Plans: Atherton c.1790–c. 1820, Atherton park 1759; Bewsey demesne c.1790; Leigh churchyard 1791; Tyldesley to Leigh bridleroad 1777, 1799; Leigh market-place 1827; Tyldesley 1825; Astley coal-mines 1887

Rentals: Atherton, Pennington, Ince, Hindley, and Ashton-in-Makerfield, with Fryton, Hovingham, Slingsby, and Scarborough, co. York 1563, Warrington, Burtonwood, and Sankey 1564, Atherton estates 1726–1893, Lancashire and Herefordshire estates 1760, Bank Hall estate 1860–93, Coppull and Duxbury 1653, 1655, Herefordshire tithes 1749–50

Accounts: Atherton and Bewsey estates 1724–1910, Bank Hall estate 1835–1910. vouchers 1792–1912; weekly labour accounts 1835–1914, Atherton domestic expenditure 1749–1837; pay-sheets 1887–1913; timber accounts 1807–62; colliery accounts 1814–40, Astley Hall estate accounts 1849–88, Langston, Herefordshire, estate accounts 1751–56

Charity Papers: Miscellaneous charities and relief funds 1799–1866, Lady Lilford charity 1841–1904, Patriotic Fund accounts 1854

Miscellaneous: Account of voyage to South America 1819, stations of British and French ships and regiments c.1756

Trappes-Lomax of Clayton-le-Moors (DDLx)

Richard Lomax of Pilsworth and Brunshaw married, about 1715, Rebecca, daughter of John Heywood of Urmston, who, as representative of the Grimshaws, brought the Clayton Hall estate to her husband. Their son, James, rebuilt the hall about 1772 and his great-grand-daughter, Helen, who was heiress of a moiety of the Clayton Hall estate and the whole of the Allsprings property in Great Harwood, married her cousin, Thomas Byrnand Trappes of Clitheroe, in 1866.

Reference should be made to *A History of . . . Clayton-le-Moors* by R. Trappes-Lomax (Chet. Soc. N.S. 85, 1926).

Title Deeds: Allithwaite 1687; Clayton-le-Moors *c*.1290–1914; Further Sparth (families of Cunliffe and Brookbank*) 1647–1849, Nearer Sparth (families of Christian of the Isle of Man, Rishton and Whalley) 1490–1830, Stanworth House 1727–76; Great Harwood 1728–1928; Hundersfield 1766–68

Family Papers: Settlements 1373–1883, wills 1696–1848, appointment of Charles Brookbank as quartermaster 1798

Estate Papers: Lease register, Great Harwood 1764, survey, Great Harwood *c*.1840, Clayton and Altham enclosure from waste 1277, licences for digging coalpits on Henfield common 1635, 1637

Correspondence: The Mosley interest in the estate 1752–80, letter from James Neville concerning a reform meeting at Burnley 1820

Legal Papers: Grimshaw *v*. Banister (Henfield common) 1596, Berry *v*. Clayton and Grimshaw (Clayton Hall) 1718–26, Lomax *v*. Walton (coal) 1778–98, rating of coalpits *c*.1784–90, division of Clayton and Altham commons *c*.1786–87, "Richard Cotthams costly lawe booke" concerning Clayton estates 1657–64, Brookbank *v*. Grimshaw (Sparth) 1728–31, Blackburn tithe case 1816–19, the child-marriage of Lord Molyneux and M. Stanley 1648, "Lord Molyneux's Case about the Rebellion" 1716

Business Papers: Coalmining in Devon, Somerset, Dorset, Gloucestershire and Yorkshire, 1767, 1773, coal agreements 1774–83, partnership of James Lomax and William Mercer in cotton-trade 1783, colliery papers 1659–1843

Official Papers: Clayton apprenticeship agreement 1772; enclosure award 1797, tithe merger 1844; Great Harwood assessments 1784–85; Harwood and Tottleworth valuation 1817, lists of constables, churchwardens, and assessments for Pilsworth 1660–1770

Ecclesiastical Papers: Faculty for gallery in Cartmel church 1710, conveyance of site of St. Hubert's church, Clayton 1859, subscription to augment curacy of Harwood 1771

Plans: Clayton coal *c*.1780, commons *c*.1785, Sparth 1779; Great Harwood moor 1762, Clayton 1797, line of road in Great Harwood 1818, Altham colliery 1892–96

Rentals and Accounts: General rentals 1817–64, Clayton rentals 1849–89, 1924–32, Allsprings rentals 1867–89, 1892–1932; paving and sewering ledgers: Clayton 1889–1925, Harwood

---

* This group contains many Brookbank documents other than title-deeds, especially relating to the curacy of Cartmel.

1895–1914, Allsprings 1896–1915, labourers' wage-book 1924–41, cash-books 1935–47; coal banksmen's weekly bills 1793–1803, Clayton colliery stock book 1848

Miscellaneous: Book of arithmetic, geometry, and mensuration 1705

Machell of Pennybridge (DDMc)

Manorial: Dunnerdale-with-Seathwaite court books 1775, 1776

Title Deeds: Allithwaite 1641, Blawith 1739, 1825, Broughton 1758, Cartmel 1640, 1712, 1797, Claife 1698–1712, 1728, Colton 1540–1899, Finsthwaite 1700, 1750–95, Haverthwaite 1567–1876, Nibthwaite 1787–1871, Dalton-in-Furness 1724–53, Dunnerdale-with-Seathwaite 1703–71, Egton-with-Newland 1574–1932, Hawkshead 1704–33, 1785, Lowick 1587–1901, Osmotherley 1850, Torver 1631, Ulverston 1699–1745, London 1681–1702, Warter, Yorkshire East Riding 1806, Windermere, Westmorland 1668–1781

Accounts: Estate and personal 1757–1822

Correspondence: Estate 1715–1891, family 1732–1913, Lord Chief Justice Dallas 1789–1832, William Wordsworth 1846, miscellaneous 1746–1881

Family Papers: Wills and settlements 1637–1876, genealogical papers c.1200–1878

Miscellaneous: Notes on Furness flora, fauna and weather 1773–1852

Marton of Capernwray (DDMa)

The manor of Capernwray in Over Kellet was owned at the beginning of the fourteenth century by the Blackburnes. In the middle of the seventeenth century it was conveyed to Sir Robert Bindloss of Borwick, but he held it for only a few years, when it was purchased by John Otway who had also bought the manor of Over Kellet. Early in the eighteenth century Oliver Marton (from Craven) became the owner and his descendants have held the property until recently.

Manorial (Malhamdale, co. York): Airton: court-rolls 1604, 1606, 1607, 1609–15, 1617, 1620–24, 1626–28, 1632, 1633, 1635–41, 1646, 1648, 1650, 1652–55, 1657; verdicts 1665, 1667, 1670, 1671, 1678–81, 1690, 1691, 1693–95, 1697–99, 1704–08; estreats 1650, 1653, 1658, 1659, 1661, 1667, 1668, 1670, 1671, 1675, 1677–80; call-books 1690–92, 1695, 1696, 1697, 1698, 1702

Calton: court-rolls 1536–41, 1543–49, 1553, 1558, 1559, 1562, 1604, 1606, 1607, 1609–15, 1617, 1620–24, 1626, 1632, 1633, 1635–39, 1648, 1650, 1652–55, 1657; verdicts 1661, 1663, 1675, 1677–81,

1690, 1691, 1693–95, 1697–99, 1704–08, 1710–11; estreats 1650, 1653, 1658, 1659, 1661, 1667, 1668, 1670, 1671, 1675, 1677–80; call-books 1690–92, 1694, 1695, 1697, 1698, 1702

Hanlith: court-rolls 1604, 1606, 1607, 1609–11, 1613–15, 1617, 1620, 1622–26, 1632, 1633–41, 1646, 1648, 1650, 1652–55, 1657; verdicts 1677–80, 1690, 1691, 1693–95, 1697–99, 1704–08, 1710, 1711; call-books 1690–92, 1694, 1695, 1697, 1698, 1702; estreats 1650–53, 1658, 1659, 1661, 1667, 1668, 1670, 1671, 1675, 1677–80

Kilnsey: court-roll 1534

Kirkby: court-rolls 1604, 1606–11, 1613–15, 1617, 1620, 1622–24, 1626, 1632, 1633, 1635–39, 1640, 1641, 1646, 1648, 1650, 1652–55, 1657; verdicts 1677–81, 1690, 1691, 1693–95, 1697–99, 1704–08, 1710, 1711; estreats 1650–53, 1658, 1659, 1661, 1675, 1677–80; call-books 1690–92, 1694, 1695, 1697, 1698, 1702

Litton: court-roll 1534

Malham East: court-rolls 1534, 1550, 1558, 1560, 1562, 1569, 1573, 1575–81, 1583, 1604, 1606–15, 1618, 1620, 1622, 1624, 1626, 1632, 1633, 1635–41, 1646, 1648, 1650, 1652–55, 1657; verdicts 1670, 1671, 1675, 1677–79, 1681, 1690, 1691, 1693–95, 1697–99, 1704–08, 1710, 1711; estreats 1650–53, 1658, 1659, 1661, 1667, 1668, 1670, 1671, 1675, 1677–80; call-books 1690–92, 1694, 1695, 1697, 1698, 1702

Malham West: court-rolls 1604, 1606–15, 1617, 1622, 1624, 1640, 1641, 1648, 1650, 1652–55, 1657; verdicts 1670, 1671, 1675, 1677, 1690, 1691, 1693–95, 1697–99, 1704–08, 1710, 1711; estreats 1650–53, 1658, 1659, 1661, 1667, 1668, 1670, 1671, 1675, 1677, 1678; call-books 1690–92, 1694, 1695, 1697, 1698, 1702

Flasby, Hinton, Threshfield, Rilstone, Hetton and Skipton: extent c.1600

Title Deeds: Arkholme 1770–1879; Bolton-le-Sands 1699; Borwick 1638–1875; Bulk 1741; Carnforth 1773–1808; Gressingham 1699–1849; Halton 1699–1808; Heysham 1699; Ireby 1744; Lancaster 1662–1796; Middleton (Lancaster) 1699–1842; Newton-with-Scales 1741; Over Kellet 1666–1871, Capernwray 1709–1854; Overton, Troughton marsh 1745–1849; Poulton-le-Sands 1699; Priest Hutton 1666–1871; Quernmore tithe 1859; Slyne-with-Hest 1699–1744; Tatham 1744; Thurnham 1708; Tunstall 1744

Other counties: London: Grays Inn 1710–40, Yorkshire: Airton 1517–1618, Calton 1517–1618, 1757–85, Kirkby Malham 1517–1618, Skipton 1517–1618, Thornton-in-Lonsdale 1751–1856

Family Papers: Marton settlements and papers 1663–1887, Curwen and Rawlinson of Cark settlements and papers 1605–77, Wharmby and Mansergh of Borwick papers 1636–1837

Appointments: John Foxcroft, exemption from parish offices 1647, Oliver Marton, deputy lieutenant 1714, steward of Lonsdale 1725, 1727, Edward Marton, steward of Lonsdale 1745, captain 1745, deputy lieutenant 1757, Oliver Marton, rector of Bentham 1748, deputy lieutenant 1762, George Richard Marton, ensign 1788, lieutenant 1788, 1789, 1790, captain 1792, 1794, major 1796, inspecting field-officer 1804, 1807, deputy-lieutenant 1806, George Marton, captain 1823, gentleman of privy chamber 1843, George Blucher Heneage Marton, captain 1862, major 1874, sheriff 1877

Estate Papers: Leases: Over Wyresdale 1741, 1756, Lancaster 1692–1779; Middleton (Lancaster) 1690, 1723, Over Kellet 1801; Ireby 1737, Tunstall 1793; leasing agreements 1772–1832; surveys and valuations: Lancashire estates 1726, Lancashire and Yorkshire estates 1858, Capernwray estate 1832, various 1760–1818; surveys and leases, Borwick 1681–1858

Correspondence: Tithe and lords' rents of Lancashire and Yorkshire estate 1859–92, letter-book 1727–1823

Legal Papers: Chaytor v. Holmes (East Scrafton moor, co. York) 1790, in re Oliver Marton (with estate accounts) 1795–1832, North v. Marton (Over Kellet moor) 1815–16, Dent common 1807, confiscation order for rebellion, Richard Norton and Leonard Metcalfe 1570

Maps and Plans: Marton estates c.1760, allotment on Aughton moor 1800, parts of Lancaster c.1820

Accounts: Compoti: honour of Middleham, co. York 1468–69, honours of Alnwick, Northumberland and Cockermouth, Cumberland 1492–93, Marton general estate and household accounts 1776–1842, Rev. Oliver Marton's accounts 1767–92, Capernwray quarry 1783–1826

Rentals: Otterburn, co. York, 1548, Craven lands 1570, Marton estates 1761, 1782–88, 1796–1818

Miscellaneous: Airton, co. York, enclosure of moor 1536, Thornton-in-Lonsdale, co. York, enclosure and land-tax papers 1814–17, subsidy roll, wapentake of Staincliffe and Ewcross 1571

Mather of Lowick (DDLk)

In the mid-fifteenth century Lowick came to the Ambrose family through marriage with the Towers heiress and it remained with them until about 1680 when it passed, again through marriage, to John Latus of Millom. Further descents through female lines brought the manor to the families of Blencowe, Everard, Gaskarth, Montagu and Mather.

Manorial: Lowick: court-rolls and books 1579, 1597, 1599, 1605, 1611–13, 1620, 1623, 1624, 1630, 1647–53, 1656, 1658, 1661, 1663, 1668–70, 1673–75, 1685–98, 1710–14, 1717, 1719, 1722–26, 1729–36, 1738–63, 1804–1910, 1921–35; admittance registers 1739–1925; call-books 1739, 1742–48, 1757–63

Conishead: court-rolls 1608–10, 1685, 1686, 1688, 1695, 1696; Kirkby Ireleth: custumal 1590

Title Deeds: Blawith 1649; Broughton-in-Furness 1703–31; Colton 1617–24; Dunnerdale-with-Seathwaite 1613–1728; Kirkby Ireleth 1561–1703; Lowick 1556–1793; Ulverston 1324–1409

Other counties: Cumberland: Carlisle 1691, Cockermouth 1711, Ulpha 1733, Whicham 1389–1720; Gloucestershire: Sudeley and Winchcomb 1603–06; Westmorland: Kendal 1699

Family Papers: Settlements 1603–1742, wills 1557–1672, bonds 1624–1781, appointments: Ferdinando Latus, deputy-lieutenant of Cumberland 1715, 1734, Sir George Fletcher, freeman of Newcastle-upon-Tyne 1682, inventory of John Ambrose 1638, inquisition *post mortem* James Ambrose 1593, Blencowe family papers 1632–1750, goods at Lowick Hall 1782

Estate Papers: Agreement on alterations at Lowick Hall 1741

Correspondence: Goathwaite Moss 1742, battle of Preston 1715

Legal Papers: Lowick manor and chapel 1601–1765, Wilson *v.* Clarke (theft of cloth between Rochdale and Archangel) 1729–31, Ambrose *v.* Fleming (Lowick tithes) *c.*1630, Latus *v.* Sidebottom (Lowick timber) 1686

Ecclesiastical Papers: Kirkby Ireleth rectory and tithes 1600–1703, Lowick chapel 1693–1806

Rentals: Lowick: *c.*1680, 1739, 1743, 1744, 1758–61, 1870–1906, 1926–47

Accounts: Work done at Lowick Hall 1744–47, repairs at Lowick mills 1752

Charity Papers: Agreement establishing Lowick school 1757, lease for Broughton-in-Furness school 1714

Election Papers: Cockermouth poll-list 1701

Miscellaneous: Warrant to keeper of Broughton Park to supply buck and doe to Ralph Latus 1612, assignment of shares in ships *Hope* and *Resolution* of Whitehaven 1727, lease for land for watch-house in Workington 1730, *A Letter in Praise of the Duke of Cumberland c.*1750

Molyneux, Earls of Sefton (DDM)

The name Molyneux is said to derive from Moulineaux in the French department of Seine Inferiure. Be this as it may, Roger of Poitou, about 1100, granted to Robert de Molyneux a large estate consisting of the manors of Sefton, Thornton, Cuerden and half of Down Litherland. Croxteth came to the family in 1473, Toxteth Park in 1605, Simonswood in 1507, as well as many other properties. Richard Molyneux was one of the first baronets created in 1611; his son Sir Richard became viscount Molyneux of Maryborough in 1628 and the eighth viscount was created earl of Sefton in 1771, both these being in the peerage of Ireland. A United Kingdom barony of Sefton of Croxteth was conferred on the second earl in 1831.

Manorial: Altcar: court books 1784–97, 1799–1806, 1808–21, 1823–
55, estreats 1761–71, 1785

Clayton-le-Woods: court rolls 1574, 1609–11, 1615, 1616, 1618,
1621–23, 1625, 1636; estreats 1674, 1676

Croxteth: court-rolls 1458, 1459, 1538

Eccleston and Heskin: court rolls 1508, 1604, 1613, 1614, 1618,
1619, 1621, 1623, 1656, 1658, 1663, 1665–67; estreats 1658,
1666, suitors roll 1656

Ellel: court books 1610-12, 1615, 1618, 1619

Euxton: court-book 1618, 1619, 1621, 1623–26

Fishwick: court roll 1594

Great Crosby: court rolls 1458, 1459, 1474, 1537, 1538

Kirkby: court books 1786, 1788–92, 1795–97, 1799, 1804, 1807–48;
estreats 1759–61, 1763, 1767

Litherland, Aintree, Orrell and Ford: court books 1786, 1788–92,
1794, 1795, 1799, 1800, 1808–53; estreats 1759–62, 1785

Liverpool: court rolls 1544, 1545

Sefton, Netherton and Lunt: court books 1785, 1786, 1788–93, 1795–
97, 1799, 1804, 1808–53, estreats 1762, 1763

Simonswood: court rolls 1459, 1538

Tarbock: court books 1785, 1788–92, 1795, 1796, 1799, 1804, 1807–
44; estreats 1759, 1764, 1765, 1783

Thornton: court books 1773–75, 1777, 1779, 1782, 1788, 1835, 1843

Toxteth Park: court rolls 1459, 1538; court book 1784

Ulnes Walton: court books 1649, 1665, 1673, 1683, 1684

West Derby: court rolls 1458, 1459, 1474, 1537, 1538; court books
1823–59

Church Minshull, co. Chester: court rolls 1485, 1487, 1490, 1497, 1503

Grant of free warren in manors of Sefton, Litherland, Orrell, Ford, Aintree, Kirkby, Tarbock, Altcar, Maghull, Euxton, Eccleston, Heskin, Fishwick, Ellel, Lydiate, Ulnes Walton, and Ince Blundell 1615, grant of manor of Altcar 1558, grant for tenants of Altcar to be toll-free 1613, confirmation of grant by Henry VI that the Molyneux manors from Hale to North Meols should be free from the jurisdiction of the Admiral of England 1528, lease for 300 years to Henry Blundell of wreck of the sea in manors of Formby, Birkdale, and Ainsdale 1671

Title Deeds (including leases): Aintree 1295–1659, leases 1670–1839; Altcar (Merivale abbey) c.1235–1563, leases 1389–1812; Ashton-in-Makerfield c.1290; Aughton (Merivale abbey) 1285–1734, leases 1345–1791; Clayton-le-Woods 1558–1736; Great Crosby c.1290–1776, leases 1337–1788; Little Crosby c.1280–1560; Croxteth 1473 (warrant by Richard, duke of Gloucester), 1508 (grant by Henry VIII), leases 1712–1803; Eccleston and Heskin 1506–1693, leases 1674–96; Ellel (Conishead priory) c.1270–1406, leases 1655–1742; Euxton c.1290–1613; Fazakerley c.1200–1529, leases 1655–1796; Halsall 1529; Much Hoole (Merivale abbey) c.1280–c.1300; Ince Blundell (Stanlaw abbey) c.1230–1588, leases 1650–1802; Kirkby c.1270–1784, leases 1443–1849; Kirkdale c.1280–1565, leases 1501–1744; Leyland c.1260; Litherland c.1250–1790, leases 1347–1845; Liverpool c.1270–1788, leases 1559–1781; Lunt leases 1743–1806; Lydiate 1403–1790, lease 1582–1783; Maghull c.1230–1660, leases 1471–1755; Melling c.1250–1542, leases 1659–1821; Netherton 1388–1763, leases 1654–1845; Orrell and Ford c.1260–1549, leases 1647–1845; Sefton c.1210–1589, leases 1343–1833; Simonswood leases 1647–1842; Tarbock 1200–1778, leases 1603–1843; Thornton c.1230–1773, leases 1653–1804; Thornton-le-Fylde 1461; Toxteth Park 1596–1832, leases 1634–1834; Walton-on-the-Hill c.1260–1589, leases 1342–1805; West Derby c.1260–1612, leases 1389–1822

Family Papers: Settlements c.1300–1746, wills 1475–1744, general pardons 1437–1626, inquisitions post mortem 1368, 1636, inventories of viscount Molyneux, London 1638, Croxteth and Preston 1745; appointments: Sir Richard Molyneux, master-forester of West Derby, steward of West Derby and Salford and constable of Liverpool castle 1446; Thomas Molyneux, likewise, 1461; Thomas Molyneux, constable and captain of Beaumaris castle 1477; Thomas Molyneux, constable of Liverpool castle, steward of West Derby and Salford, and master-forester of Simonswood, Toxteth, and Croxteth 1483; William Molyneux to levy money missing from Duchy accounts 1531; Sir Richard Molyneux, sheriff, 1565; Richard Molyneux, master-forester of West Derby, steward of West Derby and Salford, constable of Liverpool castle 1585; Sir Richard Molyneux, baronet 1611, steward of Blackburn, Tottington, Rochdale and Clitheroe 1621, deputy lieutenant 1625, viscount of Maryborough 1628; viscount Molyneux, steward of Blackburn, Tottington, Rochdale and Clitheroe, butler of Lancashire 1640, 1672, lord lieutenant 1687, lord Gerard of Brandon, constable of Liverpool castle and butler of Lancashire 1692; earl of Sefton, steward of West Derby and Salford 1786

Estate Papers (leases are included with title-deeds): Lease registers 1739, 1745, estate memoranda 1834–42, contract books 1649–1770, 1680–97, 1718–32; surveys: general 1769, 1797, 1800, Clayton-le-Woods 1660–85, Ellel 1756, Kirkby 1696, Orrel and Ford 1815, Tarbock 1616, 1755, 1766, Toxteth Park 1754, Ulnes Walton 1614, Sefton, Aintree, Altcar, Croxteth and Bradley 1579, Altcar, Ince Blundell and Little Crosby 1697, woods in Toxteth Park, Tarbock, West Derby, Kirkby, Simonswood and Ellel 1739; agreement between Stanlaw and Merivale abbeys concerning Alt pastures 1238, enclosure of Crosby marsh 1779–80, agreement concerning Great Crosby warren 1736, agreement for bridge over brook between Kirkby and Knowsley 1781, enclosure of Litherland marsh 1718, 1791, enclosures in West Derby and Wavertree 1667–1756, enclosure of Great Field in Thornton 1742

Correspondence: Bolton and Wigan railway 1845, estate matters 1828–55, sale of lands 1839–55, Toxteth estate 1769–91, Henry VIII to Sir William Molyneux, thanks for services at Flodden 1513, preparations against rebellion 1536, to raise men against the Scots 1543, Henry VIII to keeper of Toxteth Park to deliver stag to earl of Devon 1522

Legal Papers: Ireland v. Molyneux (boundaries of Simonswood) 1571, Every v. Molyneux (Receiver-General of Duchy) 1636–64, Nelson v. Brettargh (debt) 1658, Woodroffe v. Woodroffe (Walton-le-Dale, Cuerden and Clitheroe) 1669, Molyneux v. various people about Liverpool cases 1670–1800, stewardship of West Derby and Salford 1776–86, Rex. v. Robinson and Chaddock (assault on warrener of Great Crosby) 1782, Merivale abbey v. Halsall (Altcar and Halsall moss) 1532, Altcar tolls and rates 1726–67, Ballard v. Blundell (Ince Blundell waste) 1505, Molyneux v. Wilbraham-Bootle (Carr Mill Dam) 1793–94

Business Papers: Accounts, plans and papers relating to coal at Croxteth, Kirkby, Tarbock, Rainford, Winstanley, Eccleston, Maghull, and Burton-in-Lonsdale 1610–1814

Official Papers: Alt drainage: commission of sewers 1771, papers and accounts 1779–1828; West Derby Wapentake: court-books 1733–37, 1785–1806; docket-books 1738–51, 1772–80, 1794–1806, 1809–11, papers and correspondence 1786–1800, 1804–23, 1834–68; Salford Hundred court: statements of account 1844–62, correspondence 1786–1846; appointments of constables of Aughton 1785, 1790, 1792, 1794, 1795, writ for viscount Maryborough to appear in Irish Parliament 1703, subsidy-roll, Salford Hundred 1585, muster-roll at Melling 1618, Cleveley and Forton assessments 1760, 1754, petition of inhabitants of Swinton and Pendlebury concerning appointment of Justices c.1852, a volume entitled "The Earl of Sefton's Special Mission to Lisbon 1865" to invest the king of Portugal with the Garter, proceedings at Lichfield concerning Altcar tithes 1367–68 (see p. 208); conveyance of Altcar tithes 1649, licence to build seat in chancel of Aughton church 1601, agreement for Edward Law to keep a school in Huyton church 1556, conveyances of Huyton rectory and tithes 1602–08, terrier, accounts and papers concerning Kirkby chapel and school 1566–1850, grants of advowson and papers concerning Walton-on-the-Hill church, chantry and tithes 1319–1804, faculty for pew in West Derby chapel 1741

Plans: Aintree 1769, c.1800, c.1845; Aintree racecourse 1829; Altcar 1769, c.1780; Aughton 1769; Little Crosby 1769; Croxteth Park 1769, 1886; Croxteth Hall 1795; Ellel 1769; Fazakerley 1769; Ford 1769; Ince Blundell 1769; Kirkby 1769, 1809; Kirkdale 1796; Knowsley 1769, c.1810; Knowsley Brook 1796, c.1799; Linacre 1769; Litherland 1769, c.1780; Liverpool 1765, 1817; Lunt c.1850; Lydiate 1769; Melling 1769; Netherton 1769, 1801; Orrell 1769; Sefton 1769; Simonswood 1769, 1784, 1838, 1839; Tarbock 1769; Thornton 1769, c.1850; Toxteth Park 1754, c.1760, 1769, c.1780, c.1790, c.1800, c.1810; Walton-on-the-Hill 1769; West Derby 1769, Alt rabbit-warren c.1800; railway from Whiston colliery to Halebank 1802; Alt drainage 1778

Rentals: General 1509, 1515, 1523, 1529, 1568, 1672–84, 1691, 1701–08, 1716, 1718, 1739, 1745, 1755–1844; Altcar 1622, 1650–54, 1708; Aughton 1680, 1688, 1718, 1722, 1725–29, 1735–38, 1740, 1742, 1745, 1748–51, 1753; Clayton-le-Woods 1683; Clifton-with-Salwick 1520; Great Crosby 1654; Eccleston-with-Heskin 1604, 1605, 1609, 1621–24; Ellel 1724, 1725, 1761, 1763, 1768; Euxton 1506, 1508–10; Formby c.1543; Kirkby c.1650, 1705,

1718; Litherland 1708, 1710, 1716; Rainford, Mossborough 1744–54; Scotforth c.1540; Sefton 1689, 1710; Simonswood 1705; Toxteth Park 1720, c.1784; Ulnes Walton 1614, 1622, 1623, 1626–28, 1673; West Derby 1510, 1631; Thornton, co. Chester 1354; York, Clifton, Henworth, Naburn and Holtby, co. York 1443; Holme, Preston Patrick and Nether Levens, Westmorland 1673

Ecclesiastical Papers: Declaration of bishop of Coventry and Lichfield concerning Robert Mercer's presentation to Sefton 1485, induction of Alexander Molyneux to Walton-on-the-Hill 1566, presentation of Samuel Hynd to Sefton 1639, presentation of David Lloyd to Sefton 1639 presentation of Edward Morton to Sefton 1639, grant of next presentation of Sefton 1662 and of Huyton 1664, grant of advowsons of Sefton and Walton-on-the-Hill to the earl of Cardigan 1719

Accounts: Stewards' accounts (many containing rentals) 1572–75, 1577, 1578, 1580–84, 1589–91, 1598, 1603–14, 1620, 1621; 1650, 1651–86; London 1625, 1657, 1688–94, 1704, 1710, general accounts 1738–40, 1742–45, 1756, 1758, 1759, 1761–1811, household accounts 1691–92

Miscellaneous: Inquisitions *post mortem* William Langley 1594, Robert Dickson 1393, Edmund Ley 1589, Richard Ley 1599, Thomas Torbocke 1555, Thomas, earl of Lancaster 1326, "Names of suche persons as are in the Lyverey of Sir Richard Mollyneux" c.1610, agreement for horse racing at Crosby 1739, arms of the nobility and pedigrees of Northern gentry compiled by Christopher Towneley, warrant for the rendering of Liverpool castle untenable 1667, "Evidences of the Molyneux Family" transcribed by Christopher Towneley

Newall of Townhouse, Littleborough (DP400)

Title Deeds: Bacup 1624–27, Butterworth 1656, Hundersfield 1601–90; Todmorden and Walsden 1686, co. York: Langfield 1610, Northowram 1478

Accounts and receipts: 1624–1711, bonds 1556–1722, correspondence 1674–1700, legal papers 1600–98, probate papers 1628–1808, miscellanea 1627–1727

Openshaw of Hothersall (DDOp)

Title deeds and papers: Hothersall, Longridge, and Ribchester 17th to 20th c.

Parker of Browsholme (DDB)

This family first appears in the records as being of Alkincoats, Colne, at the end of the thirteenth century. A younger branch early acquired Browsholme in Bowland and the two estates came together again in 1820. They have been hereditary bow-bearers of the forest of Bowland since Elizabeth I. The marriages of Thomas Parker to Alice Blakey of Lanehead about 1720 and of Edward Parker to Ellen Barcroft of Noyna in Foulridge in 1816 brought in documents relating to those families.

The late Col John Parker made an artificial collection of manuscripts, details of which are given at the end. These include a group relating to Hesketh of Rufford.

A.—Parker MSS

Title Deeds: Colne: Alkincoats 1609–1760, Colne Edge 1625–1781, Hatherholt 1346–1789, Hobstones and Ball Bridge 1663–1792, Holt House 1533–1786, Lane Head 1622–1805, Marsden Close 1697–1807, Stone Edge 1686–1786, Wanless 1785–1846; Hindley 1575–1821; Ribchester 1853–34; Read 1781

Family Papers: Settlements 1751; wills 1717–1865; inventory of Thomas Parker 1635; "a note of all the howshold stuffes at Brousholme" 1592; pedigree of Holgate of Foulridge c.1820

Appointments: Edward Parker as deputy lieutenant 1704; Thomas Parker as captain 1714; William Brennand as surveyor of excise 1761; Thomas Lister Parker as sheriff 1804; Thomas Parker as bow-bearer of Bowland 1820; Edward Parker as master extraordinary in Chancery 1808; Thomas Parker as deputy lieutenant and bow-bearer of Bowland 1827; Edward Parker as lieutenant 1867 and captain 1868; Thomas Goulburne Parker as major 1870

Diaries and memoranda books of Elizabeth Shackleton *nee* Parker 1764–81; pocket-books of Edward Parker and Thomas Goulburne Parker 1804, 1814, 1818, 1823, 1824, 1827, 1844, 1846–57, 1859–62, 1864

Estate Papers: Ribchester survey c.1831

Correspondence: T. Forster, surgeon, requesting removal of wounded to Charles Town, U.S.A. 1781; Robert Parker to his wife, before marriage 1751–56; to Robert Parker 1752–57; to Mrs. Parker 1753–81; to Mrs. Shackleton 1765–77; to Edward Parker 1760–1819; to Robert Parker 1744–95; to Thomas Parker 1768–1819; to Ellen Parker 1833–48; to Elizabeth A. Parker 1828–46; to Edward Parker 1827–47; from Edward Parker 1814–16, 1833–49; letter-books of Edward Parker 1847–65; letter-book of Thomas E. Parker 1851–63

Ecclesiastical Papers: Repair of Whitewell chapel 1665; allotment of seats in Colne chapel 1635; faculty for gallery in Colne chapel 1733; lease of Bannisters chancel in Colne chapel 1731; papers on charges against William Norcross, curate of Colne 1740; papers on dispute about Bannisters chancel in Colne chapel 1731–78; accounts of Colne tithes 1727–29

Plans: Ribchester 1833, Bowland 1835; Parker estates 1765

Rentals: General 1832–36, 1840–62; Ribchester 1833

Accounts: Robert Parker 1745–58; Elizabeth Parker 1751–52, 1775; Thomas Parker 1758–75; John Parker 1760–76; Edward Parker 1766–79; Thomas Parker 1795–1827; Edward Parker 1840–65

Charity Papers: Account of doles in the parish of Colne 1722

Miscellaneous: Apprenticeship of William Sodd to clothmaking 1700; claim to shares in Colne Piece Hall 1837; hunting poems 18th century

A series of bound volumes: 1–6 historical writings and transcripts of documents, including Yorkshire pedigrees 1681–86; 7–8 Whalley and Salley abbeys 17th century; 9–12 letters to members of the Parker family 1591–1711; 13 genealogical memoranda c.1645–c.1770; 14–18 Lancashire and Yorkshire miscellany temp. Charles I; 19–20 speeches in Parliament and Parker letters on public affairs 1591–1720; 21 Wakefield charities c.1810; 22–24 Parker extracts from Plea rolls, etc.

B.—Barcroft MSS.

Title Deeds (including leases): Foulridge: manor and mill 1586–1679, various 1575–1788, leases 1604–1844, Clough 1607–1785; Marsden 1612–1784; Roughlee leases 1788–1830; Trawden 1716, 1784

Family Papers: Apprenticeship of Ambrose Barcroft to York merchant 1647; letter of attorney of Ambrose Barcroft "having a designe to goe byond the Sea" 1720; inquisition *post mortem* Robert Blakey 1630; Appointments: John Barcroft, stewardship of Clitheroe 1770; Ambrose William Barcroft, ensign at Philadelphia 1778 and lieutenant at New York 1780; Ambrose Barcroft, surveyor of excise 1714; settlements 1575–1683; wills 1641–1815; bonds and acquittances 1629–1783

Estate Papers (leases are included with title-deeds): Surveys: Foulridge 1742, 1761; Stonedge in Colne 1802

Correspondence: Miscellaneous letters 1654–1785 including items from Ireland 1682 and America 1723–80; letters from Capt. Ambrose William Barcroft, and concerning his death by shipwreck off Weymouth 1785–96; letters to Ellen Moon, née Barcroft, 1805–51, to Barbara Barcroft 1805–39, to Martha Barcroft 1785–1843, to John Barcroft 1772–95, to Elizabeth Barcroft 1783–1803, to E. Reynolds, née Barcroft, 1817–40, to Mary Barcroft 1817–26, and to Robert Reynolds 1823–31

Business Papers: Papers concerning coal-pits at Carry Hey 1721–24; Foulridge mill accounts 1691, 1697, 1700–06, 1718

Legal Papers: Decree relating to suit of mills and settling copyhold in honour of Clitheroe 1609

Official Papers: Appointment for repair of Colne highway 1623; nonpayers of hearth tax in Colne 1685; papers concerning stopping of highway over Piked Edge 1655–65; Foulridge assessments 1748, 1751, 1752; agreement for Foulridge constableship 1642; book of rates for Blackburn Hundred 1710; memorandum book of Ambrose Barcroft as high constable of Blackburn Hundred 1680–81*

Plans: Clough in Colne 1757; Noyna in Foulridge c.1740; Foulridge, Colne and Trawden 1781; Stonedge in Colne 1805

Rentals: Foulridge 1679–96, 1783, 1784, 1786, 1793–94

Accounts: General 1689–1732

Miscellaneous: "Orders to be Observed by Officers commanding Detachments on Board Transport Vessells" 1780; contract for building house at Roughlee 1769; "The Method of Mrs. Barcroft's Funeral" 1770

C—Artificial Collection

Hesketh of Rufford

Title Deeds: Bretherton 1649; Croston 1331–1542; Eccleston 1590; Great Harwood 1334; Howick 1612; Lancaster 1604; Mawdesley c.1300–1650; Preston rectory (Leicester college) 1531; Rishton 1306; Rufford 1639; Shevington 1517–23; Simonstone and Read 1610; Wigan 1330–1622; Wrightington c.1300–1471

Family Papers: Settlements 1361–1700; wills 1523, 1560; appointment of Sir Thomas Hesketh as steward of Bretherton 1569; ordination of Geoffrey Hesketh 1447; inquisition *post mortem* Robert Hesketh 1491

Official Papers: *Quieti* for recusancy of Jane, lady Hoghton 1658; *quietus* for shrievalty of Robert Hesketh 1614

Ecclesiastical Papers: Appointment of Richard Yate as chaplain of Rufford 1481; award concerning Rufford chantry 1489

---

* Printed by Historic Society of Lancashire and Cheshire vol. 107.

Miscellaneous: Agreement concerning services of Adam Nowell of Great Harwood 1312; deposit of deeds in Whalley abbey 1522

Various

Manorial: Woodplumpton: court-book 1816; customs of the manor of Ightenhill, Burnley and Colne 1686

Title Deeds: Abram 1656–62; Bispham-with-Norbreck 1596–1629; Bolton-le-Moors 1718, 1731; Bretherton 1715; Brindle 1768, 1812; Broughton-in-Amounderness 1602–1740; Chorley 1838; Clitheroe 1691, 1695; Dilworth 1781; Downham 1736; Eccleshill 1701–21; Farnworth 1322; Goosnargh 1770, 1772; Greenhalgh-with-Thistleton 1762; Hambleton 1712; Heskin 1483; Hoghton 1793; Little Mitton 1769; Liverpool 1749–74; Longton 1761; Lytham and Marton 1606; Penwortham 1737, 1792; Preston 1699–1809; Ribby-with-Wrea 1721–83; Tarleton 1755; Walton-le-Dale 1792; Warton-in-Amounderness c.1290–1687; Westby-with-Plumpton 1750; Whittingham 1677–1758; Wiswell 1719

Legal Papers: Writ *Ad Quod Damnum* concerning diversion of highway at Whittle-le-Woods 1782

Official Papers: Settlement of Alexander and Jennet Hutchinson in Greenhalgh 1750; solemn league and covenant signed by inhabitants of Ashton-under-Lyne 1643; oaths in support of Commonwealth taken at Manchester quarter sessions 1650–51; articles for regulating expenses of sheriff 1744; certificate of discharge of John Fort from Veevers company of York Regiment 1781; certificate of voluntary enlistment of Matthew Reddihalgh in 63rd Regiment 1794

Ecclesiastical papers: Account of Blackburn tithes 1537–38

Accounts: Account-book of Sir Francis Anderton 1746–56

Miscellaneous: Estreats of king's court at Clitheroe 1496–97; statutes of Clitheroe school 1622; inventory of Samuel Salton-stall of Kingston-upon-Hull 1613

Pedder of Finsthwaite (DDPd)

This family descends from Thomas Pedder a 17th–century Preston merchant. His grandson acquired the advowson of Garstang, a living which was held by many members of the family. By his second marriage the Rev. John Pedder obtained the Taylor estate of Finsthwaite in 1801 .

Manorial: Chorley: call-books 1753, 1754

Title Deeds: Bispham-with-Norbreck 1768–1836; Broughton-in-Amounderness 1702; Catterall 1784; Claughton 1784; Eccleston (Chorley) 1621, 1755; Fulwood 1717–1838; Larbreck 1664,

1769; Poulton, Bare, and Torrisholme 1716–1853; Preston c.1260–1835; Liverpool c.1300, 1341; Ribbleton 1727–1836; Ribchester 1310–1401; Sefton 1626; Walton-le-Dale, Clayton-le-Woods, Whittle-le-Woods, and Brindle 1677; Finsthwaite 1552–1888; Cartmel Fell 1669–1734; Colton 1603–1711; Haverthwaite 1622–1798; Kirkby Ireleth 1731–33; Lindal-in-Furness 1728; Rusland 1613–1726; Staveley 1661–1832; Ulverston 1744–1809; Upper Holker 1750; Walton-le-Dale 1722–1865; Wood Broughton 1808

Family Papers: Settlements 1600–1883; wills 1599–1885; appointments: Alexander Mawdesley, lieutenant 1789, John Rigbie Fletcher, captain 1793, Richard Pedder of Preston, attorney 1835, Roger Taylor of Finsthwaite, magistrate 1821; genealogical memoranda: Pedder of Preston 1712, 1762, Horrocks of Edgeworth and Preston 1745–1804, Crosse of Liverpool and Preston 1625–1722; papers and sketch-books of the family of Dr. William St. Clare of Preston 1779–1865; commonplace book of Richard Pedder 19th century; inventory of James Pedder 1772; diaries: Thomas Pedder 1853–63, Richard Pedder 1863–87

Estate Papers: Survey and valuation of properties in Dutton 1802–45; proposals for building in Lancaster 1783; conditions for building in Winckley Square, Preston, with articles for regulation of the square 1807

Correspondence: To John Pedder from his mother 1786; to and from Joseph Pedder, Batavia, 1834–41; to Thomas Pedder 1854–55; to various Palatinate Seal-keepers 1791–1822; to various members of the family of Hammond of Downham 1664–1748; to and from members of the family of Rigby of Middleton in Goosnargh 1724–1806; to the duchess of Saxe-Gotha 1822–40

Legal Papers: Commissions and duchy orders concerning Cadley watermill 1599 and Fulwood common 1630–1740; Taylor v. Wilson (Poulton-le-Sands) 1824–28; Poulton-le-Sands highways 1827; Preston riots 1854; Taylor v. Noble (apprenticeship) 1742

Business Papers: Walker & Pedder, tobacco-merchants, Preston: balance sheets etc., 1836–65; agreement for delivery of wood for charcoal at Cunsey works 1748; account of shares in Penny Bridge and other furnaces 1767; Finsthwaite bloomsmithy rents 1839–41, 1845–47; King & Barlow, cotton manufacturers, Bolton: deed of partnership 1787; papers concerning executorship of estate of Elizabeth Crombleholme of Kirkland 1817–30, including ordination of William Crombleholme as deacon 1723, his appointment to St. Michaels-on-Wyre 1729 and salebook of her property at Churchtown 1817

Official Papers: Preston election: registers of tallies and voters 1768; Duchy and Palatinate records: reports, etc. 1818–32; list of contributors from Garstang parish towards defence of the country 1798; Grenadier Company, Manchester and Salford Volunteers, attendance-book 1803–04

Ecclesiastical Papers: Sermon at funeral of Mary Backhouse, Finsthwaite, 1744; Finsthwaite curacy and school papers 1723–1913; Colton church and school papers 1719–1884; Garstang: advowson deeds 1569–1862; ordinations and inductions 1753–1891; appointments of parish clerks 1668, 1695; accounts 1784–91, 1798–1806, 1818–34; faculty for galleries 1822

Maps and Plans: Lands in Poulton-le-Sands c.1823; Finsthwaite Height c.1770; Rusland Pool 1805; new road from Finsthwaite to Backbarrow 1826; North America 1776; Lancaster canal 1791; Napoleon's threatened invasion 1803; inland navigations 1803; panorama of Morecambe Bay 1850

Rentals: Henry Preston's properties in Preston, Goosnargh, Liverpool and Ribchester 1489; Finsthwaite estate 1821–49, 1859–79; Poulton-le-Sands estate 1836–44, 1881–90; Whinney Fold, Woodplumpton, and Larbreck Hall (with plans) 1824–35

Accounts: Clement Taylor and Edward Taylor of Finsthwaite 1712–52, Mary Taylor 1775–80 and Roger Taylor 1833–38; Edward Taylor 1777–96; Roger Taylor 1794–1828 and 1822–32, 1838–49; general accounts, Finsthwaite 1799–1829; Finsthwaite school 1803, 1834–49; Richard Pedder 1879–83; hay sales 1860–75, cutter *Maggie* expenses 1831–32, schooner *Peg A. Ramsey* expenses 1834–35, household bills 1825–34, day book 1857–91

Miscellaneous: Apprenticeship indentures: Cartmel Fell, John Simpson to Stephen Britton, glover, 1585; Joseph Aspden of Tockholes to Zachary Leafe of Warrington, surgeon, 1736. Agreement for payment for defence of company of joiners in Kendal 1676; certificate by mayor of Newcastle-on-Tyne that Gilbert Woosey was prisoner in Martinique 1711; "list of the auncient Gentrye of the County of Lancaster with their severall coates of armes" 1681

Peel of Knowlmere (DDPl)

Papers, deeds, diaries and correspondence (including log of H.M.S. *Jupiter*) 18th and 19th c.

253

Petre of Dunkenhalgh (DDPt)

The estate of Dunkenhalgh in Clayton-le-Moors first appears in the late thirteenth century. In 1332 it came to the Rishtons who held it until it was bought by Thomas Walmesley in 1571. Walmesley —who had acquired the Shuttleworth estate of Hacking in Billington by marriage—later became a judge of the Common Pleas and built up a great estate in Lancashire and Yorkshire which passed to the Petres by marriage in 1712. (See *Dunkenhalgh Deeds*, ed. Stocks & Tait, Chetham Society, N.S. 80.)

Manorial: Billington: court-books 1542–46, 1558–66, 1578–1640, 1652–60, 1816–32, 1842–44, 1848; call-books 1815–30, 1835–44

Church: court-books 1816–32, 1842, 1843, 1847; call-books 1785–98, 1815–26, 1835–39

Rishton: court-books 1581–1683, 1713–16, 1718–31, 1734, 1738, 1739, 1746, 1784, 1785, 1816–32, 1842, 1843, 1845, 1849; court-papers 1666–83; call-books 1719–31, 1734–38, 1746, 1815–20, 1835–49

Paythorn-in-Craven, co. York: call-books 1786–94

Billington, Paythorn and Rishton: court-books 1702–12

Wakefield, co. York: court roll 1427

Selby, Brayton, Cowthorpe, Monkfryston and Hillom, Thorpe-Willowby, Wilsthorpe, and Tockwith, co. York: court-book 1702–09

Title Deeds (including leases): Accrington 1608–1715; Aighton, Bailey and Chaigley 1422–1827; Aldcliffe 1600; Alston-with-Hothersall 1608–73; Anderton 1387; Ashton-with-Stodday 1401; Ashton (Preston) 1348; Billington c.1260–1839, Ryleys estate 1652–1713, Hacking c.1290–1663, Cunliffe House 1571–99, leases 1557–1798; Blackburn 1236–1845; the Blackburne estate in Chipping 1618, Goosnargh 1427–1723, Little Crosby 1549–1705; Dutton 1587–1761; Great Eccleston 1356, 1611; Ince Blundell 1626–85; Pilling Hall 1642 and Up Holland 1634–58; Bolton-le-Sands c.1280–1314; Briercliffe 1446; Catterall 1395–1517; Chipping 1445; Church c.1250–1790, Ponthalgh 1578–1659, leases 1683–1873; Clayton-le-Moors c.1250–1488, Dunkenhalgh 1556–84; Clitheroe 1326–1761; Lower Darwen 1672–1852; Dutton 1662, 1761; Elston 1370–1616; Flixton 1752; Fulwood 1765; Grimsargh 1451; Haighton and Whittingham 1609; Great Harwood 1579, 1838; Hapton 1398; Heath Charnock 1577; Howick 1350, 1439; Huncoat 1413; Ightenhill 1554; Lancaster c.1270–1589; Livesey 1435, 1518; Longton c.1290–1435; Lytham 1712; Manchester 1292; Mellor c.1280–1524; Oxcliffe 1333; Oswaldtwistle 1376, 1512; Padiham 1423, 1595;

Parbold 1432; Pendleton 1382; Penwortham 1439; Pleasington 1404; Preston c.1260–1789, leases 1659–1784; Rawcliffe c.1290–1581; Read 1556; Ribbleton 1603–1777; Ribchester c.1280–1788, Boys House 1586–96; Rishton c.1230–1889, Cowell 1654–1771, Tottleworth 1792–1853, leases 1556–1807; Salesbury c.1270–1602, leases 1607–1774; Samlesbury, Lower Hall 1568–1696; Scotforth c.1290–1562; Simonstone c.1290–1613; Tatham, Robert Hall 1704; Tockholes 1528–86; Torrisholme 1451; Tottington 1404; Treales 1643, 1653; Wigan 1334; Wilpshire c.1230–1612, Carr Hall 1423–1708, leases 1568–1795; Worsthorne 1389

Other counties: Cheshire: Barnton 1409, Legh 1347; Denbighshire: Dyffrincloyt 1302; Durham: Hurworth 1578; Hampshire: Odiham 1907; Kent: Hadlow 1372–1587; Lincolnshire: Armeston 1597; London, 1352, 1537; Surrey: Burstow 1318, 1568, East Cheam c.1300, 1609; Warwickshire: Studley c.1260–1556, Chilvers Coton 1643, Nuneaton 1660, Whitley 1453, Wolverdington 1397; Worcestershire: Feckenham 1383; Yorkshire: Barnoldswick 1548–1672, Bashall Eaves 1581, Bowthorpe 1603, 1609, Carleton 1700–21, Cowthorpe 1587, 1654, Eastby 1342, Gisburn 1584, Kildwick 1576–1653, Paythorn 1350–1753, Pickering 1711, Selby 1612–87, Slingsby 1564, Little Sutton 1387, Waddington 1591–1636, Wilsthorpe 1697

Family Papers: Settlements 1423–1853; wills 1387–1815; bonds 1331–1727; recusancy papers 1610–27; general pardons: Ralph Rishton 1423, Henry Rishton 1460, 1479, Sir Thomas Walmesley 1603, John Dewhurst 1604, Lady Anne Walmesley 1626; inventories: Richard Walmesley 1679, Bartholomew Walmesley 1702. Appointments: Thomas Walmesley, master-forester of Wyresdale and Quernmore 1597, chief justice of Lancashire 1603; Richard Walmesley studmaster to James, duke of York 1665; Sir George Glyn Petre, envoy extraordinary to Portugal 1891; Judge Walmesley's commonplace book c.1599 with additions to 1702; contract with Isaac James of St. Martin-in-the-Fields, Middlesex, for Judge Walmesley's tomb 1613; ratification of marriage of Henry of Shuttleworth to Agnes of Hacking 1373; certificate of no record of divorce of Ralph Rishton and Ellen Towneley 1573; inspeximus (1582) of divorce of the same 1546; absolution to William Rishton for clandestine marriage to Dorothy Anderton 1637; grants of wardship of Richard Walmesley 1637, 1639, 1640; inquisition *post mortem* of Thomas Walmesley 1642; licence for Richard Walmesley to leave the realm 1678; list of persons residing at Dunkenhalgh, including those in the hospital and on charity 1706; passports to George Petre 1814, 1817

Estate Papers (leases are included with title-deeds): Lease books and registers 1694–96, 1719–50, 1788, 1793; "A true account of such additions as have accrued to the house and family of Dunkenhalgh" 1642–79; specification of rebuilding gatehouse at Dunkenhalgh 1830

Enclosure: Henfield common 1576, 1786–91; Rishton moor 1785; Clayton moor 1797; Billington, Wilpshire and Dinckley 1788–93; Ribbleton and Fulwood moors 1811–25

Surveys: general estate 1593, 1639, 1657–88, 1713, 1735, 1786; Aighton and Dinckley 1826; Goosnargh and Preston (surveyor's notes and sketches) 1787; Billington 1554, 1824; Brindle glebe 1800; Church 1712, 1824; Ribchester c.1750; Paythorn co. York 1803

Correspondence: The affairs of Ann Lacon 1638–41; to Catherine, Lady Petre, 1713–40

Legal Papers: Depositions concerning way between Huncoat and Accrington 1660–64; Walmesley v. Assheton (Chew mill) 1686; Rishton and Great Harwood boundaries 1583–98; pardon for outlawry, John of Gaunt to John Shuttleworth 1366; warrant for arrest of Thomas Colteman of Lancaster for affray 1415; exemplification (1439) of trial of Gilbert of Rishton for murder 1256; award of abbot of Whalley between Richard Rishton and William Starkey 1455; writ of *habeas corpus* for William Rishton 1585

Business Papers: Whitebirk colliery papers 1887–93; statements of coal got from Darwen colliery 1819–25; Leeds and Liverpool canal minutes and papers 1773–94, 1796–1851

Official Papers: Book of rates for Lancashire 1622

Ecclesiastical Papers: Blackburn parish tithes, papers and agreements 1599, 1793–1851; agreement between abbot of Whalley and the parishioners of Whalley concerning tithes 1334; commission to convey "criminous clerks" from Lancaster assizes to the archbishop of York's gaol at York 1470; ordination and other appointments of William Hewertson (Leck, Poulton, Marton, Blackburn) 1758–72

Plans: Clayton-le-Moors c.1680, 1780, 1785, 1796; Rishton 1785; Church 1780, 1785, 1808, 1833; Dunkenhalgh park 1785; Henfield common 1786; Accrington and Oswaldtwistle 1833

Rentals: General estate 1596, 1690–97, 1703–31, 1736–49, 1754–56, 1758, 1759, 1775, 1781, 1783–85, 1787, 1792–1826, 1832–51; Billington 1620–96, Church 1653–63, Ponthalgh 1657–58, Preston 1671, 1696, 1712, 1713, Rishton 1658–61

Accounts: Stewards' accounts 1612–40, 1657–70, 1666–75, 1680–1758, 1781, 1782, 1784, 1788–1826; Thomas Walmesley's funeral accounts 1612; Thomas Walmesley's accounts 1585–1610; accounts for quartering soldiers 1648; grain account 1695–96; Bartholomew Walmesley's executors' accounts 1701–12, almoners' accounts 1704–12; account of timber and estates sold 1793–1800; park and timber accounts 1807–26; building accounts 1829–34; stable accounts 1829–52; journals 1816–24, 1834–57; account of Bell House estate, Essex 1797–1818

Miscellaneous: Agreement of Peter de la Holte to serve the earl of Warwick 1378; inspeximus of charters of John and Henry III and private individuals to Cockersand abbey 1385; letters of confraternity, prior of Rochester to Nicholas Rixton, rector of Bishops Cleeve 1412; mandate of dean of Blackburn to warn adversaries of Henry Rishton that they risk excommunication 1414; inquisition *post mortem*, Robert Cunliffe 1551; proceedings at the Justice Seat held for the Forest of Dean at Gloucester 1634

Pilkington of Rainford and Windle (DDPk)

Title Deeds: Billinge, Rainford and Windle 16th to 19th c.; correspondence 1888–1963, account books 1910–48, farm ledgers 1889–1922, cottage rentals 1910–32; Pilkington Bold Estates Co. books and papers 1909–47

Rawstorne of Hutton (DDR, DDX/43 and DDX/103)

The manor of Hutton, which had belonged to Cockersand abbey, was sold in 1546 to Lawrence Rawstorne, of the Tottington family. Lands in Penwortham, Farington and Howick were acquired about 1800.

Title Deeds (including leases): Broughton-in-Amounderness abstracts of title 1682–1711; Farington 1393–1751, leases 1422–1776; Howick leases 1747–72, duchy grant of marsh 1860; Hutton 1546–1876, leases 1733–77, abstracts of title 1702–1811; Kirkham and Freckleton 1689; London, abstract of title 1634–1765; Longton 1492–1752; Penwortham 1479–1755, leases 1611–1735; Preston lease 1804; Rawtenstall mill lease 1832; Tarleton 1324

Family Papers: Settlements 1597–1768; wills 1639–1849; appointments: William Fleetwood, steward of Penwortham 1567; Samuel Rawstorne, deputy lieutenant of Essex 1705; Lawrence Rawstorne, deputy lieutenant 1761, 1796, lieutenant-colonel 1804, 1819, sheriff 1814; pedigrees, Rawstorne of Lumb 17th c. and 1821

Estate Papers (leases are included with title-deeds): Surveys: Farington 1751, 1754, 1767, c.1797, 1799; Hutton 1771, 1804, c.1810, 1811; London 1753; Penwortham 1375, 1766, 1815, Penwortham and Howick tithes 1768

Farington enclosure agreements 1713, 1784; Farington leasebook 1708–44

Legal Papers: Opinion on enclosure of Farington moss 1775

Ecclesiastical Papers: Grant of Penwortham and Leyland rectories and tithes 1599

Plans: Longton Lower Marsh enclosure 1838

Rentals: Hutton c.1809, 1811, 1823; General 1753–56, 1763, 1776, 1779, 1780, 1816, 1823

Charity Papers: Appointment of Lawrence Rawstorne as trustee for Marton's Longton charity 1793

Miscellaneous: Conveyance of share in ship *Happy Recovery* of London 1668; Penwortham and Howick Association for Prosecution of Felons 1801

Sanderson of Marton (DDX 506)
Deeds and papers 1596–1920

Sandys of Graythwaite (DDSa)
Manorial: Court rolls of Furness, Dalton, Colton, Hawkshead and Newby, co. York 1545–46; Ullthwaite, Westmorland 1766–1840

Title Deeds: Graythwaite 1548–1849; Cunsey 1550–1862; Esthwaite 1633–1855; Broughton-in-Furness 1731; Cartmel Fell 1528–1758; Claife 1667–1897; Colton 1667–1722; Coniston 1709–1859; Dalton-in-Furness 1622–1872; Egton-with-Newland 1625; Finsthwaite 1596–1750; Gressingham 1725–33; Hawkshead 1572–1881; Melling-in-Lonsdale 1749; Rusland 1676–1745; Satterthwaite 1621–1772; Staveley 1593–1731; Ulverston 1597–1856

Other counties: Cumberland: Corney 1661; Essex: Saffron Walden 1543–1661; Westmorland: Ambleside 1671–80, Kendal 1609, Kentmere 1589–1626, Ullthwaite 1583–1687, Underbarrow 1684, Windermere ferry and fishery 1707–14

Family Papers: Wills and settlements 1592–1879, bonds and bills 1559–1714, appointments (deputy lieutenants, militia) 1700–61

Rentals and Surveys: Satterthwaite, Hawkshead, Muchland, Urswick, Coniston, Ulverston, Graythwaite, Cunsey, Hornby 1538–1815

Legal Papers: Estates, fisheries, etc. 1641–1880

Official Papers: Shrievalty 1707–26; warrants, bonds, etc. 1610–1732

Correspondence: From John Towers, Kendal, *re* 1715 rising; Rawlinson family, especially John of Grays Inn 1671–1737

Business Papers: Partnerships and agreements *re* Cunsey and other forges 1681–1750

Scarisbrick of Scarisbrick (DDSc)

Manorial: Downholland: court-books 1807–32; Halsall 1807–12; Scarisbrick: court-books 1788–1811, estreats 1615, 1616, 1628, 1630, 1672–75, 1677–87, 1690–95, 1698–1713, 1715, 1718–25, 1727, 1730, 1731, 1734–36, 1770, call-book 1812; Shevington: court book 1561

Title Deeds (including leases): Allerton *c.*1260; Altcar leases 1741–47; Anderton lease 1472; Aughton *c.*1260–1479; Barnacre-with-Bonds lease 1712; Burscough 1709–86; Coppull 1436; Ditton 1307; Downholland 1824–39, leases 1749–1806; Eccleston (Cockersand abbey) *c.*1180–1445, leases 1598–1763; Halsall *c.*1230–1856, leases 1728–1808; Ince Blundell *c.*1210, 1402; Lathom *c.*1240–1468; Longton *c.*1200; North Meols leases 1686–1783; Ormskirk *c.*1280, leases 1745–91; Penwortham 1290; Rainhill *c.*1190; Rainford *c.*1260; Scarisbrick (Burscough priory) *c.*1200–1865, leases 1634–1802, Harleton 1229–1804, Greaves 1681–98, Pinfold House 1771–79, Shaws *c.*1260–1539; Shevington *c.*1250–1696; Skelmersdale 1507–85; Sutton leases 1663–84; Tarleton lease 1781; Tarbock 1365; Up Holland 1471; Walton-le-Dale 1350–1635; Warrington *c.*1230; Welch Whittle *c.*1260–1504; Woodplumpton leases 1683–1745; Worthington *c.*1240–*c.*1300; Wrightington *c.*1240–1547

Family Papers: Settlements *c.*1290–1735; wills 1359–1801; mortgages 1749–1814; dispensation for marriage of Richard of Scarisbrick and Maud of Birchcarr 1367; summons to Gilbert Scarisbrick and others to be knighted 1501; order to Thomas Eccleston to raise a regiment of foot 1793; Thomas Eccleston's notebook 1781–1804 and diaries 1801, 1803, 1804; licence for Robert Scarisbrick to remain in England 1698 and for him not to be summoned to quarter sessions 1701; agreement for three Dicconson boys to be educated at Douai or Paris 1738; passport for Henry Eccleston 1651; general pardons: Henry Scarisbrick 1446, Edward Scarisbrick 1640, Thomas Eccleston 1693; pedigrees: Eccleston and Scarisbrick 17th to 19th century, Scarisbrick 14th to 19th c., Dicconson 16th to 19th c.

Correspondence: Lord Stanley to James Scarisbrick requiring horsemen *c.*1480; Lord Derby to James Scarisbrick requiring horsemen to Berwick *c.*1540; various (many relating to agricultural activities of Thomas Eccleston) 1701–1809

Estate Papers (leases are included with title-deeds): Surveys: Eccleston *c.*1720, 1749, 1753; Halsall *c.*1830; Downholland 1791–1840; Scarisbrick 1790. Burscough and Scarisbrick boundaries *c.*1260, 1303, 1396, 1398; grants of ways in Scarisbrick 1386, 1577; specifications for houses in Ormskirk 1789; agreement for building Scarisbrick watermill 1699; receipt by collectors of wool 1340; valuation of livestock and implements of husbandry 1788, 1792, 1793; house repair book 1812; stud papers 1786–1818

Legal Papers: Murder of Brother Adam of Burscough 1333; declaration that Thomas Holland, earl of Kent, and others, are traitors 1401; papers (16th–18th c.) concerning Scarisbrick commons; Scarisbrick *v.* Hesketh (Aughton hall) *c.*1706; Valentine *v.* Scarisbrick (Harleton) 1729–36; Scarisbrick *v.* Skelmersdale *c.*1836; Dicconson *v.* Talbot (Wigan coal) 1864–67; Scarisbrick *v.* Leatherbarrow (Ormskirk) 1725–27; a Precedent Book *c.*1690; record of conviction of Edward Scarisbrick for recusancy 1630

Business Papers: Eccleston cotton factory papers 1784–93; Shevington coal agreements 1679, 1770

Official Papers: Scarisbrick constables' accounts 1667–68; Scarisbrick census 1798; Scarisbrick taxes 1809–10; Scarisbrick land tax assessment 1817; *quietus* of John Wrightington, subsidy-collector, 1547; William Dicconson, subsidy-collector: bond receipt and *quietus* 1640–42

Ecclesiastical Papers: Subscribers to stipend of Ormskirk priest 1366; grants of oratories 1420, 1447, 1451; indulgences from Brother Robert of Knaresborough 1471 and St. John of Jerusalem 1530; lease of tithes of Brockholes 1581

Plans: Burtonhead in Sutton *c.*1580

Rentals: Eccleston 1373, 1449, *c.*1480, 1609, 1612, 1696, 1740, 1745–56, 1789; Downholland 1751, 1789, 1790, 1792, 1798, 1805–07; Scarisbrick 1630, 1632, 1675, 1684, 1699–1724, 1732–1820; the lands of St. John of Jerusalem south of Ribble *c.*1540*; Marton and Ormskirk 1704; Standish, Wigan, Shevington, Woolston, Hutton, Warton, Garstang 1789–90; Penwortham moss 1653–68, 1671–81; Wrightington, Parbold, Whittle, Coppull, Charnock Richard 1657–60; Croston, Wigan, Eccleston, Mawdesley, Shevington Newbrough, Penwortham 1727

---

* Printed by Lancashire and Cheshire Antiquarian Society, vol. 58

Accounts: Inventory and sale accounts of John Simkin 1749; Gillar's Green coal accounts 1754–57; B. T. Eccleston's coal account 1770–73; Eccleston watermill and cottonmill accounts 1775–84; B. T. Eccleston's executors' accounts 1749–53

Miscellaneous: Grants of serfs c.1260, 1361. "The trewe report of a miraculous case of Dispossession of a young gentlman from . . . Devills . . . on Asse Wednesday, Ao.Dm. 1585;" a long religious poem headed "Jhesus Maria", c.1580; inquisitions *post mortem* Thomas Fletcher of West Derby 1585; John Wrightington of Wrightington 1559

Shuttleworth of Gawthorpe (DDKs)

Family and estate accounts 1582–1621, correspondence 16th and 17th cents.; Deeds: Padiham and district, Inskip-with-Sowerby, Myerscough, Whittingham, Goosnargh, Lancaster, Warton-in-Lonsdale, Chipping, Clitheroe, Henthorn, Mitton and Coldcotes; Great Mitton and Dent, co. York; Barbon, Westmorland 13th to 20th cents

Stanley of Cross Hall (DDCr)

The Cross Hall estate in Lathom can be traced from the early thirteenth century among the properties of Burscough priory and was among the lands granted after the Dissolution to the earl of Derby. Shortly afterwards it came to a junior branch of the Stanleys who have held it ever since.

Title Deeds: Aughton, Bradshaws mill 1548–1709, Litherland Hall 1649–1711, various 1486–1789; Catterall 1608–1713; Chipping, Crowtrees 1342–1741, Blackhouse 1545–1667, various 1636–69; Ditton 1332; Fulwood 1622–1775; Lathom, Leveldale House 1682–1764, Kekewick's lands 1378–1591; Ormskirk 1560; Preston, Swan inn 1623–1703, Church Street houses (including the King's Arms inn) 1568–1795, Friargate houses 1602–91, Minspitt Wiend property 1722–55, Becconsall chantry lands 1599–1664, various 1401–1791; West Derby 1378–1591

Other counties: Chester 1573

Family Papers: Settlements 1394–1714; wills 1617–1747

Estate Papers: Survey of Aughton, Lathom and Catterall c.1710; agreement for building house in Preston 1649; exchange of common rights in Chipping 1566; insurance of Preston house 1727

Official Papers: Appointment of Preston highway surveyors 1693; Aughton assessment 1742

Ecclesiastical Papers: Faculty for pew alteration in Ormskirk church 1739

Accounts: Work done on Leveldale estate at Lathom 1725–33; Catterall estate accounts 1721–25

Charity Papers: James Suddell's bequest to school and poor of Preston 1714–34

Miscellaneous: Inquisitions *post mortem*: William Helm of Chipping 1610, Thomas Jameson of Aughton 1642

Inventories: William Sudell, Preston 1678, Jane Sudell, Preston, 1684, Henry Abbot, Preston, 1702, Roger Sudell, Preston, 1703

Stanley, Earls of Derby (DDK)

It was by the marriage of Isabel, heiress of Sir Thomas of Lathom, to Sir John of Stanley, a Cheshire man, about 1385, that the Knowsley and Lathom estates came to the Stanleys. Other vast Lancashire properties were acquired through the forfeitures of the Wars of the Roses and the Reformation. In 1405 the lordship of Man and in 1414 the stewardship of Macclesfield came to the family. The properties of Sir Cleave Moore of Bankhall in Bootle, Kirkdale and Liverpool were acquired in 1724. A collection of Stanley documents deposited by the Bury Estate Company (DDKb) is shewn on p. 270.

Manorial: Bickerstaffe: court books 1735–1821, 1836–79; Bolton-with-Adgarley: court papers 1690, 1691, 1694, 1696–98, 1701, 1703–06, 1708–10, 1855–58, 1860, 1861, 1863–66, 1868–70, verdict books 1730–1883, 1894–1925, enrolment books 1828–66, 1868–1935; Bootle-with-Linacre: court rolls and presentments 1668, 1711–17, 1725, 1726, 1742–74; Broughton-in-Furness: estreats 1587–92; Burscough: court books 1677, 1678, 1750–85, 1788–1823, 1838–79; Bury: court books 1733–83, 1786–1809, 1823–75; Chipping: court rolls 1566, 1603, 1626, 1629, 1680–82, 1694; Halewood: court-books 1678, 1716, 1322, 1750–77; Inskip: verdict-books 1734, 1778–85, 1787–93, 1797, 1799, 1801–05, 1807, 1810, 1812, 1814–17, 1820–22, 1824–29, 1831–33, 1841, 1842, 1844, 1845, 1847–75, call-books 1731, 1847–69; Kirkdale: court-books 1624, 1740–51, 1753–59, 1761–63, 1765–67, 1769–71, 1773–75, estreats 1763–77; Knowsley: court-books 1678, 1679, 1748–78, 1795–1823; Newburgh: court-books 1624, 1675–77, 1695, 1698, 1707, 1710, 1711, 1716, 1722, 1727, 1729, 1733–57, 1763, 1769–74, 1777, 1789, 1790, 1792, 1793, 1798, 1800, 1806, 1807, 1810, 1816, 1824, 1825, 1839–79, estreats 1665, 1677, call-book 1727, stewards' fees 1733; Ormskirk: court-books 1677, 1679, 1680, 1754, 1755, 1779–1823, 1837–75; Pilkington: court-books 1675–78, 1722, 1723, 1725–27, 1731–

1821, 1823–75; Rainford: court books 1678, 1728–44, 1746–
1822, 1833–79, estreats 1781–83; Sowerby: court books 1765,
1766, 1769–72, 1778, 1780–82, 1785, 1787, 1789, 1792, 1798,
1801–06, 1808, 1810–75, call-books 1767–70, 1778, 1779, 1789,
1800, 1804, 1817, 1818, 1820, 1830, 1839–68; Thornley: court-
books 1674–85, 1710, 1713, 1714, 1716, 1717, 1719, 1727–33,
1735–61, 1766, 1767, 1770–74, 1780, 1783–85, 1787, 1792, 1798–
1800, 1802, 1804, 1806–39, 1841–74, call-books 1676–80, 1696–
1708, 1712, 1728, 1730–39, 1744–50, 1753–61, 1765–67, 1780,
1790, 1793, 1798, 1804–13, 1815, 1825–45, 1857–67, estreats
1759; Treales, Wharles, and Roseacre: court-books 1736–58,
1760–62, 1785, 1787, 1792–94, 1798, 1801–08, 1810–49, 1851–53,
1855–75, call-books 1746–60, 1777, 1782, 1783, 1800, 1801,
1819, 1824, 1829–71, estreats 1748, 1764, list of officers 1754–60,
1762, 1763; Up Holland: court-books 1650, 1678, 1679;
Weeton: court-books 1735–47, 1749–57, 1759–61, 1764–67,
1787, 1792, 1793, 1798–00, 1802–47, 1849–75, call-books 1747–
67, 1777–1825, 1834–55, 1860–71, lists of officers 1756–64

Other counties: Devon, Bradworthy court-roll 1555; Isle of Man,
court-roll 1576; Shropshire, Ellesmere estreats 1589; Sussex,
hundreds of Buttinghill, Poynings, Barcombe, Street, etc., and
borough of Lewes, court-roll 1565; Westmorland: Witherslack
and Beetham court-books 1690–93, 1695–1706, 1708, 1710,
1711, 1713–15, 1717; Yorkshire, Kirkby Malzeard court-rolls
1512, 1620, 1622, 1628, Thirsk court-roll 1424–27. Estreat roll
of manors of Broughton-in-Furness and Nether Kellett, Lancs.,
Ellesmere, Dobaston, Middle, Kynaston, Shropshire, 1588–92

Title Deeds: General grants of properties 1443–1797

Alston-with-Hothersall 1614–1723, Anderton 1610–14, Astley 1343,
Aughton 1364–1727, Bickerstaffe 1433–1833, Bispham 1607–
1798, Bolton-le-Moors 1406, Bolton-le-Sands 1485, Bolton-
with-Adgarley 1777–1803, Bootle-with-Linacre 1637–1867,
Breightmet 1597–1850, Burscough c.1300–1832, Bury 1564–
1884, Carleton 1609–1700, Charnock 1439, Cheetham 1597–
1884, Childwall 1596–1602, Chipping c.1230–1846, Chorley
1719, Claughton-in-Amounderness 1491, Little Crosby c.1280–
1501, Great Crosby 1343–1596, Croston c.1390, Cuerdley 1648–
1720, Dalton 1421–1596, Ditton 1347, Great Eccleston 1752–
1842, Euxton 1664–1709, Formby 1642, Goosnargh 1625–1834,
Greenhalgh 1723–60, Halewood 1382–1760, Halliwell 1604–14,
Harwood 1682–1886, Heap 1626–1886, Huyton-with-Roby
1372–1825, Inskip-with-Sowerby 1623–1842, Kirkdale c.1290–
1813, Knowsley and Eccleston 1628–1799, Lancaster 1346–
1658, Lathom 1586–1735, Litherland 1300, Liverpool 1308–

1825, Lydiate 1563, Maghull 1495–1662, Melling c.1290–1782, Netherton 1710, Ormskirk 1576–1810, Pemberton 1618, Penwortham 1627, Pilkington 1546–1886, Plumpton 1637–1842, Prescot 1775, Preston 1466–1862, Radcliffe 1740–1882, Rainford c.1270–1836, Rainford Mossborough c.1290–1786, Rainhill 1331, Raven Meols 1682–1717, Salford 1830–76, Scarisbrick 1723, Singleton Grange 1679, Skelmersdale 1563–1617, Thornley 1338–1837, Toxteth Park 1593, Treales, Wharles and Roseacre 1637–1885, Ulnes Walton 1596, Ulverston c.1220, Up Holland 1655, Walmersley-with-Shuttleworth 1670–1884, Walton-on-the-Hill 1729–1812, Weeton 1637–1883, Wesham 1637–1890, West Derby 1517, Wheatley 1663, Wheelton 1694–99, Whiston 1739–1836, Whittingham 1680, Wigan 1619, Much Woolton 1630, Woodplumpton 1410, Wrightington c.1250–1425

Other counties: Anglesey: Beaumaris 1353; Cheshire: Great Boughton 1638–39, Chester 1481–1664, Childer Thornton 1599–1613, Macclesfield, etc., 1416–1786, Thornton Hough 1664, Trafford 1684, Upton 1622–26, Woodchurch 1628; Devon: Bovey Tracy and Torrington 1336; Dorset: Sturminster Marshall 1597; Essex: Barndon 1556, Hedingham 1580–91; Flintshire: Hope and Mold 1570–1795; Gloucestershire: Wincote 1540; Isle of Ely: Glassmore 1721; Isle of Man: Appyn 1379; Leicestershire: Clawson 1590; Middlesex: Westminster and Isleworth 1600–1652; Northamptonshire: Burton Latimer 1810; Northumberland: Fleetham 1653–58; Nottinghamshire: Hoveringham 1367–81; Oxfordshire: Milton 1608, Eynsham 1383–1635; Surrey: Reigate 1598; Sussex: Halnaker and East Lavant 1702–21; Warwickshire: Binton 1487, Meriden 1600, Whichford and Ascot 1607; Westmorland: Burton-in-Kendal 1448, Witherslack and Beetham, 1540–1745; Yorkshire: Burton and Mewith 1718, Skeldon 1606, Thirsk and Kirkby Malzeard 1609–1717

Family Papers: Settlements 1411–1798; wills 1513–1796; genealogical papers 1632–1844; general pardons 1445–1626; inquisitions *post mortem* 1459–1612; dispensation for marriage of Thomas Stanley and Elizabeth Welles 1498; letter of confraternity, prior of Ely to earl and countess of Derby 1507

Appointments: Lord Cromwell and Sir Thomas Stanley, stewards of Macclesfield 1439, 1442; Lord Stanley, steward of Macclesfield 1462; Lord Stanley, earldom of Derby 1485; Lord Strange, constableship of Wicklow castle 1486; Richard Cantsfield, collector of subsidies in Lancashire 1488; earl of Derby, lieutenant of Lancashire, Cheshire, Salop, Flintshire and Denbighshire 1554; Thomas Tyldesley, sergeant-at-law 1604; earl of Derby, lieutenant of Lancashire, Cheshire and Chester

1625; Roger Downes, vice-chamberlain of Cheshire 1625; earl of Derby and Lord Strange, chamberlain of Cheshire 1626; Edward Stanley of Bickerstaffe, baronetcy 1627; Edward Christian, lieutenant of Isle of Man 1627; earl of Derby and others, commission to collect for repair of St. Paul's, 1632, 1633; Lord Strange, commission to raise forces and erect beacons 1640; Earl of Derby, steward of Macclesfield 1640; earl of Derby, steward of Macclesfield 1661; Richard Acton, examinership in Cheshire exchequer 1667; James Stanley, captaincy in Netherlands army 1686; William Darbishire, bailiff of West Derby 1694; James Stanley, brigadier, 1702; earl of Derby, custos rotulorum of Lancashire 1702; earl of Derby, master forester of Quernmore, Myerscough and Amoun-, derness 1702; earl of Derby, chancellor of duchy of Lancaster 1706; earl of Derby, lieutenant of Lancashire 1714; earl of Derby, summons to Parliament 1727; Lord Strange, lieutenant of Lancashire 1757, 1761; Lord Strange, chancellor of duchy of Lancashire 1762; earl of Derby, lieutenant and custos rotulorum of Lancashire 1771, 1776; earl of Derby, chancellor of duchy of Lancaster 1783, 1806; Henry Stanley, clerk of council of duchy of Lancaster 1806; earl of Derby, receiver-general of duchy of Lancaster 1806; earl of Derby, lieutenant and custos rotulorum of Lancashire 1830, 1834, 1837; earl of Derby, knight bachelor 1839

There is a collection of documents 1650–95 referring to the Heskeths of Rufford which probably came to Knowsley through a trusteeship. Many Rufford leases are included.

Estate: There is a large number of leases, extending from the middle of the sixteenth century, relating to the following places: Alston, Aughton, Barnacre, Bickerstaffe, Billinge, Bispham, Bolton-le-Moors, Bolton-with-Adgarley, Bootle-with-Linacre, Breightmet, Bretherton, Burscough, Bury, Carleton, Childwall, Chipping, Claughton-in-Amounderness, Colne, Little Crosby, Cuerdley, Eccleston, Elswick, Elton, Goosnargh, Halewood, Halliwell, Hambleton, Heap, Much Hoole, Huyton, Kearsley, Kirkdale, Knowsley, Lathom, Litherland, Liverpool, Manchester, Marsden, Marton, Melling, Ormskirk, Orrell, Pilkington, Plumpton, Prestwich, Radcliffe, Rainford, Rufford, Salford, Scotforth, Singleton, Skelmersdale, Sowerby, Thornley, Treales, Wharles and Roseacre, Up Holland, Walmersley-with-Shuttleworth, Walton-on-the-Hill, Warrington, Wavertree, Weeton, Wesham, West Derby, Whittingham, Wigan, Windle and Little Woolton

Other counties: Cheshire, Macclesfield, Northwich, Sutton, Wallasey, Wildboarclough; Flintshire, Hope, etc.; Oxfordshire,

Eynsham; Warwickshire, Meriden; Westmorland, Beetham, Witherslack; Yorkshire, Kirkby Malzeard, Thirsk

Lease registers: late-17th to mid-19th century

Surveys: Alston *c*.1630; Aughton 1713, *c*.1800; Bickerstaffe *c*.1800; Bispham 1750, 1780, *c*.1800; Bretherton 1652; Burscough 1787; Bury 1701, 1721, 1775, 1790; Carleton 1798; Cheetham 1792; Chipping 1635, *c*.1695, *c*.1800; Halewood 1784, *c*.1804; Hornby castle estate *c*.1790; Kearsley 1792; Kirkdale 1795; Knowsley 1649, 1789; Lathom *c*.1800; Linacre *c*.1700, 1781; Liverpool 1697; Ormskirk 1713, 1787; Plumpton 1703, 1798, *c*.1800; Preston 1709, 1774, 1819; Rainford *c*.1780, 1785; Roby *c*.1790; Sowerby *c*.1800; Thornley 1690, *c*.1800; Treales, Wharles, and Roseacre 1703, *c*.1800; Walton-on-the-Hill 1727; Weeton 1703, 1779, 1798, *c*.1800; Lord Petre's property in Preston 1788

Other counties: Cheshire, Macclesfield 1634, 1674, 1709, 1721, 1783, 1793, Northwich 1782; Flintshire, Hope 1702, 1767, 1794; Northumberland, Fleetham 1658; Warwickshire, Meriden 1716; Westmorland, Beetham 1736, 1813, Witherlack 1736, 1813; Yorkshire, Burton and Mewith 1652, 1708; Irish estate 1774; Isle of Man 1506, 1607, 1614

Particulars for sale of estates of James, earl of Derby 1650–52 (properties in Lancashire, Cumberland, Yorkshire, Cheshire, Flintshire); boundary between Aughton and Bickerstaffe 1733; boundary between Burscough and Rufford 1439; Martin Mere drainage papers 1694–1725; inquisition *ad quod damnum* concerning road past Knowsley hall 1777; boundary of Eccleston 1796; establishment of bow-bearers' and keepers' allowances 1650, 1680; contract for brickwork of Ormskirk town-hall 1779; agreement concerning Prescot moss 1803; division of Chipping wastes 1566; enclosure of Roby Carrs 1629; division of Little Crosby commons 1598; list of servants at Knowsley and Lathom 1702; grant of fairs at Ormskirk and Weeton 1670; grant of free warren at Lathom, Knowsley, Childwall, Roby and Anglezark 1339; boundaries of Rainford and Windle 1830; Sowerby drainage papers 1741–1874; Marton mere drainage agreement 1853; Treales, Wharles, and Roseacre crop-books 1845, 1879–88, 1894–98; Chipping, Roseacre, and Weeton land improvement books 1882

Correspondence: Stewards' letters 1746–60, 1762–64, 1780–86, 1788–96, 1802, 1803, 1808–10, 1812, 1815, 1817–32, 1835–37; letter-books 1756–65, 1796–1819, 1829–30; weekly notes of stewards' correspondence 1796–1802; boundaries and mining in Flintshire 1651–1787, 1821–25, 1843–45; Macclesfield Forest 1641–79; Sir Cleave Moore's estates 1617–1743; disturbances and riots 1842;

the Irish estates 1747–1806; the Isle of Man 1602–1781; the lieutenancy and militia 1692–1814

There are letters included in the majority of the "bundles" relating to all parts of the estate

Legal Papers: Chamberlainship of Chester 1568; Molyneux *v.* Moore (wreck) 1594; Derby *v.* Regina (succession to I.o.M.) 1598; Kelly *v.* Derby (Bidston, Ches.) 1620; Derby *v.* Fleetwood (Dalton and Up Holland tithes) 1620; Ashhurst *v.* Derby (Skelmersdale) *c.*1620; Stanley *v.* Derby (Cross Hall) 1624; Derby *v.* Lincoln (Arras hangings) 1627; Stanley *v.* Derby (Ormskirk moss) 1635; Martin *v.* Derby (debt) 1646; Parker *v.* Sherburne (Chipping) 1648; Derby *v.* Owen (Skelmersdale) 1655; Holt *v.* Derby (Burscough) *c.*1664; Athol *v.* Derby (marriage settlement) 1672; Patten *v.* Preston corporation (Marsh mill) 1662–70; recovery of estates 1673–74; Attorney-General *v.* Pickford (Macclesfield Forest) 1664–78; Rex *v.* Cutler (Blackmoor in Chipping) 1681; Patten *v.* Rhodes (Longridge common) 1684; Lund chapel 1687; Greenfield *v.* Patten (Preston church) 1700; Bishop of Chester *v.* Derby (Bury church) 1702–35; Ashburnham *v.* Derby (settlements) 1714–22; Maguire *v.* Jackson (wine in I.o.M.) 1720; Horobin *v.* Hastey (false doctrine in I.o.M) 1721; Stanley *v* Hesketh (Patten estates in Fylde) 1725; Bootle *v.* Derby (Lathom colliery) *c.*1730; Derby *v.* Lowther (Bolton-with-Adgarley minerals) *c.*1733; Athol *v.* Derby (Isle of Man) 1736–51; bishop of Man *v.* Derby (tithes of Man, etc.) 1738–58, 1810; Derby *v.* Harrison (Witherslack) 1736–44; Ann *v.* Derby (Witherslack) 1756–62; Bootle springs 1765; Derby *v.* Pearson (Witherslack timber) 1786–92; Fishwick *v.* Holmes (Sowerby) 1794; Oad *v.* Derby (Ormskirk and Burscough) 1797; Derby *v.* Ackers (Salford) 1807; Wrea Green fair 1814; Holcroft *v.* Calderbank (Ormskirk market) 1835

Record of enquiry into Derby lands in Samlesbury forfeited by Lord Lovell, 1519; affidavits concerning seawall at Walton and Clacton, Essex, 1713; proceedings before duchy council in outlawry of Lawrence of Knoll of Chipping *c.*1390; the laws of the Isle of Man 1667, 1705–26

Business Papers: Memorandum on coalmines in Eccleston 1792; papers concerning Adgarley mines 1709–1856; Bolton and Bury canal papers 1799–1804; Liverpool and Bury railway 1845–50; Lancashire and Yorkshire Railway 1830–48; London and North Western Railway 1827–47; East Lancashire Railway 1845–51; Manchester, Bolton and Bury Railway 1834–46; accounts of Liverpool Water Company 1799–1820; estimate for building Scotts Tannery, Kirkdale, 1839

Official Papers: Rainford assessment 1772; Thornley land tax assessments 1764, 1767, 1769, 1772, 1791; Ormskirk town order-book 1613–1725

Election Papers: Preston: correspondence 1706, 1784, 1788, 1789, 1794, 1796, 1797, 1813, 1818, 1819, 1820; accounts 1780, 1796, 1812–13; election of Nicholas Fazackerley 1732

Lancashire: poll-book 1702; freeholders' list 1695. South Lancashire: papers 1837; Fylde: papers 1885

Ecclesiastical Papers: Bury: new plan 1782. Chipping, erection of seat 1761. Huyton: faculty for burial 1656. conveyances of advowson 1748–56. Ormskirk: various papers 1593–1847. Scarth Hill church, papers 1848–50. Prescot and Rainford: pew papers 1634–1741. Preston: faculty and grant of gallery 1682–88. Rainford: pew plan 1634. Rainford Independent chapel agreements 1786–1820. Badsworth, co. York, list of presentations 1496–1732. Mold, co. Flint, alienation of rectory 1670. East Lavant, co. Sussex, next presentation 1749

Charity Papers: Hulme's Charity for B.A.s of Brazenose College, Oxford: appointment of trustees 1752; Boxgrove, East Lavant and Tangmere, co. Sussex: foundation of almshouses 1717

Plans: Adgarley Green 1730–38; Bury and district c.1600; Chipping 1800, Blacksticks 1821, 1875, Loudside 1875; Goosnargh 1800, Lower Core 1828; Huyton, Wheathill 1774; Irish estate 1774; Liverpool: new streets 1805, 1843; Liverpool to Northwich road 1818; Macclesfield Forest c.1800; Preston: cockpit 1790, racecourse 1813; Rainford 1666, 1765; Sowerby 1800, drainage 1847; Thornley c.1681, 1800; Treales, Wharles and Roseacre 1800, 1841, 1888; Weeton 1800, 1880; Wildboarclough 1739; Witherslack drained land 1813; Witherslack to Levens road 1819; Witherslack moss c.1780; new road north of Manchester 1804; Thornley to Longridge road 1813

Rentals: General Estate, 1728–1837

Alston, Thornley, Chipping, Chaigeley and Preston 1747–1840; Beetham 1746–1814; Bickerstaffe 1746–1849; Bolton-with-Adgarley 1730, 1745–1890; Bootle, Kirkdale and Walton 1746–1849; Burscough 1746–1849, 1910–39; Burton-in-Lonsdale and Mewith 1708; Bury 1746–1850; Fylde estate 1834–1939; Chipping 1636; Glassmore in Ely 1774–77; Halewood 1746–1849; Halnaker 1710; Hope 1746–1849; Irish estates 1748–1826, 1850–56; Isle of Man 1607; Knockin 1629; Knowsley, Eccleston, Huyton, Roby and Melling 1746–1849; Liverpool c.1390, 1724–1849; Macclesfield 1672–80, 1685, 1694, 1698, 1707–17, 1747–

1849, 1900–39; Meriden 1660, 1743–83; Newburgh and Bispham 1746–1849, 1910–39; Ormskirk 1660, 1746–1849; Pilkington 1746–1849; Preston 1819; Rainford, Mossborough and Wigan 1746–1849; Skelmersdale 1660, c.1680; Sowerby and Inskip 1745–1849; Thornley and Chipping 1745–46; Treales, Wharles and Roseacre 1640, 1660, 1745–1849; Upton c.1660; Weeton 1745–1849; Whicham and Corney c.1660; Witherslack 1628–41, 1746–1871; Much Woolton and Little Woolton 1653. Moore estates in Liverpool, Kirkdale, etc., 1509–1724; Patten estate in Thornley, Chipping, Wheatley and Whittingham 1678, 1681–83, 1685, 1690–98, 1707

Accounts: General cashbooks 1720–27, 1750–54, 1795–1831; general journals 1795–1838; general ledgers 1795–1835; yearly summaries of estate accounts 1776–1837; farm bailiffs' account-books 1711–76; stewards' accounts 1703–28; audit accounts 1702–20; accounts at Eton 1768–70

Ministers' accounts of the earldom 1512, 1514, 1517, 1518, 1524–27, 1598, 1601, 1672–95, 1714–28

Household account 1562; Knowsley bailiff 1649; Burscough priory 1537; building Ormskirk townhall 1780–81; London household accounts 1812–32; steward of the Isle of Man 1706–18

Other counties: Middlesex, Colham and Hillingdon bailiffs' accounts 1372, 1376, 1380, 1388, 1408, 1410, 1411, 1418; Oxfordshire, Milton bailiffs' accounts 1385; Shropshire, Ellesmere baliffs' accounts 1378. Ministers' accounts of Lord Lovell (counties of Lancaster, Chester, Leicester, Stafford, Northampton and York) 1446

Ministers' accounts of duchess of Exeter (counties of Bedford, Hertford, Northampton and Rutland) 1472

Bailiffs' accounts of duchess of Norfolk (Lincolnshire) 1477, 1495

Receivers' accounts of countess of Richmond (Somerset) 1504

Receivers' accounts of Sir Robert Broughton (counties of Cambridge, Huntingdon, Norfolk, Suffolk, Essex, Hertford, Northampton, Buckingham, Leicester and Oxford) 1505

Ministers' accounts of the Isle of Man 1521–23, 1622, 1623, 1673–98, 1701, 1703–35

Bailiffs' accounts: Hope 1685, 1688, 1690, 1692, 1693, 1697, 1775–78, 1781–84, 1787, 1788, 1795, 1800–03; Burscough 1693, 1697; Burton and Mewith 1637, 1682–85, 1688, 1690, 1692, 1693, 1696, 1697; Goosnargh 1636; Halewood 1685, 1688–90, 1697; Thirsk and Kirkby Malzeard 1683, 1684, 1688, 1689, 1696, 1697; Knowsley 1696, 1697; Lathom 1694, 1696; Macclesfield 1633–41, 1682, 1683, 1689, 1690, 1697; Meriden 1684, 1688,

1695; Northwich 1685, 1690, 1693, 1694, 1696, 1697; Ormskirk and Aughton 1683, 1687, 1689, 1696, 1697; Rainford 1696, 1697; Up Holland and Skelmersdale 1696, 1697; Upton 1689, 1697; Weeton, Treales, Sowerby, Bretherton, and Alston 1682, 1688–90, 1693, 1696, 1697; West Derby, Wavertree, Everton, Childwall, Woolton, Liverpool, and Speke 1693, 1696, 1697; Alston 1628

Keeper of great seal of exchequer of Chester 1682–84, 1688, 1689, 1691, 1696, 1697

Bailiff-itinerant of Cheshire 1693–96

Water-bailiffs of Isle of Man 1703–06, 1713–16, 1721, 1722, 1728–33, 1735

Miscellaneous: Grant of fair and market at Knockin 1249; will and inventory of Denis Robinson of Kirkdale 1465; agreement for building house in Liverpool 1665; agreement for building street in Liverpool 1700; Kirkdale enclosure award 1800; papers concerning sale of woods and letting the fishery at Arnside 1781–82, 1795; commission to enquire into forfeitures in Macclesfield Forest 1597; papers concerning Bootle springs 1799–1867; school on Kirkdale marsh, donations and cost 1838; grant of liberty to erect weir on Irwell in Pilkington 1546; subscription list to public walks in Manchester 1844; Preston races 1809; list of subscriptions for new road over Newton marsh 1804; rental and commonplace-book of William Moore of Bankhall 1509–72; inventory of arms in the Isle of Man 1701, 1702; Isle of Man customs rates 1677, 1692; accounts of voyages of the *Henrietta* from Liverpool to the Isle of Man 1704–18; accounts of cattle bought in the Isle of Man for the earl's use 1704–14; sales of puffins, rabbits and cattle-grazing in Calf of Man 1735; inventory of Roger Corless of Up Holland 1633; report on defence of Liverpool 1803

Bury Estate Company: plans, Bury c.1790, c.1840, 1847, c.1850; Carleton 1832; Cheetham, Temple Estate 1847; Colne 1846; Elton c.1790, c.1840, c.1845; Farnworth and Kearsley 1798; Harwood 1797; Heap c.1790, c.1840; Great Marsden c.1790; Outwood c.1790; Salford 1846; Shuttleworth 1838, c.1840, c.1845; Unsworth c.1820, 1830, 1847; Walmersley c.1790, c.1845, c.1850; West Derby 1835; Whitefield c.1790, c.1840, c.1850

Correspondence: letter-books 1845–1924; miscellaneous letters 1845–1925

Rentals: Bury 1907–23, Pilkington 1907–23

Leases: Bury, Cheetham, Elton, Farnworth, Kearsley, Harwood, Heap, Pilkington, Salford, Walmersley-with-Shuttleworth 1800– *c*.1860

Hawkshead-Talbot of Chorley (DDHk) (See also DDX/1111)

The estate of Bagganley in Chorley was in the ownership of the Parker family from at least 1443 until the marriage of Margaret Parker to William Talbot of Hindley about 1730. In 1812 James Talbot married Cecily Hawkshead of Heskin and in due course their son William succeeded to the Hawkshead properties and, dying childless, bequeathed his estate to his wife's nephew William Talbot Bretherton of Eccleston. William Hawkshead was a surveyor in the latter half of the eighteenth century.

Estate papers, Euxton township papers, Chorley and Euxton deeds, Euxton mill accounts, rentals of Liverpool and Goosnargh, High Constables' papers and documents *re* Commonwealth church survey, sequestration, Chorley workhouse and Mason and Hodgson charities 17th to 19th c., Gaskell family deeds of Stalmine, Hambleton, Out Rawcliffe, Preesall 1630–1884, grant of foreshore rights at Windley, Stalmine 1885

Manorial: Chorley court orders 1661–1738; estreats 1734

Title Deeds: Adlington 1555–1618, 1783–84; Anderton 1724–82; Aspull, Bedford and Wigan 1752–91; Aughton and Ormskirk 1499; Bispham and Carleton 1661; Burscough 1512, 1821; Charnock Richard 1582–1787; Chorley 1274–1791; Coppull 1676–1841; Dalton 1790; Duxbury 1636; Eccleston (Chorley) 1615–1823; Euxton 1616–1721; Fazakerley and Walton-on-the-Hill 1627; Heapey 1632–81; Heskin 1591–1791; Leyland 1743–1805; Mawdesley 1738–1863; Padiham 1771; Parbold, Shevington, Standish, Up Holland and Walton-le-Dale 1607–1796; Penwortham 1817–42; Preston 1725; Standish 1732–81; Ulnes Walton 1722–82; Walton-le-Dale 1785; Warton-in-Amounderness 1504; Wavertree 1771; Welch Whittle 1687–1784; Wigan 1789; Worsley 1601; Worsthorne 1582–1766; Wrightington 1587–1760

Other counties: Bedfordshire, Ravensden 1557

Family Papers: Settlements 1655–1812; bonds 1647–1809; wills and inventories 1582–1840; executorship papers 1684–1809; diaries 1741–42, 1809–20, 1824–27

Estate Papers: Leases: Cliviger 1706; Penwortham 1717–89

Enclosure papers: Chorley 1737–97; Layton Hawes *c*.1769

Horwich: footpath agreement 1774

Surveys: Leyland 1791; Rumworth colliery 1783; Orrell c.1780; Eccleston, Southart's farm 1770; Bradford, Manchester 1662; Whittle-le-Woods. Dr. Lowe's 1791; Heskin and Eccleston 1781; Martin Mere 1770; Hutton, Up Hall c.1780; Read 1771; Bowland, Lees 1773; Up Holland, Fisher's 1768; Chorley, Gillibrand's 1758; Welch Whittle, Harvey's 1790; Chorley, Hartwood Green 1824; Walton-le-Dale, Essex House 1765; Broughton, Preston, Whittingham and Goosnargh 1771; Broughton 1767; Houghton, Middleton and Arbury 1759; Wrightington c.1789; Rainford, Ribbleton, Whittle-le-Woods, Widnes, Sutton, Hindley, Abram, Windle, Little Harwood, Eccleston, Mawdesley, Heskin and Wrightington 1758; Houghton, Middleton and Arbury, Pemberton, Westhoughton, Winstanley, Orrell 1760; Eccleston (Chorley) 1777; Barton, Goosnargh, Bilsborrow and Sowerby 1770; Adlington, Orrell, Coppull and Heath Charnock 1763; Wakefield, Thorne and Horbury co. York, Southworth-with-Croft 1761; Longton, Hutton, Scarisbrick Hall and Malham co. York c.1770; Slaidburn, co. York, Cuerden Hall, Ramsgreave, Over Darwen, Much Woolton Hall, Chisnall Hall, Coppull, Wrightington, Langtree and Rivington 1769; Preston c.1770; Wigan, Ince, Abram, Heaton, Anderton, Horwich, Rumworth, Chipping, Preston, Standish, Coppull, Clitheroe, Ainsdale, Birkdale, Formby, Worden Hall, Blackrod, Cuerden Hall, Ashton, Ince Blundell, Shevington Hall and Westhoughton 1778–88; Haigh 1749; Newton-in-Makerfield 1759; Coppull, Langtree, Tockholes and Welch Whittle 1757–60; Leyland, Heskin, Chorley, Eccleston, Wrightington, Anderton, Skelmersdale, Lathom and Parbold 1790–96; Up Holland c.1770; Heath Charnock, Winwick, Broughton (Preston), Haydock, Shevington, Skelmersdale and Colne c.1770; Barton 1771; Golborne and Kenyon 1754; Burnley, Chorley, Whittle-le-Woods, Charnock Richard, Bradford, Leyland, Goosnargh, Whittingham, Briercliffe, Cliviger, Hapton, Worsthorne, Padiham, Habergham Eaves and Marsden 1782–93; Oldham and Coppull 1780; Melling, Wigan and Raven Meols 1756; Lower Darwen, Over Darwen, Eccleshill, Little Harwood and Samlesbury c.1770; Pendle, Marsden, Cliviger, Padiham, Billington, Eccleston, Euxton and Mawdesley 1777–81; Dalton, Up Holland, Skelmersdale, Ormskirk, Lathom, Orrell and Bispham 1750; Inskip, Goosnargh, Myerscough, Bilsborrow and Chipping 1772; Winstanley, Pemberton and Orrell 1764; Orrell 1763; Eccleston, Croston, Wheelton, Heskin, Billinge, Brockholes and Euxton 1758–59; Darwen, Staining, Woodplumpton, Elswick, Catterall, Carleton and Tockholes 1764; Anderton, Padiham, Clitheroe, Chorley, Inskip, Ightenhill Park, Over Darwen, Marsden, Henthorn and

Clapham, co. York 1751–70; Anderton, Charnock Richard, Welch Whittle, Heskin and Eccleston 1735; Dalton and Ashhurst c.1770; Chorley 1768

Correspondence: Parker family 1509–15, 1674–1778; Hawkshead family 1775–1842; Euxton, Pincock 1662–1726; miscellaneous 1773–1806

Legal Papers: Partington v. Briggs (debt) 1675; Calvert v. Leigh (breach of promise) c.1760; Eccleston tithes 1755

Official Papers: Chorley: assessments and township accounts 1654–1747, 1781; Euxton: surveyors' accounts 1660–1715; Leyland Hundred: high constables' warrants, receipts and bridge rolls 1616–1724

Ecclesiastical Papers: Chorley: tithe papers 1602–1731; Coppull: building and pew papers 1755–58; Croston: rectory lease 1749; Eccleston: tithe receipts 1738–1819; Hesketh-with-Becconsall: tithe lease 1739; Standish: rectory valuation 1776; Whalley: rectory rental 1767

Plans: Clayton-le-Woods, Little Dove Cote 1784; Walton-le-Dale 1765

Rentals: Barton (Preston) and Padiham 1772; Astley (Chorley) 1767–85, 1792–95; Chorley, Charnock, Whittle-le-Woods, Goosnargh, Cottam and Bradford 1793–94; Cliviger, Hapton, Briercliffe-with-Extwistle, Habergham Eaves, Pendle, Dunnockshaw, Hurstwood, Burnley, Marsden and Padiham 1741

Accounts: Chorley: Brooke family 1726–67, 1786; Parker family 1741–95; Euxton: Robinsons estate 1696–1721; Stansfields house 1694–1728; water corn-mill 1689–1727; Pincock farm 1677–1729; Pincock miscellaneous 1737–45; Welch Whittle: Nicholas Heskin 1701–29; Liverpool: Crosse estate 1706–20. Goosnargh: Crosse estate 1700–10. Townley accounts 1773–87, 1794–95. Hawkshead family school-bills 1795–1800; Thomas Hawkshead 1770–1826; general 1714–1823; account-book of Francis Walmesley of Dunkenhalgh, including expenses of his father's funeral 1702–12

Charity Papers: Peter Lathom's charity: miscellaneous papers 1700–1839; rules of Croston workhouse, 18th c.

Miscellaneous Papers: Verses about kings of England, c.1440. 18th c. gardening notes, recipes and prescriptions, essays and verses; writing-master's copy-book 1736; verses addressed to Mr. Hawkshead 1782; table of pawnbrokers' interest c.1784; leaflet on proposed Leeds and Liverpool canal c.1770

Tatton of Cuerden (DDTa)

From the early years of the fourteenth century the Cuerden estate was in the ownership of the Charnocks until sold to the Langtons, barons of Newton-in-Makerfield, with whom it remained until another sale about 1605 to Henry Banastre of Bank in Bretherton. From them it went, by the marriage of a co-heiress, to Robert Parker of Extwistle. Another marriage brought in the Brooke properties of Charnock Richard, Astley in Chorley, etc. In 1906 the estates were bequeathed by Thomas Townley-Parker to his nephew R. A. Tatton.

Manorial: Cowling, co. York: court-rolls 1624, 1625, 1631, 1715, 1721. Sutton, co. York: court-rolls 1615, 1625, 1629, 1631, 1637, 1665, 1671, 1715; call books 1715, 1736; estreats 1721

Title Deeds: Abram 1673; Aighton, Bailey and Chaigley 1567; Barton-upon-Irwell 1585, 1587; Bispham-with-Norbreck 1538; Blackburn 1653; Bolton 1357; Bradford 1719; Briercliffe-with-Extwistle (Kirkstall abbey) c.1260–1878; Broughton and Whittingham 1589–1768; Burnley 1623–1888; Charnock Richard (St. John of Jerusalem) c.1200–1874; Chipping 1498; Chorley (St. John of Jerusalem) c.1220–1891; Clayton-le-Woods 1721–1868; Clifton-with-Salwick 1751; Clitheroe 1346, 1399; Cliviger 1655–1809; Colne 1445–1881; Coppull 1597–1715; Croston 1316, 1382; Cuerden 1317–1834; Euxton 1603–1863; Farington 1419–1676; Goosnargh 1417; Lea 1787; Leyland 1616, 1617; Longton 1588–1771; Manchester 1617; Marsden 1442–1749; Mawdesley 1379, 1402; Mellor 1353–1612; Penwortham 1606–1731; Preston 1605–1797; Rochdale 1725, 1816; Rossall (Dieulacres abbey) 1533, 1538; Tarleton 1361; Trawden 1445–1513; Walton-le-Dale 1394–1815; Whittle-le-Woods 1619–1835; Worsthorne 1522–1712; Worthington (St. John of Jerusalem) c.1260–1439

Other counties: Cheshire, Malpas, 1476, 1482, Mere c.1260–1543; Staffordshire, Rickarscote, Burton and Forebridge 1631–71; Yorkshire, Conistone school 1686–1746, Cowling 1371–1816, Erringden 1586–1646, Glusburn c.1300–1817, Kirk Smeaton c.1170, Newton-by-Gargrave c.1290–1825, Osgodby c.1195, Sutton-in-Airedale 1340–1816

Family Papers: Settlements 1405–1895; wills 1555–1812; general pardons: John Banastre 1446, Robert Charnock 1605, Peter Brooke 1661. Appointments: Deputy-lieutenants of Cheshire, 1664, 1673, 1685 and of Lancashire 1676, 1685, 1688; Sir Peter Brooke, sheriff 1673; Richard Brooke, deputy-lieutenant 1703, 1704, 1711; Robert Parker, sheriff 1710; Robert Parker, captain 1714; Robert Parker, deputy-lieutenant 1714; Thomas Towneley, keeper of forest of Quernmore, Myerscough, Amounderness, Bleasdale and Wyresdale 1715; Thomas Townley, deputy-lieutenant 1761; Banastre Parker, lieutenant 1779; Thomas Townley Parker, sheriff 1793; Robert Townley Parker, constable of Lancaster castle 1874; Reginald Arthur Tatton, sheriff 1910; Thomas Barcroft, gamekeeper of honour of Clitheroe and Bowland 1662; Thomas Barcroft and Alexander Morres, collectors of subsidies 1664; Robert Townley Parker, deputy-lieutenant 1817; Richard Brooke free-burgess of Liverpool 1675; Sir Peter Brooke, deputy-lieutenant of Cheshire 1660. Grant to Nicholas Townley of exemption from jury service 1639. Inquisitions *post mortem*: William Barcroft 1623, John Eastwood 1641. Inventories: Henry Waterhouse of Sowerby 1587; Robert Charnock of Astley 1615, John Parker of Extwistle 1634, Robert Parker of Netherwood 1636, Thomas Townley of Royle 1737, Robert Parker of Cuerden 1779. Clayton pedigree *c*.1590

Estate Papers: Surveys: Lancashire and Yorkshire estates 1733, 1736, *c*.1780, *c*.1800, 1826; Chorley etc. 1800; Cuerden 1805; Briercliffe-with-Extwistle 1810; Cuerden, Clayton, Walton-le-Dale, and Farington 1817

Astley hall inventories *c*.1830, 1858. Papers concerning sale of Yorkshire estates 1817

Enclosure Papers: Burnley, Ightenhill and Marsden 1545; Cliviger 1598; Briercliffe-with-Extwistle 1605; Glusburn 1738; Cuerden 1804

Correspondence: Conistone (co. York) grammar school 1820–27

Legal Papers: Warrant for arrest of Robert Banastre for murder 1473; warrant for arrest of Richard Woodrofe of Samlesbury for threats 1426; Farington *v.* Charnock (Astley-in-Chorley tithes) 1543; Charnock *v.* Leigh (Bradford coal) *c*.1620; Hoghton *v.* Master (Astley) 1822

Official Papers: Subsidy rolls: Amounderness, Blackburn and Lonsdale 1607, Blackburn and Amounderness 1664. Precepts for repair of bridges: new bridge in Pendle 1675; stone bridge in Walton-le-Dale 1677, 1690, 1697. Books of rates 1636 (contains Privy Council letters 1607–08), 1651. Shrievalty *quietus* 1674, 1676

Ecclesiastical Papers: Report on lands of Gargrave church, co. York 1321

Rentals: Bradford 1669, 1723–26; Glusburn and Stothill, co. York 1665–1700

Accounts: Bills for building Astley hall lodges 1772

Miscellaneous: "Instruction to young travellers setting out for a tour in Turkey" c.1800.

Worsley-Taylor of Whalley (DDWt)

Estate deeds and papers, Whalley area, 17th to 20th c.

Towneley of Belfield (DDTw)

Papers, 19th c.

Towneley of Towneley (DDTo)

The Towneley pedigree can be traced back quite certainly to about the year 1200 when Roger de Lacy, constable of Chester and lord of the honour of Clitheroe, granted *Tunleia* to his son-in-law. Marriages with heiresses from time to time brought into the family estates in Nottinghamshire, Lincolnshire and many other places. Specially to be mentioned are groups of documents relating to the Middletons of Leighton in Lancashire, Pilkington of Gateford in Nottinghamshire, Wymbish of Nocton Priory in Lincolnshire and Lord Widdrington. The muniments passed to Lord O'Hagan on marriage with a daughter of Charles Towneley, the last of the family, who died in 1878.

Manorial: Silverdale court-book 1706; Warton court-rolls 1558, 1593, 1595, 1596, 1598, 1599, 1607–13; Yealand court-rolls 1385, 1495, 1609, 1623–25, 1638, 1651, 1677, 1678; Strickland, co. Westmorland court-roll 1541; Blackburnshire tenant-roll 1378–79

Title Deeds (including leases): Aighton, Baily and Chaigley 1390–1583; Alston-with-Hothersall c.1260–1590; Arkholme 1578; Barnacre-with-Bonds c.1280; Barrowford 1623; Billington 1335; Bilsborrow c.1280; Blackburnshire bailiwick 1351–1598; Borwick 1412; Briercliffe-with-Extwistle c.1230–1620; Burnley 1313–1832; Bury and Middleton 1402; Catterall c.1300; Chadderton 1622; Chipping 1383; Chorley 1402–11; Church 1546; Claughton-in-Amounderness c.1260–1491; Clitheroe c.1260; Cliviger c.1250–1858, leases 1606–1787; Colne 1444–1636; Culcheth 1351–1408; Dutton 1364–1622; Ellel c.1230–1371; Foulridge 1374–1444; Garstang c.1280; Goosnargh 1342–80; Grimsargh c.1260; Habergham Eaves 1319–1832; Hapton 1303–1810, leases 1797–1805; Little Harwood 1388–1476; Heaton-with-Oxcliffe c.1280; Heysham c.1260; Hopwood 1523; Huncoat c.1260–1826; Hundersfield 1586–1783; Kellet c.1260–1584; Lancaster 1339–1427; Marsden 1413–1534; Medlar-with-Wesham 1707–47; Middleton (Lancaster) 1393–1631; Oswaldtwistle c.1280–1566; Padiham 1584–1622; Preston

1355–1445; Ribchester 1306–1591; Rishton 1558; Rossendale 1519–1838; Salesbury 1326–1592; Samlesbury 1547; Scotforth 1459; Silverdale 1651; Southworth-with-Croft 1547; Tarleton 1330–82; Todmorden 1586–1844; Trawden 1444–48; Warrington 1391; Warton 1410–1650; Whalley *c.*1350; Whittingham 1555; Worsthorne-with-Hurstwood *c.*1200–1828; Yealand 1350–1672

Other counties: Cambridgeshire, Horseheath 1359, Longstanton 1395; Cheshire, Brindley *c.*1200–1333, Chester *c.*1280–1331, Marley 1762, Swettenham *c.*1300; Cumberland, Warwick and Wetheral 1688–1770; Derbyshire, Chesterfield 1377–1452; Devon, Bampton and Uffculme 1562; Durham, Barnard Castle 1541–1706, Coxhoe and Hunwick 1688–1729, Gainford 1617–35, Hurworth 1452, Ryton 1715–1813, Stanley *c.*1230–1854, Stella 1632–1854, Winlaton 1632–1854; Essex, Grays Thurrock 1556; Wimbish *c.*1250; Gloucestershire, Wiggold 1549–1784; Hampshire, Christchurch 1654–1720; Lincolnshire, Armston 1591, Blankney 1474–98, Bottisford 1302–57, Bracebridge 1461, Cadney 1459, Dimbleby *c.* 1260–*c.*1360, Dunston *c.* 1200–1720, Fillingham *c.*1150–1389, Haceby *c.*1260, Hanworth *c.* 1260–1305, Harpswell *c.*1250–96, Helpringham 1442, North Ingleby 1513, Metheringham 1631–57, Nocton *c.*1190–1657, Normanton *c.*1250–1309, Osburnby *c.*1280–1657, Saxilby 1481, Spridlington *c.*1240–1322, Wellingore *c.*1250; Middlesex, Cheswick 1755–93, Holborn 1562; Norfolk, Great Yarmouth 1309–60; Northumberland, Berwick-on-Tweed 1391, Dissington 1577, Newcastle-on-Tyne 1478; Nottinghamshire, Blyth *c.*1280, Canwick 1347, Caberton 1485–1531, Clarborough 1266, Dunham *c.*1230, Everton *c.*1240–1505, Flixthorp 1381, Gaitford 1335–1706, Hawksworth 1338, Warsop 1531, Worksop 1313–1441; Shropshire, Church Acton and Whitchurch 1663–1726; Somerset, Huntspill, Norton, Nunnington and Taunton 1562; Surrey, Tooting Graveney *c.*1250–1491; Westmorland, Askham 1604, Kirkby Lonsdale 1565, Strickland *c.*1250–1678; Yorkshire, Almondbury 1482–1508, Bashall Eaves 1795–1854, Bentham 1335–1403, Bolton-by-Bowland 1349–1611, Bowland 1547–1857, Bradford 1550, Broughton-in-Craven 1486, Bubwith *c.*1260–1706, Calton 1425, Grassington 1453–75, Grindleton 1521–1767, Guisborough 1275, Hartshead 1623, Heptonstall 1586–1853, Hinderwell 1558, Holgate *c.*1240, Idle 1453, Keighley 1419, Laverton 1363, Marton-in-Cleveland 1452, Newton-by-Gargrave *c.*1300–1601, Otterburn 1571, Plumpton 1382–1453, Rimington 1578–1619, Ripon 1453–1505, Selby 1353–1476, Slaidburn 1614–1850, Stansfield *c.*1250–1843, Steeton 1453, Swine-in-Holderness 1712, Whitgift 1659

277

France, Calais 1360–1482

Family Papers: Settlements 1349–1838; wills 1315–1824; inquisitions *post mortem*: Alice of the Legh 1388, John Lawrence 1513, Richard Towneley 1455, Edward Crossley 1596; pardons: John Towneley 1382, Thomas Knight 1433, Thomas Middleton 1506, John Towneley 1548, Thomas Middleton 1604, Lord Widrington 1660

Appointments: Richard Towneley, escheator of Lancashire 1371; Sir William Plumpton, chief warden of chase of Kirkby Malzeard and Nidderdale, co. York, 1461; Charles Pilkington, deputy seneschal of Allerton, Notts., Thomas Metcalf, auditor of north parts of duchy of Lancaster 1486; Thomas Middleton, bowbearer and ranger of Arnside 1610; Lord Clifford, steward of Warton 1630; George Middleton, sheriff of Lancashire 1660; deputy-lieutenants of Northumberland 1662

Thomas Middleton's recusancy roll 1595; annulment of marriage of John Towneley and Isabel Butler 1442; licence for John Towneley to hunt in New Forest 1770; confirmation of dispensation for marriage of John Radclyf and Joan Radclyf 1398; commission from John of Gaunt to Richard Towneley to hand over Lancaster castle to Sir Nicholas Harrington 1379; correspondence and drawing *re* art collections 18th and 19th c.

Estate Papers (leases are included with title-deeds): Warton boundaries 1633; Warton moss-book 1661; waste and wood papers, Yealand and Warton, 1650; enclosure of Whorlaw Pasture in Ightenhill 1597–1618; prohibition to dig slate from Extwistle waste 1604; Extwistle boundaries 1835; enclosure in Cliviger, Worsthorne and Hurstwood 1735–65; G.indleton mill papers 1591–1723; terrier of Nocton fields 1590

Correspondence: Barcroft miscellaneous letters 1640–1776, 1795–96

Legal Papers: Burnley grammar school 1622; Whitaker *v.* Towneley (Cliviger boundaries) 1576–79; Clavering *v.* Drinkerrow (Derwent river) 1745; Widdrington *v.* Simpson (Winlaton coal) 1768–75; Whalley rectory 1688; indictment of Richard Towneley for high treason 1716. Many documents relating to litigation of Sir Thomas Middleton of Leighton 17th century

Business Papers: Milnthorpe forge agreements 1658, 1663, 1664; articles concerning hard-soap makers in counties of Gloucester, Somerset, Wilts., Dorset, Devon and Cornwall 1636; Cliviger and Bradley mill accounts 1718–50; Leeds and Liverpool canal papers 19th c.; lead and coal leases and papers 17th to 19th c.

Official Papers: Rate book for Blackburn Hundred 1628. Subsidy-roll, Lonsdale Hundred *c.*1590

Ecclesiastical Papers: Yealand Roman Catholic chapel, letters and papers 1783–1803; conveyance of part of Salley abbey 1376; agreement of chapels of Burnley, Colne, Church and Haslingden with Whalley abbey concerning repair of Whalley church 1396; award between Salley abbey and Henry Pudsay 1520; indulgence (printed by Pynsen) from Boston 1519; Burnley chantry deed 1371; reply from Citeaux to Whalley abbey concerning collections on St. Lambert's day 1362; grant of Rufford chantry 1528; licence to preach in Lincoln diocese 1584; grant of priest at Chaigley 1522; agreement for priest at Burnley 1521; appointment of William Davenport to Benefield church, Northants. 1555; Warton Easter-tithe books 1624–26; tithe papers of Welsh Newton, co. Hereford, 1819–20; registration of Roman Catholic chapel, Chiswick, 1792; Edisford leper hospital cartulary 1317

Plans: Cliviger and Bacup 1576; Stanley and Stella, co. Durham 1745–88

Rentals: Bryning, Kellamergh and Warton 1440; Yealand 1527, 1705; Warton 1511; Ightenhill 1649; Blackburnshire 1599

Other counties: Chesterfield, Derbyshire 1410; Lincoln and Nocton 1527; Stella, Stanley, and Winlaton, co. Durham, 1786–94

Accounts: Whalley abbey bursar's account 1520; Sir William Stanley's executors' accounts 1786–92; Ursula Towneley's accounts 1747 (bound in flock wallpaper); accounts of expenses of journey of Charles, son of James I, from Berwick to Hampton Court 1604; Burholme-in-Bowland estate accounts 1759–1823; accounts of a stay in France 1708; Dame Anne Middleton's household accounts 1675; Yarmouth chamberlain's account 1608; Towneley estate accounts 1824–25; honour of Clitheroe accounts 1488, 1489, 1558, 1827–34; accounts for work done at Towneley 1713–39

Miscellaneous: Letters-patent to earl of Derby and others for putting into force the Act for Regulating Corporations 1664; rules for Bank marsh bowling-green 1681; various 17th and 18th c. papers relating to Great and Little Yarmouth; Henry VII frees Sir Robert Radcliffe from restraint 1491; agreement between inhabitants of Nocton and Potter Hanworth, co. Lincoln, concerning cattle on commons 1590

Townley of Townhead, Staveley (DDTy)

Title Deeds: Cartmel 1633–1944, Colton 1602–1890, Rochdale 1730–1946; Beetham, Westmorland 1633–1941

Family Papers: Mortgages, settlements, wills 1684–1951; diaries and memoranda of Sneyds of Ashcombe, co. Staffs. 1807–74 (refs. to India and Tibet); journals, sketchbooks and papers of Col. Charles Townley in Spain, Turkey, Russia 1835–59; genealogical papers of Townley and Lock 1750–1885; household accounts of Mary Townley of Belfield 1764–68

Surveys, etc.: Finsthwaite, Fell Foot, Townhead, etc. 1774–90, Spotland c.1800, Hundersfield c.1805, Stidd in Ribchester c.1820, Beetham and Cartmel 1850, Meathop and Witherslack c.1900, Staveley 1813; various estate letters and papers c.1800–1944

Correspondence: James Lock, Southampton, to John Lock, Carlisle, re French revolution 1792, William Repton, India 1843–53, Rochdale waterworks 1933, various 1844–1956

Ecclesiastical Papers: Family appointments to Upwell-with-Welney, Norfolk 1798, Stradsett, Norfolk 1827, Staveley, Lancs. 1828, Staveley school 1829, Rural Dean of Cartmel 1858, 1929, Claverdon and Norton Lindsey, co. Warwick 1872, Buckland St. Mary, Somerset 1874, Troutbeck, Westmorland 1882, Egton-cum-Newland 1893, Canon of Carlisle 1919

Plans: Yewbarrow c.1800, Wilson House, Cartmel and Beetham c.1820, c.1880, c.1900, 1941, Meathop c.1820, c.1845, Backbarrow c.1900, c.1945, Nebraska U.S.A. 1875

Accounts: Townhead estates 1809–1944

De Trafford of Trafford (DDTr and DDX 103)

In 1212 there were in the township of Stretford two manors—Stretford and Trafford—the former belonging to Hamon de Mascy the latter to Henry de Trafford. About 1250 another Hamon de Mascy gave Stretford to his daughter who later conveyed it to Richard de Trafford, with whose descendants they have remained. Extensive properties in Cheshire came into the family by the marriage of Sir Edmund Trafford in 1411 to a co-heiress of Sir William Venables. The manor of Barton-upon-Irwell was acquired in 1576 by the marriage of Edmund Trafford to Margaret Booth. Thomas Joseph Trafford was created a baronet in 1841, at which time he altered the surname to De Trafford. Many of the documents are printed in *History of Stretford Chapel*, Chetham Society, N.S. 42, 45, 51.

Manorial: Barton-upon-Irwell: court-books 1693–1733, 1756–1872, call-books 1765–80; Pilling: court-book 1670; Stretford: court-books 1700–32, 1782–1872; Bollin-with-Norcliffe, co. Chester: court-books 1724–80, 1785–1872. Liberties claimed by Sir Thomas Arderne in his manor of Aldford, co. Chester c.1340

Title Deeds: Astley *c*.1300; Barton-upon-Irwell (Dumplington, Irlam, Whittleswick) *c*.1230–1725; Croston 1325–20th c.; Culcheth (mill) *c*.1290–1806; Farnworth *c*.1240–1436; Flixton and Urmston *c*.1250–1668; Hindley 1629–20th c.; Litherland 1391–1455; Longton *c*.1290–1583; Manchester (Chorlton, Hulme, Rusholme, Withington) *c*.1202–1770; Mawdesley 1329–1558; Pemberton 1349–1468; Pilling 17th to 19th c.; Stretford *c*.1210–1840; Wigan 1346–1879

Other counties: Cheshire, Thornton 1399, Wilmslow (Chorley, Hough, Morley) *c*.1220–1879; Derbyshire, Hayfield 1339; Middlesex, Bloomsbury 1713–15; Norfolk, Bradfield 1723–1849; Westmorland, Middleton 1586–96; Yorkshire, Bennetland *c*.1300–49, Halton-on-Humber *c*.1300–1406; Wales, Beaumaris and Caernarvon 1492; Ulster, Holywood abbey 1569

Family Papers: Settlements 1371–1862; wills 1527–1852; letters of confraternity, preaching friars to John and Elizabeth Trafford 1452; Sir John Trafford to serve the earl of Warwick 1461; see also DDX/637 p. 314

Estate Papers: Stewards' diaries 1839, 1841–45, 1847, 1849, 1850

Leases: Barton-upon-Irwell 1673–1869; Croston 1529–1776; Culcheth 1775–1804; Ditton 1721; Longton 1576–1767; Mawdesley 1529–1762; Pilling 1552–1781; Stretford 1668–1849; Wilmslow 1587–1845

Croston Finney papers *c*.1600–1782; Mawdesley waste agreement 1733; Urmston heath award 1554; contract for building house at Old Trafford 1713; division of Great Lindow moss, Wilmslow 1608

Plans, ledger, rentals, surveys etc. Barton-upon-Irwell, Stretford 18th to 20th c., Croston pasturage book 1878–80

Correspondence: Stewards' letters 1786–1820, letter books 1897–1918

Ecclesiastical Papers: Trafford chapel in Manchester church 1814–18; appointment of Reynold Hobson to St. Nicholas chantry in Manchester church 1506; sale of Eccles church porch 1784

Plans: Cornbrook Field, Stretford 1825; Eccles and district 1759; Wilmslow parish 1840; Trafford lands in Wigan *c*.1800; Croston *c*.1830

Rentals: Croston 1659, 1906–37

Accounts: Stewards' accounts 1703–08; bills and vouchers 1786–1820; estate cash-books 1835–74

Miscellaneous: Mandates for John Potter, captain of H.M.S. *Marie Ragged Staff* and H.M.S. *Fortunate* to provision at any port 1568 and 1574

Inqusitions *post mortem*: Thomas Hyde of Urmston 1445, William Hyde of Urmston 1574

Walmesley of Westwood (DDWa)

The manor of Ince-in-Makerfield passed about 1400 by marriage to the Gerards with whom it remained until about 1760 when it passed, again by marriage, to a junior branch of the Walmesleys of Showley in Clayton-le-Dale. See also DDX 590, p. 313.

Title Deeds: "The Ince Roll" a 15th century enrolment of charters relating to Ince, Wigan and Aspull

Abram 1577–1811; Adlington 1570; Aspull 1627–99, 1879–84; Culcheth 1334–1561; Golborne 1615–22; Heskin 1577–1668; Hindley 1630–1785; Houghton, Middleton and Arbury 1405–1712; Ince-in-Makerfield 1607–1854; Liverpool 1566–1633; Manchester 1760–76; Newton-in-Makerfield 1373–1753; Pemberton 1652; Pendle 1676; Poulton-with-Fearnhead 1515–1660; Samlesbury 1607; Southworth-with-Croft 1519–1748; Standish 1780–93; Tarbock 1681; Up Holland 1546–1890; Warrington 1325; Wharton 1638; Westhoughton 1807; Westleigh 1661–84; Wigan 1583–1889; Winwick-with-Hulme 1631; Woolston-with-Martinscroft 1627

Other counties: Cornwall, Broadoak 1651, Liskeard 1691–92; Devon, Plymouth 1624, Plympton 1630; Durham, Murton 1622; Lincolnshire, Weston 1698–1701; Westmorland, Thornthwaite 1657; Yorkshire, Castleford 1657, Leake rectory 1662, Tickhill 1611

Family Papers: Settlements 1582–1804; wills 1568–1874; bonds 1546–1843; papers on administration of estate of John Latham of Wigan, founder 1741–1802

Estate Papers: Lease register 1840–1908; agreements for letting farms, houses, and mines 1835–82; Holt Leigh estate leases 1721–1878

Surveys: Abram, Hindley and Newton 1726, 1748; Worsley Mesnes 1851–54

Correspondence: Various 1601–1886. but principally family affairs 1849–68

Legal Papers: Gerard *v.* Stoughton (Wigan) 1657–75; Gerard *v.* Wainwright (Ince) 1663–77; Gerard *v.* Ashton (annuity) 1681–82; Gerard *v.* Robinson (Southworth) 1699; Gerard *v.* Baldwin (Wigan) 1733; various 1609–1781

Business Papers: Coal: Cross and Tetley 1886–1933; Crompton and Shawcross 1897–1905; Ince Hall Coal and Canal Company 1836–1905; Morley Colliery Company 1855–85; Pearson and Knowles 1895–98

Ashton to Platt Bridge Turnpike Trust: miscellaneous papers 1793–1803, 1813–56

Accounts and rentals: Mining accounts and rentals 1846–1942; miscellaneous accounts 1706–1926; servants' wages 1812–49. Rentals 1786–92, 1795–1816, 1818–35, 1839–55, 1877–90; pew rents 1859–67. Lord Hawarden's estates in Somerset 1797–98

Weld (Shireburne) of Stonyhurst (DDSt)

Robert of Shireburne in 1245 received the manor of Hambleton from his uncle and it remained with his descendants until 1867. Their Aighton estate, in which Stonyhurst lay, came by marriage in the early fourteenth century. Sir Nicholas, the last Shireburne, died in 1718, the estate passing to his daughter Mary, duchess of Norfolk. From here it descended to the issue of her aunt Elizabeth who had married William Weld of Lulworth in Dorset. It was through the marriage of Sir Nicholas with Catherine Charlton that Northumberland properties came into the family, her mother being a Widdrington heiress. From earlier marriages came Yorkshire and Nottinghamshire estates. See also DP 440, p. 342.

Title Deeds (including leases): Aighton, Bailey and Chaigley c.1230–1774; Aldingham 1583; Billington 1386–1581; Bleasdale 1576; Briercliffe-with-Extwistle 1685–1741; Burnley 1681–1738; Carleton c.1210–1772; Chipping 1543–1771; Chorley 1301–1702; Clayton-le-Dale c.1260; Clitheroe c.1260–1747; Cockerham rectory 1602; Dalton (Carnforth) c.1250; Darwen 1337; Dutton c.1250–1684; Ellel 1549–1812; Fishwick 1775; Formby 1351; Goosnargh 1567–1761; Greenhalgh 1291–1343; Habergham Eaves 1700–87; Hambleton 1229–1714; Henthorn c.1260; Howick 1716; Kirkham 1444; Lancaster 1357–1749; Leagram 1670–1735; Longton 1281–1761; Marton c.1190; Much Hoole 1317–1691; Newsham 1677–1759; Norbreck c.1194; Oswaldtwistle 1538; Plumpton 1330–1682; Poulton-le-Fylde 1330–1811; Preese c.1250; Ribchester c.1230–1738; Simonstone c.1260–1672; Sowerby 1249–1371; Thornley 1579; Warton (Kirkham) c.1200; Whittle-le-Woods 1641; Whittingham c.1210–1761; Wiswell c.1260–1706; Woodplumpton c.1260–1741; Worsthorne c.1250–1738; Wyresdale 1605–1759

Other counties: Durham, Gateshead 1707; Middlesex, Westminster 1682–1734; Northumberland, Alwinton, Cottenshope, Elsdon and Harbottle 1636–1706; Nottinghamshire, Auckley c.1200–1648, Finningley c.1260–1648, Misson 1540–1646; Sussex, Lewes 1574; Yorkshire, Bowland 1560–1697, Doncaster c.1260–1398, Grindleton 1665–1757, Guiseley 1635–92, Malham 1606, Mitton c.1300–1600, Newton (Slaidburn) c.1210–1698, Rishworth and Norland 1335–1578, Stainton 1705, Waddington 1680, Wigglesworth *c*.1150–1719

Family Papers: Settlements *c*.1350–1777; wills 1513–1754

Disposition of wife's jewellery by Sir Richard Shireburne 1591; account of Sir Nicholas Shireburne's debts 1724; Stonyhurst inventories 1594, 1705, 1754; catalogue of books *c*.1750; list of plate and linen 1731; duchess of Norfolk's executors' papers 1755–63; Peregrine Widdrington's executors' papers 1746–47; inventory of James Bradley of Bailey 1699; inquisitions *post mortem* John of Bayley 1389, Hugh Shireburne 1528, Richard Ashe of Cloughbank 1603, Richard Reade of Aighton 1643; general pardon to John of Baylegh 1334; valors of Sir Richard Shireburne 1594, Richard Shireburne 1630; genealogical papers and pedigrees 16th to 18th centuries

Appointments: Sir Richard Shireburne, keeper of Radom park 1558, butler of Lancashire 1559, lieutenant and captain of Isle of Man 1578. Nicholas Shireburne, baronet 1686. Sir Edward Charleton, captain of arquebusiers 1642, captain of foot 1662, captain of Admiral's regiment 1666, major and captain of Fitzgerald's regiment 1672. Sir Henry Widdrington, deputy vice-admiral of Cumberland, Westmorland, and Northumberland 1611. Roger Widdrington, scoutmaster-general 1639; various military orders to Sir Edward Charleton 1667–77

Estate Papers (leases are included with title-deeds): Agreement for building duchess of Norfolk's house in Arlington street, Westminster 1734; Stonyhurst park-books 1741, 1761; sale of Chorley oaks 1734; registers of Sir Nicholas Shireburne's estates in Lancashire, Northumberland and Yorkshire 1717

Correspondence: Concerning the Shireburne coat-of-arms 1708–13; the duke of Norfolk's imprisonment in the Tower 1722; miscellaneous 17th–18th c.

Legal Papers: Duchy order against Cuthbert Musgrave for deer-stealing in Bowland 1560; Shireburne *v*. Clark (Slaidburn) 1680; settlement of Lawrence Starky of Lancaster 1541, 1545, 1554; Weld *v*. Mackay (Thornton marsh) 1767; Cottam *v*. Shireburn (Chipping) 1683; Shireburne *v*. Hammond (Wiswell common) 1618

Ecclesiastical Papers: Presentation of William Jones to Llanfair Kilgedyn, Monmouth 1622; foundation of Mitton chantry 1546; Mitton rectory compositions, etc., 1338–1600; dispensations for marriages: Ralph Cliderowe and Joan Shireburne 1534, John Talbot and Ann Shireburne 1514; agreement with Lancaster priory for chapel at Carleton *c*.1240; masses at Salley abbey for Robert of Cliderowe, rector of Wigan 1335; licence in mortmain for lands in Ribchester and Dutton to Bailey chapel 1284; papal blessing on duke and duchess of Norfolk 1715

Plans: Wiswell c.1550; Over Hacking, Threlfalls, and Merricks in Aighton c.1780; Swinburne House and Felton House, Northumberland 18th century

Rentals and Accounts: General estate rentals and stewards' accounts 1567, 1571, 1690–92, 1695–1700, 1703, 1706, 1709–12, 1732, 1738, 1741, 1746, 1755–59, 1761–74, 1776–94, 1812–25, 1827–30, 1832, 1837

Aighton and Bailey 1373; Aighton, Bailey, and Chaigley, Dinckley, Dutton, Ribchester, and Thornley 1593; Goosnargh 1656–64, 1685

Mitton tithe-accounts 1668, 1670–72, 1711–28; accounts for wedding of Mary Shireburn to Duke of Norfolk 1709; Stonyhurst day-work accounts 1695–99; Stonyhurst wool-book 1699–1700; bills and vouchers 1776–1813

Charity Papers: Hurst Green almshouses: foundation deed 1702; account 1713

Miscellaneous: Agreement for settling disputes over Longton marsh enclosure 1717; petitions to duchess of Norfolk for workhouse in Aighton and bells at Whalley c.1730; resolutions for defence of country 1794; lease of Stonyhurst 1797; agreement for Thomas Weld to place students in Stonyhurst 1797

(DDX/388) A (typescript) history of the family of Sherborn, vol. 2 by C. D. Sherborn, 1917. A (typescript) history of the family of Sherborn of Yorkshire by C. D. and J. C. Sherborn, 1930

Whittaker of Simonstone (DDWh)

Title Deeds: Abram and Tyldesley 1710–14, Accrington 1790, Blackburn 1777, 1804, Burnley 1748, Clayton-le-Moors 1716, Clitheroe 1721, Habergham Eaves, Hapton, Foulridge and Colne 1672, Huncoat 1673–1815, Marsden 1642, 1660, Mellor 1799, Padiham 1621–70, Simonstone c.1270–1730, Pendleton 1699

Other counties: Yorkshire: Edisford 1635–99, Great Mitton 1663, Easington 1672, Malham 1675, 1683, Barnoldswick 1675, 1683,

Estate Papers: Leases 1317–1874, Padiham highways c.1600, partition of Simonstone commons 1629–1751, inventory of Simonstone hall 1807

Family Papers: Settlements, wills, etc., 1320–1901 (including Horrocks of Preston)

Correspondence: Family and estate miscellanea 1681–1886 (including Horrocks of Preston)

Legal Papers: Mainly cases referring to family or estate 1616–1788. Papers in case *re* lands of the Calders of Caithness 1758–1822

Ecclesiastical Papers: Agreement between Whalley abbey and parishioners of Burnley, Colne, Altham, Church, Haslingden, Simonstone, Padiham, Twiston, Hapton, Read, Downham, Pendleton and Chatburn on payment of tithes 1334; seat in Padiham chapel 1641, 1672, 1703–35; appointment of church-wardens for Padiham, Simonstone and Hapton 1661; repair of Whalley church 1705; Simonstone tithes 1724–26, 1851; Padiham church leys 1639, 1703, 1710

Official Papers: Allotments on Padiham common 1619, 1641; ley for building New Bridge in Pendle 1665; Padiham assessments 1663, 1689, 1698, 1702; repair of Burnley highways 1704; Padiham land tax 1733

Accounts: Executors of Henry Whitaker of Brownmoor 1730–44, executors of William Holt of Mitton 1738–49; costs of house repair 1846–49

Rentals: Burnley, Habergham Eaves, Huncoat and Simonstone 1794–95. Burnley and Simonstone 1796–99

Miscellanea: Box containing chain, with paper stating that it was on a spur of Henry VI found at Waddington 1465. Preston election addresses of Samuel Horrocks and Edmund Hornby 1818. Election verse *c*.1820

Bootle-Wilbraham of Lathom (DDLm)

The Lathom estate, after having been in possession of the Stanleys for about 350 years, was sold about 1720 by the heiress of the ninth earl of Derby, the purchaser re-selling in 1724 to Thomas Bootle of Melling. In 1758, his niece Mary, who had married Richard Wilbraham of Rode Hall, Cheshire, succeeded. Their son Edward was created Baron Skelmersdale in 1828, his son becoming earl of Lathom in 1880. The earldom became extinct in 1930 but the barony continues. Lathom House was demolished in 1929 and it is said that the contents of the muniment room were fed into the furnaces at Blaguegate colliery.

The documents indicated below were in the custody of the estate solicitors in London and are apparently all that have survived of what was a fine collection.

Title Deeds (including leases): Clayton-le-Woods: Abbots 1696–1746, Calderbanks 1683–1759, Clayton Fields 1608–1777, Cuerdens 1722–50, Harrisons 1667–1765, Lancaster House

1739–50, Laviers 1692–1740, Leylands 1691–1768, Manor House 1655–1739, Southworths 1664–1738, Starkie House 1706–27, Wrights 1609–1771; Dalton: leases 1727–1804. Lathom: Ayscoughs 1671–1757, Birchenholts 1783–1859, Blythe Hall 1489–1827, Cobbs Brow 1745–77, Dumbells 1710–41, Duttons 1603–1854, Hall Lane Farm 1640–1728, Keys 1698–1757, Lawrensons 1691–1741, Leary Hill 1721–80, Lees 1650–1786, Manor 1602–1732, Rogers 1610–1873, Taylors 1695–1779, Wainlow 1676–1720, Wainwrights 1724–60, various properties 1592–1894, leases 1668–1881; Leyland: Coopers 1613–1722, Higher Croft 1628–1754; Melling: Halsalls 1657–99, Strange Ashtons 1705–1860, various properties 1672–1847; Skelmersdale Bartons 1696–1749, Blaguegate 1744–1859, Lindleys 1718–43, Skelmersdale Hall 1715–68, various properties 1714–1882; Up Holland: Penningtons 1636–1768, school 1616–1805; Westhoughton: leases 1753–1865

Family Papers: Settlements 1699–1838; wills 1565–1879; shares in Douglas Navigation 1720

Estate Papers: Lathom valuations 1657–1725; Lathom and Skelmersdale enclosure 1779–81; stopping of footway through Lathom park 1805

Ecclesiastical Papers: Pew in Ormskirk church 1696–1741; pew in Skelmersdale chapel 1852; Clayton-le-Woods tithes 1601–1741; Lathom and Skelmersdale tithes 1709–76

Miscellaneous: Rules of Up Holland school 1711

Willis of Halsnead (DDWi)

The estate of Halsnead in Whiston passed through several families until 1684, when it was bought by Thomas Willis, a Liverpool merchant. It remained with his descendants, though twice the death of the male heir has taken it to female lines—Swettenhams and Earles—but on each occasion they changed their name to Willis.

Title Deeds: Cronton: Shaw and Lower Shaw 1661–1828, Deanes House 1597–1639, Kiln Hey 1809–26, various 1689–1809; Duxbury: Brettarghs 1654–90; Eccleston: Dentons 1665–1792; Knowsley 1781–1854; Liverpool 1708–1852; Parbold 1611; Prescot pew 1730–87; Rainhill: Penningtons 1798–1860, Garnetts 1713–1860, Fishpond estate 1713–1875, Deanes House 1597–1639; Tarbock 1678–1880; Up Holland 1602; Whiston: Halsnead 1333–1735, New Hey colliery 1659, Princes colliery 1785–1801, Woodfalls 1721–1824, Cumberlane charity school 1783–1900, Methodist chapel 1846–79, Townsends 1741–1850, Royal Oak 1866–85, various 1405–1900; Wigan 1310–1676

Cheshire: Daniell properties in Appleton, Acton, Chester, Lache, Lymm, Tabley, Tarporley and Thelwall 1349–1655

Family Papers: Settlements 1630–1902, Bradshaigh estates 1682–84; bonds 1455–1658; mortgages 1705–1904

Appointments: William Daniell, captain 1650, colonel 1660; Daniel Willis, sheriff 1745. General pardon, William Forth of Wigan 1626. Wills 17th to 19th c.

Estate Papers: Leases: Anglezarke 1672–73, Altcar 1539, Coppull 1672, Cronton 1642–59, Duxbury 1684, Eccles 1629–1758, Heath Charnock 1656–1817, Huyton 1837, Liverpool 1698–1765, Parbold 1599, Tarbock 1607–1717, Whiston 1607–1815, Wigan 1550–1666; Chester 1650

Legal Papers: Whiston coal-mines 1802; Prescot tithes 1820

Plans: Gildarts in Whiston 1770; coalmines in Huyton, Whiston and Knowsley 1800; Eccles 1797; Tarbock land to be enclosed 1814; Mullanstown, co. Louth 1850

Rental: Charnocks land in Penwortham c.1610

The Earl of Wilton (DDEg)

Manorial: Kenyon court rolls 1550–1676

Title Deeds: Ainsworth, Blackley, Crumpsall, Denton, Great and Little Heaton, Kenyon, Little Bolton, Lowton, Pilsworth, Unsworth; Farthinghoe, Northants., Wrinehill and Betley, Staffs., and Batley, Yorks. c.1200–1850

Plans: Denton 1657, 1711

Correspondence: Letter books 1871–1920, repair letters 1919–49

Rentals and Accounts: Rentals 1743–1958, rental ledgers 1825–1911, cash books 1899–1950, ledgers 1901–15, statements of account 1891–1914

Miscellanea: Militia papers 1770–90, agents' diaries 1912–40

Winckley of Preston (DDW)

Edward Winckley, descended from a cadet branch of the Winckleys of Winckley, settled in Preston about 1600, several of his descendants being prominent attornies. The line died out with the death of Thomas Winckley and the properties, principally in Brockholes, Catterall and Preston, passed to his daughter Frances who married Sir John Shelley, bart., in 1807.

Title Deeds: Balderstone 1677–1781; Brockholes 1348–1830, Catterall 1635–1831; Cuerden 1621–1705; Fishwick 1543–1640; Fulwood 1609–96; Garstang 1423–1697; Goosnaigh 1627; Great Harwood 1576–77; Hothersall 1576–1677; Kirkland

1544–1698; Little Mitton 1653–75; Penwortham 1391–1691; Poulton-le-Fylde 1670; Preston 1525–1867; Ribbleton 1682–1744; Samlesbury 1638–39; Sowerby 1679; Walton-le-Dale 1680–1791

Family Papers: Settlements 1561–1785; wills 1608–1817; bonds 1553–1793; patent of denization for Paul Moreau 1634

Ecclesiastical Papers: Grants of seats in Preston church 1607, 1663, 1671, 1709; grant of Banastre's chantry at Rufford 1610

Rentals: General estate 1733–68, 1781–90, 1807–32

Accounts: Ledger 1778–79; household expenses 1789

Miscellaneous: Inventories: Edmund Lemon of Preston 1609, goods at Little Mitton 1665, Bailey's hotel at Blackpool 1791. Order for repair of Bamber bridge 1662; order for finding footsoldier 1669; order *re* Brockholes weir 1679; petition *re* Brockholes weir 1696; papers concerning Preston to Blackburn new road 1822–24

Wright of Heysham and Gressingham (DDWr)
Deeds and papers 17th to 19th c.

SMALLER DEPOSITS

Fylde Historical Society (DDX/1). Much Hoole deeds 1760–61; bill-of-sale of ship *Ann* of Preston 1817; plans of Kidsnape estate, Goosnargh 18th century

E. B. Porter, Esq. (DDX/2). Deeds: Greenhalgh-with-Thistleton 1623–1722, Newton-with-Scales 1632–1709, Medlar-with-Wesham 1622–1738, Urswick 1610, Goosnargh 1673, 1680, Carleton 1700

R. Sharpe France, Esq. (DDX/3). Deeds: Accrington 1657, Arkholme-with-Cawood 1663–1832, Ashton-under-Lyne 1671, Blackpool 1819, Carleton 1588, Catterall 1811, Goosnargh 1689, Gorton 1611–81, Greenhalgh-with-Thistleton 1598–1623, Layton-with-Warbreck 1635, 1819, Manchester 1636, Pemberton 1686, Pilling 1820, Out Rawcliffe 1707. Samlesbury 1685, Sutton c.1190, Walton-le-Dale 1815, Widnes 1746, Whittington 1722. Opinion in dispute between parish of Bury and chapelries of Tottington over rate 1724; bond for maintenance of Margaret Dilworth of Elswick 1569; receipt for Kirkham town measures 1682; letter referring to cattle plague 1747; Bridgewater canal Acts 1760, 1762; bill of divorcement, Robert Shireburn and Grace Clitheroe, Mitton, 1512; Accrington Sunday school rules c.1845; newspaper-cuttings concerning Fleetwood floods

1927; news-film of visit of George V to Blackpool 1913. Ministers' accounts of monasteries of Alnwick, Hexham and Tynemouth, Northumberland; Coverham, Egglestone, Ellerton, Fountains, Marrick, Nunmonkton and Richmond, co. York; Durham and Neasham, co. Durham, 1538–47, Salford Hundred subsidy rolls 1663, 1664. Memoranda book of Robert Fisher of Marton 1748–1806. Particulars of sale of Kirkland hall and contents 1969. Statute roll 1235–97. Blackpool Children's Pantomime programmes 1915–63. Watercolour of cottages at Roby by Wm. Herdman 1849. Provisional catalogue of the Hackensall hoard of Roman coins 1926

Miss A. Law (DDX/6). Deeds, etc., relating to the Hartleys of White Lee in Higham and allied families 1584–1863

A. Wade, Esq. (DDX/9) Preston lease 1568

Mrs. N. L. Fielden (DDX/12). Deeds: Catterall, Claughton and Grimsargh 1459–1784

A. C. M. Lillie, Esq. (DDX/13) Croston and Mawdesley lease 1471

Procter and Birkbeck (DDX/14). Royal lease of moiety of manor of Nether Wyersdale 1569

Woosnam & Co. (DDX/15). Deeds: Great Eccleston 1691, Little Eccleston-with-Larbreck 1600–1718, Out Rawcliffe 1698–1770, Ulnes Walton 1712–85

Mrs. Makinson (DDX/16). Anderton Hall deeds 1818–65

Samuel Stockton, Esq. (DDX/17). Astley deeds 1634–1765

C. Cartmell, Esq. (DDX/18). Deeds: Layton-with-Warbreck 1596–1740, Wigan pew 1734

Mrs. E. A. Self Weeks (DDX/19). Deeds: Billington c.1280, Blackburn 1788, Briercliffe 1573, 1589, Burnley 1778–90, Chatburn 1596, Chipping 1812, Clitheroe 1601–1838, Colne 1598, 1707, Downham 1630, Foulridge 1562, Goldshaw Booth 1558–1650, Goosnargh 1713–39, Habergham Eaves 1668, Halton 1379, Hapton 1674, 1743, Higher and Lower Booths 1633–1781, Marsden 1788 Newchurch-in-Rossendale 1613, 1745, Old Laund Booth 1741, Oswaldtwistle 1512, 1647, Padiham 1666, Trawden 1697, Walton-le-Dale 1785

Miscellaneous: commission-in-bankruptcy, Hannah Aspinall of Blackburn, brazier and victualler 1820; rate-precepts for repair of Preston House of Correction 1705 and Barton Bridge 1706; proclamation concerning papists 1722; bounds of Goldshaw Booth and Pendleton 1516; inventory of Peter Ormerod of Goodshaw 1689; a horoscope 17th century; agreement for highway between Chew mill and Whalley bridge 1691; plan of Lower

Greystoneley in Bowland *c.*1760; inventory of John Dugdale of Clitheroe 1664; Darwen land-tax assessment 1778; grant of wardship of sisters of Lord Dacre of Gilsland 1569; decree concerning copyholders of manor of Slaidburn 1619; composition for building of Waddington chapel 1438

Mrs. G. Wilkinson (DDX/20). Deeds: Clitheroe 1681, Chatburn watermill 1690

E. Smallpage, Esq. (DDX/21). Letters to Robert Dall, Methodist minister 1779–1827, Mrs. Dall 1791–1805, John Wesley Dall 1805–62, Mrs. John Wesley Dall 1837–64, on religious and family matters, also James and Margaret Dall to Joseph Smallpage, Burnley 1880–82. Smallpage letters and papers 1779–1890 with references to religious matters, cotton trade, Caledonian canal, Australia, Canada, South Africa, Jamaica

Essex Record Office (DDX/23). Deeds: Bilsborrow, Claughton, Sowerby and Woodplumpton 1626, Leece 1693, Hundersfield 1565, Orrell in Sefton 1815, Gorton 1763, Popplewell charities in Blackrod, Bolton, and Hartshead co. York 1820–33

Certificate of loss by fire by John Idsforth of Clitheroe 1647; Westby estate act 1731; particulars of manor of Halton 1640, 1653; plans of Longworth estate in Euxton, Eccleston, Ulnes Walton and Skelmersdale (microfilm) 1787; case concerning Lord Dacre's title to the manor of Halton 1660; case *re* manor of Halton 1660

J. C. Kay, Esq. (DDX/24). Plans of Pilling wind and watermills *c.*1808

Miss A. Tattersall (DDX/26). John Tattersall's treatise on astrology 1826

Mrs. Trafford (DDX/27). Thornton (Sefton) leases 1706, 1713

A. Langshaw, Esq. (DDX/28). Historical and antiquarian collections towards a history of Clitheroe.
Manorial: Wiswell court verdicts 1732–35, call-book 1733; Dutton call-book 1817–27; Ribchester call-book 1817–22. Deeds: Clitheroe 1676–1859, Chatburn 1784–92, Oswaldtwistle 1743, Padiham 1834
Agreement concerning Read moor 1600; account-book of Thomas Preston of Little Mearley; wages-book of Bridgewater print-works 1830–1847; diary of John O'Neill, cotton-weaver, 1860–64* (see also DDX/636 p. 314)

---

* Printed by Historic Society of Lancashire and Cheshire. Vol. 105

Manchester Collieries Ltd. (DDX/29). Deeds: Bradshaw and Quarlton 1834, Chadderton 1885, Chorlton-upon-Medlock 1854, Clifton 1814–84, Eccleston 1823, Farnworth 1835, Kearsley 1792–1873, Great Lever, Little Lever and Darcy Lever 1807–75, Manchester 1885, Pendlebury, Pendleton and Prestwich 1823–85, Pilkington 1840, Radcliffe 1847–89, Rochdale 1845–75, Worsley 1860–75

Miss E. Hodgson (DDX/30). Deeds: Osbaldeston 1508, 1715

E. Morland, Esq. (DDX/31). Apprenticeship indenture, Samuel Crosfield to Manchester woollen-cloth finisher 1813

Yorkshire Archaeological Society (DDX/32). Deeds: Gressingham 1761, Silverdale 1879, Tatham 1578–1788, Bolton 1618–1700, Blacko 1614. Licence of Rev. John Lloyd to St. Paul's, Liverpool 1889; faculty for alterations to St. Paul's, Liverpool, 1889

Miss Cookson and Mrs. Stuart (DDX/33). Deeds: Freckleton 1590–1788, Hardhorn-with-Newton and Newton-with-Scales 1710–1823, Kirkham 1762, Warton 1747–61, Treales, Wharles and Roseacre 1724–1822

Wills: 1727–1835; licences and ordinations of James Fox of Kirkham as schoolmaster 1786, deacon 1791, priest 1792; Ribby-with-Wrea surveys 1790, 1818; inventories of James Hall of Freckleton 1660, Richard Hunt of North Meols 1816, John Hunt of Ribby 1835; accounts of John Hunt for Wrea Green school 1825–34

Edward Moss, Esq. (DDX/34). Rufford manor call-books 1869–74, 1876–87

W. N. Cookson, Esq. (DDX/35). Deeds: Freckleton 1650–1750

Edward Ashton, Esq. (DDX/36). Accounts of executors of William Goulter of Lytham 1754–62, Great Marton deed 1836

J. T. Cardwell, Esq. (DDX/38). Stalmine deed 1727, Stalmine and Preesall rental 1846–48

J. Miller, Esq. (DDX/40). Goosnargh highway division 1771; Woodplumpton pew deed 1797; Woodplumpton manor court-books 1817–18

Rev. J. A. Nairn (DDX/45). Deed: Butterworth 1662

M. Neville, Esq (DDX/46). Deeds: Penwortham 1704–18, Walton-le-Dale 1738, 1766

Mrs. Tonge (DDX/47). A *pica* or almanac 1462

H. E. Hey, Esq. (DDX/48). Survey and plans of Leyland churchyard 1932

Hankinson Crook, Esq. (DDX/49). Deeds: Clifton-with-Salwick 1723, Coppull 1738, Freckleton 1689, Lea, Ashton, Ingol and Cottam 1789–1813, Newton-with Scales 1692–1823

Highway statute work, Clifton-with-Salwick 1798; specifications for work at Scales Hall 1835; agreement concerning cart-roads in Newton-with-Scales 1850; bills of Dr. Hankinson of Warrington 1777–1810; partnership: John Hankinson and James Kendrick of Warrington, surgeon-apothecaries 1794

Mrs. A. Woods (DDX/51). Accounts for rebuilding Walton bridge 1779–82

S. Entwistle, Esq. (DDX/52). Deeds: Warton 1666–1673

G. E. Clark, Esq. (DDX/53). Deed of consecration of additional churchyard, Middleton 1787

Capt. F. B. Mitchell (DDX/54). Deeds: Accrington 1762, Chatburn 1765, Clitheroe 1555, Westleigh and Pennington 1632–66, Mearley 1639; Yorkshire, Grindleton 1607–1804, Rathmell 1550, 1637, Gisburn and Paythorn 1801

Commission in bankrupty, Samuel Martin of Gisburn, chapman 1802; lists of sheep and cattle in Crosedale, Slaidburn 1576–82; depositions concerning bounds of Crosedale pasture 1575 and concerning pasturage there 1550; papers in Aspinall v. Mitchell (pollution of Ribble) 1879–86; papers concerning paper-trade 1872–82; minutes on Clitheroe election 1780

T. Billington, Esq. (DDX/55). Historical and antiquarian collections towards a history of Westhoughton

D. Wilkinson, Esq. (DDX/57). Deeds: Fernyhalgh in Broughton 1675–1851

S. Corrs, Esq. (DDX/58). Lathom deeds 1725–1809, particulars of sale of Moor Hall, Aughton 1840

Capt. J. F. Berkeley-Weld (DDX/59). Survey and plans of Shireburne of Stonyhurst estate 1774

Dr. R. G. B. Marsh (DDX/62). Commission of lieutenancy to John Whitehead of Bolton 1812

H. E. Blundell, Esq. (DDX/63). Depositions re Moor hall, Aughton 1429

J. H. Tyrrell, Esq. (DDX/65). Apprenticeship indenture, John Garner to Barton-upon-Irwell hatter 1782

J. L. Gradwell, Esq. (DDX/66). Particulars of sale of Moston estates 1797

H. Bright, Esq. (DDX/68). Deeds: Silverdale 1595–1803, Rochdale 1718–1809

T. Rowntree, Esq. (DDX/72). Deeds: Paythorne, co. York 1710–1861

J. Morris, Esq. (DDX/73). Fees for knighting of Sir Edward Wrightington 1640

Prof. R. J. A. Berry (DDX/76). Handbills of schools at Blackburn 1800, 1805, 1809, Bacup 1800, Manchester 1802, Musbury 1818

S. Graveson, Esq. (DDX/79). Deed *re* Ashton-under-Lyne and Warrington manors 1671

W. Banks & Co. (DDX/80). Court-book of manor of Salesbury 1641–61

Miss D. Catlow (DDX/81). Deed: Goosnargh 1620

F. W. Steer, Esq. (DDX/82). Extent of Lancashire lands of duke of Suffolk 1607

W. T. Garner, Esq. (DDX/85). Patent to Joseph Eccles of Preston for improvement in looms 1877

W. Mayer, Esq. (DDX/86). Chorley coalmine deed 1846. Plan of "Mr. Harding's", Preston 1871. Particulars of sale and plans of properties in the Chorley area 1843–1919

Miss I. Aspinall (DDX/87). Various papers, handbills, etc., of Lancashire and Yorkshire Railway 1848–1909, Liverpool and Bury Railway 1846, Manchester and Leeds Railway 1830–47, Preston and Wyre Railway 1842–46, various railways 1827–1934

R. E. Threlfall, Esq. (DDX/88). Deeds: Newsham 1795, Wharles 1772, Woodplumpton 1602–1863. Agreement for erecting obelisk in Preston market-place 1782

G. Eglin, Esq. (DDX/89). Handbills: Preston concert 1762, Preston theatre 1802.

I. Jackson & Son (DDX/91). Deeds: Lancaster 1754–1874.

J. E. Hartley, Esq. (DDX/93). Deeds: Roughlee 1690–1850

F. Harris, Esq. (DDX/95). Licences and correspondence of Rev. Richard Moore, vicar of Lund, 1815–43

Miss Rothwell (DDX/97). Letters from Sydney, Australia 1880

Middlesex Record Office (DDX/99). Chart of Mersey and Dee 1764; plans of Liverpool 1765, 1768, 1769, 1803; plan of Aigburth Hall estate 1772

Mrs. D. Abbatt (DDX/100). Manor court-books: Quernmore 1740–42, Wyresdale 1737, 1740, 1742. Narrative of Isaac Sharples of Prescot and Hitchin, a Quaker, *c*.1782; licence for divine service at new church in Walton-on-the-Hill 1847

D. A. Parkyn, Esq. (DDX/101). Correspondence of Daniel Adamson, first chairman of Manchester Ship Canal Company 1882–87; various Ship Canal papers 1882–1936

T. A. Clarke, Esq. (DDX/105). Letters to Manchester: describing holiday at Llandudno 1859, and Manchester Volunteers in London 1860

D. Beardsworth, Esq. (DDX/107). Deeds: Longton 1727–1854; William Beardsworth's arithmetic exercise book 1812

J. Coulthurst, Esq. (DDX/108). Deeds: Walton-le-Dale 1635–1846. Plan of Kenyon's estate, Walton-le-Dale 1817

T. Williams, Esq. (DDX/109). Manor court rolls: Bootle 1669–1774, Great Crosby 1458–1885, Little Crosby 1557–1719 (copies). Downholland deeds 1846–1920

Whitefield U.D.C. (DDX/111). Deeds: Philips Park 1654–1840

H. Talbot, Esq. (DDX/112). Deeds: Claife 1766–1849, Great Eccleston 1601, Ingleton, co. York 1616–1803, Preston Patrick, Westmorland 1615–1752, Burton-in-Kendal, Westmorland, presentments 1690–1721; papers on Esthwaite fishery 1558–1850; plans of estates in Sawrey c.1828; genealogical memoranda of Redmaynes of Ingleton 1754–1852 and Towers of Sawrey 1759–1836; inventory of Rev. John Wright of Preston Patrick 1796

J. H. Spencer, Esq. (DDX/113). Address to the king 1682; depositions concerning Preston election 1768; letters and papers of Henry Hunt 1818–32; letter from General Burgoyne refusing to admit Mr. Prideaux to his regiment 1761; letter from William Cobbett on Poor Law 1835

J. C. Dickinson, Esq. (DDX/114). Book of rates and taxations for Lancashire 1675–78

R. J. W. Parke, Esq. (DDX/115). Deeds: Halton 1595–1728, Leck 1540–1739, Over Burrow 1682, Tunstall 1616, 1627; Kirkby Lonsdale, Westmorland 1650–1724; Hathern, co. Leicester 1796 Admittance of John Robinson as burgess of Lancaster 1700; inventory of Francis Robinson of Staunton, co. Worcester 1696; Thomas Tiffin's drawing-book 1762; farming memoranda 1785–1838; agreement for armed brigantine, the *Jenny*, of Dartmouth 1799

K. H. Docton, Esq. (DDX/116). Almanacs made at Yealand school c.1811; letter from New York describing Quakers in U.S.A. 1839. Plan shewing evolution of Glasson Dock. Deeds: Cartmel Fell and Ulverston 1668, Slaidburn 1617–1726, Spotland 1732

C. Fairclough, Esq. (DDX/117). Aughton deed 1678

Staffordshire Record Office (DDX/119). Proceedings in witchcraft at Burscough priory 1454

E. Wilkinson, Esq. (DDX/120). Deeds: Walton-le-Dale 1813, 1818

Exeter City Library (DDX/121). Deeds: Horwich 1796–1809, Ince Blundell 1804, Liverpool 1845, Rivington 1621–1785, Rumworth, Lostock, Anderton, and Horwich 1589–1884

Mrs. A. Stone (DDX/122). Deeds: Westhoughton 1758, 1803

Harris Museum, Preston (DDX/123). Deeds: Ribby-with-Wrea 1713, 1775, Warton 1760. Book of rates for Lancashire 1718. Indentures of returns of Preston M.P.s 1658–1745

Mrs. A. Tackley (DDX/124). Muster roll of Royal Lancashire Volunteers 1795

Manchester Geological Society (DDX/127). Reports to House of Commons on mines 1835–1914; papers concerning mining lawsuits 1870–1910; colliery memoranda books 1795–1903

Sir Harold Parkinson (DDX/128). Deeds: Cockerham 1698, Ellel 1757, Poulton-le-Sands 1783, 1796; letter to vicar of Claughton concerning brief for Scarborough church 1661; conditions for letting Lancaster tolls 1833

H. Bond, Esq. (DDX/131). Particulars of sale and plans of Garstang Estate 1919, Wyresdale Estate 1921, Winmarleigh Estate 1945

Liverpool City Libraries (DDX/137). Deeds: Ardwick 1808–16

R. Downs, Esq. (DDX/138). Natural history notebooks from Leagram Hall 1857–86

F. I. Harris, Esq. (DDX/139). Deeds: Bottom mill 1755–1812

R. Walmsley, Esq. (DDX/140).Love-letters of Thomas Hare of Bolton 1749–50; letters concerning the trial and transportation of Thomas Holden of Bolton 1812–16; letters from U.S.A. 1846, 1851; papers of J. W. and T. Balmforth of Clayton, ironmasters 1852–55; agreement for altering Salvation Army barracks, Wigan 1889

Preston W.E.A. (DDX/141). North Meols lease 1826. Papers *re* settlement of Alice Wareing in Inskip 1842–43

J. R. Whitfield, Esq. (DDX/144). Deeds: Ashton-under-Lyne 1660–1915

F. J. Sobee, Esq. (DDX/145). Cartmel Fell deed 1679

F. Lovat, Esq. (DDX/146). Deed: Preston 1599

T. Pape, Esq. (DDX/147). Particulars of estate of the Hon. Francis Charteris of Hornby 1786

N. S. P. Williams (DDX/154). Sale of oak-trees, Elston 1682; apprenticeship indenture, Henry Sharp to Blackburn surgeon 1831

Chester Record Office (DDX/155). Newton-in-Makerfield deed 1615

G. Sherring, Esq. (DDX/156). Deeds: Blackburn 1729–1876, Clitheroe 1821–26, Plans: Whalley 1859, 1887, Blackburn 1876, 1878, Great Harwood 1889–1904

J. Wallwork, Esq. (DDX/159). Deed: Worsley 1599

Lt.-Col. L. C. King-Wilkinson (DDX/160). Bracewell, co. York: plans 1717, 1796, surveys 1639–1750

A. Whitehead, Esq. (DDX/161). Cockersand abbey deeds: Forton c.1150–1504

Gloucestershire Record Office (DDX/162). Deeds: Heath Charnock 1616–1849, Adlington 1793, Atherton 1842

S. Marling, Esq. (DDX/163). Deeds: Whittingham 1565–1873, Preston c.1800–34

Miss Shaw (DDX/164). Rental and account-book of John Whitham of Preston 1798–1803

H. Andrews, Esq. (DDX/166). Letter *re* appointment of apothecary to Bolton Infirmary 1818

J. Brocklehurst, Esq. (DDX/167). Journal of R. Battersby, Bedford 1821–31

Judge Walmsley (DDX/168). Plaint book of Blackburn Court of Requests 1841–43

Imperial Chemical Industries Ltd. (DDX/169). Deeds: Preesall 1679–1842; plan of Higher Lickow c.1830

Sir Edward Anson, Bart. (DDX/170). Order to Col. Birch to provide a horsemen 1660; levy on Manchester and Salford for Jacobites 1745; plan of the Palace Inn, Manchester, 1745

A. W. Smith, Esq. (DDX/172). Apprenticeship indenture, Peter Dickinson to Preston watchmaker 1852

A. E. Dickson, Esq. (DDX/174). Deeds: Huddleston estates in Cumberland and Yorkshire 1717–52, Goosnargh (Rigby estate) 1554–1729, Kirkham 1719, 1726, Ribby-with-Wrea 1623–1735. Plan of Middleton demesne in Goosnargh 1742

Henry Whittaker, Phillips and Co. (DDX/176). Abstracts of title to property in Didsbury 1752–1857

Lancashire County Library (DDX/177). Petitions of Lancashire knights and recusants 1642; folders of letters, pictures, etc., towards histories of Lancashire and Liverpool 1823–75; plan of Whitemoss Gap in Staining 1813

Dr. A. S. Mellor (DDX/179). Deeds: Lverpool 1703–62

W. G. Ellison, Esq. (DDX/182). Plans of Shaw Place, Heath Charnock, c.1820, 1839, 1872

L. Pilling, Esq. (DDX/183). Deeds: Rochdale 1721–1880; valuation of steam-engine 1809; plan of land at Spotland bridge 1844

H. E. Sandwell, Esq. (DDX/184). Engineering prize-essays by J. A. Bennison, with descriptions of factories in Manchester, Rochdale, Oldham and Bolton 1868–70

L. Cotman, Esq. (DDX/186). Deeds: Leyland 1662–1785, Spaddock Hall, Bilsborrow 1700–1926; commissions: Baldwin family of Leyland 1805–61

Bury Public Library (DDX/187). Deeds: Bury 1636–1835, Little Bolton 1639, Tottington 1691–1786, Gollinrod in Walmersley c.1260–1640, Edale, co. Derby 1609, Saltcotes, co. Ayr 1555

Notes and pedigrees on Kay family of Bury 1820–98; Peter Stock's papers re Bury Local Advisory Committee of Ministry of Labour 1910–18; poor-rate assessment for Walmersley 1735; plan of Irwell House estate, Bury 1853; Holt and Hamer marriage settlement Spotland 1632

Miss D. E. Ormerod (DDX/188). Deeds: Butterworth 1770, 1776, Castleton 1820, Milnrow 1852–76. Accounts of Robert Butterworth 1767–70, John Kershaw 1796–1807, Sally Kershaw 1807–19, Thomas Clegg 1811–60, William Clegg 1861–67. Butterworth church-ley 1777–78. Liquor etc. licences for Milnrow 1782–1811. Rochdale Methodist circuit-plans 1817–25. Rules of Castleton Cow Club 1859

F. J. Rigby, Esq. (DDX/189). Plans of properties in Freckleton 1769, 1837. Letters and papers of E. J. Fallows, Manchester, concerning his appointment as engineer and draughtsman in Poland 1870–83. Preston Home Guard and Civil Defence papers 1940–55. Fallows of Preston family papers 1847–1957

The Misses Langton (DDX/190). Deeds: Preston 1658–1717. Wills 1620–1782. Correspondence from Thomas Langton of Kirkham 1771–88. Minutes, correspondence, etc., of Loyal Kirkham Volunteers 1798. Pedigree papers 17th and 18th century. Orders for ringing Preston bells 1588. Inventory of Cornelius Langton of Kirkham 1715. Memoranda book of John Langton 1717–53. Diary of Thomas Langton's tour in Ireland 1748. Order of Bury vestry concerning organist's salary 1751. Call-book of manor of Manchester 1727–31. Appointments of Thomas Langton as captain 1803, deputy lieutenant 1807. Passport of John Langton 1815–17. Scrap-books of Lancashire items c.1800–40

The Towneley Hall Committee (DDX/194). Working and fair-copy plans made in 1684: Preston, Lancaster; roads from Lancaster to Warrington, Lancaster to Cockerham, Crimbles to Pilling, Lancaster to Clougha, Preston to Haighton, Ribbleton to Inglewhite, Preston to Poulton and Pilling, Lancaster to Bolton-le-Sands and Cark; the Winster, Windermere, Leven and Cartmel shores; Wrightington Hall; Appley moor; Shevington moor

Blackhurst, Parker and Yates (DDX/195). Deeds of Lancaster St. John pews 1755–88; deeds of Forton 1672–1775, Pilling 1748–1866

D. Bush, Esq. (DDX/197). Plans of Garstang and Knott End railway 1865–70

W. Vert, Esq. (DDX/202). Royal licence to kill game in the forests of Bleasdale, Wyresdale, Myerscough and Quernmore 1775

N. J. Swarbrick, Esq. (DDX/206). Deeds: Goosnargh White Lee 1669–1884, valuations 1806–31, plan c.1830

Mrs. E. Blackburn (DDX/210). Letters to John Nuttall of Liverpool and Chester 1814–15

H. R. Hodgkinson, Esq. (DDX/211). Papers of Richard Hodgkinson, agent for the Atherton estate: correspondence 1783–1856 (references to the Napoleonic wars, Lancashire riots); bills and receipts 1791–1867; speeches at Standish school 1775–77; school exercise books 1784; Leigh theatre playbills 1789, 1804; apprenticeship indenture, Ellen Slow to Bolton mantua-maker 1815; travel diaries 1794–96, 1803, 1812, 1819, 1822, 1824, 1840; wills 1791–1850

G. Bowley, Esq. (DDX/213). Catterall deed 1806

B. Pearson, Esq. (DDX/214). Inquisition as to value of ninths and fifteenths, Leyland Hundred 1341

E. A. C. Westby, Esq. (DDX/216). Deeds: Turnover Hall, Rawcliffe 1624–35

R. Irwin, Esq. (DDX/217). Diaries of Rachel M. Irwin of Manchester, Shatton in Cumberland, and Reigate in Surrey 1901–28

R. Flintoff, Esq. (DDX/218). Preston telephone directory 1882

Sir William Ascroft (DDX/222). Letters-patent of knighthood and grant-of-arms 1908

Col. G. N. Robinson (DDX/223). Deeds: Clitheroe, Henheads, Marsden, Chatburn, Blackburn, Accrington, Haslingden, Barley, Wheatley Booth and Brindle 1571–1932. Clayton

Estates, survey and plans: Little Harwood, Blackburn, Walton-le-Dale, Abram, Colne, Foulridge, Hindley and Westleigh 1760. Chatburn plans and surveys 1823–74

Norton, Youatt & Co. (DDX/224). Deeds: Crumpsall 1622–1902

S. V. Blomeley, Esq. (DDX/225). Apprenticeship indenture, Silvester Blomeley to Pendleton ironmonger 1868

G. W. Earle, Esq. (DDX/226). Deeds: Accrington 1769, Barley 1771–1804, Clitheroe 1733, 1775, Great Mearley 1653, Marsden 1630, 1697, Oswaldtwistle 1721, 1802, Over Darwen 1791, Ribchester 1723–1803, Tatham 1678–1799, Tottington 1823, Trawden 1705, Gisburn, co. York 1682–1810, Craven, co. York 1585

East Riding Record Office (DDX/227). Plan of St. Peter's Fields, Manchester 1819; licence of Thomas Dixon of Ulverston as priest 1537. Deeds: Over Darwen 1776, Mellor and Over Darwen 1781

A. W. Chambers, Esq. (DDX/228). Deeds: (E. H. Moss estate) Ashton-under-Lyne 1707–1866, Oldham 1685–1909, Saddleworth, co. York 1657–1927.

W. D. Fairclough, Esq. (DDX/230). Letter from Sebastopol 1855

Brighouses Ltd. (DDX/231). Deeds: Ormskirk 1784–1811

North Riding Record Office (DDX/233). Deeds: Orrell 1737–88, Salwick 1780, plan of land in Orrell c.1785

R. C. Watson, Esq. (DDX/234). Photographs and plans of old buildings in the Fylde 1891–1961. Cash-book of Paul Harrison of Bankfield in Singleton 1846–49

W. T. Kay, Esq. (DDX/235). Recipe-book for human and animal sickness 1840

Stoke-on-Trent Library (DDX/236). Barton-upon-Irwell deed 1718

Preston Rural District Council (DDX/238). Deeds: Kings Fold, Penwortham 1464–1798, Goosnargh 1672

Mrs. Falkner Hill (DDX/239). Deeds: Metcalfe estate in Middleton, co. York 1662 and Dominica (slaves) 1804–35; Heseltine estate in Burton and Aysgarth, co. York 1638–1872; Letter-books of Geoarge Metcalfe (slaving) 1813–14 and Elizabeth Metcalf (slaving) 1833–36. Certificate of absolution for attempted clandestine marriage by George and Joanna Heseltine 1630; Quaker marriage certificate of George Heseltine and Isabel Gallely 1765. Papers of the Bensons of Manchester, Preston and Ulverston 1835–92

R. D. Orrell, Esq. (DDX/240). Deeds: Crompton 1774, Oldham 1798. Papers of Henry Forrer of Liverpool, merchant, 1856–86

Anonymous (DDX/243). Deeds: Caton 1579–1876, Bare 1640. Plan, Broadwood and Bell Hill c.1786

Miss Hutton (DDX/244). Subscription list for racing at Aughton 1764; correspondence and notes of William Hutton for *Church Bells of Liverpool Diocese* 1883–92

H. Bateson, Esq. (DDX/245). Deeds: Thornton-le-Fylde 1664–1901, Westby 1700, Ribby 1729

F. Cookson, Esq. (DDX/246). Memoranda book of Richard Miller of Goosnargh 1817–40; exercise-book Esprick school c.1871

J. F. Parker, Esq. (DDX/247). Admission of James Gordon to freedom of Liverpool 1736

Lt. Col. R. B. Crosse (DDX/248). Appointment of trustees of Elizabeth Lathom's charity for Charnock Richard 1777

J. D. Bickersteth, Esq. (DDX/251). The earl of Ashburnham deeds of Bretherton 1714–66

G. Higgins, Esq. (DDX/254). Plan of duke of Bridgewater's weir in Manchester c.1760. Poulton-le-Fylde property account-book 1768

R. F. C. Butler-Cole, Esq. (DDX/255). General livery to Thomas Carus of manor and advowson of Whittington 1594; settlement of Butler of Rawcliffe estates 1718; appointment of Alexander Butler as sheriff 1767 and constable of Lancaster castle 1803; shrievalty accounts 1767–68. Kirkland Hall cashbook 1756–60

Governors of Bootham School, York (DDX/257). Deeds: Leyland 1640, Walton-le-Dale 1665. Book of surrenders and inquisitions of manor and fee of Penwortham 1726–1845

Messrs. Warrens (DDX/258). Armetriding wills 1704–1832. Deeds: Bury 1821, Euxton (papermill) 1611–1766, Farington and Leyland 1620–1782; plans: Welch's land in Leyland and Farington 1737, 1854; certificate concerning shooting by Cromwell's trooper 1648; appointment of John Armetriding as ensign 1744

Mrs. Joyce (DDX/265). Deeds: Salesbury 1780–1860

Kent Archives Office (DDX/266). Deeds: Tytup Hall, Dalton-in-Furness 1582–1713

Miss Livesey (DDX/267). Deeds: Tockholes 1608–1877

Ipswich and East Suffolk Record Office (DDX/270). Survey of honour of Hornby 1662

Anonymous (DDX/273). Deeds: Burnley c.1275–1814. Apprentice-ship indenture, Richard Piccop to Rossendale woollen-weaver 1760; allotment of pews in Burnley church 1804; Burnley union (joiners and carpenters) cash-book 1873–77

Sir Peter Anson, Bart. (DDX/274). Dickenson of Manchester: commentary of current affairs 1742–60, recipe-book c.1772, letter-books 1767–79, 1785–94, account-books 1779–1853, 1810–14, tour diaries 1812, 1817, 1819, book of anecdotes 1814, diaries of John Dickenson II 1776–82, 1792–1810, John Dickenson III 1774–94, 1786–1842

J. Lee, Esq. (DDX/275). Survey of Foxdenton 1727

Norwich Public Library (DDX/276). Accrington deeds 1510–1760

Major R. O. Bridgeman (DDX/277). Canon G. T. O. Bridgeman's letter and notes concerning his *History of Wigan* 1875–89

Miss A. Bretherton (DDX/280). Deeds: Bretherton 1726–1813

Rev. S. Freshwater (DDX/282). Theatre bills: Manchester 1800, 1812, 1813; Bradford 1862

Mrs. Rodney (DDX/286): Deed: Flixton 1671

Bolton Public Library (DDX/288). Deeds: Forton 1706–1816

W. H. Robinson and Co. (DDX/289). Haydock Lodge plan 1926

The Society of Genealogists (DDX/291). Deeds: Broughton (Preston) 1602–97, Dalton-in-Furness 1630, Gorton 1768, Manchester 1813, Newton (Manchester) 1850–81, Pendleton (Salford) 1801–55, Prestwich 1761–1839, Salford 1855, Southport 1824–30, Walton-le-Dale 1648. Faculty for pew in Samlesbury chapel 1785. Dalton *v.* Fitzgerald (manor of Bulk) 1566–1896

S. Percival, Esq. (DDX/292). Lease of Rose and Crown, Warrington 1727

Capt. P. R. Chester (DDX/293). Deeds: Woolston c.1350, Rixton-with-Glazebrook 1332–1500. Perquisites of halmote of Rixton 1399; licence for Rixton chapel 1451; will of Hamon Mascy 1462; rental of Rixton and Altrincham, co. Chester, 1462

Kent Archaeological Society (DDX/294). Deeds: Ince Blundell 1382, 1424

C. H. France-Hayhurst (DDX/295). Wallace and Currie of Liver-pool, deeds and wills 1783–1818

F. L. Collins, Esq. (DDX/297). Deeds: Broughton-in-Furness 1676–1891; plan of lands in Broughton-in-Furness 1826

Dr. R. Dickinson (DDX/298). Descriptions of events in Lancashire c.1750. Ulverston deed 1875

Worcestershire Record Office (DDX/300). Great Eccleston plan 1841

Leeds City Library (DDX/301). Starkie of Huntroyde letters 1806–54

J. F. Lancaster, Esq. (DDX/309). Deeds: Extwistle 1374–1552

H. Speakman Brown, Esq. (DDX/312). Deeds: Culcheth 1687–1732, Tyldesley-with-Shakerley 1633–84, Bedford 1639–1720; Culcheth, Tyldesley, Worsley 1650–1789. Papers of William Speakman 1788–99

Miss G. N. Holme (DDX/313). Deeds: Ormskirk 1563–1621

Woods, Barton & Co. (DDX/314). Deeds: Blackleach, Woodplumpton 1420–1876

Maude and Tunnicliffe (DDX/315). Deeds: Bilsborrow (White Bull) 1726–52, Myerscough 1556–1735, Stretford 1790, Great Eccleston, Elswick and Little Eccleston 1721, Clayton-le-Dale 1725, Barnacre-with-Bonds 1725, Liverpool 1901

Neville, Rimmer & Birkett (DDX/316). Deeds: Castleton 1778–1806

Mrs. S. Cowburn (DDX/317). Amyas *v.* Champnant (Fleetwood Hall in Samlesbury) 1672–95; Amyas correspondence 1690–1769; Barton correspondence (including scientific matters) 1787–1800; appointments of Robert Brickwell as B.A., deacon, priest, etc., 1835–48; testimonial to Rev. William Harrison, headmaster of Penwortham (Hutton) school 1851

E. C. Marsden (DDX/319). Deeds: Longton 1452, Hutton 1525–88, Tockholes 1639

Dr. W. J. Elwood (DDX/321). Barton-upon-Irwell deed 1782

Miss Arminson (DDX/322). Letters between James Kenyon and John Arminson *re* their estate in Stalmine 1835–45

Lord Ashton of Hyde (DDX/323). Deeds: Didsbury 1676–1772

Lincolnshire Record Office (DDX/325). Deeds: Livesey 1449, 1452, Arkholme 1656, Billington 1564, 1613, Cockerham 1553, Forton 1553, Foulridge 1616, 1679, Trawden 1711

Shropshire Record Office (DDX/326). Deeds: Bolton 1810, Goosnargh 1704; Lees plan 1784; papers *re* estates of Ellis Fletcher in Clifton, Denton, Farnworth, Kearsley, Little Hulton, Tyldesley, etc., including coalmine plans and inventories *c.*1860–65. Manchester cathedral subscription book 1859. Papers of Sparling and Berry families—Liverpool, Bolton-le-Sands, Skerton, Carnforth, Lancaster, including Herculaneum and Harrington docks *c.* 1820–90.

R. Phillips, Esq. (DDX/327). Plan of Outerthwaite in Lower Allithwaite 1801

Harward and Evers (DDX/328). Manchester deed 1803

J. Higson, Esq. (DDX/329). Little Bolton deed 1784

Dr. R. F. W. Fisher (DDX/331). Photograph album of B. B. Gardner, Fluke Hall, Pilling 1876–1906

Anonymous (DDX/333). Deeds: Marsden 1665–1789, Briercliffe 1698, Accrington 1699, Goldshaw Booth 1719, Wheatley Booth 1719, Burnley 1830, 1864; minute-book of Burnley lodge of Operative Joiners and Carpenters 1850–73

Mrs. W. R. Hollingworth (DDX/334). Letters to Sir William Horton of Chadderton 1740–70; agreement by John of Radclif, parson of Bury, to protect and teach his ward 1357; muster papers 1577; insurance policy for Manchester theatre 1759; rules for employees of Chadderton collieries 1860

London County Record Office (DDX/335). Deeds: Rusholme 1837–38. Pedigree of Haworth of Highercroft in Darwen 1664–1865. Plans of Hindle estates in Darwen, Mellor, Blackburn and Clitheroe 1862, 1874

W. N. Whitehead, Esq. (DDX/336). Deeds: Entwistle 1730–1817, Samlesbury (boat) 1733, 1743, Whalley 1762–89; survey of Thomas Braddyll's estate in Lancashire and Yorkshire 1757, Apprenticeship indentures: John Higgin to Wiswell linen-webster 1712, Miles Burch to Rathmel, co. York, husbandman 1748, William Harrison to Billington carpenter 1762. Correspondence: review of Priestley's *Examination of Scottish Philosophy* 1775, Whalley organ from Lancaster 1813, Whalley armorial window 1816, James Northcote's picture *Christ in the garden* 1816. Licence to Adam Greenwood to teach at Whalley 1716

R. Singleton, Esq. (DDX/337). Recipes for ink 1752; Mrs. Owen's recipe book 18th–19th century

Miss D. B. Dew (DDX/342). Manchester deed 1858.

Warrington Library (DDX/343). Patent for calico-printing, John Slater of Mosney, Walton-le-Dale 1785

Dr. J. W. Grieve (DDX/348). Warton-in-Amounderness deed 1601

Mrs. W. M. Bowman (DDX/350). Institution of Henry Fairfax to Ashton-under-Lyne 1619. Three volumes of newspaper cuttings on Lancashire local government 1894–97. Plan of manor of Staley, co. Chester *c*.1580 with surveys 1650–1801. Antiquarian notebooks *re* Ashton-under-Lyne; Waterhouses plan 1773; manor court-books of Staley 1630 and Ashton-under-Lyne 1665

Miss J. Woolfenden (DDX/351). Depositions on Royton riot 1794

G. G. Horsfall, Esq. (DDX/353). Lees deeds 1778–1840. Papers *re* strike at Springhead Spinning Co., Lees 1868

Manchester Central Library (DDX/354). Photocopies: plan of Hollins in Higham, 18th c.; agreement for Little Harwood bridge 1698; plan of Walton Estate, Upper Holker 18th c.; agreement for enclosure at Woodplumpton 1573; plan of Wrightington enclosure 18th c.; Lieutenancy order book 1625–87; Towneley transcripts of Garstang and Cockerham deeds; sale particulars: Southport 1909, Myerscough Hall 1918

H. Swann, Esq. (DDX/356). Log-book of Windermere steamer *Fairy Queen* 1879 (Photo)

Wiltshire Record Office (DDX/357). Deeds of Poulton, Bare, and Torrisholme, Preston, Weeton, Kirkham and Leyland 1656–1823

J. L. Buller, Esq. (DDX/362). Letter from New York 1850

S. S. Mayfield, Esq. (DDX/364). Address of welcome to earl of Ellesmere and his reply (Worsley) 1857

Miss M. Barron (DDX/366). Kirkland Hall household account book 1792–1818

W. H. Heelis & Son (DDX/369). Deeds: Hawkshead 1597–1882, Sawrey and Wray 1710, 1729, Cockermouth, Cumberland 1649, 1685

Bolton, Jobson & Martyn (DDX/370). Settlement by John Ruskin 1876

Public Record Office of Northern Ireland (DDX/371). Augmentation of arms of Sir Piers Legh 1575, Winwick pew deed 1606

A. S. Hall, Esq. (DDX/372). Deeds: Preesall 1729, 1785

Rev. J. S. Boulter (DDX/375). Deeds: Aldingham 1767–1906

Myerscough & Green (DDX/376). J. E. W. Marsden's book of medical treatments 1892

Mrs. G. M. Scott (DDX/377). Grants of arms: James Stott of Brownwardle 1844, James Stott-Milne of Brownwardle 1844, Robert Stott of Whitworth 1854, John Stott-Milne of Castleton 1854

Radcliff & Co. (DDX/379). Dissolutions of iron-making partnerships at Ulverston and Wigan 1773

Mrs. E. H. Cliff (DDX/382). Forton deeds 1694–1880

J. Leslie, Esq. (DDX/384). Kirkham deed 1629

Mrs. G. Irwin (DDX/385). Expenditure of Dr. Charles Rothwell, Bolton, 1858–62

Mrs. R. Dixon (DDX/387). Letter of emigrant to Australia 1875

E. Hargreaves, Esq. (DDX/389). Calico-printer's recipe and pattern books c.1835

Baron de Breffny (DDX/390). Account-book of steward to Edward Parker of Browsholme 1766–79

Cheshire Record Office (DDX/391). Bolton-le-Sands rectorial manor court rolls 1799–1947

Mrs. M. K. Oldham (DDX/392). Oldham family geneaological papers

S. Herd, Esq. (DDX/393). Letters of Rev. W. D. Watson, Chorley 1900–07

Mrs. G. McCormack (DDX/394). Deeds: Newton (Manchester) 1850–94

Gateshead Public Library (DDX/395). Deeds: Parbold 1697–1718, Walton-le-Dale 1618–91, Whittle-le-Woods 1629, Wrightington 1559

Lord Shuttleworth (DDX/396). Deeds: Littledale 14th to 17th century

S. A Jackson, Esq. (DDX/397). Deeds: Little Eccleston 1608–1795

The Rothwell Estates (DDX/400). Plans of Rothwell properties in Anglezarke, Blackrod, Little Bolton, Bretherton, Broughton, Castleton, Clayton-le-Woods, Crompton, Great Crosby, Over Darwen, Didsbury, Dutton, Euxton, Failsworth, Fillingley (co. Warwick), Fulwood, Halliwell, Hindley, Much Hoole, Horwich, Hundersfield, Leyland, Lunt and Thornton, Preston and Manchester, Oldham, Rivington, Royton, Sharples, Tockholes, Turton, Up Holland, Westhoughton c.1840

R. Turner, Esq. (DDX/404). Deeds: Meg's farm, Tatham, 1714–1846

Mrs. E. M. Hill (DDX/405). Deeds: Royton 1600–1822

Mrs. E. M. Dickson (DDX/406). Dalton deeds 1665–1845

H. Horsfall, Esq. (DDX/407). Correspondence, depositions, etc., concerning the strike at Springhead, Lees 1867–68

W. R. Hodgson, Esq. (DDX/408). The papers of Mrs. Enid Taylor for a history of Silverdale

McLaren, Jeens & Seacome (DDX/409). Deeds relating to the Holt family coal-mines, etc., in Castleton, Butterworth and Walsden 1584–1889

The Stephen Marshall Documents (DDX/412). Deeds, papers and plans of the Skelwith Fold estate 1675–1888; including letters of William Wordsworth, David Wilkie, Jeremy Bentham and Thomas Carlyle; incantations to stop bleeding and to cure burns and scalds, c.1740

Pickering, Kenyon & Co. (DDX 415) Drinkwater of Prestwich MSS. Manorial: Prestwich court-books 1669, 1673, 1676, 1678, 1679, 1681–83, 1685, 1687, 1690, 1693, 1694, 1698, 1701, 1703–07, 1709, 1710, 1712–14, 1716, 1718, 1720–26, 1729, 1731, 1738, 1753, 1764, 1769, 1778, 1810, presentments 1753, 1764, 1769, 1778, call-books 1753, 1759, 1769.
Title deeds and papers: Failsworth 1734, 1815; Prestwich (including mills) 1663–1911, Tottington (including mills) 1827–62; Arkesden, Essex 1864–70; Watlington, Norfolk 1709–1878, Wormgay, Norfolk 1573–1852; Rotherhithe, Kent 1685–1882
Miscellaneous: Irwell Hall inventory 1858, plan of Prestwich parish 1830, rentals 1802–21, diversion of road at Irwell Hall 1799

T. R. Allen, Esq. (DDX/416). Deeds: Haslingden 1707–1875; Oswaldtwistle 1820–68

Longueville and Co. (DDX/417). Deeds: Bold 1847, Bootle 1843, 1854, Colton 1840, Ditton 1847, 1851, Eccleston (Chorley) 1851, Egton-with-Newland 1864, Liverpool 1786–1876, Sutton 1847, Toxteth Park 1851, Tattersall of Lower Darwen 1675–1853

May, May & Deacon (DDX/419). Plans of Heywood Hall estate 1637, 1718, 1766

G. M. Whiley, Esq. (DDX/421). Deeds: Ashton-under-Lyne, Ulverston, Nibthwaite, Furness Fells, Hundersfield, Claughton-in-Amounderness 1641–1886

Stephenson, Harwood and Tatham (DDX/422). Deeds: Broughton-in-Amounderness, and Whittingham 1592–1823, Bury 1838–1900

Frere, Cholmeley & Nicholson (DDX/426). Deeds: Peel Hall, Little Hulton 1801–45, Salford and Spotland 1865–68

Brundrett, Randall & Whitmore (DDX/427). Deeds: Great Lever 1793–96

Perry & Co. (DDX/428). Deeds: Manchester 1823, Nibthwaite 1585, Stretford 1833–55, Dominica 1804. Plans: Anglezarke 1774, Up Holland c.1800, Fleetwood 1841

T. Bradley, Esq. (DDX/436). Ribchester workhouse deed 1835

Arkle and Derbyshire (DDX/437). Liverpool deeds 1779–1830

Hackney Borough Library (DDX/439). Deeds: Hutton and Longton 1681–1805, Middleton 1614, Bolton-le-Sands 1753–1818, Lancaster 1761–83, Pilling 1752–81, Maghull 1738–61, Oldham 1671–1738. Assignment of Barrow Haematite Steel Co., Barrow-in-Furness 1866

Bowen, Cotton & Bowen (DDX/442). Deeds and settlements of Barlow properties in Barton-upon-Irwell and Manchester 1823–1921

Corbould, Rigby & Co. (DDX/443). Potter estate: deeds, Elton 1713–1823, Tottington 1783–1874, Darley, co. Derby 1734–1868. Survey, Edgworth 1778. Executorship papers 1799–1845. Settlements 1816, 1829. Genealogical data 1744–1828. Division of seats in Bury church 1776, 1780

Mrs. L. Culshaw (DDX/444). Deeds: Aughton 1582–1700, Burtonwood 1714, Huyton 1767. Lathom 1623–1806. Ormskirk 1634–96, Parr 1597–1630, Pemberton 1699, Rainford 1703, Scarisbrick c.1655, 1715; bankruptcy of Thomas Hornby, Liverpool, chapman 1705

Hereford City Library (DDX/447) Poulton-le-Sands and Skerton deeds 1668–1854

Clark and Co. (DDX/450) Deeds: Bury 1897, Liverpool 1805, Wavertree 1807

Mrs. D. King (DDX/451) Letter re thefts in Manchester 1809

S. Bannister, Esq. (DDX/452). Deeds of Shard Ferry House, Hambleton 1836–74

F. C. Lowe, Esq. (DDX/454). Droylsden constables 1844

J. E. Huddleston, Esq. (DDX/455). Roeburndale deeds 1750–57

C. C. Oman, Esq. (DDX/456). Tunstall deed 1623

Cornwall Record Office (DDX/457). Deeds: Medlar-with-Wesham 1636, Sabden 1671, Thistleton 1621–1721, Westhoughton 1641

Liverpool University Library (DDX/458). Deeds: Billinge 1393, Scholes in Eccleston-next-Knowsley 1402–1676, Prescot 1636, 1692, Up Holland and Bretherton 1669

Miss Ashworth (DDX/459). Deeds and papers re Over Darwen lands and collieries 1765–1905

J. Cowell, Esq. (DDX/461). Worsthorne deeds 1734–70

W. H. Waddington, Esq. (DDX/462). Deeds: Colne 1638–1796, Marsden 1598–1846, Livesey 1691–1895; letters re Padiham Unitarian chapel 1821–44

D. Bagnall, Esq. (DDX/464). Deeds: Chipping 1746–1831, Goosnargh 1722–75

J. Ditchfield, Esq. (DDX/468). Leagram deed 1815

Miss Winstanley (DDX/469) Parr and Lowton deed 1683

R Addie, Esq. (DDX/470). Deeds: Elswick 1866, 1879, Penwortham 1827, Preesall 1725–1831, Stalmine 1836, Thornton-le-Fylde 1721, 1805–38; mariner's certificates of John McGrindle 1870–1909

C. M. Couch, Esq. (DDX/471). Manuscript charm found in house-wall, Sabden c.1800

Derbyshire Record Office (DDX/473). Marriage licence for Gilbert of Abram and Joan of Bradshawe 1369

B. G. Pearson, Esq. (DDX/474). Torver and Blawith deeds 1626–1860, Torver rate 1733

R. Towler, Esq. (DDX/475). Preston printer's apprenticeship indenture 1878

T. Fitzsimmons, Esq. (DDX/476). Freckleton deed 1750

R. G. Shepherd, Esq. (DDX/479). Diaries 1923–70; sale particulars of Bank House Farm and Shard Hotel, Hambleton 1908

Mrs. F. A. Bailey (DDX/480). Deeds: Aldcliffe 1466, Widnes 1387, 1414, 1639, Windle 1369 and Bold, Eccleston, Prescot, St. Helens, Widnes, Whiston 1310–1914

Miss C. M. Bannister (DDX/484). Letters from the Rev. J. E. D. Bannister to Adam Sedgwick, geologist 1859–1900

A. W. Price, Esq. (DDX/486). Torver deed 1764

H. C. Irvine, Esq. (DDX/487). Deeds: Manchester 1340–1719, Moston 1630, Preston 1736, 1817; licence to teach in Tarleton 1733

E. Cowell, Esq. (DDX/489). Catterall and Claughton-in-Amounder-ness deed 1726

P. Aspinall, Esq. (DDX/491). Deeds: Bolton St. George's pew 1796, Sharples 1712, 1723

Mrs. E. Norris (DDX/492). List of closed cotton-mills, Bolton, 1957–70; stained-glass designs 1950–73; Unitarian scrapbook 1864–88

G. Berwick, Esq. (DDX/493). Dilworth deed 1614

J. Bickerstaffe, Esq. (DDX/494). Tatham deed 1603

L. B. Richardson, Esq. (DDX/495). Freckleton Marsh agreement 1772; registration of S.S. *Gem*, Preston, 1852

Darwen Public Library (DDX/496). Deeds: Darwen apprenticeship 1658, Entwistle 1658

Hodgson and Son (DDX/497). Penwortham Bridge papers *c*.1752–1885; deeds: Euxton, Ulnes Walton, and Eccleston 1617–1752, Myerscough and Weeton 1797–1887

Miss K. M. Shawcross (DDX/498). Rivington deeds and papers 1591–1950

Miss L. Carr (DDX/499). Cartmel deeds 1604–1799

E. J. Owen, Esq. (DDX/500). Ormskirk deed 1701

Caernarvonshire Record Office (DDX/501). Lancashire postcards 1905–08

D. L. Roberts, Esq. (DDX/502). Peter Pickup of Burnley and his father, coal investigators: accounts and memoranda 1818–49, work diary 1866, survey book 1787–1880

R. Cottam, Esq. (DDX/503). Photographs of Blackpool Aviation Week 1909

R. Hawkey, Esq. (DDX/505). Letters of Richard Taylor and Simon Brown, Burnley, transportees to Australia 1840–58

P. Magee, Esq. (DDX/506). Everton deed 1843

W. J. G. Boucher, Esq. (DDX/507). Croft deeds 1719–35

Miss E. Lees (DDX/508). Housekeeping accounts of Frank Lees, Prestwich 1892–94

Capt. R. L. B. Cunliffe (DDX/510). Diaries of Dolly, wife of George Clayton of Lostock Hall, Bamber Bridge 1777–1833

L. Wardle, Esq. (DDX/511). Probate papers of Topping family of Bury 1862–91

Mrs. F. L. Hirst (DDX/512). Deeds of Counthill, Oldham 1640–1881

J. D. Burton, Esq. (DDX/514). Recusancy fine on Ann Massey of Rishton 1592

H. Conolly, Esq. (DDX/515). Oldham: passports of Daniel Conolly 1848, 1858 and Charles Conolly 1868–84

W. and A. Alker (DDX/517). Blackpool deeds 1865–68, Longton apprenticeship 1898

R. Dobson, Esq. (DDX/519). Correspondence of the Rev. H. V. Koop *re* his book *Broughton-in-Furness* 1966–69; valuation of Barrow printworks, Wiswell 1855

Sir Nicholas Cheetham (DDX/520). Deeds: Butterworth 1655, Chadderton 1664, Crompton 1613–1857, Hundersfield 1750, Milnrow 1750, 1754, Oldham 1722–1845

T. Molloy, Esq. (DDX/521). Letters and papers *re* Sir John Barrow memorial, Ulverston, 1850–51

Durham Record Office (DDX/523). Pennington-in-Furness deed 1768

A. Bell, Esq. (DDX/527). Warrants for discharge of prisoners from Lancaster Castle 1794

Major Phillips (DDX/532). Coastal chart—Formby to Solway 1883

Miss E. Waller (DDX/533). Blackpool: Gynn Estate abstract of title 1897–1919

Pinsent and Co. (DDX/534). Bolton-le-Moors deeds 1815–47

H. Preston, Esq. (DDX/537). Letters of Richard Boothman, Colne, transportee to Australia 1840–46; his will 1876

Miss E. Maitland (DDX/538). Deeds and papers of Platt family of Chipping and Clitheroe, and of Dr. Thomas Platt of Oldham, 18th and 19th c.

Pilkington Bros. (DDX/539). Eccleston (Prescot) manor court books 1812–56

H. Taylor, Esq. (DDX/540). Almanac of Roger Foster of Bury 1715

B. J. N. Edwards, Esq. (DDX/541). Preston deeds 1911–24; Lancashire and Yorkshire Railway handbill 1865

B. D. Scotley, Esq. (DDX/542). School exercise book of John Briggs, Ulverston c.1820

J. Molesworth and Sons (DDX/546). Petitions of Littleborough postmen for wage increase 1895

Mrs. O. M. Etheridge (DDX/548). Hundersfield deed 1677

Mrs. M. Sunter (DDX/549). Ordinance incorporating Duchy of Lancaster as separate inheritance of king 1467; Goosnargh deeds 1657, 1770; Preston election call-book 1761; brief in Preston election dispute 1768

G. Trollope and Sons (DDX/550). Thurland Castle particulars of sale 1929

R. B. Austin, Esq. (DDX/551). Leyland deeds 1618–1900

Salford City Museum (DDX/552). Skelmersdale plan 1839

E. Penny, Esq. (DDX/554). Bills of sale for Lancaster ships 1865, 1868

Miss L. Basnett (DDX/556). Arithmetic book of Elijah Heaton of Westhoughton 1802

Edelston, Carter and Jones (DDX/557). Deed of Penwortham grammar school land in Preston 1585; papers of Penwortham grammar school 18th to 19th c.; rules of Swillbrook mill, Preston 1867; autobiography of John Jackson of Longton, apprenticeship to woollendraper 1826–28; deeds: Croston 1860,

Samlesbury mill 1784–1871, Howick school, Fulwood 1881, Hutton 1666–1786, Longton 1675–1771, Newton-with-Scales 1668–1864, Preston 1845–1969

G. R. and C. E. Wace (DDX/561). Wigan deed 1740

H. D. Lees, Esq. (DDX/562). Telephone contract 1908

H. R. Atkinson, Esq. (DDX/563). Motor-driver's licence 1904

E. C. Walsh, Esq. (DDX/564). Chipping deeds (including mill) 1544–1846; Singleton Hall estate accounts 1934–50

Skipton Public Library (DDX/567). Deeds: Ashton-in-Makerfield 1709–16, Ormskirk 1726, Scarisbrick 1742

Tallents and Co. (DDX/568). Deeds: Barton-upon-Irwell and Pendleton 1567–1740, Broughton (Salford) 1613, Butterworth and Pendleton 1613, Castleton 1779, Manchester 1628, 1635, Manchester, Blackley and Failsworth 1680

F. W. Goddard, Esq. (DDX/570). Clifton of Lytham documents *re* Kirkham 1435, Bleasdale 1601–1719, Heysham rectory 1637, 1659, Warton 1737

Veale, Benson and Co. (DDX/571). Deeds of Stopfords of Audenshaw, Gloucester and Bristol, hatters 1827–71

E. Kelsall, Esq. (DDX/572). Common-place book of Benjamin Broadbent 1827

Miss K. Happold (DDX/573). Barrow-in-Furness deeds 1872–1919

H. R. Fitton and Butler (DDX/574). Deeds: Middleton 1890–1966, Chadderton 1924–66

R. Towler, Esq. (DDX/575). Apprenticeship indenture—printer and compositor 1878

W. Sharples, Esq. (DDX/576). Diaries: Edward Cooke of Preston 1838–41, Henry Cooke of Preston and the Punjab 1870–73

Mrs. M. Atherton (DDX/577). Accounts for building house in Blackburn 1858

Miss P. Green (DDX/578). Deeds: Whitworth, Spotland and Hundersfield 1698, Windle 1751

Robson Lowe, Esq. (DDX/580). Whittington deed 1609

Sussex Archaelogical Society (DDX/581). Deeds: Ormskirk, Gorton, Broughton-in-Furness, Rochdale 1609–1835; Huyton 1864, Aughton 1706

Lindsay, Greenfield and Mason (DDX/582). Wigan deeds 1741–1822

A. E. Jennings, Esq. (DDX/586). Hundersfield deed 1722

Price and Cross (DDX/587). Ellel deed 1688

Farrer and Co. (DDX/589). Assheton of Downham deeds 1718–1917; Hornby Castle deeds 1841–47

Gregory, Rowcliffe and Co. (DDX/590). Deeds: Wigan, Blackrod and Preston 1801–46; Bedford, Pennington and Westleigh 1636–1907; deeds and papers of Walmesley family of Westwood in Ince-in-Makerfield 1627–1915

Gaultry, Goodfellow and Co. (DDX/593). Formby deeds 1770–1812

Simmons and Simmons (DDX/594). Deeds: Colne, Lancaster, St. Helens 19th and 20th c.; Chorley 1843–1919, Preston 1887–1966

Mrs. J. E. Gardner (DDX/595). Plans: Bamber Bridge, Blackpool, Calder Vale, Catterall, Fulwood, Goosnargh, Longridge, Longton, Preston and Warton-in-Amounderness 1819–c. 1910; rules of Shepherd Street Reading Room, Preston 1826; Preston political leaflets c.1830; theatre programmes: Blackpool, Liverpool, Preston 1901–33

C. Shorrock, Esq. (DDX/597). Duchy of Lancaster *compotus* concerning Lancashire charities 1619

R. Banks, Esq. (DDX/599). Croston deeds 1873–99

Miss D. Sutton (DDX/602). Southport deeds 1836, 1840

M. Campbell, Esq. (DDX/603). Book of rates, County of Lancaster 1752

Mrs. Moyers (DDX/604). Papers and apprenticeship indentures of Bispham's charity, Billinge 1728–1817; Tyrer family of Parr papers 1705–29; valuation of Bispham delf 1863

Sproth, Stokes and Turnbull (DDX/607). Halewood deed 1766

A. Leigh, Esq. (DDX/610). Deeds of Hareappletree, Quernmore 1607–1870. Plans: Swainshead vaccary 1652, Hayshaw Fell c.1652, 1849, 1871, Hareappletree 1793, Lentworth 1877

J. R. Stainer, Esq. (DDX/611). Deeds: Hades in Hundersfield 1540–1651, Todmorden 1635–1861, Spotland 1542–1718; Todmorden highway assessments 1815–16; charm for curing cows 1773

T. E. Hey, Esq. (DDX/612). Papers of Harold Hey for a history of Newton-with-Scales

Lucas and Wyllys (DDX/613). Mortgage of Rochdale and Edenfield Turnpike tolls 1796

Hemingway, Marcy and Sons (DDX/614). Papers *re* coalmines in Hurst 1778–1860; agreement *re* manager of tartaric acid works, Bury 1851; deeds and papers: Ashton-under-Lyne, Bury, Chadderton, Crompton, Kirkdale, Liverpool, Manchester, Preston, Oldham, Royton, Warrington 1650–1911

Miss Pilkington (DDX/615). Deeds: Allerton 1772, Bolton 1603–1776, Breightmet 1655–1726, Halliwell 1773, Little Lever 1669–1717, Sharples 1735, Tottington 1741

Calveley and Co. (DDX/616). Freckleton and Warton-in-Amounderness deeds 1715–83.

Colne Library (DDX/617). Deeds of Ribble Hall, Clitheroe 17th and 18th c.; Reedley mill papers 18th and 19th c.; Nelson Local Board and Gas Co. deeds and papers 19th c.

Miss C. Roskell (DDX/618). Forton deeds and papers 1645–1885, including drainage agreement 1797

Walker and Hart (DDX/619). Garstang deeds 1850–75

Mrs. E. C. Woods (DDX/621). Deeds: Euxton 1384, 1478, Ulnes Walton 1481, 1603, 1616, 1621, Heskin 1592, 1603, 1666

Miss B. K. Gaskell (DDX/623). Photographs of Maypole pit disaster, Abram 1908

Stalland and Co. (DDX/624). Deeds and papers: Harrison of Manchester and Salford 1860–1916, Mence of Rainhill 1879–84

Mrs. E. Vinden (DDX/627). Passport and papers of Hodgson family of Cockerham, Yealand and New Zealand 1847–1903

Thomas Cooper and Co. (DDX/628). Towneley estate deeds 1847–78

Major Y. R. H. Probert (DDX/629). Littleborough deed 1810

J. McHugh, Esq. (DDX/630). Plan of Leyland 1844

T. R. Clark, Esq. (DDX/631). Letters *re* Morecambe Bay railway 1840 and Fleetwood 1841

Hounslow Library (DDX/632). Volume of Cunliffe of Liverpool wills and law cases 1767–90

J. S. Horne, Esq. (DDX/633). Letters and papers of the Rev. W. Allen of Peel, Little Hulton 1815–31

Mrs. Sloane (DDX/634). Plans and papers *re* building of Lund parsonage, Clifton 1812–16, 1827

H. Davies, Esq. (DDX/636). Diaries of John O'Neill, Clitheroe 1856–60, 1872–75 (see also DDX/28 p. 291)

M. H. Kevill, Esq. (DDX/637). Reminiscences of Nurse E. F. de Trafford at Auxiliary Military Hospital, Preston 1914–19

Mrs. D. Moore-Stevens (DDX/638). Deeds and papers: Accrington 1618–1788, Altham 1747, Billington 1788, Clayton-le-Moors 1720–58, Whalley 1749–1920, Whalley rectory 1679–1866, Bashall Eaves 1581–1691; Mitton tithe 1729

J. A. Gillman, Esq. (DDX/640). Upper Allithwaite deed 1734

Northamptonshire Record Office (DDX/641). Papers of S. E. Barrow, Lancaster architect 1910–15

Mrs. E. Phillips (DDX/642). Extracts from minutes of Blackpool Tramway Committee 1891–1922

P. F. Pierce, Esq. (DDX/645). Letters Patent: Thomas Lightfoot, Accrington, cotton printing 1850; John Mercer, Clayton-le-Moors, cotton improvement 1850

Dr. J. B. Penfold (DDX/647). Halton deed 1610

Board of Trade Bankruptcy Department (DDX/648). Deeds: Caton, Claughton-in-Lonsdale, Tarleton, Halton, Hornby, Wray, and Prestwich and Westleigh coalmines 1630–1886

Rhodes and Gillman (DDX/649). Deeds of 17 New Street, Lancaster 1747–1861

J. Rawlinson, Esq. (DDX/650). Horwich plan 1620

Miss M. Spencer (DDX/652). Arithmetic copy-books of Alice Stopforth of Halsall 1835, 1836

W. Marshall, Esq. (DDX/656). Wage agreement for Preston pilots 1894

J. H. Fell, Esq. (DDX/658). Whalley church handbills 1883–1902

R. G. Chorlton, Esq. (DDX/660). Newspaper cuttings on closure of churches and chapels in Manchester area 1968–72

E. Holt, Esq. (DDX/662). Collation to St. Simon's, Salford 1878

Mrs. E. M. Stopford (DDX/664). Deeds and papers: Bispham 1598, Dalton 1746, 1779, Heskin 1687, Ince-in-Makerfield 1653–1881, Mawdesley 1816, Little Mitton 1579, Up Holland 1640–1866, Wigan 1704–1816, Wrightington 1567–1687

H. H. G. Vorley, Esq. (DDX/665). Manchester deeds 1773–79; letters and papers re Sir Thomas Hammer's property in Wigan 1780–1840

J. C. Ashburner, Esq. (DDX/667). Urswick deeds 1767–1869

Mrs. M. Shepherd (DDX/668). Pilling pew deed 1816

W. A. Bright, Esq. (DDX/672). Family correspondence 1833–45

H. M. Carrington, Esq. (DDX/674). Notes on churches in Colne district c.1850–70

Potts and Ball (DDX/677). Failsworth deed 1700

Blackpool Library (DDX/679). Brindle, Inskip and Golborne rental 1729; theatre posters: Bolton 1810, Bury 1807, Manchester 1808, 1809, Oldham 1811, Rochdale 1794–1809, Crompton 1809

Mrs. M. Wallis (DDX/680). MS. history of Dolphinholme; Up Holland deed 1750; letter from Alexander Nowell *re* chapel in Whalley church 1593

P. R. Fitzgibbons, Esq. (DDX/681). Deeds: Barrow-in-Furness 1863–79, Freckleton 1601–1779; papers of Martin family of Fleetwood and Birkenhead 1873–1923, and of Fenton family of Barrow-in-Furness 1900–21

H. Wollaston, Esq. (DDX/686). Lathom, Parr and Sutton deed 1766

Lee, Bygott and Eccleston (DDX/687). Deeds: Bacup 1875, Liverpool 1898, Oldham 1902, Preston brewery 1900, Southport 1870–82, Toxteth Park 1846

Marsh, Son and Calvert (DDX/688). Deeds: Abram, Bedford, Pennington, Westleigh 1659–1892; papers of Leigh and Astley Burial Committee 1889–1902

Waterhouse and Co. (DDX/689). Deeds and papers: Holt Leigh family of Wigan 1754–1868; awards *re* Whalley quarries 1833. Deeds: Manchester 1765–71, Wigan 1770, 1773

May and May (DDX/691). Deeds and papers of Potter family of Darwen 1695–1911

C. Sherwin, Esq. (DDX/693). Apprenticeship indenture, Manchester hooker 1888

R. Kellett, Esq. (DDX/694). Letters from J. P. Pemberton, Long Marton school, to parents at Catterall Hall 1859; Pilling pew deed 1816; particulars of sale: White Hall, Rawcliffe 1857, Rawcliffe Hall 1928

Mrs. M. L. Redfern (DDX/695). Darwen deeds: 1801, coalmine 1830

Dr. M. N. O'Riordan (DDX/696). Nether Wyresdale deeds 1764, 1773

L. Roe, Esq. (DDX/698). List of Poulton-le-Fylde special constables 1837

J. Bold, Esq. (DDX/699). Deeds: Orrell 1686–1797, Wigan 1680–1784

W. E. F. Clarke, Esq. (DDX/700). Deeds of building-club houses, Longridge 1803–1936

K. Stansfield, Esq. (DDX/703). Deeds: Burnley 1826, Goldshaw Booth 1841, Old Laund Booth 1799

Magee, Marshall and Co. (DDX/704). Papers found in Owl Inn, Up Holland: certificates of burial in woollen 1684–86, petition for brief 1693, receipt for ale duty 1699

H. Sweeten, Esq. (DDX/706). Blackpool Military Hospital magazine 1916–19

J. Brown, Esq. (DDX/708). Sketch of Bank House Academy, Warton-in-Amounderness 1844

R. M. Wood, Esq. (DDX/713). Wheelton (Brinscall mill) deed 1799

Anonymous (DDX/715). Deeds: Brockholes 1635–73, Preston 1707–1870, Walton-le-Dale 1762, Thornley 1726. 1st report of Preston National school 1816

Birchall and Yates (DDX/717). Preston deeds 1874–1970

Miss J. Thompson (DDX/719). Bond family letters from America to relatives at Aughton and Sefton 1870–99

Ewen Kerr, Esq. (DDX/721). Memoranda book of mayor of Salford 1847–48

J. R. Roper, Esq. (DDX/723). Deeds and papers: Egton-with-Newland 1805–1930, Ulverston 1772–1840, Whittington 1873

Mrs. M. H. Knowles (DDX/726). Deeds: Kirkham 1795–1808, Preston 1793–1882

The Rev. H. G. B. Folland (DDX/727). Memoranda on Crossley family of Burnley c.1883

Brig. D. C. Phelps (DDX/728). Correspondence and accounts of Bayley family of Stalybridge 1804–31

Wilson and Firth (DDX/731). Blackley deeds 1757–1800

Mrs. L. G. Blocksidge (DDX/732). Antiquarian papers of Fr. McNulty, Clitheroe area.

The Borthwick Institute (DDX/733). Culcheth deeds 1808, 1813

Denbighshire Record Office (DDX/735). Postcards: St. Helens, Liverpool, Blackpool, Manchester, Grange-over-Sands, Newton-le-Willows 1900–15

Lord & Parker (DDX/403, 737). Deeds of properties of J. R. Lord in Blackburn, Over Darwen, Euxton, Croston, Coppull, Heath Charnock, Ince-in-Makerfield, Burscough, Haigh, Billinge, Ashton-in-Makerfield, Lowton, Golborne, Wigan 1692–1915

J. Y. Brown, Esq. (DDX/739). Cotton-weaving pattern and order book of John Threlfall of Calcutta 1844–45

Mrs. P. Ormerod (DDX/743). Photographs of Burnley area c.1900

Colne Library (DDX/752). Oldham deed 1716, Parr murderer's licence of parole 1897, Roughlee plan 1808

Mrs. D'Aeth (DDX/753). Deeds: Ashton-under-Lyne 1752–1849, Chadderton 1637–1884, Royton 1622

Wright, Hassall and Co. (DDX/755). Oldham deeds 1849–85

Mrs. J. Vujovich (DDX/756). Certificates of age of children employed at Todd's factory, Wheelton 1860–64

L. Worsley, Esq. (DDX/757). Plan of Highfield Moss, Lowton c.1765

Mrs. M. Crawford (DDX/758). Receipts for money paid by John Butler of Kirkland, Esq. 1613–18

Anonymous (DDX/760). Cragg of Ortner in Wyresdale family memoranda book 1698–1816 (contains diary of Timothy Cragg 1734–1807)

C. Roberts, Esq. (DDX/763). Postcards of St. Annes-on-the-Sea c.1885

J. W. S. Utley, Esq. (DDX/765). Deeds of Midghalgh in Myerscough 1654–1845

J. E. G. Hodgson, Esq. (DDX/767). Letters and papers of Askew, Hodgson, and Irving families of Hawkshead, and of Elizabeth Smith of Coniston, authoress 1810–1946

A. Bennett, Esq. (DDX/768). Poulton-le-Fylde deeds 1663–1811

Miss E. B. Ainscow (DDX/769). Portraits: Joseph Shawe, brother-in-law of the Rev. Thomas Whitehead, rector of Eccleston 1770–1812; Richard, son of the Rev. Thomas Whitehead

Heywood and Middleton Water Board (DDX/770). Deeds: Wolstenholme 1626, Cheesden 1709

T. G. Slater, Esq. (DDX/771). Letters and papers re Loyal North Lancashire Regiment 1894–1909; apprenticeship indentures to Slaters of Dunscar 1789, 1860; letter from E. Evans of the Antarctic expedition of 1910, 1913; letter from Queensland, Australia 1899

R. H. Jenkinson, Esq. (DDX/772). Haydock Lodge Lunatic Asylum: inspectors' books 1852–66, 1930–60; post-mortem register 1896–1960; patients' books 1921–60; patients' register 1948–60; visitors' book 1930–60; admission and discharge register 1948–69

E. Jemson, Esq. (DDX/776). Mensuration book of James Gregson, Lane Head School, Great Eccleston 1858

T. Rawcliffe, Esq. (DDX/779). Kirkham lease 1766

J. Cookson and Son (DDX/781). Elswick deeds 1897–1967

Newcastle-upon-Tyne City Archives (DDX/783). Plans: Warrington St. Barnabas c.1882, Oldham St. Mary 1884–96

H. M. Allen, Esq. (DDX/785). Deeds: Altcar 1753, Chipping 1785–99, Little Crosby 1713–31, Netherton 1663, Orrell 1839, Widnes 1849–71

W. L. Gorry, Esq. (DDX/786). Pamphlets on Blackpool electricity supply 1893–1913

Sir Gilbert Laithwaite (DDX/788). Photographs of Laithwaite MSS in the Public Record Office 15th to 17th c.

Messrs. Plumb (DDX/789). Preston deeds 1845–1953

The Nature Conservancy (DDX/790). Notes on Formby birds by T. S. Williams 1914–39

Anonymous (DDX/795). Out Rawcliffe deeds 1788, 1789, 1810

H. Hopwood, Esq. (DDX/799). Reports on Thomas Hill, teacher (including Hulme St. Paul's school) 1859–83

T. D. Horn, Esq. (DDX/801). Myerscough deed 1622

Mrs. Grime (DDX/808). Deeds: Barton-upon-Irwell 1891–1907, Blackburn 1882, Denton 1891–94, Eccles 1882, 1900, 1913, Failsworth and Saddleworth 1836, Haughton and Hyde 1842, 1883, Hulme 1834, Manchester 1835–70, Newton (Manchester) 1878, Oldham 1868, Salford 1841–1900, Warrington 1876, West Derby 1870; Manchester marriage settlements 1849–1903

Lancaster Library (DDX/811). Deeds: Aighton 1750–1811, Aughton 1649–1841, Burscough 1592–1717, Downham 1623–1770, Parbold 1694, Rainford 1748, Reedley Hallows 1768, Walton-le-Dale 1676, 1680, Westby-with-Plumpton 1752, Woodplumpton 1630–43

Miss E. M. Everett (DDX/813). Deeds: Aighton 1611, Blackburn 1806, Darwen 1820, Kearsley 1834, Over Wyersdale 1854, Pilkington 1626–1764, Samlesbury 1789; Rimington survey 1804

J. G. Smith, Esq. (DDX/815). Deeds: Adlington 1694, Chorley 1563

Preston Cold Storage and Ice Co. Ltd. (DDX/816). Deeds of Main Sprit Weind and Glovers Court, Preston 1727–1923

Anonymous (DDX/818). Posters, etc. Oldham and district 1760–1858

Mrs. E. M. Gaskell (DDX/822). Photographs of Newton-le-Willows 1905–16

R. Wood, Esq. (DDX/826). Burnley historical press-cuttings 1897–1923

K. S. Himsworth, Esq. (DDX/831). Collector's register of insurance policies, Carnforth area c.1910

East Malling Research Station (DDX/833). Deeds: Colne 1837, Salford 1850, Skerton 1787

J. Whittaker, Esq. (DDX/834). Glover Street, Preston, deed 1850

Major P. I. C. Payne (DDX/835). Photocopies of legal opinions *re* Bindloss claim to Lower Brockholes, mid 17th c.

F. Simpson, Esq. (DDX/836) Press-cutting book for Clitheroe, Whalley and district 1890–1926

Northumberland Record Office (DDX/837). Blackpool electoral expenses 1886; agreement to support dissenting ministers 1730; Lancaster election correspondence 1780–1807; rentals of Dalton family estate in Thurnham, Ditton, Bulk and Lancaster 1739. Photocopies of Whittingham estate papers 1549–1790

Mrs. A. M. Pye (DDX/838). Deeds of Carleton smithy 1729–1810

G. R. Ablett, Esq. (DDX/839). Deeds and papers of Moor street, Ormskirk 1785–1878

G. Gates, Esq. (DDX/840). Order for quartering troops in Leyland 1649

F. S. Moxon, Esq. (DDX/842). Photocopies and notes *re* Preston Old Bank

R. H. Willis, Esq. (DDX/846). Singleton deeds 1679, 1700

K. A. MacMahon, Esq. (DDX/847). Deeds: Blackley 1729, Walton-le-Dale *c.*1290

J. G. Read, Esq. (DDX/848). Postcards: Blackpool, Liverpool, Manchester, Southport 1911–37

J. S. Hall, Esq. (DDX/849). Great Marton deed 1769

Nelson History Society (DDX/850). Brief for Preston to Blackburn new road 1824

K. W. Jones, Esq. (DDX/851). Droylsden deed 1717

Miss M. Dyke (DDX/853). Deeds: Aighton 1755, 1821, Claughton-in-Lonsdale 1679, Warton-in-Lonsdale 1690

D. J. Fisher, Esq. (DDX/854). Apprenticeship indenture: Lancaster painter and gilder 1825

Mrs. I. Jones (DDX/855). Hindley deed 1534

County Library, Ormskirk (DDX/856). Ormskirk deeds 1756, 1848

Mrs. E. Coope (DDX/859). Photographs of Blackpool Central Station 1916–18

Messrs. Collyers-Bristow (DDX/860). Cockerham manor: deeds and papers 1653–1899, plan 1792

The Manx Museum (DDX/861). Edgworth deeds 1612–92

Grundy, Kershaw, Farmer and Co. (DDX/862). Plans of Lower Greystoneley, Little Bowland 1803, 1811, 1834

R. P. Rigby, Esq. (DDX/865). Exercise-books of Jacksons of Lydiate 1838–53

Messrs. Foysters (DDX/871). Deeds and papers: Blackburn 1902, Chorlton-on-Medlock 1806–97, Pendleton (Salford) 1866, 1869, Salford 1805–1964, Stretford 1870, Urmston 1874–1928, Walmersley 1856, 1897

Miss N. Carbis (DDX/872). Letters from Valparaiso, Chile 1907; letters from Lancashire Territorials 1914–15

H. Varley, Esq. (DDX/873). Preston tramways timetable 1908; postcard of Preston railway accident 1903

Miss E. Williams (DDX/877). Deeds: Parbold, Wrightington and district c.1300–1836

N. V. Denwood, Esq. (DDX/878). Litherland Marsh deed 1835

J. Chew, Esq. (DDX/879). Handbill for fair at Blackpool 1881

Mrs. J. W. Wilson (DDX/880). Letters from the Rev. John Bowringe, Manchester, to the Rt. Hon. George Lamb re industrial unrest 1830

Leyland Historical Society (DDX/881). Survey and plans of Mawdesley family property in Eccleston, Euxton, Heskin, Leyland, Mawdesley and Ulnes Walton c.1837

E. S. Gardner, Esq. (DDX/882). Hutton Common deed 1770; atlas from Howick school 1846

J. Brandwood, Esq. (DDX/884). Plan of Penwortham Priory, late 19th c.

Miss M. A. Parkinson (DDX/893). Bills for house-building in Andee Road, Preston 1903–16

Radcliffe Library (DDX/895). Transcripts of deeds of Ainsworth and Radcliffe 1202–1761

The Society of Antiquaries (DDX/898). Deeds of Elswick, Farington and St. Michaels-on-Wyre 1655–1809

D. Maddox, Esq. (DDX/899). Deeds of the Foresters' Arms, Preston 1906

Mrs. M. Toulmin (DDX/900). Deeds: Preston family of Preston c.1300–1800, Dicconsons of Wrightington 17th to 18th c., and of Clitheroe, Rossendale, etc., with deeds and papers of Pedder, Rigby, Scarisbrick and Winckley families 1581–1800

Little and Shepherd (DDX/901). Papers of Briggs family of Garstang, apothecary surgeons 1695–1831

M. Pinhorn, Esq. (DDX/902). Plan of Allerton and Wavertree 1564

R. Hartley, Esq. (DDX/905). Deeds of Wycoller Hall, etc., Trawden 1841–1923

W. and R. Hodge and Halsall (DDX/906). Deeds: Pemberton 1697–1952, Orrell 1698–1911, Coppull and Duxbury 1755–1835, Up Holland and Dalton 1845–1912; specification for Hare and Hounds, Pemberton 1854

J. E. Mawdesley, Esq. (DDX/907). Adlington plan 1869

Tower Hamlets Library (DDX/908). Apprenticeship indenture: Manchester smith and farrier 1820

The Earl Peel (DDX/909). Newspaper cuttings *re* Lord Ashton in Lancaster 1906–11

C. D. Cleaver, Esq. (DDX/910). Penance for fornication, Newchurch-in-Rossendale 1737

Carter and Co. (DDX/912). Records of Parke family of Withnell, including deeds of Hoghton, Withnell, Wheelton, etc., 1672–1984

Mrs. E. Samuel (DDX/913). Commercial arithmetic exercise-book of William Beardman, Farington 1813

J. Furnell, Esq. (DDX/918). Birkacre mill plan 1926; Pleasington telephone exchange plan *c.*1934

Mrs. B. Whittle (DDX/919) Medlar deed 1716

W. Farrar, Esq. (DDX/920). Over Darwen agreement 1870; Gibraltar letters 1865, 1894

Nightingales, solicitors (DDX/921). Swinton deeds 1931–73

Town Clerk, Evesham (DDX/922). Deeds and plan, Poulton-le-Fylde 1899–1900; Liverpool warehouse lease 1856; will of Thomas Bourne of Liverpool 1879

Miss M. Carnson (DDX/925). Letters of the Rev. T. Carnson of Longridge 1862–70

G. Jenkinson, Esq. (DDX/927). Letter *re* Scots cattle-droving 1824

Mrs. A. Wilkinson (DDX/928). Exercise book of Annie Barnham at Carnforth National school 1899–1902

A. J. Wheeler, Esq. (DDX/931). Personal football scrapbook—Blackburn Rovers, Swindon, etc. 1947–57

Mrs. M. Carter (DDX/933). Pilling deeds 1691–1894

H. Sherdley, Esq. (DDX/934). Sale particulars of Lord Winmarleigh's estate at Winmarleigh 1912

F. Tyrer, Esq. (DDX/935). Blackburn deed 1890

Miss E. M. Albery (DDX/936). Letter *re* genealogy of Gladstone and Robertson of Liverpool 1918

Mrs. M. A. Cummings (DDX/937). Farming account and recipe book, Chipping area 1740–68

Mrs. M. W. L. Eaves (DDX/939). Reminiscences of M. W. L. Eaves *c.*1850–1918; family letters and papers, mainly of Leigh *c.*1850–1930

Mrs. M. Simm (DDX/941). Deeds: Leyland 1616–1851, Up Holland 1631, Whitworth cotton-mill 1854, 1877

Dr. R. Taylor (DDX/942). Letters *re* work of excise-collector in Liverpool, St. Helens and Ashton-in-Makerfield 1837

L. A. Webster, Esq. (DDX/943). Great Marton deeds 1596–1794

W. J. Blair, Esq. (DDX/944). Deeds: Bury, Lathom and Newburgh 1488, 1770

Marsh, Son, and Calvert (DDX/946). Particulars of sale of the Earl of Wilton's estate in Kenyon and Lowton 1918

T. Kay, Esq. (DDX/949). Plans of Fowden-Hindley properties in Stockport 1792–1823 and Blackburn area 1799–1832

Peake & Co. (DDX/953). Deeds of Lyon family property in Astley, Warrington and Latchford, co. Chester *c.*1730–1810

The College of Arms (DDX/957). Deeds: Marton and Layton Hawes 1768–77; case for counsel on election of Lancaster common councilmen *c.*1800

Edgley & Co. (DDX/958). Will of Henry Walmsley of Nelson 1893

Allen & Son (DDX/959). Deeds and papers of Green family of Leyland and Preston 1754–1872; Pedder of Preston deed 1782

Boodle, Hatfield & Co. (DDX/961). Penketh wharf deed 1695

Stilgoe & Sons (DDX/963). Papers *re* Lentworth, Over Wyresdale 1829–37

Bird & Bird (DDX/964). Deeds: Hoghton 1657, Prescot 1687, 1690, Preston 1657

J. Rawlinson, Esq. (DDX/967). Tally for Winter Hill colliery 1856

Miss M. Owens (DDX/968). Postcards: Southport, Liverpool, Manchester 1904–10

W. Wallace, Esq. (DDX/969). Notes and press-cuttings on history of aeronautics, mid 20th c.

A. Wilde, Esq. (DDX/971). Military papers of Alfred Wilde of Hurst 1906–15

Mrs. A. Bond (DDX/973). Slides and photographs of Walton Summit canal and tramroad *c.*1965

G. Forrest, Esq. (DDX/974). Sale particulars: Wrightington 1919, Mawdesley and Ulnes Walton 1946

Watterson, Moore and Co. (DDX/975). Fenton of Barrow probates 1860, 1900

Wilson and Sons (DDX/976). Arkholme deeds 1631–1831

J. P. Dodd, Esq. (DDX/980). Preston deed 1625

Mrs. F. Threlfall (DDX/981). Preston pew deeds 1791–1829; apprenticeship indenture—Preston millwrights 1853

D. Woodall, Esq. (DDX/983). Cotton-weaving test-papers 1902–33

The Rev. W. Porteus (DDX/985). Notes on Charnock family; deeds of Standish, Gillibrand and Fazakerley families 18th to 20th c.; Chorley plans 1734, 1769; Astley Hall estate plan 1822

G. Langton, Esq. (DDX/986). Plan of Gillibrand family lands in Adlington, Blackrod, Chorley, Duxbury and Euxton 1769

D. E. Sharples, Esq. (DDX/989). List of dead in Maypole colliery disaster, Abram 1908

Lee, Bolton and Lee (DDX/990). Hale deed 1658

H. R. Beakbane, Esq. (DDX/992). Caton and Quernmore deed 1607; wills: Richard Sidgewick of Tatham 1735, Henry Beakbane of Liverpool 1836, Ellen Parkinson of Scotforth 1853, Isaac Bradshaw of Lancaster 1876

M. Silvester, Esq. (DDX/994). Silvester deeds: Chorley 1729–1894, Whittle-le-Woods 1732–1905, Worthington 1690–1736, Adlington 1710–1802, Euxton 1789–1871, Blackrod 1748–1901, Leyland 1808–09, Charnock Richard 1772, Manchester 1869–1955; coal leases, etc., in Blackrod 1874–1910, Chorley 1891–1928, Charnock Richard 1909–22

J. Yates, Esq. (DDX/995). Lower Darwen deeds 1603–1826

Mrs. L. Davies (DDX/997). Great Crosby deeds 1840–80

Hertfordshire Record Office (DDX/1001). Agreement and plan of Grange on Ellel 1779, estate correspondence 1830–39

N. J. Tudor-Thomas, Esq. (DDX/1003). Deeds of White Carr, Ribchester 1765–1861

G. Wightman, Esq. (DDX/1004). Blackburn, etc., deeds 18th to 20th c.

Miss Mason (DDX/1006). Quernmore enclosure correspondence 1814–19, 1848

Pearman, Smith and Co. (DDX/1007). Out Rawcliffe deeds 19th c. and manor court books 1845–56

C. A. Spencer, Esq. (DDX/1008). Penwortham Hall deeds 1744–1829

T. S. H. Wordsworth, Esq. (DDX/1010). Film of Lancaster canal 1959–63

Newcastle-upon-Tyne Library (DDX/1016). Torver deed 1794

Rev. J. G. Sutcliffe (DDX/1017). Habergham Eaves deeds 1803–1918; notebook containing letters of Thomas Bowker of Lancaster from Bechuanaland c.1882

F. Beaver, Esq. (DDX/1019). Apprenticeship indenture: Fleetwood plumber and painter 1875

P. Harrison, Esq. (DDX/1020). West Bradford Cart Bridge committee report 1888–91

Miss M. H. Dobson (DDX/1021). Deeds and papers: Cartmel, Colton, Dalton-in-Furness, Kirkby Ireleth. Lancaster and Warton-in-Lonsdale 1592–1807

N. Lees, Esq. (DDX/1022). Thornton-le-Fylde deeds 1730–1920

Lawrence, Graham and Co. (DDX/1024). Deeds: Colne 1545–1884, Fishwick 1771–87, Goosnargh 1779–1877, Preston 1731–1914, Barnton, Ches. 1837–1910, Morton, Yorks. 1798–1903, Riddlesden, Yorks. 1737–1854

G. H. Riley, Esq. (DDX/1025). Carnforth deed 1857

W. Banks and Co. (DDX/1026). Deeds: Blackpool 1690–1830, Preston 1715–1920

A. D. Smith, Esq. (DDX/1028). Deeds and papers: Clayton-le-Moors, Huncoat, Mearley, Rishton, and Stansfield, co. York. 1407–1823

Ticehurst, Wyatt and Co. (DDX/1030). Deeds: Castleton, Dalton-in-Furness, Huyton, Rochdale 1820–74

Miss J. O. Kennedy (DDX/1032). Deed of Whalley, Colne and Marsden 1850

Hughes, Minton and Barker (DDX/1035). Deed of Bulk and Thurnham 1899

J. Pery, Esq. (DDX/1038). Lathom deed 1640

Sir John Ainsworth (DDX/1039). Grant of baronetcy 1917

Gwynedd Record Office (DDX/1040). Poster re building land in Southport 1887

J. E. Starkie, Esq. (DDX/1044). Plans of Shelley Arms hotel, Preston 1891–1900.

C. Green, Esq. (DDX/1056). Wilson of Eshton Hall estate-deeds and papers 18th and 19th c.

Dr. A. Bird (DDX/1057). Diary of Miss M. A. Hackey, J.P., Litherland 1932

Castle Museum, York (DDX/1058). Ulnes Walton deed 1647

St. Helens Library (DDX/1059). Service exemption certificates 1916

Mrs. E. Humphreys (DDX/1060). Army papers of James Gradwell, Leigh 1919–20

Mrs. V. Cheston (DDX/1061). Diaries of Joseph Francis Tempest of Broughton-in-Craven 1831–40

W. E. Mayer, Esq. (DDX/1063). Agents' account book of Anderton family estate in Chorley, Duxbury, Coppull, Orrell and Up Holland 1869–1930; rentals of Cunliffe and Grundy family estates in Anglezarke, Chorley, Euxton, Leyland, Shevington, Tockholes and Wheelton 1838–97; Silvester family estate rentals, etc., of Blackrod, Charnock Richard, Chorley, Euxton and Whittle-le-Woods 1875–1946 (see also DDX/994); sale particulars: Accrington, Adlington, Anderton, Anglezarke, Ashton-with-Stodday, Bamber Bridge, Barton-in-Amounderness, Bispham (Blackpool), Blackpool, Bold, Bolton, Brindle, Broughton-in-Amounderness, Burtonwood, Chorley, Clayton-le-Woods, Coppull, Cottam, Croston, Dalton, Duxbury, Eccleston (Chorley), Eccleston (Prescot), Ellel, Euxton, Farington, Fulwood, Heapey, Heath Charnock, Hesketh, Heskin, Hoghton, Huncoat, Huyton, Inglewhite, Knowsley, Lea, Leyland, Marton, Mawdesley, Orrell, Parbold, Penwortham, Preston, Rainhill, Rivington, Rufford, Shevington, Skelmersdale, Standish, Sutton, Tarleton, Torrisholme, Turton, Ulnes Walton, Up Holland, Warrington, Walton-le-Dale, Wheelton, Welch Whittle, Whittle-le-Woods, Whittingham, Whiston, Widnes, Wigan, Woodplumpton, Worthington, Wrea

Kennedy and Glover (DDX/1064). Deeds: Lathom 1684–1767, Ormskirk 1636–1794

Mrs. P. Couch (DDX/1072). Papers, pedigrees, etc., re executorship of Robert Hamilton of Manchester, merchant 1783–1933

Mrs. Rigby (DDX/1075). Deeds of Grundy family property in Bury 1765–1894

Mrs. E. Sherwin (DDX/1076). Papers of Inspector Eades of Lancashire and Leicestershire police, early 20th c. to 1976

D. Carberry, Esq. (DDX/1080). Letters and papers of Mrs. Henrietta Miller of Preston and Lytham 1874–85

Anonymous (DDX/1082). Deeds: Accrington 1771–1885, Blackburn 1722–1844, Eccleshill 1729, Salesbury 1814–45

Peachey Property Co. (DDX/1083). Darwen deeds 1823–1963

Ward, Dewhurst, Waddingham and Gartside (DDX/1084 and 1085). Anderton family of Haighton deeds and papers 17th to 19th c.; Goosnargh deeds 1695, 1714

K. Stopford, Esq. (DDX/1086). Exercise books, St. Thomas' school, Preston 1933–36

R. T. Gibbon, Esq. (DDX/1087). Accrington Academy exercise books 1870–71; prospectus of the Elms School, Ainsdale c.1885

Miss B. Green (DDX/1092). Photographs, letters and papers of Green family of Oldham and Salford 18th to 20th c.

Miss K. Cartmell (DDX/1096). Garstang estate accounts 1855–95

Burnley Library (DDX/1101). Sale particulars: Bamber Bridge, Barton-in-Amounderness, Blackburn, Blackpool, Briercliffe, Burnley, Colne, Foulridge, Fulwood, Goosnargh, Habergham Eaves, Hapton, Longridge, Preston, Ribbleton, Todmorden, Ulverston, Whalley, Wiswell 1902–42

D. Tatton, Esq. (DDX/1111). Papers re Parker, Chorley and Crosse families 1480–1853

Miss D. Hodgson (DDX/1113). Historical notes and reminiscences of St. Michaels-on-Wyre c.1975

J. B. Firth, Esq. (DDX/1114). Sale particulars: Bradshaw, Edgworth and Turton 1919

Miss M. Cooper (DDX/1137). Suffragette and women's rights papers of Mrs. Selina Jane Cooper of Nelson 1897–1968

The Rev. E. Swinneston (DDX/1152). Stalmine deeds 1634–1728

Wigan Record Office (DDX/1156). Plans re St. James Street, Burnley 1891–93

J. W. Barber-Lomax, Esq. (DDX/1165). Apprenticeship of William Ormerod of Billington, Whalley tailor 1773

Sturton and Co. (DDAi). Over Kellet: Hall Garth estate deeds 1673–1929, survey 1843, enclosure correspondence 1859–60

Witham, Weld and Co. (DDAn). Correspondence and historical memoranda of Henry Ince Anderton c.1890–1920

R. Walch, Esq. (DDAs). Ashworth of Birkenshaw in Turton family papers c.1800–50; Dobson of Gilnough in Bolton family papers 19th c.

J. Cook, Esq. (DDC). Deeds: Heysham 1627, 1661, Warton-in-Lonsdale 1597–1800, Yealand Redmayne 1748; inventory of Thomas Wilson of Silverdale 1709; apprenticeship indenture of

Thomas Moss to Preston gardener; admission of John Cook, pavior, to freedom of London 1771 with badge; large scale plans of parts of the Houses of Parliament 1842–45

Mrs. L. Drinnan (DDDr). Westleigh deeds 1617–1949

W. Diggle, Esq. (DDX3). Salford Hundred subsidy rolls 1663; early 14th c. roll of 1235–97 statutes

Sir Matthew Fell (DDFe). Correspondence: Barrow-in-Furness elections 1885–92, Liberal registration in North Lancashire 1869–75, Westmorland and Lancashire boundary 1889–1907, Grange-over-Sands foreshore 1897, licensing reform 1879–1905, Penwortham bridge 1885, North-West Lancashire Liberal candidate 1879, highways 1890–95, North Lancashire election 1868–69, appointment of magistrates 1871–1910, chairman of quarter sessions 1866–1907, Lancaster castle and assizes 1890–1909, local politics 1886–93, Lancashire county council 1882–90. Grant of office of "Keeper Conductor and Governor" of Kent Sands 1867

Taylor, Kirkham and Mainprice (DDHm). Astley manor court rolls 1564, 1569, 1571, 1572, 1608, 1623, 1654, 1744–46; Astley, Bedford and Tyldesley deeds 1385, 1522–1891

Mrs. B. E. Griffiths (DDHr). Gramophone records of John Harrison of Foulridge, operatic baritone d. 1929

King's College, Cambridge (DDKc). Prescot manor court rolls, papers and township records c.1600–1810

The Goldsmiths' Company (DDKy). Heysham quarry papers 1889; Knowlys family correspondence re Heysham estate 1859–71

The National Trust (DDN, see also p. 221). Wray Castle estate deeds 1679–1925. Deeds: Coniston 1671–1930, Hawkshead 1743–1936, Kirkby Ireleth 1895–1935, Sawrey 1777–1943, Seathwaite 1737–1895, Skelwith 1800–1935, Tilberthwaite 1729–1934

Procter, Birkbeck and Batty (DDPc). North Lancashire sale particulars 1827–1950; surveys: Claughton-in-Amounderness 1851, Halton 1799, Heaton 1857, Heysham 1744, Lancaster to Heiring Syke road 1807, Myerscough 1857, Singleton 1841; book of Lancaster canal specifications and estimates

The Misses Pilkington (DDPi). Deeds: Allerton 1663–1789, Halliwell 1778, Horwich 1617–1811, Turton 1692, 1694. Accounts: Doffcocker turnpike 1779–1819, Horwich New chapel 1817–24; various correspondence 1760–1839; diaries of Richard Pilkington of Horwich 1784–97, 1806–08, 1817–19; arithmetic exercise book of James Pilkington 1789; partnership agreement: Walmsley and Pilkington, whitesters 1793; inventory of Thomas

Preston of Horwich 1795; resolutions at Bolton on truck system 1818; management scheme for Scholes Sunday School, Wigan 1826

R. Cunliffe Shaw, Esq. (DDS). Deeds: Thornton-le-Fylde 1629–1798, Treales 1778–1822, Wharles 1838, Woodplumpton 1714–1816; family papers, certificates, etc. 1830–99; grant of arms 1936; leases: Bretherton 1668, Burscough 1747, Bury 1772, Carleton 1888, Clifton-with-Salwick 1911, Freckleton 1892, Halewood 1712, Kirkham 1843, 1894, Rainford 1721, Roseacre 1825, Roby 1794, Salford 1808, Shuttleworth 1725, Sowerby 1726, Treales 1772, 1809, 1834, Wharles 1801, 1857; rentals and surveys: Catforth, Thornton, Treales c.1800, Thornton 1867–69; Freckleton Moss agreement 1746; Treales farm inventory 1836; Kirkham subscribers' lists for Patriotic Fund 1854–55 and Jubilee 1887; petition of Earl of Derby re Isle of Man 1685; journal of Cecilia Shaw 1869; Kirkham manor court-roll 1588; Woodplumpton 1714–1816; letter from earl of Derby requiring George Kellet to be parish-clerk of Kirkham 1578; apprenticeship indenture, Edward Sharples to Preston tailor 1749; Newton, Freckleton and Clifton Marsh papers 1673–1890, minute book 1833–60; memorandum on Kirkham common 1604; memoranda book of Adam Wright of Kirkham, merchant-banker and H.M. Consul at Malta 1838–51

W. M. Spencer, Esq. (DDSp). Papers of Coldweather family of Colne 18th to 19th c.; deeds of Greenfield, Colne 18th to 19th c.; diary of Abraham Hargreaves of Colne 1784; Marsden survey 1777; papers of Leeming family of Colne 1798–1829

Sir Thomas Tomlinson (DDT). Deeds: Ashton-on-Ribble 1748–1869, Bolton-le-Sands 1631–1904, Carnforth 1719, Preston 1871

"ANCIENT DEEDS" (DX)

This class consists of some 2,000 documents which were found among the county records, probably come there owing to the fact that in the nineteenth century the deputy clerks of the peace were so frequently solicitors in private practice.

Consisting chiefly of conveyances, wills, mortgages, fines and recoveries, etc., they may be described briefly as follows:—

The Barton (Preston) Estate 1704–1855. Principally leases, but included are diaries of Roger Jacson, senior, 1829–37, and Roger Jacson, junior, 1847–55; rentals 1772, 1815; surveys 1830–33; pedigree papers 1779; railway papers 1836–42

The~Culcheth of Culcheth and Dicconson of Wrightington Estates 1522–1813, relating chiefly to Culcheth, Hindley, Manchester and Wrightington; Mrs. Mary Culcheth's accounts 1715–42; Culcheth estate accounts 1741, 1744–49; payments to Culcheth priest 1730–59; Culcheth and Hindley rental 1748; Wrightington estate accounts 1722–24 and 1731; 32 deeds of Dicconson properties in Ranby, Sturton, Sotby, Boothby, and Laughton, co. Lincoln 1611–81.

The Flitcroft and Litchford families of Manchester 1651–1766, relating to properties in Forton, Spotland, Hundersfield, Blackley, Tottington, Cheetham and Rossendale.

The Preese Hall estate in Weeton-with-Preese, 1564–1727

The Ribbleton Hall estate deeds 1552–1888; plan c.1750; inquisitions *post mortem* John Ridley 1600, Richard Ridley 1607

The Standish Family of Duxbury 1623–1845. These papers, principally relating to the succession of the estate, include accounts of Thomas Standish 1742–44, papers relating to Standish coal mine 1796–98, Hapton coal-mine 1794–1804, Anglezarke lead mines 1822–43, Whittle waste 1830–34, Culcheth tithes and Peasfurlong and Holcroft mosses 1831–38, and claims of Madame Scelerier of Perigueux on the estate 1833–57

The Tyldesley family of Myerscough and Astley 1719–60

Miscellaneous documents (mainly deeds) relating to Abram 1776, Aighton, Bailey and Chaigley 1663–1828, Ardwick 1639–1746, Ashton-in-Makerfield 1730–1827, Ashton-under-Lyne 1688–1700, Astley 1761–1815, Atherton 1720–83, Aughton 1722, Balderstone 1813, Barton-upon-Irwell 1658–1731, Bedford 1598–1789, Bispham-with-Norbreck 1772, Blackley 1621–54, Blackrod 1676–1868, Bolton-le-Moors 1669–1803, Breightmet 1754, Bretherton 1815–29, Brindle 1638–1783, Broughton-in-Amounderness 1837–40, Bryning-with-Kellamergh 1656, Cartmel Fell 1638–1702, Charnock Richard 1655, Clitheroe 1854, Clitheroe grammar school 1554–1683, Crompton 1844–59, Cronton 1659–1760, Croston 1741–1825, Crumpsall 1768–98, Culcheth 1639–1787, Over Darwen 1693, Droylsden 1614–1719, Dutton 1765–68, Duxbury 1671–1779, Eccleston, Chorley 1637–1815, Edgworth 1668, Ellel 1832–39, Euxton 1753, Everton 1714–1831, Farnworth 1736, Goosnargh 1699–1838, Gorton 1669–1724, Haigh 1848, Heap 1641–76, Heapey 1607, Heath Charnock 1626–87, Heysham 1684–1769, Hindley 1686–1798, Hoghton 1754–1831, Much Hoole 1687–1838, Little Hulton 1784, Hundersfield 1703, Huyton 1719, Irlam 1750–64, Kirkby 1714, Kirkham 1638–1729, Lancaster: property on Castle Hill 1729–1865; Leyland 1812–32, Liverpool 1695–1800, Livesey

1691, Longton 1726–1852, Longworth 1829–30, Lostock 1773–89, Lowton 1722–85, Manchester 1485–1850 including 34 letters and accounts relating to the Manchester, Bolton and Bury canal 1793–99, Mawdesley 1811, Medlar-with-Wesham 1658–1854, Middleton (Salford) 1814, Myerscough 1717–1840 including 11 letters and papers concerning tithe 1797–1840, Newton-with-Scales 1730–43, Oldham 1831–38, Parbold 1788, Parr 1727, Pendleton, Eccles 1767, Pennington, Leigh 1635–1809 including action against "improper" master of Leigh grammar school 1747, Pilling 1807, Preston 1629–1883, Prestwich 1721–25, Quernmore 1629–1842, Ribby-with-Wrea 1823–72, Rixton-with-Glazebrook 1738, Rochdale 1598, Salesbury manor 1704–60, Salford 1758, Samlesbury 1666–76, Sharples Hall 1812–33, Skelmersdale 1750–51, Standish tithes 1827–28, Stretford (flooding by canal) 1808–29, Tatham 1840, Thornton-le-Fylde 1710–1803, Tonge-with-Haulgh 1602–1719, Trafford 1804, Tyldesley-with-Shakerley 1787, Ulnes Walton 1743–1820, Up Holland 1767–1850, Walton-le-Dale 1806–43, Warrington 1764–66, Westhoughton 1674–1848, Westleigh 1766–83, Wheelton 1831–68, Whiston 1750, Whittingham, 1677–1838, Whittington 1673–1763, Wigan 1706–91 Withington 1708, Withnell 1831, Witton 1705, Woodplumpton 1740–61, Little Woolton 1807, Worsley 1693–1744, Worston 1563, Wrightington 1731–46

Volume of Acts, plans, pamphlets, broadsheets, etc., concerning Douglas Navigation and Leeds and Liverpool canal 1720–1827; letters of Richard Watson, bishop of Llandaff, 1812, 1813; scheme for division of Lancashire into ridings 1855; case concerning Ellenbrook chapel 1693; rental of Trafford estate 1790

ARTIFICIAL COLLECTIONS

The Lancashire Evening Post (DDPr)

Deeds: Accrington 1733, 1760, Altcar 1604, Bretherton 1603–1783, Brindle 1732–94, Bryning-with-Kellamergh 1691–1807, Burscough 1767, Carleton 1663–1772, Catterall 1725, 1773, Chorley 1816, Claughton and Chipping 1751, Clayton-le-Woods 1817, 1820, Clifton-with-Salwick 1777–1816, Colne 1686, Croston 1695–1819, Cuerden 1767, Dilworth 1782, Ellel 1788, Elston 1713–77, Elswick 1667–1821, Freckleton 1796–1815, Fulwood 1760, 1783, Garstang 1714, Garston 1700, Goosnargh 1659–1818, Greenhalgh-with-Thistleton 1724–1813, Habergham Eaves 1794, Haigh 1809, Hardhorn-with-Newton 1694–1815, Haslingden 1782, Heath Charnock 1816, Heskin 1815, Hoghton 1814, Horwich 1809–19, Hothersall 1788–1800, Hulton 1701, Ince-in-Makerfield 1820, Inskip-with-Sowerby 1725, Kirkby 1749,

Kirkdale 1774, Kirkham 1763–1823, Layton-with-Warbreck 1605–1876, Lea 1791–1812, Leyland 1671–1817, Little Eccleston-with-Larbreck 1786–1820, Liverpool 1656–1763, Livesey 1766, Lydiate and Maghull 1591–1702, Lytham 1789–1868, Marsden 1777, Marton 1681–1804, Myerscough 1758, Nateby 1621–1812, Newton-with-Scales 1767–1823, Pleasington 1769, Poulton-le-Fylde 1574–1796, Preston 1570–1879, Ribby-with-Wrea 1772–1819, Singleton 1746, 1815, Stalmine-with-Stainall 1741, 1799, Sutton 1693–1757, Tarleton 1762, 1772, Thornley 1696–1718, Tockholes 1692, Tottington 1775–76, Treales, Wharles and Roseacre 1746–1814, Upper Rawcliffe 1760, Walton-le-Dale 1736–1813, Warton (Kirkham) 1664–70, Weeton 1789–1814, Wesham 1777–1816, Westby-with-Plumpton 1764–1816, Wheelton 1759, 1822, Whittingham 1658–1828, Whittle-le-Woods 1785, Widnes 1730–1807, Withnell 1752–1811, Woodplumpton 1717–1835, Wrightington 1816, 1826

Apprenticeship indentures: Poulton-le-Fylde 1718–1818, Kirkham 1804, Preston 1736–1878, various 1732–1821; Preston register of apprentices 1682–1744

Appointments: Thomas Seed, clerk, cursitor, and attorney of palatinate chancery 1709; William Lucas, chief clerk and registrar of palatinate chancery 1756; Humphrey Stevens, clerk of the peace 1771; John Charles Villiers, prothonotary of palatinate common pleas 1775; William Shawe, palatinate seal-keeper 1783; Edward Falkner, sheriff 1788; Robert William Hopkins, clerk of the crown 1831

Maps and plans: battle of Preston 1715, Preston 1809, Preston Moor Park 1835, Fulwood Park c.1840, Preston Guild Hall 1845, River Ribble from Red Scar to Clifton 1756

Correspondence: coastal trade 1801, Kirkham prisoner-of-war in Arras 1807, cost of billeting troops in Preston 1843

Preston elections: various papers 1661–1868; Preston militia: various papers 1790–1860; assignments of Lancaster gaol 1779–91; Lancaster assize sermons 1749–1805; Lancaster election papers 1784–1868; papers of James Baines of Poulton-le-Fylde 1700–17; papers of William Atherton of Jamaica and Prescot 1771–1803, and Elizabeth his wife 1801–30; race-bills: Lancaster 1811–27, Liverpool 1828–35, Manchester 1820–25, Newton-le-Willows 1831, Preston 1794–1842; railway miscellanea 1834–1905; rules of societies in Accrington 1813, Blackburn 1823–88, Bolton 1821–43, Chipping 1817, Hothersall 1841, Lancaster 1838, Liverpool 1843–46, Manchester 1816–63, Preston 1806–61 Rawtenstall 1835, St. Helens 1794, Samlesbury 1839, Shaw 1829, Winmarleigh 1839

Papers in Oliver *v.* Corporation of Preston (arrears of headmaster's salary) 1767–68; certificates of admission to Preston company of smiths and company of mercers, grocers, and haberdashers 1762–82; account-book of Roger Hesketh of Tulketh 1756–89; Preston contributions for defence of the realm 1798; Preston freight-rates 1809–10; report on establishment of Preston National school 1815; minute-book of Preston committee for soup distribution 1847–66; papers on Preston lock-out 1854; Preston Guild papers 1802–82

Patents for spinning machinery 1846–52; petition for bridge at Mitton ford *c.*1720; sale catalogue of Catterall print-works 1831; Clitheroe election papers 1832, 1841; survey of Blakey Hall, Colne 1779; agreements for Arkwright's mill at Birkacre in Coppull 1777, 1780; case concerning Hoole schoolmaster *c.*1790; case concerning flooding of Martin mere, 1787; sequestration papers of Sir Edward Wrightington of Wrightington 1646–47

The R. Evans Mills Memorial Deeds (DDE)

Deeds: Barley 1869; Barnacre-with-Bonds 1811, 1853; Barrow-in-Furness 1863; Catterall 1811; Chatburn (watermill) 1797–1833; Chipping 1723–68; Colne 1815–48; Elswick 1721–1854; Forton 1749–1832; Hardhorn-with-Newton 1737; Lancaster 1784–1826; Leck 1671; Myerscough (Badsberry school) 1732–1812; Pilling 1691–1862; St. Michaels-on-Wyre 1821–34; Tatham 1709–1862; Worston 1629–33; Tunstall 1777; Up Holland 1736–97; Wray-with-Botton 1856; grant of Singleton Grange 1543

Ecclesiastical: agreement for nomination of minister of Pilling 1833

Preston Library and Art Gallery Collection (DDP)

Deeds: Accrington 1803; Anglezarke 1691; Balderstone 1671; Bispham-with-Norbreck 1755–84; Blackburn 1746; Blackrod 1722; Broughton East 1601; Burnley 1864; Carleton 1717; Chorley 1579–1683; Over Darwen 1594–1659; Great Eccleston 1637; Little Eccleston 1615; Goosnargh 1662–1804; Hambleton 1677–1780; Heapey, Heath Charnock and Chorley 1574–1705; Lancaster 1705–1808; Layton-with-Warbreck 1652, 1755; Oswaldtwistle 1694; Penwortham 1660; Preston 1657–1736; Rawcliffe 1646–1710; Ribchester 1583, 1765; Slyne-with-Hest 1800; Staveley 1695–97; Tockholes 1592; Welch Whittle 1806, 1813; Whittingham 1749–1809; Preston and Witton 1583–1739; Hindley, Wigan, Myerscough, Chorley, Blackburn, Preston, Samlesbury, Walton-le-Dale, Holcomb and Ribchester 17th to 19th c.

Plan of River Crake *c*.1760; appointments of Roger Barton 1783 and Miles Barton 1812 to Hoole rectory; lease of Ribble fisheries 1745; apprentice indentures, Thomas Gornall to Over Wyresdale feltmaker 1787 and to Kirkham feltmaker 1798; letters patent for George Marton to deliver records to Sir Robert Gerard, sheriff 1859; queries concerning Gunnolfsmore commons *c*.1580; statements on Singleton Grange freedom from tithe *c*.1750; Walton-on-the-Hill enclosure agreement and plan 1771; Preston prosecution of felons deed 1809; Hoghton manor call book 1790; County rate book 1767; deed of Blackbarrow cotton-mill 1801; deeds of John Watson's cotton business, Preston 1784–1806; miscellanea 17th to 20th c.

Rochdale Library Collection (DDRo)

Deeds: Ainsworth 1692–1750; Bamford 1665–1916; Blackley 1610–82; Broughton (Salford) 1732, 1768; Church 1617; Crompton 1767–1807; Elswick 1629; Elton 1771; Entwistle 1696–1707; Haslingden 1588–1820; Larbreck mill 1611; Lytham 1822; Manchester 1658; Middleton 1661; Oldham 1684–1762; Oswaldtwistle 1549–1736; Pennington 1291–1811; Rochdale 1611–1861; Saddleworth, co. York 1670; Salford 1701; Singleton 1777, 1786; Spotland 1650–1858; Tottington 1700, 1770; Wardleworth 1820, 1829

Family papers: Lodge of Windybank 1588–1819; Townley of Belfield 1653–1932; Clayton of Schofield 1598–1790

Ecclesiastical papers: Whitworth chapel and school 1532–1730; Rochdale church 1764–1819

Charity papers: Gartsides 1791–1874; Hills (Milnrow) 1858–79; Butterworth school 1726–1915

Miscellaneous papers: Rochdale cloth-hall 1792–1814; Tonge and Middleton highways 1733–75; inquisition *post mortem* Lambert Tyldesley 1597

The Sir Cuthbert Grundy Papers (DDX/207). (These are partly family.)

Letters and papers of Dr. George Benson, nonconformist minister, 1721–61; letters concerning the North Lancashire and Westmorland Unitarian Association 1899–1901; Grundy pedigrees and genealogical papers; journal of tour in the Netherlands 1863; meteorological findings at South Shore, Blackpool, 1855–91; letter concerning trading from New York 1782; genealogy of Strickland of Hartbarrow in Cartmel Fell; diary of Cuthbert Grundy, with autobiographical notes, 1854–57

The Henry Ogle Collection (DDX/208)

Scale drawings (many coloured) of glass, floor-tiles, churches, datestones, etc., at Ribchester, Preston, Rufford, Eccleston, Samlesbury, Penwortham, Leyland, St. Michaels-on-Wyre, Whalley, Stidd, Walton-le-Dale, Fulwood, Pickup Bank, Ribbleton, Furness abbey, Darwen, Billington, Brindle, Broughton (Preston), Chipping, Garstang, Croston, Chorley, Goosnargh, Balderstone, Longridge, Mawdesley, Osbaldeston, Hothersall, Howick, Grimsargh, Thornley and Heskin

The British Records Association (DDX/75). (Many other collections have been deposited through the good offices of the British Records Association)

Manorial: Broughton-in-Furness court-book 1819

Deeds: Arkholme 1613; Ashton-in-Makerfield 1841; Ashton-under-Lyne 1833–65; Barrow-in-Furness 1893–1903; Barton (Preston) 1729; Blackley 1832; Broughton-in-Furness 1817; Caton 1721; Chipping 1760; Cockerham 1880; Conishead 1847–93; Crompton 1766; Downholland 1824; Duxbury 1566; Egton-with-Newland 1875, 1880; Goosnargh 1770–1860; Great Crosby 1869; Halsall 1840; Hopwood 1563–69; Lathom 1838; Leigh 1723; Manchester 1473–1720, 1811; Ormskirk 1850; Pennington 1700–07; Prescot 1816; Rochdale 1807, 1819; Rusholme 1835–53; Samlesbury 1817–31; Tarbock 1858, 1866; Toxteth Park 1808, 1815; Warrington 1861; Wigan 1502; Yealand 1711–1823

Miscellaneous: commission of James Barnes as captain 1810; correspondence of members of the Barnes family of Farnworth 1832–93; journal of tour in Ireland by Alfred Barnes 1850; dispensation for marriage of Robert Waddington and Alice Orrell 1493

The Hornby Presbytery Collection (RCHy)

This collection is, properly, of two origins, *viz.*, the papers of Thomas Benison of Lancaster and Hornby, attorney (who was a trustee of the charitable will of William Penny of Lancaster) and his daughter Ann Fenwick; and a collection of early material (much of it monastic) made by Father Thomas West, the historian of Furness, with some of his own manuscripts. The correspondence of John Lingard remains at Hornby.

Benison section:

Deeds: Arkholme 1691, Bolton-le-Sands 1598–1720, Botton 1719, Broughton (Preston) 1598–1665, Bulk 1677–1730, Claughton-in-Lonsdale 1613–22, Ellel 1652–81, Haighton 1636–38, Lancaster 1553–1754, Mansriggs 1702, Nether Kellet 1718,

Poulton-le-Sands 1722, Quernmore 1693, Scotforth 1681–1703, Skerton 1698, Standish 1572, Tatham 1684, Torrisholme 1716, Widnes 1719

Other counties: Flintshire: Axton 1771, Prestatyn 1747; Westmorland: Burton-in-Kendal 1578; Yorkshire: Austwick 1637, East Dalton 1603–53, Eshton 1685, Giggleswick 1610, Mewith 1727, Rathmell 1598–1674

Accounts: Executors of William Penny of Lancaster 1716–38; Thomas Benison 1730–35; voyage of the *True Love* 1737–39; various accounts 17th and 18th century

Plans: Whittington *c.*1760; Thornton-in-Lonsdale *c.*1760; sieges of Mayence and Valenciennes 1793

Miscellaneous: Inventories: Alan Penny of Lancaster 1625, William Penny of Lancaster 1716; presentation of William Senhouse to Claughton-in-Lonsdale 1524; Burton-in-Lonsdale, co. York, rentals 1714–19; court-book of Hundred of Lonsdale 1704–06; correspondence of Thomas Benison and his daughter Ann Fenwick 18th century

West section:

Deeds: Aldingham 1284; Brockholes 1309; Catterall 1368; Chadderton (Prestwich church) *c.*1230; Coniston 1418; Lindale-in-Cartmel (St. John) 1191; Shevington *c.*1250–70; Stalmine 1367; Warton-in-Lonsdale 1345. 1423; Much Woolton 1334

Other counties: Buckinghamshire, Hardmead *c.*1300; Cumberland, Beckermet *c.*1250, Highhead castle 1412; Gloucestershire, Hucclecote 1317; Hampshire, Portsea 1268; Lincolnshire, Horwell (Nostell priory) 1538; London 1312, 1317; Nottinghamshire, Ossington (St. John) 1189; Oxfordshire, Bradwell (St. John) 1500; Yorkshire, Boroughbridge 1323, Burnsall *c.*1160, Cleveland (Guisborough priory) 1282, Dent 1290, Gipton (Kirkstall abbey) *c.*1260, Hinderwell (St. John) *c.*1200, Middlethorpe 1318, 1441, Newby (Ripon hospital) *c.*1250, 1298, Normanton 1524, Skipton 1338 Tadcaster *c.*1250, Thornton (North Riding) chantry (Newburgh priory) *c.*1280, York 1316, 1381, 1434

Bruern abbey, Oxfordshire, deeds: Broadmoor and Denchworth, Berkshire; Colesborne and Eastleach, Gloucestershire; Bunthorpe, Middleton and West Skipton, Yorkshire; *c.*1260–1361

Cockersand abbey documents: Longworth, Preesall; Newbiggin, Kirkby Lonsdale, and Sedgwick, Westmorland *c.*1195–1260. Agreements for masses for Ralph and Ingrid Bethum *c*.1220 and Henry le Waleys, rector of Wigan 1327. Rentals 1451, 1539

Watton priory, Yorkshire, deeds: Kilnwick *c*.1165–1385

Miscellaneous: Licence-in-mortmain for chantry at Tickhill, co. York 1281; confirmation by Henry I of grant to Guisborough priory *c*.1130; annulment of marriage of Constance Anderton and Gilbert Charnock 1461; agreement concerning pasture in Taddington, co. Gloucester 1196; mandate for care of Standish church during infirmity of rector 1516; licence for Leicester abbey to farm out churches and chapels 1399; admission to guild of B.V.M. at Boston, co. Lincoln 1500; confirmation to abbey of Aumale of churches in co. Lincoln 1156; pardon for crimes in Salcay forest, co. Northampton 1294; composition between Meaux abbey and Bridlington priory concerning tithes, etc., of Ottringham, co. York 1294; appointment by bishop of Carlisle of Alexander Neville as receiver-general of Leeds, etc., co. York 1431; letters of confraternity: St. Robert of Knaresborough 1422, 1453, 1483, Coverham abbey 1504

Father West's manuscripts: abstracts of deeds of Strickland of Sizergh 1785; drafts and collections for *Antiquities of Furness* and *Guide to the Lakes*

DOCUMENTS PURCHASED (DP)

1–169. Deeds, etc.: Ardwick 1727, 1746; Ashton-under-Lyne 1729; Barton-upon-Irwell 1658; Bispham-with-Norbreck 1772; Blackrod 1676; Brindle 1683–1738; Cartmel Fell 1638–1703; Charnock Richard 1655; Crumpsall 1768, 1798; Culcheth 1666, 1749; Over Darwen 1693; Duxbury 1672; Edgworth 1668; Euxton 1753; Goosnargh 1699, 1716; Heapey 1608; Heath Charnock 1626, 1687; Heysham 1684, 1769; Hoole 1687; Hundersfield 1704; Huyton 1720, Kirkby 1715; Liverpool 1695–1772; Livesey 1692; Lonsdale cattle-plague-watch assessment 1747; Manchester 1630–1786; Medlar-with-Wesham 1693–1753; Parr 1727; Prestwich 1721–25; Lordship of Salesbury (Clayton-le-Dale, Dinckley, Ribchester, Salesbury and Wilpshire) leases 1704–60; Skelmersdale 1751; Thornton-le-Fylde 1710, 1733; Tonge-with-Haulgh 1603, 1719; Ulnes Walton 1743; Up Holland 1767; Westhoughton 1828; Whiston 1750; Whittington 1674–1763; Withington 1708; Witton 1706; Woodplumpton 1741–61; Little Woolton 1807; Rochdale: valor of lands of Charles Holte of Stubley, esq. 1598

170. Rental of Burtonwood and Great Sankey late 16th c.

171. Ordinance of Parliament for William Ashhurst, esq. to be clerk of the Crown in Lancashire 1648

172. "Articles to bee given in Charge at the Sessions of the Peace" *c.*1610

173. Map of Liverpool late 19th c.

174. Settlement of manor and rectory of Middleton 1814

176–178. Little Bolton manor court-books 1698–1738

189. Buck's views of Cartmel priory, Clitheroe castle, Cockersand abbey, Furness abbey, Gleaston castle, Up Holland priory, Hornby castle, Lancaster, Lancaster castle, Liverpool, Manchester, Peel castle, Preston, Whalley abbey 1727–28

193–208. Deeds, etc.: Newton-with-Scales and Preston 1730–1815; Ribby-with-Wrea and Stainall 1823, 1872; Walton-le-Dale 1806–43

209. Bishop Gastrell's survey of the diocese of Chester (contemporary copy) 1723

217. History of Leagram park and hall *c.*1870

218. History and pedigrees of the Shireburne family 19th c.

219. History of Leagram manor, park and hall 19th c.

222. *A Letter out of Lancashire* . . . (Jacobite) printed 1694

223. *Lieutenant General Cromwell's Letter re* battle of Preston printed 1648

224. Transcripts of 14th c. Shireburn deeds of Longton, Newton, Rawcliffe, Hambleton, Sowerby, Woodplumpton and Lower Darwen

225. Aighton, Bailey and Chaigley field book 1753

226. Survey and rental of Shireburne estates *c.*1750

229. Wiswell, Leagram, Chipping, Thornley, and Little Bowland field book 1733

237. Leyland deed 1708

238. Thistleton deed 1724

239. Ardwick deed 1776

240. *The Farington Papers* Chetham Society vol. 39 with extra illustrations by Susan Maria Farington

241. Notes, letters, press cuttings, plans, etc., relating to the churches of Salford Hundred 1235–1876

242. Transcripts of deeds, etc., relating to churches and schools in Stanhill, Hollinwood, Littleborough, Quernmore, Ashton-under-Lyne, Burnley, Little Bolton, Moston, Lancaster, Stalmine, Clayton-le-Moors, Cheetham, Prestolee, Tyldesley, Bamber Bridge, Samlesbury, Manchester, Swinton, Longsight, Oswaldtwistle, Preston, Rishton, Atherton and Mossley 1726–1883

244. Hulme plan 1836

249. Map of Manchester and Salford 1857

256. Plan of lower Ribble 1738

259. Plan of Chamber House Farm, Castleton 1788

260. Chipping terrier 1733

261. Chipping deed 1765

262. Slaidburn deed 1789

264. Commission of Henry Wilson, esq. as ensign in Royal Lancashire Militia 1816

265–278. Birkett family letters from America 1833–59

279–282. Handbills, letters and papers collected by the Rev. W. Allen of Peel chapel, Little Hulton, relating to the Bolton area 1813–31

288. Documents relating to the formation of the Manchester Military Association 1780–83

290. The diary and letter book of the Rev. Thomas Brockbank, vicar of Cartmel, 1671–1709 (see Chetham Society vol. 89 N.S.)

291–293. Three sketch books by William Latham relating to all parts of Lancashire 1809–23

298. Address by Joseph Dulton *re* cotton wages dispute 1818

302. Resolutions of Committee of the Preston Religious Freedom Society 1841

322. Survey of lands of Charles Towneley, esq. 1735

326. Letters and papers *re* nonconformity in Chorley 1792–1857

327. Plan of Manchester and Salford 1808

330–344. Deeds relating to Sir Cuthbert Halsall's property in Goosnargh, Scotforth, Up Holland and Dalton 1619–23

345–350. Deposition books of Liverpool Borough Quarter Sessions 1841–42

353. Sermons of Christopher Hudson, Preston 1631–39

354. Account book of Edward Swarbrick of Nateby House 1804–46

355–361. Letters patent to John Braddyll of Whalley 1545–55; Whalley church letters and papers 1593–1747

363–370. Deeds, etc.: Rishton c.1270, Down Litherland 1328, Bickerstaffe 1470–1586

372. Pedigree of Birtwistle of Huncoat 1336–1852

373. Backbarrow and Pennybridge furnace accounts 1763–80

374. Hardhorn-with-Newton deeds 1690–1743

375. Orderly book of the Leyland and Ormskirk Local Militia 1809–13

376. Ten scrap-books relating principally to Kirkham but also including Blackpool, Bolton, Lancaster, Liverpool, Manchester, Preston, Wigan, etc. 1793–1889

378. Letters re Chartism in Lancashire 1838–40

380. Nominal roll of Loyal North Lancashire Regiment for medals 1899–1902

381. Survey of lands in Briercliffe-with-Extwistle, Burnley, Habergham Eaves, Pendle, Marsden, Worsthorne and Trawden 1821

382. Account-book of John Faithwaite of Caton 1777–1802

384. Letters and papers concerning Cartmel and Furness 1591–1885

385. Account book of Richard Latham of Scarisbrick, farmer, 1723–67

386. Sketch book of John Weld of Leagram covering a wide area of Lancashire c.1830–86

387. Lease of Skelmersdale and Ormskirk tithes 1606

388. Wigan deed 1388; lease of booths on Kersal Moor 1821

391. Cockerham survey 1653

393. Letters of Elizabeth Appleton, governess to children of John Walmsley, Esq., Castleton 1805–20

394. Ulverston plans: Swarthmoor and Oxenholme 1827

395. Kay family of Bury funeral sermons 1706–75

396. Scarisbrick small-tithe accounts 1807

397. Deeds and papers of the Standish family of Duxbury c.1220–1850

398. Deeds and papers of the manor of Culcheth c.1250–1845

399. Papers, plans and rentals of the estate of the Marquess de Rothwell: Anglezarke, Blackrod, Bolton, Crompton, Halliwell, Oldham and Westhoughton 1829–91; papers *re* Bury Improvement Act 1870–72, Padiham Waterworks 1802, Blackburn Improvement 1870, and Lancaster Waterworks and Improvement 1876–79

400. Papers of the Newall family of Lower Townhouse, Littleborough 1478–1808

401. Survey of Huyton Hey 1812; Huyton tithe accounts 1827;

404. Deed of St. Annes, Lancaster, pew 1800

405. Euxton market charter 1301

408–409. Correspondence *re* Blundell of Ince Blundell foreshore rights 1901–02; letter book of James Moore and Co., Lancaster *re* Jamaica trade 1809–17

410. Liverpool Overhead Railway papers 1899, plans 1889–1906; correspondence of Sandbach, Tinne, and Co., Liverpool merchants 1810–48

412. Letters to William Horrocks of Farnworth 1859–66

413. Inventory of W. J. Lamb, Birkdale 1895

415. German aerial photographs, etc., of Flookburgh, Formby, and Warton-in-Amounderness 1942–43

416. Deeds of Pemberton Hey 1632–99

417. Letter from Earl of Derby to Sir Thomas Gerrard *re* munitions for the Isle of Man *c.*1596

419. Field Book of estates of R. T. North, Esq. in the Lune Valley 1812

421. Papers and books of T. H. Myres, architect, of Preston and Lea 1815–1923

424. Valuation of Duke of Montagu's estate in Furness and Cartmel 1767

429. Valuation of Barrow print-works, Wiswell 1855

430. Map of Liverpool 1826

432. Railway plans 1845–1955

437. Ormskirk scrap-book *c.*1862–65

438. Account of sale of goods of James Hooton of Scarisbrick, farmer 1854

439. Cliviger deeds 1344–1718

440. Documents relating to the Stonyhurst estate, including rentals 1692, 1693, 1699, 1718, 1753, 1766, 1780, 1781, 1787–1805, 1815, 1822–27, 1830–32, 1838, 1840; Carleton and Hambleton manor court books c.1740–53; 18th c. deeds; surveys 1733, 1833; field book 1734; Longton plan 1825; Ribchester rentals 1793, 1799; Haworth, co. York, manor court estreats 1701; estate management books 1693–1751; Clitheroe commons allotment book 1786

Index

The following points should be noted in using the Index:
1. Cases where more than one reference to a heading occur on a single page are *not* indicated.
2. Individual charities are *not* indexed.
3. Individual members of families referred to in a main deposit entry are *not* indexed. This entry is in bold figures.
4. Place names *not* in Lancashire are indexed under their county or country.

Ardwick : bishops' transcripts 127; deeds 232, 296, 330, 337, 338; R.C. records 129; tithe 28

Arkholme-with-Cawood : deeds 240, 276, 289, 303, 324, 335; parish records 96; scrapbook 157; tithe 26

Arkle & Derbyshire, 307

Arkwright, Daniel, of Preston, 170

Armetriding family, 301

Arminson, John of Stalmine, 303; Miss 303

Armistead, Henry, of Sabden, 172

arms, coats of, 181, 182, 192, 202, 212, 220, 229, 253, 299, 305, 329

arms (weapons), 196, 270, 341

army : accounts 257; cavalry 57; commissions 192, 195, 196, 203, 210, 212, 216, 226, 227, 229, 238, 241, 248, 249, 252, 257, 265, 274, 275, 284, 288, 298, 335, 339; garrisons 122, 226; horsemen 221, 230, 257, 258; leave grants 227; orders 284, 320; papers 323, 326; property qualifications 57; transport 2, 250; trooper (1648) 301

Arrowsmith & Roskell, of Preston, 186

Ashburner, J. C., 315

Ashburnham, Earl of, 301

Ashcroft, Sir William, 299; Whiteside & Co., of Blackpool, 172

Ashe, Richard, of Cloughbank, 284

Ashhurst, see Dalton (Wigan)

Ashhurst, William, clerk of the crown, 338

Ashton : bounds 226; deeds 175, 254, 293, 329; leases 226; parish records 108; schools 81, 86; tithe 27; see also Lea, Ashton, Ingol and Cottam

Ashton, barons, of Hyde, 303, 322; Edward, 292

Ashton-under-Lyne, 251, 304; bishops' transcripts 126; borough records 43; coal 165; church 304; Congregational records 136; deeds 187, 227, 232, 289, 296, 300, 307, 313, 317, 330, 335, 337, 339; divisional executive committee 38; enclosure 13; Hey bishops' transcripts 126; Home Guard 58; Hurst 323, manor 294, 304; mechanics' institute 9; parish records 96; police 58; poor law guardians 63; public assistance committee 40; riots 20; R.C. records 129; societies 152, 156; terriers 128; turnpike 61; Waterhouses 304; workhouse 129

Ashton-in-Makerfield, 180, 218, 219, 323; apprentice stock 149; bishops' transcripts 126; bounds 219; chapel 219;

coal 32, 33, 174, 219; deeds 146, 173, 179, 181, 192, 218, 229, 244, 312, 317, 330, 335; Eye bridge 219; felons 174; free warren 219; manor 218; mill 219; parish records 96; rental 237; schools 68; Society of Friends records 146; survey 272; terrier 126; tithe 27; turnpike 283

Ashton-with-Stodday : deeds 206, 254, 326; tithe 26

Ashworth : bishops' transcripts 127; deeds 227; parish records 96; school 68; tithe 28

Ashworth family, of Birkenshaw, Turton, 327; Miss 308

Askam, see Dalton-in-Furness

Askew family, of Hawkshead, 318

Aspden, Joseph, of Tockholes, 253

Aspinall, Hannah, of Blackburn, 290; Miss I. 294; P. 309

Aspinwall family, 193

Aspull : deeds 173, 181, 218, 221, 232, 271, 282; enclosure 174; manor 211; R.C. records 129; schools 68; tithe 27

Assheton family, of Downham, 191, 313

assizes, 176, 223, 234, 328, 332; rolls 24; and see under individual towns

Associations (1696), 19

Astley, 274, 275; bishops' transcripts 127; burial committee 316; coal 32, 33, 237; deeds 51, 206, 209, 232, 263, 281, 290, 323, 328, 330; enclosure 13, 14; hall 237, 275, 324; Hulme trust 94; manor 94, 328; rentals 273; school 68; terrier 128; tithe 28, 275

Astley family, 182

astrology, 291

asylums, 5, 6-7, 8, 317; committees of county council 39, 41; and see hospitals, lunacy

Atherton, 235, 299; bishops' transcripts 127; Chowbent chapel 236, 237; coal, 32, 33, 165, 236; cotton mills 169, 236; deeds 235, 297, 330, 339; estate papers 236, 237; manor 235; plans 237; rentals 237; schools 68; tithe 28, 237

Atherton family, of Atherton, 174, 235; Lucy 185; Mrs. M. 312; Peter, of Liverpool 187; William and Elizabeth, of Prescot and Jamaica 332

Atkinson, H. R., 312

auctioneers 163; and see surveyors

Audenshaw, 312; schools 68; urban district 47

Aughton, 246, 317; accounts 270; assessment 261; bishops' transcripts 124;

bounds 266; charity 149; church 246; *compoti* 178; deeds 173, 175, 194, 196, 206, 211, 215, 218, 221, 244, 259, 261, 263, 271, 295, 308, 312, 319, 330; hall 260; leases 265; Moor Hall 293; parish records 96-7; plans 198; races 158, 301; rentals 246; R.C. records 129, 134; schools 68; surveys 198, 261, 266; terriers 126; tithe 27

Aughton, James, of Adlington, 176

Aughton-in-Halton : bishops' transcripts 121; plans 185, 241; school 68, 77

Austin, R. B., 311

Australia, 291, 306, 310, 311; Queensland 318; Sydney 294

Austria : Vienna 207

Backbarrow : cotton mill 203, 334; iron company 167; plans 280; and Penny Bridge furnace 167, 340; road 253; school *see* Upper Holker

Backhouse, Mary, of Finsthwaite, 253

Bacup : bishops' transcripts 122; borough records 43; deeds 189, 247, 316, mechanics' institute 153; plans 279; plumber 168; police 7, 8, 58; schools 66, 68, 294; terrier 123

badgers, 11

Badsberry, *see* Myerscough

Bagganley, *see* Chorley

Bagnall, D., 308

Bailey, 284; chapel 285; deeds 179; *and see* Aighton, Bailey, and Chaigley

Bailey, Mrs. F. A., 309

Baines, James, of Poulton-le-Fylde, 332

baker, 163

Balderston, 335; bishops' transcripts 121; deeds 186, 201, 209, 288, 330, 333; parish records 97, 98; rental 210; schools 69

Balldock, David (1682), 232

Baldwin family, of Aldingham, 181; of Leyland 298; Weeks & Baldwin, of Clitheroe 172

Balmforth, of Clayton, 296

Balshaw, Thomas, of Walton-le-Dale, 180

Bamber, Joshua & Co., of Bolton, 169

Bamber Bridge : bishops' transcripts 121; bridge 289; deeds 326, 327, 339; Lostock Hall 30, 310; parish records 98; plans 313; R.C. records 129; trade union 159

Bamford, *see* Birtle-with-Bamford

Banastre family, of Bretherton, 235, 274-5, 289; Christopher, of Bretherton 235; Robert (1167) 229

Bank, *see* Bretherton

Bankes family, of Winstanley, **191-2**

Bankhall, *see* Bootle

bankruptcy, 15, 172, 179, 181, 223, 290, 293, 308, 185, 186, 315

Banks, R., 313; W. & Co. 294, 325

banks, 9, 163-4, 183, 186, 320

Bannister family, 249; Miss C. M., 309; Rev. J. E. D. 309; John, of Bentham 176; S. 308

Barber-Lomax, J. W., 327

Barcroft family, **249-50,** 278; Ellen, of Noyna, Foulridge 248; Thomas (1664) 275; William (1623) 275

Bardsea : bishops' transcripts 124; deeds 218; enclosure 219; rental 219; school 69

Bare, *see* Poulton-le-Sands

Barley Booth, *see* Barley-with-Wheatley Booth

Barley-with-Wheatley Booth : Barley Booth 182; deeds 182, 299, 300, 333; Methodist records 141; parish records 97; Wheatley Booth 299, 304

Barlow family, 308

Barnacre-with-Bonds : deeds 259, 276, 303, 333; enclosure 13; leases 265; Lingart 207; parish records 97; tithe 26

Barnes family, of Farnworth, 335

Barnham, Annie, of Carnforth, 322

barrister, 168

Barron, Miss M., 305

Barrow, Rev. John, of Claughton, 130; Sir John 310; Spencer, E., architect 163, 315

Barrow-in-Furness, 156, 157, 316; Congregational records 136; court records 21; deeds 186, 312, 316, 333, 335; elections 328; Haematite Steel Co. 308; insurance committee 30; police 59; schools 69; tontine 153; trades union 159; Walney Island 190

Barrowford, 184; bridge 182; Congregational records 136; deeds 128, 182, 276; Industrial & Commercial Co. 171; Methodist records 141; mill 182; parish records 97; pensions committee 32, 39; plans 183; rentals 183; R.C. records 129; schools 66, 69, 183; urban district 47

Barton family, 303; of Preston 329; Miles and Roger, rectors of Hoole, 334; Thomas, of Barton-in-Amounderness 186

Barton-in-Amounderness, 186; bishops' transcripts 122; bridge 290; deeds 100, 179, 186, 326, 327, 335; felons 156;

manor 186; Newsham deeds 202, 283, 294; Newsham R.C. records 83, 133; parish records 97; rental 273; surveys 272; tithe 26, 180

Barton-upon-Irwell, 293; bishops' transcripts 127; deeds 229, 232, 274, 281, 300, 303, 308, 312, 319, 330, 337; enclosure 13; leases 281; manor 280; parish records 97; plans 281; poor 63; R.C. records 129, 131; rural district 54; South, highway board 61; tithe 28

Bashall, William, & Co., of Farington, 170

Basnett, Miss L., 311

bastardy, 21-3

Bateson, H., 301

Bath, earl of, 210

bathing machines, 195

Batho, Taylor, & Ogden, of Manchester, 168

Battersby, R., of Bedford, 297

Battinson & Whitaker, of Colne, 168

Bayley family, of Stalybridge, 317; John of 284; Mr. Justice 223

beacons, 265

Beakbane, H. R., 324; Henry, of Liverpool 324

Beardman, William, of Farington, 322

Beardsworth family, 211; D. 295; William (1812) 295

Beaver, F., 325

Becconsall : chapel 224; chantry 261; and see Hesketh-with-Becconsall

Bedford, 230, 297; bishops' transcripts 127; deeds 51, 94, 235, 271, 303, 313, 316, 328, 330; R.C. records 134; school 69, 81; tithe 28, 234

Bedfordshire, 269; Cardington 207; Ravensden 271

beerhouses, 23; and see alehouses

beggars, 12

Bela, river, 177

Belfield, see Butterworth

Belfield, Adam, of Rochdale, 231

Bell, A., 311

Bell Hill, see Caton

Belmont : bishops' transcripts 126; parish records 115; school board 66

Benison, Thomas, of Lancaster, 335, 336

Bennett, A., 318

Bennison, J. A., engineer, 298

Benson family, 300; Dr. George 334

Bentham, Jeremy, 307

Bentinck, Lord William, 226

Bentley & Harrison, of Clitheroe, 166

Berkshire : Broadmoor 336; Denchinworth 336; Eton College 269

Berry family, 303; R. H. & Sons, of Colne; Prof. R. J. A. 294

Berwick, G., 309

Beswick : school 71; tithe 28

Bethum, Ralph and Ingrid, 336-7

Bewsey, 235, 237; manor 235; plans 237

Bickershaw : coal, 32

Bickerstaffe, 265; bounds 266; charity 149; deeds 194, 196, 263, 340; felons 156; leases 265; manor 262; parish records 97; rentals 268; school 69; survey 266; terrier 126; tithe 27

Bickerstaffe, J., 309

Bickersteth, J. D., 301

Bigland, see Upper Holker

Billinge : bishops' transcripts 126; Carr Mill 219, 245; charity 192, 313; coal 219; deeds 51, 192, 194, 196, 218, 229, 257, 308, 318; enclosure 13; free warren 219; leases 265; parish records 97; quarry 169; road 219; schools 69, 98; survey, 272; tithe 27

Billington, 304, 327, 335; Chew Mill 256, 290; deeds 184, 199, 200, 232, 254, 276, 283, 290, 303, 314; enclosure 13, 98, 256; Hacking 254; manor 200, 254; parish records 97; poor stock 149; rentals 200; 234, 256; R.C. records 129; school 69; society 153; surveys 256, 272

Billington, T., 293

Bilsborrow : deeds 186, 200, 206, 221, 232, 276, 291, 298, 303; parish records 98, 105; scrapbook 156, 157; surveys 272; tithe 26

Bindloss family, 320; Sir Robert, of Borwick 239

Birch, Col. (1660), 297

Birchall, Thomas, clerk of the peace, 20; & Yates 317

Birchcarr, Maud of, 259

Birchley : R.C. records 129, 134; school 69

Bird, Dr. A., 326; & Bird 323

Birkacre, see Coppull

Birkdale, 341; common 197; deeds 189, 196, 206; foreshore 198; manor 196, 244; parish records 98; pensions committee 32, 39; plans 198; rentals 198; surveys 198, 272; school 197; tithe 27

Birkett family, 339

Birley family, 175

Birtle-with-Bamford : Bamford 334; deeds 187, 227, 232; hearth tax 18; leases 188; parish records 98; tithe 28

Bold family, 174, 225; J. 316

Bolton (Bolton-le-Moors), 230, 232, 252, 293, 296, 328, 339, 340; bishops' transcripts 126; Breightmet 263, 265, 314, 330; canal 267, 331; charity 149; churches 231, 309; Congregational records 136-7; cotton mills 169-70, 309; county court 22; deeds 175, 179, 200, 232, 251, 263, 265, 274, 291, 292, 303, 311, 314, 326, 330; division of Salford hundred 18; Doffcocker 328; engineering 298; Gilnough 327; Haulgh 184, 200; Infirmary 297; insurance committee 31; militia 7; plans 200, 341; police 7; poor 231; Quarlton 187, 292; railway 245, 267; riots 20; R.C. records 129, 134; schools 70; Society of Friends records 147; societies 156, 332; terriers 128; theatre 315; Unitarian records 146; vicarage 197

Bolton, John, of Colne, 167; Robert, of Wigan 174; Jobson & Martyn 305; & Hargreaves, of Colne 167-8, 183

Bolton Public Library, 302

Bolton-with-Adgarley, 267; Adgarley Green 268; Adgarley mines 267; deeds 263; leases 265; manor 262; rentals 268; school see Urswick

Bolton-le-Sands, 303; bishops' transcripts 121; church 220; deeds 178, 240, 254, 263, 308, 329, 335; rectory manor 306; road 299; school 220; terriers 123; tithe 26, 220

Bond family, 317; Mrs. A. 323; H. 296

Bonds, see Barnacre-with-Bonds

Boodle, Hatfield, & Co., 323

books, 212, 284; club 158

Boote, Edgar, & Co., of Manchester, 172-3

Booth, Margaret (Trafford), 280

Bootham School, York, 301

Boothman, Richard, transportee, 311

Boothstown, see Worsley

Bootle, 262; Bankhall 262, 270; bishops' transcripts 125; Congregational records 137; deeds 307; insurance committee 31; manor 295; rentals 268; schools 70; springs 267, 270

Bootle-cum-Linacre : deeds 206, 263; leases 265; Linacre 246, 266; manor 262; tithe 27

Bootle-Wilbraham family, of Lathom, **286-7**

boroughs : quarter sessions 15; records 42-7, 172; relations with county 5; treasures 156; *and see* individual boroughs, *and* municipal officers

Borthwick Institute, York, 317

Borwick, 239; deeds 178, 240, 276; enclosure 13; surveys 241; tithe 26

Bottom Mill, see Melling-with-Wrayton

Botton, see Wray-with-Botton

Boucher, W. J. G., 310

Boulter, Rev. J. S., 305

boundary commissions, 12

Bourne family, of Stalmine, **198-9;** Thomas, of Liverpool 322

Bouth, see Colton

Bowen, Cotton, & Bowen, 308

Bowers & Peate, of Openshaw, 164

Bowker, John, of Salford, 227; Thomas, of Lancaster 325

Bowland Forest, 248; parish records 99; schools 70; Trough of 209

Bowland-with-Leagram, 65, 284; Browsholme 248, 306; deeds 187, 283; honour 275; plans 249, 290-1; rental 200; rural district 55; survey 272; tithe 200; *and see* Leagram, Little Bowland

Bowley, G., 299

bowling, 158, 230, 279

Bowman, Mrs. W. M., 304

Bowringe, Rev. John, of Manchester, 321

boy scouts, 156, 158

Braddyll family, of Portfield, Whalley, **199-200;** John, of Brockhall 199, 340; Thomas (1757) 304

Bradford : coal 275; deeds 274; rentals 273, 275; R.C. records 129; school 71; survey 272; tithe 28

Bradford, earl of, **200**

Bradkirk, Richard (1720), 175

Bradley, see Eccleston (Prescot)

Bradley family, 220; Mrs. Greene 220; James, of Bailey 284; T. 307

Bradshaigh family, 288

Bradshaw : bishops' transcripts, 126; church 231; deeds 232, 292, 327; parish records 99

Bradshaw family, 212; Isaac, of Lancaster 324; Richard, of Swinton 228

Bradshawe, Joan of (1369), 309

Brandwood, J., 321

brassfounders, 174, 184, 290

Brathay : bishops' transcripts 124; school 90

Breffney, Baron de, 306

Breightmet, see Bolton-le-Moors

Brennand, William, surveyor of excise, 248

Bretherton, 212, 235, 250; accounts 270; Bank Hall 235, 236, 237, 274; Bank marsh bowling green 279; bishops'

Bulk : deeds 217, 240, 325, 335; manor 302; rental 320; tithe 26
Buller, J. L., 305
Burch, Miles, apprentice husbandman, 304
Burdett, P. P., of Derby, 225
Burgoyne, General John, 295
Burma, 195
Burnage : deeds 179; school 71; tithe 28
Burnett, John, of Rufford, 223, 224
Burnley 172, 183, 310, 317, 319; bishops' transcripts 122; borough records 43; Brunshaw 237; chantry 279; church 183, 184, 234, 279, 302; coal 34, 35, 165; Congregational records 137; cotton mill 172; curacy 182, 183; deeds 182, 189, 274, 276, 283, 285, 290, 302, 304, 316, 327, 333, 339; employers' association 162; enclosure 275; highways 286; Home Guard 58; joiners 304; hospital 29; hospital board 29; insurance committee 31; manor 251; mechanics' institute 9; Methodist records 142; militia 7, 182; poor law guardians 63; public assistance 40; reform 238; rentals 273, 286; R.C. records 130; Royle 275; rural district 55; schools 7, 184, 225, 278; societies 156, 158; surveys 272, 340; terrier 123; tithe 26, 286; Towneley 187, 276, 279; trades unions 161, 302, 304
Burnley Library, 327
Burrow-with-Burrow : deeds 175, 178; Over Burrow 295; parish records 100; tithe 26
Burscough, 267; accounts 269; bounds 260, 266; charities 149; deeds 174, 193, 259, 263, 271, 317, 319, 331; hospital board 30; leases 265, 329; manor 262; Martin Hall 223; moss 173; parish records 100; priory 197, 259, 261, 269, 296; rentals 268; R.C. records 130, 134; schools 71; survey 266; tithe 27; turnpike 60
Burscough, Brother Adam of, 260
Burton, J. D., 310
Burtonwood, 235; bishops' transcripts 125; deeds 173, 235, 308, 326; manor 173, 236; minister 174; parish officers 237; rentals 237, 337; schools 66, 71, 174; tithe 27
Bury, 340; bishops' transcripts 126; borough records 43; breweries 164, 188; canal 267, 331; charities 149, 188; churches 187, 231, 233, 267, 268, 298, 304, 308; cotton mills 188; deeds 172, 181,

187, 215, 232, 263; 276, 298, 301, 307, 308, 313, 323, 326; engineering 165; foundry 187; Improvement Act 341; insurance committee 31; leases 189, 265, 271, 329; manor 262; militia 7; mills 189; Ministry of Labour 298; parish records 100; plans 188, 268, 270, 298; police 7; poor law guardians 63; public assistance 40; railways 188, 267, 294; rectory estate 128; rentals 188, 268, 270; school 71; surveys 266; tartaric acid works 171, 313; terriers 128; thearte 315; tithe 28; turnpike 61; woollen mill 171
Bury Bros., of Accrington, 169
Bury Estate Co., 262, **270-71**
Bury Public Library, 298
Bush, D., 299
Bussel, William, of Penwortham, 225; Robert, of Leyland, 210
butcher, 224
Butler family, of Rawcliffe, 198, 301; John, of Kirkland 318; Isobel (Towneley) 278; Margaret (Blundell) 196
Butler-Cole, R. F. C., 301
Butter family, of Garstang, 105
Butterworth : Belfield 276, 280; church-ley 298; Clegg Hall 181; coal 306; deeds 229, 232, 247, 292, 298, 310, 312; hearth tax 18; parish records 100; Schofield 334; schools 71, 334; tithe 28
Butterworth, Robert (1767), 298
Byrom family, 228

Cabus : parish records 100, 105; tithe 26
Cadley, see Fulwood
Caernarvonshire Record Office, 310
Caine, Allen, of Liverpool, 228
Calder, river, 62, 158; Vale : parish records 105; plans 313; scrapbook 157
Calder family, of Caithness, 286
Calderbrook, see Blatchingworth and Calderbrook
calico-printers, 169, 180, 304, 306
Calvely & Co., 314
Calvert family, of Broughton and Preston, **202**
Cambridgeshire, 269; Crawden 193; Glassmore 264, 268; Horseheath 277; Isle of Ely 264, 268; Longstanton 277; Sawston 211
Campbell, M., 313
Canada, 291; Nova Scotia 190
canals, 15, 16, 46, 56, 158, 164, 176, **182**, 199, 207, 223, 230, 253, 256, 267, 273,

278, 282, 287, 289, 291, 323, 325, 331; *and see* individual canals

Cannon Bros., of Bolton, 170

Cantsfield, 218; deeds 175, 182; parish records 101; plan 182; survey 181; tithe 26; Thurland Castle 311

Cantsfield, Richard (1488), 264

Capernwray, *see* Over Kellet

Carberry, D., 326

Carbis, Miss N., 321

Cardigan, earl of, 247

Cardwell, J. T., 292

Cardwell's brewery, of Preston, 164

Cark-in-Cartmel, *see* Upper Holker

Carleton, 52; chapel 284; deeds 176, 184, 199, 202, 206, 263, 271, 283, 289, 331, 333; leases 265, 329; manor 342; parish records 101; plans 270; school 71; smithy 320; surveys 266, 272; tithe 26

Carlyle, Thomas, 307

Carnforth, 303, 319; bishops' transcripts 122; deeds 178, 186, 232, 240, 325, 329; enclosure 13; gas company 166; manor 48; school 72, 322; tithe 26; turnpike 61; urban district 48

Carnson, Miss M., 322; Rev. T., of Longridge 322

carpenters, *see* woodworkers

Carr, John, of York, 203; Miss L. 310; Rev. Wilfred, of Formby 131

Carr Mill, *see* Billinge

Carrington, H. M., 315

Carry Hey, *see* Colne

Carter, Mrs. M., 322; & Co. 322

Cartmel 340; Bible association 152; bishops' transcripts 124, 341; Broughton East 176, 333; church 238, 339; deeds 176, 203, 239, 279, 310, 325; enclosure 13, 203; highway board 61; history 177; manor 203; parish records 101; plans 204, 280, 299; priory 202, 231, 338; rectory 203, 204; rentals 204; rural dean 280; school 72; scrapbook 157; survey 280; terriers 124; tithe 204; Wood Broughton 252

Cartmel Fell, 253, 334; bishops' transcripts 124; deeds 252, 258, 295, 296, 330, 337; Hartbarrow 334; Height Society of Friends records 124; school 72, 203; Thorphinsty 177

Cartmel family, 177

Cartmell, C., 290; Miss K. 327

cartularies, 187, 193, 234, 279, 282

Carus, Thomas, of Whittington, 301

Castle Museum, York, 326

Castlereagh, viscount, 226

Castleton, 228, 305, 340; coal 306; Congregational records 137; cow club 298; deeds 172, 187, 232, 298, 303, 312, 325; hearth tax 18; parish records 101; plans 306, 339; school 72; survey 236

Catforth : rental 329; R.C. records 130; schools 94

Cathay, emperor of, 210

Catlow, Miss D., 294

Caton, 340; bishops' transcripts 122; Bell Hill 301; bounds 216; bridge 217, 218; Broadwood 301; church 217; Congregational records 137; deeds 173, 178, 179, 185, 206, 214, 216, 301, 324, 335; enclosure 13, 216; felons 156, 217; forge 177; Gresgarth (Grassyard), 216, 217; highway rates 217; land tax 217; Littledale 306; manor 185, 216; moor 216; parish records 101; plans 185, 217; rate assessments 217; roads 216; school 72; tithe 26, 217; workhouse 216

Catterall : accounts 262; deeds 174, 175, 202, 206, 232, 251, 254, 261, 276, 288, 289, 290, 299, 309, 331, 333, 336; hall 316; mills 174; parish records 101; plans 313; printworks 333; surveys 261, 272; tithe 26

Catterall, Paul, of Preston, 168

cattle, 227, 270, 293, 322; plague *see* animals, diseases of

Cavendish family, of Brindle and Inskip, **205**; of Holker **202-4**

Cawood, *see* Arkholme-with-Cawood

Cawthorne, J. F., forester of Wyresdale, 216

census returns, 44, 180, 236, 255, 260

Ceylon, 214

Chadderton, 227; bishops' transcripts 127; coal 165, 304; deeds 187, 227, 232, 233, 276, 292, 304, 310, 312, 313, 317, 336; Fox Denton 302; school 72; Stockfield 165; tithe 28; urban district 48

Chadwick family, of Preston, 186

Chaigley : Congregational records 137; priest 279; rentals 268; *and see* Aighton, Bailey and Chaigley

Chaloner, Thomas, Irish King-of-Arms, 193

Chambers, A. W., 300

chantries, 198, 224, 228, 235, 246, 250, 261, 279, 281, 284, 289, 336, 337

Chapman, Charles & Sons, of Manchester, 166

chapmen, 227, 293, 308

charcoal, 177, 252

charities, 215, 237; education 94; prison 6; records 8-9, 149-52, 215; returns 8-9; societies 153-5; war 41; *and see under* individual parishes

Charles I, 213, 279

Charlton, Catherine (Shireburne), 283; Sir Edward 284

charm, manuscript, 309

Charnock family, 211-12, 324; of Cuerden 274-5; Gilbert 337

Charnock Richard, 274; charity 301; coal 324; deeds 179, 190, 206, 209, 263, 271, 274, 324, 330, 337; parish records 101; Park Hall 190; rentals 260, 273, 326; schools 72; surveys 190, 272, 273; tithe 26

Charteris, Hon. Francis, of Hornby, 296

chartism, 340

Chatburn : bishops' transcripts 122; charity 149; deeds 220, 290, 291, 293, 299; mill 291, 333; parish records 101; school 72; surveys 300; tithes 26, 286

Cheesden, *see* Spotland

cheese factors, 164; sellers 11

Cheetham : bishops' transcripts 127; deeds 187, 232, 263, 330, 339; leases 271; plans 188, 270; railway 188; R.C. records 130; school 72 ;survey 266; tithe 28

Cheetham, Sir Nicholas, 310

chemists, 154, 164, 224

Chesham, lords, 205

Cheshire, 196, 207, 236, 264, 265, 269, 270, 274, 275, 280; Acton 288; Aldford 280; Altrincham 302; Anderton 174; Antrobus 205; Appleton 288 *and see* Widnes; Barnton 255, 325; Beeston 233; Betchton 233; Bidston 205, 267; Birkenhead 316; Birtles 233; Bollin-with-Norcliffe 280; Bowdon (Congregation recs.) 136; Bredbury 230; Brindley 277; Buglawton 233; Buntley 210; Capesthorne 233; Chester, 180, 299; abbey 211, 224; bishop 203, 223, 338; chamberlain 267; constable 276; customer 234; deeds 146, 197, 233, 261, 264, 277, 288; diocese : probate records 25, visitations 124; exchequer 270; friary 193; palatinate court 13; prisoners at 234; Society of Friends 146; Childer Thornton 264; Church Minshull 244; Cogshall 205; Crowley 201; Cuddington 195; Disley 233; Drakelow 233; Dukinfield 9; Great Boughton 264; Guilden Sutton 222; Halton (honour) 205, 236;

Haughton 210; Holmes Chapel 154; Hyde 319; Kelsall 205; Lache 288; Latchford 323; Ledsham 219; Legh 254; Lymm 288; Macclesfield 136, 233, 262, 264, 265, 266, 267, 268, 269, 270; Malpas 274; Marley 277; Mellor 233; Mere 274; Middlewich 233; Mobberley 233; More 205; Mottram 233; Nantwich 233; Noctorum 195; Norley 210; Norton Abbey 222; Northwich 265, 266, 268, 270; Odd Rode 210; Over Whitley 201; Partington 234; Ravenscroft 234; Rode Hall 286; Runcorn 38, 205; Staley 4, 304; Stanlaw Abbey 197, 244, 245; Stockport 136, 233, 323; Stretton 233; Sutton 265; Swettenham 277; Tabley 288; Tarporley 288; Thelwall 288; Thornton 247, 281; Thornton Hough 264; Upton 264; Vale Royal 234; Wallasey 265; Warmingham 215; Whitley 205, 236; Wildboarclough 265, 268; Wilmslow 281; Wincle 233; Wirral 163; Woodchurch 264

Cheshire Record Office, 306

Chester, Capt. P. R., 302

Chester Record Office, 297

Cheston, Mrs. V., 326

Chew, J., 321

Chew mill, *see* Billington

children : committee of county council, 37; employment of 318

Childwall : accounts 270; bishops' transcripts 124; deeds 194, 263; enclosure 13; free warren 266; highway board 61; leases 265; rectory 174, 196, 218; terriers 126; tithe 27, 174

China, 218

Chipping, 266, 284, 323, 335; bishops' transcripts 121; Blackmoor 267; church 268; deeds 172, 179, 185, 186, 196-7, 254, 261, 263, 276, 283, 290, 308, 311, 312, 318, 331, 333, 335, 338, 339; enclosure 13; leases 265; manor 262; mill 312; parish records 101; plans 268; rentals 228, 268, 269; roads 182; societies 154, 332; surveys 198, 266, 272; terriers 132, 339; tithe 26; waste 266

Chishall, *see* Coppull

Chorley, 181, 284, 306, 326, 335, 339; Bagganley 271; bishops' transcripts 121; borough records 43; charities 149, 271; church 179, 210; coal 186-7, 294, 324; *compoti* 178; Congregational records 137; court records 23; deeds 175, 179, 209, 211, 229, 232, 251, 263, 271, 276, 283, 313, 319, 324, 326, 331, 333; divi-

354

355

Connolly, Charles and Daniel, of Oldham, 310; H. 310
Conservative associations, 155
constables, high, 2, 3, 250, 271, 273; petty 2, 10, 19
Constancon, M. (1785), 212
Cook, J., 327; John, pavior 328
Cooke, Edward and Henry, of Preston, 312; Henry, canon of York 212
Cookson, F., 301; J. & Sons 318; Miss 292; Richard, of Goosnargh 180; W. N. 292
Coope, Mrs. E., 320
Cooper, Edwin, of Bolton, 170; John, of Walton-le-Dale 180; Miss M. 327; Selina Jane, of Nelson 327; Thomas & Co. 314
cooperative societies, 165
coopers, 172
Copeland deanery, 120; probate records 25
Copley, Edward and Beatrix, of Batley, 234
Coppull, 326; Birkacre mill 322, 333; Blainscough coal 32; bishops' transcripts 122; church 273; Chisnall Hall 272; deeds 181, 194, 232, 235, 259, 271, 274, 293, 317, 322, 326; leases 288; manor 235; parish records 102; rentals 237, 260; schools 74; surveys 236, 272; tithe 26
Corbould, Rigby & Co., 308
Corless, Roger, of Up Holland, 270
corn : merchant 172; mills see mills; rents 13; sellers 11; tax 18
Cornwall, 278; Broadoak 282; Grampound 231; Liskeard 282
Cornwall Record Office, 308
coroners, 2, 15, 20, 44; court records 23-4, 173, 179, 193, 198
Corrs, S., 293
Cotman, L., 298
Cottam, 81; deeds 175, 293, 326; parish records 108; rental 273; tithe 27; see also Lea, Ashton, Ingol, and Cottam
Cottam, John, of Fleetwood, 165; R. 310; Richard, of Whalley 199
Cottham, Richard (1657), 238
cotton industry : 228, 236, 238, 252, 291, 315, 324, 339; famine 190; firms 169-71, 172, 184, 188; mills 180, 181, 203, 236, 260, 261, 309, 311, 323, 334 and see mills; pattern book 317; power-loom 180, and see inventions and printworks
Couch, C. M., 309; Mrs. P., 326
Coulthurst, J., 295

Council for the Preservation of Rural England, 157
county council, 202, 328; records 36-42
county court records, 24
Cow Hill, see Haighton
Cowburn, Mrs. S., 303
Cowell, E., 309; J. 308
Cowpe-with-Lench : deeds 189; Hall Carr tithe 28; Longholme 88, 145; school 88; tithe 28
Cragg family, of Wyresdale, 318
Crake, river, 334
Crawford, Mrs. M., 318
Crawshaw, lord, of Crawshaw, **209**
Crawshawbooth, 209; plans 189; school 79; Society of Friends records 147
cricket, 158
Crimbles, see Cockerham
Crimean War, letter from, 300; Patriotic funds 184, 234, 329
Croft, 74; deed 310; parish records 102; plans 219; R.C. records 130; school 74, 90; see also Southworth-with-Croft
Crombock, John, of Clerk Hill, 220
Crombocke, Richard, of Clerk Hill, 220
Crompton : bishops' transcripts 127; coal 165; deeds 222, 227, 233, 301, 310, 313, 330, 334, 335; parish records 103; plans 306, 341; R.C. records 130; schools 74; theatre 315; tithe 28; urban district 49
Crompton family, 180; & Shawcross, coal co. 282
Cromwell, lord, 264; Oliver 220, 338
Cronton : charities 149; deeds 51, 173, 201, 209, 287, 330; leases 288; parish records 103; school 74; tithe 27
Crook, Hankinson, 293; William, of Nelson 165, 184
Crosby, 155, 247; church 195; deeds 187; enclosure 13; hall 196; manor 187; marsh 245; parish records 103; R.C. records 135; schools 74
Crosfield, Samuel (1813), 292
Cross Hall, see Lathom
Cross, Adam of the, 209; H. & Co., of Prescot 173-4; Richard Assheton, viscount **209**; & Tetley, coal co. 282
Crosse family, 327; of Liverpool 252, 273; of Shaw Hill **209-10**; Lt. Col. R. B. 301
Crossley family, of Burnley, 317; Edward 278
Croston, 195, 223, 224, 335; bishops' transcripts 121; charities 149; court records 23; deeds 49, 175, 179, 181, 202, 211, 222, 250, 263, 274, 281, 311, 313,

356

357

debtors, insolvent, 3, 24

Dee, river, 294

deeds, enrolled, 13, 14; of married women 15; registers, of county council 36

defence : acts 10; contributions to 253; invasion map 253; records 56-8; resolutions 285

Denbighshire Record Office, 317

Dendron : bishops' transcripts 123; school 67

Denmark : Copenhagen, 225

Denton, 156, 230; bishops' transcripts 127; deeds 49, 229, 232, 288, 303, 319; Home Guard 58; plans 288; rentals 231, 234; schools 75; survey 233; tithe 28; urban district 49

Denwood, N. V., 321

Derby, earls of, 205, 210, 214, 221, 223, 226, 234, 259, 261, 262-70, 279, 286, 329, 341

Derbyshire : Aske 219; Blackwell (R.C. records) 129; Chesterfield 277, 279; Darley 308; Edale 298; Etwall 219; Hardwick 219; Hayfield 281; Hope 233; New Mills 186; Repton school 218, 219

Derbyshire Record Office, 309

Derwent, river, 278

Despard, General, 223

Devon, earl of, 245

Devonshire, 238, 278; Bampton 277; Bovey Tracy 264; Bradworthy 263; Dartmouth 295; Plymouth 282; Plympton 282; Sturminster Marshall 264; Syon abbey 207; Torrington 264; Uffculme 277

Devonshire, dukes of, 202, 205

Dew, Miss D. B., 304

Dewhurst, G. & R. Ltd., of Preston, 171; John, of Padiham 184

Dicconson family, of Wrightington, 259, 321, 330; William (1640) 260

Dick, Kerr & Co., of Preston, 169

Dickenson family, of Manchester, 302

Dickinson, J. C., 295; Peter, apprentice watchmaker 297; Dr. R., 302

Dickson, A. E., 297; Mrs. E. M. 306; Robert (1393) 247; W. J. & Sons, of Kirkham 174-5

Diconson, Bishop Edward, 134

Didsbury : bishops' transcripts 127; deeds 175, 297, 303; graveyard inscriptions 128; plans 306; R.C. records 131; school 75; tithe 28

Diggle, W., 328

Dilworth : charity 150; deeds 175, 179, 232, 233, 251, 309, 331; parish records 104; plans 180; tithe 26

Dilworth, Margaret, of Elswick, 289

Dinckley : deeds 182, 211, 222, 232, 337; enclosure 13, 98, 256; rentals 200, 285; survey 256

diocesan records, 120-28

Disraeli, Isaac, 219

dissenters, 17; places of worship 2, 17-18, 226

Ditchfield, J., 309

Ditton, 196; deeds 173, 194, 200, 201, 259, 261, 263, 307; leases 281; parish records 104; rentals 175, 320; surveys 195; tenants' books 195; tithe 27

Dixon, Mrs. R., 306; Thomas, of Clitheroe 172; Rev. Thomas, of Ulverston 300

Dobson family, of Gilrough, Bolton, 327; Miss M. H. 325; R. 310; Richard, apprentice sailor 173

docks and harbours, 16, 199, 207, 295, 303

Docton, K. H., 295

Dodd, J. P., 324

Doffcocker, see Bolton-le-Moors

Dolphinholme, see Nether Wyresdale

Donishope, see Accrington

Dorset, 238, 278; Dorchester 224; Lulworth 283; Weymouth 250

Douglas : bishops' transcripts 121; parish records 111; school 85

Douglas Navigation, 287, 331; river 62

Dowdale family, 195

Down Litherland, see Litherland

Downes, Roger, vice-chamberlain of Cheshire, 265

Downham, 191, 252; bishops' transcripts 123; deeds 220, 232, 251, 290, 319; friendly society 154; plan 234; school 75; scrapbook 157; tithe 26, 199, 286

Downholland : charity 150; deeds 197, 206, 215, 259, 295, 335; hall 215; manor 259; moss 198; parish records 104; plans 216; rentals 260; surveys 260; tithe 27

drainage, 36, 53, 173, 180, 185, 207, 216, 223, 224, 226, 236, 246, 266; authority records 62-3; plans 16, 180, 246, 268

drapers, 165, 174, 179, 184

Drinkwater family, of Prestwich, 307

Drinnan, Mrs. L., 328

Driver family, 182

Droylsden, 308; Congregational records 137; deeds 232, 320, 330; Kirkmanshulme tithe 28; R.C. records 131; schools 75; tithe 28; urban district 49

Duddon : ironworks, see Egton-with-Newland; river 177

Dugdale, John, of Clitheroe, 291

Ellenbrook : bishops' transcripts 127; chapel 233, 331; terrier 128
Ellesmere, earl of, 305
Ellison, W. G., 298
Elston, 297; deeds 254, 331; tithe 26
Elswick, 289; deeds 174, 175, 194, 206, 303, 309, 318, 321, 331, 333, 334; leases 165; survey 272; tithe 26
Elton : bishops' transcripts 126; census 100; deeds 149, 187, 227, 308, 334; leases 188, 265, 270; plans 188, 271; schools 76; surveys 188; tithe 28; turnpike 188, 215
Elwood, Dr. W. J., 303
emigration, 12, 228, 306
employers' associations, 162-3
enclosure awards, 13-14; and see under individual parishes
engineering, 165-6, 177, 298
England family, 182
Entwistle, 233; deeds 232, 304, 309, 334; enclosure 14; parish records 104
Entwistle, S., 293
Ermen & Engels, of Manchester, 171
Esprick, see Greenhalgh-with-Thistleton
Essex, 186, 257, 269; Arkesdon 307; Barndon 264; Bell House estate 257; Clacton 267; Felsted School 230; Goldhanger 197; Grays Thurrock 277; Hedingham 264; Little Totham 197; Lees 230; Saffron Walden 258; Southminster 197; Walton 267
Essex, earl of, 198
Essex Record Office, 291
estate agents, see auctioneers
Esthwaite, see Hawkshead
Etheridge, Mrs. O. M., 311
Euxton, 273; accounts 273; bishops' transcripts 122; deeds 190, 206, 211, 232, 244, 263, 271, 274, 310, 314, 317, 324, 326, 330 ,337; manor 243, 244; market 341; mills 271, 273, 301; parish records 104, 271, 273; plans 291, 306, 324; rentals 208, 246, 326; R.C. records 131, 135; school 76, 210; surveys 272, 321; tithe 26
evacuation, 39, 53, 56
Evans, Edward, Antarctic explorer, 318; Richard & Co. 33; trust (Congregational) 135
Everard family, 242
Everett, Miss E. M., 319
Everton : accounts 270; bishops' transcripts 125; deeds 179, 310, 330; militia 7; schools 76; tithe 27
Evesham, town clerk of, 322

excise : collector 323; duties 234, 270; surveyors 248, 249
Exeter, duchess of, 269
Exeter City Library, 296
explosives, 22, 167
Extwistle, 274, 275; bounds 278; deeds 303; waste 278; and see Briercliffe-with-Extwistle

Failsworth : deeds 307, 312, 315, 319; plans 306; police 7; R.C. records 131; school 76; tithe 28; urban district 49
Fairclough, C., 295; W. D. 300
Fairfax, Rev. Henry, 304
fairs, 221, 234, 266, 267, 270, 321
Faithwaite, John, of Caton, 340
Falkner, Edward, sheriff, 332
Fallows family, of Preston 298; E. J., of Manchester 298
Farington, 170, 180, 257, 322; bishops' transcripts 122; cotton mills 170, 171; deeds 211, 214, 232, 257, 274, 301, 321, 326; enclosure 14, 258; gas company 166; leases 258; moss 258; parish records 104; plans 301; schools 76; surveys 258, 275; tithe 26
Farington family, of Worden, 210-14; Susan Maria 338
Farleton, see Melling-with-Wrayton
farming records, 166, 172, 174, 186, 195, 197, 204, 207, 215, 223, 225, 236, 253, 257, 260, 266, 269, 273, 295, 323, 329, 340, 341; and see agriculture
Farnworth, 335, 341; bishops' transcripts 127; Britannia Works 172; Congregational records 136; deeds 187, 197, 200, 229, 251, 281, 292, 303, 330; divisional executive committee 38; enclosure 14; Halshaw Moor 230; leases 271; parish records 118; plans 200, 270; R.C. records 131; schools 76, 94; tithe 28
Farrar, W., 322
Farrer family, 182; & Co. 313
Fazakerley : deeds 179, 209, 244, 271; enclosure 14; plans 180, 246; tithe 27
Fazakerley family, 181, 324; Nicholas, M.P., 268
Fearnhead, see Poulton-with-Fearnhead
Fell family, of Ulverston, 214; J. H. 315; Sir Matthew 328
felons, prosecution of, 13, 97, 156, 174, 217, 258, 334
feltmakers, 334
Fence : bishops' transcripts 123; school 84

361

Foulds family, 182

Foulridge, 184, 248; assessments 250; constable 250; deeds 182, 249, 276, 285, 290, 303, 327; mill 249, 250; Noyna 248, 250; plans 250; rentals 185, 250; schools 76; surveys 249, 300; tithe 26, 182

Fowden-Hindley family, 323

Fox, Cornelius, of Stalmine, 198; James, of Kirkham 292

Fox Denton, see Chadderton

Foxfield, see Broughton-in-Furness

Foyster, Messrs., 321

France, 279; Aumale 337; Calais 278; Citeaux 279; Douai 259; emperor 219; Mayence 336; Meaux abbey 337; Moulineaux 243; Paris 259; St. Omer 219; Valenciennes 336

France, R. Sharpe, 289

France-Hayhurst, C. H., 302

Francis & Co., of Cambridge, 176

Fraser, Col. and Mrs., of Ravenhead, 174

Freckleton, 292; deeds 83, 172, 174, 175, 179, 184, 186, 194, 202, 206, 257, 292, 293, 309, 314, 316, 331; felons 156; leases 329; marsh 309, 329; Methodist records 143; moss 329; parish records 105; plans 298; school 76; Society of Friends records 148; tithe 26

Free Church Councils, 146

freemasons, 9

French revolution, 280

Frere, Cholmeley, & Nicholson, 307

Freshwater, Rev. S., 302

friars, 5, 193, 224, 231, 281

friendly societies, 153-5, 170, 172, 179, 181

Friends, Society of, 75, 294, 295, 300; records 146-8

Fulwood, 152, 335; bishops' transcripts 122; Cadley 76, 252; common 252; deeds 174, 186, 192, 254, 261, 288, 326, 327, 331; divisional executive committee 39; enclosure 14, 256; garrison bishops' transcripts 122; parish records 105; plans 198, 306, 313, 332; police 7; race-course 158; schools 76; tithe 26; urban district 50

furnaces, 177, 234, 252; see also bloomeries, forges, iron industry

Furnell, J., 322

Furness, 217, 218, 335, 340, 341; abbey 203, 335, 338; dean 207; deanery 120; probate records 25; deeds 232; estates 203, 204; Fells 220, 307; High Furness, highway board 62; historical collec-

tions 337; manor 204, 258; Plain 233, 234; rentals 204, 234; and see Low Furness

furnishings 181, 196, 197, 210, 212, 242, 248, 267, 275, 284, 285, 289, 307

Fylde, 267; buildings 300; Congregational district 139; drainage board 63; elections 268; Horsebreeding Co. 207; hospital board 30; poor law guardians 63; public assistance committee 40; rentals 268; rural district 55; Society of Friends records 148; Water Board 65

Fylde Historical Society, 289

Gaisford family, of Gresgarth, **216-17**

Galgate, see Ellel

Gallely, Isabel (Heseltine), 300

game, 181, 212, 217, 236, 242, 245, 299; duty 19; keepers 10, 275; poaching 172; tax 217; and see hunting, rabbits

gaols, 2, 4, 5-6, 8; and see under individual parishes and prisoners

gardeners, 225, 328; gardening notes 273

Gardiner family, 220-21

Gardner, B. B., of Pilling, 304; E. S. 321; Mrs. J. E. 313

Garner, John, apprentice hatter, 293; W. T. 294

Garnett family, of Quernmore, **217-18**

Garstang, 202, 253, 335; accounts 327; bishops' transcripts 121; borough records 45; chapel 105; church 251, 253; Churchtown 253; court records 22; deeds 175, 202, 222, 276, 288, 305, 314, 321, 331; gas company 166; highway board 61; parish records 105; plans 296; police station 8; poor law guardians 63; Primrose League 155; public assistance committee 40; railways 299; rectory 173; rental 260; R.C. records 131; rural district 55; Stout House 105; terriers 123; turnpike 61

Garston : Aigburth 76, 294; bishops' transcripts 124; deeds 193, 218, 222, 331; district nurses 157; schools 76; tithe 27

Garswood, 219; coal 33; R.C. records 131, 135

Gartside, Capt. Thomas, of Manchester, 185; charity 334

gas companies 44, 46, 48, 51, 52, 53, 58, 166, 183, 186, 189, 314; inspector 174; plans 16; records 65

Gaskarth family, 242

Gaskell family, 271; Miss B. K. 314; Mrs. E. M. 319

Gastrell, Francis, bishop of Chester, 338

Gates, G., 320
Gateshead Public Library, 306
Gaultry, Goodfellow & Co., 313
Gawthorpe, *see* Habergham Eaves
Genealogists, Society of, 302
genealogy, *see* pedigrees
Gerard family, 205, 282; of Ashton-in-Makerfield **218-19**; Joan, of Wigan 228; lord, of Brandon 245; Sir Robert 334
German, William, of Charnock Richard, 190
Germany : Lubeck, 230
Gerrard, Sir Thomas, 341
Gibbon, R. T., 327
Gibraltar, 322
Gibson family, 176, 217, 218; Charles, of Preston 217, 218; William of Beckhead 169
Gillar's (Gillas) Green, *see* Eccleston
Gillibrand family, 324
Gillman, J. A., 314
Gillmoss, *see* Kirby
girdlemaker, 227
girl guides, 157
Gladstone family, of Liverpool, 323
glass, heraldic, 234; manufacturer 174
Glasson : bishops' transcripts 122; dock 295; school 91
Glazebrook, *see* Rixton-with-Glazebrook
Glazebury, *see* Culcheth
Gleaston : castle 338; deeds 203; enclosure 14; survey 203
Gloucestershire, 238, 278; Bishops Cleeve 257; Bristol 312; Colesborne 336; Eastleach 336; Forest of Dean 257; Gloucester 214, 257, 312; Hucclecote 336; Little Compton 222; Sudeley 242; Taddington 337; Wiggold 277; Winchcomb 242; Wincote 264
Gloucestershire Record Office, 297
glover, 253
Goathwaite, *see* Lowick
Goddard, F. W., 312
Golborne : bishops' transcripts 126; charities 150; deeds 51, 179, 181, 282, 317; enclosure 14; police 60; rental 315; school 77; survey 272; tithe 27
Goldshaw Booth : bounds 290; deeds 182, 290, 304, 316
Goldsmiths' Company, 328
Goodshaw Booth, 290; bishops' transcripts 123; deeds 172; parish records 105; school 77, 88; terrier 123
Goore, John, of Lydiate, 198

Goosnargh-with-Newsham, 180, 226, 252, 335; accounts 269, 273; bishops' transcripts 121; church-ley 180; deeds 100, 130, 174, 175, 179, 185, 186, 202, 206, 208, 232, 251, 254, 261, 263, 274, 276, 283, 288, 289, 290, 294, 297, 299, 300, 303, 308, 311, 313, 325, 327, 330, 331, 333, 335, 337, 339; highways 292; history 180; Inglewhite 299, 326; Kidsnape 289; leases 265; mill 180; parish records 105, 180; plans 209, 268, 297, 299; rate book 180; R.C. records 131; schools 77, 180; surveys 256, 272; Threlfall chapel 226; tithe 26, 180; valuations 299; White-chapel bishops' transcripts 121
Gordon, James, freeman of Liverpool, **301**
Gornall, Thomas, apprentice feltmaker, 334
Gorry, W. L., 319
Gorton : bishops' transcripts 127; deeds 232, 289, 291, 302, 312, 330; R.C. records 131; rental 234; schools 77; terrier 128; tithe 28
Goss, Alexander, R.C. bishop of Liverpool, 128
Gould, Wright, & Davies, of Manchester, 167
Goulter, William, of Lytham, 292
Gradwell, Rev. Henry, of Claughton, 130; J. L. 293; James, of Leigh 326; Rev. Robert, of Claughton (1800) 130; Rev. Robert of Claughton (1860) 130
Graham, Mr., of Warrington, 215
Grand Junction railway, 228
Grange-over-Sands, 317; bishops' transcripts 124; foreshore 328; police 60
Grassendale : bishops' transcripts 124
Grassyard (Gresgarth), *see* Caton
Graveson, S., 294
Graythwaite, 190, 258; deeds 258; surveys 258
Great Crosby, 196; bishops' transcripts 125; church 195; deeds 195, 197, 215, 244, 263, 324, 335; halmote 194; manor 243, 295; parish records 105; plans 306; R.C. records 131; rental 246; schools 74, 77, 195; terrier 126; tithe 27; warren 245
Great Eccleston : bishops' transcripts 122; deeds 83, 174-5, 254, 263, 290, 295, 303, 333; parish records 105; plan 303; R.C. records 131; schools 77, 318; tithe 26
Great Harwood, 224, 251; Allsprings 237, 238, 239; assessments 238; bishops' transcripts 121; bounds 256; coal 224;

commons 223; cotton mill 170; curacy 238; deeds 184, 222, 232, 238, 250, 254, 288; employers' association 162; enclosure 14, 222; leases 238; manor 221; Martholme 223; Methodist records 143; moor 223, 238; parish records 98, 105; paving and sewering 238-9; plans 189, 238, 297; police 60; rental 224; schools 77; surveys 223, 238; terrier 123; trades unions 160; urban district 50; valuation 238
Great Heaton : deeds 187, 288; tithe 28
Great Lever : deeds 200, 232, 292, 307; plans 200; tithe 28
Great Marsden : bishops' transcripts 123; plans 270
Great Marton : deeds 292, 320, 323; mill 172; plans 208; school 77; *and see* Little Marton *and* Marton
Great Mearley, *see* Mearley
Great Sankey : bishops' transcripts 125; deeds 172, 194, 236; rental 337; schools 66, 77; tithe 27
Green family, of Leyland, 323; of Oldham 327; Miss B. 327; C. 325; Miss P. 312
Greene family, 187, 193
Greenhalgh-with-Thisleton, 77; Congregational records 138; deeds 172, 175, 184, 220, 251, 263, 283, 289, 331; Esprick school 77, 301; parish records 106, 251; Thistleton 83, 308, 338; tithe 26, 206
Greenodd, *see* Egton-with-Newland
Greenwood family of Clerk Hill, **220-21**; Adam, schoolmaster 304
Gregge, Edward (Hopwood), of Werneth 227; Joseph (1680) 227
Gregory, John, of Rochdale, 228; Rowcliffe & Co. 313
Gregson, James, of Great Eccleston, 318; John, of Liverpool 185; William, of Liverpool 185
Gresgarth (Grassyard), *see* Caton
Gressingham, 289; bishops' transcripts 122; deeds 240, 258, 292; school 77; scrapbook 157; tithe 26
Grieve, Dr. J. W., 304
Griffiths, Mrs. B. E., **328**
Grime, Mrs., 319
Grimsargh-with-Brockholes, 335; deeds 186, 202, 254, 276, 290; parish records 56, 106; tithe 26; *and see* Brockholes
Grimshaw family, 237
Grizedale, *see* Satterthwaite
grocers, 166-7, 224
grooms, 225
Grundy family, 326, 334; Cuthbert (1854)

334; Sir Cuthbert 334; Kershaw, Farmer & Co. 320
Grymesdiche, Thomas, of Warrington, 201
Gunnolfsmore, *see* Houghton
gunpowder, *see* explosives
Gwillym, Robert, of Herefordshire, 235
Gwynedd Record Office, 325
Gynn family, of Blackpool, 311

Habergham Eaves, 187; coal 34; deeds 182, 187, 189, 276, 283, 285, 290, 325, 327, 331; Gawthorpe 261; parish records 106; rentals 273, 286; schools 77; surveys 272, 340; tithe 26
Hackensall, *see* Preesall-with-Hackensall
Hacking, Agnes of (1373), 255
Hackney, Miss M. A., of Litherland, 326
Hackney Borough Library, 308
Haigh : charity 213; deeds 179, 232, 317, 330, 331; R.C. records 131; survey 272; tithe 28
Haighton, 327; Cow Hill 180; deeds 100, 175, 179, 181, 206, 254, 335; enclosure 14, 180; road 299; tithe 26
hairpowder duty, 19
Hale, 244; bishops' transcripts 124; chapel 193; coroner 24; deeds 193, 194, 197, 324; enclosure 14; manor 193; parish records 106; terrier 126; tithe 28
Halebank, *see* Halewood
Halewood : accounts 269; bishops' transcripts 124; *compoti* 178; deeds 194, 197, 202, 209, 263, 313; enclosure 14; Halebank 246; leases 265, 329; manor 262; parish records 106; rentals 268; schools 77; surveys 266; tithe 28
Hall, A. S., 305; James, of Freckleton 292; Robert & Sons, of Bury 165
Hall Carr, *see* Cowpe-with-Lench
Hallé Orchestra, 185
Halliwell : bishops' transcripts 127; deeds 187, 227, 229, 232, 263, 314, 328; leases 265; plans 306, 341; schools 77; Smithills 197; tithe 28
Halsall, 193, 315; bishops' transcripts 124; charities 150; church 194; deeds 197, 206, 244, 259, 335; felons 156; manor 259; Methodist records 143; moss 245; parish records 106; poor 208; rectory 208; school 77, 208; surveys 260; terriers 126; tithe 28
Halsall, Sir Cuthbert, 339; Hugh, rector of Halsall 208
Halshaw Moor, *see* Farnworth
Halsnead, *see* Whiston

Haydock family, 134
Hayley, William, poet, 220
Hayshaw Fell, *see* Over Wyresdale
Heald family, 212
health committee of county council, 38
Heap : deeds 187, 263, 330; leases 188, 265, 271; parish records 106; plans 188, 270; poor rates 188; surveys 188; tithe 28
Heapey : bishops' transcripts 122; bounds 226; chapel 209; deeds 271, 326, 330, 333, 337; parish records 106; school 78; tithe 26
hearth tax, 18, 250
Heath Charnock : deeds 173, 175, 197, 209, 254, 297, 317, 326, 330, 331, 333, 337; leases 288; plans 298; roads 179; surveys 272; tithe 26
Heathwaite, Robert, rural dean of Richmond, 207-8
Heaton, 201; deeds 202, 218, 229, 232; highways 56; manor 201; parish records 103; rentals 202, 234; school 78; surveys 272, 328; tithe 28
Heaton, Elijah, of Westhoughton, 311
Heaton Norris : bishops' transcripts 127; deeds 211; R.C. records 131; terrier 128; tithe 28
Heaton-with-Oxcliffe : deeds 276; Oxcliffe 254; tithe 26
Heelis, W. H. & Son, 305
Height, *see* Cartmel Fell
heirlooms, *see* furnishings
Heirs House, *see* Colne
Helm, William, of Chipping, 262
Helmshore, *see* Haslingden
Hemingway, Marcy & Sons, 313
Henfield, *see* Clayton-le-Moors
Henheads, *see* Haslingden
Henry VIII, letters 230, 231, 245
Henthorn, *see* Little Mitton
heraldry, 234, 247, 253, 284; *and see* arms, coats of
Herd, S., 306
Herdman, William (1849), 290
Hereford City Library, 308
Herefordshire, 235, 236, 237; Langston 237; Welsh Newton 279
Heron family, 181
Hertfordshire, 269; Hitchin 294
Hertfordshire Record Office, 324
Heseltine family, 300
Hesketh family, of Mains, 201; of Rufford 221-5, 235, 248, 250-51, 265; of Tulketh 215; Roger 333; Sir Thomas & Lady 212; William of 221

Hesketh-with-Becconsall : bishops' transcripts 121; deeds 179, 211, 222, 326; drainage 62; enclosure 14, 222; fishery 224; manor 221; plans 224; school 78; surveys 223; tithes 26, 273; *and see* Becconsall
Heskin, 271, 335; deeds 179, 181, 206, 244, 251, 271, 282, 314, 315, 326, 331; manor 243, 244; plans 180; rentals 246; surveys 272, 273, 321; tithe 26
Heskin, Nicholas, of Welch Whittle, 273
Hest, *see* Slyne-with-Hest
Hewartson, Rev. William, of Poulton-le-Fylde, 256
Hey, *see* Ashton-under-Lyne; *for* The Hey *see* Newton-in-Makerfield
Hey, H. E., 292; Harold 313; T. E. 313
Heyhouses, *see* Lytham
Heysham, 289, 328; bishops' transcripts 121; borough records 45; deeds 173, 178, 182, 240, 276, 327, 330, 337; free church council 146; harbour 179; Methodist records 143; parish records 106; quarry 328; rectory 206, 312; survey 328; terriers 123; tithe 26
Heywood : bishops' transcripts 126; borough records 45; church 231; deeds 172, 184; hall 307; leases 188; parish records 106, 107; R.C. records 131; schools 78; turnpike 61; water board 318; woollen mill 171
Heywood, John, of Urmston, 237; Rebecca 237
Higgin, John, apprentice linen-webster, 304
Higgins, G., 301
High Furness, *see* Furness
High Wray, *see* Claife
Higham-with-West Close Booth : deeds 172; Hollins 305; Methodist records 143; parish records 107; schools 78; White Lee 290
Higher Booths : deeds 172, 182, 290; land tax 172; Loveclough Methodist records 145; school 79
Higher Lickow, *see* Preesall-with-Hackensall
Higher Walton : bishops' transcripts 121; cotton mill 171; school 92
highwaymen, 3
highways, 2, 4, 10, 15, 22, 36, 189, 217, 250, 251, 252, 261, 285, 286, 289, 290, 292, 293, 313, 328, 334, *and see* 43-54; boards 61-2; committee of county council 38; *see also* roads

Higson, J., 304
Hill, Mrs. E. M., 306; Mrs. Falkner 300; Thomas, schoolmaster 319; & son, of Ormskirk 177-8
Hilton family, 203
Himsworth, K. S., 319
Hindle family, 304
Hindley, 219, 271; bishops' transcripts 126; coal 188; deeds 175, 181, 187, 194, 201, 218, 229, 232, 248, 281, 282, 320, 330; enclosure 14; plans 306; police 7; R.C. records 132, 135; rentals 237, 330; schools 79; surveys 272, 282, 300; tithe 28
Hindsford, see Tyldesley-with-Shakerley
Hirst, Mrs. F. L., 310
Hobson, Reynold, chantry priest, 281
Hodder, river, 62, 158
Hodge, Henry, of Bretherton, 164; W. & R., of Halsall, 322
Hodges, William, of Bretherton, 166
Hodgkinson, H. R., 299; Richard, of Atherton, 299
Hodgson family, of Cockerham and Yealand, 314; of Hawkshead 318; Mrs. D. 327; Miss E. 292; J. E. G. 318; W. R. 306; & Son 310
Hoghton, 225; accounts 226, bishops' transcripts 122; bounds 226; cotton mill 180; deeds 179, 225, 251, 322, 323, 326, 330, 331, 333; drainage 226; Gunnolfsmore commons 334; manor 334; Moulden Brow 226; Moulden mill 225; parish records 107; plans 180; school 79, 225; tithe 26, 179
de Hoghton family, of Hoghton, 190, 225-6; Sir Gilbert 212; Sir Henry 223; Jane, Lady 250
Holcome : bishops' transcripts 126; church 231; deeds 333
Holden, Thomas, of Bolton, 296; Thomas and John, of Blackburn 164; & Wilson, of Lancaster 178-9
Holgate family, of Foulridge, 248
Holker, 202; assessments 204; coal 203; deeds 203; Parkhead 203; rentals 204; roads 203, 204; and see Upper Holker
Holleth : parish records 107; tithe 26
Hollin Hall, see Trawden
Hollinfare : bishops' transcripts 125; chapel 193; parish records 107; terrier 126
Hollingworth, Mrs. W. R., 304
Hollinwood : bishops' transcripts 127; deeds 339; R.C. records 133; school 72

Holme : bishops' transcripts 123; Independent registers 188; parish records 102; school 73; and see Cliviger
Holme, Miss G. N., 303
Holmeswood, see Rufford
Holt family, 306; of Bispham 192; of Spotland 298; E. 315; William, of Mitton 286; William, hatter 234
Holt Leigh family, of Wigan, 282, 316
Holte, Charles, of Stubley, 337; Peter de la (1378), 257
Home Guard, 57-8, 298
Hoole : bishops' transcripts 121; church 334; deeds 337; parish records 107; school 333; terrier 123
Hooton, James, of Scarisbrick, 341
Hopkins, Gerald Manley, 129; Robert William, clerk of the crown, 322
Hopkinson family, 147
Hopwood, 226, 228; bishops' transcripts 127; deeds 227, 232, 276, 335; enclosure 14; school 79; tithe 28; valuation 227
Hopwood family, of Hopwood, 226-8, and see Gregge, Edward; H. 319; William of (1277) 226
Hornby, 296, 335; bishops' transcripts 122; castle 266, 313, 338; charity 150; court records 22; enclosure 14; honour 173, 301; manor 185; parish records 107; R.C. records 132; surveys 258, 266; terriers 123; tithe 26
Hornby family, 181; Edmund (1818), 286; John, archdeacon of Lancaster 120; Newsham & Haworth, of Blackburn 184; Thomas, of Liverpool 308; & Kenworthy, of Blackburn 184
Horner, J. S., 314
horoscope, 290
Horrocks family, of Preston, 252, 285, 286; Samuel 286; William, of Farnworth, 341
horses : breeding, 36, 37, 207, 255, 260; on canals 164; gin 230
Horsfall, G. G., 305; H. 306
Horton, Sir William, of Chadderton, 304
Horwich, 271, 328; bishops' transcripts 127; chapels 103, 328; Congregational records 138; deeds 187, 197, 232, 296, 328, 331; enclosure 14; hospital board 30; Methodist records 143; parish records 107; plans 306, 315; school 79; survey 272; terrier 128; tithe award 28
hosiers, 167
Hospitallers of St. John of Jerusalem, 197, 206, 260, 274, 336

hospitals, 53, 208, 236, 314, 316; insurance committees 30-31; records 29-30; voluntary 42

hotels, 167, 289, 325; *see also* inns

Hothersall, 247, 335; deeds 247, 288, 331; societies 332; tithe 26; *and see* Alston-with-Hothersall

Houghton, Middleton, and Arbury : deeds 282; parish records 107; survey 272; tithe 28; *see also* Arbury, Middleton

Houghton family, of Lowton, **228;** Craven & Co., of Preston, 179-80, 211; Daniel, African traveller 226

Hounslow Library, 314

household accounts, 202, 208, 213, 214, 218, 237, 247, 253, 269, 279, 280, 283, 289, 301, 305, 310; *see also* furnishings

houses of correction, *see* gaols

Howick, 257, 335; deeds 211, 222, 250, 254, 257, 283; enclosure 14, 222; felons 156, 258; marsh 257; schools 79, 312, 321; tithe 26, 258

Hoyle, James, of Bashall, 172

Huddleston family, 211, 214, 297; J. E. 308

Hudson, Christopher, of Preston, 339

Hughes, John, of Downholland, 104; Mitton & Barker 325

Hulme : bishops' transcripts 127; deeds 281, 319; plan 339; R.C. records 132; schools 79, 319; tithe 28

Hulme trust, *see* Astley

Hulton, 229, 230; coal 34, 165; deeds 229, 331; Middle, rental 234; tithe 28; rental 234; school 79; *and see* Little Hulton

Hulton family, of Hulton, **229-32;** Richard of (1312) 230

Humphreys, Mrs. E., 326

Huncoat, 256, 340; deeds 254, 276, 285, 325, 326; hearth tax 18; rental 286; schools 79

Hundersfield : deeds 229, 232, 238, 247, 276, 291, 307, 310, 311, 312, 313, 330, 337; plans 306; survey 280

Hunt, Henry (1818), 295; John, of Ribby 292; Richard, of North Meols 292

hunting, 158, 202, 209, 228, 249, 284, 299; *see also* game

Huntingdonshire, 269; Alconbury 219

Huntroyde, *see* Simonstone

Hurst, *see* Ashton-under-Lyne

Hurst Green, *see* Aighton, Bailey, and Chaigley

Hurstwood, *see* Worsthorne-with-Hurstwood

Hutchinson, Alexander and Janet, 251

Hutton, 257; common 321; deeds 184, 199, 211, 222, 257, 303, 308, 312; plans 213; rentals 258, 260; school 79; surveys 258, 272

Hutton, Miss, 301; William, campanologist, 301

Huyton : bishops' transcripts 125; builder 164; church 246, 247, 268; coal 288; deeds 173, 187, 194, 209, 263, 308, 312, 325, 326, 330, 337; leases 265, 288; plans 268; rectory 246; rentals 268; schools 79, 246; survey 341; terrier 126; tithe 28, 246, 341; urban district 50

Hyde, Thomas and William, of Urmston, 282

Hynd, Samuel, minister of Sefton, 247

Idsworth, John, of Clitheroe, 291

Ightenhill (Park) : deeds 232, 254; enclosure 275, 278; manor 251; plans 279; survey 272; tithe 26

Ikin family, 210

Imperial Chemical Industries, 297

improvement plans, 16

Ince, Arthur, of Wigan, 228

Ince Blundell, 196; bounds 197; deeds 194, 197, 206, 244, 254, 259, 296, 302; flooding 197; highways 10; manor 244; parish records 107; plans 198, 246; rentals 198; R.C. records 132, 135; surveys 198, 245, 272; tithe 28, 197; townfield 198; waste 245; windmill 198

Ince Hall Coal & Canal Co., 282

Ince-in-Makerfield, 282; deeds 200, 201, 209, 215, 229, 232, 282, 315, 317, 331; enclosure 14; manor 282; Platt Bridge turnpike 283; police 7; rental 237; riots 20; R.C. records 132, 135; schools 79; survey 272; tithe 28; Westwood 313

income tax, 15, **228**

India, 180, 196, 225, 226, 280; Calcutta 317; Punjab 312

indulgences, 201, 224, 260, 279

Inghamite church records 140-41

Inglewhite, *see* Goosnargh-with-Newsham

Ingol, 81; deeds 175, 293; parish records 108; tithe 27; *and see* Lea, Ashton, Ingol, and Cottam

innkeepers, 172, 175; *see also* alehouses, beerhouses, inns

inns, 49, 167, 176, 177, 183, 186, 231, 261, 297, 302, 303, 316, 322, 325; *see also* alehouses, beerhouses, hotels, licensing, public houses

inquisitions *post mortem*, 176, 194, 186, 197, 227, 229, 242, 244, 247, 249, 251,

255, 257, 261, 262, 264, 275, 278, 282, 284, 334
Inskip-with-Sowerby, 180, 205, 296; bishops' transcripts 122; deeds 205, 261, 263, 331; manor 262; parish records 107; plans 205; rentals 269, 315; school 205; surveys 272; tithe 26, 205; *see also* Sowerby
insurance, 212, 228, 361, 304; committees 30-31; companies 167, 184; policy collector 319
inventions (patents), 174, 180, 187, 209, 214, 228, 294, 296, 308, 315, 333
inventories, 172, 180, 181, 184, 185, 196, 197, 203, 208, 213, 227, 229, 231, 242, 244, 248, 251, 252, 255, 261, 262, 270, 271, 275, 284, 289, 290, 291, 292, 295, 298, 327, 328, 336, 341
Iorwerth, son of Bleiddyn, 229
Ipswich and East Suffolk Record Office, 301
Ireby (Thornton-in-Lonsdale), deeds 197, 240, 241
Ireland, 234, 249, 266, 267, 268, 298, 335; Bryan's Town 229, 230; Conge abbey 219; Drogheda 195; Dundalk 195; Dysart 195; Galway 226; Holyrood abbey 281; Maryborough 243, 245 : viscount, *see* Molyneux; Mullanstown 288; parliament 246; Westmeath 229, 230; Wicklow 264
Ireland family, 193, 236; Thomas 235, 236
Ireland Blackburne family, of Hale, 193
Irlam : deeds 232, 330; Home Guard 57; R.C. records 132
iron industry, 167, 177, 179, 186, 236, 305; cinders 191; hammerman 191; mining 177, 204, 227, 267; ore owners 203; *see also* bloomeries, forges, furnaces
ironmongers, 168, 300
Irvine, H. C., 309
Irving family, of Hawkshead, 318
Irwell : hall 307; reservoirs 171; river 42, 62, 270
Irwin, Mrs. G., 306; R. 299; Rachel M., of Manchester 299
Italy : Leghorn 207; Venice 207

Jackson family, of Lydiate, 321; I. & sons 294; John, of Longton 311; R. R., of Blackburn 169; S. A. 306; Stephenson & Swainson, of Walton-le-Dale 180
Jacobites, 195, 234, 338; (1715) 198, 259; (1745) 227, 297

Jacson, Roger, senior and junior, of Preston, 329
James III (Old Pretender), 220
James, Isaac, of St. Martins-in-the-Fields, London, 255
Jameson, Thomas, of Aughton, 262
Jeffreys, John, father of Judge Jeffreys, 236
Jemson, E., 318
Jenkinson, G., 322; R. H. 318
Jennings, A. E., 312
Jessop family, 229, 230; Ann (Hulton) 229, 230; William, clerk of the council 229, 230
Jesuits, 135, 203
Johnson & Kay, of Preston, 180; Taylor & Chadwick, of Blackburn 164, 184
joiners, 167, 253, 302, 304; *see also* woodworkers
Jolly family
Jollybrand, Hugh, of Latham, 178; Richard, of Lathom 178
Jones, Mrs. I., 320; Jabey & Son, of Preston 163; K. W. 320; Rev. William 284
Joyce, Mrs., 301
jurors, 2, 10, 24, 58, 228
justices of the peace, 19-20; clerks 8
juvenile courts, 21-3; offenders 12

Kay family, of Bury, 188, 298, 340; J. C. 291; T. 323; W. T. 300; & Birley, of Kirkham 175
Kearsley : chemist 154, 164; coal 33; deeds 172, 187, 200, 229, 230, 292, 303, 319; divisional executive committee 39; enclosure 14; friendly society 154; leases 265, 271; Methodist records 143; moss 187; plans 188, 270; schools 79; surveys 266; tithe 28
Keck, James Anthony, of Leicestershire, 235
Keighley family, 205
Kellamergh, *see* Bryning-with-Kellamergh,
Kellet, *see* Over Kellet
Kellet, George, of Kirkham, 329
Kellett, R., 316
Kelsall, E., 312
Kendrick, John, surgeon, of Warrington, 293
Kennedy, Miss J. D., 325; & Glover, 326
Kent, 219; Canterbury, archbishops' lands in Lancs. 184; Dover 226; Greenwich 197; Hadlow 255; Rochester 257; Rotherhithe 307
Kent, river, 177; sands 203, 328

369

371

marsh 245, 321; parish records 108; plans 246; rentals 247; schools 81; tithe 28; urban district 50

Little Bolton : deeds 175, 288, 298, 304, 339; manor 338; plans 306; tithe 28

Little Bowland, 320, 338

Little Crosby, 194, 196; commons 266; deeds 195, 197, 244, 254, 263, 318; flooding 197; Harkirk burial ground 196; leases 265; manor 194; plans 246; R.C. records 132; surveys 195, 245; tenants' books 195; tithe 28

Little Eccleston-with-Larbreck : deeds 83, 202, 290, 303, 306, 332, 333; Larbreck 175, 176, 251, 253, 334; tithe 27, 206

Little Harwood : bridge 305; deeds 276; enclosure 14, 98; parish records 108; surveys 97, 272, 300

Little Heaton : deeds 227, 288; parish records 108; tithe 28

Little Hoole : schools 81; tithe 27

Little Hulton, 232; church 231; deeds 187, 232, 303, 330; parish records 108; Peel (Kenyon Peel) Hall 232, 233, 234, 307, 314, 339; Peel terrier 128; school 81; smithy 188; tithe 28; Wharton 282

Little Lever, 230; bishops' transcripts 126; deeds 187, 292, 314; divisional executive sub-committee 39; police 60; schools 81

Little Marsden : bishops' transcripts 123; deeds 182; parish records 109

Little Marton : deeds 206; manor 205, 206; plans 208; and see Great Marton and Marton

Little Mitton, 289; Coldcotes 261; deeds 251, 289, 315; Henthorn 261, 272, 283; and see Mitton

Little Sankey, see Warrington

Little & Shepherd, 321

Little Urswick, see Urswick

Little Woolton : deeds 331, 337; leases 265; rental 269; school 81; tithe 28;see also Much Woolton and Woolton

Littleborough, 247, 311; bishops' transcripts 128; Congregational records 138; deeds 189, 314, 339; gas co. 166; Lower Townhouse 341; police 7; schools 66, 81; Stubley 337; Townhouse 247; urban district 51; Windybank 334

Littledale, see Caton

Littlewood, see Royton

Liverpool, 187, 198, 215, 223, 227, 245, 252, 262, 270, 287, 299, 301, 302, 303, 317, 320, 322, 323, 324, 332, 338, 340, 341; accounts 270 273; archdeaconry 120; beggars 12; bishops' transcripts

125; canal 182; castle 244, 245, 247; churches 215, 292; Congregational records 135, 138, 153; corporation 207; cotton brokers 170; Daily Post & Journal 168; deeds 146, 175, 179, 181, 182, 185, 186, 187, 193, 194, 197, 199, 206, 209, 235, 244, 251, 252, 263-4, 282, 287, 296, 298, 303, 307, 308, 313, 316, 330, 332, 337; diocese 95, 124-6, 301, probate records 26, tithe awards 27; estate agent 163; freemen 215, 275, 301; gaol 5; history 297; industrial school 130; leases 265, 288, 322; manor 243; maps 338, 341; Medical Institution 9; militia 7; overspill 41; Picton's Academy 81; plague 207; plans 246, 268, 294; quarter sessions 339; railways 169, 228, 267, 294, 341; rentals 210, 253, 268, 269, 271; roads 38, 268; R.C. diocese 130, records 135; schools 194, 215; Sessions House committee 8; Societies 153, 332; Society of Friends records 146; solicitors 168; survey 266; surveyors 163; terrier 126; theatre 313; townfield 210; turnpike 61

Liverpool City Libraries, 296

Liverpool University Library, 308

livery, 247

Livesey : Congregational records 138; deeds 184, 254, 303, 308, 330-31, 332, 337; friendly society 154; parish records 108; schools 81

Livesey, Miss, 301

Llandaff, bishop of, 203

Lloyd, David, minister of Sefton, 247; Rev. John, of Liverpool 292

loan societies, 9

Lock family, 280

Lodge family, of Windybank, 334

Lomax family, of Clayton-le-Moors, 237-8; James, of Clayton-le-Moors, 170

London, 217, 219, 229, 244, 247; accounts 213; deeds 193, 239, 255, 257, 336; Derby household 269; freedom of 328; Gracechurch St. 200; Grays Inn 240; Hatten Garden 200; Midland & Scottish railway 58; North-Eastern railway 58; & North-Western railway 228, 267; St. Paul's 264; Savoy hospital 198; survey 258

London County Record Office, 304

Longholme, see Cowpe-with-Lench

Longridge, 322, 335; bishops' transcripts 122; building societies 152, 180, 186; charity 150; common 267; deeds 247, 316, 327; gas co. 166; parish records

108; plans 313; railway 169; roads 268; R.C. records 132; schools 81; society 157; trades union 160; urban district 51

Longsight : deeds 339; R.C. records 132; school 77

Longton, 223, 310, 311; bishops' transcripts 122; charity 258; deeds 100, 179, 181, 211, 222, 251, 254, 257, 259, 274, 281, 283, 295, 303, 308, 312, 331, 338; drainage 62; enclosure 14, 222, 258; leases 281; manor 180; marsh 181, 258, 285; moss 223; parish records 108; plans 313, 342; schools 81; survey 272; terrier 123; tithe 27, 213; workhouse 224

Longueville & Co., 307

Longworth : deeds 229, 331, 336; Hackin 230; parish records 109, 231; plans 231; rental 231; survey 233

Longworth family, 291; Frank, J. P. 162; S. & Co., of Whalley 171; Solomon, of Clerk Hill 220

Lonsdale deanery, 120; probate records 25

Lonsdale hundred : assessments 337; bridge assessment 217; bridges (North) 4; court records (North) 23; court record (South) 23; court book 336; land tax 11; land tax (North) 204; steward 241; subsidies 177, 275, 278

Lord, J. R., 317; & Parker 317

Lostock : deeds 197, 232, 296, 331; enclosure 14; hall see Bamber Bridge; parish records 109; tithe 28

Lotherington, Miss, of Mossley, 82

lotteries, 228

Lovat, F., 296

Loveclough, see Higher Booths

Lovell, lords, 267, 269

Low Furness : deeds 190; highway board 62; Muchland 177, 204, 258

Lowde family, 207

Lowe, F. C., 308; Robson, 312

Lower Allithwaite : land tax 177; Outerthwaite 304; see also Allithwaite and Upper Allithwaite

Lower Booths, see Whalley

Lower Brockholes, see Brockholes

Lower Darwen : bishops' transcripts 121; deeds 220, 254, 307, 324, 338; enclosure 14, 98; parish records 98; survey 272

Lowick, 241; bishops' transcripts 124; chapel 242; deeds 177, 239, 242; Goathwaite Moss 242; hall 242; manor 242; mills 242; rentals 242; school 81; terrier 124; timber 242; tithe 27, 242

Lowther family, of Holker, 202, 203; of Marske 202; Anthony (1677) 204; Hon. William 207

Lowton, 228; bishops' transcripts 126; charities 150; deeds 51, 181, 183, 206, 228, 288, 309, 317, 323, 331; enclosure 14; felons 156; Highfield Moss 318; Lanehead 248; plan 228; rental 234; school 81; terrier 126; tithe 28

Loxham, William, of Kirkham, 169

Lucas, William, clerk in palatinate chancery, 332; & Wyllys 313

Lumb, see Tottington Higher End

lunacy, 6-7, 8, 22, 236; also see asylums, hospitals

Lund : bishops' transcripts 121; chapel 208, 267; parish records 102; parsonage 314; vicar 294

Lune, river 173; byelaws 15; fishery 185; plans 185, 217; Steam Fishing Co. of Fleetwood 166; Valley, fieldbook 341

Lunesdale : poor law guardians 64; rural district 56

Lunt : deeds 244; manor 243; plans 246, 306; tithe 28

Lydiate, 193, 321; bishops' transcripts 124; charities 150, 198; deeds 197, 206, 222, 232, 244, 264, 332; manor 244; plans 198, 246; R.C. records 135; rentals 198; school 81; surveys 198; tithe 28

Lyon family, 323

Lytham, 205, 326; accounts 208; bishops' transcripts 122; borough records 45; charities 208; common 206, 208; cottagers 207; deeds 175, 184, 185, 186, 206, 251, 254, 292, 332, 334; divisional executive committee 39; dock 207; drawing 208; Easter rolls 208; enclosure 14; farm-books 207; Heyhouses 233; school 78; invalids' home 208; manor 205, 206; mills 207; parish records 109; plans 208; priory 207; railway 207; rentals 208; R.C. records 132; sea defences 207; schools 82; surveys 207; terriers 123; tithe 27; and see St. Annes-on-the-Sea

McCormack, Mrs. G., 306

McGrindle, John, mariner, 309

McGuffogg, T. & W., of Preston, 170

McHugh, J., 314

MacKay, West & Holt, glass manufacturers, 174

McLaren, Jeens & Seacome, 306

MacMahon, K. A., 320

McNulty, Father, 317

Machell family, of Penny Bridge, **239**

machine-makers, 180, 187
Maddox, D., 321
Madoc, son of Bleiddyn, 229
Magee, P., 310; Marshall & Co. 316
Maghull : bishops' transcripts 124; charity 150; coal 246; deeds 197, 206, 215, 218, 244, 264, 308, 332; manor 244; parish records 109; plans 216; school 82; survey 215; terriers 126; tithe 28
magistrates, 6, 328; *and see* justices of the peace
Mains, *see* Singleton
Maitland, Miss E., 311
Makinson, Mrs., 290
Malta, 329
Man, Isle of, 193, 232, 234, 238 ,262, 263, 265, 266, 267, 268, 269, 270, 284, 329, 341
Manchester, 292, 297, 299, 300, 302, 308, 314, 316, 317, 320, 321, 322, 323, 326, 332; assize court 4; bishops' transcripts 127; brewer 164; canal 331; cathedral 303; chantry 281; charity 150; churches 231, 281, 315; coal 34; concert hall 9; Congregational records 138-9; cotton mills 170; county court records 23; deeds 146, 172, 184, 186, 187, 189, 227, 229, 232, 254, 274, 281, 282, 289, 292, 302, 304, 307, 308, 309, 312, 313, 315, 316, 319, 330, 331, 334, 335, 337, 339, 340; diocese 120, tithe awards 28; engineering 166, 298; Grammar School 230; graveyard inscriptions 128; grocers 167; hearth tax 18; hospital 237; house of correction 5; insurance co. 184; Jacobite trial 194; leases 265; manor 198, 298; map 339; Military Association 57, 339; militia 7; milliner 168; parish records 126-8; pawnbrokers 12; plans 297, 300, 306; police 7, 60; poor law guardians 64; public walks 270; quarter sessions 228, 251; railways 228, 267, 294; rental 234; riots 20; roads 268; R.C. records 132, 135; Royal Exchange library 9; School of Design 176; schools 82, 294; Chip Canal 164, 295; societies 9, 157, 332; Society of Friends records 146; Strangeways gaol 5; tailors 169; terriers 128; theatres 302, 304, 315; thread manufacturer 171; tithe 28; trades, various 171; trades union 160; turnpike 61; volunteers 253, 295; weir 301
Manchester Central Library, 305
Manchester Collieries Ltd., 291

Manchester Geological Society, 296
manors, lord of, 10
Mansergh family, 240
Mansriggs, *see* Ulverston
Manx Museum, 320
markets, 16, 44, 221, 234, 267, 270, 341
Marling, S., 297
Marriott family, 182
Marsden : bishops' transcripts 123; Bradley mill 278; deeds 182, 220, 249, 274, 276, 285, 290, 299, 300, 304, 308, 325, 332; enclosure 275; leases 265; parish records 109; plans 183; school 82; surveys 272, 329, 340; Society of Friends records 146-7; tithe 27
Marsden, E. C., 303; J. E. W. (1892) 305
Marsh family, 173; Dr. R. G. B. 293; & Francis, of Manchester 171; Son & Calvert 316, 323
Marshall, Stephen, 307; W. 315
Marsland family, 187
Martholme, *see* Great Harwood
Martin family, of Fleetwood, 316; Samuel, of Gisburn 293
Martin Hall, *see* Burscough
Martin mere, 180, 223, 266, 272, 333
Martinscroft, *see* Woolston-with-Martinscroft
Marton, 258, 290; bishops' transcripts 122; charities 150, 258; church 256; deeds 175, 176, 184, 202, 251, 283, 323, 326, 332; mere 173, 266; moss 208; parish records 109; plans 208; school 70; Spen Dyke 36, 207; surveys 207, 236; tithe 27; *see also* Great Marton, Little Marton; *for* Marton (Furness) *see* Dalton-in-Furness
Marton family, of Capernwray, 239-41; George (1859) 335
de Mascy, Hamon (1250), 280; Hamon (1462) 302
Mason, Hugh and Isobel, of Lathom, 178; Miss 324
Massey, Ann, of Rishton ,310
Mather family, of Lowick, 241-2; Henry and John, of Billinge 169
Matthews family, 212; Wilkinson (1834) 212
Maude & Tunnicliffe, 303
Mawdesley family, 321; Lt. Alexander 252; J. 322
Mawdsley, 335; bishops' transcripts 121; church 223; deeds 130, 175, 197, 218, 222, 229, 250, 271, 274, 281, 315, 324, 326, 331; leases 281, 290; parish records

375

109; plans 224; rental 260; R.C. records 132, 135; schools 82; surveys 223, 272, 321; tithe 27; waste 281

Maxwell, Henry & Co., of Blackpool, 168

May & May, 316; May & Deacon 307

Mayer, W., 294; W. E. 326

Mayfield, S. S., 305

Maykin, of Kenyon, 210

Mearley, 291; deeds 293, 325; Great Mearley 300; school 82, 85

Meath, Richard of, 193

mechanics' institutes, 9

medical committees, 65

Medlar-with-Wesham : deeds 276, 289, 308, 322, 331, 337; Mowbreck 199; tithe 27, 206; and see Wesham

Melling (Halsall), 215, 287; bishops' transcripts 124; commons 207; Cunscough 198; deeds 197, 206, 244, 264; leases 265; muster-roll 246; plans 198, 246; rentals 178, 268; surveys 198, 272; terriers 126; tithe 28, 178

Melling-with-Wrayton : bishops' transcripts 122; Bottom mill 296; deeds 222, 258; Farleton tithe 26; felons 156; parish records 109; terriers 123; tithe 27

Mellings Ltd., of Fleetwood, 166

Mellor (Mellor Brook), 55; deeds 69, 189, 232-3, 254, 274, 285, 300; parish records 98, 109; plans 304; school 69

Mellor, Dr. A. S., 298

Mence family, of Rainhill, 314

Mercer, John, of Clayton-le-Moors, 315; Robert, minister of Sefton 247; William, of Clayton-le-Moors 170, 238

Mersey, river, 15, 42, 62, 294

Metcalf, Thomas, duchy auditor, 278

Metcalfe family, 300; Leonard (1570) 241

meteorological records, 203, 213, 239, 334

Methodist church records, 140-46

Middle Hulton, see Hulton

Middlesex : Bloomsbury 281; Chiswick 277, 279; Colham 269; Edmonton 193; Hendon 219; Hillingdon 269; Holborn 277; Isleworth 264; Tottenham 200; Westminster 264, 283, 284

Middlesex Record Office, 294

Middleton (with Houghton and Arbury), 219; deeds 282, 334; parish records 107; plans 219; survey 272; tithe 28; see also Arbury, Houghton

Middleton (Lancaster), 252; deeds 240, 241, 276; tithe 27

Middleton (Salford), 228, 230; bishops' transcripts 127; borough records 45; charity 150; church 227, 228, 293; county court records 23; deeds 187, 200, 228, 232, 276, 308, 312, 331; hearth tax 18; highway 334; manor 338; rentals 234; school 82; terriers 128; tithe 28

Middleton family, of Goosnargh, 297; of Leighton 276; Thomas (1595) 278

midwives, 39; and see hospitals

militia, 2, 4, 7, 8, 44, 47, 56, 57, 174, 182, 185, 216, 218, 234, 237, 258, 267, 288, 332, 339, 240; see also army, regiments

Miller, Henrietta, of Preston, 326; J. 292; Richard, of Goosnargh 301; Thomas, of Preston 170; W., of Preston 223

millers, 168

milliners, 168

Mills, R. Evans, memorial deeds, 333

mills, 54, 174, 176, 179, 181, 182, 183, 185, 188, 189, 199, 207, 209, 211, 223, 225, 228, 242, 249, 250, 256, 257, 261, 267, 271, 278, 307, 312, 314, 317, 322, 334; see also cotton industry, water-mills, windmills

millwrights, 171, 324

Milnes, John, of Gloucester, 214

Milnrow, 298; bishops' transcripts 128; charity 334; deeds 172, 298, 310; schools 82; terrier 128; urban district 51

mining, see coal, iron, lead

Mitchell, Capt. F. B., 293

Mitton : deeds 261; enclosure 13; ford 333; tithe 314; and see Little Mitton

Molesworth, J. & Sons, 311

Molloy, T., 310

Molyneux family, earls of Sefton, 205, 207, 238, 243-7; Agnes (Blundell) 194; Alexander, minister of Walton-on-the-Hill 247; Sir Richard (c. 1550) 198; viscount, of Croxteth 208

Molyneux Seel family, 187

Monk Coniston : enclosure 14; parish records 106; tithe award 27; and see Coniston

Monks, E. H., of Wigan, 167

Montague family, 242; duke of 341; of Beaulieu, lord 191

Moon, Ellen (Barcroft), 250

Moore family, 269; Sir Cleave, of Bankhall 262, 266; James & Co. of Lancaster 341 Mrs. Mary (1859) 218; Rev. Richard 294; William, of Bankhall 270

Moore-Stevens, Mrs. D., 314

Moreau, Paul (1634), 289

Morecambe : borough court records 23; borough records 45; deeds 173, 178; gas company 166; and Heysham Free Church Federal Council 146; Methodists 143; sailing 166; schools 82; tramways 179

Morecambe Bay : Congregational records 139; panorama 253; railway 314

Morland, E., 292

Morley Colliery Co., 282

Morres, Alexander, collector of subsidy, 275

Morris family, 228; J. 294

Mort, Adam (1631), 94; Thomas (1638) 94

mortality, bills of, 236

Morton, Edward, vicar of Sefton, 247

Mosley family, 238

Moss, E. H., 300; Edward 292

Moss Hall, see Wigan

Moss Side : bishops' transcripts 127; tithe 28

Mossborough, see Rainford

Mossley : bishops' transcripts 126; borough records 46; deeds 339; R.C. records 133; schools 82

Moston, 293; deeds 227, 233, 309, 339; parish records 109; R.C. records 133; school 82; tithe 28

motoring, 47, 312; taxation 37; and see coachbuilders

Mowbreck, see Medlar-with-Wesham

Moxon, F. S., 320

Moyers, Mrs., 313

Much Hoole : deeds 179, 202, 222, 244, 283, 289, 330; leases 265; plans 306; school 82; tithe 27

Much Woolton : bishops' transcripts 124; deeds 194, 197, 206, 264, 336; hall 272; mechanics' institute 153; rental 269; school 83; tithe 28; see also Little Woolton and Woolton

Muchland, see Low Furness

Muirhead & Percival, of Manchester, 169

Munday & Munday, of Preston, 180

municipal officers : town clerks' society 155; treasurers and accountants' society 156; see also boroughs

Musbury : deeds 71, 179, 189; roads 189; school 83, 294

Musgrave, Cuthbert (1560), 284

music, licensing 22; societies 155

musters, 213, 246, 296, 304

Myers, Joseph, of Preston, 179

Myerscough, 216, 265, 275; Badsberry 232, deeds 202, 261, 303, 310, 319, 330, 331, 332, 333; forest 216, 265, 275, 299; hall 305; manor 232; Midghalgh 318; parish records 109; rentals 202; school 232, 333; surveys 272, 328; tithe 331

Myerscough & Green, 305

Myres, T. H., architect, of Preston, 341

Nairn, Rev. J. A., 292

Nasmyth, Gaskell & Co., of Eccles, 166

Nateby : deeds 202, 332; House 340; parish records 109; school 83; tithe 27

National Coal Board : records 32-4; and see coal

National Trust, 328

natural history records, 239, 296, 319; society 9

Nature Conservancy, 319

navigations, see canals

navy, 10, 177, 231, 237; see also shipping

Naylor family, of Up Holland, 117

Nelson, 184, 323, 327; borough records 46; draper 165; employers' association 163; flour millers 168; gas co. 314; local board 314; Methodist records 143-4; parish records 109; R.C. records 133; schools 66, 83; trades unions 160; water bills 183; water board 65

Nelson History Society, 320

Nether Kellet : deeds 220, 335; enclosure 14; manor 263; parish records 109; survey 185; tithe 27

Nether Wyresdale : deeds 209, 316; Dolphinholme 316; Congregational records 138, school 83; manor 290; parish records 109; tithe 27; see also Over Wyresdale and Wyresdale

Netherlands, 334

Netherton : deeds 244, 264, 318; manor 243; plans 246; tithe 28

Neville, James (1820), 238; M. 292; Rimmer & Birkett 303

New Hall Hey : deeds 189; plans 189; tithe 28

New Laund Booth : deeds 182; highway plans 183

New Zealand, 314

Newall family, of Littleborough, 247, 341

Newburgh (Lathom) : deeds 323; manor 262; rentals 269; schools 80; tithe 28

Newcastle-upon-Tyne City Archives, 318

Newcastle-upon-Tyne Library, 325

Newchurch-in-Culcheth : bishops' transcripts 126; parish records 109; terrier 126

377

Newchurch-in-Pendle : bishops' transcripts 123; parish records 110; school 83; terrier 123

Newchurch-in-Rossendale 322; bishops' transcripts 123; chapel 189; Cloughfold 88, 145; deeds 182, 187, 189, 215, 290; parish records 110; plans 183, 189; school 83; terrier 123

Newland, see Egton-with-Newland

Newsham, see Barton-in-Amounderness, and Goosnargh-with-Newsham

newspapers, 168

Newton (Manchester) : bishops' transcripts 127; deeds 227, 302, 306, 319; enclosure 14; Heath 155; manor 232; school 83; tithe 28

Newton (Poulton-le-Fylde), see Hardhorn-with-Newton

Newton family, of Whitchurch, co. Salop. 210

Newton-in-Makerfield, 200, 228, 274; bishops' transcripts 126; deeds 51, 179, 192, 201, 228, 282, 297; election 201; The Hey 200-201; parish records 110; schools 83; surveys 272, 282; tithe 28

Newton-with-Scales : deeds 83, 172, 175, 179, 186, 194, 206, 222, 240, 289, 292, 293, 312, 313, 331, 332, 338; felons 156; marsh 152, 175, 270, 329; parish records 110; roads 293; Scales Hall 293; school 83

Newton-le-Willows, 317, 319, 332; urban district 51

Nibthwaite, see Colton

Nicholson, M. & Co., of Manchester, 168

Nightingale, solicitors, of London, 322

nonconformists, see dissenters, and under individual churches

Norbreck, see Bispham-with-Norbreck

Norcross, William, curate, of Colne, 249

Norfolk, 269; Bradfield 281; Great Yarmouth 277, 279; Stradsett 280; Upwell-with-Welney 280; Walsoken hospital 216; Watlington 307; Wormgay 307

Norfolk, duchess of (Mary Shireburne), 269, 283, 284, 285; duke of 284, 285

Norris family, 181; Clemence (Hulton) 231; Mrs. E. 309; Letitia (Cross) 210

North, R. T. (1812), 341

North Meols 244, 292; bishops' transcripts 125; deeds 259, 296; fishery 224; parish records 110; rural deanery 95; schools 83; smuggling 210; terriers 126; tithe 28

North Ribble, see Ribble

North Riding Record Office, 300

North-Western Railway Co., 216

Northamptonshire, 269; Benefield 279; Burton Latimer 264; Farthinghoe 288; Salcay Forest 337; Whittlebury 195

Northamptonshire Record Office, 315

Northcote, James, painter, 304

Northern Ireland, Public Record Office of, 305

Northscale, see Dalton-in-Furness

Northumberland, 278, 283, 284; Alnwick 241, 290; Alwinton 283; Berwick-on-Tweed 260, 277; Cottenshope 283; Dissington 277; Elsdon and Harbottle 283; Felton House 285; Fleetham 264, 266; Flodden 245; Hexham 296; Newcastle-upon-Tyne 242, 253, 277; Swinburne House 285; Tynemouth 290

Northumberland Record Office, 320

Norton, Richard (1570), 241; Youatt & Co., 300

Norwich Public Library, 302

Nottinghamshire, 219, 276, 283; Allerton 278; Auckley 283; Caberton 277; Canwick 277; Clarborough 277; Durham 277; Everton 277; Finningley 283; Flixthorp 277; Gateford 276, 277; Hawksworth 277; Hoveringham 264; Misson 283; Ossington 336; Warsop 277; Worksop 277

Nowell family, 212; Adam, of Great Harwood 251; Alexander, dean of St. Paul's 316; Richard 213

nursing 314; associations 51, 156, 157, 158; district 38, 157; and see hospitals, midwives

Nuttall, see Tottington Lower End

Nuttall, John, of Liverpool, 299; & Fox, of Ramsbottom 189

oaths, 12, 15, 16-17, 20, 22, 57, 181, 251

Oddfellows, 154, 155

Ogle family, cartulary 187; Henry, church drawings 335

O'Hagan, lord, 276

Old Laund Booth : deeds 182, 290, 316; school 84

Oldham, 311, 319, 327; bishops' transcripts 127; brickworks 164; building societies 152; church 227, 228, 318; coal 165, 227; Congregational records 136, 139; cotton mills 170; Counthill 310; deeds 172, 227, 229, 233, 300, 301, 308, 310, 313, 316, 317, 319, 331, 334; enclosure 14, 227; engineering works 298; graveyard inscriptions 128; Horsedge 227; insurance committee 31;

insurance company 167; parish records 110; plans 306, 341; poor law guardians 64; printer 168; R.C. records 133; schools 83; Shaw chapel 228; societies 158, 332; Society of Friends records 146, 147; survey 272; theatres 166, 315; turnpikes 183

Oldham family, 306; Mrs. M. K., 306

Oman, C. C., 308

O'Neill, John, of Clitheroe, 291, 314

Openshaw: bishops' transcripts 127; chemists 164; deeds 232; parish records 110; rental 234; school 84; tithe 28

Openshaw family, of Bury, 188; of Hothersall, 247; W. A. & Co., of Bolton 170

oratories, 260

Ordsall, see Salford

O'Reilly, Bernard, R.C. bishop of Liverpool, 128

O'Riordan, Dr. M. N., 316

Ormerod family, 188; Miss D. E. 298; Mrs. P. 317; Peter, of Goodshaw 290; William, of Billington 327

Ormskirk, 260, 267, 341; accounts 270; bishops' transcripts 125; church 260, 262, 268, 287; Congregational records 139; coroners' court 24; county court plan 23; deeds 193, 197, 202, 211, 215, 222, 259, 261, 264, 271, 300, 303, 308, 310, 312, 320, 326, 335; fair 266; highway board 62; historical collection 51; hospital board 30; land tax commissioners 31; leases 265; manor 178, 222, 262; market 267; militia 57, 340; moss 267; order book 268; parish records 110; pensions committee 32, 39; police 7; poor law guardians 64; public assistance 40; rentals 260, 269; R.C. records 135; rural deanery 95; rural district 56; schools 84; surveys 266, 272; terriers 126; tithes 28, 340; town hall 266, 269; urban district 51; workhouse 97

Ormskirk County Library, 320

Orrell, 326; deeds 181, 192, 194, 233, 291, 300, 316, 318, 322, 326; enclosure 14; leases 215, 265; plans 246, 300; R.C. records 133, 135; schools 84; survey 272; tithe 28

Orrell, Alice (Waddington), 335; R. D. 301

Orrell-with-Ford: deeds 244; manor 243, 244; survey 245; tithe 28; see also Ford

Osbaldeston, 335; deeds 179, 185, 202, 292; R.C. records 133

Osmotherley: deeds 177, 239; enclosure 14; schools 84; tithe 27

Oswaldtwistle: bishops' transcripts 123; coal 221, 256; cotton mill 170; deeds 199, 202, 233, 254, 276, 283, 290, 291, 300, 307, 333, 334, 339; enclosure 14; Methodist records 144; nursing associations 157; plans 256; R.C. records 133; schools 72, 84; Stanhill 339; tithe 234; trades union 160; urban district 339

Otway, John, of Over Kellet, 239

Out Rawcliffe: bishops' transcripts 122; deeds 173, 175, 206, 271, 289, 290, 319, 324; manor 324; parish records 110

outlawry, 256, 267

Outwood: coal 33; parish records 111; plans 270

Over Burrow, see Burrow-with-Burrow

Over Darwen: bishops' transcripts 121; coal 308; deeds 179, 182, 227, 300, 308, 317, 322, 330, 333, 337; enclosure 14; gas company 183; plans 306; railway station 185; surveys 272

Over Hulton, see Deane

Over Kellet: bishops' transcripts 121; Capernwray 239, 240, 241; compoti 178; deeds 178, 189, 220, 240, 241, 276; enclosure 14, 327; Hall Garth 327; parish records 110; plans 183, 185; school 84

Over Wyresdale, 334; deeds 175, 179, 241, 319; Hayshaw Fell 313; highways 56; improvement society 153; Lentworth 313, 323; parish records 110; school 84; Swainshead 313; see also Nether Wyresdale and Wyresdale

Overton: bishops' transcripts 122; deeds 173, 178, 202, 214, 240; drainage 36; parish records 110; school 84; Troughton marsh 240

Owen, E. J., 310

Owens, Miss M., 323

Oxcliffe, see Heaton-with-Oxcliffe

Oxfordshire, 269; Bradwell 336; Bruern abbey 336; Eynsham 264, 266; Milton 264, 269; Oxford: Christ Church 175, 207, Brazenose College 268

Padgate, see Poulton-with-Fearnhead

Padiham, 184; assessments 286; bishops' transcripts 123; chapel 286; church 286; common 286; Congregational records 139; deeds 182, 184, 254, 261, 271, 276, 285, 290, 291; district nurses 157; employers' association 163; gas co. 166; gas, light & coke co. 65; highways 285;

parish records 111; plans 213; priory 211, 321; rectory 258; rentals 213, 260, 288; schools 85, 303, 311; society 157; stewards 212; surveys 212, 258; terrier 123; tithe 27, 258; turnpike 61

Percival, S., 302

Perry & Co., 307

Persia, 218

Pery, J., 325

Petre family, of Dunkenhalgh, **254-7**, 266

Petty family, 177

Phelps, Brig. D. C., 317

Phillips, Mrs. E., 315; Major 311; R. 304

Pickering, Kenyon & Co., 307

Pickup, James, of Burnley, 172; Peter, of Burnley 165, 310

Pickup Bank, 335; deeds 182; plans 183; tithe 27; *and see* Yate

Picop, Richard, apprentice weaver, 302

Pierce, P. F., 315

Piked Edge, *see* Colne

Pilgrim & Badgery, of Colne, 182-4

Pilkington, 270; coal 33; deeds 187, 233, 264, 292, 319; gas co. 186; leases 188, 265, 271; manor 262-3; mechanics' institute 9; parish records 111; plans 188; Prestolee 339; railways 188; rentals 269, 270; school 85; tithe 28

Pilkington family, of Rainford and Windle, 187, **257;** Bros. 311; Charles, of Allerton, Notts. 278; James (1789) 328; Miss 314, 328; Richard, of Horwich 328

Pilling : bishops' transcripts 121; church 315, 316, 333; deeds 175, 176, 184, 199, 206, 254, 281, 289, 299, 308, 322, 331; enclosure 14; Fluke Hall 304; hall 254; leases 281; manor 280; mills 291; parish records 111; road 299; schools 85, 333; tithe 27

Pilling, L., 298

Pilling Lane, *see* Preesall-with-Hackensall

pilots, 46, 315

Pilsworth, 237; deeds 227, 288; parish records 238; tithe 28

Pinhorn, M., 321

Pinsent & Co., 311

Pippard family, 195; Frances (Blundell), 194

plague, 207, 230

planning committee of county council, 39; *see also* 43-7

Plant, Abbot, & Plant, of Poulton-le-Fylde, 184

Platt family, of Chipping, 311; Dr. Thomas, of Oldham 311

Platt Bridge, *see* Ince-in-Makerfield

Pleasington, 322; deeds 179, 184, 255, 332; parish records 111; rental 180; R.C. records 133; schools 66, 85

Plumb, Messrs., 319

Plumbe family, 174

plumbers, 168, 325

Plumpton, *see* Egton-with-Newland, *and* Westby-with-Plumpton

Plumpton, Sir William, 278

Poitou, Roger of (c. 1100), 243

Poland, 298

police, 4, 5, 316, 326; joint standing committee 42; in quarter sessions 7-8; records 58-60

political societies, 155-6

poll tax, 18

Polland, John, of Foulridge, 184; Matthew, of Lower Bradley, 184

Ponthalgh, *see* Wiswell

Pooley, Giles, of London, 171, 204

poor law : commissioners 15; guardians 6, 63-4; house 230; overseers 43-54; prisoners 22, 208; rates 5, 188; relief 2, 231; unions 15; *and see* individual parishes

Popplewell family, 291

Porter, E. B., 289

Porteus, Rev. W., 324

Portugal, 255; Lisbon 130, 246

Postgate, Rev. Nicholas, 132

postmen, 311

Potter family, 308; of Darwen 316; John, R.N. 281; & Co., of Darwen 168

pottery : earthenware manufacturers 174; stoneware merchant 171

Potts & Ball, 315

Poulton-with-Fearnhead : deeds 51, 193, 233, 282; Fearnhead 219; Padgate bishops' transcripts 125; school 85; plans 219; tithe 28

Poulton-le-Fylde, 172, 332; accounts 301; bishops' transcripts 122; charity 150; deeds 172, 173, 175, 176, 184, 201, 206, 283, 289, 318, 322, 332; divisional executive committee 39; gas co. 166; Methodist records 144; parish records 111-12; police 316; R.C. records 133, 135, 202; road 299; schools 85, 94; survey 236; terriers 123; tithe 27; urban district 52

Poulton-le-Sands, 252; Bare deeds 178, 252, 301, 305; tithe 27; bishops' transcripts 122; deeds 173, 178, 240, 252, 296, 305,

308, 336; highways 252; plans 253; rentals 253; school 82; terrier 123; tithe 27

precedent books, 20, 260

Preesall-with-Hackensall : deeds 173, 178, 199, 271, 297, 305, 309, 336; Hackensall 173, 198, 290; Higher Lickow 297; Knott End 299; Methodist records 144; mill 199; parish records 112; railway 299; rentals 199, 292; Pilling Lane 27, 157; society 157; tithe 27, 199; tontine 154; urban district 52

Preese, see Weeton-with-Preese

Prescot, 294, 332; bishops' transcripts 125; church 174, 268, 287; coroners 24, 173; deeds 51, 173, 174, 255, 257, 264, 308, 309, 313, 317, 323, 335; gas co. 166, 174; felons 156, 174; highway board 62; lieutenancy 57; manor 173, 328; market house 174; militia 174; moss 266; papists 17; parish records 112; plans 174; police 7; poor 262; poor law guardians 64; public assistance 40; rural deanery 95; rural district 56; schools 66, 86, 262; societies 152, 158; tithe 28, 174, 288; turnpike 61; urban district 52; watchmaker 174

Prescott, Rev. Richard, of Up Holland, 176

Prestolee, see Pilkington

Preston, 164, 179, 180, 185, 197, 202, 233, 244, 252, 261, 288, 289, 297, 298, 299, 300, 309, 313, 315, 321, 324, 326, 328, 329, 332, 333, 335, 340, 341; apprentice register 332; Ashton Park 128; auctioneers 163; banks 164, 186, 320; Barton estate 329; battle 242, 332, 338; bishops' transcripts 122; borough court 23, 172; borough records 46; brewers 164; builder 164; census 120; charities 151, 333; Church St. 46; churches 181, 210, 226, 227, 267, 268, 281, 324; coachbuilder 164; cockpit 268; companies 333; concert 37; Congregational records 139; coroners' court 23; cotton mills 170-71, 334; court house 37; deeds 46, 128, 172-3, 175, 178, 179, 181, 184, 186, 197, 202, 206, 211, 214, 217, 218, 220, 222, 251, 252, 261, 264, 271, 274, 276-7, 289, 296, 297, 298, 305, 311, 312, 313, 316, 319, 321, 323, 324, 325, 326, 327, 329, 331, 332, 333, 338; dispensary 185; divisional sub-committee 37; elections 12, 180, 253, 267, 268, 286, 295, 311, 322; electrical engineers 169; engineers 166;

felons 334; foundry 186; friary 5, 224; gaol 5, 6; garrison 226; gas co. 166; grocer 167; guild 185, 333; highways 10; Home Guard 57; house of correction 5, 290; hunt 158; inns 186; insurance committee 31; lease 290; market place 294; medical committees 65; M.P.s 296; Methodist records 144-5; military hospital 314; militia 7, 185; mill 267; millwrights 171; parish records 112-3, 261; plans 23, 56, 180, 181, 198, 224, 294, 299, 306, 313, 325, 332; pleasure ground 185; police 60; poor law guardians 64; public houses 23; quarter sessions 3, 4, 181; races 268, 270; railways 294, 321; reading room 313; rectory 250; rentals 253, 256, 268, 269; riots 252; roads 289, 299, 320; R.C. records 135; rural district 56; schools 86-7, 317, 327, 333; sessions 21; sessions house 21; Sharoe Green hospital 30; shipping 35, 181; societies 9, 153, 154, 156, 157-8, 332, 339; Society of Friends records 147, 148; solicitors 168; suffragettes 156; surveys 180, 256, 266, 272; Swillbrook mill 311; telephone 171; terrier 123; theatres and cinemas 23, 166, 186, 294, 313; tithe 27; trades unions 159-61; tramway 321; turnpikes 61, 176; Unitarian records 146; volunteer training corps 57; Winckley Square development 185, 252

Preston family, of Holker, 202-4; of Preston 321; H. 311; Henry, of Preston 253; Sir Thomas, of Furness 202-3, 217; Thomas, of Horwich 328-9; Thomas, of Little Mearley 291; W. E. A. 296

Preston Cold Storage and Ice Co., 319

Preston Library and Art Gallery, 333-4

Preston Rural District Council, 300

Prestwich, 3, 233, 310; asylum 6-7; bishops' transcripts 127; borough records 46; church 336; coal 315; deeds 173, 233, 292, 302, 307, 331, 337; leases 188, 265; manor 307; mills 307; plan 307; Polefield Hall hospital 30; railway 188; schools 9, 87; society 155; terriers 128, 234; tithe 28, 233, 234

Price, A. W., 309; & Cross 312

Prideaux, Mr. (1761), 295

Priest Hutton : deeds 178, 240; parish records 113; tithe 27

Priestley, Joseph, 304

Primrose league, 155, 202

printing, 168, 177, 179, 291, 309, 310, 312, 333, 341

printworks, 291, 310, 312, 333, 341; *see also* cotton

prisoners, 2, 6, 22, 24, 208, 231, 234, 311

prisons, *see* gaols

Pritt family, 178

prize-fighting, 3

probate records, 25-6; *and see* wills

probation, 8, 21-3, 42

Probert, Major Y. R. H., 314

Procter & Birkbeck (& Batty), 290, 328

public assistance committees, 40; health and housing committee 40; houses 6, 23, *and see* alehouses, beerhouses, inns, licensing; undertakings 16 *and see* individual subjects; utilities 15

Pudsay, Henry (1520), 279

Pugin, Edward Welby, 129

Pye, Mrs. A. M., 320

Pynsen, Richard, printer, 279

Quakers, *see* Friends, Society of

Quarlton, *see* Bolton-le-Moors

quarries, 169, 241, 316, 328

quarter sessions, **1-21**, 57, 134, 178, 220, 224, 228, 234, 328; borough 15; *and see* individual places

Quernmore, 216, 255, 265, 275; accounts 218; bishops' transcripts 122; church 217; deeds 178, 187, 216, 217, 313, 324, 331, 336, 339; enclosure 14, 324; forest 216, 255, 275, 299; manor 294; mill 185; parish magazines 218; parish records 113; park 217; plans 218, 220, 313; rentals 218; Scarthwaite 185; schools 87, 217; surveys 217; tithe 27, 217, 240; waste 217

rabbits, 191, 223, 246, 270

racing, 158, 246, 247, 268, 301, 332

Radclif, John, of, parson of Bury, 304

Radcliff & Co., 305

Radcliffe : bishops' transcripts 128; borough records 46; bridge 4; cotton mill 171; deeds 46, 227, 264, 292, 321; enclosure 14; gas co. 186; leases 265; mechanics' institute 9; militia 7; railway 188; rentals 234; schools 87; Society of Friends records 147; terriers 128; tithe 28

Radcliffe, Sir Robert (1491), 279

Radcliffe Library, 321

Radclyf, John and Joan, 278

railways, 15, 16, 46, 55, 169, 179, 182, 183, 185, 186, 188, 207, 216, 228, 230, 236, 246, 267, 294, 298, 311, 314, 320, 321, 329, 332, 341; *see also* individual railways

Rainford, 219, 257; accounts 270; assessment 268; bishops' transcripts 125; bounds 266; chapel 268; church 268; coat 165, 246; deeds 173, 181, 194, 218, 222, 257, 259, 264, 308, 319; leases 265, 329; manor 263; Mossborough 247, 269; parish records 113; plans 268; rentals 269; school 87; social club 158; surveys 266, 272; tithe 28; urban district 52

Rainhill, 201, 314; asylum 7; Congregational records 139; deeds 173, 174, 194, 200, 201, 259, 287, 326; Ogle cartulary 187; parish records 113; tithe 28

Ramsbottom 189; bishops' transcripts 126; calico printers 169; deeds 189; divisional executive committee 39; graveyard inscriptions 128; police 7; schools 66, 67, 88; urban district 52

Ramsden, William & Sons, 34

Ramsgreave : deeds 189; survey 272; tithe 27

rates, county, 3, 5, 8, 37, 41, 172, 256, 275, 295, 313

Rathbone, William, of Liverpool, 129

Raven Meols : bounds 215; deeds 215, 264; survey 272; tithe 216

Ravenhead, *see* Sutton

Rawcliffe, 198, 301; deeds 199, 202, 255, 333, 338; enclosure 14, 222; hall 316; rentals 199; Turnover Hall 299; White Hall 316

Rawcliffe, T., 318; & Baines, of Preston, 167

Rawlinson family, 177; of Cark 241; of Graythwaite 190, 258; J. 315, 323; John, of Grays Inn 259

Rawstorne family, of Hutton, **257-8**; of Lumb 257; William, of Preston 223

Rawtenstall : bishops' transcripts 123; borough records 46-7; deeds 189, 257; Home Guard 58; Methodist records 145; plans 189; R.C. records 133; schools **88**; societies 332; survey 47; trades unions 161; waterworks 171, 189

Read, 212; deeds 172, 211, 233, 248, 250, 255; moor 291; parish records 113; school 88; survey 272; tithe 286

Read, J. G., 320

Reade, Richard, of Aighton, 284

recipes, 234, 273, 302, 304, 323; medicinal 218, 300, 305, 306, 307

reclamation : plans 16

records, *see* archives

recusancy, 12, 195, 201, 219, 234, 250, 255, 260, 278, 297, 310; *see also* papists, Roman Catholics

Reddihalgh, Matthew, of 63rd Regiment, 251

Reddish : school 88; tithe 28

Redfern, Mrs. M. L., 316

Redmayne family, of Ingleton, 295

Reed, E. J. and son, of Preston, 163

Reedley Hallows : deeds 319; mill 314; parish records 113

regiments: 63rd 251; Admiral's 284; Fitzgerald's 284; General Burgoyne's 295; Leyland and Ormskirk Local Militia 57, 340; Loyal Kirkham Volunteers 57, 298; Loyal North Lancashire 318, 340; Major Preston's Company 203; Manchester Military Association 57, 339; Manchester & Salford Volunteers 253, 295; Royal Field Artillery 57; Royal Lancashire Militia 174, 218, 339; Royal Lancashire Volunteers 57, 218, 296; York 251; *and see* army, militia

relief committee (1843), 236; funds 237

reminiscences, 157, 323, 327

Repton, William (1843), 280

Reynolds, E. (Barcroft), 250; F. W. & James, of Warrington; Robert (1823) 250

Rhodes & Gillman, 315

Ribble, river, 260, 293; bridges 4, 172; Brockholes weir 179, 185, 289; chart 224; drainage commission 62; fisheries 158, 179, 213, 334; joint committee 42; navigation 46, 207, 223; North, pensions committee 32, 39; plans 332, 339; railway 46

Ribbleton, 223, 335; deeds 186, 202, 222, 252, 255, 289, 327; enclosure 14, 256; hall 330; parish records 113; plan 330; road 299; surveys 180, 272; tithe 27

Ribby-with-Wrea, 292; deeds 172, 175, 193, 206, 251, 296, 297, 301, 331, 332, 338; parish records 113-14; schools 88; surveys 292; tithe 27; *see also* Wrea

Ribchester, 285, 335; bishops' transcripts 122; bridge 4; chantry 228; charities 151; church 226, 228; Cloughbank 284; deeds 184, 186, 199, 233, 247, 248, 252, 255, 277, 283, 300, 333, 337; enclosure 13; manor 291; mill 227; parish records 114; plans 249; rentals 249, 253, 285, 342; R.C. records 133; schools 88, 186; Seed Green 186; Stidd 280, 335; surveys 248, 256; terriers 123; tithe 27; White Carr 324; workhouse 307

Richardson, J. H. (1788), 204; L. B. 309

Richmond : archdeaconry 120, probate records 25; commissary 207-8; countess of 269; rural dean 207; *see also* Yorkshire : Richmond

Ridley, John, of Ribbleton, 330; Richard, of Ribbleton 330

Rigby family, 252, 297, 321; of Peel 232-4; F. J. 298; Mrs. 326; R. P. 321

Rigge family, 177; Charles Gray, R. N. 177

Riley, Edward & Pickles & Co., of Colne, 170; G. H. 325

Ringley, 9; bishops' transcripts 127; chapel 234

riots, 3, 20, 252, 266, 299, 305

Rishton, 310; bounds 256; common 223; deeds 184, 222, 250, 255, 277, 325, 339, 340; divisional executive committee 39; enclosure 256; manor 254; Methodist records 145; parish records 114; pensions committee 32, 39; plans 256; police 60; rentals 256; R.C. records 133; schools 88; surveys 223; Tottleworth 221, 238, 255; urban district 52

Rishton family, 238, 254-7; Elizabeth and William, of Accrington 185

rivers, 15, 236; authorities 41; committees 42; *and see* individual rivers

Rivington : bishops' transcripts 126; church 197, 231; deeds 187, 209, 296, 310, 326; parish records 114; plans 306; schools 70, 88-9; survey 272; terrier 128; tithe 28

Rixton, Nicholas, rector of Bishops Cleeve co. Gloucester, 257

Rixton-with-Glazebrook : chapel 302; deeds 302, 331; Glazebrook drainage 36; halmote 302; parish records 114; rental 302; tithe 28

roads, 2, 16, 179, 181, 182, 188, 189, 190, 202, 203, 204, 212, 215, 216, 219, 237, 250, 251, 252, 253, 266, 268, 270, 293, 307, 328; safety committee of county council 42; *see also* highways

Roberts, C., 318; D. L. 310

Robertson family, of Liverpool, 323

Robinson, Denis, of Kirkdale, 270; Francis, of Staunton Co. Worcs., 295; Col. G. N. 299; John, of Holker 204; John, of Lancaster 295; W. H. & Co. 302; & Cooks, of St. Helens 166; & Sons, of Blackburn 184-5

Roby : deeds 201, 263; enclosure 266; free warren 266; hall 174; leases 329; rentals

384

sessions : (1610), 338; annual general 21, *and see* 'sheriff's table'; petty 21-23; *see also* quarter sessions
sewerage, 43, 45, 49, 50, 52, 53, 55, 208, 238
Shackleton, Elizabeth (Parker), 248
Shakerley, *see* Tyldesley-with-Shakerley
Shakeshaft, William, of Rufford, 223, 224
share prices, 183
Sharp family, 178; Henry, apprentice surgeon 297; Fletcher & Co., ironfounders 179
Sharples : deeds 128, 232, 309, 314; Hall 331; Higher End 115; parish records 115; plans 306; rental 234; schools 90; Winter Hill colliery 323
Sharples, D. E., 324; Edward, apprentice tailor 329; Isaac, of Prescot 294; Nicholas, of London 175; W. 312
Shaw, *see* Oldham
Shaw family, 188, 329; Cecilia (1869) 329; Miss 297; R. Cunliffe 329; Thomas, of Kirkham 169
Shaw Hill, *see* Whittle-le-Woods
Shawcross, Mrs. K. M., 310
Shawe, Joseph (c. 1800), 318; William, sealkeeper 332
Shawes family, 181
Sheldon, W. L., of Salford, 140
Shelley family, 223
Shepherd family, 186; Miss M. 315; R. G. 309; Robert, of Bury 188; Robert, of Oldham 184; Swire & Markham, of Bacup 168
Sherborn family, 285
Sherdley, H., 322
sheriffs, *see* shrievalty
'sheriff's table, 21
Sherring, G., 297
Sherwin, C., 316; Mrs. E. 326
Shevington, 223; brickmaking 223; coal 165, 190, 223, 224, 260; deeds 175, 181, 222, 250, 259, 271, 326, 336; hall 272; manor 259; milldam 223; moor 299; parish records 115, 223, 224; rentals 260, 326; school 90; tithe 27; waste 223
shipping, 16, 35, 44, 46, 56, 166, 171, 181, 194, 230, 233, 250, 304, 311; *see also* seamen, ships
ships : *Alice* of Ulverston 173; *Ann* of Preston 289; *Bee* 177; *Britannia* 204; *Dolphin* 73; *Fairy Queen* 305; *Fortunate* 281; *Foudroyant* 172; *Gem* of Preston 309; *Happy Recovery* 258; *Henrietta* 270; *Hope* of Whitehaven 242; *Jenny* of

Dartmouth 295; *Jupiter* 253; *Maggie* 253; *Marie Ragged Staff* 281; *Mischief* 190; *Peg A. Ramsey* 253; *Resolution* of Whitehaven 242; *St. John* 230; *True Love* 336
Shireburn, Robert (1512), 289
Shireburne family, of Stonyhurst, **283-5,** 293, 338
Shireshead : bishops' transcripts 121; parish records 115
shoemaker, 185
Shorrock, C., 313
shorthand, 230
Shovelton, Henry, of Leigh, 166-7
shrievalty, 179, 193, 213, 217, 228, 231, 234, 250, 251, 259, 334; appointments 15, 210, 217, 227, 229, 241, 245, 248, 257, 258, 274, 275, 278, 301, 332; records 58
Shrigley & Williamson, of Lancaster, 168
Shropshire, 264; Bishops Castle 195; Church Acton 277; Dobaston 263; Drayton 210; Ellesmere 222, 263, 269; Gravenhanger 210; Hodnet 222; Kenwick 222; Knockin 268, 270; Kynaston 263; Middle 263; Northwood 222; Oswestry 210; Walcot 195; Whitchurch 210, 277; Woore 210
Shropshire Record Office, 303
Shuttleworth, *see* Walmersley-with-Shuttleworth
Shuttleworth family, of Gawthorpe, **254-6,** 261; Henry of 255; lord 306; Dallas & Crombleholme, of Preston 185-6; & Hopkins, of Preston 223
Sidgewick, Richard, of Tatham, 324
Silverdale, 306, 327; bishops' transcripts 122; charity 151; deeds 206, 220, 277, 292, 293; enclosure 14; historical collections 306; manor 276; parish records 115; school 90; tithe 27
Silvester family, 324, 326; M. 324
Simkin, John (1749), 261
Simm, Mrs. M., 323
Simmons & Simmons, 313
Simonstone, 285, 286, 303; common 285; deeds 250, 255, 283, 285; hall 285; Huntroyde 303; rentals 286; school 90; tithe 286
Simonswood, 243, 245; bounds 245; deeds 244; forest 245; manor 243; parish records 115; plans 246; rental 247; school 80, 90; survey 245; tithe 28
Simpson, F., 320; John, apprentice glover 253

387

Singleton : Bankfield 300; deeds 173, 185, 202, 206, 264, 320, 332, 334; Grange 333, 334; hall 312; leases 265; Mains 201, 202; R.C. records 133; survey 328; tithe 27

Singleton, R., 304

Skelmersdale, 267; accounts 270; Blaguegate 90, 286; chapel 287; coal 165, 286; deeds 181, 218, 259, 264, 287, 326, 331, 337; enclosure 14, 287; leases 265; manor 178; Methodist records 145; park 287; plans 291, 311; rentals 178, 269; schools 66, 90; surveys 272; tithe 28, 287, 340; urban district 52

Skelmersdale, lords, 286

Skelwith : deeds 328; enclosure 14; Fold 307; parish records 106; school 90; tithe 27

Skerton, 303; bishops' transcripts 122; deeds 173, 178, 179, 217, 220, 308, 319, 336; Methodist records 143; police 7; school 80; tithe 27; weir 185

Skipton Public Library, 312

slatequarrying, 203, 216, 278

Slater, John, of Walton-le-Dale, 304; T. G. 318; Heelis & Co., of Manchester 186-7

slave trade, 173, 300

slitting mill, 234

Sloane, Mrs., 314

Slow, Ellen, apprentice mantua-maker, 299

Slyne-with-Hest : building land 179; deeds 220, 240, 333; manor 219; tithe award 27; Valley drainage board 63

smallholdings, 36, 37, 40; and see allotments

Smallpage family, of Burnley, 291; E. 291

Smeedon, see Toxteth Park

Smiles, Samuel, 177

Smith, A. D., 325; A. W. 297; Elizabeth, of Coniston 318; F. (1840) 195; J. G. 319; James, of Ashton-in-Makerfield 180; Philip (1661) 196; Thomas (1805) 201

Smithills, see Halliwell

smuggling, 210

Smythe family, 220; Agnes (1842) 195

Sneyd family, of Ashcombe, co. Stafford, 280

soap-makers, 278

Sobee, F. J., 296

social services committee of county council, 41

societies, 9, 22, 23, 29, 151-8, 170, 172, 175, 179, 181, 182, 258 298 332

Society of Antiquaries, 321

Sodd, William, apprentice clothmaker, 249

solicitors, 172-90, 175, 183, 184, 189

Solway, river, 311

Somerset, 238, 269, 278, 283; Buckland St. Mary 280; Cothelstone 215; Huntspill 277; Newton-in-Martock 207; Norton 277; Nunnington 277; Taunton 277; West Monkton 215

Somerville, J. J., of Liverpool and Preston, 168

Sorocold family, 228

Soulby, Stephen, of Ulverston, 177

South Hill, see Whittle-le-Woods

South Sea Company, 175

Southern & Southern, drapers, 174

Southport, 208, 305, 320, 323, 325; bishops' transcripts 125; boy scouts 158; Congregational records 140; deeds 146, 181, 302, 313, 316; highway board 62; insurance committee 31; parish records 115; police 60; railway 169; schools 90; Society of Friends' records 146; waterworks 188

Southworth-with-Croft, 282; bishops' transcripts 126; deeds 277, 282; manor 219; plans 219; schools 66, 74, 90; survey 272; tithe 28; and see Croft

Sowerby, 267; accounts 270; deeds 100, 283, 289, 291; drainage 266, 268; leases 265, 329; manor 263; plans 268; rentals 269; surveys 266, 272; and see Inskipwith-Sowerby

Spain, 280

Spark Bridge, see Egton-with-Newland

Sparling family, 303

Sparth, see Clayton-le-Moors

Speakman, William (1788), 303

Speke : accounts 270; bishops' transcripts 124; deeds 209; parish records 115; tithe 28

Spen Dyke, see Marton

Spencer, C. A., 325; J. H. 295; Miss M. 315; Thomas, earthenware manufacturer 174; W. M. 329

sports and pastimes, 158

Spotland, 190, 298; bishops' transcripts 128; bridge 298; Cheesden 318; deeds 187, 189, 215, 222, 227, 229, 295, 307, 312, 313, 330, 334; enclosure 14; leases 118; parish records 115; plans 189, 298; school 90; survey 280; tithe 28; Wolstenholme 318

Springhead Spinning Co., of Lees, 305, 306

Sproth, Stokes, & Turnbull, 313

Staffordshire, 202, 269; Ashcombe 280; Ashmore 219; Betley 288; Burton-on-Trent 274; Chillington 220; Dieulacres abbey 274; Forebridge 274; Lichfield 246, 247; Newcastle-under-Lyme 195; Rickarscote 274; Stafford 201; Wrinehill 288

Staffordshire Record Office, 296

Stainall, see Stalmine

Stainer, J. R., 313

Staining : charity 184; survey 272; tithe 210; Whitemoss Gap 297

Stainton-with-Adgarley, see Urswick

Stalland & Co., 314

Stalmine-with-Stainall, 174, 198, 271; bishops' transcripts 122; church 199; customs 176; deeds 175, 199, 206, 271, 292, 303, 309, 327, 332, 336, 339; enclosure 14; foreshore 271; mill 199; parish records 115; plans 199; rentals 199, 292; school 90; Stainall deeds 338; terriers 123, 199; tithe 27; Windley 271; wrecks 199

Stalybridge, 317; bishops' transcripts 126; riots 20

Stand : bishops' transcripts 127; schools 85

Standish family, 187, 324; of Duxbury 330, 340; Thomas, of Ormskirk 224

Standish-with-Langtree, 187, 219; bishops' transcripts 122; church 337; coal 330; deeds 181, 200, 206, 233, 271, 282, 326, 336; parish records 115; rectory 273; rental 260; R.C. records 134, 135; school 90, 299; terriers 123; tithe 27, 331; see also Langtree

Stanhill, see Oswaldtwistle

Stanley family, of Cross Hall, 261-2; of Knowsley 210, 214, 262-70, 286 and see Derby, earls of; Joan (Standish) 224; lord (1460) 178, 259; M. (1648) 238; Sir William 279

Stansfield, K., 316

Stanworth, see Withnell

Stapleton family, 203

Stapleton-Bretherton family, of Rainhill, 201

Starkey, James, minister of Inskip, 205; Lawrence, of Lancaster 284; William (1455) 256

Starkie family, of Huntroyde, 303; J. E. 325

statute rolls, 290, 328

Staveley : bishops' transcripts 124; charity 151; church 203, 280; deeds 252, 258, 333; parish records 115; school 90, 280; surveys 280; Townhead 279, 280

steam engine, 298

Steer, F. W., 294

Stephenson, William, of Preston, 179; Harwood, & Tatham 307

Stevens, Humphrey, clerk of the peace, 332

Stidd, see Ribchester

Stilgoe & Sons, of Manchester, 323

Stock, Peter, of Bury, 298

Stockdale, James, of Cartmel, 177

Stockton, Samuel, 290

Stodday, see Ashton-with-Stodday

Stoke-on-Trent Library, 300

Stone, Mrs. A., 296; J. & R. & Co. 35

Stonyhurst, see Aighton, Bailey and Chaigley

Stopford, Mrs. E. M., 315; K. 327

Stopfords, of Audenshaw, hatters, 312

Stopforth family, 222; Alice, of Halsall 315

Stott-Milne family, 305

Strange, lords, 214, 264, 265

Stretford : bishops' transcripts 127; borough records 47; canal 331; Congregational records 140; deeds 227, 281, 303, 307, 321; leases 281; manor 280; parish records 115; plans 281; R.C. records 134; school 90; tithe 28

Strickland family, of Cartmel Fell, 334; of Sizergh co. Westmorland, 337

Stuart, Mrs., 292

Stubley, see Littleborough

Sturton & Co., 327

Subberthwaite, see Ulverston

Suddell family, of Preston, 262

Suffolk, 269; duke of 294; Orford 192

suffragettes, 156, 327

Sunter, Mrs. M., 311

surgeons, 169, 196, 248, 253, 293, 297, 321

Surrey : Burstow 255; East Cheam 255; Reigate 264, 299; Tooting Graveney 277

surveyors, 163, 224, 236, 256, 271

Sussex : Barcombe hundred 263; Boxgrove 268; Buttinghill hundred 263; East Lavant 264, 268; Eastbourne priory 222; Halnaker 264, 268; Lancing 207; Lewes 263, 283; Poynings hundred 263; Street hundred 263; Tangmere 268

Sussex Archaeological Society, 312

Sutcliffe, Rev. J. G., 325

Sutton : bishops' transcripts 125; Burton-head 260; coal (Sutton Heath, Sutton Manor, Lea Green) 35; deeds 173, 210, 222, 236, 259, 289, 307, 316, 326, 332; enclosure 174; plans 74; Ravenhead 174; schools 90; survey 272; tithe 28
Sutton, Miss D., 313
Swainshead, see Over Wyresdale
Swann, H., 305
Swarbrick, Edward, of Nateby, 340; N. J. 299
Swarthmoor, see Ulverston
Sweeten, H., 316
Swettenham family, 287
Swinneston, Rev. E., 327
Swinton, 246; bishops' transcripts 127; deeds 322, 339; hearth tax 18; industrial school 64, 90; R.C. records 134

Tackley, Mrs. A., 296
tailors, 169, 172, 327, 329
Talbot, H., 295; James (1812) 271; John (1514) 284; Sir Thomas, of Blackburn 213; William, of Hindley 271
Tallents & Co., 312
tanners, 12, 169, 175, 267
Tarbock : coal, 246; deeds 206, 244, 259, 282, 287, 335; leases 288; manor 243, 244; parish records 116; plans 246, 288; surveys 245; tithe 28
Tarleton, 223, 309; bishops' transcripts 121; chapels 237; coastal traders 171, 204; deeds 222, 236, 251, 257, 274, 277, 315, 326, 332; manor 221; moss 223; parish records 116; schools 91; society 155; terrier 123; tithe 27
Tarnacre, see Upper-Rawcliffe-with-Tarn-acre
tartaric acid works, 171, 313
Tasburgh family, 218, 219
Tatham, 324; bishops' transcripts 122; deeds 182, 202, 214, 218, 240, 255, 292, 300, 306, 309, 311, 333, 336; enclosure 14, 182; Hipping Hall 176; manor 185; parish records 116; R.C. records 134; school 91; terriers 123
Tatham Fells : bishops' transcripts 122; parish records 116; terriers 123
Tattersall family, of Lower Darwen, 307; Miss A. 291; John (1826) 291
Tatton family, of Cuerden, 274-6; D. 327
tax, 18, 213; commissioners 18; see also corn, hearth, income, land, poll, and window tax

Taylor family, of Finsthwaite, 251-3; Mrs. Enid, of Silverdale 306; H. 311; J. R. of Penwortham 167; Dr. R. 323; Richard, transportee 310; Kirkham & Mainprice 328
teachers' union, 159
technical instruction committee of county council, 41
Teebay family, 186
telephones, 171, 299, 312, 322
temperance societies, 156, 157, 158
Tempest, Charles, of Broughton, 195; Joseph Francis, of Broughton-in-Craven 326
tennis, 158
textiles : employers' associations 162-3; trades unions 158-61; weavers' society 153; see also calico, cotton, linen, wool
theatres, 23, 166, 183, 186, 290, 299, 304, 314, 315; and see under individual parishes
Thistleton, see Greenhalgh-with-Thistleton
Thomasson family, 147
Thompson, Richard & Son, of Blackburn, 164; William & John, of Great Harwood 170; & Marshall, of Manchester 171
Thornber, Thomas, of Vivary Bridge, 184
Thornborrow, Adam, of Berbice, West Indies, 173
Thornham : deeds 227; enclosure 14; Hathershaw Moor 227; hearth tax 18; parish records 116; rental 320; tithe 28
Thornley-with-Wheatley, 335; deeds 185, 233, 264, 283, 317, 332, 338; land tax 268; leases 265; manor 263; plans 268; R.C. records 134; rentals 269; road 268; school 91; surveys 266; Wheatley 264, 269
Thornton (Sefton) : charity 151; deeds 194, 199, 206, 244; enclosure 14, 245; leases 291; manor 243; parish records 116; plans 246, 306; tithe 28; windmill 197
Thornton family, 181
Thornton-le-Fylde : bishops' transcripts 122; deeds 173, 175, 176, 184, 202, 244, 301, 309, 325, 329, 331, 337; divisional executive committee 39; enclosure 14; marsh 284; Methodists 146; parish records 116; rental 329; Rossall 274; schools 66, 91, 184; Thornton Cleveleys urban district 52
Thornyholme, see Roughlee Booth
Thorphinsty, see Cartmel Fell
thread manufacturers, 171

31; deeds 51, 233, 236, 277, 282, 302, 313, 319, 323, 326, 331, 335; garrison 226; insurance committee 31; jurors 10; land tax 31; leases 265; library 39; Little Sankey 236; manor 235, 236, 294; mechanics' institute 9; militia 7; museum 9; parish records 117, 237; police 60; poor 236-7; poor law guardians 64; rental 237; roads 299; R.C. records 134, 135; rural district 56; schools 92-3, 236; tanners 169; terriers 126; tithe 28; tobacconists 174; Trinity chapel 236

Warrington Library, 304

Warton-in-Amounderness, 341; Bank House academy 317; bishops' transcripts 121; church 208; deeds 83, 175, 202, 206, 251, 271, 282, 283, 292, 296, 304, 312, 314, 332; highways 56; parish records 118; plans 208, 313; rental 260; sea defences 207

Warton-in-Lonsdale : bishops' transcripts 122; bounds 278; charity 151; deeds 178, 261, 277, 278, 320, 325, 327, 336; enclosure 14; Lindeth 14; manor 276; moss 278; rental 279; schools 93; scrapbook 157; tithe 27, 279; waste 278

Warwick, earls of, 257, 281

Warwickshire : Ascot 264; Binton 264; Brockhurst 210; Berkswell 210; Chilvers Coton 255; Claverdon 280; Fillingley 306; Meriden 264, 266, 269; Merivale abbey 197, 206, 207, 244, 245; Norton Lindsey 280; Nuneaton 255; Studley 255; Whichford 264; Whitley 255; Wolverdington 255

watching, 189, 242

watchmakers, 174

water undertakings, 43, 44, 46, 49, 50, 51, 53, 55, 56, 233, 280; plans 16; records 65, 171, 183, 188, 189, 205, 267

Waterhead (Oldham) : bishops' transcripts 127; school 83

Waterhouse, Henry, of Sowerby, 275; & Co. 316

watermills, 172, 203, 219, 221, 227, 252, 260, 261, 273, 291, 333; and see mills

Watson, John, of Preston, 334; R. C. 300; Richard, bishop of Llandaff 331; Rev. W. D. 306

Watt, James, 177

Watterson, Moore & Co., 324

Wavertree : accounts 270; bishops' transcripts 124; deeds 173, 209, 271, 308; enclosure 14, 245; leases 265; plan 321; schools 93; tithe 28

Weaste, see Pendleton (Salford)

Webster, L. A., 323

Weeks, Mrs. E. A. Self, 290

Weeton-with-Preese, 266; accounts 270; deeds 83, 172, 185, 206-7, 264, 305, 310, 332; fair 266; leases 265; manor 263; parish records 118; plans 268; Preese 283, 330; hall 330; rentals 269; school 93; surveys 266; tithe 27

Welch Whittle, 273; deeds 190, 259, 271, 326, 333; surveys 272, 273; tithe 27

Weld (Shireburne) family, of Stonyhurst, **283-5**

Weld, John, of Leagram, 340; Thomas, of Lulworth co. Dorset 197; and see Blundell

Weld Bank, see Chorley

Weld Blundell family, 187; Hubert, African traveller 187

Welles, Elizabeth (1498), 264

Wellington, duke of (marquis Wellesley), 220, 226

Wennington : deeds 178; tithe 27

Werneth : bishops' transcripts 127; Chamber Hall 227

Wesham, 176; deeds 264, 332; leases 265; R.C. records 134; schools 80, 93; see also Medlar-with-Wesham

West, Father Thomas, 335, 337; William (1653) 220

West Close Booth, see Higham-with-West Close Booth

West Derby, 261, 265; accounts 270; bishops' transcripts 125; chapel 246; coroners' court 24; deeds 193, 207, 209, 236, 244, 261, 264, 319; divisional subcommittee 38; enclosure 14, 245; leases 265; manor 243; plans 180, 246, 270; police 7; rentals 247; rural district 56; schools 93; survey 245; terrier 126; tithe 28; wapentake 246

West Derby hundred : bridges 4; farmleases 225; forest 244, 245; stewards 244, 245; subsidy rolls 208, 230

West Indies, 177, 181, 226; Berbice 173; Bermuda (Barmodas) 229; Dominica 300, 307; Jamaica 217, 291, 332, 341; Martinique 253

Westby family, 199; E. A. C. 299

Westby-with-Plumpton 208; deeds 172, 184, 207, 251, 301, 319, 332; estate act 291; manor 205, 206; parish records 118; plans 208; R.C. records 134; school 93; sea defences 207; surveys 207; tithe 27

Westhoughton, 230, 293, 311; bishops' transcripts 127; chapel 231; coal 187; deeds 146, 181, 187, 201, 233, 236, 282, 287, 296, 308, 331, 337; enclosure 14; hospital board 30; parish records 118; plans 306, 341; police 60; rentals 178, 231, 234, 341; road 179; schools 13; surveys 233, 272; terrier 128; tithe 28, 197; waste 230

Westleigh, 219; coal 315; deeds 207, 218, 236, 282, 293, 313, 316, 328, 331; parsonage 236; schools 81, 93; survey 300; tithe 28

Westmorland, 234, 284, 328, 334; Ambleside 258; Arnside 270, 278; Askham 277; Barbon 186, 261; Beckhead (Kirkby Lonsdale) 169; Beetham 207, 263, 264, 266, 268, 279, 280; Burton-in-Kendal 204, 264, 295, 336; Heiring Syke 328; Heversham 203; Holme 247; Kendal : deanery probate records 25, records 120, deeds 242, 258, joiners' co. 253, rental 224, Kentmere 258; Kirby Lonsdale 277, 295, 336; Levens 268; Long Marton 316; Middleton 281; Meathop 175, 280; Milnthorpe 278; Nether Levens 247; Newbiggin 336; Preston Patrick 185, 247, 295; Sedgewick 336; Sizergh 337; Strickland 276, 277; Thornthwaite 282; Troutbeck 280; Ullthwaite 258; Windermere 239, 258; Witherslack 263, 264, 266, 267, 268, 269, 280

Westwood, *see* Worsley

Whalley, 199, 276, 320, 327, 335, 340; abbey 200, 220, 222, 224, 225, 249, 251, 256 279, 286, 338; bells 285; bishops' transcripts 122; bridge 4, 290; Brockhall 199; builder 164; charities 151; church 200, 279, 286, 304, 315, 316, 340; Clerk Hill (Snelleshow) 199, 220, 221; cotton mill 171; deeds 184, 199, 220, 233, 270, 304, 314, 325, 327; Fiendsforth bridge 4; freeholders 221; glebe 172; highway 290; Lower Booths 187, 189, 290; Methodist records 146; parish records 118; Parkhead 234; plans 297; police 60; Portfield 199; quarries 316; rectory 273, 278, 314; rentals 200, 234; schools 93, 304; surveys 221; tithe 184, 256; turnpike 61; Twiston tithe 27, 286; vicarage 200; watermills 221

Whalley family, of Sparth, 220, 238; James, of Clerk Hill 199; John (1733) 221; John, of Trawden 184; Thomas (1693) 221

Wharles, 266; deeds 264, 292, 294, 329, 332; leases 265, 329; manor 263; plans 268; rentals 269; surveys 266; tithe 27; *and see* Treales *and* Roseacre

Wharmby family, 241

Wharton, *see* Little Hulton

Wheatley, *see* Thornley-with-Wheatley

Wheatley Booth, *see* Barley-with-Wheatley Booth

Wheatley Carr Booth : parish records 118

Wheeler, A. J., 322

Wheelton : deeds 176, 179, 187, 264, 322, 326, 331, 332; mills 317; parish records 118; rentals 326; school 93; survey 272; Todd's factory 318

wheelwright, 224

Whiley, G. M., 307

Whiston, 215; bishops' transcripts 125; chapel 287; charities 151, 187; coal 246, 287, 288; deeds 173, 174, 187, 264, 287, 309, 326, 331, 337; Halshead 93, 185, 215, 287; leases 288; parish records 118; plans 288; rural district 56; schools 93, 287; tithe 28

Whitacker, Robert, of Walton-le-Dale, 176

Whitaker, Henry, of Brownmoor, 286

Whitechapel, *see* Goosnargh-with-Newsham

Whitefield : deeds 176; parish records 111; Philips Park 295; plans 270; school 93; urban district 295

Whitehead, A., 297; John, of Bolton 293; Rev. Thomas, of Eccleston and Richard, son of 318; W. N. 304

Whiteside, Thomas, R.C. bishop of Liverpool, 128

whitesters, 328

Whitfield, J. R., 296

Whitham, John, of Preston, 297

Whittaker family, of Simonstone, 285-6; Henry, Phillips, & Co. 297; J. 319; J. & Son, of Huyton 164

Whittingham : deeds 176, 185, 186, 211, 251, 254, 261, 264, 274, 277, 283, 297, 307, 326, 331, 332, 333; Easter roll 180; estate papers 320; hospital 30; leases 265; plans 186; poor tax 180; rentals 269; survey 272; tithe 180

Whittington, 219; bishops' transcripts 123; church 301; deeds 220, 289, 312, 317, 331, 337; enclosure 14; hall 220; manor 219, 301; moss 220; parish records 118; plans 336; rectory 219; school 93; surveys 220; terriers 123

Whittle, Mrs. B., 322

395

Whittle-le-Woods : charity 151; deeds 179, 209, 211, 252, 274, 283, 306, 324, 326, 332; parish records 118; rentals 260, 273, 326; road 251; R.C. club 158; schools 93; Shaw Hill 209, 210, 212; South Hill R.C. records 134; surveys 272; tithe 27; waste 330

Whitrigg, see Dalton-in-Furness

Whitworth, 305; bishops' transcripts 128; chapel 334; cotton mills 171, 323; deeds 187, 312; manufacturing co. 188; parish records 118; schools 93, 334; societies 158

Widdrington family, 283; lords 276, 278; Peregrine (1746) 284; Roger, scout-master-general 284

Widnes, 219; bishops' transcripts 125; bridge 38; charities 152; deeds 194, 218, 289, 309, 318, 326, 332, 336; engineers 116; manor 205; parish records 118-9; R.C. records (Appleton) 135; schools 94; survey 272; tithe 28; Upton 269; rental 270

Wigan, 174, 185, 191, 209, 282, 288, 296, 302, 316, 340; bills of mortality 236; bishops' transcripts 126; church 290, 336; coal 32, 34, 35, 260; coal & iron co. 35, 165, 167, 236; compoti 178; deeds 146, 176, 181, 192, 211, 218, 222, 227, 229, 233, 250, 255, 264, 271, 281, 282, 287, 312, 313, 315, 316, 317, 326, 331, 333, 335, 340; garrison 226; grocer 167; historical collections 302; insurance committee 31; iron 305; Junction Co. 35; land tax commissioners 31; leases 265, 288; mining & technical college 42; Moss Hall 34; plans 281; police 60; poor law guardians 64; public assistance 40; railway 245; rector 285; rentals 260, 269; riots 20; R.C. records 134, 135; Scholes Sunday school 329; schools 94; society 153; surveys 233, 272; terriers 126; tithe 28; turnpikes 61, 176

Wigan Record Office, 327

Wightman, G., 324

Wilbraham family, 286; and see Bootle-Wilbraham

Wilde, A., 323; Alfred, of Hurst 323

Wilkes & Peel, cotton manufacturers, 184

Wilkie, David, 307

Wilkinson, Mrs. A., 322; D. 293; E. 296; Mrs. G. 291; John, ironmaster 177

William IV, 210

William the Botyler (Boteler) (c. 1264), 193, 235

Williams, Miss E., 321; N. S. P. 297; T. 295; & Sutclife, of Liverpool 163

Williamson, James, & Son, of Lancaster, 168

Willis family, of Halsnead, 287-8; R. H. 320; Richard, of Halsnead 185, 215

wills, 182, 184, 188, 195, 199, 200, 203, 207, 210, 214, 215, 217, 220, 221, 225, 227, 228, 229, 233, 236, 238, 239, 242, 244, 248, 249, 250, 252, 255, 257, 258, 259, 261, 264, 270, 271, 274, 278, 280, 281, 282, 285, 289, 292, 302, 311, 314, 324; Roman Catholic 14; and see probate records

Wilpshire : deeds 211, 222, 255, 337; enclosure 13, 98, 256

Wilson family, of Eshton Hall, 325; Henry, ensign 329; Mrs. J. W. 321; Thomas, of Silverdale 327; & Frith 317; & Sons 324; Rawstorne & Wilson, of Preston 168

Wilton, earls of, 288, 323

Wiltshire, 278; Baverstock 221; Broad Hinton 236; Clack 221; Dunhead 201; Ham 201; Quidhampton 236; Salthorp 236; Swindon 322

Wiltshire Record Office, 305

Winckley family, 321; of Preston 288-9; of Winckley 288

Winder & Holden, of Bolton, 187

Windermere, lake : ferry 258; fishery 258; plan 299; steamer 305

Windle, 257; bishops' transcripts 125; Blackbrook R.C. records 129, 135; bounds 266; coal 219; deeds 173, 208, 218, 222, 257, 309, 312; Hardshaw 146; leases 265; manor 218; parish records 119; plans 209; school 94; surveys 209, 272; tithe 28

windmills, 197 ,198, 215, 291; and see mills

window tax, 44, 204

Windybank, see Littleborough

wine merchants, 179, 181

Winmarleigh : boundaries 173; deeds 222, 233, 322; parish records 119; plans 296; school 94; societies 332; tithe 27

Winmarleigh, lord, 322

Winstanley : coal 165, 192, 246; deeds 192, 207; hall plans 192; manor 191-2; parish records 119; surveys 272; tithe 28; wagon road 219

Winstanley family, 191; Rev. Calvin, of Liverpool 215; Miss 309

Winster, river, 177, 299

Winter Hill, see Sharples

Winwick-with-Hulme, 181; bishops' transcripts 126; church 201; deeds 201, 218, 282, 305; parish records 117; survey 272; terriers 126; tithe 28, 201; *see also* Hulme

Wiswell, 304, 338; Barrow printworks 310, 341; common 284; deeds 197, 199, 220, 251, 283, 327; enclosure 14; manor 291; parish records 119; plans 285; Ponthalgh 254, 256; schools 94

witchcraft, 296

Witham, Weld, & Co., of Liverpool, 187, 327

Withington : bishops' transcripts 127; deeds 173, 233, 281, 331, 337; school 94; tithe 28

Withnell : bishops' transcripts 122; deeds 176, 179, 322, 331, 332; leases 226; manor 225; Methodist records 146; Stanworth House 238; tithe 27; urban district 54

Witton : deeds 202, 331, 333, 337; parish records 98

Wollaston, H., 316

Wolstenholme, *see* Spotland

Womens' Institutes, 156, 157

Wood, R., 319; R. M. 317

Wood Broughton, *see* Cartmel

Woodall, D., 324

Woodcock family, 190, 212; William, of Preston 181; & Sons, of Bury 187-8; & Sons, of Haslingden 189-90

Woodland, *see* Kirkby Ireleth

Woodplumpton, 180; bishops' transcripts 122; church 292; deeds 100, 172, 175, 179, 185, 186, 202, 211, 259, 264, 283, 291, 294, 303, 319, 326, 329, 331, 332, 337, 338; enclosure 305; manor 251, 292; parish records 119; schools 94; survey 272; terriers 123; tithe 27

Woodrofe, Richard, of Samlesbury, 275

Woods, Mrs. A., 293; Mrs. E. C. 314; Barton & Co., 303

woods, 245, 270; *and see* charcoal, timber

woodworkers, 224, 304; unions 161; *and see* joiners

Woolfenden, Miss J., 305

woollen industry, 171, 227, 242, 249, 260, 285, 292, 302, 311

Woolston-with-Martincroft : deeds 282, 302; enclosure 14; R.C. records 134; tithe 28

Woolton : accounts 270; deeds 236; enclosure 13; rental 260; R.C. records 135; *and see* Little Woolton *and* Much Woolton

Woosey, Gilbert (1711), 253

Woosnam & Co., 290

Worcestershire, 186; Evesham abbey 211, 213; Feckenham 255; Staunton 295

Worcestershire Record Office, 303

Worden, *see* Leyland

Wordsworth, T. S. H., 325; William 239, 307

workhouses, 213, 216, 224, 271, 273, 285, 307; *see also* poor law guardians

Worsley, 305; bishops' transcripts 127; Boothstown remand home 37, 38; deeds 227, 232, 233, 271, 292, 297, 303, 331; enclosure 14; friendly society 155; hearth tax 18; parish records 119; survey 282; Westwood 282

Worsley, L., 318

Worsley-Taylor family, of Whalley, 276

Worsthorne-with-Hurstwood : deeds 188, 255, 271, 274, 277, 283, 308; enclosure 14, 278; Hurstwood 273; schools 67, 94; surveys 272, 340

Worston : deeds 182, 199, 232, 331, 333; parish records 119; plan 234

Worswick family, 182

Worthington : coal 165; deeds 176, 181, 218, 259, 274, 324, 326; parish records 119; tithe 27

Wray, *see* Claife

Wray-with-Botton : deeds 214, 315, 333; parish records 119; school 94; tithe 27

Wrea (Wrea Green) : deeds 215, 326; fair 267; manor house 182; school 292; scrapbook 157; *and see* Ribby-with-Wrea

wreck, 187, 199, 215, 244, 267

Wright family, of Heysham and Gressingham, **289**; Adam, of Kirkham 329; Rev. John, of Preston Patrick co. Westmorland 295; Hassall & Co. 317

Wrightington, 223, 261, 330, 333; accounts 330; Appley moor 299; bishops' transcripts 121; coal 224; deeds 207, 211, 220, 222, 250, 259, 264, 271, 306, 315, 321, 324, 330, 331, 332; enclosure 305; hall 181, 299; manor 221; parish records 119; plans 224; R.C. records 134, 135; school 94; scrapbook 157; surveys 223, 272; tithe 27; turnpike 61

Wrightington, Sir Edward, 294, 333; John, subsidy-collector 260, 261

Wrigley, Henry, of London, 227

Wuerdle-and-Wardle : bishops' transcripts 128; Brownwardle 305; Wardle urban district 54

Wyatt, Lewis, architect, 192